Patent Case Management Judicial Guide

Third Edition

2016

Volume II

Trial Case Management

ANDA/Biosimilars

Design Patents

Plant Patents

Court of Claims

Primer

Chapters 7–14

Patent Case Management Judicial Guide

Third Edition

Peter S. Menell
Koret Professor of Law
Berkeley Center for Law & Technology
University of California, Berkeley School of Law

Lynn H. Pasahow
Fenwick & West LLP

James Pooley
Orrick, Herrington & Sutcliffe LLP

Matthew D. Powers
Tensegrity Law Group LLP

Steven C. Carlson
Kasowitz, Benson, Torres & Friedman LLP

Jeffrey G. Homrig
Latham & Watkins LLP

George F. Pappas
Covington & Burling LLP

Carolyn Chang
Fenwick & West LLP

Colette Reiner Mayer
Morrison & Foerster LLP

Marc David Peters
Morrison & Foerster LLP

in collaboration with

Anita Choi
Morrison & Foerster LLP

John Fargo
U.S. Department of Justice

Michael Sawyer
Covington & Burling LLP

Allison A. Schmitt
University of California, Berkeley

Michael R. Ward
Morrison & Foerster LLP

Patricia Young
Latham & Watkins LLP

Federal Judicial Center 2016

email: pmenell@law.berkeley.edu

A print version of *Patent Case Management Judicial Guide* (3d ed. 2016), including all appendices, is available through Clause 8 Publishing (Clause8Publishing.com). The treatise is also available through the Lexis online database.

Summary Table of Contents

Table of Contents

Chapter 7 Pretrial Case Management

Chapter 10 ANDA and Biologics Cases: Patent Infringement Actions Involving FDA-Approved Drugs

Chapter 14 Patent Law Primer

Chapter 7
Pretrial Case Management

Close judicial management of the preparations for trial is integral to ensuring smooth proceedings during trial. As discussed in previous chapters, early judicial management can help narrow the issues that require resolution by trial. There are many procedural and substantive issues that can be resolved in the weeks preceding trial to refine issues and avoid delay during trial. This chapter discusses the considerations that should be given to pretrial preparations to promote efficient proceedings during trial, with particular discussion of the patent case pretrial conference, jury instructions, limitations on expert testimony, and motions *in limine*. Note that in some cases sound case management may require that some issues be addressed well *before* the pretrial conference.

7.1 Pretrial Conference

The complexity of patent cases creates a particular need for pretrial preparation to minimize jury downtime and increase jury comprehension. The pretrial conference represents the final opportunity to anticipate and resolve problems that would otherwise interrupt and delay trial proceedings. Having an effective pretrial conference is best guaranteed by requiring counsel to confer on a series of issues and then identifying and briefing the areas of disagreement.

As will be apparent from the sample order that is provided as Appendix 7-1, most of these issues arise in any complex case. However, in patent litigation they can take on special dimensions. In this section, we explore the pretrial conference process.

7.1.1 Timing

The pretrial conference should be held sufficiently in advance of trial, but long enough after claim construction and dispositive motion practice so that the court and counsel have a good idea of the boundaries of the trial and the interplay of issues that may need to be tried. Usually, the conference is set six to eight weeks before trial.

7.1.2 Participation

Because of the importance of the issues to be determined at the pretrial conference, the court should conduct this proceeding in person rather than telephonically. Lead trial counsel should be required to attend.

7.1.3 The Pretrial Order

The objective of the pretrial conference is to generate an order that will govern the issues for trial and establish the ground rules for the conduct of the trial. Because of the special issues that often arise in patent cases, it is helpful to provide counsel in advance with a draft form of order that leaves blanks where appropriate, effectively providing a checklist of issues to consider. The form should include provisions that reflect the court's typical view on many aspects of the trial. However, counsel should be allowed to suggest deviations from those typical procedures where circumstances warrant.

7.1.4 Motions at the Pretrial Conference

Patent cases are characterized by large numbers of motions directed at excluding or limiting the use of evidence, including *Daubert* motions attacking expert opinions. It is common practice, and very sensible, to resolve such issues substantially in advance of trial so that the parties return with their presentations appropriately honed in accordance with the court's limiting orders. The sample pretrial order includes instructions for identifying and briefing *in limine* motions. Of course, circumstances may justify making additional such orders during the trial. Frequently, however, a great deal of delay and confusion can be avoided by making these determinations in advance. Even where the court determines that certain disputes are best resolved during trial, the briefing and arguments often help the court and the parties by distilling the issues before trial. This enables the court to evaluate the evidence in that context as it comes in and causes the parties to self-regulate during trial. Pretrial conferences can also produce the collateral benefit of settlement, by giving the parties a clearer picture of what evidence will or will not be accepted. The sections that follow provide detailed advice on the most frequent pretrial motions directed at expert testimony and other evidence.

7.2 Trial and Disclosure Schedule

Before any trial can begin, the court and the parties must settle on the schedule governing trial proceedings. While the overall trial schedule can be determined at the pretrial conference, the exact process and order of witnesses typically evolves during trial as a result of adjustments to evidence admitted, refused, or withdrawn, or one party responding to the emergent witness list of the other. The parties can and should be required to disclose well in advance of trial the universe of trial witnesses and trial exhibits that they may present and objections thereto. *See, e.g.*, Appendix 7.1 and Appendix 7.2 (requiring pretrial disclosure of will-call and may-call trial witnesses, trial exhibits, and objections). It is nevertheless impractical to finalize and commit the parties before trial to a fixed schedule identifying which of those witnesses and exhibits will actually be presented and the exact order in which they will occur. Likewise, while parties can and should be required to identify in advance which depositions they will or may use at trial, requiring the parties to identify weeks or months in advance of trial the *specific portions* of deposition testimony that they plan to present at trial is often inefficient—in typical cases, the parties spend vast amounts of time and money making deposition designations, counter-designations, and objections for *preservation* purposes in the pretrial stage. But these have little value because these designations cover broad swaths of testimony, and the parties redo them completely (selecting a much narrower set of testimony) once they decide, during trial, which designations to actually play. The court should, however, encourage the parties to stipulate to a protocol for disclosing the order in which witnesses will be called, the trial exhibits associated with each witness, and deposition designations during trial (collectively, "trial disclosures").

Because the parties are in a better position to determine how much time is needed to finalize cross-examinations and objections to exhibits, the court should allow the parties to stipulate to a mutually agreeable schedule for trial disclosures (so long as it affords the court time to rule on objections). In a typical patent case, a one- or two-day advance disclosure of the witnesses and exhibits to be used on a specific day usually suffices. For example, a party intending to call a witness on Monday would disclose the witness and the exhibits to be used with the witness by a specified time on Saturday. The non-disclosing party would identify any objections to the exhibits by the next day. For deposition designations, a somewhat longer disclosure period (e.g., three or four days in advance) is usually warranted to allow sufficient time for counter-designations and resolution of objections. Whether more or less time is appropriate depends on the complexity of the particular case. These trial disclosures should notify the opposing party of the order in which previously identified trial witnesses and exhibits will be presented, not circumvent the court's pretrial witness and exhibit disclosure requirements.

Any established trial disclosure protocol should also cover the disclosure of demonstrative exhibits that may be used with a particular witness. However, demonstratives should be disclosed with sufficient time to allow the opposing party to raise objections prior to the presentation to the jury. The court should also develop and share with the parties a default schedule for trial disclosures so that it can (1) avoid agreements that unduly burden the court (e.g., a deposition designation schedule that does not afford the court a meaningful opportunity to resolve objections) and (2) impose that default schedule if the parties cannot agree.

7.3 Jury Instructions

7.3.1 Preliminary Instructions

Many jurors are called to service without much understanding of trial practice or the legal system. Usually, their understanding of the patent system is particularly limited. The problem is exacerbated because, unlike many other legal frameworks (such as negligence), principles of patent law often do not line up with jurors' moral or "common sense" reasoning, especially without explanation. For example, some find it illogical that a defendant can be liable even if it did not know about a patent. Some wrongly assume that a defendant's product cannot infringe the plaintiff's patent if the defendant has its own patent. Some believe that a device that was not patented cannot be "prior art" to a patent.

It is, therefore, good practice to give the jury preliminary instructions regarding their duties and the trial process before the start of trial. Providing the jurors with a legal framework before the presentation of evidence will help them understand what information they should consider once trial begins. Many of the available model jury instructions contain examples of useful preliminary instructions.[1] Preliminary instructions should, at a minimum, set forth the duty of the jury, explain what constitutes evidence, explain the varying burdens of proof in a civil trial, and outline trial proceedings. They should also include a non-argumentative description of the technology involved, the accused products, and the patents.

Because jurors usually understand the patent system even less than they understand the general legal system, it is important to provide the jury with a short explanation of the patent system, the particular patents at issue, and an overview of the patent law applicable to the contentions of the case. The Federal Judicial Center (FJC) has prepared a video that has often been used to provide a basic primer on the patent system. The video, together with a sample mock patent, is designed to be shown to prospective jurors in patent trials and provides background information on what patents are, why they are needed, how inventors get them, the role of the USPTO, and why disputes over patents arise.

The FJC updated the video in 2013 to address changes in patent law, including the enactment and implementation of the American Invents Act (AIA). This 2013 video, "The Patent Process: An Overview for Jurors," can be found here:

---

1. *See, e.g.*, Benchbook for U.S. District Judges (Federal Judiciary Center 6th ed. 2014), § 6.06 Preliminary Jury Instructions in Civil Case; Fifth Circuit Pattern Jury Instructions—Civil (http://www.lb5.uscourts.gov/juryinstructions/); Eighth Circuit Manual of Model Jury Instructions (http://www.juryinstructions.ca8.uscourts.gov/civil_instructions.htm); Ninth Circuit Manual of Model Jury Instruction—Civil (http://www.akd.uscourts.gov/docs/general/model_jury_civil.pdf); Eleventh Circuit Pattern Jury Instructions—Civil (http://www.ca11.uscourts.gov/documents/pdfs/civjury.pdf).

https://www.youtube.com/watch?v=ax7QHQTbKQE. The original video, which had been used to educate patent juries for many years, is now out of date and should not be used. The 2013 video will be appropriate for most patent-infringement cases, but the court should confirm this in each case by discussing with the parties whether to play it. Given the rapid evolution of the substantive law in many areas, the court should also proactively inquire whether any aspects of the video that are relevant to the issues that the jury will be asked to decide are inaccurate or misleading in light of applicable law.

As an alternative to the FJC video, the court can address these issues in its preliminary instructions, for example by using preliminary instruction A.1 ("What A Patent Is and How One Is Obtained") promulgated by the Northern District of California in its Model Patent Jury Instructions (June 14, 2014). These instructions can be found in Appendix E. *See also* Federal Circuit Bar Association, Model Patent Jury Instructions (January 2016) (contained in Appendix E). Preliminary instructions should also include an instruction setting forth the court's construction of patent claim terms. The jurors should be instructed that they must accept the court's constructions and are not allowed to construe terms on their own. *See Structural Rubber Prods. Co. v. Park Rubber*, 749 F.2d 707, 723 (Fed. Cir. 1984).

7.3.2 Final Instructions—Timing

In addition to preliminary instructions, the court should also instruct the jurors before they begin deliberations. While the court has discretion to instruct the jury before or after closing arguments are given, it is usually preferred to give instructions beforehand. Fed. R. Civ. P. 51, 1987 Advisory Committee Notes (delineating benefits of instructions before closing arguments). This is especially true in a patent case. Jurors are usually more focused and in a better position to listen to instructions before closing arguments. Jurors better understand the arguments advanced during the closings when they have been instructed on the law applicable to the case. Instructing the jury before closing arguments can also lead to more effective arguments by the parties. Closing arguments can be tailored to meet the specific language of the instructions, enabling the parties to highlight the significance of particular evidence. Thus, instructing the jury before closing argument is recommended.

If the jury will be instructed after closing argument, some of the benefits listed above can be retained if jury instructions are finalized before closing argument and provided to the parties. This allows the parties to tailor their closing arguments to the instructions that will be given, which is especially helpful to the jury. Thus, we recommend that the court finalize the instructions and provide them to the parties before closing arguments begin if the court chooses to instruct the jury after closing arguments.

7.3.3 Final Instructions—Substance

Patent law is complex, and so, typically, are jury instructions in patent cases. Fortunately, several organizations and courts have prepared model patent jury instructions. They serve as useful resources on which the parties can base their proposed instructions. *See* Appendix E. The model instruction sets differ stylistically. Moreover, the patent law has changed and continues to change in important ways, and at any given time some instructions may have been updated to reflect a recent Supreme Court or Federal Circuit decision while others may have not.

As a result, it generally makes sense to start from one of these sets of model instructions and modify or add to it as needed to address the issues in a particular case and the subsequent changes in law. One approach is for the court to select the set of model jury instructions it prefers and require the parties to prepare proposed instructions based on that set. This allows the court to become familiar with one set of instructions, while allowing the parties to propose changes based on changes in the law or the needs of the case. This approach has potential drawbacks, however, because some sets of model instructions do not address some issues, and as stated above, some sets of instructions will better reflect recent changes in the law. Another approach is to allow the parties to select which set of instructions makes the most sense to use as a model for a particular case.

The parties also often amend instructions to highlight the law particularly relevant to the arguments they intend to advance during trial. Allowing them to revise the model instructions to the particulars of the case can lead to argumentative and objectionable instructions, however. It is usually helpful to require the parties to submit "redlines" that show how they have revised the model instructions and provide any authority justifying their revisions.

7.3.4 Final Instructions—Common Disputes

Experience has shown that many of the same disputes over jury instructions arise repeatedly. This section discusses the most common disputes regarding jury instructions.

7.3.4.1 Integration of Case-Specific Contentions

Many disputes result from the integration of a party's particular contentions into model jury instructions. Such particularized jury instructions may or may not be helpful to the jury. Generally, the court should attempt to exclude argumentative statements proposed by either side from the jury instructions. The "redline" mentioned above—which will show where any alterations have been made—is particularly helpful in avoiding this issue.

7.3.4.2 Claim-Construction Instruction

The instruction on claim construction is important and part of virtually every patent case. If the court has held a claim-construction hearing and issued a claim-construction order, those constructions should be restated as a jury instruction. The parties may not argue a contrary construction. One common problem is that, in an effort to preserve their claim-construction positions for appeal, parties will often reargue rejected claim constructions during the process of drafting jury instructions. This is inefficient. The court should streamline this process by instructing the parties to put the claim-construction order in the form of a jury instruction, and allowing them to reserve their objections to any constructions on the record. *See* § 5.1.6.

7.3.4.3 The "Presumption" of Validity Instruction

As most patent trials involve claims of invalidity, the patent owner will often try to incorporate into the instruction on invalidity a statement that patents are presumed to be valid. *See* 35 U.S.C. § 282. The defendant usually objects.

In 2011, the Supreme Court squarely addressed the question of the appropriate burden of proof for validity challenges in *Microsoft Corp. v. i4i Ltd. Partnership*, 131 S. Ct. 2238, 2251 (2011). In that case, the Court held that the "clear and convincing evidence" standard applied to all factual questions underlying the issue of invalidity, regardless of whether the United States Patent and Trademark Office (PTO) was aware of the prior art on which the validity challenge is based.

At the same time, the Court recognized that "if the PTO did not have all material facts before it, its considered judgment may lose significant force . . . And, concomitantly, the challenger's burden to persuade the jury of its invalidity defense by clear and convincing evidence may be easier to sustain." *Id.* at 2251. The Court noted that

> although we have no occasion to endorse any particular formulation, we note that a jury instruction on the effect of new evidence can, and when requested, most often should be given. When warranted, the jury may be instructed to consider that it has heard evidence that the PTO had no opportunity to evaluate before granting the patent. When it is disputed whether the evidence presented to the jury differs from that evaluated by the PTO, the jury may be instructed to consider that question. In either case, the jury may be instructed to evaluate whether the evidence before it is materially new, and if so, to consider that fact when determining whether an invalidity defense has been proved by clear and convincing evidence.

Id. For this reason, where a defendant challenges the validity of a patent based on prior art that either (1) was not before the PTO or (2) was before the PTO but was not discussed or otherwise given substantive attention, the Court should consider instructing the jury that it may take this fact into consideration in evaluating whether the defendant has met the clear and convincing evidence standard. *See, e.g.*, *AbbVie Deutschland GmbH & Co., KG v. Janssen Biotech, Inc.*, 759 F.3d 1285 (Fed. Cir. 2014) (finding acceptable an instruction explaining that the defendant's burden may be easier to meet when the jury considers evidence of invalidity that is materially new, rephrasing the Supreme Court's "materially new" as "additional information [that] would have been 'material' to the PTO's decision to grant the patents," stating that something is "material" if "there is a substantial likelihood that a reasonable patent examiner would consider it important in deciding whether to allow the application to issue as a patent," and including the additional language that "if the additional information was not material, or it would not have carried significant weight, [the defendant's] burden may be more difficult to meet").

A concurrence from Justices Breyer, Scalia, and Alito emphasized that many invalidity disputes turn "not upon factual disputes, but upon how the law applies to facts as given." *i4i*, 131 S. Ct. at 2253. The Justices pointed out that where questions of this nature arise (such as in questions about whether the facts show that the invention was novel and nonobvious) the clear and convincing standard "has no application." *Id.* They noted further that:

> Courts can help to keep the application of today's "clear and convincing" standard within its proper legal bounds by separating factual and legal aspects of an invalidity claim, say, by using instructions based on case-specific circumstances that help the jury make the distinction or by using interrogatories and special verdicts to make clear which specific factual findings underlie the jury's conclusions. *See* Fed. R. Civ. Proc. 49 and 51. By isolating the facts (determined with help of the "clear and convincing" standard), courts can thereby assure the proper interpretation or application of the correct legal standard (without use of the "clear and convincing" standard).

Id. Although this concurrence is not the opinion of the Court, it strongly suggests that courts should confine the applicability of the "clear and convincing" standard to factual questions and avoid their improper application to legal determinations.

Finally, it is also generally agreed that while juries should be instructed on the higher burden of proof required to prove invalidity, they should not be instructed that there is a presumption of validity, which would be redundant and likely confusing. As the National Jury Instruction Project explains: "In light of the procedural role of the presumption of validity, instructing the jury on the presumption in addition to informing it of the highly probable burden of proof may cause jury confusion as to its role in deciding invalidity." Committee Note to National Jury Instruction Project, Model Patent Jury Instructions 5.1. In line with this approach, the Federal Circuit Bar Association's Model Patent Jury Instructions, the Northern District of California Model Patent Jury Instructions and American Intellectual Property Law Association's Model Patent Jury Instructions also omit any reference to the presumption of validity in their instructions. *See also Chiron Corp. v. Genentech, Inc.*, 363 F.3d 1247, 1258–59 (Fed. Cir. 2004) (finding district court did not err in declining to instruct jury on the presumption of validity because the jury had applied the clear and convincing evidence standard); *Avia Group Int'l, Inc. v. L.A. Gear Cal., Inc.*, 853 F.2d 1557, 1562 (Fed. Cir. 1988) (the presumption of validity "does not constitute 'evidence' to be weighed against a challenger's evidence").

7.3.4.4 The Obviousness Instruction

The Supreme Court's decision in *KSR International Co. v. Teleflex, Inc.*, 550 U.S. 398 (2007), was a significant change in the law that has had a significant direct effect on jury instructions. *KSR* reversed the Federal Circuit's requirement that the evidence contain a "teaching, motivation, or suggestion" to combine the prior art used to show obviousness. *KSR* emphasized the need for courts to apply an "expansive and flexible" common-sense approach in evaluating validity, rather than being constrained by the rigid requirement of "motivation to combine." *Id.* at 415.

KSR also reemphasized the long-standing law that the question of obviousness is a legal question for the court. *Id.* at 426–27. Prior to *KSR*, the obviousness inquiry under § 103 was generally treated as secondary to the anticipation analysis under § 102, and was generally submitted to the jury for resolution along with anticipation. Often, the verdict form did not even separate the questions of obviousness and anticipation, including instead a single yes/no box for the question of validity. *KSR*'s insistence that obviousness was a legal determination for the court—one that should be made by the court when the obviousness of the claim is "apparent" even despite disputes about underlying facts—calls that practice into doubt. *Cf. Agrizap, Inc. v. Woodstream Corp.*, 520 F.3d 1337, 1343 n.3 (Fed. Cir. 2008) ("While a special verdict that asks a jury whether a patent claim is obvious provides more insight than one which simply asks whether the patent is invalid, the former still does not provide any detail into the specific fact findings made by the jury"); *see also Richardson-Vicks Inc. v. Upjohn Co.*, 122 F.3d 1476, 1484–85 (Fed. Cir. 1997) (noting that the "preferred route [to make a jury verdict on obviousness more amenable to appellate review] would have been to submit the underlying factual issues to the jury in the form of a special verdict under [R]ule 49(a)"); Paul J. Zegger et al., *The Paper Side of Jury Patent Trials: Jury Instructions, Special Verdict Forms, and Post-Trial Motions,* 910 PLI/PAT 701, 716 (2007) ("By compelling a jury to consider factual issues individually, special verdicts and interrogatories may improve the consistency of jury verdicts as well as the underlying decision-making processes that produce them."). This is reflected, for example, in the Northern District of California's model patent jury instructions, which provide two alternative model instructions on obviousness, one to be used when seeking an advisory verdict on the ultimate question of obviousness, and one to be used when only seeking resolution of the relevant factual questions. The AIPLA and FCBA model instructions have likewise been updated to reflect *KSR*, but were drafted to address only the situation in which the jury is asked to reach an advisory verdict on obviousness.

7.3.4.4.1 Background: Pre-*KSR* Obviousness Law and Jury Instructions

In *Graham v. John Deere*, 383 U.S. 1 (1966), the Supreme Court laid out the basic test for obviousness that remains the law today. It held that:

> [u]nder § 103, the scope and content of the prior art are to be determined; differences between the prior art and the claims at issue are to be ascertained; and the level of ordinary skill in the pertinent art resolved. Against this background the obviousness or nonobviousness of the subject matter is determined. Such secondary considerations as commercial success, long felt but unsolved needs, failure of others, etc., might be utilized to give light to the circumstances surrounding the origin of the subject matter sought to be patented.

Id. at 17–18. These three factual predicates, along with the "secondary considerations," are known as the *Graham* factors. Evaluation of each of the *Graham* factors is a question of fact.

Traditionally, the question of obviousness has been submitted to the jury with instructions to consider the *Graham* factors and reach a conclusion as to obviousness. An instruction on the "nexus" requirement for secondary considerations is also sometimes given. Secondary considerations only support nonobviousness (or, in the case of a contemporaneous invention, obviousness) if they are tied to the alleged invention (i.e., have a "nexus"). *See Ormco Corp. v. Align Tech., Inc.*, 463 F.3d 1299, 1311–12 (Fed. Cir. 2006) (holding that if the feature responsible for a claimed invention's commercial success was in the prior art, that success is irrelevant for purposes of determining obviousness); *Dippin' Dots, Inc. v. Mosey*, 476 F.3d 1337, 1345 (Fed. Cir. 2007) (same). Because "nexus" is a legal question, an alternative to a "nexus" instruction is the exclusion of "secondary considerations," evidence not shown to have the required "nexus."

7.3.4.4.2 Post-*KSR* Obviousness Law and Jury Instructions

Since *KSR* emphasized that obviousness is a legal determination for the court, the Federal Circuit has exhibited a much greater proclivity to find patents invalid under § 103. *See Allergan, Inc. v. Apotex, Inc.*, 754 F.3d 952 (Fed. Cir. 2014) (finding both patents-in-suit obvious and reversing district court's bench trial determination of nonobviousness); *Novo Nordisk A/S v. Caraco Pharm. Labs., Ltd.*, 719 F.3d 1346 (Fed. Cir. 2014) (affirming district court's bench trial determination of obviousness, reversing on other grounds); *I/P Engine, Inc. v. AOL, Inc.*, 576 F. App'x 982, (Fed. Cir. 2014) (reversing district court's post-jury-trial determination that asserted claims were nonobvious) (unpublished); *Tokai Corp. v. Easton Enters., Inc.*, 632 F.3d 1358 (Fed. Cir. 2011) (affirming summary judgment of obviousness); *Odom v. Microsoft Corp.*, 429 F. App'x 967 (Fed. Cir. 2011) (affirming summary judgment of obviousness) (unpublished); *Bayer Schering Pharma AG v. Barr Labs, Inc.*, 575 F.3d 1341 (Fed. Cir. 2009) (affirming finding of obviousness after bench trial); *In re Trans Tex. Holdings Corp.*, 498 F.3d 1290 (Fed. Cir. 2007); *Pharmastem Therapeutics, Inc. v. Viacell, Inc.*, 491 F.3d 1342 (Fed. Cir. 2007) (reversing denial of judgment as a matter of law (JMOL) to find obviousness); *Leapfrog Enters., Inc. v. Fisher-Price, Inc.*, 485 F.3d 1157 (Fed. Cir. 2007) (affirming finding of obviousness after bench trial); *In re Icon Health & Fitness, Inc.*, 469 F.3d 1374 (Fed. Cir. 2007); *Frazier v. Layne Christensen Co.*, 239 F. App'x 604 (Fed. Cir. 2007) (affirming JMOL of obviousness) (unpublished).

It is the court's responsibility to reach a conclusion on the ultimate issue of obviousness. However, any obviousness finding requires that the fact finder consider all of the "objective evidence presented by the patentee." *WMS Gaming Inc. v. Int'l Game Tech.*, 184 F.3d 1339, 1359 (Fed. Cir. 1999); *see also Rothman v. Target Corp.*, 556 F.3d 1310, 1322 (Fed. Cir. 2009) (approving district court's charge "that the jury 'must consider' objective indicia of nonobviousness, such as . . . licensing activity"). The renewed emphasis on the role of the court casts doubt on the practice of submitting the ultimate question of obviousness to the jury. It may now be better practice to limit the jury's consideration of obviousness to the factual disputes as to the *Graham* factors, as reflected in the Northern District of California Model Patent Jury Instruc-

ences, and we must defer to this factual finding because it is supported by substantial evidence.").

In *Kinetic Concepts*, the Federal Circuit applied this framework to review the district court's grant of judgment as a matter of law (JMOL) of obviousness. 688 F.3d at 1356–57. There, the parties disputed the form and content of the verdict form and the district court created a verdict form consisting of yes-or-no questions regarding the *Graham* factors, a chart pertaining to whether secondary considerations were present, and a question on the ultimate question of obviousness. *Id.* at 1354. Despite submitting the obviousness question to the jury, the judge stressed that the jury's final determination would only be "advisory." *Id.* at 1357. The jury subsequently determined that (1) there were other differences between the claims and the prior art in addition to those listed, (2) most of the objective considerations favoring nonobviousness were present, (3) infringement was proven, and (4) the asserted patents were not obvious. *Id.* at 1354. The district court, however, found the asserted claims obvious and granted the defendant's motion for JMOL. In so doing, the district court gave the jury's "advisory" determination of nonobviousness no deference. *Id.* at 1355–56.

The Federal Circuit reversed, noting that the court must presume that the jury resolved the underlying factual disputes in favor of the verdict, "leave those presumed findings undisturbed if . . . supported by substantial evidence," and then examine the district court's legal conclusion of obviousness de novo. *Id.* at 1356–57 (internal citation omitted). Importantly, even though the jury was specifically asked to decide certain factual issues and not others, the existence of the advisory verdict on the ultimate question of obviousness requires the court to presume that the jury found for the patentee on all underlying factual issues that it did *not* explicitly decide. Thus, when examining the legal conclusion of obviousness, the court must consider the jury's explicit *and* implicit factual findings.

The Federal Circuit also rejected the defendant's claim that the "advisory" status of the jury's verdict on the ultimate question of obviousness affected the presumed factual findings. It held instead that, in this context, "advisory" simply meant that the jury resolved a legal issue for the court, which is permissible because the judge remains the ultimate arbiter of obviousness through the drafting of the jury's legal instructions and the consideration of motions for a judgment notwithstanding the verdict or new trial. *Id.* at 1357–59. After gathering the jury's explicit and implicit findings, the Federal Circuit reexamined the ultimate nonobviousness conclusion de novo and held that the district court erred in granting Smith & Nephew's motion for JMOL because Smith & Nephew did not prove that the asserted claims were obvious. *Id.* at 1371.

The question of obviousness is often essential to the judgment. Unless the evidence meets the JMOL standard for finding obviousness or nonobviousness, resolution of the underlying factual disputes is necessary, and each party has a right to have a jury resolve such disputes if they are material. The losing party at trial will typically seek JMOL on the issue of obviousness, which joins the issue of how the jury resolved the material underlying factual disputes. If the court then draws conclusions about how the underlying factual disputes were resolved, it runs the risk of having those conclusions challenged on Seventh Amendment grounds. Consider also the scenario where a jury finds that there is anticipation and obviousness, and either the district court or the Federal Circuit reverses the finding of anticipation because a specific limitation in one claim is not present in one of the references. At this point, with a single-question verdict form, it is not clear whether the jury's error on anticipation affects its conclusion as to obviousness. Avoiding these situations, as well as helping the court perform its duty of drawing a legal conclusion as to obviousness, are good reasons for the recommendation in the Northern District of California's model verdict form that "the verdict form should require the jury's finding on each factual issue so that the trial judge may make the final determination on the obviousness question." *See* Appendix E.

Requiring the jury to make specific findings on the *Graham* factors does, however, have drawbacks. The most serious is that it is likely to lead to a complex verdict form. This is apparent from the Northern District of California's model verdict form. Some courts may find that such a verdict form is simply too complex to be practicable, notwithstanding the risks discussed above.

Certainly, if a form like the Northern District of California's form is used, it needs to be available to the parties before closing to give them the opportunity to tell the jury how their arguments and positions connect to the verdict form. Asking only about the factors where the court believes there is a *material* dispute can simplify the verdict form used to ask the jury to make specific findings as to the *Graham* factors. While this could simplify the form, it poses the same risk of a new trial described above. It may be better simply to urge the parties to reach agreement on what the material disputes are. This is the approach contemplated by the Northern District of California's model form.

7.3.4.5 Willfulness

Proving willful infringement has long played a significant role in patent litigation. The Federal Circuit had long held that such proof served as a trigger for enhanced damages and award of attorneys' fees. The Supreme Court's decisions in *Octane Fitness LLC v. Icon Health & Fitness Inc.*, 134 S. Ct. 1749 (2014), and *Halo Electronics, Inc., v. Pulse Electronics, Inc.*, No. 14-1513 (Supreme Court June 3, 2016), loosened, although did not entirely dislodge, that connection. The ramifications for case management remain in flux, although some aspects of the analysis are clearer.

The *Halo* decision reshaped the contours of enhanced damages law. In rejecting the Federal Circuit's "unduly rigid" two-prong test for determining that the Federal Circuit adopted in *In re Seagate Technology, LLC*, 497 F.3d 1360 (Fed. Cir. 2007), the Supreme Court grounds the enhanced damages inquiry in equitable remedies jurisprudence dating back to the nineteenth century. *See Tilghman v. Proctor*, 125 U.S. 136, 143–144 (1888) (characterizing enhanced damages as "vindictive or punitive"); *Topliff v. Topliff*, 145 U.S. 156, 174 (1892) (infringer knowingly sold copied technology of his former employer); *Cincinnati Siemens-Lungren Gas Illuminating Co. v. Western Siemens-Lungren Co.*, 152 U.S. 200, 204 (1894) (requiring some showing of wanton or willful conduct). The Court noted that § 284 "contains no explicit limit or condition" on the award of enhanced damages. The statute merely states that the court "may increase the damages up to three times the amount found or assessed." The Court emphasized the centrality of the trial court's discretion.

In so doing, the Supreme Court noted that subjective bad faith alone could warrant award of enhanced damages. The Federal Circuit's second prong of "objective recklessness" unduly limits the trial court's discretion. At the same time, the Court cautioned that "'the channel of discretion [for enhanced damages] ha[s] narrowed'" over the past two centuries, *Halo*, 579 U.S. at ___ (quoting Friendly, *Indiscretion About Discretion*, 31 Emory L.J. 747, 772 (1982)), with the result that "such damages are generally reserved for egregious cases of culpable behavior." *Id.* Thus, damages should not be enhanced in "garden-variety" infringement cases. They are "generally ... reserved for egregious cases typified by willful misconduct," such as "deliberate or wanton" infringement, "malicious pira[cy]," or objective recklessness. Nonetheless, willfulness is not a per se requirement for enhanced damages and enhanced damages need not follow a finding of egregious misconduct. "[C]ourts should continue to take into account the particular circumstances of each case in deciding whether to award damages, and in what amount." *Id.* Willful infringement must be proven by a preponderance of evidence, *id.* at 12, and usually is based on the infringer's knowledge and conduct at the time of infringement, not, for example, the merit of arguments later asserted in litigation, *id.* at 10.

Although the Supreme Court did not expressly address whether there remains any role for the jury in the determination of enhanced damages, the Federal Circuit held in *WBIP, LLC v. Kohler Co.*, __ F.3d __ (Fed. Cir. July 19, 2016), that "[w]e do not interpret [the Supreme Court's decision in *Halo*] as changing the established law that the factual components of the willfulness question should be resolved by the jury." Several of the factors affecting that discretion turn on historical factual predicates that could be disputed.

The *Halo* decision leaves no doubt that the ultimate exercise of discretion is for the trial judge. Thus, even if a jury finds willful infringement, the court may still decide that the conduct is not sufficiently egregious to warrant enhancement of damages. *See WBIP, LLC,* __ F.3d at __, n.13. Furthermore, the amount of any enhancement is for the district judge to decide.

Whether an advisory verdict on willfulness is appropriate (or even helpful to the court), and if so, what guidance to give the jury in making such a determination, remains an open question. But a jury's responses to special interrogatories on underlying issues—for example, whether the defendant's conduct falls within accepted norms in the industry, whether and when the defendant learned of the patent before the lawsuit, and whether the defendant believed in good faith that it did not infringe or the patent was invalid—may in many cases help the court exercise its discretion. Parties will no doubt disagree about the utility and content of such special interrogatories and the instructions that accompany them in many cases.

One further observation bears mention. Balancing providing clear instructions to (and questions for) the jury, on the one hand, with preventing substantial prejudice to the accused infringer, on the other hand, can be difficult. The *Halo* decision is likely to exacerbate this tension. If the court permits the patentee to present willfulness generally, or the facts underlying willfulness, to the jury, it may well be that the simplest and most effective way to balance these issues fairly is to phase or bifurcate willfulness such that it is tried after a jury has reached a verdict on liability.

7.3.4.6 Inducement of Infringement

In 2011, the Supreme Court resolved a long-standing ambiguity in indirect infringement law when it held that "induced infringement under § 271(b) requires knowledge that the induced acts constitute infringement" of the asserted patent. *Global-Tech Appliances, Inc. v. SEB S.A.*, 131 S. Ct. 2060, 2068 (2011). This decision harmonizes the required mental states for both forms of indirect infringement—inducement under § 271(b) and contributory infringement under § 271(c). *Id.* at 2067–68 (discussing its prior decision in *Aro II* and holding that § 271(b) and (c) require the "same knowledge"); *Aro Mfg. Co., Inc. v. Convertible Top Replacement Co., Inc.* (*Aro II*), 377 U.S. 476 (1964) ("[Section] 271(c) does require a showing that the alleged contributory infringer knew that the combination for which his component was especially designed was both patented and infringing."). This standard requires proving that the alleged infringer had a specific intent to induce acts it knew would infringe the asserted patent, as opposed to simply having the intent to induce acts that happen to infringe. The Supreme Court also recognized that the accused infringer, therefore, cannot induce infringement unless it knew of the patent. *Global-Tech*, 131 S. Ct. at 2068.

In reaching this result, the Supreme Court expressly rejected the standard set forth in *DSU Medical Corp. v. JMS Co.*, 471 F.3d 1293 (Fed. Cir. 2006) (en banc). In reviewing the district court decision underlying *Global-Tech*, the Federal Circuit found that "Pentalpha deliberately disregarded a known risk that SEB had a protective patent," and that this was sufficient to satisfy *DSU*'s "knew or should have known" standard. *Global-Tech*, 131 S. Ct. at 2064–65. But the Supreme Court made clear that this standard is not viable: "deliberate indifference to a known risk that a patent exists is not the appropriate standard under § 271(b)." *Id.* at 2068 (describing "should have known" as a simple negligence standard); *see also Commil USA, LLC v. Cisco Sys., Inc.*, 720 F.3d 1361, 1367–68 (Fed. Cir. 2013) (vacating induced infringement verdict where jury instruction included improper language that the jury could find inducement where Cisco "should have known that its actions would induce actual infringement").

In situations where an accused infringer is alleged to have deliberately avoided knowledge of the patent, the Supreme Court found that the appropriate touchstone is the doctrine of "willful blindness." This doctrine varies somewhat between circuits, but all formulations contain "two basic requirements: (1) the defendant must subjectively believe that there is a high probability that a fact exists and (2) the defendant must take deliberate actions to avoid learning of that fact." *Global-Tech*, 131 S. Ct. at 2070.

Regarding requisite specific intent, the Federal Circuit commented that "it is clear that a good-faith belief of noninfringement is relevant evidence that tends to show that an accused inducer lacked the intent required to be held liable for induced infringement." *Commil*, 720 F.3d at 1367–68. The same standard does not, however, apply to a good-faith belief that a patent is invalid. In *Commil USA, LLC v. Cisco Systems, Inc.*, 135 S. Ct. 1920 (2015), the Supreme Court ruled that because induced infringement and validity are separate issues and have separate defenses under the Patent Act, belief regarding validity cannot negate § 271(b)'s scienter requirement of "actively induce[d] infringement." Otherwise, the Act's presumption of validity, § 282(a), would be undermined, permitting circumvention of the high bar—the clear and convincing standard—that defendants must surmount to rebut the presumption.

It is also worth noting that in amending the law governing the use of legal opinions, the AIA not only prevents plaintiffs from using the lack of a legal opinion to show willfulness, but also prevents plaintiffs from arguing that the lack of a legal opinion can be used "to prove . . . that the infringer intended to induce infringement of the patent." § 298. Thus, the absence of an opinion cannot be used to infer the "specific intent" necessary to support a claim of inducing infringement.

Further, *see* § 6.2.1.2.6, where an accused infringer does not itself perform all the steps of an accused method, it cannot be liable for infringement unless it controls or directs performance of each step of the accused method. *Muniauction, Inc. v. Thomson Corp.*, 532 F.3d 1318 (Fed. Cir. 2008) (reversing a jury verdict of infringement). "There can only be joint infringement when there is an agency relationship between the parties who perform the method steps or when one party is contractually obligated to the other person to perform the steps." *Akamai Techs., Inc. v. Limelight Networks, Inc.*, 629 F.3d 1311, 1320 (Fed. Cir. 2010), *rev'd on other grounds*, 692 F.3d 1301 (Fed. Cir. 2012) (en banc) (per curiam), *rev'd*, 134 S. Ct. 2111 (2014). And "a defendant is not liable for inducing infringement under § 271(b) when no one has directly infringed under § 271(a) or any other statutory provision." *Limelight Networks, Inc. v. Akamai Techs., Inc.*, 134 S. Ct. 2111 (2014).

The Northern District of California model jury instructions and the Federal Circuit Bar Association 2016 model jury instructions have been updated to reflect the Supreme Court's decisions in *Global-Tech* and *Akamai*. The Federal Circuit Bar Association's 2016 instructions have also been updated to reflect the Supreme Court's decision in *Commil*.

7.3.4.7 Damages

One of the most vexing issues in patent law is the proper measure of damages. Crafting an appropriate jury instruction on compensatory damages for patent infringement is difficult. The first paragraph of § 284 provides that "the court shall award the claimant damages *adequate to compensate* for the infringement but in no event less than a reasonable royalty for the use made of the invention by the infringer . . ." (emphasis added). Thus, this provision aims to put the patent holder in the financial position it would have enjoyed but for the infringement. It calls for the court to determine the patent holder's lost profits. As the Supreme Court has stated, the question to be asked is: "Had the infringer not infringed, what would the patent holder . . . have made?" *Aro II*, 377 U.S. at 507; *see also Pall Corp. v. Micron Separa-*

tions, Inc., 66 F.3d 1211, 1223 (Fed. Cir. 1995) ("the purpose of compensatory damages is not to punish the infringer, but to make the patentee whole");[2] *State Indus., Inc. v. Mor-Flo Indus., Inc.*, 883 F.2d 1573, 1577 (Fed. Cir. 1989) (damages shall compensate the patentee for its pecuniary loss because of the infringement).

Depending on the circumstances, a patentee's compensatory damages can include: lost direct sales; price erosion (lost profits resulting from the lower price resulting from competition from the infringer); increased costs; and lost "convoyed sales"—parts, accessories, and repair or maintenance services that are functionally related to the patented products. *See generally* § 14.4.3.2. The Federal Circuit has developed exacting standards of proof for lost profits. To establish lost sales, the patent holder must ordinarily prove demand for the patented product, absence of acceptable noninfringing substitutes, manufacturing and marketing capability to exploit the demand, and the amount of per-unit profit. *See Rite-Hite Corp. v. Kelley Co.*, 56 F.3d 1358, 1545 (Fed Cir. 1995) (en banc) (endorsing the test articulated in *Panduit Corp. v. Stahlin Bros. Fibre Works, Inc.*, 575 F.2d 1152 (6th Cir. 1978)).

Owing to relatively strict standards of proof, lost profits can be difficult to establish in practice. Moreover, some entities cannot prove lost sales. Their injury is better characterized as lost licensing revenue. Thus, as an alternative to determining lost profits, § 284 sets a floor for compensatory damages: "in no event [shall the compensatory award be] less than a reasonable royalty for the use made of the invention by the infringer."

In recent years, reasonable royalty jurisprudence has developed rapidly. Analyzing a hypothetical negotiation is the most common, although not the only, way to determine a reasonable royalty. In a typical case, the parties will put forward economic experts to opine on the payment that would have resulted from a hypothetical arms-length negotiation between the patent holder and the infringer prior to the infringing activity. The hypothetical negotiation is based on the assumptions that the patent was valid, would be infringed by the defendant's conduct, and the parties were truly willing and able to negotiate a license. Most often, this testimony examines the wide range of factors set forth in *Georgia-Pacific Corp. v. U.S. Plywood Corp.*, 318 F. Supp. 1116 (S.D.N.Y. 1970).[3]

In theory, reasonable royalty testimony should establish three items: (1) the date of the hypothetical negotiation and when the royalty obligation begins; (2) the royalty base; and (3) the royalty rate per unit (or lump sum amount, where appropriate).[4]

---

2. Pecuniary damages are not meant to punish for infringement because treble damages are available for punishing willful infringement.

3. Not all *Georgia-Pacific* factors apply in every case. In *Ericsson, Inc. v. D-Link Systems, Inc.*, 773 F.3d 1201, 1235 (Fed. Cir. 2014), in a case involving a RAND-encumbered patent, the Federal Circuit noted that "a district court must instruct the jury only on factors that are relevant to the specific case at issue." "There is no *Georgia-Pacific*-like list of factors that district courts can parrot for every case involving RAND-encumbered patents." *Id.*

4. Not all royalty agreements require a rate per unit sold. Some royalty agreements require a fixed payment per unit of time. Such agreements trade flexibility for a guaranteed income stream. They can also be easier to administer and audit. In some fields, such

The jury instruction regarding the date of the hypothetical negotiation is usually relatively straightforward. The royalty base and royalty rate instructions have generated substantial controversy because of concerns about the reliability of economic experts' analysis and juror comprehension.

7.3.4.7.1 Royalty Base

One common dispute concerns the royalty base against which the royalty rate is applied. In cases in which the patented technology represents the primary basis for demand for the defendant's infringing product, such as a pharmaceutical case in which the patent claims a new drug, the reasonable royalty appropriately extends to the accused product's entire revenue. In cases where the patent covers only one component of a multicomponent product, such as one feature of a complex microcomputer, the reasonable royalty determination requires more scrutiny to ensure that the damage award measures the harm to the patent holder attributable to the infringing component or feature and not the contribution from other components of the product, the defendant's good will in the marketplace, and other factors unrelated to the patent. "Where small elements of multi-component products are accused of infringement, calculating a royalty on the entire product carries a considerable risk that the patentee will be improperly compensated for non-infringing components of that product." *LaserDynamics, Inc. v. Quanta Computer, Inc.*, 694 F.3d 51, 67 (Fed. Cir. 2012). Indeed, even where a patentee bases the royalty on the "smallest salable patent-practicing unit," there may still need to be further constraint on the selection of the base. *VirnetX, Inc. v. Cisco Sys., Inc.*, 767 F.3d 1308, 1327 (Fed. Cir. 2014) (holding that where the smallest salable unit is a multicomponent product containing several noninfringing features, the patentee must do more to estimate what portion of the value of that product is attributable to the patented technology). Instead, the requirement that the patentee identify damages associated with the smallest salable patent-practicing unit is simply a step toward meeting the requirement of apportionment. *Id.*

The "entire market value rule" is a "narrow exception" to the general rule. When claims are drawn to an individual component of a multicomponent product, it is the exception, not the rule, that a patentee can recover "damages as a percentage of revenues or profits attributable to the entire product." The exception applies only when the patentee can show that the "patented feature drives the demand for an entire multi-component product." *LaserDynamics*, 694 F.3d at 67–68 (holding that LaserDynamics' use of the entire market value rule was impermissible where patentee did not show that the patented method drove demand for the entire product and that it was not enough to merely show that the method is valuable, important, or even essential to the entire product). "The entire market rule allows for the recovery of damages based on the value of an entire apparatus containing several features, when the feature patented constitutes the basis for customer demand." *Lucent*

---

agreements are more common and may provide the basis for an alternative royalty rate calculation.

Techs., Inc. v. Gateway, Inc., 580 F.3d 1301 (Fed. Cir. 2009) (quoting *TWM Mfg. Co. v. Dura Corp.*, 789 F.2d 895, 901 (1986)) (finding that a $358 million damages award was not supported by substantial evidence and remanding for new trial).

Even in cases in which the accused device incorporates many components beyond the patented technology, patent holders will typically advocate using the entire market value of the defendant's product as the baseline for the reasonable royalty determination. They typically request a general instruction indicating that the patent holder is entitled to a reasonable royalty based on the list of *Georgia-Pacific* factors. *Georgia-Pacific* Factor 13 expressly considers the value of other components in the accused device to the overall market value of the accused device: "The portion of the realizable profit that should be credited to the invention as distinguished from non-patented elements, the manufacturing process, business risks, or significant features or improvements added by the infringer." *Georgia-Pacific Corp. v. U.S. Plywood Corp.*, 318 F. Supp. 1116, 1120 (S.D.N.Y. 1970) (Factor 13). However, simply relegating this important issue to a long list of factors risks placing undue importance on the patented technology in suit relative to the value of other components in the accused device. Essentially, this approach provides the jury with little genuine guidance about how to resolve the battle of the economic experts and can lead to results that defy the economic logic that undergirds real-world licensing negotiations.

In weighing Factor 13, the *Lucent* court observed that "numerous features other than the [accused feature] appear to account for the overwhelming majority of the consumer demand and therefore significant profit." *Lucent*, 580 F.3d at 1333. Consequently, "[t]he only reasonable conclusion that can be drawn" from the factual evidence presented at trial is that the accused feature "is a minor aspect of a much larger software program and that the portion of the profit that can be credited to the infringing use of the [accused feature] is exceedingly small." *Id.*

Further, in *LaserDynamics*, the Federal Circuit emphasized that "the requirement to prove that the patented feature drives demand for the entire product may not be avoided by the use of a very small royalty rate." *LaserDynamics*, 694 F.3d at 67; *see also Uniloc USA, Inc. v. Microsoft Corp.*, 632 F.3d 1292, 1318–21 (Fed. Cir. 2011).

Moreover, "[r]egardless of the chosen royalty rate, one way in which the error of an improperly admitted entire market value rule theory manifests itself is in the disclosure of the revenues earned by the accused infringer associated with a complete product rather than the patented component only." *LaserDynamics*, 694 F.3d at 68 (referring to *Uniloc*, where the disclosure of a $19 billion damages theory based on the entire market value caused unfair prejudice). "Admission of such overall revenues, which have no demonstrated correlation to the value of the patented feature alone, only serve to make a patentee's proffered damages amount appear modest by comparison, and to artificially inflate the jury's damages calculation beyond that which is 'adequate to compensate for the infringement.'" *Id.* It is also important, therefore, to take care to avoid misleading the jury by placing undue emphasis on the value of the entire product, over the value of the infringed feature.

To ensure that the jury appreciates the narrow "entire market value rule" exception, the Court should educate the jury about the importance of evaluating the relationship between the accused feature and other aspects of the commercial product or service in its instructions in determining the value of that feature. The Northern District of California Model Patent Jury Instructions provide a helpful example. The Model Instruction that explains a reasonable royalty states in relevant part:

> If the patent covers only part of the product that the infringer sells, then the base would normally be only that feature or component. For example, if you find that for a $100 car, the patented feature is the tires which sell for $5, the base revenue would be $5. However, in a circumstance in which the patented feature is the reason customers buy the whole product, the base revenue could be the value of the whole product. Even if the patented feature is not the reason for customer demand, the value of the whole product could be used if, for example, the value of the patented feature could not be separated out from the value of the whole product. In such a case, however, the rate resulting from the hypothetical negotiation would be a lower rate because it is being applied to the value of the whole product and the patented feature is not the reason for the customer's purchase of the whole product.

N.D. Cal. Model Patent Jury Inst. 5.7 ("Reasonable Royalty—Definition") (June 17, 2014) (*see* Appendix E).

The most recent version of the Federal Circuit Bar Association's Model Instructions (January 2016) take a different approach to making the same point. Speaking of a "reasonable royalty" generally, without calling out the specific issues of rate and base, the instruction simplifies the *Georgia-Pacific* factors into three foundational considerations:

> (1) The value that the claimed invention contributes to the accused product.
> (2) The value that factors other than the claimed invention contribute to [the accused product].
> (3) Comparable license agreements, such as those covering the use of the claimed invention or similar technology.

FCBA Model Instructions § 6.7 (January 2016). In general, this instruction seeks to focus the jury on the core issues by highlighting just three considerations framed in language that is relatively easy to comprehend and apply (in place of the fifteen *Georgia-Pacific* factors, many of which are opaque). The first two considerations guide the jury to consider the relative value and significance of the claimed invention when determining the royalty arising from the alleged infringement.

As the Supreme Court recognized long ago, it would be "very grave error to instruct a jury 'that as to the measure of damages the same rule is to govern, whether the patent covers an entire machine or an improvement on a machine.'" *Seymore v. McCormick*, 57 U.S. 480, 491 (1853); *see also Westinghouse Elec. & Mfg. Co. v. Wagner Co.*, 225 U.S. 604, 614–15 (1912) ("[The] invention may have been used in combination with valuable improvements made, or other patents appropriated by the infringer, and each may have jointly, but unequally contributed to the profits. In such case, if plaintiff's patent only created a part of the profits, he is only entitled to recover that part of the net gains."); *Garretson v. Clark*, 111 U.S. 120, 121 (1884) ("When a patent is for an improvement, and not for an entirely new machine or contrivance, the patentee must show in what particulars his improvement has added to the usefulness of the machine or contrivance. He must separate its results distinctly from those of the other parts, so that the benefits derived from it may be distinctly seen and appreciated. . . . 'The patentee' . . . must in every case give evidence tending to separate or apportion the defendant's profits and the patentee's damages between the patented feature and the unpatented features, and such evidence must be reliable and tangible, and not conjectural or speculative; or he must show, by equally reliable and satisfactory evidence, that the profits and damages are to be calculated on the whole machine, for the reason that the entire value of the whole machine, as a marketable article, is properly and legally attributable to the patented feature.'" (quoting the lower court)). It is incumbent upon the district court to ensure that this important issue is not overlooked.

Another consideration in determining the value of an accused feature is the extent to which that feature could have been replaced with a noninfringing alternative and, if so, the value of that feature over its replacement. The Federal Circuit has recognized the relevance of noninfringing alternatives in the context of reasonable royalty determinations:

> *Shell* also urges that a reasonable royalty may not exceed the cost savings between its proposed non-infringing alternative installation . . . and the patented method. . . . Upon remand, the district court is free to entertain additional evidence by the parties on this fact issue in its re-determination of the damage award. The trial court may also consider any other evidence about non-infringing alternatives.

Riles v. Shell Exploration & Prod. Co., 298 F.3d 1302, 1313 (Fed. Cir. 2002). Yet this critical consideration, too, can be difficult for a jury to appreciate in the context of the long list of *Georgia-Pacific* factors.

The following supplemental instruction ensures against this oversight by explaining the significance of noninfringing alternatives in determining the value of the accused feature:

> [Patent holder] claims a reasonable royalty based on [alleged infringer's] sales of the [accused device/system] rather than sales of the [component] in the [accused device/system]. In these circumstances, a reasonable royalty should reflect the portion of the revenue from sales of the [accused device/system] that result from the improvement provided by the [xxx] patent over alternatives to the patented technology available to the [alleged infringer] at the time that the infringement began.

Where the patentee has claimed both a component and the previously known apparatus or system in which it is used, the instruction should direct the jury to the patented improvement, as explained typically in the patent specification or prosecution history.

This supplemental language should be used to augment the court's general instructions regarding reasonable royalty. *See, e.g.*, Model Patent Jury Instructions for the Northern District of California, Instruction 5.7 (Reasonable Royalty—Definition) (June 17, 2014) (*see* Appendix E). We note that this specific language regarding noninfringing alternatives has not been formally adopted in any model jury instructions. Nonetheless, it comports with general principles of damages apportionment law and the specific concerns emerging in patent cases involving accused devices incorporating multiple technologies and features.

Consistent with these principles, courts should afford defendants adequate leeway to offer evidence relating to prior judgments or to licenses covering attributes of the accused product not covered by the patent(s) in suit, where the defendants can show that there is a basis for comparing their value to the value of the hypothetical license (e.g., the relative value or importance of the accused and non-accused features covered by the licenses, the relative scope of the licenses, or the like). Thus, if the defendant has licensed other technologies in order to bring the accused product to market, then such licenses may bear on the relative value of the accused product attributable to the patent(s) in suit. Courts should also permit the introduction of evidence relating to the value of different components of an accused device to consumers of the product. This can come in the form of direct testimony of customers, survey evidence, and expert testimony from marketing professionals and economists. Such evidence directly addresses Factor 13 of the *Georgia-Pacific* test and helps to determine whether the patented technology in suit or another component or factor drives demand for the accused product.

7.3.4.7.2 Royalty Rate

The Federal Circuit has recognized that estimating a reasonable royalty is not an "exact science," and that there may be more than one reliable method. *Apple Inc. v. Motorola, Inc.*, 757 F.3d 1286, 1315 (Fed. Cir. 2014). "For example, a party may use the royalty rate from sufficiently comparable licenses, value the infringed features based upon comparable features in the marketplace, or estimate the value of the benefit provided by the infringed features by comparing the accused product to non-infringing alternatives." *Id.* Each approach has "strengths and weaknesses," and each approach may be appropriate and may produce admissible testimony depending on the facts of the case. *Id.*

In *Apple*, the Federal Circuit noted that a "fact finder may award no damages only *when the record supports a zero royalty award.*" *Id.* at 1327–28 (emphasis added) (noting that "[i]f a patentee's evidence fails to support its specific royalty estimate, the fact finder is still required to determine what royalty is supported by the record," whereas, if a patentee fails to meet its burden on lost profits, then no award of lost profits is justified).

The Federal Circuit has in recent years substantially enhanced the court's gatekeeping role to ensure that a party's proof of damages is not based on improper "principles and methodology, or legally insufficient facts and data." *Id.* at 1314. The court rejected the use of general, simplistic apportionment rules. *See id.* at 1324–25; *VirnetX, Inc.*, 767 F.3d at 1331–34 (rejecting the Nash Bargaining Solution); *Uniloc*, 632 F.3d at 1312 (rejecting the "25% Rule"). Thus, *Daubert* motions play a substantial role in screening royalty rate methodologies. *See* § 7.4.3.3.2.1.

7.4 Substantive Limitations on Expert Testimony

Critical to managing a patent trial is the court's ability to control expert testimony. Of course, expert testimony of various forms is used in a variety of cases, and hence judges are familiar with both the concerns and the safeguards reflected in Federal Rule of Evidence 702 and the Supreme Court's decision in *Daubert v. Merrell Dow Pharms.*, 509 U.S. 579 (1993). But patent cases present special challenges for at least three reasons. First, because the factual evidence is often technically complex and difficult to understand, juries may place undue weight on expert testimony, especially when it simplifies (or purports to simplify) the issues that the jury has to decide. Second, many of the legal tests used to evaluate liability and damages incorporate—expressly or implicitly—concepts that largely, if not exclusively, depend upon expert testimony. Thus, experts are aggrandized in patent cases in ways not typical of other types of litigation. Finally, as discussed more fully below, the role that experts play in patent cases does not always fit squarely within the Rule 702/*Daubert* framework. Consequently, managing the scope and content of the experts' testimony is a critical component of trial management. This section explores issues that courts are likely to confront when evaluating the proper substantive limits of expert testimony in patent cases.

7.4.1 The Role of Experts in Patent Cases

Expert testimony in patent cases may be categorized into at least two distinct types. One, common to most other types of litigation, involves applying an accepted technical or scientific methodology to facts established during the trial to reach conclusions about factual issues. An expert might testify, for example, about the results of her analysis to determine the chemical composition of the accused product. Because this type of testimony is directed to an analysis that the expert regularly performs outside of a litigation context, it falls squarely within the Federal Rule of Evidence 702/*Daubert* framework. Consequently, it presents few distinctive or novel issues and should be familiar to the court.

The second type of testimony presents more challenges. In patent cases, an expert is often asked to use her scientific, technical, or specialized knowledge to evaluate a hypothetical legal construct. For example:

- Who is a "person having ordinary skill in the art"?
- Would a "person having ordinary skill in the art" believe at the time of alleged infringement that differences between the patent claim and the accused product are "insubstantial"?
- At the time the patent application was originally filed, would a "person having ordinary skill in the art" have had a motivation to combine known ideas to create the claimed invention? (Note that, although a patent challenger is not required to show that one of ordinary skill in the art would have had a specific motivation to combine prior art references, such a showing may be helpful to the obviousness analysis. *See KSR*, 550 U.S. at 418; § 14.3.5.2.)
- What royalty rate would the patentee and the infringer have agreed upon had they participated in a negotiation at the time of first infringement knowing that the patent was valid and infringed?

Obviously, it is more difficult for a court to perform its gatekeeping function effectively when this type of testimony is at issue. Because it reflects a hypothetical le-tion 4.3b (Alternative 1) and Sample Verdict Form § F (Alternative 1). *See* Appendix E.

Of course, courts remain free to seek an advisory verdict from the jury. The Northern District of California Model Patent Jury Instruction 4.3b (Alternative 2) and Sample Verdict Form § F (Alternative 2) provide this option. If the traditional advisory verdict approach is taken, however, courts should not rely on pre-*KSR* jury instructions. *KSR* criticized pre-2007 Federal Circuit decisions in the area of obviousness and effected a substantial change in the law. Both the Northern District of California and Federal Circuit Bar Association Model Patent Jury Instructions have been updated to reflect the *KSR* decision. Another is the Patent Office's detailed set of guidelines describing how to evaluate obviousness under *KSR*. 72 Fed. Reg. 57526-57535 (Oct. 10, 2007). These guidelines explain the law in a more operational manner and provide seven different rationales that can be used to support a finding of obviousness as well as the factual elements needed to support each of the seven rationales. They also provide examples of actual cases finding obviousness under each of the seven rationales. *See* § 14.3.5.3.5 (Tables 14.5–14.8) (reproducing the PTO's charts). While the Patent Office's guidelines cannot be directly used as jury instructions, they are a useful resource for crafting instructions. Whatever instruction is adopted, it needs to reflect *KSR*'s mandate that an "expansive and flexible" approach be employed.

If the advisory verdict approach is taken, courts should carefully consider the structure of the verdict form. If the verdict form merely asks for the final conclusion on obviousness without specifying its underlying factual determinations, it can be difficult or impossible to understand what the advisory verdict implies. This can hinder the court's ability to perform its duty of reaching a conclusion regarding obviousness. Moreover, it can easily create a need for a new trial, especially if the jury's decisions on the *Graham* factors (the factual underpinnings of obviousness) cannot be discerned from the verdict. *See, e.g., Agrizap, Inc. v. Woodstream Corp.*, 520 F.3d 1337, 1343 n.3 (Fed. Cir. 2008); *see also Wyers v. Master Lock Co.*, 616 F.3d 1231, 1248 (Fed. Cir. 2010) (Linn, J. concurring) ("To facilitate review and reveal more clearly the jury's underlying factual findings, this Court has encouraged trial court judges to provide juries with special interrogatories on obviousness."). This risk is mitigated, however, by the court's general practice when faced with a verdict in which the jury was not asked to answer special interrogatories. The court presumes the existence of factual findings necessary to support the jury's verdict. *See Wyers*, 616 F.3d at 1248 (Linn, J., concurring).

> Our review of a general verdict on obviousness thus entails two steps. We first presume that the jury resolved the underlying factual disputes in favor of the verdict winner and leave those presumed findings undisturbed if they are supported by substantial evidence. Then we examine the legal conclusion de novo to see whether it is correct in light of the presumed jury fact findings.

Id. (quotations omitted); *see also Kinetic Concepts, Inc. v. Smith & Nephew, Inc.*, 688 F.3d 1342, 1367 (Fed. Cir. 2012) ("Significantly, whether there is a reason to combine prior art references is a question of fact . . . [and] [i]n light of the jury's verdict, we must assume that it determined there was no reason to combine the prior art refergal construct, it necessarily departs from the type of generally accepted, peer-reviewed methodology contemplated by Federal Rule of Evidence 702 and *Daubert*. This second type of expert testimony forms the bulk of expert testimony in patent cases. As a result, the majority of issues discussed in this section arise from this type of analysis.

7.4.2 Timing and Procedure: When and How Should the Court Exercise Its Gatekeeping Role?

The first step for the court to take in managing expert testimony in patent cases is to decide when to exercise its gatekeeping role and the process by which to do so. Although many courts permit parties to raise *Daubert* challenges in summary judgment or *in limine* motions, courts are most effective when they establish a separate mechanism for resolving *Daubert* challenges.

One problem with addressing *Daubert* issues as part of summary judgment or *in limine* briefing is that neither provides an adequate means for fleshing out the record on the factual and legal issues relevant to the sufficiency of expert testimony. Summary judgment briefing is inadequate for this purpose because there is little overlap between either the facts or the legal standards for deciding summary judgment and *Daubert* issues. Because both issues are substantial, there typically is not room in a summary judgment brief to do justice to both. The *Daubert* challenge usually gets short shrift: either as a conclusory statement, paragraph, or section tacked on to justify the court overlooking what might otherwise be a question of fact created by expert testimony; or as a series of essentially thematic statements that seek to underscore the purported flaws in the opposing party's position, but nevertheless fail to assist the court because they do not squarely address the legal standard for excluding the expert's opinions.

Dealing with *Daubert* issues at the *in limine* stage presents different challenges, but usually reaches the same result: an insufficient record for thoughtful analysis. *In limine* motions reflect the harried environment in which they are prepared and decided. Briefing is typically sparse and argument short. Although this provides an efficient way to resolve simple evidentiary disputes, it is not an effective way to resolve the more complicated issues presented by a *Daubert* challenge. At a minimum, the court should have thorough, summary-judgment-length briefs from each party, but even this may not be enough in some cases. The court may also need to hear directly from the expert during an evidentiary hearing. This is true whether the motion is styled as a *Daubert* motion or, as is often the case, as a motion *in limine* asking the court to preclude an expert from testifying for a purportedly simple, straightforward reason that, when considered carefully, implicates an issue related to reliability. *See, e.g.*, discussion of conclusory expert opinions in § 7.4.3.3.1.

A more effective way for courts to consider these issues is to include a specific briefing/hearing schedule for *Daubert* motions in its case-management order. *See* §§ 2.4, 2.6.6. The schedule should be timed such that the motions are filed after experts are deposed on their reports, but well before the pretrial conference. Many courts hear *Daubert* challenges at the same time as, but separate from, summary judgment motions. Timing the briefing and hearing this way will ensure that a full record is available, but also give the court adequate time to consider the merits of each challenge.

In addition, early consideration of *Daubert* challenges prevents the risk of a party being denied any expert at trial, which in some circumstances can be a harsh sanction for a correctable error. For example, discussed in § 7.4.3.3.2.1.3, a common *Daubert* challenge to a damages expert is based on an alleged incorrect date for the hypothetical negotiation for the determination of a reasonable royalty. Determining that date can be challenging, not only because it depends on technical information related to infringement that is usually beyond the purview of damages experts, but also because the trial court's summary judgment rulings can have a profound effect on that date. So it can happen that while a damages expert's *methodology* can be perfectly adequate, the *factual basis* for the analysis is incorrect as a matter of law. Of course, once informed by the court's summary judgment rulings, the expert can revise her analysis to include the correct information, so if the question is raised through an *in limine* motion on the eve of trial, it may seem unjust to grant the motion and strike the expert. Because of scenarios like this one, and because *Daubert* issues are usually known to the parties through expert reports and depositions well in advance of trial, resolving *Daubert* challenges well before the pretrial conference is good practice.

Expert opinions regarding damages warrant special mention in this context. As discussed in § 2.6.6, district courts frequently wrestle with complex issues related to the reliability and admissibility of damages-related opinions. A variety of factors generate frequent challenges to damages-related theories and evidence, and lead those disputes to be raised with the court at the very end of the case:

- Damages law is evolving rapidly, which generates disputes about the viability of damages theories and expert methodologies.
- Unlike the typical expert opinion on patent liability issues, damages opinions implicate and can draw from economic, mathematical, and financial valuation methodologies that are peer-reviewed and testable, as well as industry experience in patent valuation in the licensing and acquisition context. The interplay between this body of established non-patent-litigation valuation methodologies and the *Georgia-Pacific* factors commonly used to calculate damages in patent cases creates myriad disputes.
- Neither patent local rules nor case-management orders typically require disclosure of damages contentions, as is done with infringement and invalidity.
- Parties tend to focus less extensively on theory development and discovery for damages than they do on liability issues.
- Challenges to damages theories most often come in the form of *Daubert* motions, which are filed after the close of all discovery and, unfortunately, in some instances contemporaneously with motions *in limine*.

As noted, such disputes are almost always raised with the court at the end of the case. As a result, a court that believes that an expert's opinions may not be reliable is typically faced with imperfect options: (1) excluding the expert and leaving the party with no expert testimony regarding damages at trial; (2) continuing the trial date and providing the party proffering the expert a do-over; or (3) allowing the testimony, despite the court's reservations, with the belief that the jury will see the weakness in the opinions and the intent that, if not, the court will correct the outcome through remittitur, JMOL, or a motion for new trial. In our experience, most courts take the third option (allowing the opinion at trial with the intent to address deficiencies later). Unfortunately, while there are some notable examples of district courts overturning high damages awards based on inadequate expert opinions (*see, e.g.*, *Mirror Worlds LLC v. Apple, Inc.*, 784 F. Supp. 2d 703 (E.D. Tex. 2011)), courts that opt for this approach are too often uncomfortable correcting reliability problems with an expert's trial testimony in view of a jury verdict. In most situations, the second option (excluding the opinions but allowing a new report) is the fairest of these imperfect options. However, courts that follow this path should in most circumstances give the party one chance, and no more, to correct the deficiencies so as to prevent abuse. Allowing multiple do-overs encourages parties to game the system, drains judicial and party resources, and wreaks havoc on the trial schedule.

Of course, the best course is to avoid these problems by resolving the disputes that lead to *Daubert* challenges to damages opinions earlier in the litigation process. Section 2.6.6 discusses some case-management tools that may be used to identify and resolve challenges to damages theories and evidence earlier in the case.

7.4.3 Specific Substantive Limitations on Expert Testimony

This section explores substantive limitations on expert testimony that either arise from the unique attributes of a patent case or have a significant or unusual impact on patent cases. Motions invoking these limitations typically fall into one of three broad categories: (1) they allege that the expert opinions are directed to improper subject matter; (2) they allege that the expert is unqualified to render the opinion in question; or (3) they allege that the expert's analysis is insufficiently reliable to be admissible under Federal Rule of Evidence 702.

7.4.3.1 Improper Subject Matter

Motions to preclude expert testimony directed at "improper" subject matter, which commonly arise when experts offer opinions about the research and development (R&D) leading to the patent or the prosecution of the application, usually make one of two allegations: (1) that the expert improperly speculates about what another person was thinking at a given time; or (2) that the expert is giving an opinion on a matter of law, which usurps the role of the judge. Each of these bases presents distinct issues for the court to consider.

7.4.3.1.1 State of Mind of Another Person, Usually an Inventor, Prosecutor, or Examiner

An objection that an expert improperly speculates about what another person thought, believed, or knew most frequently arises when an expert gives an opinion about why the inventor took a particular course of action during the R&D that led to the patent-in-suit. Perhaps the most common example is where an expert offers opinions that an inventor was motivated by a particular goal or found some aspect of the research particularly challenging. A less common, but real-world example is that an expert might review documents describing the inventor's field of study and then offer an opinion that the inventor would have known that a particular laboratory had expertise in that field. This issue also arises in expert testimony about patent prosecution. For example, an expert might offer opinions about why a prosecutor elected not to submit a reference or why an examiner cited or did not cite a piece of prior art when that information is not stated explicitly in the prosecution history.

The moving party generally argues that the expert is simply speculating about the state of mind of the inventor, prosecutor, or examiner. As a result, the opinion is not based on scientific, technical, or specialized knowledge and is not the proper basis for an opinion. Indeed, it is an argument that a lawyer, not an expert, should make. If asserted as fact, it should be presented through a witness with personal knowledge, such as the prosecutor or inventor himself. In response, the party offering the testimony typically argues that the expert does not seek to offer an opinion as to what the inventor, examiner, or prosecutor actually thought. Instead, the expert is opining, based on her expertise in the relevant field, what was typical or standard practice for someone in that situation to do.

The court should evaluate this type of motion on a case-by-case basis. Whether the testimony is appropriate will depend in part upon whether the expert stops short of testifying about what the inventor, examiner, or prosecutor actually believed. If so, the court should also evaluate whether knowledge about the standard practice among similarly situated people will help the jury answer the question at hand or inappropriately distract the jury and affect the result for an inappropriate reason.

7.4.3.1.2 Matters of Law

This type of objection to expert testimony arises when the expert intends to testify about what legal requirements apply to a particular person or situation. Most commonly, this occurs when an expert testifies about the prosecution of the patent in suit. For example, the expert might seek to inform the jury that the law requires a prosecutor to disclose all material prior art of which she is aware. The expert may wish to testify about the standard for materiality. Although most common in connection with testimony about patent prosecution, this issue may arise in other contexts as well. For example, an expert might attempt to offer testimony that a class of conduct is legally actionable by stating that offering a warranty on a product sold before the patent issued can constitute active inducement of infringement.

The moving party typically argues that an opinion about the state of the law inappropriately usurps the role of the judge, whose duty it is to instruct the jury about the law. Because the moving party is correct that an expert generally may not testify about the state of the law, *see, e.g.*, *Hygh v. Jacobs*, 961 F.2d 359, 363–64 (2d Cir. 1992); *United States v. Wilson*, 133 F.3d 251, 265 (4th Cir. 1997); *Aguilar v. Int'l Longshoremen's Union Local 10*, 966 F.2d 443, 447 (9th Cir. 1992); *United States v. Brodie*, 858 F.2d 492, 496 (9th Cir. 1988), the party offering the testimony typically argues that the expert is offering testimony about a permissible subject, such as Patent Office practice and procedure. *See, e.g.*, *Buckley v. Airshield Corp.*, 116 F. Supp. 2d 658, 662 (D. Md. 2000). If the court determines that the proffered opinion purports to set forth the governing law, it should exclude the testimony.

7.4.3.2 Inadequate Qualifications

Challenges to an expert's credentials typically present the same issues in a patent case that they do in any other case. As a result, most issues related to these motions do not merit special treatment in patent litigation. But one patent-specific issue does arise with some frequency: whether a technical expert must have experience in the specific technology that is accused of infringement. For example, in a case in which a certain type of car door is the subject of the infringement claim, the expert may have a Ph.D. in mechanical engineering and computational and applied mathematics, but no experience in the automotive industry and no experience designing car doors. Should the expert be precluded from testifying on aspects of automotive door design?

The movant will typically argue that although the expert may have education, training, and experience that qualifies her as an expert in other fields, her lack of experience with the accused technology prevents her from having the specialized knowledge necessary to offer reliable opinions about the accused products. The party offering the expert will usually argue that experience with the accused technology is not a per se requirement, and that the witness's education and training—although not specific to the accused product—provide the requisite foundation for the opinion. This issue, the argument goes, should be directed to the weight that the jury gives to the testimony, not its admissibility.

Although experience with the technology at issue is not a per se requirement, it may be necessary to provide a foundation for the opinions being proffered in some cases. *Compare Tormenia v. First Investors Realty Co., Inc.*, 251 F.3d 128, 136 (3d Cir. 2000), *with United States v. Marler*, 614 F.2d 47, 50 (5th Cir. 1980). Consequently, the specific opinions that the expert intends to offer should determine the outcome. For example, the expert with a Ph.D. in mechanical engineering mentioned above may be sufficiently qualified to compare the mechanical aspects of the accused door with the patent claims, but may not have the requisite knowledge to testify about manufacturing standards applicable in the automotive industry. Thus, the court will need to resolve this issue on a case-by-case basis, above all by applying its common sense to determine whether the expert has sufficient foundation to offer the opinions in question.

7.4.3.3 Unreliable Analysis

The third category of disputes about the substantive admissibility of expert opinions centers on whether the analysis leading to the opinions was reliable. Generally, the party challenging the expert's opinion makes one of two assertions: (1) that the expert's opinion is conclusory or (2) that the expert misapplied an accepted methodology. The first type of motion most often arises with technical experts; the latter with damages experts, survey experts, and those testing or analyzing accused products.

7.4.3.3.1 Conclusory Expert Opinions

Disputes about conclusory expert opinions often take the form of motions *in limine* that seek to preclude a technical expert from offering an opinion about a general issue because the expert provided only a conclusory opinion about that issue in the expert's report. Motions of this nature are most commonly filed to exclude opinions about obviousness and infringement under the doctrine of equivalents. The "conclusory" opinions sought to be excluded typically take one of two forms. One is a bald statement at the beginning or end of the expert's report offering the expert's conclusion about the ultimate issue, such as the following, after a discussion of literal infringement:

> Moreover, to the extent that there are any differences between the accused product and Claim 1, they are insubstantial and the accused products infringe under the doctrine of equivalents.

The other is an opinion that, although addressing a specific claim element and product, does no more than parrot an accepted test for determining the ultimate issue, such as the following:

> Although Claim 1 requires "a layer" that performs both functions, the combination of two layers in the accused product achieves substantially the same functions in substantially the same way to achieve substantially the same result as would a single layer.

In both cases, the opinion sought to be excluded is usually preceded or followed by a discussion of the general technology of the patent-in-suit, a discussion of the accused product (or asserted prior art reference), and a detailed discussion of literal infringement (or of anticipation), but there is no other mention of equivalents (or obviousness).

The moving party typically argues that the only discussion in the expert report related to equivalents (or obviousness) is a single conclusory opinion such as the ones set forth above. As a result, it is impossible to determine the basis for or test the reliability of the expert's conclusions. Citing a wealth of case law, the party argues that the conclusory opinion is insufficient. *See, e.g., Dynacore Holdings Corp. v. U.S. Philips Corp.*, 363 F.3d 1263, 1278 (Fed. Cir. 2004). Because conclusory opinions devoid of analysis are indeed inadmissible, the party offering the testimony usually counters that the statement is merely a summary of the conclusion, which is based on the detailed discussions found elsewhere in the report.

To evaluate this dispute in the context of the doctrine of equivalents, the court should keep in mind the differences between an analysis of literal infringement (where the test is whether the claim limitation matches the accused instrumentality exactly) and of infringement under the doctrine of equivalents (where the test is whether the differences between the claim limitation and the accused instrumentality are insubstantial—typically measured by whether one skilled in the art would consider them to be interchangeable, or whether they perform substantially the same function, substantially the same way, to achieve substantially the same result). Because the tests are different, an expert opinion discussing why the claim limitation matches exactly the accused instrumentality often does not, but may in some cases, provide foundation for a conclusion that any differences are (or are not) insubstantial.

To evaluate this dispute in the obviousness context, the court should likewise keep in mind the differences between an analysis of anticipation (where the test is whether a single prior art reference discloses all the limitations of a claim exactly) and obviousness (where the test is whether a single reference fails to disclose every element, but nevertheless, by itself or in combination with other references, renders the specific claimed combination of limitations obvious to one of ordinary skill in the art at the time of invention, in view of the *Graham* factors and *KSR*). *See* § 14.3.5.

Opinions discussing literal infringement typically do not contain the additional material necessary to support a doctrine of equivalents opinion, because that additional subject matter is not, in most cases, germane to whether or not the literal infringement test is satisfied. An expert who elects not to include that material in a separate doctrine of equivalents opinion typically also elects not to include it in the literal infringement opinions. Likewise, the differing standards means that an opinion seeking to establish anticipation by showing the disclosure of each claim element in a prior art reference does not need to include the types of information pertinent to evaluating obviousness. Experts who do not address the underlying factors in detail in their obviousness opinions also typically do not address that subject matter in their anticipation opinions. Practices vary widely, however, from expert to expert and, even with the same expert, from case to case, so the court must assess for each dispute whether the specific opinions in question provide the requisite foundation for the proffered conclusion.

As this discussion illustrates, this type of motion generally requires more than a cursory review of the expert's report and provides a good example of why *in limine* motion practice is not a good vehicle for deciding *Daubert* issues. Although seldom styled as a *Daubert* motion, this dispute implicates the court's gatekeeping role under Federal Rule of Evidence 702. Indeed, the court must determine whether the other sections of the report reflect the reliable implementation of a reliable methodology that provides a foundation for the challenged opinion. Instead of a thorough analysis of these sections under Rule 702 and *Daubert*, the court is almost always presented with a bare excerpt from the report, a few stern quotations from the Federal Circuit, and no time to dig deeper before deciding the motion. An effective strategy for addressing this issue is for the court to set a separate briefing schedule for *Daubert* motions. In any event, the outcome should be determined on a case-by-case basis and will depend on whether the other sections of the report do, indeed, support the opinion alleged to be conclusory.

7.4.3.3.2 Unreliability of the Methodology or Its Application

Although disputes of this nature could arise with respect to any expert, they most commonly arise in patent cases in connection with the computation of damages. *See generally* § 14.4.3.2. Consequently, all of the examples discussed here relate to methods for calculating damages. The law requires that a patentee be awarded damages "adequate to compensate for infringement, but in no event less than a reasonable royalty for the use made of the invention by the infringer." § 284. In practice, this means damages based on a "reasonable royalty" will be an issue in almost every patent case because a "reasonable royalty" is the "floor below which damage awards may not fall." *Rite-Hite Corp. v. Kelley Co.*, 56 F.3d 1358, 1544 (Fed. Cir. 1995) (en banc). Expert testimony supporting a reasonable royalty analysis raises two clusters of issues. The first cluster concerns the methodology used to calculate the royalty; the second concerns the scope of the base to which the royalty rate is applied. In addition, a growing number of cases use surveys to establish the value of an accused feature and to show the volume of use for purposes of establishing direct infringement by third parties that underlies a claim of indirect infringement or proving damages, among other reasons. Because the surveys are litigation-driven and often involve modifications to peer-reviewed methodologies or limited or allegedly non-representative sample sizes, experts proffering opinions based on such surveys are commonly the subject of *Daubert* challenges. For general background on survey methodology, see Shari Seidman Diamond, *Reference Guide on Survey Research, in* Reference Manual on Scientific Evidence 361 (Federal Judicial Center and National Research Council of the National Academies, 3d ed. 2011).

7.4.3.3.2.1 Misapplication of the *Georgia-Pacific* Factors

Courts have generally accepted the multifactor analysis set forth in *Georgia-Pacific*, 318 F. Supp. at 1120, as the framework for calculating a reasonable royalty. *See, e.g.*, *Fromson v. W. Litho Plate & Supply Co.*, 853 F.2d 1568 (Fed. Cir. 1988), *overruled on other grounds by Knorr-Bremse Systeme Fuer Nutzfahrzeuge GmbH v. Dana Corp.*, 383 F.3d 1337, 1343 (Fed. Cir. 2004). Under this framework, the proffered expert attempts to determine what the royalty would have been had the parties conducted a negotiation at the time of first infringement, with both parties willing to enter into a license, having knowledge that the patent was valid and infringed. (The negotiation is, of course, hypothetical and counterfactual, as the existence of the suit shows.) *Georgia-Pacific* (*GP*) lays out fifteen factors to be considered as part of this hypothetical negotiation. Because the framework is so widely used, most *Daubert* challenges to expert opinions on damages stem from a purported misapplication of the *GP* factors.

Indeed, damages issues are heavily fact-dependent and are far from one-size-fits-all. It takes significant effort on the part of each party and experts to find and use the proper data, analyses, and damages framework that fits the available facts and that properly falls within the bounds of the legal requirements. *See, e.g.*, *Apple Inc. v. Motorola, Inc.*, 757 F.3d 1286, 1315–26 (Fed. Cir. 2014) (except for one minor exception, reversing the district court's exclusion of proposed damages testimony, noting that "estimating a 'reasonable royalty' is not an exact science," that there may be more than one reliable method, and that "one approach may better account for one aspect of a royalty estimation does not make other approaches inadmissible"); *ResQNet.com, Inc. v. Lansa, Inc.*, 594 F.3d 860, 870–72 (Fed. Cir. 2010) (vacating a damages award where expert had relied on re-bundling licenses that had no relationship to the claimed invention and finding that in this instance the most reliable licenses arose out of litigation, whereas in most other occasions, the court had found that litigation itself could skew the results of the hypothetical negotiation).

7.4.3.3.2.1.1 Consideration of Factors Not Specified in *Georgia-Pacific*

Although application of the fifteen *GP* factors is nearly universal, some experts rely on other factors in some cases. For example, an expert with years of licensing experience in a particular industry may elect to consider additional factors used in that industry when calculating a reasonable royalty for patents in that industry. As another example, if the patent-in-suit was purchased from the patentee by the plaintiff, an expert might consider the value attributed to that patent during the acquisition. Alternatively, an expert might offer an opinion that takes into consideration the cost to design around the patent, the cost of removing the infringing feature from the accused product, the value attributed to the technology by respondents to marketing surveys, or myriad other factors.

When an expert does this, the opposing party often seeks to exclude the opinion on the basis that the expert departed from the accepted methodology by considering additional factors. The party offering the testimony usually counters that the specific factors outlined in *GP* are an accepted, *but not required*, tool for evaluating the outcome of a hypothetical negotiation. Indeed, the *GP* factors are not exclusive. *Georgia-Pacific*, 317 F. Supp. at 1120. If the expert can provide information that shows that the additional factor considered is generally accepted as relevant to valuation and was reliably applied in this instance, the court should allow the opinion. *See, e.g.*, *Apple*, 757 F.3d at 1315 ("a party may . . . estimate the value of the benefit provided by the infringed features by . . . comparing the accused product to non-infringing alternatives") (citations omitted); *Open Text S.A. v. Box, Inc.*, 2015 U.S. Dist. LEXIS 8783, 2015 WL 393858, *3–4 (N.D. Cal. Jan. 29, 2015) (citing and distinguishing *Mars, Inc. v. Coin Acceptors, Inc.*, 527 F.3d 1359, 1373 (Fed. Cir. 2008)) (allowing expert opinion regarding noninfringing alternative and noting that "*Mars* is not a blanket prohibition on expert testimony about non-infringing alternatives as a damages measure. As the Federal Circuit has held [in *Apple*] . . . basing a reasonable royalty estimate on the cost of implementing non-infringing alternatives is an allowable methodology . . . . That *Mars* only forbids 'courts, not experts, imposing caps based on expected profits as a matter of law' is a reading endorsed by other district courts.").

7.4.3.3.2.1.2 Selective Use of the *Georgia-Pacific* Factors

Similarly, experts often combine several of the *GP* factors or decline to apply one or more factors in a given case. The issue is essentially the same—*GP* provides the core framework and factors that may be used in evaluating a royalty within that framework, but there is no express requirement that every factor be applied in every case. In considering a motion brought on this ground, the court should evaluate the totality of the analysis to determine whether it reflects the overall framework, rather than evaluate the expert's consideration (or lack of consideration) of each factor in isolation.

7.4.3.3.2.1.3 Use of an Incorrect Date for the Hypothetical Negotiation

Another commonly brought motion seeks to exclude an expert opinion on the grounds that the expert used the wrong date for the hypothetical negotiation. This most often arises where multiple patents are asserted. For example, a common approach when multiple patents are at issue is to assume that the royalty for all patents is determined during a single negotiation that occurred at the time of first infringement of the earliest-infringed patent. This is especially true when the patents are part of the same patent family.

The movant usually argues either that the expert's use of an incorrect date conflicts with the legal standard or that it renders the analysis unreliable. Of course, the party offering the testimony disagrees, arguing that it is the jury's province to determine which of the factual scenarios that undergird the expert's analysis is more accurate. Thus, the issue goes to weight, not admissibility. The non-movant usually has the better argument. If the expert can identify a plausible explanation for the date selected that is consistent with the flexible hypothetical construct (e.g., the opinion covers a multiple-patent scenario, or reflects one party's contention about when infringement began), then the motion should be denied. *See Brunswick Corp. v. United States*, 46 U.S.P.Q.2d 1446 (Fed. Cir. 1998) (unpublished). In the case where the date used bears no logical relationship to the date of first infringement, however, the court should grant the motion. *See Unisplay, S.A. v. Am. Elec. Sign Co., Inc.*, 69 F.3d 512, 518 (Fed. Cir. 1995); *Hanson v. Alpine Valley Ski Area, Inc.*, 718 F.2d 1075, 1079 (Fed. Cir. 1983) ("the key element in setting a reasonable royalty . . . is the necessity for return to the date when infringement began").

7.4.3.3.2.1.4 Use of Facts that Post-Date the Hypothetical Negotiation

A fourth frequently filed motion concerns the extent to which experts can rely on events that occurred after the date of first infringement in their analysis of the *GP* factors. The movant typically contends that the analysis is legally deficient or unreliable because it relies exclusively or partially on such facts. In response, the party offering the testimony typically argues that considering the post-infringement facts is helpful and sometimes necessary to ensure that the result of the hypothetical negotiation does not stray too far from actual events. Here, both parties can have legitimate points and the resolution depends on a subtle distinction: the expert must base her opinion on facts that predate the hypothetical negotiation, but may look to post-negotiation facts as a reality check.

In *Fromson v. Western Litho Plate & Supply Co.*, the Federal Circuit discussed the role that facts occurring after the date of the hypothetical negotiation can play in the analysis:

> The methodology encompasses fantasy and flexibility; fantasy because it requires a court to imagine what warring parties would have agreed to as willing negotiators; flexibility because it speaks of negotiations as of the time infringement began, yet permits and often requires a court to look to events and facts that occurred thereafter and that could not have been known to or predicted by the hypothesized negotiators.

853 F.2d 1568, 1575 (1988), *overruled on other grounds by Knorr-Bremse Systeme Fuer Nutzfahrzeuge GmbH v. Dana Corp.*, 383 F.3d 1337, 1343 (Fed. Cir. 2004). This language in *Fromson* flows from the Supreme Court's discussion of post-infringement facts in *Sinclair Ref. Co. v. Jenkins Petroleum Co.*:

> But a different situation is presented if years have gone by before the evidence is offered. Experience is then available to correct uncertain prophecy. Here is a book of wisdom that courts may not neglect. We find no rule of law that sets a clasp upon its pages, and forbids us to look within. . . . To correct uncertain prophecies in such circumstances is not to charge the offender with elements of value non-existent at the time of his offense. It is to bring out and expose to light the elements of value that were there from the beginning.

289 U.S. 689, 697 (1933). Nevertheless, an expert is not free to disregard entirely the date of first infringement and base her opinion entirely upon post-infringement facts:

> Burns was not discussing what royalty rate a hypothetical negotiation would have yielded *at the time infringement began*. Instead, Burns was testifying to what the parties might arrive *at the time of trial*. Such testimony was not directed to the proper reasonable royalty criteria and therefore cannot support the jury's verdict.

Unisplay, S.A. v. Am. Elec. Sign Co., Inc., 69 F.3d 512, 518 (Fed. Cir. 1995). *See also Hanson*, 718 F.2d at 1081 ("The issue of the infringer's profit is to be determined not on the basis of a hindsight evaluation of what actually happened, but on the basis of what parties to the hypothetical license negotiations would have considered at the time of the negotiations.").

From this medley of pronouncements about the relevance of post-negotiation facts, the conclusion emerges that an expert who uses the hypothetical negotiation framework must ground his or her opinion in facts that would have been known on the date of the hypothetical negotiation, but may also consider post-negotiation facts to color his or her analysis such that it does not depart dramatically from actual events. Thus, if the court finds that the analysis is based primarily or exclusively upon post-negotiation facts, the opinion should be excluded. On the other hand, the opinion should be admitted if the court finds that the expert merely uses post-negotiation facts to supplement his or her analysis of prenegotiation facts.

7.4.3.3.2.2 Use of an Incorrect Base for Damages

Another damages-related dispute that merits discussion concerns the appropriate base from which damages are to be measured. Most commonly, this dispute arises in one of two situations: (1) where the patentee accuses a component of a larger system or product of infringement but seeks a royalty base that includes the entire system or product; or (2) where the patentee seeks to include products sold in connection with the infringing product (allegedly "convoyed sales") in the royalty base. Typically, this dispute takes the form of a motion *in limine* to preclude the patentee from presenting evidence or argument concerning damages based on the entire system or on "convoyed sales."

Some such disputes are not directed at the reliability or helpfulness of expert testimony per se, but rather focus on whether the patentee has a legal basis for seeking damages that extend beyond the infringing component or product. Such disputes are best presented through summary judgment (in cases where the theory has been developed through discovery) or motions *in limine* (in cases where the accused infringer seeks to prevent argument or testimony that has been hinted at, but not developed, through discovery). In other cases, parties seek to challenge the methodology by which an expert apportions the value of an accused feature in a multifeature product and, therefore, raise such issues in a *Daubert* motion.

In its *Lucent* decision, the Federal Circuit held that in the reasonable royalty context, the base can be the entire product so long as the rate accounts for the relative contribution of that feature in comparison with other features. *See* § 7.3.4.7. The Federal Circuit subsequently explained that "consideration of the entire market value of accused products for minor patent improvements simply by asserting a low enough royalty rate" is impermissible. *Uniloc USA, Inc. v. Microsoft Corp.*, 632 F.3d 1292, 1320 (Fed. Cir. 2011). The majority of disputes of this nature in the reasonable royalty context are likely to focus on the methodology or reliability of the analysis and thus to be brought in a *Daubert* motion.

7.4.3.3.2.3 Reliance on a Legally Insufficient Methodology

The principal area in which this is likely to arise in patent cases is with respect to the improper use of "rule of thumb" methodologies, such as use of the so-called "25% Rule" or an inappropriate application of the Nash Bargaining Solution used by some experts in calculating reasonable-royalty damages.

The essence of the "25% Rule" is that a patentee should recover 25% of the profits garnered by the accused infringer from its sale of an accused product. In *Uniloc*, the Federal Circuit held as a matter of law that the "25% Rule" is an unreliable methodology by which to calculate a reasonable royalty:

> This court now holds as a matter of Federal Circuit law that the 25 percent rule of thumb is a fundamentally flawed tool for determining a baseline royalty rate in a hypothetical negotiation. Evidence relying on the 25 percent rule of thumb is thus inadmissible under Daubert and the Federal Rules of Evidence, because it fails to tie a reasonable royalty base to the facts of the case at issue.

632 F.3d at 1315.

The Nash Bargaining Solution suggests that where two persons bargain over a matter, there is a "solution" to the negotiation problem in which each bargainer gets the same money profit, such that they will split 50/50 the incremental profits that are associated with the use of the patented technology. The Federal Circuit rejected this methodology unless the party "sufficiently establish[es] that the premises of the theorem actually apply to the facts of the case at hand," because such use would be an "inappropriate 'rule of thumb.'" *VirnetX*, 767 F.3d at 1332–34 ("The Nash theorem arrives at a result that follows from a certain set of premises. It itself asserts nothing about what situations in the real world fit those premises. Anyone seeking to invoke the theorem as applicable to a particular situation must establish that fit, because the 50/50 profit-split result is proven by the theorem only on those premises.").

In the wake of these cases, two types of disputes are likely to arise. First, a party might assert that an expert is surreptitiously relying on the 25% Rule in his or her analysis. Second, and more commonly, a party might assert that the expert is relying on some other "rule of thumb" (e.g., IBM's historical 1%-per-patent rate) or is applying a methodology in a manner that fails to take the specific facts of the case into account. The misapplication of the Nash Bargaining Solution is the prime, but not only, example—similar criticisms could arise with respect to any methodology if the expert does not tie the methodology or model to the specific facts of the case.

In both types of disputes, the court should evaluate the methodology underlying the expert's opinions, as well as the manner in which the expert applies that methodology. It should consider the Federal Circuit's explicit basis for excluding the expert opinions in *Uniloc* and *VirnetX*: that the "rule of thumb" failed to weigh the specific facts of a given case to reach the royalty that would be reasonable in light of that specific fact pattern. Applying this reasoning, other methodologies—or applications of methodologies—that fail to draw their conclusions from the specific facts of the case at hand should be excluded.

7.4.3.3.2.4 Litigation Surveys

In recent years, it has been more common for a party—typically the patentee—to proffer expert testimony based on a survey conducted specifically for the litigation to support its damages calculation or other contentions. For example, a survey might show the alleged value of the accused feature or the alleged invention, estimate the percentage or overall volume of use of the accused feature or product, or estimate the extent to which a feature drives sales of the product into which it is incorporated. *See, e.g., Lucent*, 580 F.3d at 1333–34. The opposing party often objects to the reliability of the survey on the grounds that it does not comply with generally accepted and peer-reviewed methodologies for conducting surveys. For example, the party opposing the survey may argue that the questions were not properly formulated or balanced, that the process by which responses were tabulated were subjective or were otherwise unreliable, that the sample was not representative, that the sample size was too small, and the like. *See, e.g., Lucent Techs., Inc. v. Microsoft Corp.*, 837 F. Supp. 2d 1107, 1122–24 (S.D. Cal. 2011).

Unlike much of the expert testimony offered in patent cases, survey-based opinions arise from a field with well-documented and peer-reviewed methodologies on which a court can and should rely to evaluate the reliability of the particular survey in question. *See generally* Shari Seidman Diamond, *Reference Guide on Survey Research, in* Reference Manual on Scientific Evidence 361 (Federal Judicial Center and National Research Council of the National Academies, 3d ed. 2011). Moreover, provided that the survey accords with accepted, peer-reviewed methodologies, criticisms of the particular methodology used, the survey design, its reliability, and the conclusions drawn typically go to the weight, not the admissibility, of the survey results. *See, e.g., Microsoft Corp. v. Motorola, Inc.*, 904 F. Supp. 2d 1109, 1120 (W.D. Wash. 2012) (applying Ninth Circuit standards for admissibility of survey material). This principle, however, has limits. Irrational results, especially when presented without a reasonable explanation of the criteria used to design the survey, may in some circumstances be sufficient for exclusion. *See, e.g., Oracle Am., Inc. v. Google, Inc.*, 2012 U.S. Dist. LEXIS 33619, 2012 WL 850705, at *11 (N.D. Cal. Mar. 13, 2012) (excluding conjoint analysis where the expert included three patented features among the seven studied features, failed to include important non-patented features among the seven tested features, and failed to provide any reasonable criteria for the selection). Moreover, simply confirming that the expert reliably applied an accepted, peer-reviewed methodology is not sufficient to determine admissibility—the other requirements for admissibility of expert testimony must also be met. This is especially important to keep in mind, because expert opinions relating to surveys are typically layered—for example, one might have an underlying survey showing how respondents ranked certain tested features (first layer), an opinion interpreting those results and offering a conclusion about the extent to which the tested features drive customer demand (second layer), and an opinion relying on the conclusions about the extent to which the *tested features* drive customer demand to draw conclusions about the extent to which the *patented features* are the basis for consumer demand for the allegedly infringing product (third layer). Even if the first- and second-layer opinions are reliable, the third-layer opinion may not be. For example, valid survey results and valid conclusions about features tested in the survey may not support conclusions about the use, value, or effect on customer demand of the *patented* feature if the features *tested* do not match the features *patented*. As one district court observed:

> At some point, a description of a patent in a survey may vary so much from what is claimed that the survey no longer "relate[s] to any issue in the case" and is "not relevant and, ergo, non-helpful." *Daubert*, 509 U.S. at 591. Such survey evidence would not "help the trier of fact" and therefore must be excluded under Rule 702(a). Moreover, at some point, discrepancies between the scope of the patent claims and the survey questions may be so confusing to the jury as to substantially outweigh the survey's probative value, thus requiring the Court to exclude such material under Rule 403.

Apple Inc. v. Samsung Elecs., Co., 2014 U.S. Dist. LEXIS 24506, 2014 WL 794328 (N.D. Cal. Feb. 25, 2014) (holding, based on the particular facts of the case, that the disparity between the scope of the claims and the scope of the survey questions did not warrant exclusion of the conclusions the expert drew from the survey results).

Thus, a court considering a *Daubert* challenge to "survey opinions" should consider carefully not just the methodology used to conduct the survey, but also whether the conclusions drawn by the survey expert (and experts relying on the opinion of the survey expert) about the data are both consistent with the issues that the survey was designed to measure and genuinely helpful to evaluate the ultimate factual or legal issue in support of which it is proffered. To assist them with this fact-intensive and context-specific exercise, courts should require the party challenging the "survey opinion" to identify what precisely is being challenged (i.e., in the example above, the survey data (first layer), the intermediate conclusions about the tested features (second layer), or the ultimate conclusions about the patented invention (third layer)) and require the party proffering the testimony to identify how precisely the challenged material is proposed to be used.

7.4.4 Motions Seeking to Prevent Lay Witness Opinions and Expert Witness Fact Testimony

Because of the multifaceted role that expert witnesses play in patent cases, it can be difficult to draw the appropriate distinction between a technical expert witness and a technically skilled fact witness, such as an inventor. In addition to her opinions, an expert witness may have personal knowledge of facts relevant to disputed issues. Further complicating trial management, fact witnesses may be just as credentialed as expert witnesses and all too willing to offer their opinions about a multitude of subjects.

To manage this situation, the court should employ a simple guiding principle: the relationship between fact testimony and expert testimony does not change simply because a fact witness has a technical background or the expert witness has personal knowledge of relevant facts. To the extent that the witness has personal knowledge of relevant facts, she may testify about them whether or not they are technical in nature, so long as the fact-witness disclosure requirements are met. She may also testify as to lay witness opinions, but may not offer opinions of an expert nature unless she is disclosed as an expert witness. If a witness is to offer expert opinions at trial, she must satisfy both the disclosure requirements (Fed. R. Civ. P. 26(a)(2)(B) for retained experts, and 26(a)(2)(C) for other witnesses offering expert opinions, including most employee witnesses) and the reliability standards for expert testimony.

7.5 Managing Patent Trials Through Motions *In Limine*

As discussed throughout this guide, active management of patent cases is crucial at every stage of the litigation. But nowhere is such management more important than during a jury trial—just ask a befuddled juror required to apply an infringement analysis to a multiplicity of claims and accused products amid a bewildering set of technical facts. Motions *in limine* provide the court with an opportunity to establish procedures and substantive limitations that will streamline the evidence, shorten the trial, and reduce jury confusion.

Courts should consider a number of questions with respect to each motion:

- Is this a motion that needs to be decided now, or should it wait for additional context and information to be elicited at trial?
- What is the relationship between the substantive issue for which the party seeks to exclude evidence and other substantive issues in the case?
- Is the evidence sought to be excluded potentially relevant to multiple issues?
- Is the motion effectively dispositive?
- Should the motion have been brought at the summary judgment stage?

The court should bear in mind that although substantive to some degree, these motions largely implicate procedural requirements and the balancing test of Federal Rule of Evidence 403. For this reason, some courts choose to hear motions *in limine* at the outset of a trial so that they are better acquainted with the disputes that are likely to arise, and then continue some portion of them until the issues are fleshed out during the course of the proceeding. If the court takes this path, it should admonish counsel to ask for a sidebar before introducing evidence that was the subject of a continued motion. In addition, courts should be wary of simply deferring *all* evidentiary decisions because resolving them during trial can extend and interrupt the proceedings and place additional burdens on the jury.

7.5.1 Maintaining the Integrity of the Infringement/ Validity Framework

Patent cases incorporate a number of legal standards that can be difficult for an advocate to explain and even more difficult for a jury to apply. For example, as discussed in § 14.4.1.4, to determine whether an accused product infringes a particular claim, one must compare each limitation of that claim with the accused product to assess whether the limitation is satisfied, either literally or under the doctrine of equivalents. *See, e.g., Aquatex Indus., Inc. v. Techniche Sols.*, 419 F.3d 1374, 1382 (Fed. Cir. 2005). This analysis must be applied to each accused product and for each claim. In the context of a complex technology, this exercise is virtually guaranteed to confuse at least some members of a jury. No wonder, then, that parties make significant efforts to identify shortcuts to proving infringement and validity.

The first constellation of frequently filed, patent-specific motions arises as a response to these efforts. Typically styled, in whole or in part, as seeking to focus the evidence on the required legal standard, these motions ultimately seek to close shortcuts to proving infringement and invalidity. Because these issues arise in nearly every patent case, a substantial portion of pretrial filings, including motions *in limine*, is often pitched to the court as attempts to require the opposing party to adhere to the proper legal standard. But, of course, not all motions pitched that way actually aim to maintain the integrity of the legal standards. Indeed, they often seek to preclude legitimate evidence relevant to a different issue by contending that it improperly alters the infringement or validity analysis. This section highlights four commonly brought motions implicating these issues.

7.5.1.1 Motion to Bar a Comparison Between the Accused Product and an Embodying Product (or Between Prior Art and an Embodying Product)

This motion is typically brought by the accused infringer to prevent the patentee from comparing the accused product to the patentee's product, but not exclusively so. The movant generally argues that the comparison should be barred under Federal Rule of Evidence 403 because the comparison has no probative value as to infringement, and there is a substantial risk of jury confusion resulting in an improper infringement analysis.

From a substantive standpoint, a party clearly cannot be permitted to argue that a comparison between commercial products shows that the patent is or is not infringed. Of course, no sophisticated litigant would openly offer the comparison for this purpose. Instead, the respondent typically argues that the comparison has probative value for an issue other than infringement. For example, a patentee may argue that the comparison is probative of whether the infringement was willful because it shows that the accused infringer copied the patentee's product. Alternatively, after putting on evidence concerning differences between the accused products and claim limitations, an accused infringer might argue that the comparison will help the jury understand the evidence that has already been presented.

In either case, the risk of confusion is high because it is easier in most cases to compare two products than to compare the product with the often-confusing language of a patent claim. For this reason, allowing comparisons with an embodying product creates an especially high risk of confusion. Thus, at a minimum, the party that wishes to make such a comparison must be instructed that it cannot argue or attempt to imply that the comparison itself bears on infringement. Note that one or both of the parties may appropriately refer to embodying products in other contexts that do not implicate the concerns and potential confusion outlined above. For example, a patentee may refer to a commercial embodiment to argue that the alleged invention was commercially successful, thus rebutting an argument that the alleged invention was obvious. Likewise, an accused infringer may refer to a commercial embodiment to argue that the asserted claims are invalid, because a product or process embodying them was offered for sale in the United States more than a year before the application for the patent was filed.

Because of the risks of confusion, the court should consider deferring its ruling on a motion to exclude a comparison between the accused product and an embodying product until it can fully appreciate the context in which the jury will see the comparison. If the court elects to defer this or any other motion *in limine*, it should impose strict conditions on how the motion will be addressed during trial. For example, it should bar the parties from using the comparison in opening statements, and it should instruct the parties that the dispute over this evidence absolutely will not be addressed in the presence of the jury. Instead, the party offering the evidence should be required to notify the court on the day preceding the trial day when it will offer the evidence. The court should hear the motion before trial begins for that day. If the offering party or the court believes that testimony yet to be elicited will provide relevant context, the court should require the offering party to provide an offer of proof rather than hear the motion in the middle of the trial day. These measures, strictly enforced, will help prevent the disputed evidence from being "inadvertently" elicited in the jury's presence.

7.5.1.2 Motion to Bar Presentation of Embodying Products as Physical Exhibits

A more extreme version of the motion discussed above is to ask the court to bar introduction of the embodying product as a physical exhibit. The movant typically argues that the embodying product should be excluded under Federal Rule of Evidence 403 because it has no probative value for infringement, but this risks confusing the jury and resulting in an improper infringement analysis. The party seeking to offer the embodiment as a physical exhibit typically responds with one of two arguments. One typical argument is that the sample is relevant to an issue other than infringement. For example, a patentee might argue that the physical sample is a prototype corroborating prefiling development work and is thus highly relevant to the patent's priority date, which is in turn relevant to invalidity. Another typical argument is that a physical embodiment will help the jury understand the technology and thus understand the infringement and invalidity issues that it will have to decide.

Even if the embodying product has no legal relevance, this does not mean that it should be excluded, per se. The court should not discount the importance of providing the jury with a mechanism that will help it understand the technology and technical issues in dispute. It is entirely appropriate to admit a physical sample for this purpose. Whether the physical sample in question will help illuminate the relevant technical issues for the jury depends entirely on the context in which it is offered. In addition to evaluating the difficulty of the technology and the issues in dispute, the court may find it helpful to evaluate the quality of the other tools offered to the jury. The court should attempt to gauge the jury's response to these tools before admitting this evidence solely for understanding the surrounding technology. As a result, the court should consider deferring resolution of the motion until it is in a position to evaluate these factors.

7.5.1.3 Motion to Bar Evidence that the Accused Infringer Has Patents of Its Own

This motion is brought by the patentee to prevent the accused infringer from introducing its own patents into evidence. The typical argument is that there is no legitimate purpose for introducing the patents because they are not relevant to any disputed issue. Thus, their introduction is a "frolic and detour" that will waste time. Moreover, the argument typically points to the risk that the jury will be confused by the introduction of the new patents and the technologies they claim. This risk is heightened dramatically, patentees typically argue, when the patents in question claim improvements over the patent being asserted (e.g., the asserted patent claims a car with round wheels and the improvement patents claim a car with round *rubber* wheels). In such a case, there is a risk that the jury will misinterpret the existence of an improvement patent as grounds for finding no infringement. Juries can fail to grasp the fundamental concept that multiple patents can cover a single product, and thus fail to appreciate that the existence of an improvement patent does not shield its holder from liability for infringement of a more basic patent. *See, e.g., Bio-Tech. Gen. Corp. v. Genentech, Inc.*, 80 F.3d 1553, 1559 (Fed. Cir. 1996).

Of course, this argument founders if the accused infringer identifies a legitimate purpose for introducing its own patents. For example, a patent in which the accused infringer described its products as being different from the asserted patent may be relevant to the reverse doctrine of equivalents or to a lack of the intent required for inducement. In addition, the figures or description contained in an accused infringer's patent may help the jury understand aspects of the accused products better than any other piece of evidence available. This may be important where the technology is particularly complex or abstract.

Depending on the argument for relevance advanced by the accused infringer, the court may benefit from deferring the motion until some evidence has been elicited so that it may better gauge whether the purpose advanced is legitimate or pretextual. If legitimate, the court can head off jury confusion by including in its instructions the admonition that a patent gives its holder the right to exclude others from making the invention, not the right to practice it, and illustrating this point with concrete examples.

7.5.1.4 Motion to Bar Argument that Patent Is Not Infringed Because It Is Invalid

In this motion, the patentee seeks to prevent the accused infringer from arguing that it does not infringe the patent because the patent is invalid or unenforceable. Infringement and validity are separate issues that should be decided separately. *See, e.g., Cardinal Chem. Co. v. Morton Int'l*, 508 U.S. 83, 96 (1993); *Spectra-Physics, Inc. v. Coherent, Inc.*, 827 F.3d 1524, 1535 (Fed. Cir. 1987); *see also MedImmune, Inc. v. Genentech, Inc.*, 549 U.S. 118, 131 n.10 (2007). Likewise, infringement and enforceability are distinct issues. *Gardco Mfg., Inc. v. Herst Lighting Co.*, 820 F.2d 1209, 1213 (Fed. Cir. 1987). As a result, this motion should be granted.

7.5.2 Untimely Disclosures

The second constellation of frequently made motions *in limine* concerns evidence that is asserted to have been disclosed in an untimely fashion. Untimely disclosures, whether relating to documents, expert opinions, or fact witnesses, are certainly not unique to patent cases. Indeed, tardy disclosures in patent cases often result from the same root causes, and have the same effects, as tardy disclosures in other cases. But one characteristic sets patent cases apart—the relativity of the parties' basic contentions.

In patent cases, there is a fundamental tension between infringement and invalidity: the broader the claim, the more likely it is to be infringed, but the less likely it is to be valid, and vice versa. This tension causes parties to take positions that are relative to the other party's positions. For example, a defendant may argue that an asserted claim does not cover its products because claim limitation X is different from product element Y, but that if Y is within the scope of X as the patentee asserts, then the claim is invalidated by prior art that also contains element Y. Likewise, a patentee may argue that a claim element is missing from a prior art reference, but if present as the defendant asserts, additional products containing that element infringe. More subtly, the products and prior art at issue determine which disputes are joined at the claim construction, summary judgment, and trial stages. As a result, the discovery (or exclusion from evidence) of a single prior art reference, for example, may fundamentally affect the invalidity and infringement arguments of both parties. For this reason, several jurisdictions have established local rules that require parties to exchange infringement and invalidity contentions at certain points during discovery. *See* Appendix D (summary of districts with Patent Local Rules or standard practices that affect patent cases). Courts in jurisdictions that have not adopted such rules should consider implementing similar procedures through a standing or scheduling order.

The relativity of the parties' contentions affects the way that courts should evaluate and redress complaints of untimely disclosed evidence in several ways. First, it is important that the court resolve these motions as quickly as possible—in any event before opening statements. Whether a belated disclosure is justifiable and/or excusable depends on facts that should be available to the court before trial, and so trial evidence is not likely to shed light on the proper result. Moreover, because the admission or exclusion of the evidence could fundamentally alter both parties' trial strategies, it is important that the court resolve such disputes before the parties lay out their trial themes during opening statements.

Second, a seemingly untimely disclosure may be justified in light of the circumstances. For example, the discovery and production of a prior art reference on the day before discovery closes may be timely, depending on the court's rules, but it also may warrant supplementation of interrogatory responses or disclosure of additional evidence by the opposing party after discovery closes. In cases in which the court holds claim-construction proceedings after discovery closes, an unexpected construction may trigger a cascade of new contentions and evidence.

A third, related, point is that the court should treat each belated disclosure independently. Indeed, it is often inequitable to treat both parties' disclosures the same way. For example, one party's belated expert report may be justified in light of the circumstances, while the opposing party's belated report is unjustified. Not only would applying parity to this situation be unfair, but the addition of new facts may also create new inequities. Instead, the court should first determine which belated disclosures, if any, will be excused, and then evaluate what, if any, remedial disclosures are necessary to prevent prejudice to the receiving party. For example, the court may find that it is equitable to allow a party to rebut the other party's belated report, but not to allow it to supplement its existing reports on other issues.

Finally, although the standards for disclosure vary between districts, a court should remember that the general purpose of infringement contentions and invalidity contentions is not to provide a level of detail on par with an expert report. *See, e.g.,*

Fenner Invs., Ltd. v. Hewlett-Packard Co., 2010 U.S. Dist. LEXIS 17536, 2010 WL 786606 (E.D. Tex. Feb. 26, 2010). Rather, the purpose of infringement and validity contentions is to provide notice of infringement and invalidity theories and identify evidence sufficient to illustrate how the party intends to apply those theories to the evidence, with the full scope of proof and evidence of infringement and invalidity being set forth in expert reports—prepared and served after the completion of fact discovery. *Id.*

With these principles in mind, we turn to three commonly filed motions *in limine* arising from belated disclosures.

7.5.2.1 Motion to Preclude Undisclosed Fact Witnesses

This motion seeks to exclude witnesses identified on a party's trial witness list who were not disclosed in that party's initial/supplemental disclosures or interrogatory responses. It largely implicates the same issues as do similar motions in other types of cases and should typically be handled the same way. The court should nevertheless consider the above discussion in evaluating whether the witness disclosure was timely in light of the circumstances.

7.5.2.2 Motion to Preclude Undisclosed Prior Art

In evaluating a patentee's motion to exclude undisclosed or belatedly disclosed prior art, the court should be aware of at least two patent-specific issues. The first, which derives from the Patent Act itself, is that an accused infringer must disclose the prior art that it intends to assert at trial at least 30 days prior to the first day of trial. § 282(c).[5] The second is the substantial effect that admitting or excluding even one reference could have on the litigation. These issues are discussed in turn.

Accused infringers attempting to inject new prior art into evidence after the close of discovery typically invoke § 282(c) as justification for allowing the reference despite the late disclosure. Patentees typically respond that § 282(c) does not excuse compliance with federal rule, local rule, and court-imposed deadlines. Patentees have the better argument. "[A]lthough § 282 sets a minimum period for the identifi-

---

5. Section 282(c) provides, in pertinent part, that:

> In an action involving the validity or infringement of a patent the party asserting invalidity or noninfringement shall give notice in the pleadings or otherwise in writing to the adverse party at least thirty days before the trial, of the country, number, date, and name of the patentee of any patent, the title, date, and page numbers of any publication to be relied upon as anticipation of the patent in suit or, except in actions in the United States Court of Federal Claims, as showing the state of the art, and the name and address of any person who may be relied upon as the prior inventor or as having prior knowledge of or as having previously used or offered for sale the invention of the patent in suit. In the absence of such notice proof of the said matters may not be made at the trial except on such terms as the court requires.

cation of prior art to be introduced as evidence of anticipation, a specific judicial directive for the timing of discovery establishes the procedures to which the parties are bound." *ADT Corp. v. Lydall, Inc.*, 159 F.3d 534, 551 (Fed. Cir. 1998). Thus, the court should evaluate this failure to comply with its discovery schedule through the same lens as it would any other transgression to determine whether the circumstances justified the belated disclosure.

Accused infringers attempting to excuse a failure to serve a § 282(c) disclosure complying with the statute typically argue that the prior art was disclosed sufficiently through earlier discovery responses. Patentees typically argue that this is insufficient because compliance with judicially established deadlines cannot excuse a failure to comply with a statutory requirement. The patentees typically have the better of this argument, too, although it can be a much closer case. A failure to comply with § 282(c) may be grounds for exclusion, even if the prior art was produced in discovery or identified in discovery responses. *Ferguson-Beauregard v. Mega Sys. LLC*, 350 F.3d 1327, 1347 (Fed. Cir. 2003). But exclusion is not required. *See, e.g., Eaton Corp. v. Appliance Valves Corp.*, 792 F.2d 874, 879–80 (Fed. Cir. 1986); *but see Applera Corp. v. MJ Research, Inc.*, 389 F. Supp. 2d 344, 351 (D. Conn. 2005) (excluding prior art for failure to comply with § 282 and noting that the Federal Rules have tightened since *Eaton* was decided). In this situation, the court should measure whether the purpose of the rule—that the patentee be advised that the prior art will be *asserted at trial*—has been served. *Eaton*, 792 F.3d at 879 ("What counts is notice of intent to rely."). If the patentee knew of the accused infringer's intent to rely on the art at trial, then it *may be* equitable, depending upon the circumstances, to excuse the failure to comply with § 282(c). For example, in a jurisdiction that requires invalidity contentions by local rule, it does not seem equitable to require a later document specifically titled "Section 282 Notice" to admit a prior art reference that had been identified earlier in the case as part of those contentions. A court may well find that the invalidity contentions serve the purposes of the statute.

This motion implicates broader issues, as well: whether the belated disclosure is justifiable in light of some action on the part of the patentee or the court, and the extent to which allowing the reference will have downstream effects. Like a newly disclosed theory of infringement, a newly identified prior art reference could potentially drive the parties to refine or outright alter their positions on any issue, to add or drop claims, and to affect expert testimony presented at trial. As a result, allowing the addition of even one new prior art reference after the close of discovery can trigger a cascade of new evidence or arguments. For example, a new piece of prior art asserted as part of a combinatorial obviousness attack can require new arguments about motivations to combine, secondary considerations of nonobviousness, and the proper application of *Georgia-Pacific* factors in a damages analysis. This, in turn, can cause experts to stray beyond the bounds of their reports (to comment on evidence presented at trial) and can spawn a whole host of related evidentiary issues. In light of this follow-on effect, the court might reasonably require substantial justification before excusing the belated disclosure of prior art.

On the other hand, allowing supplemental art can be an appropriate remedy to counterbalance discovery violations on the part of the patentee. For example, in many cases patent owners will (either with or without permission) change their infringement theories after claim construction, during expert depositions (and after expert reports), or as trial approaches. Where those changes have been either allowed or tolerated, it might be appropriate to allow the defendant to inject new prior art into the proceedings. This is true because, in many cases, a defendant's invalidity theory will depend on how the plaintiff intends to read the asserted claims on the accused product. Late changes to an infringement theory present particular difficulties where the defendant intends to make a "practicing the prior art" defense. The equities will vary with every fact pattern, so there is no "best" approach other than to consider carefully how the decision is likely to affect the trial as a whole.

7.5.2.3 Motion to Preclude Untimely Expert Opinions

The third type of commonly filed motion centers around whether and to what extent experts are permitted to testify at trial beyond the expert reports prepared according to the schedule set forth in Federal Rule of Civil Procedure 26 or by the court's scheduling order. Typically, this motion comes in one of three forms.

7.5.2.3.1 Opinions Not Disclosed in Reports

The first variant seeks to preclude experts from testifying about issues that were not identified in any timely served report. Commonly, these opinions come to light through a declaration filed in support of a summary judgment motion or a supplemental report served after the close of expert discovery.

Although the court should address this type of motion as soon as possible, many courts do not address the untimeliness of opinions included in summary judgment declarations at the summary judgment stage. Instead, they keep silent on the issue or explicitly defer a ruling until later in the case. The danger in this approach is that it effectively decides the issue in favor of admissibility: without guidance from the court, the receiving party deposes the expert, the prejudice argument is weakened, and the court ultimately allows the opinions, either alone or in connection with a trade-off that allows both parties to disclose opinions outside the normal schedule. Although a one-for-one exchange of reports may appear fair on its face, for the reasons discussed above, it may significantly handicap the receiving party. It also allows the disclosing party to circumvent the court's schedule and undermines the court's ability to manage its docket.

When belated opinions are styled as "supplemental reports," the danger is that the court will treat supplemental reports as interchangeable and adopt an "all-in or all-out" approach. While sometimes appropriate, this approach risks significant prejudice—the scope of opinions set forth in supplemental reports may differ significantly, one report may have downstream effects while the other does not, and one belated disclosure may be justified while the other is not.

7.5.2.3.2 Affirmative Opinions Disclosed in Rebuttal Reports

The second variant seeks to exclude affirmative opinions that were disclosed for the first time in "rebuttal" reports served pursuant to Federal Rule of Civil Procedure 26(a)(2)(C) or the court's scheduling order. As Rule 26(a)(2)(C) states, these "rebuttal" disclosures are made "solely to contradict or rebut" expert opinions disclosed by the other side. Thus, it is clearly improper to label affirmative opinions as "rebuttal" in nature and to evaluate them under that standard. Instead, the court should treat such disclosures for what they are: "supplemental" opinions, which should be evaluated according to the principles set forth in § 7.5.2.3.2.

7.5.2.3.3 Limit Experts to Their Reports

The third variant seeks to prevent experts from testifying on direct examination about opinions that go beyond their reports. In principle, this motion should be granted. But, in practice, it is often difficult to draw a clear line. On the one hand, experts should not be limited to a recitation of their reports. On the other hand, the more flexibility the expert has to restate her opinions, the more likely it is that the ultimate opinion will contain substantive differences that prejudice the other party. Furthermore, context can be important to discern which departures from the report are appropriate and which are not.

For these reasons, the court should attempt to resolve this motion early, but may need to defer decision concerning certain issues until trial. Rather than grant a blanket motion stating that experts are limited to reports, which will encourage objections during the expert's testimony, the court should address this general subject on an issue-by-issue basis. It can do so in several ways. First, if a party has concerns directed at certain issues—e.g., a function-way-result analysis of potential equivalents—before trial, the party should be required to brief these issues specifically in its motions *in limine*. If specific concerns arise during trial, but before the expert is put on the stand (e.g., through exchange of graphics or witness binders), the party opposing the testimony should be required to raise the issue in advance, outside the presence of the jury, to allow the court to evaluate the issue before the expert is called to testify. Finally, parties calling an expert should be encouraged to resolve potential disputes in advance. One way to do so would be to require an expert to move on to a completely different subject when an objection about scope is made so that the objection can be resolved outside the presence of the jury. By implementing these procedures, the court can prevent surprise testimony and reduce the number of disputes that are joined in the jury's presence.

7.5.3 Precluding Claims/Defenses

A third constellation of motions seeks to preclude a party from presenting evidence concerning a particular claim or defense. Four examples illustrate common issues:

Doctrine of Equivalents: The accused infringer brings a motion to preclude the patentee from presenting any evidence concerning the doctrine of equivalents. The thrust of the argument is often that there is no expert testimony (or no expert testimony that is sufficiently detailed to be admissible, *see* § 7.4.3.3.1) explaining why the element of the accused product has "insubstantial differences" from the relevant claim limitation. Without such testimony, so the argument goes, there is no evidence to show that the differences are insubstantial and, therefore, no way to prove infringement under the doctrine of equivalents. Thus, evidence or argument directed at the doctrine should be precluded as prejudicial and likely to confuse the jury.

Prosecution History Estoppel: Another common motion is predicated on prosecution history estoppel. Under that doctrine, a plaintiff who makes a narrowing amendment during prosecution is barred from relying on the doctrine of equivalents to "recapture" the scope that he surrendered. *See Trading Techs. Int'l, Inc. v. eSpeed, Inc.*, 595 F.3d 1340, 1355 (Fed. Cir. 2010) ("Under prosecution history estoppel, a patentee may not seek to recapture as an equivalent subject matter surrendered during prosecution."); *PODS, Inc. v. Porta Stor, Inc.*, 484 F.3d 1359, 1367 (Fed. Cir. 2007) ("prosecution history estoppel limits the range of equivalents available to a patentee by preventing recapture of subject matter surrendered during prosecution of the patent") (internal citations omitted). In many cases, prosecution history estoppel arises when an applicant adds a limitation in an attempt to distinguish prior art. It can also arise, however, where an applicant makes an express disclaimer of claim scope in an argument to the examiner. *See Medtronic Inc. v. Guidant Corp.*, 465 F.3d 1360, 1373 (Fed. Cir. 2006) ("unmistakable assertions made to the Patent Office in support of patentability can give rise to a surrender for purposes of the recapture rule") (internal citations omitted).

Obviousness: The patentee brings a motion to preclude the accused infringer from presenting evidence that a claim is obvious in light of one or more prior art references. Typically, the patentee makes one of two arguments:

- that the accused infringer identified no evidence that one of ordinary skill in the art had a motivation to combine the references (note that evidence of a specific motivation to combine reference for obviousness purposes is no longer required, although the Supreme Court has stated that it may be helpful to the analysis; *see KSR*, 550 U.S. at 418; *see also* § 14.3.5.2); or
- that the accused infringer identified no adequate expert testimony to explain the elements of obviousness. Thus, evidence or argument directed at the specific obviousness combination—or obviousness generally—would be irrelevant, prejudicial, and likely to confuse the jury. But note that obviousness is a legal issue that does not always require expert testimony, although it may be helpful. *Moleculon Res. Corp. v. CBS, Inc.*, 793 F.2d 1261, 1270 (Fed. Cir. 1986) (argument that expert testimony is required "borders on the frivolous").

Damages: The accused infringer brings a motion to preclude any evidence of damages prior to the filing of the lawsuit (or the date on which the patentee provided notice of the patent, if earlier). Typically, the accused infringer argues that § 287 bars pre-notice damages unless the patentee marks products covered by the patent with the patent number, and that the patentee has identified no evidence of the required "marking." Therefore, evidence concerning pre-notice damages would be irrelevant and prejudicial. The patentee may argue in response that a reasonable royalty analysis depends on the "time of first infringement," and pre-notice activities must be addressed as part of that analysis.

As these examples illustrate, there is often no clean line between a true motion *in limine* and a summary judgment motion in disguise. One way to resolve this question is to focus on the differences between the motion *in limine* and summary judgment processes. At the summary judgment stage, the briefs are longer, contain more factual detail, and present a fuller explication of the relevant legal standards than at the motion *in limine* stage. Likewise, summary judgment arguments tend to be longer, and the court typically takes much more time to resolve a summary judgment motion than it does a motion *in limine*. When presented with a borderline motion *in limine*, the court should consider whether the issue would benefit from fuller examination. In most cases it will and the court should deny the motion. *See Kimball ex rel. Kimball v. RJ Reynolds Tobacco Co.*, 2006 U.S. Dist. LEXIS 27138, 2006 WL 1148506 (W.D. Wash. Apr. 26, 2006) ("The court assumes that counsel is aware of the differences between dispositive motions and motions *in limine*. The court is thus surprised and disappointed to find numerous dispositive motions pending only days before trial.").

Merely denying the motion, though, deprives the court of an opportunity to weed out issues for which a party will not be able to carry its burden of proof. As a result, the court should advise parties during the initial case-management conference that it will treat certain exclusion/preclusion motions, such as those identified above, as summary judgment motions. *See* § 2.5; Appendix 2.1; Appendix 2.2a. With fair warning, parties may elect to bring these motions at the summary judgment stage, giving the court an opportunity to resolve these disputes with adequate time for evaluating the record.

7.5.4 Miscellaneous Patent-Related Motions

In addition to the three constellations of motions discussed above, several other motions *in limine* with patent-specific implications arise in many cases.

7.5.4.1 Motion to Bar Evidence/Argument Inconsistent with Claim Construction

This motion can be brought by either party and asserts that the opposing party seeks to reargue, or present evidence that conflicts with, the court's construction of a particular claim term. Typically, the moving party argues that claim construction is an issue of law to be decided by the court and that arguing or presenting inconsistent evidence to the jury intrudes into the province of the court. Consequently, the argument goes, a party should not be permitted to ask the jury to construe a claim term or to present evidence that clearly implicates a contrary construction.

Taken at face value, the movant's argument is sensible—claim construction is a legal exercise that must be performed by the court. *See Markman v. Westview Instruments, Inc.*, 517 U.S. 370, 391 (1996); § 5.2. This motion is often more complicated, however, because parties also employ this reasoning to exclude legitimate arguments and evidence directed at issues that do not rely on claim construction. For example, a written description defense is premised on a comparison between the construed claim and the originally filed specification to determine whether the patentee was in possession of the claimed invention at the time the application was filed. *See, e.g., Moba, B.V. v. Diamond Automation, Inc.*, 325 F.3d 1306, 1320–21 (Fed. Cir. 2003). Even if an accused infringer were to argue that the inventor was not in possession of the invention as claimed because the construed claim lacks a limitation corresponding to a feature of the embodiments discussed in the specification, the jury should not rewrite the court's claim construction, at least expressly. The argument is directed to a different issue. Likewise, a noninfringement defense based on the reverse doctrine of equivalents is premised on a comparison of the accused product to the originally filed application. *See, e.g., Scripps Clinic & Research Found. v. Genentech*, 927 F.2d 1565, 1581 (Fed. Cir. 1991). Therefore, an accused infringer offering evidence of that comparison is not seeking to rewrite the court's claim construction, but rather to satisfy a different legal standard.

Because the argument that an alleged infringer is seeking to diverge from the court's claim construction is so easily used to thwart a genuine defense, it is important that the court evaluate carefully whether there is a legitimate purpose for introducing the evidence or making the argument, and not simply take the motion at face value. Moreover, because the decision may have far-reaching effects (especially if the court's ruling has the effect of precluding a defense), the court should rule on this motion before trial begins.

7.5.4.2 Motion to Preclude Reference to an Expert's Contrary Claim-Construction Opinion

Experts in patent cases are often asked to provide opinions at multiple stages in the case. They will, for example, often be asked at the claim-construction stage to offer an opinion directed to explaining how a person having ordinary skill in the art would have understood a term at the time the patent application was filed. Once the court has construed the claims, the experts will be asked at the "expert discovery" stage to offer opinions applying the court's construction to reach conclusions related to infringement and validity. When multiple experts offer conflicting opinions about claim construction, at least one expert's opinion is necessarily at odds with the court's ultimate construction.

This motion is brought to prevent one party from cross-examining the other party's expert based on statements made to support a losing claim-construction position. Typically, the argument is that the opinion has no relevance to infringement or validity. Moreover, the jury is likely to misunderstand why the expert is "changing" positions—because she must apply the court's construction—and might unfairly discount the expert's credibility. One counter-argument is that the substance of the claim construction reveals inconsistencies beyond the meaning applied to the claim term. For example, an expert might opine at the claim-construction stage that a prior art technique was widely known, but opine later in the case that the technique was known only to a few artisans. In this example, the inconsistency—and the blow to credibility—has nothing to do with the ultimate conclusion that the expert reached about claim construction; the testimony is simply inconsistent. As a result, the court should consider allowing the use of such prior opinions based on a case-by-case balancing of probative value and potential prejudice. In some instances, the court should consider deferring decision on the motion until the direct examination of the expert is complete so as to better appreciate the import of the alleged inconsistency.

7.5.4.3 Motion to Bar Evidence/Argument About Dropped Claims/Patents

This motion is brought by the patentee and seeks to preclude any reference to the fact that the patentee initially asserted more claims or patents than it is pursuing at trial. Typically, the patentee argues that the claims/patents were dropped for efficiency and that this change does not reflect the merits of the liability arguments concerning those claims/patents in any way. As a result, the argument goes, this fact has no probative value. Moreover, there is a substantial risk of prejudice because the jury is likely to assume that the claims were dropped because the patentee believed them to be invalid or not infringed.

Accused infringers typically argue that the fact that the patentee dropped claims or patents does have probative value, at least when willful infringement or an antitrust counterclaim is asserted. In the former situation, the fact that the patentee initially asserted additional/different patents or claims before pursuing the patents/claims asserted at trial may affect the reasonableness of the accused infringer's response. Therefore, as the argument goes, this fact is relevant to whether the accused infringer reasonably believed that it had a right to continue its allegedly infringing conduct. In the antitrust counterclaim scenario, the counterclaim plaintiff may seek to show that the patentee has engaged in an unwarranted campaign to instill fear, uncertainty, and doubt into the marketplace by falsely asserting patent infringement.

There is no clear-cut way to resolve this motion. The outcome is highly fact-dependent. The accused infringer may in some cases legitimately seek to use the information to rebut willfulness or for some other purpose. Even so, this motion should be decided before opening statements. In most cases, waiting for testimony to be elicited during trial will not provide additional clarity about which side has the better argument. For antitrust counterclaims, this issue weighs in favor of bifurcating the trial (affirmative patent infringement claims tried first; antitrust counterclaims addressed in a second trial phase) so as to avoid confusing the jury.

7.5.4.4 Motion to Bar Disclosure that the Patentee Seeks an Injunction

This motion is brought by the patentee and seeks to preclude any evidence or argument to the jury disclosing that the patentee seeks an injunction. Because a request for an injunction seeks equitable relief, it is decided by the court, rather than by the jury. Typically, the patentee argues that disclosing the request for an injunction has no probative value and would prejudice the plaintiff by potentially generating sympathy that could affect the jury's decision on liability. The accused infringer often responds that mentioning the possibility of an injunction is no more prejudicial than disclosing the size of the damages award sought (which, of course, is disclosed, unless the case is bifurcated), and that the information may be relevant to other issues in the case, such as the accused infringer's state of mind for willfulness (e.g., that the accused infringer evaluated the patent seriously because it knew the plaintiff would be seeking an injunction). If the relevance to an issue before the jury is shown, the motion should generally be denied. But the court should evaluate the motion carefully to discern whether, given the specific facts of the case, the risk of prejudice trumps the probative value of the argument or evidence.

7.5.4.5 Motion to Preclude Reference to Related Proceedings in the Patent Office

This motion is often, although not always, brought by the patentee who seeks to preclude any reference to a pending reexamination or reissue involving the patent-in-suit. Typically, the argument is that the parallel proceedings have no relevance until they are completed—when the claims are ultimately issued intact, modified, or rejected. Moreover, there is considerable risk that the jury will misunderstand the significance of the proceedings and will inappropriately weigh this evidence. In response, the opposing party typically counters that the parallel proceeding has substantial probative value concerning invalidity or inequitable conduct. For example, if the Patent Office decides to reexamine the patent-in-suit because of a particular prior art reference, that fact supports the argument that the reference is material, which is relevant to inequitable conduct. Conversely, if the Patent Office reissued a patent over a prior art reference, this supports the argument that the reference is not material. *See, e.g., Bristol-Myers Squibb Co. v. Rhone-Poulenc Rorer, Inc.*, 326 F.3d 1226, 1237 (Fed. Cir. 2003).

One common dispute that has arisen since the passage of the AIA concerns the admissibility of Patent Trial and Appeal Board (PTAB) decisions to institute, or not institute, an *inter partes* review (IPR) or covered business method review (CBMR). In this context, a patentee typically argues that a non-institution decision is probative of the patent's validity because the standard for institution (effectively, more likely than not that one or more claims is invalid) is lower than the burden for proving invalidity at trial (clear and convincing evidence of invalidity). While this argument has some surface appeal, its ultimate persuasiveness depends on the specific positions being advanced before the district court in comparison with those advanced in the IPR/CBMR petition. It is strongest where the prior art and positions being advanced at trial overlap exactly with those made in the IPR/CBMR petition; it is weakest where the prior art and positions do not overlap at all. Where, as in most cases, there is some but not complete overlap, the district court should conduct typical Rule 403 balancing based on the specific facts. Weighing the factors, district courts have come down on both sides of admissibility. Some permitted the patentee to refer to the denial. *See, e.g.*, *Universal Elecs. Inc. v. Universal Remote Control Inc.*, 2014 U.S. Dist. LEXIS 182754, 2014 WL 10253110 (C.D. Cal. Apr. 21, 2014) (denying defendant's motion *in limine* to preclude any evidence regarding the USPTO's decision not to institute *inter partes* review of one of the patents-in-suit and rejecting defendant's argument that "introducing evidence of the PTO's rejection of [d]efendant's *inter partes* review petition would be irrelevant because the legal standards applicable to an *inter partes* review are different than those that apply here, and that it would increase the complexity of the trial and confuse the jury" because "[a]ny potential confusion can be addressed by appropriate jury instructions on the standard of proof applicable to patent invalidity defenses and counterclaims."). Others precluded the use of the IPR/CBMR denial. *See, e.g., Rembrandt Wireless Techs., LP v. Samsung Elecs. Co., Ltd.*, 2015 U.S. Dist. LEXIS 20306, *19, 2015 WL 627430 (E.D. Tex. Jan. 30, 2015); *Interdigital Commc'ns, Inc. v. Nokia Corp.*, 2014 U.S. Dist. LEXIS 182856, 2014 WL 8104167 (D. Del. Sept. 19, 2014) (holding that the PTAB's decision not to institute trial—"made by lawyers who are not persons of ordinary skill in the art"—was of marginal relevance and should be excluded under Federal Rule of Evidence 403).

Courts typically preclude defendants from referencing decisions to institute IPR/CBM proceedings on the basis that a finding that one or more of the claims is likely invalid says little or nothing about whether there is clear and convincing evidence that the patent is invalid. *See, e.g., Intellectual Ventures I LLC v. Symantec*, 2015 U.S. Dist. LEXIS 2841, at *3, 2015 WL 82052 (D. Del. Jan. 6, 2015). But in both the institution and noninstitution contexts, courts should distinguish between allowing a party to reference the Patent Office's decisions or the existence of the IPR/CBMR process on the one hand from referencing statements made by a party (whether the patentee or the challenger) on the other hand. For example, even where a court elects to preclude a defendant from mentioning the existence of an IPR or reexamination proceeding, the purpose of that proceeding, or decisions by the Patent Office or PTAB during that proceeding, courts should—and typically do—permit the defendant to introduce statements made by the patentee in the course of those proceedings that bear on arguments being made by the parties in litigation. *See, e.g.*, *id.* (precluding reference to reexamination proceedings but permitting introduction of "portions of the reexamination history or us[e of] same for impeachment, provided, however, that such evidence or use must be done in such a way as not to reference any reexamination").

Regardless of the district court's initial posture as to the use of materials related to, requested for, or instituted during post-issuance proceedings, a party might introduce evidence or make arguments that could open the door to their use at trial. For example, a patentee's statements about prior art already having been considered by the Patent Office or excessive discussion of the presumption of validity *might* open the door to evidence showing that asserted claims currently stand rejected by the Patent Office or the PTAB in view of prior art asserted at trial. Likewise, a defendant's statements about the Patent Office not having all the relevant information, or having not considered a specific prior art reference, during the original prosecution *might* open the door for the patentee to present evidence showing that the

PTAB denied a request to institute an IPR on the prior art asserted at trial. But in all cases, whether the statements genuinely open the door to the use of the material depends on precisely what was argued or presented and precisely how the material proffered rebuts that evidence or argument. In other words, it is highly fact-specific.

As this discussion illustrates, evidence related to post-issuance Patent Office proceedings will often have some probative value, but also some potential for prejudice. Accordingly, the court should consider carefully what evidence relating to the parallel proceedings can be used and for what exact purpose. In many instances, this judgment may be better informed once trial has begun, when the court can evaluate the precise context in which the evidence will be presented.

7.5.4.6 Motion to Preclude Evidence Concerning Undisclosed Opinions of Counsel

When it enacted the AIA in 2011, Congress revised § 298 to specify that

> The failure of an infringer to obtain the advice of counsel with respect to any allegedly infringed patent, or the failure of the infringer to present such advice to the court or jury, may not be used to prove that the accused infringer willfully infringed the patent or that the infringer intended to induce infringement of the patent.

In light of this provision, the court should grant a motion *in limine* that seeks to exclude evidence that an accused infringer failed to obtain, or to disclose in the litigation, an opinion of counsel regarding the asserted patent, when that evidence is proffered for the purpose of establishing willful infringement or indirect infringement. If such evidence is proffered for some other purpose, the court should weigh carefully whether the asserted probative value of such evidence outweighs the prejudice that led Congress to enact this prohibition.

7.5.4.7 Motion to Preclude Evidence Based on Estoppel Resulting from Postgrant Proceedings

In the AIA, Congress enacted two new postgrant proceedings to replace *inter partes* reexaminations: postgrant reviews (which must be filed within nine months of issuance or reissuance of a patent) and *inter partes* review. Both new proceedings carry with them provisions that estop the party that brought them against the patent (or the real party in interest or privy) from asserting—either in a civil action in district court or in an action brought before the International Trade Commission—"that the claim is invalid on any ground that the petitioner raised or reasonably could have raised during that [postgrant review or *inter partes* review]." *See, e.g.*, AIA §§ 315 (*inter partes*), 325 (postgrant); § 14.2.5.8.1. Congress also enacted a third postgrant review process directed at business method patents (covered business method review (CBMR)), which has a more limited estoppel provision: it estops the party bringing the challenge from relitigating any issue that it actually raised in the CBMR. For all of these proceedings, the estoppels take effect once a "final written decision" has been issued in the proceeding. Because these new postgrant proceedings were not instituted until September 16, 2012, the first wave of estoppels arising from postgrant proceedings was expected in 2014. Because the success rate for instituted proceedings has thus far been high, courts have not yet seen a substantial number of estoppel issues arising from postgrant proceedings. We expect, however, that the incidence of these issues will rise over time.

In the estoppel context, courts are likely to be presented with motions *in limine* brought by a patentee seeking to exclude argument and evidence related to invalidity arguments that were presented, or allegedly should have been presented, during a postgrant proceeding. Resolving motions directed to prior art or other invalidity arguments that were explicitly considered by the Patent Office during the proceeding should be straightforward. Motions directed to prior art or argument that the patentee alleges *should have been* raised during the proceedings will be more difficult. Although no specific standard has yet been delineated, courts should consider, among other facts, whether the basis of invalidity now asserted could actually have been raised in the postgrant proceeding (note that postgrant reviews consider a different universe of invalidity arguments than *inter partes* reviews); whether the prior art or another basis for invalidity was actually known by the requesting party when the request was made; if it was not known, the efforts made to discover bases for invalidity and the difficulty of uncovering, at that time with the resources available, the basis for invalidity now asserted; and whether expert testimony, discovery, positions taken by the patentee during litigation, and other aspects of litigation were reasonably necessary to discover the basis for invalidity or appreciate its significance.

As a practical matter, this last point is especially important. Often in litigation, the accused infringer makes the argument that prior art discloses the asserted patent claims only as those claims are interpreted by the patentee in furtherance of its infringement allegations. In other words, if properly construed, the patent claims cover neither the accused product nor the prior art, but if construed as broadly as the patentee contends, then the patent claims cover the prior art. This type of conditional argument may not arise until litigation because the patentee may not take such positions until well into the case, and long after a request for a postgrant proceeding is filed. Similarly, what diligence may be reasonable to expect of an accused infringer engaged in litigation, for example in the context of preparing patent local rule invalidity contentions, may well be unreasonable to expect of an entity before litigation begins. Conversely, reserving for potential litigation prior art that the accused infringer had identified and knew was significant to the validity of the patent claims at the time it filed the postgrant proceeding request conflicts with the clear purpose of the statute, which is to reduce the likelihood of parallel litigation. As this discussion illustrates, motions of this kind are likely to be fact-intensive. The court should weigh these and other factors pertinent to the given situation and evaluate such motions on a case-by-case basis.

7.5.4.8 Motion to Preclude Reference to Presumption of Validity

As previously noted, it is now generally considered improper to instruct a jury on the presumption of validity aside from instruction on the "clear and convincing" burden of proof. *See* § 7.3.4.3. For this same reason, defendants often ask courts to enter an order forbidding a plaintiff from mentioning the presumption of validity. The court has broad discretion to decide for itself whether such a reference is likely to be confusing or to undermine the court's efforts to clarify concepts through its jury instructions. Courts have granted this motion to align better the arguments presented by the attorneys with the court's jury instructions. *See, e.g., Alloc, Inc. v. Pergo, Inc.*, 2007 U.S. Dist. LEXIS 5183, 2007 WL 5289735 (E.D. Wis. Nov. 21, 2007) ("In the interest of making concepts as clear to the jury as possible, the court will direct that the parties refrain from referring to the 'presumption of validity,' since the parties may refer to the same concept as the Alloc Parties' burden of proof."); *Voda v. Cordis Corp.*, 2006 U.S. Dist. LEXIS 97321, 2006 WL 5347777 (W.D. Okla. May 10, 2006) ("The court will instruct the jury on the appropriate burden of proof. Defendant's motion to preclude plaintiff from referring to the presumption of validity is therefore GRANTED.").

7.5.4.9 Motion to Preclude Use of "Patent Troll" and Other Pejorative Terms Related to Nonpracticing Entities

As public and political discourse regarding nonpracticing entities expands, evidentiary disputes regarding the propriety of referring to nonpracticing entities as "patent trolls" and related monikers are increasing. District courts will sometimes grant motions to preclude the accused infringer from referring to a nonpracticing entity by such terms. Plaintiffs will typically argue that such references are derogatory, prejudicial, and confusing to the jury. Accused infringers will respond that such terms convey to the jury aspects of a nonpracticing entities' characteristics that are relevant to secondary considerations of nonobviousness and damages calculations.

In a recent case, a district court granted the plaintiff's motion *in limine* to preclude the accused infringer from using at trial the terms "patent troll," "pirate," "bounty hunter," "bandit," "paper patent," "stick up," "shakedown," "playing the lawsuit lottery," "corporate shell game" or "a corporate shell." *GPNE Corp. v. Apple, Inc.*, ECF No. 319 at 2:17-24, No. 5:12-cv-02885-LHK (N.D. Cal. June 24, 2014). The district court also ruled, however, that, at trial, the accused infringer could refer to the plaintiff, the asserted patent, and the patentee's activities as a "nonpracticing entity," "licensing entity," "patent assertion entity," "a company that doesn't make anything" or "a company that doesn't sell anything." Citing Fed. R. Evid. 403, the district court found that its ruling "strikes the balance" between such competing considerations. *Id.* Similarly, the district court in *Intellectual Ventures I LLC v. Symantec Corp.*, ruled that the defendant was precluded from disparaging the plaintiff's business model and practices, but was permitted to present evidence and argument that the plaintiff does not practice the patents-in-suit, "which is relevant to damages" and for which issue the "concerns of Federal Rule of Evidence 403 do not outweigh the probative value of the evidence." 2015 U.S. Dist. LEXIS 2841, 2015 WL 82052 (D. Del. Jan. 6, 2015).

Appendix 7.1
Sample Pretrial Order for Patent Cases

IN THE UNITED STATES DISTRICT COURT
FOR THE ________ DISTRICT OF ________

________________________,	
Plaintiff,	Civil Action No.__________
vs.	
________________________,	
Defendant.	

PROPOSED PRETRIAL ORDER

[Instructions to parties and counsel provided in this document are enclosed within brackets and should be omitted from the document when the Proposed Pretrial Order is prepared for submission.]

Trial Counsel for the Parties

[Each party shall identify the names, law firms, addresses, telephone numbers, and email addresses for the attorneys who will try the case on behalf of that party.]

Jurisdiction

[The parties shall identify the basis for the Court's jurisdiction.]

Nature of the Action

[The parties shall provide a brief description of the nature and background of the action.]

The Parties' Contentions

[Plaintiff shall provide an identification and brief description of its contentions. In a patent-infringement case, Plaintiff's statement (or in a declaratory judgment action, Defendant's statement) shall include at least the following information:

(1) The specific patent claims to be asserted at trial (i.e., the set or subset of previously-identified asserted claims);

(2) The specific products to be accused of infringement at trial (i.e., the set or subset of previously-identified accused products);

(3) Whether the patentee intends to rely at trial on the doctrine of equivalents to establish infringement for any claim;

(4) Whether the patentee intends to assert indirect infringement at trial and, if so, under what theory (i.e., contributory infringement and/or inducement) and as to which claims and products;

(5) The type of infringement damages to be sought at trial (i.e., lost profits, reasonable royalty, or both); and

(6) If the accused infringer asserts that one or more of the asserted patent claims is obvious, whether the patentee intends to rely on any "secondary indicia" of nonobviousness to rebut this contention and, if so, which specific indicia (e.g., commercial success of ______ (product), recognition as shown by ______ (award), etc.).

Defendant shall provide an identification and brief description of its contentions. In a patent-infringement case, Defendant's statement (or in a declaratory judgment action, Plaintiff's statement) shall include at least the following information:

(7) Whether the accused infringer intends to assert at trial that one or more of its products does not infringe one or more asserted claims; and

(8) Whether the accused infringer intends to assert at trial that one or more of the asserted patent claims is invalid. If so, the accused infringer shall provide at least the following additional information:

(9) The specific patents, publications, devices, or other prior art to be asserted at trial as anticipating or rendering obvious one or more of the asserted claims (i.e., the set or subset of previously-identified asserted prior art);

(10) Whether the accused infringer will assert at trial that one or more asserted claims is invalid under 35 U.S.C. § 101; and

(11) Whether the accused infringer will assert at trial that one or more asserted claims is invalid under 35 U.S.C. § 112 and, if so, the specific grounds to be asserted (i.e., written description, lack of enablement, and/or indefiniteness).]

Uncontested Facts and Stipulations

[The parties shall identify undisputed facts that are relevant to their contentions, as set forth in Section IV, and stipulations regarding trial procedures (e.g., exchange of demonstratives, disclosure of deposition designations and objections, and the like), the subject matter to be tried, or that otherwise bear on the trial.]

Contested Legal and Factual Issues

[Each party shall identify the specific issues of fact and law that are relevant to their contentions, as set forth in Section IV, and are contested.]

Jury and Non-Jury Issues

[The parties shall identify whether they request trial by a jury or by the Court. If the case is to be tried to a jury, the parties shall identify any equitable, legal, or other issues that they contend should be decided by the Court, through a bench trial or otherwise.]

List of Witnesses

[Each party shall submit with the Proposed Pretrial Order a list of witnesses that it will call or may call at trial, and specify for each such witness: a) whether that witness is expected to testify live or by deposition; b) whether the witnesses will provide factual or expert testimony; and c) any objections that have been made to the witness being called to testify. Plaintiff's witness list shall be submitted as Exhibit 8A to the Proposed Pretrial Order; Defendant's witness list shall be submitted as Exhibit 8B.]

List of Exhibits

[Each party shall submit with the Proposed Pretrial Order a list of exhibits that it may seek to offer into evidence at trial, along with the objections, if any, that have been made to each such exhibit. Plaintiff's exhibit list shall be submitted as Exhibit 9A to that proposed order; Defendant's exhibit list shall be submitted as Exhibit 9B.]

List of Pending Motions

[Each party shall identify the motions that it has filed that remain pending with the Court.]

Jury Instructions

[If the case is to be tried to a jury, the parties shall submit a joint set of preliminary instructions as Exhibit 11A to the Proposed Pretrial Order and a joint set of final instructions as Exhibit 11B to the Proposed Pretrial Order. The Court may use these proposed instructions to charge the jury, or may modify them or use other instructions as is warranted. The parties should exchange proposed preliminary instructions and proposed final instructions in accordance with the Court's scheduling order, and, in any event, well in advance of the submission of the Proposed Pretrial Order. The parties should meet-and-confer as necessary to reach agreement regarding a joint set of instructions. In Exhibits 11A and 11B submitted with the Proposed Pretrial Order, each instruction shall be separately numbered and no more than one instruction may be included on a single printed page (though some instructions may span multiple pages). Where the parties disagree about whether a particular instruction should be given, or about the specific language to be used in an instruction, the party proposing the instruction shall include it in the set, in the place in which it would appear if adopted, with the notation "PROPOSED BY PLAINTIFF [OR DEFENDANT] and shall provide a brief (i.e., 1 to 2 paragraph) explanation why this instruction should be adopted, including citations to all relevant authority. Immediately following this proposed instruction, the party opposing the instruction shall include on a separate page a similarly brief explanation why the proposed instruction should not be adopted, including citations to all relevant authority. Where the parties propose competing language for an instruction, this same procedure shall be followed consecutively for each proposed version of the instruction, such that the consecutive pages for that instruction appear as follows: 1) Instruction X, Proposal A; 2) Objection to Proposal A; 3) Instruction X, Proposal B; 4) Objection to Proposal B.]

Verdict Form

[If the case is to be tried to a jury, the parties shall submit as Exhibit 12 to the Proposed Pretrial Order a proposed verdict form. If the parties are unable to agree on a verdict form, each party shall submit a proposed verdict form, along with a short (no more than 2 pages) explanation why its proposed form should be adopted, including citations to all relevant authority. Plaintiff's proposed verdict form and accompanying argument shall be submitted as Exhibit 12A to the Proposed Pretrial Order; Defendant's proposed verdict form and accompanying argument shall be submitted as Exhibit 12B to that proposed order.]

Trial Length and Logistics

[Each party shall specify the number of hours that it contends is appropriate for each party for each of the following: a) voir dire, b) opening statements, c) presentation of evidence, and d) closing arguments. If any party intends to request phasing, bifurcation, or other procedure concerning the trial length or ordering of evidence, that party shall include such request in its statement herein, along with a short explanation of the basis for the request. A party opposing the request may include a similarly short statement explaining briefly its opposition to the request. If the request is the subject of a motion presently pending before the Court, the parties shall identify that request in this section, but omit the short statements concerning that request.]

Dated: ___________.

____

[Counsel Signatures]

Appendix 7.2
Proposed Final Pretrial Order—Patent

(Chief Judge Leonard P. Stark, District of Delaware)
REVISED June 2014

[Note: Throughout, material in brackets is provided as guidance to counsel as to the Court's practices and/or matter that needs to be addressed in the Proposed Final Pretrial Order.]

PROPOSED FINAL PRETRIAL ORDER- PATENT

This matter comes before the Court at a final pretrial conference held pursuant to Rule 16 of the Federal Rules of Civil Procedure.

Plaintiff(s) Counsel: [List name, address, telephone number, and e-mail address][6]

Defendant(s) Counsel: [List name, address, telephone number, and e-mail address][7]

I. Nature of the Case

[The parties should prepare a brief statement of the nature of the case including identification of the parties and their claims. This statement may be used by the Court to explain the case to prospective jurors during the process of jury selection.]

II. Jurisdiction

This is an action for [state the remedy sought, such as damages or injunctive or declaratory relief].

The jurisdiction of the Court is not disputed [or, if the issue has not previously been raised, the basis on which jurisdiction is contested] and is based on [state the statutory, constitutional, or other basis of jurisdiction].

III. Facts

A. Uncontested Facts

Any party, with prior notice to all other parties, may read any or all of the uncontested facts to the jury or Court, and will be charged for the time used to do so.

The following facts are not disputed or have been agreed to or stipulated to by the parties:

[This section should contain a comprehensive statement of the uncontested facts which the parties intend to make part of the evidentiary record, either by reading to the jury, or in a bench trial reading to the Court and/or filing with the Court in conjunction with posttrial briefing.]

B. Contested Facts

[Identify the facts in issue, with a brief statement of what each party intends

---

6. For simplicity, "Plaintiff(s)" refers throughout this form order to the party asserting infringement of its patent(s).

7. For simplicity, "Defendant(s)" refers throughout this form order to the party accused of infringement.

to prove in support of its claims and/or defenses. These summaries should be sufficient to identify for the Court the essential facts in issue and to fairly notify the other parties of what counsel expects to prove at trial.]

IV. Issues of Law

[Include a statement of the issues of law which any party contends remain to be litigated, and a citation of authorities relied upon by each party.]

[The Court will preclude a party from seeking relief based on claims and defenses not described in the draft pretrial order.]

V. Witnesses

[Indicate which witnesses will testify in person and which by deposition. Indicate if there are any objections to a witness and, if so, briefly state the basis for the objection.] Any witness not listed will be precluded from testifying, absent good cause shown.

In the absence of an alternative agreement between the parties, fact witnesses will be sequestered. Also, unless the parties reach an alternative agreement, the order of the presentation of evidence will follow the burden of proof.

[The presumptive order of proof is:

Phase I: Plaintiff case-in-chief on infringement and damages

Phase II: Defendant response on infringement and damages, and case-in-chief on invalidity

Phase III: Plaintiff rebuttal on infringement and damages, and response on validity

Phase IV: Defendant rebuttal on invalidity]

A. List of Witnesses the Plaintiff Expects to Call

1. Expert witnesses

[For any expert witness, the Plaintiff shall indicate the precise subject matter on which it will ask the Court to recognize the witness's expertise. At trial, the Plaintiff should offer the witness as an expert on that same subject matter. No deviations as to the described subject matter will be permitted without approval of all parties or the Court, on good cause shown.]

2. Non-expert witnesses

B. List of Witnesses Defendant Expects to Call

1. Expert witnesses

[For any expert witness, the Defendant shall indicate the precise subject matter on which it will ask the Court to recognize the witness's expertise. At trial, the Defendant should offer the witness as an expert on that same subject matter. No deviations as to the described subject matter will be permitted without approval of all parties or the Court, on good cause shown.]

2. Non-expert witnesses

C. List of Witnesses Third Parties Expect to Call

[If there are any third parties to the action, they should include a list of witnesses like those contained in Parts A and B above.]

D. Testimony by Deposition

[Counsel should confer prior to the pretrial conference to determine which testimony will be offered by deposition (including videotape depositions), to agree on the designation of those portions of the depositions to be offered into evidence, and to identify objections.] This pretrial order contains the maximum universe of deposition designations, counter-designations, and objections to admission of deposition testimony; none of the foregoing shall be supplemented without approval of all parties or leave of the Court, on good cause shown.

If there are objections that remain to be resolved, the party calling the witness by deposition shall, no later than two (2) calendar days before the witness is to be called at trial, submit, on behalf of all parties: (i) a copy of the entire deposition testimony of the witness at issue, clearly highlighting the designations, counter-designations, and pending objections; and (ii) a cover letter clearly identifying the pending objections as well as a brief indication (i.e., no more than one sentence per objection) of the basis for the objection and the offering party's response to it. Failure to comply with these procedures, absent an agreement by the parties and approval by the Court, will result in waiver of the use of the deposition testimony or waiver of objection to the use of the deposition testimony.

All irrelevant and redundant material, including colloquy between counsel and objections, will be eliminated when the deposition is read or viewed at trial.

When the witness is called to testify by deposition at trial, the party calling the witness shall provide the Court with two copies of the transcript of the designations and counter- designations that will be read or played. The parties will be charged for all time that elapses from the time the witness is called until the next witness is called, according to the proportions to be provided by the parties.

E. Impeachment with Prior Inconsistent Testimony

[The parties shall provide their position(s) as to whether the Court should allow objections to the use of deposition and other prior testimony for impeachment purposes, including objections based on lack of completeness and/or lack of inconsistency.]

F. Objections to Expert Testimony

[The parties shall provide their position(s) as to whether the Court should rule at trial on objections to expert testimony as beyond the scope of prior expert disclosures, taking time from the parties' trial presentation to argue and decide such objections; or whether the Court should instead defer ruling on all such objections unless renewed in writing following trial, subject to the proviso that a party prevailing on such a posttrial objection will be entitled to have all of its costs associated with a new trial paid for by the party that elicited the improper expert testimony at the earlier trial.]

VI. Exhibits

A. Exhibits

[The parties are to provide a list of pre-marked exhibits which each party intends to offer at trial, along with citations to the Federal Rules of Evidence to note any objections thereto lodged by any other party.] This pretrial order contains the maximum universe of exhibits to be used in any party's case-in-chief, as well as all objections to the admission of such objections, neither of which shall be supplemented without approval of all parties or leave of the Court, on good cause shown. Exhibits not listed will not be admitted unless good cause is shown.

No exhibit will be admitted unless offered into evidence through a witness, who must at least be shown the exhibit. At some point before the completion of the witness' testimony, any party that has used an exhibit with the witness and wishes that exhibit to be admitted into evidence must formally move the exhibit into evidence, by exhibit number. Exhibits may not be published, displayed, or otherwise shown to the jury until after they have been admitted into evidence. Once admitted, counsel may publish exhibits to the jury without requesting to do so.

A party will provide exhibits to be used in connection with direct examination by 6:00 p.m. the day before their intended use, and objections will be provided no later than 8:00 p.m. the night before their intended use. If good faith efforts to resolve the objections fail, the party objecting to the exhibits shall bring its objections to the Court's attention prior to the witness being called to the witness stand. Failure to comply with these procedures, absent an agreement by the parties and approval by the Court, will result in waiver of the use of an exhibit or waiver of objection to the exhibit.

Exhibits not objected to will be received into evidence by the operation of the Final Pretrial Order without the need for additional foundation testimony, provided they are shown to a witness.

On or before the first day of trial, counsel will deliver to the Courtroom Deputy a completed AO Form 187 exhibit list for each party.

B. Demonstrative Exhibits

The parties will exchange demonstratives to be used in opening statements by 8:00 p.m. two nights before opening statements. The parties will provide any objections to such demonstratives by 12:00 p.m. (noon) on the day before opening statements.

A party will provide demonstrative exhibits to be used in connection with direct examination by 6:00 p.m. the night before their intended use, and objections will be provided no later than 8:00 p.m. the night before their intended use. If any of the demonstratives change after the deadline, the party intending to use the demonstrative will promptly notify the opposing party of the change(s).

The party seeking to use a demonstrative will provide a color representation of the demonstrative to the other side in PDF form. However, for video or animations, the party seeking to use the demonstrative will provide it to the other side on a DVD or CD. For irregularly sized physical exhibits, the party seeking to use the demonstrative will provide a color representation as a PDF of 8.5 x 11 copies of the exhibits.

This provision does not apply to demonstratives created during testimony or demonstratives to be used for cross-examination, neither of which need to be provided to the other side in advance of their use. In addition, blow-ups or highlights of exhibits or parts of exhibits or testimony are not required to be provided to the other side in advance of their use.

If good faith efforts to resolve objections to demonstrative exhibits fail, the objecting party shall bring its objections to the Court's attention prior to the opening statements or prior to the applicable witness being called to the witness stand. Failure to comply with these procedures, absent an agreement by the parties and approval by the Court, will result in waiver of the use of an exhibit or waiver of objection to the exhibit.

VII. Damages

[Include an itemized statement of all damages, including special damages.]

VIII. Bifurcated Trial

[Indicate whether the parties desire a bifurcated trial, and, if so, why.]

IX. Motions in Limine

Motions in limine shall not be separately filed. All in limine requests and responses thereto shall be set forth in the proposed pretrial order. Each SIDE shall be limited to three (3) in limine requests, unless otherwise permitted by the Court. The in limine request and any response shall contain the authorities relied upon; each in limine request may be supported by a maximum of three (3) pages of argument and may be opposed by a maximum of three (3) pages of argument, and the side making the in limine request may add a maximum of one (1) additional page in reply in support of its request. If more than one party is supporting or opposing an in limine request, such support or opposition shall be combined in a single three (3) page submission (and, if the moving party, a single one (1) page reply), unless otherwise ordered by the Court. No separate briefing shall be submitted on in limine requests, unless otherwise permitted by the Court.

X. Discovery

Each party has completed discovery.

XI. Number of Jurors

There shall be eight jurors. The Court will conduct jury selection through the "struck juror" method, beginning with the Court reading voir dire to the jury panel in the courtroom, continuing by meeting with jurors individually in chambers or at sidebar and there addressing any challenges for cause, and concluding with peremptory strikes.

XII. Non-Jury Trial

[If the parties desire a detailed opinion from the Court posttrial, counsel should include a proposed posttrial briefing schedule, including page limits, in the draft pretrial order.]

Along with their initial briefs, each party shall provide proposed Findings of Fact, separately stated in numbered paragraphs, constituting a detailed listing of the relevant material facts the party believes it has proven, in a simple narrative form, along with citations to the record. The proposed Findings of Fact shall be limited to a maximum of ___ pages. No separate Conclusions of Law shall be filed.

XIII. Length of Trial

The trial will be timed. Unless otherwise ordered, time will be charged to a party for its opening statement, direct and redirect examinations of witnesses it calls, cross-examination of witnesses called by any other party, closing argument, its argument on any motions for judgment as a matter of law, and all sides' argument on objections a party raises (outside the presence of the jury) to another party's exhibits and demonstrative exhibits.

The Courtroom Deputy will keep a running total of trial time used by counsel. If any party uses all of its allotted trial time, the Court will terminate that party's trial presentation.

Considering the Court's procedures for counting time, and considering the nature and extent of the parties' disputes, the parties request __ hours for their trial presentation. [Indicate the number of hours the parties request for their trial presentations. On days other than those involving jury selection, jury instructions, or deliberations, a typical day involves between 5 ½ and 6 ½ of trial time. In a typical bench trial, each day will involve between 6 and 7 hours of trial time. If the Court has previously set a maximum number of days that will be reserved for trial in this matter, the Court will not, absent good cause shown, allocate more hours for trial presentations than can be accommodated within the number of days reserved.]

XIV. Motions for Judgment as a Matter of Law

[The parties shall provide their position(s) as to how they will make motions for judgment as a matter of law, whether it be immediately at the appropriate point during trial or at a subsequent break, whether the jury should be in or out of the courtroom at the time such motions are made and/or argued, and whether such motions may be supplemented in writing.]

XV. Amendments of the Pleadings

[Indicate any amendments of the pleadings desired by any party, along with a statement whether the proposed amendment is objected to and, if objected to, the grounds for the objection.]

XVI. Additional Matters

[List any additional issues requiring resolution prior to trial, including whether the parties anticipate requesting that the courtroom be closed to the public for a portion of any specified witness' testimony.]

XVII. Settlement

[Provide a certification that the parties have engaged in a good faith effort to explore the resolution of the controversy by settlement, including a description of the overall extent of such efforts and identification of the date of the most recent substantive discussions regarding settlement.]

IT IS HEREBY ORDERED that this Final Pretrial Order shall control the subsequent course of the action, unless modified by the Court to prevent manifest injustice.

DATED: ______________

____
UNITED STATES DISTRICT JUDGE

APPROVED AS TO FORM AND SUBSTANCE:

____
ATTORNEY FOR PLAINTIFF(S)

____
ATTORNEY FOR DEFENDANT(S)

Chapter 8
Trial

In previous chapters, we discussed approaches for managing patent cases during the various stages of pretrial litigation. While case management during the pretrial phase goes a long way in ensuring smooth proceedings during trial, patent trials present their own distinctive challenges.

In a patent case, the involvement of a lay jury, which typically lacks knowledge concerning the complex and highly technical issues in question, colors almost all aspects of trial. Inherent complexity and inappropriate argumentation can result in unsupportable or inconsistent findings of fact by a confused jury. An inordinate amount of time and resources after trial may be spent trying to unravel and remedy such findings. Thus trial, like all other phases of a patent case, benefits from early and close judicial management to assist the fact finder to evaluate the merits.

As the Federal Circuit has remarked, a court's "discretion is at its broadest on matters of trial management." *Mass. Inst. of Tech. v. Abacus Software*, 462 F.3d 1344, 1367 (Fed. Cir. 2006). This chapter reviews the procedural and substantive considerations that factor into the exercise of the court's discretion and discusses approaches for structuring proceedings and narrowing issues to facilitate the jury's and the court's fact-finding role.

8.1 Procedural Issues

Before any trial can begin, the court must define the scope of trial and the ground rules governing its proceedings, including bifurcation and trial logistics. And when a jury is involved, the court should also establish procedures for assisting the jury's comprehension of the technologies involved. These issues must be addressed to some degree in all civil trials, but are of particular import in the patent litigation context, where cases often involve numerous complex and technical claims and defenses.

This section discusses the advantages and disadvantages of particular approaches to these process issues. Specifically, we explore when to hold separate trials for the different issues disputed in patent cases. We discuss under what circumstances particular trial schedules and organizations work best. We then consider what procedures a court can adopt to assist the jury in understanding a patent case's often highly technical trial presentations.

8.1.1 Separate Trials

The first question in any patent trial is whether all the issues involved should be resolved in a single proceeding. The trial court has broad discretion with regard to trial management. Federal Rule of Civil Procedure 42(b) provides:

> [f]or convenience, to avoid prejudice, or to expedite and economize, the court may order a separate trial of one or more separate issues, claims, crossclaims, counterclaims, or third-party claims. When ordering a separate trial, the court must preserve any federal right to a jury trial.

Nonetheless, the court's discretion is not without limits. Even if multiple actions involving the same or similar issues, such as infringement of the same patent, have been consolidated for pretrial purposes, they nevertheless must be separately tried unless:

> (1) any right to relief is asserted against the parties jointly, severally, or in the alternative with respect to or arising out of the same transaction, occurrence, or series of transactions or occurrences relating to the making, using, importing into the United States, offering for sale, or selling of the same accused product or process; and,
>
> (2) questions of fact common to all defendants or counterclaim defendants will arise in the action.

§ 299; *see* §§ 2.2.2.1.1, 5.1.3.8. More generally, when deciding whether issues should be separately tried, trial courts must ensure that a litigant's constitutional right to a jury is preserved. "Maintenance of the jury as a fact-finding body is of such importance and occupies so firm a place in our history and jurisprudence that any seeming curtailment of the right to a jury trial should be scrutinized with the utmost care." *Dimick v. Schiedt*, 293 U.S. 474, 486 (1935).

It is generally more efficient to have one trial and one appeal. *See Johns Hopkins Univ. v. CellPro*, 160 F.R.D. 30, 35 (D. Del. 1995). Thus, bifurcation in patent cases is the exception, not the rule, and appropriate only if it will promote judicial economy and not be inconvenient or prejudicial to the parties. *See F & G Scrolling Mouse L.L.C. v. IBM Corp.*, 190 F.R.D. 385 (M.D.N.C. 1999) (burden on moving party to show bifurcation will (1) promote greater convenience to parties, witnesses, jurors, and the court, (2) be conducive to expedition and economy, and (3) not result in undue prejudice to any party); *Spectra-Physics Lasers, Inc. v. Uniphase Corp.*, 144 F.R.D. 99, 101 (N.D. Cal. 1992) (denying motion to bifurcate trial into separate liability and damages phases where defendant failed to meet its burden).

Patent cases are often complex, however, sometimes involving different technologies, nonpatent claims with overlapping facts, and various legal and equitable claims and defenses. Whether all these issues should be resolved in a single trial depends on the facts and circumstances of the particular case. Factors to be considered when deciding whether to bifurcate include: whether the issues, and the evidence required for each issue, are significantly different; whether they are triable by jury or the court; whether discovery has been directed to a single trial of all issues; whether a party would be prejudiced by a single or separate trials; and whether a single trial would create the potential for jury confusion. *McDaniel v. Anheuser-Busch, Inc.*, 987 F.2d 298, 305 n.22 (5th Cir. 1993); *Angelo v. Armstrong World Indus., Inc.*, 11 F.3d 957, 964 (10th Cir. 1993); *Hirst v. Gertzen*, 676 F.2d 1252, 1261 (9th Cir. 1982); *Kimberly-Clark Corp. v. James River Corp.*, 131 F.R.D. 607, 608–09 (N.D. Ga. 1989).

Ultimately, considerations regarding the manageability and comprehensibility (particularly for jurors) of the various issues presented in the case should govern the decision to bifurcate and hold separate trials. From a case-management standpoint, bifurcation can assist the court in segregating from juror consideration evidence that may be integral for one issue, but irrelevant and prejudicial for another issue in the case. Bifurcation can also assist jurors by focusing jurors' attention on one issue at a time, helping to avoid confusion that can result from overwhelming jurors with multiple complex issues as once. At the same time, there are efficiencies that result from resolving all issues in one proceeding that should not be disregarded when deciding whether to bifurcate or even trifurcate patent cases.

8.1.1.1 Bifurcating Legal and Equitable Issues

Many of the defenses to a patent infringement action are equitable in nature. In addition to noninfringement and invalidity, many defendants assert inequitable conduct, patent misuse, laches, or equitable estoppel that would render an asserted patent unenforceable. There are also affirmative patent issues, such as joint inventorship, that are equitable in nature. While the facts underlying the merits of infringement and invalidity issues and defenses are within the province of a jury, equitable issues and defenses are exclusively within the court's purview.

8.1.1.1.1 When to Bifurcate

Because legal and equitable issues are decided by different fact finders, it is common and appropriate to hold separate jury and bench trials on the different issues. Separate trials are particularly appropriate where the equitable issues involve facts that are irrelevant or only marginally relevant to the liability issues to be decided by the jury, or which may prejudice a party's case on infringement or validity. For example, allegations of inventor misconduct before the USPTO relevant to an inequitable conduct defense, while irrelevant to infringement, may influence a jury's decision on that issue by suggesting that the inventor is untrustworthy. Separating the equitable issues for the court will avoid jury confusion and ensure that the jury's decision is based on proper and relevant evidence.

Moreover, a separate and early trial on the equitable defenses can sometimes promote resolution of the case. *See Agfa Corp. v. Creo Prods. Inc.*, 451 F.3d 1366, 1371–75 (Fed. Cir. 2006) (affirming trial court's discretion to conduct a bench trial on the equitable issue of unenforceability before infringement or validity are tried to a jury (citing *Gardco Mfg., Inc. v. Herst Lighting Co.*, 820 F.2d 1209, 1213 (Fed. Cir. 1987)). Where the alleged infringer has a strong, equitable defense, a trial on those issues may lead to an early unenforceability finding, obviating the more expensive and technically involved jury trial phase on infringement and validity.

While holding two separate proceedings can be more burdensome, there are procedures for increasing the efficiency of multiple trials. Jury trials and bench trials can be conducted in parallel to reduce the burden on witnesses who may have relevant testimony for both phases. By trying the legal issues to the jury in the morning sessions, and then conducting the bench trial in the afternoon, the court can coordinate the availability of witnesses and conserve both judicial and party resources.

Bifurcating legal and equitable claims can, however, implicate Seventh Amendment concerns if the bench trial is held prior to a jury determination of legal claims. In this circumstance, care must be taken not to impinge on a party's right to a full jury trial on its legal claims when trying equitable claims separately. *Beacon Theatres, Inc. v. Westover*, 359 U.S. 500, 508 (1959). Facts relevant to a party's legal claims must be decided by a jury. To the extent there is significant factual overlap between the legal and equitable issues, it may be improper for the court to decide the equitable issues before a jury determines the legal issues. For example, the Federal Circuit found it improper to hold a bench trial on the equitable issue of correction of inventorship before the jury could decide the state-law fraud issue of whether the patentee misrepresented being the sole inventor of the patent to the USPTO and third parties. *See Shum v. Intel*, 499 F.3d 1272, 1277–79 (Fed. Cir. 2007). The relationship between the equitable and legal issues is the determinative factor: whether there is commonality between the factual disputes underlying the equitable and legal issues such that determination of the equitable issue by the court effectively denies a party the right to a jury trial on the legal issues. Thus, bench trials on equitable issues can be held before a jury trial on legal issues without violating the Seventh Amendment if resolution of the respective questions turns on different factual foundations. *See generally Ethicon v. U.S. Surgical Corp.*, 135 F.3d 1456 (Fed. Cir. 1998) (upholding district court's finding of improper inventorship and dismissal of infringement issue because infringement question did not share common factual foundation with the inventorship issue); *Paragon Podiatry Lab., Inc. v. KLM Labs., Inc.*, 984 F.2d 1182, 1190 (Fed. Cir. 1993) ("The defense of inequitable conduct in a patent suit, being entirely equitable in nature, is not an issue for a jury to decide . . . . A patentee has no right to a jury trial respecting the factual element of culpable intent as part of the defense of inequitable conduct.").

Efficiency is another consideration in deciding whether to bifurcate legal and equitable issues. It may be more efficient to present all the evidence in one proceeding. For example, evidence of patent misuse, an equitable issue for determination by the judge, is often the same evidence used to support antitrust allegations, where it is used to determine factual issues by the jury. Courts should consider whether evidence that otherwise should be limited to a court hearing on equitable issues is also relevant to issues that the jury will determine. While not dispositive of the question of bifurcation, it is appropriate to consider whether efficiencies can be achieved by having the same evidence presented simultaneously to the jury and the court. Courts should continue to consider and weigh the potential benefits of efficiency against the potential for prejudicial misuse of evidence by the jury.

8.1.1.1.2 Use of an Advisory Jury

Although reserved for the court, equitable issues need not be tried separately. All issues can go to the jury by consent of the parties. Fed. R. Civ. P. 39(c). Even without consent, the court may try the equitable issues with an advisory jury. *Id.* The jury's verdict on the equitable issues is merely advisory, and a court may consider it but is not bound by the decision. The advantage of an advisory jury is that it enables all issues to be presented within one proceeding; a major disadvantage is that it risks contaminating the jury's consideration of the legal issues (for example, invalidity) with evidence relevant only to the equitable claim (for example, inequitable conduct). Moreover, a jury's fact-finding can constrain the court's determination on equitable issues, and courts need to be conscientious not to disregard findings of fact—explicit or implicit—that implicate legal claims. *See, e.g., Kinetic Concepts, Inc. v. Smith & Nephew, Inc.*, 688 F.3d 1342 (Fed. Cir. 2012) (implied jury factual findings within verdict of obviousness).

In light of these considerations, it is often preferred to have equitable issues, such as inequitable conduct, tried separately to the court following the jury's consideration of the legal issues. A separate proceeding after the jury's fact-finding provides the court the benefit of the jury's factual determinations (avoiding any Seventh Amendment issues), while eliminating the risk of juror confusion or prejudicial misuse of evidence relevant only to the equitable issues. Only the evidence relevant to the equitable issues and not presented to the jury need be presented during the separate court proceeding. As a result, a separate court trial on inequitable conduct, for instance, typically only requires an additional one or two days. The additional time needed for a separate court trial on inequitable conduct is often counterbalanced by not having to present this additional evidence to the jury or spend time during the jury phase discussing possible limiting instructions regarding evidence relevant only to equitable issues.

8.1.1.2 Separate Proceeding on Willfulness

The Supreme Court in *Halo Electronics, Inc. v. Pulse Electronics, Inc.*, No. 14-1513 (Supreme Court June 3, 2016), removed the ultimate determination of enhanced damages from the jury, leaving the issue exclusively to the court to decide. *See* § 7.3.4.5. The Federal Circuit has since held that the factual components of the willfulness question should be resolved by the jury. *See WBIP, LLC v. Kohler Co.*, ___ F.3d ___ (Fed. Cir. July 19, 2016). As with other issues for determination by the court, proof of factors bearing on the award of enhanced damages may include evidence not relevant to the issues to be decided by the jury, such as evidence relating to the subjective intent of the alleged infringer, which may be prejudicial to a party if admitted during the jury trial. Using the analysis described above (§ 8.1.1.1.1), the court should determine whether this prejudice justifies bifurcation of the enhanced damages factors in view of the evidence the parties propose to present in a particular case. If a court does bifurcates these issues, it may delay determination of this issue until after resolution of an appeal of the liability determination. *Robert Bosch, LLC v. Pylon Mfg. Corp.*, 719 F.3d 1305 (Fed. Cir. 2013) (en banc).

8.1.1.3 Bifurcating Damages

Liability and damages issues frequently are susceptible to bifurcation. *F & G Scrolling Mouse L.L.C v. IBM Corp.*, 190 F.R.D. 385, 388 (M.D.N.C. 1999). The determination of damages presents its own set of issues separate and apart from the complexity of the liability aspects of most patent cases. Proof of lost profits or a reasonable royalty can involve voluminous data and complicated financial analysis by economic experts. This evidence can be difficult to understand and may have little relationship to patent liability issues. Separating these issues can sometimes reduce the complexity of the case while increasing the jury's ability to understand the evidence presented.

Bifurcation of damages can also expedite a trial if the alleged infringer prevails on liability. Even if the patentee prevails on liability, there is a chance that the parties will settle the remainder of the case without the need for a damages phase. The likelihood of needing to try damages may be further diminished if the court enters judgment following the liability trial, thereby allowing an appeal of the liability issues before damages are taken up. *See Robert Bosch, LLC v. Pylon Mfg. Corp.*, 719 F.3d 1305 (Fed. Cir. 2013) (en banc).

Often, however, the patentee will seek to pursue adjudication of damages following the liability stage, which results in significant duplication of effort in staging a second trial. Furthermore, patentees have a legitimate argument that bifurcating damages can skew the verdict against them, since the jury knows it can go home earlier if it rules for the accused infringer on liability. In practice, most courts decline requests to bifurcate damages.

In some cases, resolving the damages issue likely would lead to a settlement, eliminating the need to try the lengthy panoply of liability issues. This has led some commentators and parties to suggest employing "reverse bifurcation," in which damages are bifurcated from liability and tried first. *See, e.g., In re Innovatio IP Ventures, LLC Patent Litig.*, 956 F. Supp. 2d 925, 929 (N.D. Ill. 2013); *STC UNM v. Intel Corp.*, 2011 U.S. Dist. LEXIS 15439, 2011 WL 7562686 (D.N.M. Dec. 22, 2011); J. Rantanen, *Reverse Bifurcation Practice*, http://www.patentlyo.com/patent/2011/07/reverse-bifurcation-1.html (July 31, 2011).

8.1.1.4 Bifurcating Different Patents

Patent cases often involve counterclaims for patent infringement. While a plaintiff may assert one set of patents, a defendant may counterclaim for infringement of its own patents. Often the technologies between the plaintiff's asserted patents and the defendant's asserted patents are the same, such that trial on both sets of infringement claims would involve the same expert witnesses and the same fact witnesses. In those cases, it may be more efficient to have both the patent infringement claims and counterclaims go forward in one trial. *See Hilleby v. FMC Corp.*, No. C-91-0568 FMS (CW), 1992 U.S. Dist. LEXIS 20835, 1992 WL 455436, at *3 (N.D. Cal. May 13, 1992).

Where the patents asserted in the counterclaim implicate different technology, different facts, different defenses, and different witnesses, trying all these issues together in one proceeding may be inappropriate. Sorting through different technologies and the different related claims and defenses can be unmanageable for both the court and the jury. In such cases, the court should consider bifurcating the plaintiff's patent action from the defendant's patent counterclaims and holding separate trials.

Typically, the plaintiff's case should proceed first, with trial on defendant's patents following. The second trial should proceed immediately after the first to avoid any unfair advantage that may result from resolving one set of patent infringement allegations before the other.

8.1.1.5 Bifurcating Nonpatent Causes of Action

In addition to patent causes of action, parties often assert related causes of action, such as antitrust, contract, and trade secret. Separate trials for the nonpatent causes can help streamline the case and make issues more comprehensible. Whether bifurcation is appropriate depends on the interrelationships of the causes of action asserted and the specifics of the case.

Antitrust counterclaims in patent infringement actions often are bifurcated. While equitable defenses to patent infringement, such as patent misuse, can implicate antitrust issues, antitrust claims often involve a different body of law and a different factual inquiry than patent infringement or invalidity. The Federal Circuit has recognized that bifurcating antitrust claims is a common and accepted practice. *See In re Innotron Diagnostics*, 800 F.2d 1077, 1086 (Fed. Cir. 1986). When bifurcating antitrust claims, it is usually advisable to try the patent allegations first. The outcome of the antitrust trial will often depend on the resolution of the patent cause of action. Moreover, parties often assert antitrust claims in patent cases for the purpose of gaining leverage in the litigation. Resolution of the patent case will often lead the parties to settle the antitrust suit, eliminating the need for the court to expend time and resources considering claims that are of collateral or secondary importance.

Nonpatent causes of action based on contract and trade-secret law are sometimes less amenable to bifurcation. When patents are the subject of a licensing agreement or some other contract, resolution of the patent cause of action is often dispositive or at least relevant to the contract cause of action. And where a trade secret claim involves arguments that either one of the parties misappropriated closely related technology, it will usually make sense to try the causes of action together. However, if the collateral cause of action is that the patent itself resulted from a theft of secrets, it may be more sensible to try the trade-secret-misappropriation cause of action first.

8.1.1.6 Bifurcating to Aid Juror Comprehension

As discussed in §§ 8.1.1.1–8.1.1.5, the decision to bifurcate any particular issue should balance the interests of the parties, the efficiencies in holding one proceeding, the court's ability to manage the case, and the practical ability of the jury to comprehend the complex issues in the case. Not only is the number of patent cases increasing in recent years, but so is the number of defendants named as alleged infringers in each case. As this trend continues, concerns over the jury's ability to keep track of the patent technology and the technology of each of the many accused products will weigh more heavily in the bifurcation calculus. Naturally, the more complex the case, the more bifurcation will become a necessity to ensure manageability and juror comprehension. In very complex cases (involving multiple defendants and multiple patents), courts are now considering bifurcating not only the issues discussed in §§ 8.1.1.1–8.1.1.5, but also the issue of infringement and validity, as well as holding separate trials for separate defendants. Note that the AIA now restricts the defendants who can be joined in a single infringement case. *See* § 299; § 2.2.2.1.1.

In a one-patent, one-defendant case, the overall balance of interests usually disfavors bifurcating the jury's determination of infringement from its determination of patent validity. When multiple defendants and multiple patents are involved, however, a jury will be asked to evaluate the various patented inventions against numerous accused products. That undertaking, combined with the introduction of numerous prior art references relevant to the validity inquiry, can be overwhelming, particularly when the asserted patents implicate complicated technology. In such cases, any economic benefit to having only one proceeding is significantly outweighed by the likelihood of juror confusion. In many complex cases, courts are now considering trying infringement separate from validity. The court can maintain some degree of consistency and efficiency by trying the issues to the same jury while allowing the jury to focus on one issue at a time through separate proceedings. With the same jury impaneled, the parties need not duplicate presentation of evidence relevant to both infringement and validity. In addition, this process may encourage settlement, as it affords the parties an opportunity to evaluate their case at each stage.

Similarly, in cases in which a plaintiff has named multiple defendants, courts may elect to hold separate trials, especially on infringement issues for individual defendants or separate groups of defendants with similar infringement issues. This will assist the jury in keeping track of the various accused products and technologies implicated by the lawsuit. Moreover, codefendants can disagree on trial strategies, and separate proceedings will enable each defendant to control its defense.

While bifurcating or trifurcating cases into more manageable units assists in juror comprehension, the associated costs to holding separate trials make bifurcation a practice best reserved for the most complex cases.

8.1.2 Trial Logistics

Whatever the scope of the trial, it is the court's responsibility to set and enforce the guidelines that govern its proceedings. Effective management of patent trials includes establishing reasonable time limits, maintaining a daily trial schedule, and outlining the order of the parties' presentations. With an established protocol, the parties are better able to structure and streamline their presentations to fit the court's schedule, resulting in a more understandable and efficient dispute resolution process.

8.1.2.1 Time Limits

A trial court's inherent power to control cases includes the broad authority to impose reasonable time limits during trial to focus the parties' presentation of evidence and prevent undue delay, waste of time, or needless presentation of cumulative evidence. Fed. R. Civ. P. 16(c)(15); *see also Applera Corp. v. MJ Research Inc.*, 389 F. Supp. 2d 344, 348 (D. Conn. 2005); *Motorola v. Interdigital Tech. Corp.*, 930 F. Supp. 952, 983 (D. Del. 1990) ("The Court's inherent power to control cases before it includes the power to set time limits for a trial."). Time limits have been recognized as a trial technique that enhances the quality of justice and improves the administrative aspects of any civil trial. *Amgen, Inc. v. Hoechst Marion Roussel, Inc.*, 339 F. Supp. 2d 202, 298 (D. Mass. 2004) (citing *The Vanishing Trial*, Discussion at the ABA Section on Litigation Symposium (Dec. 12–14, 2003)). They force the parties to evaluate what is and is not important to their case. Time limits are particularly appropriate in patent cases, where the issues are complex, and an unduly long trial would unnecessarily burden jurors and the court. *Applera*, 389 F. Supp. 2d at 348.

8.1.2.1.1 Determining the Length of Trial

What is a reasonable time for trial depends on the particulars of a case. The number of patents at issue, the complexity of the technology, the nature and number of any associated nonpatent claims, and whether issues are being bifurcated should all be taken into consideration when determining the length of trial.

To account for all these factors, a court's limits on the length of trial should be set after an informed analysis based on a review of the parties' proposed witness lists and proffered testimony, as well as their estimates of trial time. *See Duquesne Light Co. v. Westinghouse Elec. Corp.*, 66 F.3d 604, 610 (3d Cir. 1995). Time limits that are reasonable are (1) established in consultation with the parties; (2) allocated evenhandedly; (3) allotted to whatever evidence the parties deem appropriate; and (4) applied flexibly. *Id.*

Whatever the specifics of the case, a limit on the total amount of time for trial is advisable in almost every patent case. An open-ended case schedule quickly can become unmanageable in the face of so many complex issues, and imposes an unnecessary and unreasonable burden on the jury impaneled to hear the case. Therefore, the court should adopt an absolute limit on the length of trial based on input from the parties and the court's own evaluation of the case. Experience has shown that most patent cases can be fully tried within two weeks, allocating approximately twenty hours to each side, beginning with opening statements and continuing through closing arguments. (Procedures conducted by the court, mainly voir dire and instructions, typically are not clocked.)

8.1.2.1.2 Allocation of Trial Time

In general, trial time should be split evenly between the parties. The nature of patent cases is such that the burden of presenting evidence falls roughly equally on the parties. The presumed equal allocation can be adjusted for any demonstrable difference in the complexity of issues. Any time spent questioning witnesses, either on direct or cross-examination, should be counted against the questioning party, as would time spent reading that party's designated deposition transcripts into the record. *Duquesne Light Co.*, 66 F.3d at 610 (expressing concern over the district court's "puzzling" calculation of time by attributing the defendant's cross-examination of plaintiff's witnesses against plaintiff's trial time); *Applera*, 389 F. Supp. 2d at 347–48.

The key is to provide some temporal framework to motivate the parties to use trial time efficiently. How structured of a framework is required depends on the specifics of the case. In some cases, it is enough to inform the parties of their total time for trial and leave it to their discretion to determine how to utilize their time. In other cases, it may be appropriate for the court to allocate time for each phase of trial, placing time limits on opening and closing statements and each witness examination.

8.1.2.1.2.1 Time Limits on Witness Examinations

A highly managed approach with set time limits for each witness examination should be reserved for the most complex cases involving multiple patents and multiple different claims and defenses. These cases are often lengthy and have the greatest risk of jury confusion. Extending trial beyond the initial estimate can pose an undue hardship on jurors. Limiting the time for each phase of trial helps to regulate the parties' use of time, ensuring that they will stay within the time allotted for trial. Setting and requiring the parties to meet interim time limits also compels them to assess their case and the importance of each witness for each phase of the trial, which leads to clearer and more targeted presentations and examinations for the fact finder.

The difficulty with this approach, however, is that trial is a fluid process. Rigid time limits restrict the parties' ability to react to events and revelations that occur during the trial. During trial, the parties often drop witnesses or make changes to their examinations. It is harder to adapt to these changes in a case that has already divided the trial time for different witnesses. Indeed, the imposition of time limits for individual witnesses often invites additional disputes and requests during trial for adjustment of time allotments. As a result, a tool that should help a trial proceed more smoothly will, in fact, stymie the orderly progression of trial.

In almost all cases, it is sufficient to allow the parties to determine how much time to spend examining particular witnesses from their general time allotment. Permitting flexibility in witness examinations allows the parties to adjust their presentations to highlight witnesses that prove more critical and to follow up on testimony elicited during trial. Counsel in patent cases are often litigators with enough experience to manage their time without the need for limits on individual witness examinations. Thus, this type of high-level management is far more likely to promote an efficient trial and avoid ongoing requests for time adjustments.

8.1.2.1.2.2 Time Limits on Opening and Closing Statements

Time limits on opening and closing statements are more common and more feasible than trying to predict how much time is necessary and appropriate for each witness. Many courts have established time limits for opening and closing statements.

Typical time limits are less applicable in the patent context, however. Due to the complexity and the number of issues involved, opening and closing statements in a patent case usually require more time than those in a typical civil case. It is not unusual for the parties in a patent case to spend from one to two hours on an opening or closing statement. More commonly, opening arguments in patent cases fall within the thirty- to forty-five-minute range and closings from forty to sixty minutes (including rebuttal).

Thus, the ten- to thirty-minute time limit sometimes imposed in civil cases is generally not appropriate in a patent trial. The amount of time needed for useful opening and closing statements in patent cases approaches the practical time limit dictated by a jury's attention span. Thus, a fair and appropriate time limit on opening and closing statements is often superfluous, as parties rarely extend statements beyond that.

8.1.2.1.3 Modification of Time Limits

Whatever approach is taken, time limits should not to be applied so rigidly as to "sacrifice justice in the name of efficiency." *Navellier v. Sletten*, 262 F.3d 923, 941 (9th Cir. 2001). Strict adherence to time limits that prejudice a party's case can lead to new trial motions and grounds for appeal.

To ensure that the time limits imposed are reasonable, the court should monitor how much time is charged to each party and provide periodic updates to the parties. Giving periodic updates allows the parties to reassess case strategy and their allocation of time, if necessary.

It is advisable to have court staff act as the official timekeepers to avoid disputes or uncertainty that can result if the parties are left to the task. Court oversight of the trial clock enables the court to evaluate the progress of the case and ensure that the parties are on schedule. Based on the continued reassessment of the case, the court can determine if a party's request for additional time is warranted. Courts should exercise some flexibility in modifying time limits where the parties have been conscientious and expeditious in their use of time. Where, however, the lack of time available at the end of the case is the consequence of a party's mismanagement, it is not an abuse of discretion to refuse additional time. *See, e.g., Gen. Signal Corp. v. MCI Telecomms. Corp.*, 66 F.3d 1500, 1508–09 (9th Cir. 1995).

While the court need not grant additional time, it should not reduce a party's time without good cause. "[A]n allocation of trial time relied upon by the parties should not be taken away easily and without warning." *Duquesne*, 66 F.3d at 610. The parties plan trial strategy based on their time allotment. Action taken to reduce the allotment during trial leaves little opportunity to reassess trial plans. Therefore, modifications of time limits that reduce time allotment should rarely be made, and only when a party is abusing trial time. Even then, a party should be given clear warning and indication of the consequences of its trial behavior before action is taken.

As time estimates are subject to modification, the jury should not be informed of specific time limits. It is usually advisable to inform the jurors of how long the trial is expected to last to determine whether they will be able to serve and to allow them to make necessary arrangements. *See* Ninth Circuit Jury Trial Improvement Committee, *Second Interim Report: Recommendations and Suggested Best Practices, Recommendation II* (October 2006). Discussions regarding specific interim time limits, however, are not information jurors need to perform their duty.

While it can be a tactic used to motivate the parties to operate within time limits, making the jury conscious of time can draw attention away from the merits of the presentation. Clocks can become a distraction and interfere with the jury's role as a neutral fact finder. Furthermore, the jury may become biased against a party that uses or requests more time. Accordingly, discussions regarding time should also be conducted outside the presence of the jury.

8.1.2.2 Procedures for the Presentation of Evidence

In addition to time limits, the court must also determine how the presentation of evidence is going to proceed during trial. The court needs to set a schedule that will facilitate the timely completion of trial. It also needs to establish the order in which the parties will use their time to present the various issues. The court should consider what will assist the jury in understanding the evidence to ensure that presentations and arguments are helpful.

8.1.2.2.1 Trial Schedule

The trial schedule adopted by the court will affect how long trial will last, and should be taken into consideration when setting time limits for trial. The trial schedule should also take into consideration the jury's attention span. Many factors go into determining an appropriate trial schedule: the potential burden on the jury, the court's availability, witness availability, holidays, and the issues being tried.

It may seem most efficient to complete trial by holding all-day proceedings five days a week. The court's obligation to other matters, however, may make it difficult to accommodate such a demanding schedule. Furthermore, many other practical considerations may make a full-time schedule infeasible, and in some cases less efficient.

Later in this chapter, we discuss the types of evidentiary issues that may arise during a patent trial. These issues must be resolved outside the presence of the jury. A full-day trial schedule leaves little time available for the court to consider disputes that arise during the course of trial. As a result, with full-day schedules, the jury may have to be kept waiting while the court resolves evidentiary or legal disputes. A half-day schedule allows the court to consider legal issues in the afternoon without wasting juror time. A court can also use the afternoon to try equitable issues without the jury. Having the jury and bench trials proceed in parallel can help conserve resources as equitable issues often involve overlapping facts and witnesses. The advantages and disadvantages of holding parallel proceedings versus a separate bench trial following the jury trial are discussed more fully in the section on bifurcation. *See* § 8.1.1.1.

There are several additional benefits to adopting a half-day schedule that increase both the overall efficiency and quality of proceedings. The real advantage of a half-day schedule is that it allows jurors to arrange their schedules so that they can serve on the jury and still attend to their jobs or family responsibilities, reducing the hardship that would otherwise result from lengthy trials. The attention of the jury also wanes during long trial days. A half-day schedule also gives the parties more time to make their disclosures and prepare their presentations. In an abundance of caution, parties are often overinclusive in their presentations. Having more time to refine their case can eliminate a lot of needless evidence and corresponding disputes, increasing the overall efficiency of proceedings. *See* Ninth Circuit Jury Trial Improvement Committee, *Second Interim Report: Recommendations and Suggested Best Practices, Recommendation III*. Judges report that they accomplish as much, if not more, in a compressed scheduled day as in a regularly scheduled trial day, and that attorneys are usually better prepared.

Whether court is in session for four or five days a week, the goal of a trial schedule is to balance efficiency with quality. Holding full-day proceedings can certainly help to complete the trial faster. Such a rigorous schedule is best suited for shorter trials. Full-day schedules, however, can become overly demanding and burdensome for longer trials. In practice, it is rare for a typical patent trial to last for more than two weeks, particularly in light of the time limits that are becoming more common. Even for a trial that lasts two weeks or less, it is often advisable to hold as least one or two half-days during the trial week so that the court and the parties have built-in time to address evidentiary and trial logistics issues outside the presence of the jury.

8.1.2.2.2 Order of Trial Presentations

Once the trial time and schedule are set, the court should establish guidelines on how the time will be used. The court has discretion to control the order in which the parties will present proof. In typical cases, the plaintiffs go first because they bear the burden of proof. In patent cases, however, the burden of proof is shared by the parties. While plaintiffs bear the burden of proof on infringement, for example, defendants bear the burden of proof on invalidity. Therefore, the order of trial presentation and closing statements should take into account the various issues being tried.

8.1.2.2.2.1 Evidentiary and Witness Presentation

The parties' presentations should begin with the patentee's case-in-chief. As some cases are declaratory judgment actions, the patentee may not always be the plaintiff in the action. It nonetheless makes sense to have the patent owner's infringement case presented first as it is the rights conferred to a patentee that form the basis of all patent suits. The patentee must present all of its evidence on matters on which it bears the burden of proof in its case-in-chief, including evidence of infringement and any other additional nonpatent claims.

At the close of the patentee's case, the alleged infringer will put on its case. In addition to responding to the patentee's evidence on infringement and willfulness, the alleged infringer must also present evidence on the claims on which it bears the burden of proof, such as invalidity and inequitable conduct (if tried together). Where infringement is not disputed, the defendant should usually proceed first on its invalidity defenses.

After the alleged infringer rests its case, the patentee should be allowed to present evidence restricted to responding to the alleged infringer's affirmative case (i.e., invalidity and/or inequitable conduct).

8.1.2.2.2.2 Closing Statements

Closing arguments should be structured similarly to the order of trial presentation. It is customary for the party with the burden of proof to open and close the arguments. *See, e.g., Moylan v. Meadow Club, Inc.*, 979 F.2d 1246, 1251 (7th Cir. 1992). With the burden of proof shifting for different claims, patent cases usually require four closing statements.

Again, the patentee usually begins, summarizing the evidence presented on its affirmative claims of infringement and damages, along with any other nonpatent causes of action. The alleged infringer then presents its closing remarks, summarizing its response to the patentee's claims and presenting its arguments on invalidity. The patentee then rebuts on infringement and damages and responds on invalidity. In some courts, the alleged infringer is allowed a final statement, restricted to rebuttal on invalidity.

8.1.2.2.2.3 Openness of Courtroom

8.1.2.2.2.3.1 Exclusion of Witnesses

The court's power to control and shape trial includes the power to sequester witnesses before, during, and after their testimony. *Geders v. United States*, 425 U.S. 80, 87 (1976). At the request of a party, the court must exclude witnesses so that they cannot hear the testimony of other witnesses. Fed. R. Evid. 615. The purpose is to prevent witnesses who have yet to testify from tailoring their testimony to that of earlier witnesses, and to increase the likelihood that testimony will be based on a witness's own recollection. *Id.*; Advisory Committee Notes.

The Federal Rules of Evidence, however, exempt a party or party representative from exclusion. *Id.* Therefore, a witness who has been designated as a company's corporate representative at trial is not excludable. The court should have the parties designate corporate representatives before the start of trial so that any issues regarding the designee's possible role as a witness can be resolved prior to trial.

The Federal Rules of Evidence also provide that a person whose presence is shown to be essential to the presentation of the party's cause should not be excluded. *Id.* This exception is most often applied to expert witnesses, but a showing that the expert's presence is essential to the case is still required. *See Malek v. Fed. Ins. Co.*,

994 F.2d 49, 53–54 (2d Cir. 1993); *Morvant v. Constr. Aggregates Corp.*, 570 F.2d 626, 629–30 (6th Cir. 1978). To avoid disputes, the court should encourage the parties to reach an agreement as to whether expert witnesses can remain in the courtroom during testimony of other witnesses.

8.1.2.2.2.3.2 Exclusion of Public

Separate from the issue of witness exclusion is the issue of whether the public will be excluded from the courtroom during trial. Patent cases often require presentation of confidential and proprietary technical information of a company, sometimes including third-parties' information. Protective orders governing the use of confidential competitive information are in place in almost all patent cases. Before trial begins, the court should decide what protective orders are necessary to protect trade-secret evidence introduced at trial.

While the public has a limited interest in information produced by parties during discovery, it has a strong right of access to information and documents introduced at trial. *See In re Adobe Sys., Inc. Sec. Litig.*, 141 F.R.D. 155, 165 (N.D. Cal. 1992). In general, trials should remain open and accessible to the public.

A courtroom should not be closed simply because a company's proprietary technology is involved. The public should be excluded only where there is a showing of a compelling interest in maintaining the confidentiality of documents or revelation of proprietary information through testimony. To the extent confidential documents or information are extensively and genuinely part of the case, they should be part of the public record. *Id.* at 161. The court should, however, protect against the entry of confidential information into the trial record for the sole purpose of damaging an opponent's business.

In contrast to some other areas of law in which secrecy is sought, the kind of information that the parties may want to protect in patent litigation is much more likely to be legitimate technical data that should be protected. If the court makes clear that it will grant sealing requests only when the requesting party has made an effort to "cluster" the offered evidence (so that the courtroom has to be cleared a minimum number of times), the problem becomes self-enforcing and inappropriate closure is avoided.

8.1.2.3 Procedures for Managing the Jury

While the court's decisions regarding trial logistics should always take into consideration the role of the jury, there are specific procedural mechanisms by which the court can directly address the issues of ensuring jury comprehension and guiding the conduct of the jury.

8.1.2.3.1 Jury Selection and Voir Dire

Like any other civil trial, patent jury trials are governed by the Federal Rules of Civil Procedure, which require that a jury be impaneled with a minimum of six and a maximum of twelve jurors. *See* Fed. R. Civ. P. 48. The decision as to how many jurors will be impaneled should be finalized prior to the first day of trial and the start of the jury selection process.

As patent trials can take longer than other civil trials and are often more complex, it may prove difficult to find jurors able to commit the necessary time and attention. Such considerations weigh against impaneling a twelve-member jury. On the other hand, it is advisable to impanel more than the minimum six jurors to ensure a verdict can be taken if one or two jurors become unable to serve during trial.

The voir dire process in a patent trial is largely similar to that in other civil cases. However, given the specialized nature of the case, it is appropriate to question prospective jurors on their experience with the technology underlying the patents, experience with the patent system, and their feelings regarding patent protection.

Because both parties are likely to be interested in eliciting such information, the voir dire process can be streamlined by having the prospective jurors complete questionnaires ahead of time. The court should encourage the parties to settle on a juror questionnaire covering the information both sides are interested in eliciting before the start of trial. The parties and the court can determine whether any jurors should be excused for cause based on the responses to the juror questionnaire.

Thereafter, the court should explain the voir dire process to the prospective jurors, and allow each side a reasonable amount of time to conduct focused voir dire.

8.1.2.3.2 Timing of Jury Instructions

In the previous chapter, we discussed the process of preparing jury instructions for patent trials. Jury instructions are designed to explain the trial process to the jury and educate jurors on the law governing the issues they will be deciding. The parties have a right to have the jury instructed on the general law applicable to the case. *See Williams v. Jader Fuel Co., Inc.*, 944 F.2d 1388, 1402 (7th Cir. 1992); *H.H. Robertson Co., Cupples Prods. Div. v. V.S. DiCarlo Gen. Contractors, Inc.*, 950 F.2d 572, 578 (8th Cir. 1991). Indeed, the court has an independent duty to instruct the jury. *Belotte v. Zayre Corp.*, 531 F.2d 1100, 1102 n.1 (1st Cir. 1976).

Jury instructions must be set before closing arguments begin. Fed. R. Civ. P. 51(b). The court must allow the parties to object to instructions before the jury is instructed and before closing arguments. *Id.* Indeed, a party must object to an instruction before it can later claim an instruction was given in error. *Id.* In the past, this general rule was applied to jury instructions pertaining to the court's claim constructions. *See, e.g., Serio-US Indus., Inc. v. Plastic Recovery Techs. Corp.*, 459 F.3d 1311, 1317 (Fed. Cir. 2006) (holding that appellant failed to timely object to claim-construction jury instruction); *NTP, Inc. v. Research in Motion, Ltd.*, 418 F.3d 1282, 1312 (Fed. Cir. 2005) (recognizing defendant made a timely objection to claim-construction jury instruction) (citing *Advanced Display Sys., Inc. v. Kent State Univ.*, 212 F.3d 1272, 1281 (Fed. Cir. 2000)). The Federal Circuit has since held that a party need not renew its objections to the court's claim construction when the claim-construction jury instruction is given if the party's position was previously made clear to the court. *O2 Micro Int'l Ltd. v. Beyond Innovation Tech.*, 521 F.3d 1351, 1359 (Fed. Cir. 2008).

The court otherwise has discretion as to when it instructs the jury. Fed. R. Civ. P. 51. The timing of jury instructions can affect how useful the instructions are in educating the jury and assisting them in understanding the case.

Particular issues concerning preliminary and final jury instructions on substantive issues of law, including the requirement to instruct the jury on the court's claim constructions, are discussed in the previous chapter. *See* § 7.3. Here, we discuss jury management issues and techniques that can be employed during trial to assist the jury and improve their comprehension, including admonitions, jury binders and note-taking, and allowing juror questions and transitional statements by counsel.

8.1.2.3.2.1 Jury Admonitions

Besides preliminary and final jury instructions, there are limited instructions that the court should give to the jury during the presentation of evidence. Occasionally, evidence will be introduced for a limited purpose or through means other than witness testimony. During trial, the court should explain when the parties stipulate to testimony or facts or introduce evidence through discovery. In addition, instructions regarding the limited purpose of evidence should be given during trial at the time the evidence is introduced.

Other than that, the main instructions given during trial are admonitions to the jury. The court should inform the jurors that whenever they are allowed to separate (during breaks or at the end of each day), they should not discuss the case with anyone and should immediately inform the court if approached by anyone regarding the case. Typically, the admonition is given as part of the preliminary instructions. It is useful to remind the jury of this duty once trial begins, although it may not be necessary to admonish the jurors before each separation.

The prohibition against communications regarding the case typically extends to discussions between the jurors as well, barring any discussions of evidence until formal deliberations. The concern is that jurors may form an opinion before consideration of all evidence. Adherence to early formed beliefs is thought to prejudice defendants as plaintiffs put their case on first.

Recent studies, however, indicate that discussions before final deliberations do not lead to early verdicts. *See* Ninth Circuit Jury Trial Improvement Committee, Second Interim Report: Recommendations and Suggested Best Practices, Recommendation XV. Permitting jurors to discuss evidence during the course of trial can improve juror comprehension and reduce requests for read-back of testimony. Interim discussions also allow the jurors to clarify misunderstandings when they arise. Because private conversations between small groups of jurors can become divisive, interim discussions should only be allowed when all jurors are present.

Jury comprehension is of particular concern in patent matters. For that reason, interim jury deliberations can be a useful tool in maximizing jury comprehension. *See* Comments to Instruction 1.12, *Ninth Circuit Model Jury Instructions*. As the risk of prejudice falls more on one party than another, however, the court should consider the parties' positions on the matter before allowing interim jury discussions. In any event, the court should caution jurors to remain open-minded and not to make a decision until all the evidence is presented. *United States v. Klee*, 494 F.2d 394 (9th Cir. 1974).

8.1.2.3.3 Juror Binders

The court can also improve the jury's understanding of the case by providing written information for the individual jurors to take with them to the jury room. The information presented in a patent case can be difficult to digest and remember. Providing jurors with binders containing key information can enhance jurors' memory and their deliberations. *See* Ninth Circuit Jury Trial Improvement Committee, *Second Interim Report: Recommendations and Suggested Best Practices*, Recommendation X.

The information contained in the binders should include a copy of the preliminary jury instructions. Having a copy of the preliminary instructions enables the jurors to refer back to the rules that guide their conduct and outline their duties during trial. The binders can also be updated with the final jury instructions once they are given, so that the jurors will have them as reference during deliberations. The binders can also be used as a tool to aid the jurors' memory. The parties may often refer back to the testimony of certain witnesses. Having photographs of the witnesses in the jury binders will help the jurors remember who the parties are talking about.

In a patent trial, it is also helpful to include copies of the patent at issue so that the jurors may review it during testimony or when otherwise necessary. The meaning of the terms in the patent claims are determined by the court and central to many of the issues the jury must resolve. Accordingly, a copy of the court's claim construction should also be included to assist the jurors' reading of the patent. The patent and the parties' presentations will likely include other technical terminology. It is therefore advisable for the parties to identify and prepare jointly a glossary of technical and legal terms to be included as reference.

Jury instructions, photographs, the patents, and a glossary are relatively nonpartisan items that the parties can agree to include in the jury binders. The inclusion of key trial exhibits can also be helpful to the jury. Reaching agreement on a reasonable set of exhibits to include, however, may be difficult. Individual exhibits can be voluminous, and narrowing down specific exhibits can become contentious as each side will want to ensure its preferred exhibits are included. Identification and inclusion of the principal prior art references can be similarly challenging. If the parties can agree to a reasonable set, then exhibits and prior art should also be included in the binders. Otherwise, it may be best to limit the juror binder items to less controversial information.

8.1.2.3.4 Jury Note-Taking

The court should allow, even encourage, the jurors to take notes by providing notepads and pencils. Given the length and technical nature of most patent trials, having notes to review will help the jurors understand and remember the case. *See, e.g.*, Ninth Circuit Jury Trial Improvement Committee, *Second Interim Report: Rec-*

ommendations and Suggested Best Practices, Recommendation X. It also helps to focus the jurors' attention during the proceedings.

Juror notes are confidential and should not leave the courtroom during trial. The court should instruct the jury to leave their notes in the jury room when court is not in session. The jurors should also be discouraged from sharing their notes with one another. *See United States v. Balsam*, 203 F.3d 72, 86 (1st Cir. 2000). Notes reflect individual impressions and jurors should not rely on other people's interpretation of the evidence. Indeed, jurors should be admonished not to put too much emphasis on even their own notes. *United States v. Rhodes*, 631 F.2d 43, 46 (5th Cir. 1980); Ninth Circuit Model Jury Instruction 1.11. With proper restrictions in place, however, juror note-taking can be a useful and beneficial practice in a patent jury trial.

8.1.2.3.5 Allowing Juror Questions

Courts can also allow jurors to submit questions to improve the jury's level of attentiveness and comprehension during trial. *United States v. Huebner*, 48 F.3d 376, 382 (9th Cir. 1994), *cert. denied*, 516 U.S. 816 (1995). Some courts discourage juror questioning as it risks the jury's neutrality. *See, e.g.*, *United States v. Richardson*, 233 F.3d 1285, 1290 (11th Cir. 2000); *United States v. Ajmal*, 67 F.3d 12, 14 (2d Cir. 1995); *United States v. Sutton*, 970 F.2d 1001, 1005 (1st Cir. 1992); *DeBenedetto v. Goodyear Tire & Rubber Co.*, 754 F.2d 512, 516 (4th Cir. 1985). Allowing questions also risks the jurors' making premature decisions regarding the evidence.

If the court allows juror questioning, it should establish procedures to protect against these concerns. The court can ensure the propriety of juror questions by requiring any questions the jury may have for a witness to be submitted to the court in writing first. *See, e.g.*, Ninth Circuit Model Jury Instruction 1.15. The questions should then be submitted to counsel outside the presence of the jury so that the jury will not attribute any changes to, or rejection of, their questions to a particular party. The court should hear from counsel before deciding whether to ask the question, reject the question, or modify it as appropriate.

The procedures for juror questions, if permitted, should be included in the preliminary jury instructions. The court should make clear that questions should be reserved for extraordinary circumstances, and that numerous questions can slow down proceedings.

8.1.2.3.6 Transition Statements by Counsel to the Jury

The court can allow counsel to make interim statements to the jury to help explain the significance of the evidence and testimony presented. The presentation of evidence in a jury trial cannot always be organized discretely by the issues the jurors must decide. It can, therefore, be difficult for jurors to synthesize information and identify the significance of evidence presented, particularly in lengthy and complex cases.

Interim attorney statements can serve as signposts for the jury, explaining the purpose of testimony and how the evidence fits into a party's overall case. Allowing counsel before or after a witness examination to clarify the purpose of the testimony will help jurors understand the facts. This approach can be especially helpful when there is extensive expert testimony broken up into different infringement and invalidity issues.

To guard against misuse of attorney argument, the court should limit the amount of time the parties can use for such statements and should caution against argument. *See, e.g.*, Ninth Circuit Jury Trial Improvement Committee, *Second Interim Report: Recommendations and Suggested Best Practices*, Recommendation XV (recommending fifteen minutes per side to use as they wish during trial).

8.1.2.3.7 Jury Education and Tutorials

Because of the complexity of patent and technological issues at play, jury education is a serious concern in patent trials. Not only must the jury be educated in the applicable patent law, but it must also learn about the technology of the patents involved. To the extent the parties can agree on neutral tutorials, the court should encourage their use.

As noted in § 7.3.1, a video produced by the Federal Judicial Center, which provides an overview of the patent process, together with a mock sample patent for distribution to prospective jurors, has been used as part of the preliminary jury instructions to introduce patent procedure and patent law to the jury. The FJC updated that video in 2013 to address changes to patent law and implementation of the America Invents Act. This video, "The Patent Process: An Overview for Jurors," can be found here: https://www.youtube.com/watch?v=ax7QHQTbKQE.

Alternatively, the court might consider requiring the parties to prepare a preliminary instruction that provides a fair and accurate overview of the current state of the law. The parties and the court can use the Northern District of California's Preliminary Instruction A.1 ("What A Patent Is And How One Is Obtained") as a guide in crafting such an instruction. *See* Model Patent Jury Instructions (May 2014). These instructions can be found in Appendix E. *See also* Federal Circuit Bar Association, Model Jury Instructions (Jan. 2016) (contained in Appendix E).

Neutral technology tutorials have historically been difficult to procure. Parties are rarely able to prepare and agree on nonargumentative technology tutorials. Even when the parties agree on a joint tutorial, there is risk that one party is being taken advantage of and that the tutorial is not neutral. More often, the parties will insist on presenting separate tutorials. Competing tutorials are not any more helpful to the jury than having the parties explain the technology through their witness examinations.

8.1.2.4 Special Masters, Court-Appointed Experts, or Technical Advisors

Often in patent litigation a judge needs help understanding the technology involved. The simplest solution is for the parties' attorneys or experts to provide a tutorial on the technology. If this is not sufficient, the court has several means of obtaining more direct expert assistance: appointing a special master, appointing a court expert, or appointing a technical advisor. We previously touched on this topic with regard to claim construction in § 5.1.2.2.2.

A special master renders initial decisions for the court on technical matters. The special master is appointed pursuant to Federal Rule of Civil Procedure 53 and can hear evidence and argument from the parties and render an initial decision on substantive matters, such as claim construction or summary judgment. The initial decision is made in the form of a report or recommendations, which are provided to the parties and the court. The parties then must be given an opportunity to make objections to the special master's report, and the report and any objections are reviewed by the court. In this process, the court may, but is not required to, receive additional evidence. The court finally adopts, rejects, or modifies the special master's report, applying a de novo standard to factual and legal decisions and an abuse-of-discretion standard to procedural decisions.

A court expert, like party experts, ultimately provides the court with expert testimony to be taken into account along with other evidence in rendering a decision. The court expert is appointed pursuant to Federal Rule of Evidence 706 and, as required by that rule, must be provided with initial written instructions by the court. *See generally Regents of the Univ. of Cal. v. Oncor Inc.*, No. C-95-3084-VRW, 1997 U.S. Dist. LEXIS 15068, 1997 WL 670674, at *18 (N.D. Cal. Aug. 19, 1997). After completing an analysis, the expert provides findings to the parties and the court, much like any expert's report. Any party may then depose the expert. Finally, the expert provides the court and, if present, the jury with the results in the form of expert testimony, subject to the same cross-examination as party experts. The Federal Circuit affirmed a district court's use of a court-appointed expert pursuant to Federal Rule of Evidence 706 in *Monolithic Power Sys., Inc. v. O2 Micro Int'l Ltd.*, 558 F.3d 1341 (Fed. Cir. 2009). The district court had allowed the parties to show cause why an expert should not be appointed, allowed the parties to mutually agree on an expert, provided detailed written instructions to the expert, and ordered the expert to make himself available for depositions and examination at trial. In addition, the court allowed the parties to continue to have their own experts and specifically instructed the jury not to assign the court-appointed expert any greater weight. Because the district court properly administered the standards set by Federal Rule of Evidence 706, the Federal Circuit held there was no abuse of discretion. The Federal Circuit noted, however, that the "predicament inherent in court appointment of an independent expert and revelations to the jury about the expert's neutral status trouble [the] court to some extent," and admonished that use of court-appointed experts should be limited to the rare and exceptional cases. For similar reasons, parties usually will not favor allowing a court-appointed expert to testify to a jury, and if the expert does testify, will not favor identifying the expert as "court-appointed" or "neutral."

A technical advisor functions as an advisor to the judge on technical matters in a manner often analogized to a law clerk, although case law views the analogy as imperfect. The advisor is appointed pursuant to the court's inherent power. It is a power to be used "sparingly," but appointment is proper in any highly technical case where the science or technology is well beyond the experience of the judge. Importantly, if the advisor provides no evidence to the court, Federal Rule of Evidence 706 does not apply and, as a result, the parties have no right to a deposition or other disclosure of the advisor's opinions or communications with the court. Alternatively, a person can be appointed as both a court expert and an advisor, in which case Federal Rule of Evidence 706 applies.

Best practices for use of technical advisors are set out in a quartet of appellate court cases: *FTC v. Enforma Natural Products, Inc.*, 362 F.3d 1204, 1213–15 (9th Cir. 2004); *TechSearch LLC v. Intel Corp.*, 286 F.3d 1360, 1378–79 (Fed. Cir. 2002) (applying Ninth Circuit law); *Association of Mexican-American Educators v. California*, 231 F.3d 572, 611–14 (9th Cir. 2000) (en banc) (Tashima, J., dissenting); and *Reilly v. United States*, 863 F.2d 149 (1st Cir. 1988). *See generally* § 5.1.2.2.2.1. These cases focus on several procedural aspects of the technical advisor process to ensure the technical advisor does not improperly introduce new evidence unknown to the parties or influence the court's resolution of factual disputes. First, the court should assure a fair and open procedure to appoint a neutral advisor. Second, the advisor explicitly should be given a clearly defined, proper role that ensures there is no impingement on the court's role as fact finder. Third, the court should provide some assurance that the advisor remains within that proper role. Use of these procedures also facilitates appellate review of the propriety of the technical advisor's role.

To ensure fairness in the appointment, the court should identify the proposed advisor to the parties in advance of the appointment. This process can involve inviting the parties to propose advisors, either separately or together after consultation. If the parties are asked to provide potential advisors, the court should establish, in advance, limits on the contact the parties may have with prospective advisors. Alternatively, the court can identify a proposed advisor to the parties—potentially, an advisor the judge worked with previously—without prior consultation. In either case, the parties should be allowed to challenge the advisor's bias, partiality, or lack of qualification. If any challenge is raised, the court should address it on the record.

The proper role of the advisor is to be a sounding board or tutor who aids the judge's understanding of the technology. This includes an explanation of the jargon used in the field, the underlying theory or science of the invention, or other technical aspects of the evidence presented by the parties. The advisor can also assist the judge's analysis by helping think through critical technical problems. In this latter function, case law admonishes that the court must be careful to assure that the decision making is not delegated to the advisor. Although in form much like the interaction between a judge and law clerk, the situation is different in that, because of a judge's knowledge of law, a clerk cannot usurp the judicial role; in contrast, a technical advisor in an area of science unfamiliar to the judge potentially could.

Within these parameters, the advisor properly can aid the judge's understanding and analysis throughout a patent case. This can include helping the judge understand the patent specification and claims, expert affidavits and testimony provided by the parties, and scientific articles that may be offered as prior art. Proper subjects for consultation with the advisor include whether technical facts are in dispute in a summary judgment motion, claim interpretation, validity and infringement questions, the proper articulation of technical issues for jury instructions, and the admissibility of proffered scientific evidence under *Daubert*. The advisor, however, may not provide evidence, either documentary or testimony, without compliance with Federal Rule of Evidence 706. The advisor's advice therefore cannot be based on extra-record information (except the use of technology-specific knowledge and background used to educate the judge), and the advisor cannot conduct any independent investigation. Particularly in situations in which the advisor assists the judge's efforts to resolve factual conflicts, the judge and advisor should be vigilant to avoid the advisor unduly influencing the judge's decision making. In no circumstance, of course, should the advisor become an advocate for any party or position.

The court or advisor should confirm that the advisor's work is done within proper parameters for the benefit of both the parties and appellate review. There is no fixed requirement how this should be accomplished. Proper means include supplying a transcript of the advisor's communications with the judge, providing a report by the advisor of the work performed and any communications had with the judge, or obtaining an affidavit from the advisor at the outset of the work committing to perform within a description of a proper scope of work and procedures (as outlined above) and obtaining a second affidavit at the conclusion attesting to compliance with the job description in the initial affidavit.

8.2 General Evidentiary Issues

In every trial, it is inevitable that the court will have to resolve evidentiary issues. The parties may dispute whether a witness's testimony is appropriate, whether certain exhibits should be admitted, and the proper use of demonstratives. In this section, we discuss the typical evidentiary issues that arise in a patent case and the considerations the court should keep in mind when deciding these issues.

8.2.1 Witnesses

8.2.1.1 Patent Law Experts

Parties sometimes propose presenting expert testimony regarding patent law, procedures of the USPTO, patent terminology, the prosecution history, and specific substantive (e.g., anticipation) and procedural (e.g., what a "reasonable patent examiner" would find material) issues through a patent attorney or former USPTO employee. In support of this testimony, parties often point out that the evidence rules specifically permit opinions on ultimate issues (Fed. R. Evid. 704) and the presentation of testimony without first specifying underlying facts or data (Fed. R. Evid. 705).

Testimony on issues of law by a patent law expert—as contrasted with a general description of how the patent process works—is usually deemed inadmissible. Just as in any other field, it is exclusively for the court, not an expert, to instruct the jury regarding underlying law. *See, e.g.*, *Burkhart v. Wash. Metro. Area Transit Auth.*, 112 F.3d 1207, 1213 (D.C. Cir. 1997). Testimony regarding the procedures and terminology used in patents and file histories, on the other hand, often is allowed. *See, e.g.*, *Bausch & Lomb, Inc. v. Alcon Labs., Inc.*, 79 F. Supp. 2d 252, 255–58 (W.D.N.Y.

2000). In many cases, however, this testimony might be redundant in light of a preliminary jury instruction explaining those procedures. Because a jury instruction is likely to be more neutral, it usually will be a preferable means of providing this information to the jury. An instruction, however, may lack sufficient specificity to explain a USPTO procedural event relevant in a particular case, and in that circumstance, expert testimony is more likely to be appropriate and helpful to the jury.

The admissibility of proffered patent expert testimony on ultimate issues will often depend on whether the expert is doing anything more than applying patent law to a presumed set of facts, essentially making the jury's determination. This particularly is true if the proffered patent expert has no relevant technical expertise. Thus, a patent expert's opinion regarding such matters as infringement, obviousness, and anticipation based on technical conclusions that are assumed or provided by a different expert is usually improper. Similarly, testimony applying patent law to issues intertwined with patent procedure, but dependent on technical conclusions supplied by others, such as the appropriate priority date of a claim in a continuation application, is usually inappropriate. On the other hand, if the patent expert also has relevant technical expertise, he or she should be equally able to provide expert testimony within that expertise as would be any nonlegal expert with similar technical expertise.

In trials to the court, when there is no concern regarding jurors' overreliance on expert testimony, courts more freely admit the testimony of patent law experts. This includes, for example, testimony regarding whether a reasonable patent examiner would deem particular prior art or statements important in an inequitable conduct determination. Courts have found such testimony helpful and allowed it. *See, e.g.*, *Bristol-Myers Squibb Co. v. Rhone-Poulenc Rorer, Inc.*, 326 F.3d 1226, 1238 (Fed. Cir. 2003); *PerSeptive BioSystems, Inc. v. Pharmacia Biotech, Inc.*, 12 F. Supp. 2d 69, 74 (D. Mass. 1998), *aff'd*, 225 F.3d 1315 (Fed. Cir. 2000).

Finally, testimony is sometimes offered regarding the abilities of patent examiners, their workloads, time spent on applications, or similar matters. This testimony, which is meant to bolster or undermine the statutory presumption of validity, is improper. § 282; *see also Applied Materials, Inc. v. Advanced Semiconductor Materials Am., Inc.*, No. 92-20643, 1995 U.S. Dist. LEXIS 22335, 1995 WL 261407 (N.D. Cal. Apr. 25, 1995). The deference the jury should give to the actions of the patent examiners is an issue of law like any other. *See A & L Tech. v. Resound Corp.*, Case No. C 93-00107 CW, 1995 U.S. Dist. LEXIS 22443, at *11, 1995 WL 415146 (N.D. Cal. June 29, 1995) ("As a matter of law, a patent examiner is presumed to have conducted her own independent analysis of the prior art and drawn her own conclusions."); *see also Al-Site Corp. v. VSI Int'l Inc.*, 174 F.3d 1308, 1323 (Fed. Cir. 1999); *Am. Hoist & Derrick Co. v. Sowa & Sons, Inc.*, 725 F.2d 1350, 1359 (Fed. Cir. 1984). The appropriateness of that deference is not an issue for jury resolution.

8.2.1.2 Inventor and Other Technical Party Employee Testimony

Inventors and other technical employee witnesses often testify at trial regarding the invention and other technical matters. These witnesses frequently qualify as experts, and if properly disclosed as testifying experts, appropriately may provide expert testimony. Because their duties likely do not "regularly involve giving expert testimony," no expert report is required by such employees absent special order; however, ordering such a report usually is appropriate and is a provision that might be included in the case-management conference order. *See* Fed. R. Civ. P. 26(a)(2)(B); § 2.6.

If inventors and other technical employees are not disclosed as experts, difficult line-drawing can arise regarding their testimony. For example, when an inventor or co-employee testifies regarding the invention to a jury, it usually is necessary to accompany the testimony regarding historical acts with an explanation of the technology involved. These explanations are sometimes challenged as undisclosed expert testimony. Other testimony that often draws a challenge is inventor or employee testimony regarding the nature of the prior art at the time the invention was made. While testimony about the invention and about the prior art may be highly technical, it may involve the description of historical facts without the expression of opinion. In that event, the testimony is proper without expert disclosure. Such testimony, however, is sometimes employed to attempt to introduce undisclosed opinion testimony. A similar issue is presented by testimony aimed at teaching the relevant science to a jury; this, too, may be appropriate testimony without expert disclosure, but also is an opportunity sometimes used to attempt to introduce undisclosed expert testimony.

8.2.2 Exhibits

Due to the technical nature of patent cases, the number of potential exhibits can be substantial. Parties tend to be overinclusive with their exhibit lists to minimize the risk that they will later be precluded from using a particular document during trial. A final decision on whether an exhibit will be used is often not made until the middle of trial. The sheer volume of exhibits makes it difficult for the parties and the court to arrive at any meaningful refinement of exhibits prior to trial.

In general, resolving all evidentiary issues and preadmitting exhibits prior to trial saves trial time and reduces the burden on the jurors who would otherwise have to wait while the court resolves exhibit disputes with the parties. One way the court can achieve this end is by placing the burden of agreeing on exhibits on the parties. The court can deem all exhibits admitted, unless a party raises specific objections with the court in advance of trial. The burden of having to articulate specific and defensible objections to the court often compels parties to act reasonably when conferring with the opposing side, leaving only genuine disputes for the court.

This approach, however, requires the parties and the court to expend a significant amount of time deciding the admissibility of an exhibit that the parties may ultimately never use at trial. Another approach is to defer decision on exhibits until a party intends to introduce them. The court should have the parties adopt an exhibit disclosure schedule that provides enough time for the parties to confer over objections and raise issues with the court in advance. Typically, a party should identify the exhibits it intends to use two days in advance, giving the court a day to consider the issue if the parties cannot resolve it on their own.

A copy of any exhibits admitted into evidence should be provided to the jurors during deliberations. The court should keep a record of exhibits admitted into evidence and order the parties to prepare a set for the jury room.

Another issue that often arises in patent cases in the context of trial exhibits is the authentication of exhibits used as prior art. With the proliferation of information on the Internet, litigants often rely on prior art references located on the Internet. These prior art references are still subject to usual rules of authentication. *In re Wyer*, 655 F.2d 221, 227 (C.C.P.A. 1981) (party seeking to introduce a reference as prior art must "produce sufficient proof of its dissemination or that it has otherwise been available and accessible to persons concerned with the art to which the documents relates").

As litigants increasingly rely on the Internet to uncover articles, papers, manuals, and other publications that they intend to rely on as prior art, disputes over authenticity are becoming more frequent. Typically publication in a scientific journal is enough to establish a reference's date of availability to the public and status as prior art. *Duramed Pharm. Inc. v. Paddock Labs, Inc.*, 644 F.3d 1376, 1382 n.2 (Fed. Cir. 2011), *citing In re Lister*, 583 F.3d 1307, 1313 (Fed. Cir. 2009). Other types of publications retrieved from Internet sources, however, require authentication of the date of publication. A date on a document, with nothing more, is usually insufficient to authenticate the document as prior art. *See ResQNet.com, Inc. v. Lansa, Inc.*, 533 F. Supp. 2d 397, 414 (S.D.N.Y. Feb. 1, 2008) (disregarding a publication as prior art where no witness testified and no evidence was presented as to date of publication other than a date on the document itself). Some evidence from a witness or a library setting forth procedures and date of cataloging is needed for authentication. *In re Enhanced Security Research, LLC*, 739 F.3d 1347, 1354–55 (Fed. Cir. 2014) (dated software manual authenticated as prior art only when taken into consideration with declaration of software company's CEO attesting to date of publication); *In re NTP, Inc.*, 654 F.3d 1279, 1294–96 (reference was authenticated based on attestation of university library that date-stamped and catalogued the reference).

In recent years, there has been an increased reliance on early webpages retrieved from the Wayback Machine (available at http://archive.org/web/) to establish prior art systems or disclosures. The Wayback Machine is operated by a company called the Internet Archive which seeks to catalogue all websites on the Internet. Party attestations as to the retrieval of screenshots, disclosures, or webpages from the Wayback Machine is insufficient to authenticate such exhibits as prior art. Instead, most courts require an affidavit from a representative of the Internet Archive with personal knowledge of the specific contents of the Internet archive at issue. *See Specht v. Google, Inc.*, 758 F. Supp. 2d 570, 580 (2010); *see also United States v. Bansal*, 663 F.3d 634, 667–68 (3d Cir. 2011) (requiring testimony on how the Wayback Machine works, its reliability, and comparison of screenshots before authenticating screenshots obtained from the Wayback Machine as evidence).

8.2.3 Demonstratives

Demonstratives can be especially useful tools in patent cases. They help the parties explain background technology to the court and the jury. Because demonstratives are not evidence, however, they are not admitted into the record and do not need to meet admissibility requirements. There must, nonetheless, be a foundation for the use of demonstratives. Specifically, demonstratives can be used if they are fair representations and assist the jury in understanding a witness's testimony.

A court has broad discretion in managing the use of demonstratives. A court can preclude the use of a demonstrative if its utility in illustrating concepts to the jury is outweighed by the risk of unfair prejudice, confusion to the jury, or undue delay of time. Fed. R. Evid. 403. As with exhibits, the court should require the parties to exchange demonstratives in advance of their intended use in court. If the parties cannot resolve any objections, the court can then decide whether any proposed demonstratives advance inappropriate arguments or are unduly prejudicial before they are presented to the jury.

Because demonstratives are not evidence, they are excluded from the jury room during deliberations. A party may, on occasion, ask that a demonstrative be admitted into evidence. Courts have discretion to admit into evidence demonstratives that summarize admissible evidence. Fed. R. Evid. 1006. The court should encourage the parties to confer about what demonstratives can be admitted into evidence.

8.2.4 Limits on Attorney Argument

Because patent trials typically are longer and more complex than most other cases, the court should take proactive measures to discourage the parties from prolonging trial with unnecessary and contentious arguments. Owing to the massive amounts of evidence involved in patent cases, disputes over arguments and objections to evidence during trial is unavoidable. The court can, however, make efforts to minimize sidebars and improper attorney argument.

To discourage extended attorney argument while the jury is present, the court should charge any time spent in sidebars and arguing objections to the party that loses the argument. The court should also remind the parties to refrain from extended argument when making objections. Giving the parties an outlet to make interim attorney arguments can reduce the likelihood that they will make improper or protracted arguments at other times during the trial.

During the course of a witness's testimony, a party may object to a particular subject of examination. The court should encourage the examining party to focus on another topic, if possible, until the jury is released. The court can then resolve the issue with the parties without wasting the jury's time.

8.3 Specific Substantive Issues

In addition to general evidentiary issues, patent trials present the court with substantive issues unique to patent law. The court must be familiar with considerations that arise in the context of proving infringement or invalidity. The patent law also provides a patent owner with remedies other than compensatory damages that are within the court's discretion to award. This section will discuss substantive proof issues that the court should be aware of when presiding over a patent trial.

8.3.1 Limitations on the Number of Asserted Claims

Patent cases can sometimes involve dozens of patents with hundreds of claims asserted against multiple defendants. Because management of such cases can be unwieldy, the court should consider limiting the number of claims that a patentee may assert. *See Fenster Family Patent Holdings, Inc. v. Siemens Med. Sols.*, Case No. 04-0038, 2005 U.S. Dist. LEXIS 20788, 2005 WL 2304190 (D. Del. Sept. 20, 2005) (reducing number of asserted claims from ninety to ten); *Verizon Cal., Inc. v. Ronald A. Katz Tech. Licensing, L.P.*, 326 F. Supp. 2d 1060, 1066 (C.D. Cal. 2003) (requiring plaintiff to select three representative claims per asserted patent); *Auto Wax Co. v. Mark V Prods.*, Case No. 99-cv-0982, 2001 WL 292597 (N.D. Tex. Mar. 14, 2001) (limiting claims to be tried from eighty-six to nineteen); *see also LML Patent Corp. v. JPMorgan Chase & Co.*, Case No. 08-cv-448, 2010 U.S. Dist. LEXIS 136452, 2010 WL 5140823 (E.D. Tex. Oct. 12, 2010) (court's scheduling order limiting plaintiff to ten asserted claims).

While limiting the number of asserted claims may be necessary for effective and efficient case management, care must be given to avoid violating a patentee's due process rights with respect to nonselected claims. Specifically, where nonselected claims present distinct issues of infringement and invalidity not addressed by the asserted claims, a patentee should be given an opportunity to litigate those patent claims on the merits. *See In re Katz Interactive Call Processing Patent Litig.*, 639 F.3d 1303, 1312–13 (Fed. Cir. 2011) (suggesting that an order refusing to allow a plaintiff to add claims after a showing that such claims presented unique issues as to liability or damages may be subject to review or reversal). A plaintiff should furthermore be afforded sufficient opportunity to determine (through discovery or otherwise) whether particular claims may raise distinct issues of infringement and invalidity before the court imposes any claim selection order. *Id.* at 1313 n.9.

Where a plaintiff is given an opportunity, but fails either to assert or demonstrate that the nonselected claims raised issues that are not duplicative of the issues raised by the selected claims, a court is free to enter final judgment as to all claims based only on adjudication of the selected claims. *Id.* at 1313.

Where a plaintiff demonstrates that nonselected claims present unique liability or damages issues, however, the court should either sever and stay proceedings with respect to the nonselected claims or dismiss the nonselected claims without prejudice to plaintiff's ability to reassert them in a subsequent lawsuit. In the event a plaintiff decides to pursue the unselected claims, it may be more judicially efficient to sever and stay proceedings, allowing the parties and the court to retain the benefit of earlier proceedings in adjudicating the unselected claims. The parties may furthermore be able to resolve issues involving the unselected claims as part of resolution of the rest of the case.

In contrast, dismissal of unselected claims without prejudice may remove the threat of those claims from the immediate litigation, but may lead to redundant proceedings if the plaintiff elects to pursue claims in a subsequent lawsuit. With the unselected claims removed from the scope of the litigation, they are also less likely to be useful as leverage in resolving the case at hand.

8.3.2 Indirect Infringement

Patent infringement must be proven by a preponderance of evidence. The Federal Circuit requires proof of infringement to include an element-by-element analysis for each asserted claim in the patent and the accused product. In many patent cases, patent owners not only allege direct infringement, but that a defendant contributes to or induces another's infringement. The direct infringement underlying a contributory infringement or inducement claim is usually committed by a nonparty to the action. Disputes can arise during trial as to whether the evidence of the underlying direct infringement is sufficient to submit the issue to the jury.

While there must be evidence of underlying direct infringement, a nonparty's direct infringement can be proven through direct or circumstantial evidence. *Moleculon Research Corp. v. CBS, Inc.*, 793 F.2d 1261, 1271 (Fed. Cir. 1986). Circumstantial evidence of the indirect infringer's sales and dissemination of instructions for operation in an infringing manner can support a finding of direct infringement by customers. *Id.* Furthermore, there need not be evidence showing that every customer infringes; it is sufficient that the patentee present evidence from which the jury can infer that at least one customer directly infringes.

Inducement of infringement also requires proof that the alleged infringer intended to induce infringement by others. This includes proof of the infringer's actual knowledge or "willful blindness" to the existence of the patent and that the induced acts constitute infringement. *Global-Tech Appliances, Inc. v. SEB S.A.*, 131 S. Ct. 2060 (2011). Whether the infringer deemed the patent valid, however, is irrelevant. *Commil USA, LLC v. Cisco Sys., Inc.*, 135 S. Ct. 1920 (2015). Proof of intent can be inferred from the conduct of the alleged infringer. As a result, evidence that may otherwise be prejudicial for purposes of proving infringement may be admissible to show intent. If such evidence is admitted, the court should take care to give limiting instructions explaining the purpose of such evidence. Similarly, the alleged infringer may attempt to disprove an intent to infringe a valid patent with evidence from incomplete proceedings in the USPTO in which an interim ruling has found the relevant claims invalid. Evidence of such interim PTAB rulings generally is inadmissible to prove invalidity, because its probative value is substantially outweighed by the risk of unfair prejudice to the patentee (*see* § 7.5.4.5), and for the same reason it may be excluded as evidence of an alleged inducer's lack of intent. *See VirnetX, Inc. v. Cisco Sys., Inc.*, *767* F.3d 1308, 1324–25 (Fed. Cir. 2014).

8.3.3 Invalidity

8.3.3.1 Presumption of Validity

Like infringement, proof of invalidity must include an element-by-element analysis. Invalidity, however, must be shown by clear and convincing evidence as the law provides that patents are presumed valid. § 282; *Microsoft Corp. v. i4i Ltd. P'ship*, 131 S. Ct. 2238, 2242 (2011) (holding that § 282 requires an invalidity defense to be proved by clear and convincing evidence); § 7.3.4.3. This is often phrased as requiring evidence that convinces the trier of fact that it is "highly probable" that the patent is invalid. *See, e.g., Buildex, Inc. v. Kason Indus., Inc.*, 849 F.2d 1451, 1463 (Fed. Cir. 1988).

The jury does not have the discretion to disregard the presumption of validity. During trial, it is the alleged infringer's burden to present evidence and argue that the presumption is rebutted. A party cannot argue that the presumption should not apply. *See Am. Hoist*, 725 F.2d at 1360 (stating that the statutory presumption of validity imposes a burden that "is constant and never changes and is to convince the court of invalidity by clear evidence").

Where the prior art in question was before the USPTO during prosecution, the patent holder will argue that the presumption of validity is "especially difficult" to rebut. *See Glaxo Group Ltd. v. Apotex, Inc.*, 376 F.3d 1339, 1348 (Fed. Cir. 2004). Where the prior art in question was not considered by the USPTO during prosecution, the alleged infringer will argue that the presumption carries little weight. The burden of proof, however, remains the same regardless of whether the prior art reference was before the USPTO during prosecution. *See Microsoft Corp. v. i4i*, 131 S. Ct. at 2250 (rejecting fluctuating standard of proof based on whether evidence was considered by USPTO during prosecution). Where the evidence being considered was not before the USPTO during prosecution, it may "carry more weight" in meeting a defendant's burden of proof, but it does not change the standard. *Id.* at 2251. Therefore, in both circumstances, the court should instruct the jury that an alleged infringer has the burden of presenting clear and convincing evidence before a patent can be found invalid. However, as discussed in § 7.3.4.3, the court should not instruct the jury about the presumption of validity itself—the court's instruction that the jury is to weigh invalidity evidence according to a clear-and-convincing standard incorporates this presumption and is itself sufficient; advising the jury that there is a presumption risks jury confusion that the presumption is a separate hurdle, in addition to the burden of proof, that must be overcome to establish invalidity.

8.3.3.2 Obviousness

Claims of invalidity based on obviousness, in particular, often raise unique issues that require court resolution during trial. The ultimate conclusion of obviousness is a question of law, but it is premised on underlying findings of fact. *See KSR Int'l, Co. v. Teleflex, Inc.*, 550 U.S. 398, 404 (2007) ("The ultimate judgment of obviousness is a legal determination."); § 7.3.4.4. Thus, while the ultimate conclusion rests with the court, resolution of the factual inquiries rests with the jury. The most common factual questions, known as the *Graham* factors, are: (1) the scope and content of the prior art; (2) the differences between the prior art and the claims at issue; (3) the level of ordinary skill in the art; and (4) objective evidence of nonobviousness. *Graham v. John Deere Co.*, 383 U.S. 1, 17–18 (1966). Establishing trial procedures that will assist the court in rendering a decision on obviousness will help to resolve later disputes regarding the propriety of the jury's verdict on obviousness.

The Federal Circuit has held that submission to the jury of a question of law that is based on underlying facts, like obviousness, is proper when accompanied by appropriate instructions. *White v. Jeffrey Mining Co.*, 723 F.2d 1553, 1558 (Fed. Cir. 1983). Many courts follow this course in determining obviousness. When the jury is asked to determine obviousness, it is preferred that the jury be provided with special interrogatories regarding the *Graham* factors relevant to the case so that the jury's underlying factual findings are known. *See Agrizap, Inc. v. Woodstream Corp.*, 520 F.3d 1337, 1343 n.3 (Fed. Cir. 2008). With the benefit of the answers to the special interrogatories, the district court on a renewed motion for judgment as a matter of law and the Federal Circuit on appeal can then review the jury's ultimate conclusion on obviousness in light of its underlying factual determination. As explained by Justice Breyer:

> Courts can help to keep the application of [the] "clear and convincing" standard within its proper legal bounds by separating factual and legal aspects of an invalidity claim, say, by using instructions based on case-specific circumstances that help the jury make the distinction or by using interrogatories and special verdicts to make clear which specific factual findings underlie the jury's conclusions . . . . By isolating the facts (determined with help of the "clear and convincing" standard), courts can thereby assure the proper interpretation or application of the correct legal standard (without use of the "clear and convincing" standard). By preventing the "clear and convincing" standard from roaming outside its fact-related reservation, courts can increase the likelihood that discoveries or inventions will not receive legal protection where none is due.

Microsoft Corp. v. i4i Ltd., 131 S. Ct. 2238, 2253 (Breyer, J., concurring); *see* § 7.3.4.3. Formulating special interrogatories regarding all the relevant *Graham* factors sometimes can be difficult, for example, if multiple prior art references are asserted in multiple combinations. Because the alleged infringer usually will greatly prefer submitting special interrogatories to the jury, however, it generally is possible to negotiate with the parties a manageable number of special interrogatories for submission.

Alternatively, the court can submit only the relevant *Graham* factors to the jury for its determination through special interrogatories, with or without an advisory verdict on the legal question of obviousness, and then determine the ultimate question of obviousness itself based on the jury's factual determinations. The model instructions of the Northern District of California (*see* Instruction No. 4.3b),[3] for example, adopt this approach.

---

3. The Northern District of California's Model Patent Jury Instructions are available online at http://www.cand.uscourts.gov/cand/ForAttys.nsf/d07d1927bb07c86c88256d6e005ce658/4ed41e5a5972b27a88256d6e005cee5d/$FILE/NDmodel.101007.pdf.

8.3.4 Patent Damages

A patent owner is entitled to monetary damages to compensate for the infringement, as well as to the court's consideration of equitable remedies to prevent further infringement. In cases of willful infringement, the court has further discretion to increase damages to punish the infringer. Each of these remedies presents unique issues for the court. This section focuses on evidentiary issues relating to patent damages that may arise at trial. A fuller discussion of patent damages is set forth in §§ 14.4.3.2, 7.3.4.7, 7.4.3.3.2.2. We discuss enhanced damages for willful infringement or bad faith in § 9.2.2, which is addressed through a posttrial motion.

Section 284 provides that a patent owner is entitled to "damages adequate to compensate for the infringement, but in no event less than a reasonable royalty." Even if both parties' damages evidence is rejected, the fact finder must still determine what constitutes a reasonable royalty from the evidence. *Apple, Inc. v. Motorola, Inc.*, 757 F.3d 1286, 1327–28 (Fed. Cir. 2014) (*quoting Dow Chem. Co. v. Mee Indus., Inc.*, 341 F.3d 1370, 1381–82 (Fed. Cir. 2003)); *see also Info-Hold, Inc. v. Muzak LLC*, 783 F.3d 1365 (Fed. Cir. 2015) (reversing a summary judgment of zero damages even though the patentee's damages expert's report properly was struck "because there was no evidence of record supporting a zero royalty and the evidence of record which could be used to determine a non-zero royalty was ignored").

The jury has wide discretion in awarding monetary damages within the evidentiary bounds set by the court. While the Federal Circuit has emphasized that any factual disputes relating to damages—including disputed facts within expert testimony, an expert's choice of one of several acceptable methodologies, and issues relating to an expert's credibility—are to be resolved by the jury, *Apple Inc. v. Motorola, Inc.*, 757 F.3d at 1313–20, the court has in recent years substantially enhanced the court's gatekeeping role to ensure that a party's proof of damages is not based on improper "principles and methodology, or legally insufficient facts and data," *id.* at 1314, or a royalty base that is likely to mislead a jury, *see Ericsson, Inc. v. D-Link Sys., Inc.*, 773 F.3d 1201, 1226–27 (Fed. Cir. 2014). A patent owner can recover lost profits or a reasonable royalty or, in appropriate circumstances, a combination of the two.

8.3.4.1 Lost Profits

As set forth more fully in § 14.4.3.2.1.1, the patentee must prove a causal relationship between the infringement and its lost profits, encompassing the so-called DAMP factors: (1) demand for the patented product; (2) absence of acceptable noninfringing substitutes; (3) manufacturing and marketing capability to exploit the demand; and (4) profit he or she would have made. *Rite-Hite Corp. v. Kelley Co.*, 56 F.3d 1538, 1545 (Fed. Cir. 1995) (en banc) (citing *Panduit Corp. v. Stahlin Bros. Fibre Works, Inc.*, 575 F.2d 1152, 1156 (6th Cir. 1978)). The loss can include convoyed sales (nonpatented products and services) and price erosion owing to competition from the infringing products.

The first factor focuses on economic analysis of market conditions for the patented product. The second factor examines market definition and patent scope. With regard to the second factor, the Federal Circuit has cautioned against allowing lost profits analyses to turn into separate full-blown infringement analyses on numerous other collateral products. *See Micro Motion, Inc. v. Kane Steel Co.*, 894 F.2d 1318, 1324 (Fed. Cir. 1990). Thus, while there needs to be at least some circumstantial evidence of the absence of noninfringing alternatives, such evidence need not include testimony by technical experts. *Dow Chem. Co. v. Mee Indus.*, 341 F.3d 1370, 1372 (Fed. Cir. 2003); *Northlake Mktg. & Supply, Inc. v. Glaverbel, S.A.*, 72 F. Supp. 2d 893, 898–99 (N.D. Ill. 1999). The question for the court is whether there is some evidence from which a jury can reasonably infer that there are no noninfringing alternatives, and that lost profits therefore are appropriate. Inventor testimony and claim charts, evidence that the alleged infringer failed to switch to noninfringing alternatives, and customer motivation to purchase the patented features have all been held sufficient. *Standard Havens Prods., Inc. v. Gencor Indus., Inc.*, 953 F.2d 1360, 1373 (Fed. Cir. 1991); *Kaufman Co. v. Lantech, Inc.*, 926 F.2d 1136, 1141–42 (Fed. Cir. 1991); *Datascope Corp. v. SMEC, Inc.*, 879 F. Supp. 820, 825 (Fed. Cir. 1989) (inventor testimony and claim charts sufficient for the jury to infer that substitutes were infringing).

The third factor focuses on engineering and marketing capacity.

The fourth factor—profit that would have been made, but for the infringement—is relatively straightforward when a single patent covers the entirety of a product, such as a drug, but can become complicated when the patent relates to but one component of a multicomponent product and is not the sole or predominant basis for consumer demand. In the latter circumstance, the loss to the patent holder must be apportioned between the patented and other features using "reliable and tangible" evidence. *See Ericsson, Inc. v. D-Link Sys., Inc.*, 773 F.3d 1201, 1226 (Fed. Cir. 2014) (*citing Garretson v. Clark*, 111 U.S. 120, 121 (1884)).

8.3.4.2 Reasonable Royalty

The reasonable royalty measure provides a floor for patent damages. It is typically the sole measure of monetary damages in cases involving nonpracticing entities, but can also arise in litigation between competitors where lost profits are difficult to prove or are an incomplete measure of the harm.

Patent law has long struggled to deal with apportioning patent value where a patent covers only one component of a larger product. *See Cincinnati Car Co. v. New York Rapid Transit Corp.*, 66 F.2d 592, 593 (2d Cir. 1933) (Learned Hand, J.) (observing that the allocation of profits among multiple components "is in its nature unanswerable"). The problem has become particularly acute in modern patent litigation as a result of the growing use of juries called on to apportion value based on complex and often widely divergent economic expert analyses.

As set forth more fully in § 14.4.3.2.1.4, a reasonable royalty may be derived from an established royalty (if one exists) or, more commonly, a hypothetical negotiation between the patentee and the infringer when the infringement began. The hypothetical negotiation, during which the asserted patent claims are assumed to be valid, infringed, and enforceable, seeks "to recreate the *ex ante* licensing negotiation scenario and to describe the resulting agreement." *Lucent Techs., Inc. v. Gateway,*

Inc., 580 F.3d 1301, 1325 (Fed. Cir. 2009). For nearly half a century, courts have employed the vague and open-ended fifteen-factor test set forth in *Georgia-Pacific Corp. v. U.S. Plywood Corp.*, 318 F. Supp. 1116 (S.D.N.Y. 1970). *See* § 14.4.3.2.1.4.

The Federal Circuit has sought to prevent outsize damage awards by enhancing the judge's gatekeeping role along several dimensions: focusing the jury's attention on a royalty base that is closely connected to the patented component of a product, excluding unreliable damage theories, scrutinizing the admissibility of various forms of evidence, and providing limiting jury instructions.

In general, a patent holder seeking a reasonable royalty must provide substantial evidence supporting both its choice of royalty base and royalty rate. "[W]here multi-component products are involved, the governing rule is that the ultimate combination of royalty base and royalty rate must reflect the value attributable to the infringing features of the product, and no more." *Ericsson, Inc. v. D-Link Sys., Inc.*, 773 F.3d 1201, 1226 (Fed. Cir. 2014) (citing *VirnetX, Inc. v. Cisco Sys., Inc.*, 767 F.3d 1308 (Fed. Cir. 2014)). "As a substantive matter, it is the 'value of what was taken' that measures a 'reasonable royalty' under § 284. What is taken from the owner of a utility patent (for purposes of assessing damages under § 284) is only the patented technology, and so the value to be measured is only the value of the infringing features of an accused product." *Ericsson*, 773 F.3d at 1226 (quoting *Dowagiac Mfg. Co. v. Minn. Moline Plow Co.*, 235 U.S. 641, 648 (1915)).

8.3.4.2.1 Royalty Base

The royalty base has emerged as a critical part of reasonable royalty analysis. Where a single patent is the sole or predominant basis for consumer demand for a product, the royalty base is the value of the entire market for the product. *See Fonar Corp. v. Gen. Elec. Co.*, 107 F.3d 1543, 1552 (Fed. Cir. 1997) (citing *Rite-Hite Corp. v. Kelley Co.*, 56 F.3d 1538, 1549 (Fed. Cir. 1995) (en banc)).

Problems arise when the patent covers but one component of a complex product that cannot be shown to be the predominant driver of consumer demand for the product. In theory, the court could use the entire market value as the base and apply a sufficiently discounted royalty rate. But as the Federal Circuit has warned, "reliance on the entire market value might mislead the jury, who may be less equipped to understand the extent to which the royalty rate would need to do the work in such instances." *Ericsson*, 773 F.3d at 1227 (citing *LaserDynamics, Inc. v. Quanta Computer, Inc.*, 694 F.3d 51, 67, 68 (Fed. Cir. 2012) (barring the use of too high a royalty base—even if mathematically offset by a "'low enough royalty rate'"—because such a base "carries a considerable risk" of misleading a jury into overcompensating, stating that such a base "'cannot help but skew the damages horizon for the jury'" and "make a patentee's proffered damages amount appear modest by comparison" (quoting *Uniloc USA, Inc. v. Microsoft Corp.*, 632 F.3d 1292, 1320 (Fed. Cir. 2011))). The plaintiff's expert in *Uniloc* posited a royalty base of $19.28 billion (the entire market for Microsoft Office and Windows) to justify a reasonable royalty of over half a billion dollars for a patent on a product activation method.

To cabin the risk of outsize awards in multicomponent cases, the Federal Circuit has pushed the royalty base toward the smallest salable patent-practicing unit (SSP-

PU). In *Cornell University v. Hewlett-Packard Co.*, 609 F. Supp. 2d 279 (N.D.N.Y. 2009), the patent at issue related to software that issued multiple processor instructions at once, thereby increasing processor performance. It functioned as part of the instruction record buffer of a processor within a central processing unit (CPU) module of a CPU brick within a server—much like the flea on the hair of the tail of the dog. The plaintiff's damages expert used the CPU brick as the royalty base, resulting in a royalty base of $184 million. Judge Rader, sitting by designation, issued judgment as a matter of law reducing the jury's damage award on the ground that the trial record contained "insufficient evidence to establish the required nexus between the patented aspect of the infringing processors and the entire CPU brick." *Id.* at 292. Judge Rader remitted the jury award based on a royalty base derived from the market for the processor ($53.4 million). While still above the instruction record buffer, the processor was the smallest saleable component relating to the patented invention.

The Federal Circuit embraced the SSPPU framework in *LaserDynamics Inc. v. Quanta Computer, Inc.*, 694 F.3d 51 (Fed. Cir. 2012), holding that "it is generally required that royalties be based not on the entire product, but instead on the 'smallest salable patent-practicing unit.' . . . The entire market value rule is a narrow exception to this general rule." *Id.* at 67; *see also Commonwealth Scientific and Indus. Research Organisation v. Cisco Sys., Inc.*, 809 F.3d 1295, 1301–04 (Fed. Cir. 2015) ("CSIRO"); *VirnetX, Inc. v. Cisco Sys., Inc.*, 767 F.3d 1308, 1328–29 (Fed. Cir. 2014); *LaserDynamics, Inc. v. Quanta Computer, Inc.*, 694 F.3d 51, 66–70 (Fed. Cir. 2012); *Uniloc USA, Inc. v. Microsoft Corp.*, 632 F.3d 1292, 1320 (Fed. Cir. 2011); *Lucent Techs., Inc. v. Gateway, Inc.*, 580 F.3d 1301, 1336 (Fed. Cir. 2009).

More generally, the ultimate award "must be based on the incremental value that the patented invention adds to the end product." *Ericsson*, 773 F.3d at 1226. Therefore, the patent holder must provide evidence that the claimed royalty base is a reasonable estimate—using such approximation as is necessary—of the value directly attributable to the elements of the product infringing one or more of the asserted patents, whether or not separately saleable. *See id.* at 1226–27; *CSIRO*, 809 F.3d at 1301–02; *VirnetX*, 767 F.3d at 1327–29; *Apple, Inc. v. Motorola, Inc.*, 757 F.3d at 1317–18. To avoid misleading the jury by placing undue emphasis on the value of the entire product, evidence of the loss to the patent holder or the gain to the alleged infringer from the entire market value of the product usually is inadmissible. *See Ericsson*, 773 F.3d at 1226–27; *LaserDynamics*, 694 F.3d at 68; *Uniloc*, 632 F.3d at 1320. This rule, however, is inapplicable when prior negotiations of a royalty rate for the patent at issue or comparable patents is offered, and those rates are based on the end product. *CSIRO*, 809 F.3d at 1302–04.

8.3.4.2.2 Royalty Rate

Beyond calibrating the royalty base to the scale of the patent practicing unit, the court must also ensure that the royalty rate is based on sound economic methodology and grounded in reliable and pertinent evidence. To establish an appropriate royalty rate, the patent owner often will "posit a 'hypothetical negotiation' between the patentee and adjudicated infringer and . . . 'attempt[] to ascertain the royalty upon which the parties would have agreed had they successfully negotiated an agreement just before infringement began.'" *Aqua Shield v. Inter Pool Cover Team*, 774 F.3d 766, 770 (Fed. Cir. 2014) (*quoting Lucent Techs., Inc. v. Gateway, Inc.*, 580 F.3d 1301, 1324 (Fed. Cir. 2009)). The proof of an appropriate royalty rate using this method allows for necessary "approximation and uncertainty." *Id.* at 771 (*quoting Lucent Techs.*, 580 F.3d at 1325). Nevertheless, it must be supported by substantial evidence, which usually will be based on the application of the *relevant*, but not necessarily the complete, list of fifteen *Georgia-Pacific* factors. *See WhitServe, LLC v. Computer Packages, Inc.*, 694 F.3d 10, 31–32 (Fed. Cir. 2012).

The open-ended *Georgia-Pacific* framework affords economic experts substantial leeway in determining a royalty rate. The most pertinent evidence is analogous license agreements. In many cases, however, the technology either has not been previously licensed or the licenses cover a broader range of technologies than the patented invention and/or multiple products or product components.

The most pertinent evidence for establishing a royalty rate will be past licenses to the infringing or comparable technology, the value of comparable features in the marketplace, an estimate of the value of the benefit provided by the infringed features by comparison to noninfringing alternatives, or an estimate of the cost to design around the patent. *See Ericsson*, 773 F.3d at 1227 (*citing Monsanto Co. v. McFarling*, 488 F.3d 973, 978 (Fed. Cir. 2007) ("An established royalty is usually the best measure of a 'reasonable' royalty for a given use of an invention . . . .")); *Georgia-Pacific Corp. v. U.S. Plywood Corp.*, 318 F. Supp. 1116, 1120 (S.D.N.Y. 1970) (finding that "royalties received by the patentee for the licensing of the patent in suit" is a relevant factor for the jury to consider); *VirnetX*, 767 F.3d at 1330–31; *Apple, Inc. v. Motorola, Inc.*, 757 F.3d at 1315, 1329; *ResQNet.com, Inc. v. Lansa, Inc.*, 594 F.3d 860, 871 (Fed. Cir. 2010); *Lucent Techs.*, 580 F.3d at 1327–28. The Federal Circuit noted, however, that "[p]rior licenses . . . are almost never perfectly analogous to the infringement action," *Ericsson*, 773 F.3d at 1227 (*citing VirnetX*, 767 F.3d at 1330), but such differences "generally go[] to the weight of the evidence, not its admissibility," *id.* (citing *Apple*, 757 F.3d at 1326).

Substantial evidence must explain why a license is sufficiently analogous to associate its royalty rate to a hypothetical license solely to the infringing technology if a purportedly comparable license is not to the infringing technology; it also includes other patents, other intellectual property, or physical products; or it was entered based on different economic circumstances. *See Ericsson*, 773 F.3d at 1227–28; *Uniloc*, 632 F.3d at 1316; *WordTech Sys. Inc. v. Integrated Networks Sols.*, 609 F.3d 1308, 1322, 1327 (Fed. Cir. 2010); *Lucent Techs.*, 580 F.3d at 1327–28. A prior license to the infringed patent with a royalty rate based on the entire market value of the product must be supported by testimony explaining how to discount the rate to account only for the value attributed to the licensed technology. Moreover, when such a license is admitted, if requested, the court should give a cautionary instruction explaining that it is for the limited purpose of helping to determine an appropriate royalty rate after apportionment to the incremental value of the product's patented features. *See Ericsson*, 773 F.3d at 1227–28.

A license resulting from settlement of prior litigation usually is not admissible, but it can be admitted in the limited circumstance that it is the most reliable evidence available. *See LaserDynamics*, 694 F.3d at 77–78; *ResQNet.com*, 594 F.3d at 870–72. An example of this exception is a settlement that occurred after a finding that the patent is infringed. Such a settlement may be highly probative of a reasonable royalty, because its circumstance duplicates the hypothetical royalty assumptions that a patent is valid and infringed. *AstraZeneca AB v. Apotex Corp.*, 782 F.3d 1324, 1336–37 (Fed. Cir. 2015).

8.3.4.2.2.1 Rejection of General, Simplistic Apportionment Rules

As an alternative or shortcut to considering the *Georgia-Pacific* factors, some patentees have put forward general royalty theories such as the 25% rule and the Nash bargaining solution (50% split of net product value). The Federal Circuit has rejected the application of these generalized "rules of thumb." *See Apple*, 757 F.3d at 1324–25; *VirnetX*, 767 F.3d at 1331–34 (rejecting the Nash bargaining solution); *Uniloc*, 632 F.3d at 1312 (rejecting the "25% rule"). Such evidence is inadmissible.

8.3.4.2.2.2 Consumer Surveys and Conjoint Analysis

Damages experts have begun to deploy consumer surveys to allocate value within multicomponent patented products. *See* Zelin Yang, Note, *Damaging Royalties: An Overview of Reasonable Royalty Damages*, 29 Berkeley Tech. L.J. 647, 664 (2014); S. Christian Platt & Bob Chen, *Recent Trends and Approaches in Calculating Patent Damages: Nash Bargaining Solution and Conjoint Surveys*, 86 Patent, Trademark & Copyright J. (BNA) 909 (Aug. 30, 2013). Marketing researchers have long used "conjoint analysis" to differentiate value within product configurations. *See* Paul E. Green, Abba M. Krieger & Yoram Wind, *Thirty Years of Conjoint Analysis: Reflections and Prospects*, 31 Interfaces 56 (2001); Paul E. Green and V. Srinivasan, *Conjoint Analysis in Marketing: New Developments with Implications for Research and Practice*, 54(4) J. of Marketing 3 (1990).

Conjoint analysis draws on consumer ranking of products with different features. Researchers use statistical methods to estimate consumers' willingness to pay for particular attributes. While these methods provide a logical framework for differentiating value, the technique can be limited in practice. *See* Patricia Dyck, *Beyond Confusion—Survey Evidence of Consumer Demand and the Entire Market Value Rule*, 4 Hastings Sci. & Tech. L.J. 209, 226 (2012) (noting sensitivity to data collection methods and algorithms and the problem of combinatorial explosion); Lisa Cameron, Michael Cragg & Daniel McFadden, *The Role of Conjoint Surveys in Reasonable Royalty Cases*, Law360 (Oct. 16, 2013), http://www.law360.com/articles/475390/the-role-of-conjoint-surveys-in-reasonable-royalty-cases.

Courts have shown cautious receptivity to conjoint analysis. While recognizing the general admissibility of consumer surveys, Judge Alsup nonetheless rejected some of the expert's conjoint analysis as unreliable while allowing some of it to be admitted in *Oracle America, Inc. v. Google, Inc.*, No. C 10-03571 WHA, 2012 U.S.

Dist. LEXIS 33619, 2012 WL 850705, at *10–14 (N.D. Cal. Mar. 13, 2012). In *TV Interactive Data Corp. v. Sony Corp.*, 929 F. Supp. 2d 1006 (N.D. Cal. 2013), Magistrate Judge Joseph Spero held the patentee's expert testimony using conjoint analysis to be admissible. *Id.* at 1019–25.

8.3.4.2.2.3 FRAND/Standard Essential Patents

A growing number of technologies arise within the context of network industries in which standard protocols and interfaces promote technological innovation and greater consumer value. Industry standard-setting organizations such as the Institute of Electrical Electronics Engineers (IEEE) and the International Telecommunication Union (ITU) bring together company representatives to develop industry standards. To ensure that the industry standards reflect the best technologies while avoiding (or at least postponing) licensing disputes, the participants typically commit to license standard essential patents (SEPs) on "reasonable and non-discriminatory" ("RAND") or "fair, reasonable and non-discriminatory" ("FRAND") terms. The standard setting organizations have typically left the parameters for determining FRAND license terms undefined, *see* Mark A. Lemley, *Intellectual Property Rights and Standard-Setting Organizations*, 90 Cal. L. Rev. 1889, 1906 (2002), leaving courts with the difficult task of determining licensing rates for highly complex products involving potentially hundreds of patents.

The valuation of SEPs presents distinct problems. Industry standards can encompass hundreds of patented technologies of varying significance. Not surprisingly, owners of patents within a SEP pool often see their patents as particularly valuable, thereby risking hold-up and undue royalty-stacking. The challenge lies in separating the value of the particular technology from the often tremendous value of standardization. Once consumers adopt a product, they become locked into the standard to varying degrees. This could provide the patentee tremendous leverage in a negotiation. With potentially hundreds of SEPs and dozens of patent owners, the problem becomes intractable if patent owners stake out aggressive positions or refuse to propose licensing terms.

In a series of recent cases, courts have surmounted this challenge by interpreting the principal goal of standard-setting agreements to be widespread adoption of the standard by barring RAND licensors from capturing the coordination and network value of the standard. *See* § 14.4.3.2.1.4.2; *Microsoft Corp. v. Motorola, Inc.*, No. C10-1823JLR, 2013 U.S. Dist. LEXIS 60233, 2013 WL 2111217 (W.D. Wash. Apr. 25, 2013); *see also Ericsson*, 773 F.3d at 1229–35; *In re Innovatio IP Ventures LLC Patent Litig.*, No. 11 C 9308, 2013 U.S. Dist. LEXIS 144061, 2013 WL 5593609 (N.D. Ill. Oct. 3, 2013). The courts have adapted the *Georgia-Pacific* factors to serve the standard-setting context.

In such cases, the jury should be instructed as to what FRAND commitments have been made by the patent holder and the jury's obligation to take those commitments into account when determining the royalty award, the need to apportion the value of the patented feature from any value added by adoption of the standard, those *Georgia-Pacific* or similar factors relevant (but *only* those relevant) in light of the evidence presented, and, if supported by the evidence, the issues of potential royalty-stacking and patent hold-up. This might include directing the jury to consider a hypothetical negotiation date prior to adoption of the standard rather than at the time infringement began.

8.3.4.2.2.4 Indirect Infringement

There also are further complications when a patentee's damages are based on indirect infringement—such as the use of the patented invention by the alleged infringer's customers—particularly when the accused product is capable of non-infringing modes of operation. To recover damages based on use by customers, there need not be a one-to-one correspondence between the number of accused products sold and direct infringement by customers. *Lucent Techs.*, 580 F.3d at 1323–24; *Hilgraeve, Inc. v. Symantec Corp.*, 272 F. Supp. 2d 613, 621 (E.D. Mich. 2003); *Imagexpo, L.L.C. v. Microsoft Corp.*, 284 F. Supp. 2d 365, 370 (E.D. Va. 2003); *Black & Decker v. Bosch*, No. 04 C 7955, 2006 U.S. Dist. LEXIS 94556, at *6, 2006 WL 3883286 (N.D. Ill. Dec. 18, 2006). The patent owner, however, must present evidence sufficient for a jury to extrapolate or infer the extent of the customers' direct infringement. *Imagexpo*, 284 F. Supp. 2d at 370. Whether a party's experts' opinions comply with the requirements to prove or disprove damages often is—and may be required to be (*see Versata Software, Inc. v. SAP, Inc.*, 717 F.3d 1255 (Fed. Cir. 2013)) tested in a pretrial *Daubert* motion. *See* § 7.4.3.3.2.1. Whether as the result of such a motion or at trial, however, if a party fails to adhere to these standards, a court must be prepared to preclude testimony—including all of an expert's testimony, if necessary—or correct an award. *See Ericsson*, 773 F.3d at 1229–35; *ePlus, Inc. v. Lawson Software, Inc.*, 700 F.3d 509, 522–23 (Fed. Cir. 2012); *LaserDynamics*, 694 F.3d at 66–71; *Whitserve, LLC v. Comput. Packages, Inc.*, 694 F.3d 10 (Fed. Cir. 2012); *Uniloc*, 632 F.3d at 1319–20.

8.4 Motions for Judgment as a Matter of Law

As in any jury trial, once a party has completed its case-in-chief as to an issue, the party's opponent can move for judgment as a matter of law as to the issue. Fed. R. Civ. P. 50. Such motions are decided under the law of the circuit in which the district court sits. *See, e.g., Orion IP, LLC v. Hyundai Motor Am.*, 605 F.3d 967, 973 (Fed. Cir. 2010). The usual standard is that judgment will be denied if, "viewing the evidence in the light most favorable to the nonmoving party, and giving the non-movant the benefit of all reasonable inferences, there is sufficient evidence of record to support a jury verdict in favor of the non-movant." *Honeywell Int'l Inc. v. Hamilton Sundstrand Corp.*, 370 F.3d 1131, 1139 (Fed. Cir. 2004) (en banc). These motions and their appellate implications, however, take on special significance in patent cases where each side has important claims and defenses as to which it bears the burden of proof, and where claim-construction issues often play a pivotal role.

The Federal Circuit applies the usual rule that, absent a Rule 50 motion before the case is submitted to the jury, specifically addressed to an issue, no argument can be made in posttrial motions or on appeal that the evidence is insufficient to support the jury's verdict as to that issue. *Unitherm Food Sys., Inc. v. Swift-Eckrich, Inc.*, 546 U.S. 394, 398 (2006) ("A post-trial motion for judgment can be granted only on grounds advanced in the pre-verdict motion"); *Microsoft Corp. v. i4i Ltd. P'ship*, 598 F.3d 831, 857 (Fed. Cir. 2010), *aff'd on other grounds*, 131 S. Ct. 2238, (2011). The specificity of the predeliberations motion must be sufficient to alert the opponent as to the evidence that is omitted so that, if necessary, it may seek to reopen and provide that evidence. In the patent law context, this may require, for example, that a Rule 50 motion by an accused infringer specify the particular claim or claims as to which it asserts no infringement has been proven or the particular prior art references it contends render the patent obvious or anticipated, and that a motion by a patent owner specify the particular invalidity bases it asserts have not been proven. *Duro-Last, Inc. v. Custom Seal, Inc.*, 321 F.3d 1098, 1105–09 (Fed. Cir. 2003); *Union Carbide Chems. & Plastics Tech. Corp. v. Shell Oil Co.*, 308 F.3d 1167, 1187 (Fed. Cir. 2002); *Sw. Software, Inc. v. Harlequin Inc.*, 226 F.3d 1280, 1290 (Fed. Cir. 2000).

Circumstances in particular cases, however, may make much more cryptic motions sufficient if, in context, it is clear that the court and opposing party understood what was intended. *See, e.g.*, *Western Union Co. v. MoneyGram Payment Sys.*, 626 F.3d 1361, 1367–68 (Fed. Cir. 2010) (holding that even a cursory motion suffices so long as it alerts the court and opposing party to the party's position); *Orion IP, LLC*, 605 F.3d at 973–74 ("[W]e seek partial judgment as a matter of law based on prior art. And the Court has heard testimony and the argument about that" sufficient given context of motion.); *Blackboard, Inc. v. Desire2Learn, Inc.*, 574 F.3d 1371, 1379–80 (Fed. Cir. 2009) (cursory motion for anticipation and obviousness sufficient given context and court's prompt that the motions would be taken under advisement). A predeliberations motion challenging the sufficiency of damages evidence is necessary for a posttrial objection to the reasonableness of a jury's royalty award. *Compare Lucent Techs., Inc. v. Gateway, Inc.*, 580 F.3d 1301, 1311–16 (Fed. Cir. 2009), *with Wordtech Sys., Inc. v. Integrated Networks Sols., Inc.*, 609 F.3d 1308, 1318 (Fed. Cir. 2010), *and i4i Ltd. P'ship v. Microsoft Corp.*, 598 F.3d 831, 856–57 (Fed. Cir. 2010).

8.5 Jury Deliberations

Once the case is submitted to the jury for deliberations, there is little for the court or the parties to do except to reduce the hardship on the jury and make sure it has all the information it needs to make its decision.

8.5.1 Schedule of Deliberations

While the jury is deliberating, court is not in session. Therefore, the court should be open to modifying the daily schedule for deliberations to meet the needs of the jurors. There is no longer the need to maintain time outside the jury's presence to resolve legal issues. Therefore, if the jurors agree, the court can allow full-day deliberations even when trial proceeded on a half-day schedule. The jurors, however, should be informed that they are under a continuing duty to serve, and the court should not adopt irregular schedules.

In multiphase trials, issues are usually phased to separate presentation of issues to prevent jury confusion. If the jury did not deliberate until all phases were conducted, that would defeat much of the purpose of separating the proceedings. The jury should deliberate immediately after each phase of the trial.

8.5.2 Claim-Construction Considerations

Jury deliberations are restricted to issues of fact. Therefore, the court should make clear that the jury is not to make any determination regarding claim construction. *Markman v. Westview Instr., Inc.*, 52 F.3d 967, 976 (Fed. Cir. 1995), *aff'd*, 517 U.S. 370 (1996). Indeed, the parties cannot even argue claim-construction disputes to the jury. *Cytologix Corp. v. Ventana Med. Sys., Inc.*, 424 F.3d 1168, 1172 (Fed. Cir. 2005). Claim-construction arguments may confuse jurors and lead them to believe they should be making claim-construction determinations. The court should instruct the jury on the proper construction of claims and emphasize that it is bound by the court's construction. *Structural Rubber Prods. Co. v. Park Rubber*, 749 F.2d 707, 723 (Fed. Cir. 1984).

8.5.3 Jury Access to Evidence

During deliberations, the jurors may need additional information to arrive at a decision, whether it is exhibits, testimony, or further instructions on the law. All juror communications should be conducted through the courtroom deputy in writing, with requests passed on to the judge. Before acting on any request, the court should inform the parties and allow them to be present.

8.5.3.1 Exhibits and Demonstratives

As noted above, access to evidence admitted during trial can assist the jurors in their deliberations. A copy of the exhibits introduced at trial should be provided to the jurors in the jury room. Demonstratives, however, are not evidence. Therefore, the jurors should not be given access to them. Only demonstratives admitted into evidence as an exhibit during trial should be considered by the jurors during deliberations.

8.5.3.2 Testimony

As memories fade and disagreement may arise between jurors regarding a witness's testimony, jurors may sometimes request to have testimony read during deliberations. While allowing testimony to be read to the jury is in the court's discretion, the practice can be problematic and should not be exercised routinely. *See Dabney v. Montgomery Ward & Co., Inc.*, 761 F.2d 494, 499 (8th Cir. 1985); *Mayeaux v. Am. Mut. Liberty Ins. Corp.*, 409 F.2d 508, 509 (5th Cir. 1969).

Unlike exhibits, which are complete and available in their entirety for review, reading portions of testimony is incomplete and may give a skewed presentation of evidence. It becomes difficult to draw the line as to what testimony should be read to the jury. Jurors are often unable to articulate clearly what specific testimony they are interested in, which can lead to requests for testimony on broad subject matters. Catering to such requests is neither practical nor helpful.

Testimony should be read to jurors only in circumstances when the jurors can identify the specific testimony in which they are interested to resolve a disagreement between the jurors. In such cases, the parties should be informed of the request and the court should consider counsels' request to have other portions of testimony read for fairness.

8.5.3.3 Juror Questions During Deliberations

Questions may arise during jury deliberations. The court should be wary of providing answers to requests for factual information and should only do so in the presence of and after consultation with the parties. Fact-finding is reserved for the jury, and neither the court nor the parties should usurp that role.

Courts are duty-bound to provide jurors with further legal instructions when requested to do so. The court should inform the parties of the question and give the parties an opportunity to jointly propose an appropriate instruction. It may be appropriate to give additional instructions or clarifying instructions to provide a full and fair response. Care should be taken, however, to avoid overinstructing and confusing the jury.

8.5.4 Verdict Forms

8.5.4.1 General Verdict Forms

Use of general verdict forms in patent cases is discouraged. The jury is charged with deciding several interrelated and complex issues. General verdict forms do not assist the jury in understanding the applicable law and maintaining consistency in its findings. A general verdict is inseparable; a single error completely destroys it. *Richardson-Vicks v. Upjohn Co.*, 122 F.3d 1476, 1485 (Fed. Cir. 1997). As a result, a significant amount of resources is spent reviewing decisions made by general verdict.

8.5.4.2 Special Verdict Forms and Special Interrogatories

The court can help guide the jury in proper application of the law and ensure consistency in its findings by using special verdict forms. Fed. R. Civ. P. 49(a). Special verdicts require a jury to make specific findings of fact from which the court applies the applicable law. Patent cases are particularly well suited for special verdicts. *Richardson-Vicks*, 122 F.3d at 1485, *citing Warner-Jenkinson Co. v. Hilton Davis Chem. Co.*, 520 U.S. 17, 39 (1997). For example, if the jury finds that an independent claim of a patent is not infringed, then it cannot find the dependent claims infringed. Use of a special verdict form allows the court to ensure consistency between findings on independent and dependent claims. A model sample verdict form for patent cases is now available as Appendix C.3 to the Model Patent Jury Instructions for the Northern District of California.

A court can also use a general verdict form with special interrogatories. Fed. R. Civ. P. 49(b). Use of special interrogatories differs from special verdicts only in that the jury, rather than the court, makes the ultimate decision when general verdicts with special interrogatories are used. There is still risk that the jury will make a decision inconsistent with its findings. In such cases, the federal rules permit the court to enter judgment consistent with the jury's findings notwithstanding the verdict. *Id.* Where the findings are inconsistent and do not support the verdict, the court can recall the jury for further consideration or order a new trial.

8.6 Bench Trials

A court may try a patent case without a jury where the parties have waived the right to a jury trial or when equitable issues have been bifurcated for the court's consideration. Waiver is rare. Most often, bench trials are held to try equitable defenses such as inequitable conduct, laches, and estoppel.

As the court is the fact finder in bench trials, there is less of a need for extensive judicial management. The court must make specific findings of facts and conclusions of law when rendering its decision. Fed. R. Civ. P. 52. It can, however, be less stringent with issues of admissibility and evidentiary objections as it is both the arbiter of those issues and the ultimate fact finder. There is less of a concern that the court will be prejudiced by certain evidence.

Chapter 9
Posttrial

The court's duties do not cease after a verdict is rendered. Even following entry of judgment, the court is responsible for resolving posttrial motions and issues relating to appeal. This chapter examines the posttrial considerations that courts face in patent trials.

9.1 Entry of Judgment

In patent cases, as in every case, after a jury renders its verdict or after the court makes its decision, judgment must be entered. The federal rules require that every judgment be entered in a separate document to make clear when the time to file posttrial motions and appeal begins to run. Fed. R. Civ. P. 58. The clerk may enter judgment when a jury returns a general verdict. Where special verdicts are used, the court, not the clerk, must enter the judgment.

The court has some flexibility in the timing for entry of judgment. One option is to enter judgment in accordance with the jury's verdict soon after the verdict is rendered. While the verdict may be altered by resolution of posttrial motions, the court's ruling on the posttrial motions need not be entered in a separate document. Fed. R. Civ. P. 58(a)(1)–(4). Therefore, early entry of judgment leads to quicker resolution of posttrial motions, without the need for the court to enter a second judgment and therefore without creating additional administrative duties for the court.

In cases of willful infringement, however, the patent owner will likely move for enhanced damages. Judgment entered on the verdict will need to be amended in a separate document, should the court decide to increase damages. In such cases, it may be more efficient to set a briefing schedule with the parties for posttrial motions, as well as motions for enhanced damages, prejudgment interest, and attorneys' fees. Once all motions are resolved, the court can then enter one judgment that reflects the verdict and the rulings on posttrial motions. *Larez v. Los Angeles*, 946 F.2d 630, 636 (9th Cir. 1991) (noting that nothing in the Federal Rules prohibits filing posttrial motions before entry of judgment); *Dunn v. Truck World, Inc.*, 929 F.2d 311, 313 (7th Cir. 1991) (same).

9.2 Posttrial Motions

In patent cases, as in most cases, trial is usually followed by a series of posttrial motions. Where there is a finding of infringement, patent owners almost always seek a permanent injunction. In cases of willful infringement, the patent owner will also typically move for enhanced damages. Because the patent statute authorizes the award of attorneys' fees in exceptional cases, posttrial motions often seek attorneys' fees. In addition, parties will likely bring motions for judgment as a matter of law and/or new trial motions on the liability issues. In this section, we discuss the particular considerations that arise in conjunction with these posttrial motions in patent cases.

9.2.1 Permanent Injunctions

In addition to monetary relief, many patentees seek entry of a permanent injunction after a finding of infringement. *See* § 283 ("[A court] may grant injunctions in accordance with the principles of equity to prevent the violation of any right secured by patent, on such terms as the court deems reasonable."). Historically, courts entered injunctions as a matter of course following an infringement finding. Following the Supreme Court's decision in *eBay Inc. v. MercExchange, L.L.C.*, 547 U.S. 388, 391–92 (2006), however, an injunction may be issued only if the patent holder satisfies a four-factor injunction test.

9.2.1.1 Issuing a Permanent Injunction

In *eBay*, the Supreme Court stated that to obtain an injunction a party "must demonstrate: (1) that it has suffered an irreparable injury; (2) that remedies available at law, such as monetary damages, are inadequate to compensate for that injury; (3) that, considering the balance of hardships between the plaintiff and defendant, a remedy in equity is warranted; and (4) that the public interest would not be disserved by a permanent injunction." *Id.* at 391. Subsequently, the Federal Circuit held that *eBay* eliminates any presumption of irreparable injury to a patent holder after a judgment of infringement and no invalidity. *Robert Bosch LLC v. Pylon Mfg. Corp.*, 659 F.3d 1142, 1149 (2011). The Federal Circuit also has also held that there must be a "causal nexus" between any such irreparable injury and patent infringement. *Apple Inc. v. Samsung Elecs. Co. (Apple III)*, 735 F.3d 1352, 1360 (Fed. Cir. 2013). In a case in which the harm stems from lost sales to a competitor's infringement, this requires proof that "the patented features impact consumers' decisions to purchase the accused devices" even if they are not "the exclusive or predominant reason why consumers bought . . . [the infringing] products." *Apple Inc. v. Samsung Elecs. Co.*, 801

F.3d 1352, 1360 (Fed. Cir. 2015). Additionally, the Federal Circuit has noted that, "[a]lthough injunctions are tools for prospective relief designed to alleviate future harm, by its terms the first *eBay* factor looks, in part, at what has already occurred." *i4i Ltd. P'ship v. Microsoft Corp.*, 598 F.3d 831, 862 (2010), *aff'd on other grounds*, 131 S. Ct. 2238 (2011). "Past harm to a patentee's market share, revenues, and brand recognition is relevant for determining whether the patentee '*has suffered* an irreparable injury.'" *Id.* at 861 (quoting *eBay*, 547 U.S. at 391; emphasis in original). *But see Monsanto Co. v. Geertson Seed Farms*, 561 U.S. 139, 142 (2010) (explaining that an injunction was not warranted under the *eBay* test because, "[m]ost importantly, respondents cannot show that they *will* suffer irreparable injury" (emphasis added)).

Although *eBay* generally forbids "broad classifications" of cases for purposes of determining when an injunction is proper or improper, *id.* at 393, courts have shown tendencies to grant or deny motions for permanent injunctions in certain types of situations. Courts often find the *eBay* test satisfied and issue an injunction in cases between direct or indirect competitors, or where, as a result of an infringing feature, the infringer's product supplants the market for the patent holder's product. *See Broadcom Corp. v. Emulex Corp.*, 732 F.3d 1325, 1338 (Fed. Cir. 2013); *Presidio Components, Inc. v. Am. Tech. Ceramics Corp.*, 702 F.3d 1351, 1363 (Fed. Cir. 2012); *Edwards Lifesciences AG v. CoreValve, Inc.*, 699 F.3d 1305, 1315 (Fed. Cir. 2012) ("Courts awarding permanent injunctions typically do so under circumstances where plaintiff practices its invention and is a direct market competitor"), *quoting Advanced Cardiovascular Sys. v. Medtronic Vascular, Inc.*, 579 F. Supp. 2d 554 (D. Del. 2008); *Robert Bosch LLC v. Pylon Mfg. Corp.*, 659 F.3d 1142, 1156–57 (Fed. Cir. 2011); *i4i Ltd. P'ship v. Microsoft Corp.*, 598 F.3d 831, 861–63 (Fed. Cir. 2010), *aff'd on other grounds*, 131 S. Ct. 2238 (2011); *Acumed LLC v. Stryker Corp.*, 551 F.3d 1323, 1328–29 (Fed. Cir. 2008); *Broadcom Corp. v. Qualcomm Inc.*, 543 F.3d 683, 702–03 (Fed. Cir. 2008); *Verizon Servs. Corp. v. Vonage Holdings Corp.*, 503 F.3d 1295, 1310–11 (2007). Even if the patent owner does not practice the patent, but sells a competing product, an injunction against a competitor may be proper. *Presidio Components*, 702 F.3d at 1363. Additionally, an injunction against a competitor may be proper even when the patent holder previously licensed the patent to another competitor or its customer, when other unlicensed competitors employ the patent, or when the patented product is not core to the patent holder's business or the injunction may put an infringer out of business. *Robert Bosch LLC*, 659 F.3d at 1150–1152 (additional infringing competitors; noncore nature; small competitor potentially put out of business); *Acumed*, 551 F.3d at 1328–29 (competitor); *Broadcom Corp. v. Qualcomm Inc.*, 543 F.3d at 703 (although patent licensed to customer, injunction issued that infringing party argued could preclude it from continuing in relevant business) (citing *Windsurfing Int'l, Inc. v. AMF, Inc.*, 782 F.2d 995, 1003 n. 12 (Fed. Cir. 1986) ("One who elects to build a business on a product found to infringe cannot be heard to complain if an injunction against continuing infringement destroys the business so elected")). In some cases, to ameliorate hardship on the infringer, the court will include a "sunset provision" that allows continued sales of the infringing product pursuant to a royalty to allow the infringer time to eliminate the disputed features from its product. *See, e.g.*, *Broadcom Corp. v. Qualcomm Inc.*, 543 F.3d 683,

704 (Fed. Cir. 2008) (injunction allowing continued sales by infringer for twenty months). The broad use of injunctions in these competitive cases, when properly supported by other factors, stems from the fundamental nature of patents as a grant to the owner of the right to exclude. *Id.* at 1338; *Robert Bosch*, 659 F.3d at 1149–50.

Following *eBay*, courts have denied permanent injunctions in cases where the patentee merely licensed its technology and did not offer its own commercial embodiment, where only the patentee's licensee competes with an infringer, where the scope of the requested injunction was overly broad, or where an injunction created important public health concerns. *See, e.g.*, *ActiveVideo Networks v. Verizon Commc'ns*, 694 F.3d 1312, 1337–41 (Fed. Cir. 2012) (no irreparable harm or inadequate legal remedy based on licensee's competition with infringer); *Bard Peripheral Vascular, Inc. v. W.L. Gore & Assocs.*, 670 F.3d 1171 (Fed. Cir. 2012), *on reh'g*, 682 F.3d 1003 (Fed. Cir. 2012) (injunction would preclude use of important medical devices); *Voda v. Cordis Corp.*, 2006 U.S. Dist. LEXIS 63623, 2006 WL 5347777 (W.D. Okla. Sept. 5, 2006), *aff'd*, 476 F.3d 887 (Fed. Cir. 2007) (licensor of technology); *Praxair, Inc. v. ATMI, Inc.*, 479 F. Supp. 2d 440, 442–44 (D. Del. 2007) (proposed injunction required defendant to recall products already sold to third parties); *z4 Techs., Inc. v. Microsoft Corp.*, 434 F. Supp. 2d 437, 440–41 (E.D. Tex. 2006) (licensor of technology). Also, the Federal Circuit has stated that where the jury's damages award includes monetary compensation for future infringing sales, a patent holder cannot show irreparable harm and is, therefore, not entitled to an injunction. *Innogenetics, N.V. v. Abbott Labs.*, 512 F.3d 1363, 1380 (Fed. Cir. 2008).

In connection with standard-setting proceedings and otherwise, patent owners sometimes commit to provide a fair, reasonable and nondiscriminatory ("FRAND") license to any potential licensee. While there is no per se rule precluding an injunction to such a patent owner, an injunction is unlikely. Establishing irreparable harm is difficult, and allowing the use of a standard resulting from a FRAND commitment better serves public interest. *See Apple Inc. v. Motorola, Inc.*, 757 F.3d 1286, 1331–32 (Fed. Cir. 2014) (noting that absent unusual circumstances, such as an infringer refusing a FRAND royalty or unreasonably delaying negotiations, it will be difficult for a patent owner subject to a FRAND commitment to establish irreparable harm or that damages are not an adequate remedy; and that even when an infringer has refused to accept any license offer, that does not necessarily justify injunctive relief).

Table 9.1 summarizes how courts have applied common fact patterns presented in cases to the four-factor test for issuing permanent injunctions.

Table 9.1
Permanent Injunction Considerations (*eBay* Factors)

Irreparable Harm (In situations in which the relevant patent(s) encompass only one or some features of a multifeature product, the factor is applicable only to those infringing feature(s) with a sufficiently close causal nexus to the harm (*see* § 3.2.2.2.4))	
Facts Tending to Establish Irreparable Harm	**Facts Weighing Against Irreparable Harm**
• Infringer is competitor • Loss of market share owing to infringement by competitor • Price erosion due to direct competition by infringer • Harm to goodwill, brand recognition, or reputation as innovator because of presence of infringer in the market • Customers are unlikely to switch in the future, and therefore infringement causes long-term loss • Patent holder's decision not to license or attempt to license patent to the infringer • Economic harm suffered by licensees of research institutes and universities; adverse effect on institution's ability to license intellectual property to finance further research and development • Economic harm to licensor by competitor even though licensor did not practice the invention	• Loss of licensing revenue by a patent holder that does not compete with infringer or practice the invention • Award of money damages to patent holder that includes compensation based on future sales of infringing product • Harm to licensees • The patent holder agreed to provide FRAND licenses
Inadequate Remedy at Law	
Facts Tending to Establish Inadequate Remedy at Law	**Facts Weighing Against Inadequate Remedy at Law**
• Loss of market share, harm to reputation, price erosion • Infringer's inability to pay damages, including lack of U.S. assets with which to satisfy judgment for money damages • Patent holder's refusal to grant license, or willingness to grant license only in exceptional circumstances, and its engagement in lengthy litigation to protect that business decision	• Loss of bargaining leverage by patent holder that does not practice the invention • Patent holder's willingness to license the patent to the infringer • Patent holder's policy to license the patent to others in circumstances similar to the infringer, or to obtain maximum monetary returns • Patent holder's ability to pay damages award is irrelevant (unlike its *inability* to pay)

Balance of Hardships	
Facts Tending to Establish Balance of Hardships Favoring Injunction	**Facts Weighing Against Balance of Hardships Favoring Injunction**
• Infringing product is but one of many products offered by infringer • Parties' relative size • Infringer's ability to offer a design-around • Where infringer is direct competitor, loss of right to exclude is a greater hardship than loss to infringer from interruption or even cessation of its business • Court establishes adequate time for work-around before injunction effective • Injunction not applicable to infringer's customers who purchased before injunction's effective date • Providing a provision in the injunction delaying its effective date to allow infringer to modify its product	• Patented feature is but a small component of the infringing product • Harm to infringer that practices invention is greater than harm to licensing business of nonpracticing patent holder • Consequences and costs to infringer of ceasing sales of infringing product or creating design-around, except little weight if business built primarily on infringing product
Public Interest	
Facts Tending to Establish Public Interest Favoring Injunction	**Facts Weighing Against Public Interest Favoring Injunction**
• Public interest served by enforcement of patents	• Lower prices for public access to pharmaceuticals not sufficient • Harm failing to rise to level of adverse public health consequences not sufficient • Precluding access to a large number of desired, noninfringing features

9.2.1.2 Ongoing Royalty After Denial of a Permanent Injunction

Consideration of the four permanent injunction factors articulated in *eBay* does not always end the inquiry. Where a court determines that a permanent injunction is not warranted, it might determine an appropriate ongoing royalty for the infringer's continued use of the patented invention (unless the jury explicitly awarded damages for future infringement).

In setting an ongoing royalty in lieu of a permanent injunction, the district court is first "encouraged[] to allow the parties to negotiate a license." *Telcordia Techs., Inv. v. Cisco Sys.*, 612 F.3d 1365, 1378 (Fed. Cir. 2010); *see also Paice LLC v. Toyota Motor Corp.*, 504 F.3d 1293, 1315 n.15 (Fed. Cir. 2007). In the event the parties are unable to reach an agreement, the court may impose an ongoing royalty. *Telcordia Techs.*, 612 F.3d at 1379; *Paice*, 504 F.3d at 1315. There is no Seventh Amendment right to have a jury determine the issue of an ongoing royalty. *Paice*, 504 F.3d at 1316. Indeed, even the jury's determination of a reasonable royalty does not bind the court in setting an ongoing royalty. *Amado v. Microsoft Corp.*, 517 F.3d 1353, 1361–62 (Fed. Cir. 2008). This is because, as the Federal Circuit has recognized, there is a difference between a reasonable royalty for pre-verdict infringement and damages for postverdict infringement, given the change in the parties' legal relationship and other economic factors. *Id.* Where the jury's royalty damages award is a lump sum that includes a royalty for future sales, however, the court should not provide an ongoing royalty; the jury's royalty determination precludes any further award. *Summit 6, LLC v. Samsung Elecs. Co.*, 802 F.3d 1283, 1300–01 (Fed. Cir. 2015). In any event, the court should provide a reasoned explanation for any ongoing royalty it imposes. In particular, the court may take additional evidence into account for any additional economic factors relevant to establishing a royalty for ongoing use of the patented invention postverdict. *Paice*, 504 F.3d at 1315.

In determining the amount of an ongoing royalty, the Federal Circuit has indicated that a district court should consider

> the change in the parties' bargaining positions, and the resulting change in economic circumstances, resulting from the determination of liability—for example, the infringer's likelihood of success on appeal, the infringer's ability to immediately comply with the injunction, . . . etc.—as well as the evidence and arguments found material to the granting of the injunction and the stay.

Amado, 517 F.3d at 1362. Some district courts determining ongoing royalties under this standard have used the *Georgia-Pacific* factors, *see* § 14.4.3.2.1.4, but modified the usual factors to assume that the hypothetical negotiation occurred after the determination of the patent's validity and infringement, when the infringer must consider the possibility that the patent holder could force it off the market absent a license. *See, e.g.*, *Boston Sci. Corp. v. Johnson & Johnson*, 2009 U.S. Dist. LEXIS 35372, at *7, 2009 WL 975424 (N.D. Cal. Apr. 19, 2009); *but see Amado v. Microsoft Corp.*, 2008 U.S. Dist. LEXIS 110152, at *32–33, 2008 WL 8641264 (C.D. Cal. Dec. 4, 2008) ("By not including any reference to the *Georgia-Pacific* factors [in *Amado*, 517 F.3d at 1362], the Federal Circuit implicitly rejected this approach."). In doing so, some courts have noted that, since the pre-verdict analysis assumed the patent's validity and infringement, this change will not alter the prejudgment running royalty set by the verdict. *See, e.g.*, *Presidio Components, Inc. v. Am. Tech. Ceramics Corp.*, 2010 U.S. Dist. LEXIS 79039, at *16–17, 2010 WL 3070370 (S.D. Cal. Aug. 5, 2010); *Ariba, Inc. v. Emptoris, Inc.*, 567 F. Supp. 2d 914, 918 (E.D. Tex. 2008); *Orion IP, LLC v. Mercedes-Benz USA, LLC*, 2008 U.S. Dist. LEXIS 108683, at *9, 2008 WL 8856865 (E.D. Tex. Mar. 28, 2008). Other courts, relying on the Federal Circuit's citation of the "change in the parties' bargaining positions, and the resulting change in economic circumstances, resulting from the determination of liability" (*Amado*, 517 F.3d at 1353), have believed that the hypothetical negotiation should reflect a negative posttrial impact on the infringer's position. *See, e.g.*, *Boston Sci. Corp.*, 2009 U.S. Dist. LEXIS 35372 at *16; *Joyal Prods. v. Johnson Elec. North Am., Inc.*, 2009 U.S. Dist. LEXIS 15531, *39–40, 2009 WL 512156 (D.N.J. Feb. 26, 2009); *Creative Internet Advert. Corp. v. Yahoo! Inc.*, 674 F. Supp. 2d 847, 861 (E.D. Tex. 2009). Also, some district courts have suggested that the rate of the ongoing royalty should be increased because posttrial the infringement is "willful." However, the Federal Circuit has indicated in the analogous circumstance of determining a royalty for the period when an injunction is stayed pending appeal that "willfulness, as such, is not the inquiry when the infringement is permitted by a court-ordered stay." *Amado*, 517 F.3d at 1362. Finally, while recognizing that the ultimate determination of the ongoing royalty is a legal issue to be determined by the court, some courts nevertheless submit the question to the jury for an advisory verdict, citing the efficiency of doing so. *See, e.g., Cummins-Allison Corp. v. SBM Co., Ltd.*, 669 F. Supp. 2d 774, 778 (E.D. Tex. 2009); *Amgen, Inc. v. F. Hoffmann-La Roche Ltd.*, 581 F. Supp. 2d 160, 210 n.12 (D. Mass. 2008), *vacated in part on other grounds*, 580 F.3d 1340 (Fed. Cir. 2009)

9.2.1.3 Motion for Contempt

Following entry of a permanent injunction, an infringing party often will modify the product or process found to infringe to design around the patent, and begin marketing the modified product. If the patent owner believes that the redesigned product infringes, it can challenge the design-around by commencing a second patent-infringement action. In limited circumstances, the patent owner alternatively can seek to have an enjoined party held in civil contempt for violating the injunction.

To prove contempt, the patent owner must provide clear and convincing evidence both that the newly accused product is not more than colorably different from the product found to infringe and that the newly accused product actually infringes. *TiVo Inc. v. Echostar Corp.*, 646 F.3d 869, 882 (Fed. Cir. 2011) (en banc). To resolve this first, and "primary," element, the court must determine "whether the newly accused product is so different from the product previously found to infringe that it raises 'a fair ground of doubt as to the wrongfulness of the defendant's conduct.'" *Id.* at 882, *quoting Cal. Artificial Stone Paving Co. v. Molitor*, 113 U.S. 609, 618 (1885). In making this determination, the court should focus on "those aspects of the accused product that were . . . a basis for the prior finding of infringement, and the modified features of the newly accused product." If an element previously found to infringe has been modified or removed, the court should determine whether that modification is significant. *Id.*; *see also Proveris Sci. Corp. v. Innovasystems, Inc.*, 739 F.3d 1367, 1370–71 (Fed. Cir. 2014). Usually, if the change is nonobvious, it should be found to be a significant difference. *TiVo*, 646 F.3d at 883. If the product's modification does render it more than colorably different, whether or not it still infringes the patent, there is no contempt; instead, infringement must be proven in a new jury trial. *Id.*

The test's second, independent element is that the accused product still infringes. In making this assessment, the court should determine that each element of a claim is infringed using any claim constructions decided during the liability case. *Id.* at 883. It, however, must construe any additional claims necessary to determine the infringement issue. *Id.* at 883; *Proveris Sci. Corp.*, 739 F.3d at 1372. Finally, the court must determine whether there is clear and convincing evidence that the specific provisions of the injunction were violated. In making this determination, the injunction must be construed narrowly, with any ambiguity resolved against the patent owner.

Abbott Labs. v. Torpharm, Inc., 503 F.3d 1372, 1382–83 (Fed. Cir. 2007). The propriety of the injunction or its specific provisions, however, is not subject to challenge during the contempt proceeding. *See TiVo*, 646 F.3d at 886.

In assessing the appropriate penalty for contempt, the court has wide discretion. In exercising this discretion, it may consider the infringer's "diligence and good faith efforts" to create a noninfringing product. While neither diligence nor good faith is a defense to contempt, these factors are relevant to the appropriate penalty. *TiVo*, 646 F.3d at 800.

As part of or following a contempt proceeding, the court may be asked to modify its injunction to assure that similar future infringement does not take place by adding a provision requiring that any subsequent claimed design-around be submitted to the patent holder or the court before public distribution. Such an order is allowed if the court determines that it is reasonably necessary to obtain compliance with the prior injunction. *See Additive Controls & Measurement Sys., Inc. v. Flowdata, Inc.*, 154 F.3d 1345, 1356 (Fed. Cir. 1998) ("Although such broad injunctions should be used only in exceptional cases, the district court reasonably concluded that such measures were necessary in this case to compel compliance with the court's orders").

9.2.2 Enhanced Damages

The patent statute authorizes a court to increase a damages award up to three times. § 284. The statute "contains no explicit limit or condition" as to when damages can be increased. The Supreme Court explained, however, that increased damages only should be awarded for "egregious cases of misconduct beyond typical infringement," such as "cases typified by willful conduct," or "deliberate or wanton" infringement. *Halo Electronics, Inc. v. Pulse Electronics, Inc.*, No. 14-1513, slip op. at 9–11, 15 (Supreme Court, June 3, 2016). Under this test, "intentional or knowing [infringement] may warrant enhanced damages." *Id.* at 10. Willful infringement must be proven by a preponderance of evidence (*id.* at 12) and usually is based the infringer's knowledge and conduct at the time of infringement, not, for example, the merit of arguments later asserted in litigation (*id.* at 10). Even following a finding of egregious misconduct or other circumstances that may merit an award of enhanced damages, any award of such damages, including the amount of any enhancement, remains fully in the sound discretion of the court based on the particular circumstances of the case. *Id.* at 11.

Absent other circumstances, increased damages should not be awarded to further compensate the patent holder. *Id.* at 3–4. And, because of § 298, "failure of an infringer to obtain advice of counsel . . . may not be used to prove that the accused infringer willfully infringed."

9.2.2.1 Timing

Naturally, damages can be increased only after damages and willfulness have been determined. Courts can be inundated with various motions after a verdict is returned. Therefore, the court should set a briefing schedule for a motion for enhanced damages, as well as posttrial motions, following the jury's verdict.

A motion for enhanced damages can be brought before or after entry of judgment. If brought after entry of judgment, the court should amend the judgment to reflect any increased damages. It is often more manageable to consider an enhanced damages motion at the same time as posttrial motions. The court's ruling on posttrial motions can affect the amount of enhancement. In addition, ruling on all the motions together allows the court to enter a single judgment reflecting all its rulings.

9.2.2.2 Standard

The decision of whether to enhance damages is based on the egregiousness of the infringer's conduct in light of the totality of the circumstances. *Jurgens v. CBK, Ltd.*, 80 F.3d 1566, 1570 (Fed. Cir. 1996); *Read Corp. v. Portec, Inc.*, 970 F.2d 816, 826 (Fed. Cir. 1992). Prior to its decision in *In re Seagate Tech., LLC*, 497 F.3d 1360 (Fed. Cir. 2007) (en banc), the Federal Circuit articulated nine factors to consider when evaluating the degree of the infringer's culpability and deciding whether to increase damages:

> (1) whether the infringer deliberately copied the ideas or design of another
>
> (2) whether the infringer, when he knew of the other's patent protection investigated the scope of the patent and formed a good-faith belief that it was invalid or that it was not infringed
>
> (3) the infringer's behavior as a party to the litigation
>
> (4) the defendant's size and financial condition
>
> (5) the closeness of the case
>
> (6) the duration of defendant's misconduct
>
> (7) remedial action by the defendant
>
> (8) the defendant's motivation for harm
>
> (9) whether the defendant attempted to conceal its misconduct

Read Corp., 970 F.2d at 827. Following *Seagate*, the Federal Circuit confirmed that these factors are appropriate to determine enhancement, noting that "[t]he [*Seagate*] test for willfulness is distinct and separate from the [*Read*] factors guiding a district court's discretion regarding enhanced damages." *i4i Ltd. P'ship*, 598 F.3d at 859; *see also Funai Elec. Co., Ltd. v. Daewoo Elecs. Corp.*, 616 F.3d 1357, 1376 (Fed. Cir. 2010). In particular, it is still appropriate to consider that the infringer timely obtained and relied on an opinion of counsel that the patent is not infringed or invalid. *See Aspex Eyewear, Inc. v. Clariti Eyewear, Inc.*, 605 F.3d 1305, 1313 (Fed. Cir. 2010); *Finisar Corp. v. DirecTV Grp., Inc.*, 523 F.3d 1323, 1339 (Fed. Cir. 2008). For patents issued on or after September 16, 2012, however, it is improper to consider that the infringer did *not* obtain such an opinion, or that the infringer did not present the opinion at trial. § 298 ("The failure of an infringer to obtain the advice of counsel with respect to any allegedly infringed patent, or the failure of the infringer to present such advice to the court or jury, may not be used to prove that the accused infringer willfully infringed the patent . . . ").

The court may also consider the size of the damages award in ruling on enhancement. *Riles v. Shell Expl. & Prod. Co.*, 298 F.3d 1302, 1314 (Fed. Cir. 2002). While the court is not required to enhance damages, it must state its reasons for not doing so. *Tate Access Floors, Inc. v. Maxcess Techs., Inc.*, 222 F.3d 958, 972 (Fed. Cir. 2000); *Jurgens*, 80 F.3d at 1572.

Not only does the court have discretion in determining whether to enhance damages, but it also has discretion with respect to the amount of enhancement. *SRI Int'l v. Advanced Tech. Labs., Inc.*, 127 F.3d 1462, 1468–69 (Fed. Cir. 1997) (citing *Nat'l Presto Indus. Inc. v. W. Bend Co.*, 76 F.3d 1185, 1193–94 (Fed. Cir. 1996)); *Amsted Indus., Inc. v. Buckeye Steel Castings Co.*, 24 F.3d 178, 183 (Fed. Cir. 1994). While it is common to double or triple the damages amount, courts can use a wide range of multipliers in setting the amount of enhancement, including using a non-integer or percentage calculation. *Advanced Cardiovascular Sys., Inc. v. Medtronic, Inc.*, 265 F.3d 1294, 1310–11 (Fed. Cir. 2001) (affirming 30% enhancement); *Va. Panel Corp. v. MAC Panel Co.*, 133 F.3d 860, 866–67 (Fed. Cir. 1997) (affirming 10% enhancement).

9.2.3 Attorneys' Fees

The patent statute also authorizes the award of reasonable attorneys' fees in exceptional cases. § 285. The purpose is to give the court the power to shift the burden of unnecessary and vexatious litigation onto the party responsible for it. Even in exceptional cases, however, an award of attorneys' fees is not automatic. *Nat'l Presto*, 76 F.3d at 1197. Like enhanced damages, the award of attorneys' fees lies in the trial court's discretion. *Modine Mfg. Co. v. Allen Grp., Inc.*, 917 F.2d 538, 543 (Fed. Cir. 1990). An award of fees for violation of Rule 11 instead of, or in addition to, an award pursuant to § 285 is also possible.

9.2.3.1 Timing

Attorneys' fees motions can be brought before or after entry of judgment, but no later than fourteen days after entry of judgment. Fed. R. Civ. P. 54(d)(2)(B). Unlike enhanced damages, separate judgment does not have to be entered upon postjudgment disposition of a motion for attorneys' fees. Fed. R. Civ. P. 58(a)(1)(C). When brought by a patent holder, however, a motion for attorneys' fees usually is brought together with a request for enhanced damages, as the same facts usually support both motions. The court should set a briefing schedule for these motions as well as posttrial motions. Again, it is advisable where issues overlap to consider attorneys' fees and enhanced damages motions at the same time as posttrial motions.

9.2.3.2 Standard

Attorneys' fees may be awarded by the court to the "prevailing party" in cases it finds "exceptional." § 285. Rejecting previous Federal Circuit law defining this standard, the Supreme Court in *Octane Fitness, LLC v. Icon Health & Fitness, Inc.*, 134 S. Ct. 1749 (2014), held that "an 'exceptional' case is simply one that stands out from others with respect to the substantive strength of a party's litigating position (considering both the governing law and the facts of the case) or the unreasonable manner in which the case was litigated." *Id.* at 1756. The court should make this determination in its discretion based on the "totality of the circumstances." *Id.* In making this assessment, it may consider, as a "'nonexclusive' list of 'factors'": "frivolousness, motivation, objective unreasonableness (both in the factual and legal components of the case) and the need in particular circumstances to advance considerations of compensation and deterrence" as well as "either subjective bad faith or exceptionally meritless claims." *Id.* at 1756 n. 6, 1757, quoting *Fogerty v. Fantasy, Inc.*, 510 U.S. 517, 534 (1994) (describing appropriate considerations for the fee provision in the Copyright Act). The district court also has discretion to decline to award fees even in exceptional cases. *See Octane Fitness, LLC v. Icon Health & Fitness, Inc.*, 576 F. App'x 1002 (Fed. Cir. Aug. 26, 2014) (nonprecedential); *Gardco Mfg., Inc. v. Herst Lighting Co.*, 820 F.2d 1209, 1215 (Fed. Cir. 1987); *S.C. Johnson & Son, Inc. v. Carter-Wallace, Inc.*, 781 F.2d 198, 201 (Fed. Cir. 1986). The district court should, however, set forth its reasons for declining to award fees despite the finding of litigation misconduct and exceptional case status. *See Oplus Techs., Ltd. v. Vizio, Inc.*, 782 F.3d 1371, 1375–76 (Fed. Cir. 2015) (stating "when, as here, a court finds litigation misconduct and that a case is exceptional, the court must articulate the reasons for its fee decision"). All aspects of the district court's determination are reviewed under an abuse-of-discretion standard—a standard that permits "an appellate court's correction of a district court's legal or factual error," but not for mere disagreement with the district court's judgment. *Highmark Inc. v. Allcare Health Mgmt. Sys., Inc.*, 134 S. Ct. 1744, 1748–49 & n.2 (2014).

Since *Octane Fitness*, the Federal Circuit affirmed a fees award when the patentee's allegation of infringement was ill-supported, particularly in light of communications from the alleged infringer explaining its product and the parties' proposed claim constructions, *Lumen View Tech. LLC v. Findthebest.com, Inc.*, 2016 U.S. App. LEXIS 1087 (Fed. Cir. Jan. 22, 2016), and the patentee could not provide credible evidence of infringement in response to a summary judgment motion. *Homeland Housewares, LLC v. Sorensen Research & Dev. Tr.*, 581 F. App'x 877 (Fed. Cir. 2014). Table 9.2 summarizes the factors district courts have considered when awarding fees in light of *Octane Fitness*.

Table 9.2
Facts Considered When Awarding Fees Under § 285

Factors Considered in Awarding Fees to Alleged Infringer	Factors Considered in Awarding Fees to Patent Holder
Objectively baseless or unreasonable infringement claims, including (*e.g.*, *Bayer Cropscience AG v. Dow Agrosciences LLC*, No. 12-256, 2015 U.S. Dist. LEXIS 30752,	• Objectively baseless or unreasonable invalidity or noninfringement arguments (*e.g.*, *Romag Fasteners, Inc. v. Fossil, Inc.*, No. 10-cv-1827, 2014 U.S.

Factors Considered in Awarding Fees to Alleged Infringer	Factors Considered in Awarding Fees to Patent Holder
2015 WL 1197436 (D. Del. Mar. 13, 2015); *IPVX Patent Holdings, Inc. v. Voxernet LLC*, No. 13-cv-1708, 2014 U.S. Dist. LEXIS 158037, 2014 WL 5795545 (N.D. Cal. Nov. 6, 2014)): • Lack of evidentiary support for claims (*e.g.*, *Medtrica Sols. Ltd. v. Cygnus Med. LLC*, No. 12-cv-538 (W.D. Wash. July 11, 2014)) • Knowledge that not all method steps were performed in the U.S. (*e.g.*, *Home Gambling Network Inc. v. Piche*, No. 05-cv-610, 2014 U.S. Dist. LEXIS 71071, 2014 WL 2170600 (D. Nev. May 21, 2014)) • Lack of or inadequate prefiling investigation (*e.g. UltimatePointer, LLC v. Nintendo Co. Ltd.*, No. 14-cv-00865, 2015 U.S. Dist. LEXIS 83625, 2015 WL 3822577 (W.D. Wash. Mar. 9, 2015)) • Alleged infringer was licensed (*e.g.*, *Summit Data Sys., LLC v. EMC Corp.*, No. 10-749, 2014 U.S. Dist. LEXIS 138248, 2014 WL 4955689 (D. Del. Sept. 25, 2014)) • Filing suit on expired patent combined with failure to mark (*e.g.*, *Universal Elecs., Inc. v. Universal Remote Control, Inc.*, No. 12-cv-329, 2015 U.S. Dist. LEXIS 91403 (C.D. Cal. Mar. 10, 2015)) • Finding of inequitable conduct (*e.g.*, *Intellect Wireless, Inc. v. HTC Corp.*, No. 09-C-2495, 2015 U.S. Dist. LEXIS 2864, 2015 WL 136142 (N.D. Ill. Jan. 8, 2015)) Litigation misconduct, including: • Propounding overbroad and burdensome discovery (*e.g.*, *Cambrian Science Corp. v. Cox Commc'ns Inc.*, No, 11-cv-01011, 2015 U.S. Dist. LEXIS 4415, 2015 WL 178417 (C.D. Cal. Jan. 6, 2015)) • Failure to provide discovery or proving false information (*e.g.*, *Digital Reg of Tex., LLC v. Adobe Sys., Inc.*, No. 12-1971, 2015 U.S. Dist. LEXIS 29328, 2015 WL 1026226 (N.D. Cal. Mar. 9, 2015))	Dist. LEXIS 113061, 2014 WL 4073204 (D. Conn. Aug. 14, 2014)) • Flawed, nonsensical expert reports and relitigating rejected claim construction (*e.g.*, *Intex Recreation Corp. v. Team Worldwide Corp.*, No. 04-cv-01785, 2015 U.S. Dist. LEXIS 2847, 2015 WL 135532 (D.D.C. Jan. 9, 2015)) • Finding of willful infringement (*Comaper Corp. v. Antec, Inc.*, No. 5-cv-1103 (E.D. Pa. July 14, 2014)) Litigation misconduct, including: • Failure to provide discovery or false discovery responses (*e.g.*, *Integrated Tech. Corp. v. Rudolph Tech., Inc.*, No. 06-cv-2182 (D. Ariz. Aug. 8, 2014)) • Baseless motion practice (*e.g.*, *Cognex Corp. v. Microscan Sys., Inc.*, No. 13-CV-2027, 2014 U.S. Dist. LEXIS 91203, 2014 WL 2989975 (S.D.N.Y. June 30, 2014)) • Disregard of deadlines and case-management order (*Ultimate Combustion Co., Inc. v. Fuecotech, Inc.*, No. 12-cv-60545 (S.D. Fla. June 24, 2014))

Factors Considered in Awarding Fees to Alleged Infringer	**Factors Considered in Awarding Fees to Patent Holder**
• Baseless motion practice (*e.g.*, *Wave Loch, Inc. v. Am. Wave Machs., Inc.*, No. 08-cv-00928 (S.D. Cal. Jan. 26, 2015)). • Baseless or shifting claim-construction positions (*e.g.*, *Pure Fishing, Inc. v. Normack Corp.*, 10-cv-2140, 2014 U.S. Dist. LEXIS 153272, 2014 WL 5474589 (D.S.C. Oct. 28, 2014)) • Practice of filing lawsuits with the strategy of extracting modest settlement fees from multiple parties (*e.g.*, *TechRadium, Inc. v. FirstCallNetwork, Inc.*, No. 13-2487, 2015 U.S. Dist. LEXIS 23796, 2015 WL 862326 (S.D. Tex. Feb. 27, 2015); *Lumen View Tech., LLC v. Findthebest.com, Inc.*, 63 F. Supp. 3d 321 (S.D.N.Y. 2014)) • Failure to comply with local rules (*e.g.*, *Logic Devices, Inc. v. Apple Inc.*, No. 13-2943, 2014 U.S. Dist. LEXIS 168380, 2014 WL 6844821 (N.D. Cal. Dec. 4, 2014)) • Misrepresentations about or inconsistencies with positions taken in the Patent Office (*e.g.*, *Kilopass Tech., Inc. v. Sidense Corp.*, No. 10-cv-2066, 2014 U.S. Dist. LEXIS 112321, 2014 WL 3956703 (N.D. Cal. Aug. 12, 2014))	

On the other hand, courts since *Octane Fitness* also have indicated that there are continuing limitations on the availability of fee awards. In considering what knowledge a patent holder needs to justify suit, the Federal Circuit has reaffirmed that "tests or experiments on the actual accused products are not always necessary to prove infringement. In some instances, circumstantial evidence alone may suffice." *Checkpoint Sys. v. All-Tag Sec. S.A.*, 572 F. App'x 988, 989 (Fed. Cir. 2014). Table 9.3 summarizes the factors considered by some district courts when denying fees under § 285.

Table 9.3
Facts Considered When Denying Fees Under § 285

Factors Considered in Denying Fees to Alleged Infringer	Factors Considered in Denying Fees to Patent Holder
• Infringement claims were reasonable, nonfrivolous, or made in good faith (*e.g.*, *Site Update Sols. LLC v. Accor North America Inc.*, No. 11-cv-03306, 2015 U.S. Dist. LEXIS 17603, 2015 WL 581175 (N.D. Cal. Feb. 11, 2015)) • Case was a "close call" (*e.g.*, *Eon Corp. IP Holdings LLC v. Cisco Sys. Inc.*, No. 12-cv-1011, 2014 U.S. Dist. LEXIS 101923, 2014 WL 3726170 (N.D. Cal. July 25, 2014)) • Court had to conduct extensive analysis to find in favor of alleged infringer (*e.g.*, *Calypso Wireless v. T-Mobile USA Inc.*, No. 08-cv-00441, 2015 U.S. Dist. LEXIS 26871, 2015 WL 1022745 (E.D. Tex. Mar. 5, 2015)) • Adequate prefiling investigation (*e.g.*, *CreAgri, Inc. v. Pinnaclife, Inc.*, No. 11-cv-6635, 2014 U.S. Dist. LEXIS 77484, 2014 WL 2508386 (N.D. Cal. June 3, 2014)) • Reasonable belief in patent's validity (*e.g.*, *Collectors Universe, Inc. v. Blake*, No. 14-cv-333 (C.D. Cal. Mar. 18, 2015)) • Patent holder prevailed on some claim-construction issues (*e.g.*, *CreAgri, Inc. v. Pinnaclife, Inc.*, No. 11-cv-6635, 2014 U.S. Dist. LEXIS 77484, 2014 WL 2508386 (N.D. Cal. June 3, 2014)) • Claims dismissed for reasons other than the merits of claim (*e.g.*, *Robinson v. Bartlow*, No. 12-cv-24, 2014 U.S. Dist. LEXIS 75105, 2014 WL 2468817 (W.D. Va. June 3, 2014)) • Denial of alleged infringer's motion for summary judgment (*e.g.*, *SFA Sys., LLC v. 1-800-Flowers.com, Inc.*, No. 09-cv-340, 2014 U.S. Dist. LEXIS 184311 (E.D. Tex. July 7, 2014)) • Alleged infringer's failure to move for summary judgment (*e.g.*, *Stragent, LLC v. Intel Corp.*, No. 11-cv-421, 2014 U.S.	• No finding of willful infringement (*e.g.*, *Ateliers de la Haute-Garonne v. Broetje Automation-USA, Inc.*, No. 09-cv-598, 2015 U.S. Dist. LEXIS 39850, 2015 WL 1022745 (D. Del. Mar. 30, 2015)) • No finding of exceptional or unreasonable conduct (*e.g.*, *Transperfect Glob., Inc. v. Motionpoint Corp.*, No. 10-cv-2590, 2014 U.S. Dist. LEXIS 159805, 2014 WL 6068384 (N.D. Cal. Nov. 13, 2014)) • Both parties shifted theories throughout the case (*e.g.*, *L.C. Eldridge Sales Co., Ltd. v. Jurong Shipyards PTE, Ltd.*, No. 11-cv-599 (E.D. Tex. Sept. 23, 2014))

Factors Considered in Denying Fees to Alleged Infringer	Factors Considered in Denying Fees to Patent Holder
Dist. LEXIS 169080, 2014 WL 6756304 (E.D. Tex. Aug. 6, 2014)) • Case litigated in an efficient and cooperative manner (*e.g., The Tawnsaura Grp. LLC v. Maximum Human Performance LLC*, No. 12-cv-7189 (C.D. Cal. Sept. 4, 2014)) • Patent holder voluntarily dismissed claims (*e.g., Chao Tai Electron Co. Ltd. v. Ledup Enter., Inc.*, No. 12-10137 (C.D. Cal. Sept. 18, 2014)) • Alleged infringer's winning argument was presented late in the case (*e.g., Robert Bosch LLC v. Snap-On Inc.*, No. 12-cv-11503 (E.D. Mich. Sept. 25, 2014))	

An attorneys' fees award under the patent statute usually is restricted to the patent portion of the case. *Monolith Portland Midwest Co. v. Kaiser Aluminum & Chem. Corp.*, 407 F.2d 288, 297 (9th Cir. 1969). To the extent a case involves patent and nonpatent causes of action, no award of fees can be allowed under § 285 for the nonpatent theories unless the nonpatent theories are intertwined with the patent issues. *Id.*; *Beckman Instruments, Inc. v. LKB Produckter AB*, 892 F.2d 1547, 1552 n.2 (Fed. Cir. 1989). Therefore, unless the exception applies, in considering attorneys' fees under this provision, the court should require the moving party to separate out fees attributable to other causes of action in the case. The fees award, however, is not limited to costs of responding to "conduct found to be exceptional, . . . because it is the 'totality of the circumstances,' and not just discrete acts of litigation conduct, that justify the court's award of fees." *Homeland Housewares, LLC*, 581 F. App'x at 881.

9.2.4 Motion for a New Trial

Within twenty-eight-days after entry of judgment in a jury or court trial, with or without a motion for judgment as a matter of law, a party can move for a new trial. Fed. R. Civ. P. 59(b). As with Rule 50(b) motions, the time limit is jurisdictional and may not be extended. Fed. R. Civ. P. 6(b)(2). The motion is judged under the law of the regional circuit court of appeals, and in a patent case can be based on the same grounds as any trial. *See, e.g., Minton v. Nat'l Ass'n of Sec. Dealers, Inc.*, 336 F.3d 1373, 1378–79 (Fed. Cir. 2003). These include: (1) that the judgment is contrary to the weight of the evidence; (2) misconduct by an attorney or witness that denies an opponent fair consideration; (3) jury misconduct; (4) erroneous rulings regarding evidence, jury instructions, or trial conduct issues; (5) excessive (with or without a remittitur) or inadequate (with or without an additur) damages; and, (6) new evidence that could not have been discovered during trial. To merit granting a new trial, the subject of the motion must have caused substantial prejudice and, in virtually all cases, have been the subject of a timely objection. *See generally* 12 Moore's Federal Practice § 59.13 (3d ed. 2007).

In patent cases, a motion for new trial is often used to challenge the claim construction provided in jury instructions. Typically, the jury instruction will simply adopt the claim construction set forth in the court's *Markman* order. Although it is usually clear from the *Markman* proceeding when a party disagrees with the court's construction, a party may still need to object to the jury instruction embodying the construction, depending on the circuit in which the trial court sits. Because regional circuit law governs Federal Rule of Civil Procedure 51 and the propriety of jury instructions, in some circuits, claim-construction briefing may not satisfy a party's obligation to object. *Serio-US Indus., Inc. v. Plastic Recovery Techs. Corp.*, 459 F.3d 1311, 1317 (Fed. Cir. 2006) (holding that appellant failed to timely object to claim construction under Fourth Circuit law even though the subject had been briefed); *Ecolab, Inc. v. Paraclipse, Inc.*, 285 F.3d 1362, 1369–70 (Fed. Cir. 2002) (deciding issue on merits (that there was no error), but noting that it would be "uncomfortable" to conclude that the Eighth Circuit would allow a futility exception in this case).

9.2.5 Renewed Motion for Judgment as a Matter of Law

Provided that a motion for judgment as a matter of law was made at the close of all the evidence (*see* § 8.4), a party may renew that motion within twenty-eight days after entry of judgment. *Jurgens v. McKasy*, 927 F.2d 1552, 1557 (Fed. Cir. 1991); *see also Wilson Sporting Goods Co. v. David Geoffrey & Assocs.*, 904 F.2d 677, 681 (Fed. Cir. 1990) (the law of the regional court of appeals determines whether the motion must be filed with the court or only served by the rule's deadline); Fed. R. Civ. P. 50(b). The rule's time limit for making the motion is jurisdictional and cannot be extended. Fed. R. Civ. P. 6(b); *see also U.S. Leather, Inc. v. H&W P'ship*, 60 F.3d 222, 224 (5th Cir. 1995). A renewed motion must be based on the same claimed failure of proof as the initial motion, and in judging it, the court should apply the same standard (*see* § 8.4). *Honeywell Int'l Inc. v. Hamilton Sundstrand Corp.*, 370 F.3d 1131, 1139 (Fed. Cir. 2004) (en banc); *Duro-Last, Inc. v. Custom Seal, Inc.*, 321 F.3d 1098, 1105–09 (Fed. Cir. 2003). The motion may be, and often is, joined with a motion for a new trial. Fed. R. Civ. P. 50(b). A joint motion permits the court to grant the new trial motion as an alternative, should the order granting judgment be reversed on appeal. Fed. R. Civ. P. 50(c)(1).

A renewed motion for judgment as a matter of law is the preferred mechanism by which the court can review the jury's decision on questions of law that are encompassed by a jury's verdict. "Many claims of invalidity rest, however, not upon factual disputes, but upon how the law applies to facts as given. . . . Where the ultimate question of patent validity turns on the correct answer to legal questions—what these subsidiary legal standards mean or how they apply to the facts as given— . . . [the clear-and-convincing burden of] proof has no application." *Microsoft Corp. v. i4i Ltd.*, 131 S. Ct. 2238, 2253 (2011) (Breyer, J., concurring). Rather, the court must decide such embedded legal issues without any deference to the jury verdict.

For example, obviousness is a question of law, but it is often submitted to the jury because the ultimate conclusion is based on findings of fact (the *Graham* factors). If the jury was given special interrogatories addressing each of the *Graham* factors, the court can assess the propriety of the jury's findings based on the evidence presented at trial through a renewed motion for judgment as a matter of law. But even if the jury returns a general verdict of nonobviousness without further explanation, as explained in §§ 7.3.4.4.2, 14.3.5.3.5, the court must determine whether the ultimate legal conclusion is correct in light of disputed facts, implicit as well as explicit, that the jury necessarily determined. *See Kinetic Concepts, Inc. v. Smith & Nephew, Inc.*, 688 F.3d 1342 (Fed. Cir. 2012) (judging jury's implicit factual findings in general verdict of obviousness under substantial evidence standard). See also § 8.3.3.2 for a discussion regarding submission of the issue of obviousness to the jury.

9.2.6 Motion to Vacate Judgment in Connection with Settlement

Following the entry of final judgment, parties are sometimes able to settle before any appellate disposition. As part of the settlement agreement, the patentee and the accused infringer may agree to jointly ask the district court to vacate its judgment finding the patent invalid, not infringed, or unenforceable, as well as certain subsidiary rulings such as claim-construction orders that limit the patent's scope. In some cases, the parties will even make the settlement contingent upon the grant of vacatur. The motivation of the patentee in seeking vacatur is to strip any potential preclusive effect (for collateral estoppel purposes) associated with an adverse ruling regarding the patent's validity, scope, or enforceability. For the accused infringer, on other hand, this cost-free concession presumably helped it obtain monetary or other consideration from the patentee as part of the settlement. Vacatur allows it to share the anticompetitive benefits resulting from the deterrent effect of the restored patent, which could be asserted against its competitors.

Notwithstanding the fact that both parties to the litigation agree that a vacatur motion should be granted, the public interest and considerations of judicial economy often weigh against this outcome. *See* Jeremy W. Bock, *An Empirical Study of Certain Settlement-Related Motions for Vacatur in Patent Cases*, 88 Ind. L. J. 919 (2013) (synthesizing case law and analyzing empirical data on settlement-related motions for vacatur in patent cases over a five-year period); *cf. Lear, Inc. v. Adkins*, 395 U.S. 653, 674 n.19 (1969) (noting "the public's interest in the elimination of specious patents"); *Cardinal Chem. Co. v. Morton Int'l*, 508 U.S. 83, 100 (1993) ("[O]ur prior cases have identified a strong public interest in the finality of judgments in patent litigation."); Jill E. Fisch, *Rewriting History: The Propriety of Eradicating Prior Decisional Law Through Settlement and Vacatur*, 76 Cornell L. Rev. 589, 593 (1991) ("[T]he effect of vacatur on the litigation process extends beyond judicial waste; it perverts the judicial decision into a negotiable commodity, engendering distortion of, and disrespect for, the role of the courts.").

The alleged benefit of approving the vacatur request is that it will buy peace and reduce the costs of further judicial proceedings, such as appeal. These benefits, however, are speculative at best and more likely illusory. The empirical evidence, *see* Bock, 88 Ind. L. J. 919, and anecdotal evidence indicate that the parties will likely settle the matter even if the vacatur request is denied. More significantly, vacating the court's decisions construing the patent claims and/or ruling claims invalid or not infringed could well result in satellite litigation against other parties—possibly even competitors of the defendant.

Vacating any judgment based on the parties' settlement is an "extraordinary remedy" that should be granted only in "exceptional circumstances" that go beyond the parties' desire to include such a remedy in their settlement. *U.S. Bancorp Mortg. Co. v. Bonner Mall P'ship*, 513 U.S. 18, 26, 29 (1994). This is because "[j]udicial precedents are presumptively correct and valuable to the legal community as a whole. They are not merely the property of private litigants and should stand unless a court concludes the public interest would be served by a vacatur." *Id.* at 26 (citations omitted). Indeed, Federal Rule of Civil Procedure 60(b)(6), under which a settlement-related motion for vacatur is typically brought, requires a showing of "extraordinary circumstances." *See Liljeberg v. Health Servs. Acquisition Corp.*, 486 U.S. 847, 864 (1988) (observing that Rule 60(b)(6) "should only be applied in 'extraordinary circumstances'") (internal citations and quotation marks omitted). Moreover, a party that voluntarily declines to pursue an appeal by reason of settlement is not entitled to relief under Rule 60(b)(6). *See Ackermann v. United States*, 340 U.S. 193, 200 (1950) (holding that petitioner was not entitled to relief under Rule 60(b)(6) because of his "voluntary, deliberate, free, untrammeled choice . . . not to appeal"). Thus, absent exceptional circumstances, a motion to vacate a final judgment that is filed in connection with a settlement should be denied. *See Ohio Willow Wood Co. v. Thermo-Ply, Inc.*, 629 F.3d 1374, 1376–77 (Fed. Cir. 2011) (Moore, J., concurring).

9.3 Appeal

After resolution of posttrial motions and entry of final judgment, a party may choose to appeal the judgment. While a notice of appeal to the Federal Circuit removes a patent matter from the district court's jurisdiction, there are a few issues a court must take up in conjunction with an appeal.

9.3.1 Stay of Injunction Pending Appeal

Injunctions are an often-requested remedy in patent cases. When an injunction has been issued and an appeal taken, the defendant will often request that the injunction be stayed pending appeal. Federal Rule of Civil Procedure 62(c) authorizes a district court, in its discretion, to stay an injunction when an appeal is taken. Moving for a stay of injunction in the district court pursuant to the Federal Rules is a prerequisite to requesting a stay in the Federal Circuit. Fed. R. App. P. 8.

While the literal reading of Rule 62(c) contemplates a request for a stay of injunction to be made following the filing of a notice of appeal, a court can, as a matter of judicial economy, consider a stay at the same time as the motion for permanent injunction. *See, e.g., A & L Tech. v. Resound Corp.*, 1995 U.S. Dist. LEXIS 22442, at

*9, 1995 WL 415146 (N.D. Cal. Mar. 15, 1995) (citing *Moxness Prods., Inc. v. Xomed Inc.*, 1988 U.S. Dist. LEXIS 16060, 1988 WL 193213 n.1 (N.D. Fla. 1988)); *Polaroid Corp. v. Eastman Kodak Co.*, 641 F. Supp. 828 (D. Mass. 1985), *aff'd*, 833 F.2d 930 (Fed. Cir. 1986).

In considering whether to grant a stay, the court must apply four factors:

(1) whether the stay applicant has made a strong showing that he is likely to succeed on the merits

(2) whether the applicant will be irreparably injured absent a stay

(3) whether issuance of the stay will substantially injure the other parties interested in the proceeding

(4) where the public interest lies

Standard Haven Prods., Inc. v. Gencor Indus., 897 F.2d 511, 512 (Fed. Cir. 1990); *E.I. DuPont deNemours & Co. v. Phillips Petroleum Co.*, 835 F.2d 277, 278 (Fed. Cir. 1987). The four factors should be weighed using a flexible balancing approach. *Standard Haven*, 897 F.2d at 512; *Arthrocare Corp. v. Smith & Nephew, Inc.*, 315 F. Supp. 2d 615, 619 (D. Del. 2004).

The requirement of showing irreparable injury to obtain a stay of an injunction is applied stringently because the court has already conducted an analysis finding an injunction appropriate. *See Malarkey v. Texaco, Inc.*, 794 F. Supp. 1248, 1250 (S.D.N.Y. 1992); *Crucible, Inc. v. Stora Kopparbergs Bergslags AB*, 594 F. Supp. 1249, 1264 (W.D. Pa. 1985), *aff'd in relevant part*, 793 F.2d 1565 (Fed. Cir. 1986) ("[The] plaintiff now is entitled to its injunction and [the defendant], therefore, should not be heard to complain of that which it had every reason to anticipate would be the result if it lost its gamble."). Thus, irreparable harm for the purposes of a stay of injunction usually is not found unless the injunction will put the defendant out of business in the period pending appeal. A stay of injunction may be more appropriate if the defendant has a design-around, particularly if the patented feature is but one component in a multicomponent product. Under those circumstances, a court may stay the injunction and impose an ongoing royalty for the interim period to allow the defendant to continue its business while transitioning to the release of its design-around. The ongoing royalty amount should expressly take into account the fact that any ongoing use of the patented invention takes place following the grant of an injunction. *Amado*, 517 F.3d at 1362.

In the event that the district court denies a stay pending appeal, a party likely will ask the Federal Circuit to grant the stay. *See generally* Fed. R. App. P. 8. In conjunction with the request to the Federal Circuit, the party also may request that the district court grant a short stay allowing time for the party to prepare and obtain a ruling on its request from the Federal Circuit. In the event the district court does not grant this request, the party likely also will seek an interim stay from the Federal Circuit. *Id.*

9.3.2 Remands

Following review by the Federal Circuit, cases are often returned to a district court with more to do than simply enter an affirmed or other specified judgment. Rather, explicitly or implicitly, matters often are remanded to the district court for further unspecified proceedings consistent with the appellate court's mandate and opinion.

A remand not setting forth any specified action has the effect of broadly returning jurisdiction of the case to the district court. While anything encompassed explicitly or implicitly by the Federal Circuit's mandate must be followed, any action by the district court beyond the scope of the mandate is largely unfettered. In those proceedings, the district court can decide any issue not decided by the Federal Circuit. Even as to explicit direction given by the appellate court in the mandate, compliance is subject to a general rule of flexibility under the general law of the courts of appeal. A district court's action generally will not be reversed if the result is within that contemplated by the general terms of the mandate and not contrary to its explicit terms. *See, e.g.*, *United States v. Kellington*, 217 F.3d 1084, 1095 n.12 (9th Cir. 2000).

Many remands from the Federal Circuit are essentially directions to the district court to reconsider its decision in light of the law as set out in the Federal Circuit's opinion. No outcome is implied by such a remand. It is entirely appropriate that further district court proceedings following a remand lead to an ultimate outcome other than that which would result from solely complying with the appellate mandate, or even a result reversed by an explicit mandate. For example, following reversal of a finding of patent invalidity based upon specified prior art, it is entirely proper for the district court to consider and find the patent invalid based upon other prior art, or otherwise in further proceedings to reach the result that the patent is invalid and enter judgment for the defendant. Similarly, for example, it is proper following reversal of a verdict of infringement for the district court in further proceedings to allow the addition of another patent to the suit and enter a judgment of infringement based upon it. Even as to the claims specifically considered by the Federal Circuit, further proceedings sometimes may result in entry of a judgment the same as that reversed: for example, an appellate reversal of a summary judgment does not preclude the district court's granting a second summary judgment motion based upon an altered claim construction or additional evidence; an appellate ruling that a claim or defense lacks sufficient evidence does not preclude hearing further evidence and finding the missing element is met.

In addition to the appellate mandate, an important limit on further district court proceedings following a remand is the "law of the case" rule. This rule provides that, once a case has been decided on appeal, the decision explicitly or implicitly adopted by the appellate court (excluding dicta) is to be applied, right or wrong, absent exceptional circumstances, in all subsequent proceedings of the lawsuit. *See, e.g.*, *Gindes v. United States*, 740 F.2d 947, 949 (Fed. Cir. 1984). One important example of application of this rule is provided by claim constructions adopted by the Federal Circuit, including those of the district court affirmed by the Federal Circuit, which govern further proceedings whether within or outside the appellate court's mandate. *See, e.g.*, *Ethicon Endo-Surgery, Inc. v. U.S. Surgical Corp.*, 149 F.3d 1309, 1315 (Fed.

Cir. 1998). Even here, however, while the district court may not alter the Federal Circuit's claim constructions, it properly may elaborate on the meaning intended by the Federal Circuit in further proceedings. *See, e.g., E-Pass Techs., Inc. v. 3Com Corp.*, 473 F.3d 1213, 1217–20 (Fed. Cir. 2007).

The limiting law-of-the-case rule does not apply when one of three exceptional circumstances exist: (1) the evidence in a subsequent trial is substantially different; (2) controlling authority has since made a contrary decision of the law applicable to the issues; or (3) the earlier ruling was clearly erroneous and would work a manifest injustice. *Ormco Corp. v. Align Tech., Inc.*, 498 F.3d 1307, 1319 (Fed. Cir. 2007). These departures from the law of the case properly are rare. *Toro Co. v. White Consol. Indus.*, 383 F.3d 1326, 1336–37 (Fed. Cir. 2004). For new evidence to justify a departure, it must be substantial and previously unavailable, a test the Federal Circuit has equated with that required for new evidence to justify a new trial pursuant to Federal Rule of Civil Procedure 60(b). *See Smith Int'l v. Hughes Tool Co.*, 759 F.2d 1572, 1579 (Fed. Cir. 1985). The law-of-the-case rule also does not apply to Federal Circuit opinions regarding preliminary injunctions; claim constructions, along with all other findings of fact and conclusions of law made or affirmed at the preliminary injunction stage, are subject to change by the district court as the case progresses. *See, e.g., Guttman, Inc. v. Kopykake Enters.*, 302 F.3d 1352, 1361 (Fed. Cir. 2002).

Chapter 10
ANDA and Biologics Cases: Patent Infringement Actions Involving FDA-Approved Drugs

The interplay of FDA regulation of pharmaceutical products and the Patent Act produces several distinctive issues for patent case management. (It also produces its own distinctive vocabulary, glossed in Appendix 10.1.) Most issues result from Congress's efforts to streamline generic drug manufacturers' competition with drugs encompassed only by expired or invalid patents in the Drug Price Competition and Patent Term Restoration Act of 1984 (more commonly known as the Hatch-Waxman Act). Prior to the passage of the Hatch-Waxman Act, a generic drug manufacturer that wanted to challenge a patent encompassing a marketed drug typically needed first to obtain marketing approval from the FDA. Once this was allowed, it could begin to manufacture and sell the generic drug in this country, and thus create the basis for federal jurisdiction to adjudicate a pharmaceutical patent's validity, enforceability, and scope. The cost of obtaining such approval, as well as the uncertainty regarding a patent's validity and scope, discouraged entry by generic manufacturers until after a patent expired. The FDA approval process thus extended the effective term of patents encompassing an innovative drug for several years after the patents' expiration.

To address this unintended patent-term extension, the Hatch-Waxman Act established a unified framework to coordinate drug approval and resolution of patent rights relating to generic versions of patented drugs. *See* 21 U.S.C. § 355(j). The Act expedites litigation regarding potential patent infringement of generic drugs to quickly resolve validity and infringement issues. It thereby helps generic drug manufacturers to begin marketing noninfringing products sooner. Understanding this statutory and policy scheme and the economic effects it exerts on the pharmaceutical industry can assist the management of cases involving pharmaceutical patents.

In 2010, Congress supplemented this legislation with the Biologics Price Competition and Innovation Act to provide a similar scheme for biologics litigation. Unlike the identical, small-molecule generic drugs the Hatch-Waxman Act governs, biologics are "highly similar." *See* § 10.3 below.

10.1 Hatch-Waxman Act Statutory Scheme

Congress passed the Hatch-Waxman Act to strike "a balance between two competing policy interests: (1) inducing pioneering research and development of new drugs, and (2) enabling competitors to bring low-cost, generic copies of those drugs to market." *Andrx Pharm., Inc. v. Biovail Corp.*, 276 F.3d 1368, 1371 (Fed. Cir. 2002); *see also In re Barr Labs., Inc.*, 930 F.2d 72, 76 (D.C. Cir. 1991) ("Congress sought to get generic drugs into the hands of patients at reasonable prices—fast."). To meet these objectives, the Act rewards pioneering drug companies with protection of their patent rights. However, it also encourages generic drug companies to enter the market at the earliest possible time consistent with these patent rights by providing for a potentially shortened and cheaper regulatory approval process for generic drugs. The key move legislators made in developing Hatch-Waxman was to permit the ANDA filer to rely on the pioneering drug company's clinical data. Before Hatch-Waxman, few generics were available on the market because there is little economic incentive in generating data and completing clinical trials on a product that cannot be patented.

A pioneering pharmaceutical company seeking FDA approval of a new drug must submit a New Drug Application (NDA) that includes extensive test data, usually from a series of human clinical trials, proving the safety and efficacy of the drug. 21 U.S.C. § 355(b). The FDA designates a drug approved based on human clinical trials as a Reference Listed Drug (RLD). Generic competitors instead are permitted to submit an Abbreviated New Drug Application (ANDA) that shortcuts this process by relying on the clinical trial data submitted for the NDA. The ANDA applicant need not conduct independent human trials or other tests. It can prove the safety and efficacy of the generic drug through evidence that it is equivalent to the pioneering drug. 21 U.S.C. § 355(j)(2)(A). The Hatch-Waxman Act motivates generic drug manufacturers to challenge any applicable patent rights held by the NDA-holder, by granting the first ANDA filer a 180-day market exclusivity period following the ANDA's approval by the FDA if the patent challenge succeeds. During this exclusivity period, only the first ANDA challenger, the NDA-holder and companies licensed by the NDA-holder may market their drugs. 21 U.S.C. § 355(j)(5)(B)(iv).

Resolution of patent rights is an important element of ANDA proceedings. The Hatch-Waxman Act protects the pioneering drug company's patent rights by providing that the act of filing an ANDA that challenges an NDA-holder's patent rights is an "artificial act of infringement" that "enables the judicial adjudication" of claims for infringement and patent invalidity. *Eli Lilly & Co. v. Medtronic, Inc.*, 496 U.S. 661, 678 (1990); *see also* § 271(e)(2)(A). Under normal circumstances, no ANDA will be approved until approximately thirty months after a patent infringement suit has been filed by the NDA holder against the ANDA applicant under § 271(e). 21 U.S.C. § 355(j)(5)(B)(iii). This provision encourages any dispute about the validity and applicability of an NDA-holder's patent rights to be adjudicated before the FDA approves a generic company's ANDA.

The statutory scheme envisions that ANDA patent litigation will be resolved before the thirty-month stay expires. Often, however, the litigation extends beyond the thirty-month stay. If the thirty-month stay expires while litigation remains pending, some ANDA-holders may attempt to launch, although they risk infringing the drug's patent. Likewise, NDA-holders will often seek a preliminary injunction to prevent an at-risk launch when the stay period expires. Launching at risk substantially changes an ANDA case because now the eventual trial could occur before a jury because postlaunch damages will be available to the plaintiff/NDA holder. When only prospective injunctive relief is in play, before the "at-risk" launch, the case would be tried before a judge.

The Hatch-Waxman Act also allows some ANDA applicants to reach the market without litigation. Under § (viii) of the statutory scheme, an ANDA applicant can carve out applicable method-of-use patents from its proposed drug label. It thereby avoids the "artificial act of infringement" under § 271(e), so long as there also are other, unpatented uses of the drug substance. 21 U.S.C. § 355(j)(2)(A)(viii); *see generally AstraZeneca Pharm. LP v. Apotex Corp.*, 669 F.3d 1370, 1376–80 (Fed. Cir. 2012). If a drug's label does not include an infringing use, the drug's manufacturer does not infringe or induce infringement of a method-of-use patent simply by making and selling the drug. *See Warner-Lambert Co. v. Apotex Corp.*, 316 F.3d 1348 (Fed. Cir. 2003). Even with a carve-out, however, if a generic drug manufacturer makes statements on its labels or engages in other actions that promote the infringing use of the drug, the generic company can be liable for inducing infringement. *See AstraZeneca LP v. Apotex, Inc.*, 633 F.3d 1042 (Fed. Cir. 2010). A § (viii) ANDA filer is not subject to the thirty-month stay in approval, but neither is it entitled to the 180-day exclusivity period.

10.1.1 Abbreviated New Drug Applications (ANDA) and Paragraph IV Certifications

Before an ANDA filer can obtain FDA approval of its application, it must establish that its generic drug will not infringe valid patents for the equivalent pioneering drug. To accomplish this, the Hatch-Waxman Act provides that a pioneering drug company's NDA must disclose all patents that cover the drug or a method of using the drug in a manner encompassed by the NDA. 21 U.S.C. § 355(b)(1), (c)(2). The FDA lists all such patents in a publication (available online at www.fda.gov/cder/ob/default.htm), commonly referred to as the "Orange Book," providing notice of the pioneering drug company's patents to the public. For patented methods of use, the NDA holder also must submit a "use code description," for the FDA-approved uses or indications of the drug that are patented. 21 C.F.R. § 314.53. The FDA determines whether a carve-out under § (viii) (21 U.S.C. § 355(j)(2)(A)(viii)) is appropriate based on the use-code description supplied by the NDA holder. NDA filers may not list methods of manufacturing the drug in the Orange Book. 21 C.F.R. § 314.53. The FDA does not audit what the NDA filer lists on the Orange Book in any way; this position has been upheld by courts. 21 C.F.R. § 314.53(f); *see, e.g., aaiPharma, Inc. v. Thompson*, 296 F.3d 227, 235–44 (4th Cir. 2001).

As part of an ANDA filing, a generic drug manufacturer must submit certifications addressing each of the patents listed in the Orange Book that cover the relevant listed drug. 21 U.S.C. § 355(j)(2)(A)(vii); *see Eli Lilly*, 496 U.S. at 677. Specifically, the ANDA filer must certify:

> (i) that the [NDA-required] patent information has not been filed;
>
> (ii) that such patent has expired;
>
> (iii) the date on which such patent will expire; or
>
> (iv) that such patent is invalid or will not be infringed by the manufacture, use, or sale of the new drug for which the ANDA application is submitted.

21 U.S.C. § 355(j)(2)(A)(vii). Alternatively, the ANDA filer may file a § (viii) statement certifying that a method of use patent listed by the pioneering drug company "does not claim a use for which the applicant is seeking approval." 21 U.S.C. § 355(j)(2)(A)(viii)); *AstraZeneca*, 669 F.3d at 1374. The ANDA filer may also split a particular patent, making a Paragraph IV certification as to a particular listed use and a § (viii) carve-out statement as to a second listed use.

A certification that an Orange Book–listed patent is invalid or not infringed is commonly known as a Paragraph IV certification. For each patent as to which an ANDA filer makes a Paragraph IV certification, it must provide "a detailed statement of the factual and legal basis for the opinion of the applicant that the patent is invalid or will not be infringed" or is unenforceable to both the patent owner and the NDA holder. 21 U.S.C. § 355(j)(2)(B)(iv)(II); *see* 21 C.F.R. 314.95(c)(6). Only by filing such a Paragraph IV certification can an ANDA filer obtain FDA approval to market a generic version of a listed drug for a patented use before the expiration or invalidation of an Orange Book–listed patent. *Eli Lilly*, 496 U.S. at 677. Because the Hatch-Waxman Act requires a detailed legal statement, it does not waive privilege, even when drafted by or based on the opinion of an attorney. *See Nycomed, Inc. v. Glenmark Generics Ltd.*, 2009 U.S. Dist. LEXIS 95780, 2009 WL 3334365, at *2 (E.D.N.Y. Oct. 14, 2009).

The Patent Act makes the filing of a Paragraph IV certification an act of patent infringement and allows the Orange Book–listed patent holder to initiate an infringement suit before the generic manufacturer sells any product. § 271(e)(2); *AstraZeneca*, 669 F.3d at 1377; *Glaxo Grp. Ltd. v. Apotex, Inc.*, 376 F.3d 1339, 1351 (Fed. Cir. 2004). A § (viii) filing, however, does not create a cause of action, and therefore, a patent holder cannot initiate suit in response. *See AstraZeneca*, 669 F.3d at 1379–80. If the Orange Book–listed patent holder files an infringement action within forty-five days of receiving notice of a Paragraph IV certification for any patent listed in the Orange Book prior to when the ANDA was filed, then the effective date of the FDA's approval of the generic company's ANDA application is automatically stayed for up to thirty months from the date of receipt of notice of the application to the patent owner and NDA holder. For patents filed by the NDA holder in the Orange Book after the ANDA is filed, the ANDA holder still must submit a Paragraph IV certification or § (viii) statement (21 C.F.R. § 314.94(12)(viii)(C)), but the late-listed, or "pop-up," patent does not trigger an automatic stay. *See Eli Lilly & Co. v. Teva Pharm. USA*, 557 F.3d 1346, 1351 n.1 (Fed. Cir. 2009).

Filing an ANDA is only a "technical act of infringement," as noted above, that establishes jurisdiction under § 271(e). To prove actual infringement, an NDA holder has the burden to prove the product to be sold will infringe patent claims. *See Ferring B.V. v. Watson Labs., Inc.*, 764 F.3d 1401 (Fed. Cir. 2014). Courts analyze the product to be sold against the asserted patent claims, and drug manufacturers must sell only products that comply with the ANDA drug description. *Id.* at 1408. Sometimes the ANDA specification will describe a drug that meets every claim limitation, But where the ANDA specification does not establish infringement outright, the Federal Circuit has endorsed the use of evidence such as tests of the product (in *Ferring*, tests submitted to the FDA). *Id.* at 1408–09. Evaluation of infringement focuses only on the final product complying with the terms of the ANDA—not on test drugs—because only the final product can be sold. *Id.* at 1409 (*see also Tyco Healthcare Grp. LP v. Mutual Pharm. Co.*, 762 F.3d 1338, 1344 (Fed. Cir. 2014) (finding that a patent owner may "allege infringement under § 271(e)(2)(A) if the patent owner has evidence that the as-marketed commercial ANDA product will infringe, even though the hypothetical product specified in the ANDA could not infringe")).

When the ANDA does not describe the potentially infringing product, the patentee must demonstrate by a preponderance of the evidence that the ANDA applicant "would likely sell an infringing composition pursuant to an approved ANDA." *Ferring*, 764 F.3d at 1388 (quoting *Glaxo, Inc. v. Novopharm, Ltd.*, 110 F.3d 1562, 1570 (Fed. Cir. 1997)).

If the applicant files an amended ANDA during the course of the FDA's consideration, the "application" consists of the ANDA as filed and all amendments allowed by the FDA during the litigation. *Id.* at 1390. Allowing an amendment "is within the discretion of the district court." *Id.* at 1390–91. But where an amendment has been allowed, and where the original ANDA literally infringed a patent at issue, but the amended ANDA and product to be sold do not infringe, there is no infringement. *Id.*

Any FDA approval of the ANDA during the thirty-month stay period is "tentative," and does not become a "final approval" allowing actual marketing of the drug unless prior to expiration of the thirty months, all the relevant patents expire, the ANDA applicant obtains a favorable district court or Federal Circuit judgment, or the suit is settled with an agreement that the ANDA applicant's marketing can commence. 21 U.S.C. § 355(j)(5)(B)(iii). A district court also has discretion to shorten or extend the thirty-month stay if "either party to the action failed to reasonably cooperate in expediting the action." *Id.*; *see Eli Lilly & Co. v. Teva Pharm. USA*, 557 F.3d 1346 (Fed. Cir. 2009) (affirming six-month extension of automatic stay following generic manufacturer's alteration of its product just before and production of samples and records of the altered product after close of discovery). Alternatively, a court can enjoin marketing of the ANDA filer's generic drug under the usual preliminary injunction standards. § 271(e)(4)(B); *see, e.g.*, *Altana Pharma AG v. Teva Pharm. USA, Inc.*, 566 F.3d 999, 1005 (Fed. Cir. 2009); *see generally* Chapter 3. And the thirty-month stay on final FDA approval will be extended if the NDA holder's drug is either: (1) a new chemical entity (NCE), that is, a chemical compound not previously approved for marketing by the FDA, in which case the stay is extended to seven and a half years after the NCE was approved for marketing (21 U.S.C. § 355(j)(5)(F)(ii)); or (2) a drug with pediatric-specific labeling supported by a clinical trial involving children, in which case the stay is extended six months (which may be added to the NCE period for a total of eight years) (21 U.S.C. § 355a(b)).

If no infringement action is filed during the 45-day period after the ANDA filer provides notice of its filing, the FDA may approve the ANDA within 180 days after the ANDA application was filed (a period which is often extended by agreement between the FDA and ANDA filer), and the approval is immediately effective. 21 U.S.C. § 355(j)(5)(A), (B)(iii). In that circumstance, the ANDA first-filer may be entitled to the 180 days of market exclusivity described in the next section.

Under this statutory scheme, "'Orange Book listing elevates every patent as a potential source of delay to generic competition,' because listing gives 'the patentee/NDA holder almost automatic injunctive relief for even marginal infringement claims.'" *Andrx Pharm.*, 276 F.3d at 1378 n.6. The potential delay sometimes has motivated questionable conduct by NDA holders, such as listing in the Orange Book patents of doubtful validity or applicability to the listed drug. *See generally Caraco Pharm. Labs. v. Novo Nordisk*, 132 S. Ct. 1670, 1678 (2012). If an ANDA applicant disputes an Orange Book listing to the FDA, the agency will do no more to determine the propriety of a listing of a patent or its indicated use code than to require the NDA holder to confirm the correctness of the listing. *See* 21 C.F.R. § 314.53(f); *Bayer Schering Pharma AG v. Lupin, Ltd.*, 676 F.3d 1316, 1324 (Fed. Cir. 2012) (FDA does not determine whether patents should be listed); *Apotex, Inc. v. Thompson*, 347 F.3d 1335, 1347–50 (Fed. Cir. 2003) (the FDA is not required to determine the correctness of patent listings). As a result, to obtain correction the ANDA applicant must make a Paragraph IV certification and litigate the listed patent's scope. The Orange Book listing's potential for delay also has encouraged some NDA owners to attempt to "evergreen" the delay of generics by listing patents sequentially obtained on additional uses of the same basic drug over several years. *See Andrx Pharm.*, 276 F.3d at 1378 n.6. As long as an added patent is listed in the Orange Book before the relevant ANDA application is filed, it will result in a thirty-month stay of FDA approval if litigation is filed.

10.1.2 Approval of ANDAs and First ANDA Filer's 180-Day Exclusive Marketing Period

The effectiveness of a tentative FDA approval of a second or later-filed ANDA application also can be substantially delayed by the Hatch-Waxman Act's 180-day exclusive marketing period granted to the first ANDA applicant filing a Paragraph IV certification challenging the validity or infringement of Orange Book–listed patents encompassing a product. This delay can be substantially longer than 180 days, and potentially can become an indefinite period before later ANDA filers can obtain FDA approval and begin marketing their drugs. *See, e.g.*, *Dey Pharma, LP v. Sunovian Pharm. Inc.*, 677 F.3d 1158, 1164–65 (Fed. Cir. 2012); *Caraco Pharm. Labs., Ltd. v. Forest Labs. Inc.*, 527 F.3d 1278, 1285 (Fed. Cir. 2008); *Apotex, Inc. v. Pfizer Inc.*, 385 F. Supp. 2d 187, 190 (S.D.N.Y. 2005) ("Some brand name drug manufacturers have succeeded in 'parking' the 180-day marketing exclusivity period, indefinitely delaying ANDA approvals and bottlenecking the market. Federal Trade Commission, 'Generic Drug Entry Prior to Patent Expiration,' vi–vii (July 2002)."), *aff'd*, 159 F. App'x 1013 (Fed. Cir. 2005), *cert. denied*, 549 U.S. 970 (2006).

This 180-day period of market exclusivity is provided to encourage a generic drug company to take on the potential burden and expense of challenging an Orange Book–listed patent via a Paragraph IV certification, helping to open the door for itself and other generic drug companies to enter the market with lower-cost drugs. 21 U.S.C. § 355(j)(5)(B)(iv). The period of exclusivity is effected by delaying the effective date of an FDA approval of any later-filed ANDA's generic drug based on the same NDA until the expiration of the first ANDA filer's period of exclusivity. *Id.* § 355(j)(5)(B)(iv)(II)(bb). Thus, the ANDA first-filer has exclusivity, but only against subsequent Paragraph IV filers. Its exclusivity does not prevent competitive drugs sold by the patentee, entities licensed by the patentee, or (if the FDA concludes a carve-out is available) § (viii) filers.

For ANDA applications filed before December 8, 2003, the period of exclusivity began either on the date the first Paragraph IV ANDA filer began marketing its generic or on the date of a final court decision finding the relevant Orange Book–listed patents invalid or not infringed (a decision that could occur either in a suit brought by the initial or a later ANDA filer (*see Minn. Mining & Mfg. Co. v. Barr Labs., Inc.*, 289 F.3d 775, 780 (Fed. Cir. 2002)), whichever is first. 21 U.S.C. § 355(j)(5)(B)(iv) (2000). This exclusivity period applies regardless of whether the first ANDA filer is successful in establishing the Orange Book–listed patents as invalid or not infringed.

For ANDA applications filed after December 8, 2003, the first Paragraph IV ANDA filer's marketing of the generic is the only trigger for the exclusivity period. 21 U.S.C. § 355(j)(5)(B)(iv) (2003). The exclusivity period, however, can be surrendered under certain circumstances. Most importantly, the exclusivity period is forfeited if the first ANDA filer fails to begin marketing its drug before the later of two statutorily defined dates. 21 U.S.C. § 355(j)(5)(D)(i)(I). The first of these dates is the earlier of:

> (i) 75 days after effective FDA approval of the first ANDA filer's application; or,
>
> (ii) 30 months after submission of the first ANDA application.

Id. The second of the statutorily defined dates is seventy-five days after the date one of the following occurs as to all the patents in the first ANDA filer's Paragraph IV certification:

> (i) a decision, final except for possible review by the Supreme Court, in a suit by the first or a later, tentatively-FDA approved ANDA filer that each Orange Book–listed patent in the first ANDA filer's Paragraph IV certification (the relevant patents) is invalid or not infringed;
>
> (ii) entry of an agreed judgment, pursuant to a settlement agreement, that each of the relevant patents is invalid or not infringed; or,
>
> (iii) withdrawal by the NDA holder of the relevant patents from listing in the Orange Book.

Id. Because the statute specifies that marketing must commence before the *later* of the two defined dates, if no event in the second group of dates occurs (because, for example, the NDA holder and ANDA applicant reach a settlement agreement that does not include entry of a judgment regarding the status of the patents), the FDA has taken the position that there is no forfeiture of the 180-day marketing period even though the first date has passed. *See* Teva North America, FDA Decision Letter: ANDA 77-165: Granisetron Hydrochloride Injection, 1mg/mL, Docket No. 2007N-0389 (Jan. 17, 2008), *available at* http://www.fda.gov/ohrms/dockets/DOCKETS/07n0389/07n-0389-let0003.pdf. As a result, the period by which the first ANDA filer must begin marketing to avoid forfeiture of the 180-day exclusivity period can be extended indefinitely under this provision.

The exclusivity period can also be forfeited by other events, although they are relatively rare: (1) withdrawal of the first ANDA application; (2) amendment of the first ANDA filer's Paragraph IV certification to remove all the relevant patents; (3) failure of the first ANDA filer to obtain approval of its application within thirty months of filing; (4) the first ANDA filer entering into an agreement found by the FTC or Attorney General, and affirmed in a judgment final except for possible Supreme Court review, to violate the antitrust laws; or (5) expiration of all the relevant Orange Book–listed patents. *See* 21 U.S.C. § 355(j)(5)(D). The FTC and Justice Department take the position that settlement agreements between first ANDA filers and holders of an NDA involving reverse payments violate the antitrust laws, and the Supreme Court implicated antitrust scrutiny for reverse payments in the 2013 *FTC v. Actavis, Inc.* decision. *See* § 10.2.4 below.

A further complication is that there can be multiple "first" ANDA filers as to a particular NDA. While only one "first" ANDA application can be filed per "drug," 21 U.S.C. § 335(j)(5)(B)(iv)(bb), each different dose, for example, is considered a different "drug." *See* 21 C.F.R. § 314.3 ("Drug product means a finished dosage form, for example, tablet, capsule, or solution, that contains a drug substance, generally, but not necessarily, in association with one or more other ingredients."). Thus, it is possible to have multiple first ANDA filers with 180-day exclusive marketing periods for dosages or forms of the same underlying drug product that originally was approved under a single NDA. Multiple ANDA filers can share exclusivity on the same drug if they file on the same day and also file a Paragraph IV certification on at least one of the patents. Guidance for Industry: 180-Day Exclusivity Window When Multiple ANDAs Are Submitted on the Same Day (July 2003), http://www.fda.gov/downloads/drugs/guidancecomplianceregulatoryinformation/guidances/ucm072851.pdf. Multiple subsequent ANDA filers may challenge patents within the first ANDA filer's Paragraph IV certifications.

10.1.3 The § 505(b)(2) Pathway for Drug Approval

As described above, most drug manufacturers seek FDA approval to market their drugs through either the NDA pathway for branded drugs, or through the ANDA pathway for generics. The Hatch-Waxman Act provides a third way for manufacturers to seek FDA approval to market a drug, the § 505(b)(2) pathway, if the drug is not entirely "new" but is also not a generic version of a branded drug. Typically, these drugs may have changes from the branded version and are not ANDA-eligible, but these changes (such as different dosage, strength, route of administration or substitution of one ingredient of a combination product) are slight, such that the manufacturer can rely in part on the "full reports of investigations" into the original drug on safety and efficacy issues. 21 U.S.C. § 355(b)(1). A manufacturer of such a drug is permitted to file an NDA under § 505(b)(2) on the drug even though the manufacturer did not conduct the original investigations on the drug, and the manufacturer "has not obtained a right of reference or use" from the original investigator(s). 21 U.S.C. § 355(b)(2).

A manufacturer submitting a § 505(b)(2) NDA application must provide the FDA with additional information showing that any differences between the original and § 505(b)(2) drugs will not affect the safety or efficacy of the § 505(b)(2) drug. A major advantage of this pathway is that the applicant can usually avoid certain types of clinical trials required for full NDA applications. 21 C.F.R. § 314.54(a). Finally, a § 505(b)(2) NDA applicant must certify whether its drug will infringe Orange Book–listed patents. 21 U.S.C. § 355(b)(2)(A). Like the filing of an ANDA application (*see*

§ 10.1.1), the filing of a § 505(b)(2) application for the purpose of commencing commercial manufacture, use or sale of a patented drug while a listed patent is in effect constitutes a technical act of infringement, allowing the patent owner to immediately commence suit before commercial activity begins.

10.2 The Hatch-Waxman Act's Impact on Patent Litigation

The substantive rights granted under the Hatch-Waxman Act greatly influence the litigation and marketing strategies of pharmaceutical companies. The statutory provisions significantly affect not only the litigation and market relationship between the pioneering drug NDA filer and the first generic drug ANDA filer, but also subsequent ANDA filers (i.e., later generic drug companies seeking entry into the market after the 180-day period of exclusivity). Drug companies have developed litigation strategies that attempt to take advantage of the benefits granted by the Hatch-Waxman Act while circumventing the countervailing purposes of the statute. Management of ANDA cases should take these issues into consideration. These strategies often have involved attempted manipulation of the ability of ANDA filers to obtain the requisite effective FDA approval of their applications and begin marketing by (1) avoiding resolution of all relevant Orange Book–listed patents, and thus the effective date of FDA approval of an ANDA with a Paragraph IV certification relating to those patents; and (2) extending, potentially indefinitely, the commencement of the first ANDA filer's 180-day exclusivity period.

The Hatch-Waxman Act also alters patent litigation in that suits under the Act usually involve no damages (*see* § 271(e)(4)(C); 21 U.S.C. § 355(j)(5)(c)(iii)), and thus, there is no right to a jury trial. *See Tegal Corp. v. Tokyo Electron Am. Inc.*, 257 F.3d 1331, 1339–41 (Fed. Cir. 2001); *In re Andrx Pharm., Inc.*, 399 F. App'x 582, 584 (Fed. Cir. 2010); *In re Apotex, Inc.*, 49 F. App'x 902, 903 (Fed. Cir. 2002).

10.2.1 Personal Jurisdiction to Resolve Patent Issues in ANDA Cases

Chapter 2.3.1 notes that under *Daimler AG v. Bauman*, ANDA plaintiffs must establish that a defendant is "essentially at home" in the forum state. *See* 134 S. Ct. 746 (2014).

This decision may cause more generic company defendants to challenge personal jurisdiction in jurisdictions that are neither the generic's place of incorporation or principal place of business. This decision may affect the distribution of ANDA cases nationally.

Since *Daimler*, district courts have continued to find personal jurisdiction in ANDA cases, either through specific contacts related to the filing of the ANDA or by consent. For example, in *AstraZeneca AB v. Mylan Pharmaceuticals*, No. 14-664-GMS, 2014 WL 5778016 (D. Del. Nov. 5, 2014), Judge Sleet found that there was specific personal jurisdiction. The court reasoned that the lawsuit arose out of Mylan's Paragraph IV certification sent to AstraZeneca in Delaware, and that Mylan should have "reasonably anticipate[d] being haled into court" in Delaware. *Id.* at 7.

Moreover, the court found that AstraZeneca "would be substantially burdened if forced to bring lawsuits against each ANDA filer in the defendants' home states." *Id.* As of the time of this publication, the issue of personal jurisdiction in this case has been certified for interlocutory appeal. *AstraZeneca AB v. Aurobindo Pharma Ltd.*, No. 14-664-GMS, 2014 WL 7533913, at *1 n.1 (D. Del. Dec. 17, 2014); *see also Eli Lilly & Co. v. Mylan Pharm.*, No. 14-cv-00389-SEB-TAB, 2015 WL 1125032 (S.D. Ind. Mar. 12, 2015) (finding specific personal jurisdiction in Indiana because of Mylan's act of filing an ANDA and directing a Paragraph IV notice letter to Eli Lilly in Indiana, and because Eli Lilly would be burdened to bring suit in each ANDA filer's home state).

A number of district court cases have adopted, to varying degrees, the reasoning that compliance with business registration statutes indicated consent to personal jurisdiction. *See Acorda Therapeutics, Inc. v. Mylan Pharm. Inc.*, 1-14-cv-00935-30, 2015 WL 186833 (D. Del. Jan. 14, 2015) (finding specific personal jurisdiction as well as finding that Mylan had consented to personal jurisdiction by complying with Delaware's business registration statutes); *see also Forest Labs., Inc. v. Amneal Pharm.*, No. CV 14-508-LPS, 2015 WL 880599 (D. Del. Feb. 26, 2015) (finding Mylan had consented to personal jurisdiction by complying with business registration statutes); *Otsuka Pharm. Co. v. Mylan, Inc.*, No. Civ.A. 14-4508 JBS, 2015 WL 1305764, *12 (D.N.J. Mar. 23, 2015) (finding that certain Mylan entities consented to personal jurisdiction by complying with business registration statutes); *Senju Pharm. Co. v. Metrics, Inc.*, Civ. No. 14-3962 (JBS/KMW), 2015 WL 1472123 (D.N.J. Mar. 31, 2015) (finding Metrics had consented to personal jurisdiction by not only complying with New Jersey's business registration statutes, but also by accepting service in New Jersey).

10.2.2 Subject-Matter Jurisdiction to Resolve Patent Issues in ANDA Cases

10.2.2.1 Jurisdiction over Infringement Actions by NDA Holders Arising from Paragraph IV Certifications

The Hatch-Waxman Act, in conjunction with the Patent Act, creates an artificial patent infringement cause of action and grants federal courts jurisdiction over that action once a Paragraph IV ANDA filer provides notice to a patent holder that the ANDA applicant believes the relevant Orange Book–listed patents are invalid or not infringed. 28 U.S.C. § 1338(a); § 271(e)(2); *see AstraZeneca Pharm. LP v. Apotex Corp.*, 669 F.3d 1370, 1376–77 (Fed. Cir. 2012). If the patent holder files an infringement suit within forty-five days of the ANDA filing, the Hatch-Waxman Act delays the effectiveness of FDA approval of the ANDA application for thirty months unless the litigation is ended earlier than that. 21 U.S.C. § 355(j)(5)(B). Not surprisingly, holders of Orange Book–listed patents often initiate patent infringement suits upon the filing of ANDA applications. They have strong incentives to delay the resolution of such litigation to prolong the stay of FDA approval for generic versions of patented drugs for the full thirty months of possible delay. *See* FTC, Generic Drug Entry Prior to Patent Expiration: An FTC Study 49 (July 2002).

10.2.2.2 Declaratory Judgment Jurisdiction Arising from Paragraph IV Certifications

While it has always been clear that suit can be filed as to patents listed in a Paragraph IV certification, disputes over jurisdiction arise when the Paragraph IV certification implicates more than one Orange Book–listed patent and the NDA patent holder brought suit on fewer than all of them. Furthermore, although NDA patent holders have a strong incentive to file suit to trigger the thirty-month stay, they also have a strong incentive to avoid a litigation result that may allow the first ANDA filer to enter the market and start the 180-day period, after which subsequent ANDA filers may flood the market with generics.

Consequently, in cases where multiple Orange Book–listed patents are implicated, NDA patent holders sometimes initiate suit on fewer than all of the listed patents, typically the patent or patents with the earliest expiration date. By initiating suit, the NDA holder usually obtains an automatic thirty-month stay before FDA approval of the generic is effective. And even if the litigated patent or patents are found invalid or not infringed, the first ANDA filer still runs the risk of infringing the NDA-holder's other, unlitigated patents if it goes to market. This may discourage the first ANDA filer from beginning to market, and the 180-day period before other subsequent ANDA filers can enter the market will not be triggered by market entry. Nor is a finding of invalidity or noninfringement as to less than all of the Orange Book patents enough to trigger the start or potential forfeiture of the 180-day exclusivity period; this requires that all the relevant Orange Book–listed patents be found invalid or not infringed. 21 U.S.C. § 355(j)(5)(D)(i)(I); *Caraco Pharm. Labs., Ltd. v. Forest Labs. Inc.*, 527 F.3d 1278, 1287 (Fed. Cir. 2008). As a result, this strategy enables NDA holders to take advantage of the provisions for a thirty-month stay of effectiveness of FDA approval of generics without the corresponding risk of losing their market position. *See Teva Pharm. USA, Inc. v. Novartis Pharm. Corp.*, 482 F.3d 1330, 1343 (Fed. Cir. 2007) (patent holder suing on less than all its listed patents "has tried to simultaneously leverage the benefits provided to a patentee under the Hatch-Waxman Act and avoid the patentee's accompanying responsibilities," by "invok[ing] the statutory automatic 30-month stay and . . . concurrently insulating the . . . patents [not sued upon] from a validity challenge" or "any judicial determination of the metes and bounds of the scope of the claims").

To prevent this strategy, Congress amended the Hatch-Waxman Act in 2003 to include a "civil action to obtain patent certainty" provision (CAPC) that allows an ANDA filer to file a declaratory judgment claim regarding all relevant Orange Book–listed patents if the NDA holder fails to sue upon all of them within the forty-five-day period. ANDA filers can use the CAPC provision to initiate declaratory judgment actions with respect to any relevant, unasserted Orange Book patent. If the declaratory judgment action asserts noninfringement, as opposed to solely invalidity, the ANDA filer must first make an "offer for confidential access," allowing the NDA patent holder confidential access to its ANDA application to allow the patent holder to determine whether to bring suit. 21 U.S.C. § 355(j)(5)(C)(i); *see Teva Pharm.*, 482 F.3d at 1330 (holding that in such circumstances there exists a justiciable case or controversy).

Also, if an NDA holder does file suit on a patent, an ANDA filer can file a declaratory judgment counterclaim to require the NDA holder to correct its NDA to remove an improperly listed patent or change its use code to describe more accurately the scope of a listed patent. 21 U.S.C. § 355(j)(5)(C)(ii); *Caraco Pharm. Labs. v. Novo Nordisk*, 132 S. Ct. 1670 (2012). Whether the Hatch-Waxman Act's counterclaim provision extends beyond requiring corrections in FDA listings and use codes is unsettled.[1]

10.2.2.2.1 Declaratory Judgment Actions by First ANDA Filers

First ANDA filers desiring to take their generic drugs to market without the risk of infringement may use the CAPC provision to counterclaim or initiate actions for declaratory judgment of invalidity or noninfringement with respect to the relevant Orange Book patents not asserted by the NDA holders. *See Teva Pharm. USA, Inc. v. Novartis Pharm. Corp.*, 482 F.3d 1330, 1346 (Fed. Cir. 2007) (approving such suits). Among the reasons for the Federal Circuit's decision was that the NDA holder's suit on less than all the relevant patents was contrary to the intent of the provisions of the Hatch-Waxman Act. *Id.* at 1342–43. Specifically, the Federal Circuit found that the NDA holder was trying to "simultaneously leverage the benefits provided to a patentee under the Hatch-Waxman Act and avoid the patentee's accompanying responsibilities." *Id.* at 1343.

10.2.2.2.2 Declaratory Judgment Actions by Subsequent ANDA Filers

Subsequent ANDA filers also have an interest in early resolution of patent rights due to the 180-day exclusivity period afforded to a successful first ANDA filer. Indeed, when first ANDA filers are unable or unwilling to bring their generics to market or obtain a court judgment of invalidity or noninfringement with respect to all relevant Orange Book patents, the only way a subsequent ANDA filer can start the 180-day exclusivity period is by obtaining its own court judgment of invalidity or noninfringement through a declaratory judgment action.

The Federal Circuit first addressed the issue of a subsequent ANDA filer's standing to bring declaratory judgment actions in *Caraco Pharmaceutical Laboratories, Ltd. v. Forest Laboratories, Inc.*, 527 F.3d 1278 (Fed. Cir. 2008). Forest (the NDA

---

1. District courts have held that the Hatch-Waxman Act's counterclaim provision only authorizes counterclaims seeking to delist patents from the Orange Book, and does not authorize other counterclaims (such as patent misuse) based on improper Orange Book listings. *See BrainTree Labs., Inc. v. Amruthan, Inc.*, Case No. 11-01854 (E.D. Pa. Feb. 24, 2012).

holder) sued on one of its Orange Book patents, but not the other. *Id.* at 1286. When the first ANDA filer failed to bring a declaratory judgment action regarding the other patent, Caraco, a subsequent ANDA filer, brought one. *Id.* at 1286–88. In an attempt to remove any case or controversy, Forest unilaterally granted Caraco a covenant not to sue. *Id.* at 1288. The Federal Circuit nevertheless found that even with Forest's covenant not to sue, Caraco had standing to bring the action. *Id.* at 1291–92. Specifically, by seeking to prevent the FDA from approving ANDAs of generic drug manufacturers, Forest was effectively excluding Caraco from offering what it claimed to be a noninfringing generic drug. *Id.* at 1292. The Federal Circuit found this to be a restraint from the free exploitation of noninfringing goods, which has been recognized as a cognizable injury. *Id.* (*citing Red Wing Shoe Co. v. Hockerson-Halberstadt, Inc.*, 148 F.3d 1355, 1360 (Fed. Cir. 1998)). Subsequently, the Federal Circuit held that the same rule applied even if the declaratory judgment action alone was insufficient to allow the ANDA filer to market its drug, and it additionally would have to prevail in separate litigation brought by the NDA holder over other Orange Book patents. *Dey Pharma, LP v. Sunovian Pharm. Inc.*, 677 F.3d 1158 (Fed. Cir. 2012). By contrast, the Federal Circuit has held there is no jurisdiction for a subsequent ANDA filer's declaratory judgment suit seeking only to eliminate the 180-day exclusivity period of the first ANDA filer. *Janssen Pharmaceutica, NV v. Apotex, Inc.*, 540 F.3d 1353 (Fed. Cir. 2008).

10.2.3 Case Management

10.2.3.1 Scheduling and Timing of Judgment

The Hatch-Waxman statutory framework affects not only the incentives for bringing suit but also the conduct of the parties during the litigation.

A Paragraph IV certification requires an ANDA filer to provide the NDA holder with a detailed statement of the factual and legal basis for its invalidity, unenforceability or noninfringement opinions. 21 U.S.C. § 355(j)(2)(B)(iv)(II); 21 C.F.R. § 314.95(c)(6). The parties to a patent lawsuit brought under the Hatch-Waxman Act therefore usually have more information at the start of the litigation than what is available at the start of a typical patent suit. For this reason, courts should be able to push for quicker resolution of issues than in a typical patent case.

An approach to case management that recognizes and utilizes the early availability of information is particularly important because NDA holders have strong motivation to delay resolution of the litigation at least until the thirty-month stay expires. During the thirty-month stay period, unless there is a final court judgment that the relevant Orange Book–listed patents are invalid or not infringed, the first ANDA filer cannot obtain FDA approval and take its generic to market. Therefore, by delaying resolution of the litigation until after the stay expires (and perhaps then seeking a preliminary injunction to prevent an at-risk launch), the NDA holder can delay market entry by the first ANDA filer and delay the start of the 180-day period before any subsequent ANDA filers can bring their generics to market. This has the effect of extending the NDA-holder's monopoly on sales of the listed drug.

First ANDA filers may not necessarily oppose this delay. A court judgment of invalidity or noninfringement will start the clock on a first ANDA filer's 180-day exclusivity period. The first ANDA filer will want to delay that start until it is ready to market its drug to maximize its time as the sole generic provider. Subsequent ANDA filers, in contrast, are almost always interested in a speedy resolution to ensure an early trigger of the 180-day exclusivity period and thus an earlier time to entry of subsequent generic filers. Thus, in cases between an NDA holder and the first ANDA filer, a court may be required to manage a lawsuit in which neither party is interested in early resolution but are using the litigation to advance other objectives.

Courts can combat the strong incentive to delay by adopting expedited case schedules that take advantage of the invalidity, unenforceability and noninfringement contentions already available to the parties in the Paragraph IV certification and notice. Unlike many patent defendants, ANDA filers should be able to exchange their invalidity and noninfringement positions almost immediately upon commencement of the lawsuit, having prepared their required notice to the NDA holders. NDA holders similarly should be able to exchange their infringement and validity contentions at the commencement of litigation having had notice, usually for forty-five days before the suit is filed.

Courts can also directly combat attempts by the parties to delay litigation. The Hatch-Waxman Act explicitly grants courts the discretion to adjust the thirty-month stay period based on the parties' conduct during litigation. 21 U.S.C. § 355(j)(5)(B)(iii). Where a patent holder attempts to extend its patent exclusion through extensive litigation, a court may shorten the thirty-month period. *See Allergan, Inc. v. Alcon Labs., Inc.*, 324 F.3d 1322, 1337 n.5 (Fed. Cir. 2003) (Schall, J., concurring). Similarly, where an ANDA filer delays and fails to cooperate in discovery for example, the court may extend the period before the FDA may approve the ANDA. *See Eli Lilly & Co. v. Teva Pharm. USA, Inc.*, 557 F.3d 1346 (Fed. Cir. 2009). In exercising this discretion, the court should limit its considerations to the conduct of the parties in the litigation and not to positions taken before the FDA. *See Andrx Pharm., Inc. v. Biovail Corp.*, 276 F.3d 1368, 1376 (Fed. Cir. 2002). With this in mind, courts can establish disclosure and discovery deadlines that promote early resolution of ANDA cases.

10.2.3.2 Order of Trial Presentation

ANDA cases differ from most other patent cases in that, while the patent owner typically is the plaintiff, it is the ANDA defendant—the generic drug company—that bears the burden of proof on the issues that will be tried. This is because the gist of the usual ANDA case is invalidity or unenforceability, not noninfringement. The ANDA generic drug and associated label must be identical to the NDA-holder's drug and label, so if the patent covers the NDA-holder's drug, it very likely also covers the ANDA drug. Because of this reversal of the usual burden of proof (as discussed in § 8.1.2.2.2), it also may be appropriate to reverse the order of proof.

10.2.3.3 Remedies in ANDA Litigation

In many circumstances, courts are required to provide no remedy beyond a declaratory judgment at the conclusion of an ANDA case. If, before any final FDA approval, the NDA holder wins and the patent is declared valid and infringed, the FDA will not approve the ANDA application until the patent expires (§ 271(e)(4)(A)). This is accomplished by switching the ANDA filer's Paragraph IV certification to a Paragraph III certification. *See, e.g.*, *Mylan Labs., Inc. v. Thompson*, 389 F.3d 1272, 1282–83 (D.C. Cir. 2004). If the district court judgment comes after the thirty-month stay expired and the ANDA holder began marketing its drug in an at-risk launch, the FDA will revoke the final approval and instead tentatively approve the ANDA drug, which has the effect of precluding further sales. Notwithstanding that the FDA's action precludes lawful sale of the ANDA applicant's drug, some courts additionally grant an injunction. *See, e.g.*, *Sanofi-Synthelabo v. Apotex Inc.*, 294 F. Supp. 2d 353, 397 (S.D.N.Y. 2007), *aff'd*, 5590 F.3d 1075 (Fed. Cir. 2008), *cert. denied*, 130 S. Ct. 493 (2009).

If, on the other hand, the ANDA applicant wins in the district court, upon entry of the judgment any remaining part of the thirty-month stay is terminated, and, without more, the FDA will change its tentative approval of the ANDA to a final approval allowing the drug to be marketed. 21 U.S.C. § 355(j)(5)(B)(iii)(I)(aa). The FDA will grant this final approval even if the district court judgment is "stayed" pending appeal. *Sanofi-Aventis LLC v. Sandoz, Inc.*, 345 F. App'x 594 (Fed. Cir. 2009). If, following FDA approval, the ANDA holder markets its drug and the Federal Circuit subsequently reverses the district court judgment, finding infringement of a valid patent, the usual patent remedies—injunctive relief and damages—apply. Similarly, if the ANDA holder began marketing upon receiving FDA approval at the conclusion of a thirty-month stay before any district court judgment and the district court subsequently finds infringement of a valid patent, these usual remedies apply.

10.2.3.4 Local Patent Rules in Hatch-Waxman Act Cases

As discussed previously in Chapter 2, one way to facilitate the early resolution—or at least efficient resolution—of patent cases is the adoption or use of specialized local rules, which have proven to be a powerful case-management tool. Several courts have adopted patent local rules specific to Hatch-Waxman litigation. *See* D.N.J. L. Pat. R. 3.6; E.D. Tex. P. R. 3-8; N.D. Ohio L. P. R. 3.9; Dist. Idaho Loc. Patent R. 3-6; D. Md. Pat. L. R. 805.3; E.D. Mo. Local Patent R. 3-1(a)(viii); W.D. Tenn. LPR 3.10 (all printed in Appendix 10.3). The rules of these courts recognize the different availability of information in ANDA cases, and therefore reverse the typical order and timing for disclosure of infringement and invalidity contentions.

Ordinarily, plaintiff-patent holders have the initial advantage in patent litigation, controlling the timing of the litigation and having the opportunity to prepare and plan the infringement case well in advance of filing suit. Defendants, on the other hand, must investigate and develop noninfringement and invalidity positions while already in the throes of litigation. Consequently, typical local patent rules (including the District of New Jersey and Eastern District of Texas's rules governing non-ANDA patent cases) require the plaintiff early in the litigation to provide detailed infringement contentions first, allowing the defendant some reasonable time thereafter to prepare and serve invalidity contentions.

The situation is somewhat reversed in Hatch-Waxman cases, however. It is the defendant in Hatch-Waxman cases that dictates the timing and scope of litigation through its ANDA filing. In addition, unlike a typical defendant, a defendant in a patent case brought under the Hatch-Waxman Act already has a "detailed statement of the factual and legal basis for the opinion of the applicant that the patent is invalid or will not be infringed" or is unenforceable prepared as part of its Paragraph IV certification. *See* 21 U.S.C. § 355(j)(2)(B)(iv)(II); 21 C.F.R. § 314.95(c)(6). Moreover, unlike the usual situation, a Hatch-Waxman plaintiff—the patent owner—may have little information about the defendant's generic drug. There usually is no publicly available product from the generic company, so often the plaintiff knows only the information about the generic product required to be included in the Paragraph IV certification—that the generic is bioequivalent, has the same dosage, and uses the same route of administration.

Because a defendant in an ANDA case already has detailed invalidity and non-infringement contentions by the time suit is filed, the ANDA local patent rules require the defendant to provide its invalidity contentions first. *See* D.N.J. L. Pat. R. 3.6; E.D. Tex. P.R. 3-8. In addition, they impose a new obligation on an ANDA defendant to also provide its noninfringement contentions. Specifically, District of New Jersey Local Patent Rule 3.6 requires ANDA defendants to:

> (1) produce the entire ANDA that is the basis of the case by the initial scheduling conference;
>
> (2) provide the written basis for their "Invalidity Contentions" within 14 days after the initial scheduling conference; and
>
> (3) provide the written basis (including claim charts) for their "Non-Infringement Contentions" within 14 days after the initial scheduling conference.

Id. Forty-five days thereafter, the plaintiff is required to provide its infringement contentions. *Id.* Eastern District of Texas Local Rule 3-8 contains similar requirements on the same timetable.

In addition, both New Jersey Local Patent Rule 3.6(j) and Eastern District of Texas Local Patent Rule 3-8(e) amend the disclosure requirements for Hatch-Waxman cases. Both rules require parties with pending ANDA applications that form the basis for a litigation to notify the FDA of motions for injunctive relief no later than three business days after filing the motion. These parties must also provide a copy of correspondence between the FDA and any party regarding the ANDA application to each party bringing an infringement claim, or must "set forth the basis of any claim of privilege" for the correspondence, no later than seven days after receiving or sending correspondence. This rule is intended to aid in the coordination of FDA proceedings and district court litigation, and to avoid discovery issues about the production of FDA correspondence during litigation proceedings.

Apart from these changes in the disclosure order and times, ANDA cases are subject to the remaining patent local rules in both New Jersey and the Eastern District of Texas. The ANDA rules, for example, are silent with regard to the order of proof at trial.

The reversal of disclosure obligations and the additional requirement to provide noninfringement contentions was the subject of much discussion during the comment period for the District of New Jersey's local patent rules. Critics questioned the practice of requiring ANDA defendants to provide noninfringement contentions before knowing a plaintiff's theory of infringement, particularly when plaintiffs bear the burden of proving infringement. The requirement imposes an obligation on ANDA defendants to address patent claims that ultimately may not even be asserted by the plaintiff. Proponents argued the rules appropriately accounted for the special nature and availability of information in Hatch-Waxman cases. Because generics are not available on the market for a patent holder to conduct a thorough infringement analysis, plaintiffs should not be required to provide infringement contentions without full-disclosure of the ANDA filing and noninfringement arguments required by the local rules.

The District of New Jersey local patent rules were adopted after consideration of these concerns, and serve as a helpful guideline for management of Hatch-Waxman patent cases. Whether or not a disclosure schedule similar to the one proposed by the District of New Jersey is adopted, an understanding of the mechanics of the Hatch-Waxman Act can help courts fashion case-management techniques to take advantage of and address the particular incentives and interests of the parties and assist in the early resolution of ANDA cases.

10.2.3.5 Scheduling Orders in Hatch-Waxman Case Management: Chief Judge Stark, District of Delaware

Chief Judge Stark of the District of Delaware issued ANDA-specific scheduling orders on July 1, 2014. He elected to not apply several of the July 2014 patent procedures (printed in Appendices 7.1 and E) to ANDA cases, and thus these orders differ from his standard patent scheduling orders in several ways. First, the ANDA scheduling order removes the disclosures section present in the July 2014 patent instructions, and instead specifies dates by which the plaintiff and defendant shall produce or provide information such as identification of accused products, production of core technical documents, production of initial claim charts, and production of initial invalidity, final infringement, and final invalidity contentions.

In addition, the court will not hear case-dispositive motions in ANDA cases, absent agreement between the parties (this reflects how bench trials are typically handled in the District of Delaware). The ANDA-specific instructions also do not include any specific discussion about jury instructions, voir dire, and special verdict forms, given that typically these ANDA cases are bench trials. These instructions do not include a specific section on judgment on the verdict, or posttrial status reports. Finally, the orders do not give standard posttrial briefing instructions or page limits because these instructions and limits are determined on a case-by-case basis, usually at the end of the trial. Both sides must attend posttrial briefing. A full copy of these rules is included in Appendix 10.2.

10.2.4 Settlement of Hatch-Waxman Patent Infringement Lawsuits

10.2.4.1 Reverse Payments (Pay-for-Delay Settlements)

Other than the automatic thirty-month stay on FDA approval of the ANDA, an NDA holder has little incentive to engage in litigation. Because the generic drug company is not yet selling a competing drug, an NDA holder cannot receive any damages, yet it still runs the risk of having its patents invalidated. In the best-case scenario, the NDA holder is in the same position it would be in without a lawsuit. And in the worst-case scenario, it loses its patent rights. For a generic ANDA holder, however, litigation is a low-risk proposition. In the worst-case scenario, apart from litigation expenses, the generic company is in the same position it was without litigation. In the best-case scenario, it can enter the market before expiration of the Orange Book–listed patents with a period of market exclusivity. Thus, in Hatch-Waxman patent lawsuits, the NDA holder bears the majority of the risk, creating risk-assessment that differs greatly from other patent cases. *See In re Ciprofloxacin Hydrochloride Antitrust Litig.*, 544 F.3d 1323, 1338, (Fed. Cir. 2008), *cert. denied*, 129 S. Ct. 2828 (2009).

In particular, NDA filers are highly motivated to settle in a manner that avoids the first ANDA filer's early market entry, not only to avoid the risk of having its patents found invalid or not infringed, but also because it has the incentive to delay market entry by all other generics. Because of the 180-day exclusivity period granted to first ANDA filers, by delaying a first ANDA filer's generic entry, the NDA holder can delay entry by all generics. As a result of this dynamic, NDA holders and first ANDA filers have economic incentives to reach settlement agreements that run counter to the goals of the Hatch-Waxman Act.

In the 1990s, NDA holders started entering into settlement agreements with first ANDA filers known as reverse-payment settlements. In contrast to typical patent case settlements in which payments flow from the alleged infringer to the patent holder, a reverse-payment settlement involves the patent owner (NDA holder) making payments[2] to the alleged infringer (the first ANDA filer) to settle the patent in-

2. Early reverse-payment settlements (those conducted before the mid-2000s) generally consisted of cash payments as considerations. Settlements since this time have become far more complicated. Settlements may use such terms as additional contract terms, agreements regulating other pharmaceutical products, or no cash used as consideration. Other provisions may include an intellectual property license, supply and distribution agreements, or co-promotion of brand-name products. One particular type of agreement under current investigation in several pending actions is the "no authorized generic" ("No-AG") agreement, in which the brand-name company agrees to not market its own generic brand against a generic manufacturer's product. *See* C. Scott Hemphill, *An Aggregate Approach to Antitrust: Using New Data and Rulemaking to Preserve Drug Competition*, 109 Colum. L. Rev. 629 (2009); C. Scott

fringement. The reverse payment would be made in exchange for the first ANDA filer's promise not to enter the market for a time period negotiated by the parties. Because of the exclusivity provisions of the Hatch-Waxman Act, such settlements allow NDA holders to pay one ANDA filer to delay entry by all other ANDA filers, effectively extending the term of protection for the NDA holder.

This scheme allows the NDA holder to avoid litigation risk and to guarantee market exclusivity for a period of time regardless of the merits of its patents. At the same time, the first ANDA filer is compensated for its delayed market entry and still enjoys a 180-day period of generic exclusivity once it enters the market.

10.2.4.2 Antitrust Issues with Reverse Payments Pre-*Actavis*

Prior to 2013, courts of appeal were deeply divided over the legality of reverse-payment settlements of Hatch-Waxman lawsuits under the antitrust laws. The Federal Trade Commission, joined by the United States Attorney General, continued to challenge such settlements as violations of the antitrust laws.[3]

In *In re Schering-Plough Corp.*, 136 F.T.C. 956 (2003), the FTC challenged a settlement whereby the NDA holder agreed to pay $60 million in return for the generic's agreement not to enter the market for four years, even though the thirty-month stay (before the FDA could approve the generic) would expire in only one year. The commission found that the settlement agreement amounted to an unlawful restraint on trade. *Id.* at 1061. The Eleventh Circuit, however, reversed that decision, finding that the FTC failed to consider the exclusionary power of the patent, and the relative risk assessments created by the Hatch-Waxman Act, in assessing whether the settlement violated antitrust laws. *Schering-Plough Corp. v. FTC*, 402 F.3d 1056 (11th Cir. 2005). What must be considered is "the extent to which the exclusionary effects of the agreement fall within the scope of the patent's protection." *Id.* at 1076.

The Third Circuit reached a different conclusion in a later civil suit arising from the same agreement as *Schering-Plough. In re K-Dur Antitrust Litig.*, 686 F.3d 197 (3d Cir. 2012). In the Third Circuit's view, any payment from a patent-holding pharmaceutical company to a generic maker which agrees to hold off on entering the market is a prima facie restraint of trade and therefore evidences an antitrust violation. *Id.* at 218. Similar results were reached in decisions by the D.C. and Sixth Circuits. *In re Cardizem CD Antitrust Litig.*, 332 F.3d 896 (6th Cir. 2003); *Andrx Pharm., Inc. v. Biovail Corp. Int'l*, 256 F.3d 799 (D.C. Cir. 2001).

In contrast, decisions from the Second, Ninth, Eleventh, and Federal Circuit Courts of Appeals have upheld reverse-payment agreements in the face of antitrust challenges. *See In re Tamoxifen Citrate Antitrust Litig.*, 429 F.3d 370 (2d Cir. 2005)

Hemphill, *Drug Patent Settlements Between Rivals: A Survey* 1–49 (Columbia Law School, Working Paper, 2007), *available at* http://papers.ssrn.com/sol3/papers.cfm?abstract_id=969492.

3. The Federal Trade Commission can investigate and stop certain behaviors that violate the Sherman and Clayton Acts under the Federal Trade Commission Act. The FTC Act authorizes the FTC to bring suit against parties who enter into anticompetitive reverse-payment settlements. *FTC v. Brown Shoe Co.*, 384 U.S. 316, 322 (1966).

(holding that reverse-payment settlements are not necessarily unlawful restraints on commerce and do not represent anticompetitive agreements, particularly when the scope of the agreement falls within the coverage of the relevant patents); *Ark. Carpenters Health & Welfare Fund v. Bayer AG*, 604 F.2d 98 (2d Cir.) (applying *Tamoxifen* to affirm summary judgment against challengers of reverse-payment settlement), *reh'g denied*, 625 F.3d 779 (2d Cir. 2010); *Kaiser Found. Health Plan Inc. v. Abbott Labs., Inc.*, 552 F.3d 1033 (9th Cir. 2009) (jury finding of no antitrust injury from reverse-payment settlement agreement; independent *Walker Process* claim allowed to proceed); *FTC v. Watson Pharm., Inc.*, 677 F.3d 1298, 1311 (11th Cir. 2012), *rev'd sub nom. FTC v. Actavis, Inc.*, 133 S. Ct. 2223 (2013) (holding that reverse-payment agreement is valid, reiterating its view that "absent sham litigation or fraud in obtaining the patent, a reverse-payment settlement is immune from antitrust attack so long as its anticompetitive effects fall within the scope of the exclusionary potential of the patent"); *In re Ciprofloxacin Hydrochloride Antitrust Litig.*, 544 F.3d 1323 (Fed. Cir. 2008).

10.2.4.3 *FTC v. Actavis, Inc.*: Reverse-Payment Settlements May Be Anticompetitive

In June 2013, the Supreme Court held in a five-to-three decision that the FTC's *FTC v. Watson Pharmaceuticals* lawsuit in the Eleventh Circuit should have proceeded, as reverse-payment settlements may be anticompetitive in some situations. *FTC v. Actavis, Inc.*, 133 S. Ct. 2223, 2225 (2013).

The decision mandated the use of a modified version of the antitrust "rule-of-reason" but did not hold that reverse-payment settlements are always presumptively unlawful. *Id.* at 2236–37. Instead, the Court ordered lower courts to apply a modified "rule-of-reason" antitrust analysis to these cases. *Id.* at 2237–38. The rule-of-reason test requires the plaintiff to demonstrate agreement between two or more persons intended to restrain or harm competition, actual injury to competition, and that the restraint or harm is "unreasonable." *Cal. Dental Ass'n v. FTC*, 224 F.3d 942, 947 (9th Cir. 2000). The unreasonableness factor is determined by balancing injury against pro-competitive effects of the restraint. *See id.* Defendants bear the burden of proving any justifications or pro-competitive effects of a settlement; plaintiffs bear the burden of proving that the anticompetitive effects of a settlement outweigh any pro-competitive effects. *See id.*

The Court left development of the application of the "rule-of-reason" in reverse-payment cases to the lower courts, directing that lower courts should focus on the "basic question" of whether a settlement has "significant unjustified anticompetitive consequences." *Actavis*, 133 S. Ct at 2237.

10.2.4.4 Hatch-Waxman Litigation Post-*Actavis*: Disputed Terms and Settlements

Post-*Actavis*, lower courts have struggled to interpret the decision in a consistent manner, largely because the Court left much of the interpretation of the decision to them. This area of the law is under constant development, and a number of cases not discussed below will have upcoming rulings that shape the law and interpretation in this field. Judges should make a thorough survey of the current state of the field at the outset of such a case, particularly since how courts should apply the rule of reason in these cases is a hotly debated issue.

10.2.4.4.1 Legal Definitions of "Reverse Payment" and "Large"

Much of the debate thus far has been over what the meaning of a "reverse payment" is under *Actavis*—in particular, whether nonmonetary compensation settlements implicate *Actavis*-based antitrust liability and what a "large" payment is. In addition, the Federal Trade Commission has shown renewed interest in bringing litigation actions in these types of cases. Finally, a few cases already have addressed the intersection of federal and state antitrust law in reverse-payment cases. These issues are discussed below.

As noted earlier, the *Actavis* decision did not specify what types of settlements qualify as "reverse payments." In particular, the decision did not give guidance on whether the modified rule-of-reason analysis should apply to cases in which the settlements under consideration do not consist solely of cash payments. Courts have diverged significantly on whether nonmonetary compensation falls under the *Actavis* regime.

Only two district court decisions, one of which has been reversed, have restricted the definition of "reverse payment" to include settlements wherein only cash constituted the consideration. *In re Lamictal Direct Purchaser Antitrust Litig.*, No. 12-cv-995, 2014 WL 282755, at *1 (D.N.J. Jan. 24, 2014), *vacated*, *King Drug Co. of Florence, Inc. v. Smithkline Beecham Corp.*, No. 14-1243, 2015 WL 3967112 (3d Cir. June 26, 2015); *In re Loestrin 24 Fe Antitrust Litig.*, No. 1:13-md-2472-S-PAS, 2014 WL 4368924 (D.R.I. Sept. 4, 2014).

Most of the decisions thus far applying *Actavis* have acknowledged there may be antitrust liability for settlements including nonmonetary compensation. *See In re Nexium (Esomeprazole) Antitrust Litig.*, 968 F. Supp. 2d 367, 392 (D. Mass. 2013) (finding that the Supreme Court did not require that a reverse-payment settlement include a monetary exchange, noting that a "broader interpretation" of "payment" better reflected the current reality of settlements that oftentimes include terms beyond cash); *In re Niaspan Antitrust Litig.*, No. 13-MD-2460, 2014 WL 4403848 (E.D. Pa. Sept. 5, 2014) (holding that *Actavis* applies to reverse-payment settlements whether they involve cash or noncash payments); *In re Effexor Antitrust Litig.*, No. 11-cv-5479 (PGS), 2014 WL 4988410 (D.N.J. Oct. 6, 2014) (granting defendants' motion to dismiss, as the plaintiff's allegations failed to properly estimate the value of the alleged reverse payment, and thus the allegations were not plausible); *In re Lipitor Antitrust Litig.*, No. 3:12-cv-02389 (PGS), 2014 WL 4543502 (D.N.J. Sept. 12, 2014) (dismissing the claims after finding that plaintiffs had not reasonably estimated the cash value of the settlement at issue); *United Food & Commercial Workers Local 1776 & Participating Emp'rs Health and Welfare Fund v. Teikoku Pharma USA, Inc.*, No. 14-md-02521-WHO, 2014 WL 6465235, at *11 (N.D. Cal. Nov. 17, 2014) (interpreting the *Actavis* discussion on reverse payments to encompass nonmonetary settlement terms).

In June 2015, the Third Circuit became the first circuit court to rule on the applicability of *Actavis* to a nonmonetary payment in a reverse-payment settlement. *King Drug Co. of Florence, Inc. v. Smithkline Beecham Corp.*, No. 14-1243, 2015 WL 3967112 (3d Cir. June 26, 2015). The court examined the 2014 *Lamictal* decision mentioned earlier to determine whether *Actavis* liability applied to a settlement term in which the brand-name company agreed to relinquish its right to produce an authorized generic as a settlement term, and found that in this case, *Actavis* liability should apply. *Id.* at *1–2. The panel ruled that "this [no-authorized generic] agreement falls under *Actavis*'s rule because it may represent an unusual, unexplained reverse transfer of considerable value from the patentee to the alleged infringer and may therefore give rise to the inference that it is a payment to eliminate the risk of competition," thereby implicating the *Actavis* rule-of-reason analysis for the settlement term. *Id.* at *2. The decision agreed with the majority of district court decisions that have found that the *Actavis* holding "can[not] be limited to reverse payments of cash." *Id.* at *10.

The *Actavis* decision also did not define the term "large" in the context of payments; lower courts have begun to interpret this term. *See In re Lipitor*, 2014 WL 4543502, at *22 (holding that the plaintiffs did not provide "a measure of damages accepted within the industry and a discussion of the settlement factors relating to the claim."); *In re Effexor*, 2014 WL 4988410, at *12 (holding that a loss estimate from an unrelated drug did not "specifically value the monetary amount of the no-authorized generic agreement in the instant case"). Finally, some courts have required complaints to meet the *Twombly* and *Iqbal* pleading standard by defining the value of the settlement. *In re Lipitor*, 2014 WL 4543502, at *25; *In re Effexor*, 2014 WL 4988410, at *15, *23.

10.2.4.4.2 FTC's Role in Reverse-Payment Settlement Cases

Although the *Actavis* decision did not uphold the FTC's preferred "presumption of illegality" standard from *In re K-Dur*, the Court's rejection of the "scope of the patent" test encouraged the FTC to further investigate settlements and begin litigation.

The Federal Trade Commission has expressed its approval of the *Actavis* decision, stating that it would reexamine settlements in light of *Actavis* to determine whether further investigation was warranted. *Prepared Statement of the Federal Trade Commission on Pay-for-Delay Deals: Limiting Competition and Costing Consumers Before the United States Senate Comm. on the Judiciary, Subcomm. on Antitrust, Comp. Policy and Consumer Rights*, 113th Cong. 3 (July 23, 2013). Interestingly, the FTC reported that in fiscal year 2013, fewer potential reverse-payment settlements were reported than in the previous year. *FTC Bureau of Competition, Agreements Filed with the Federal Trade Commission under the Medicare Prescription Drug, Improvement, and Modernization Act of 2003, Overview of Agreements Filed in FY 2013.* But no good data are available yet on the frequency of reverse-payment settlements post-*Actavis*.

The FTC has pursued several actions post-*Actavis* against parties who allegedly entered into illegal reverse-payment settlements. *FTC v. Actavis, Inc.*, 133 S. Ct. 2223

(2013); *FTC v. Cephalon, Inc.*, No. 2:08-cv-02141 (E.D. Pa. 2014) (settled between the FTC and Cephalon by disgorgement for $1.2 billion and an agreement to not settle patent disputes using pay-for-delay settlements in the future, 2015 WL 1724597 (E.D. Pa. Apr. 15, 2015)); *FTC v. AbbVie Prods., Inc.*, No. 14-5151 (E.D. Pa. 2014) (partially dismissed because the agreements at issue did not amount to pay-for-delay settlements, No. 14-5151, 2015 WL 2114380 (E.D. Pa. May 6, 2015)). Prior to *Actavis*, the FTC had brought suit in *FTC v. Cephalon*, an alleged reverse-payment settlement deal on Provigil, and it continued its activities in litigating the remand of the *Actavis* case itself. In September 2014, the FTC brought its first post-*Actavis* reverse-payment settlement suit against AbbVie and others based on an alleged agreement to delay the launch of generic Androgel. *AbbVie Prods., Inc.*, No. 14-5151 (E.D. Pa. 2014). On March 31, 2016, the FTC brought a suit against Endo Pharmaceuticals and multiple generic companies, alleging that the no-authorized generic settlement terms in agreements settling litigation on painkillers Opana ER and Lidoderm are reverse-payments prohibited under *Actavis*. *FTC v. Endo Pharms. Inc.*, No. 16-cv-1440-PD (E.D. Pa. 2016).

10.2.4.4.3 State Antitrust Law's Interaction with *Actavis*

In a state antitrust law class action based on an alleged reverse payment, the court ruled that no federal question jurisdiction arose because the resolution of the plaintiffs' *Actavis*-based claims did not require the litigation of patent law issues. *Time Ins. Co. v. AstraZeneca AB*, No. 14-4149, 2014 WL 4933025, at *1 (E.D. Pa. Oct. 1, 2014). Here the court did not find it necessary to litigate the validity of AstraZeneca's patents in order to determine whether state antitrust law had been violated. *Id.* at *2.[4]

10.3 Biologics and the BPCIA

10.3.1 Patent Infringement Actions Involving Biosimilar Products Under the BPCIA

The Public Health Service Act (PHSA), as amended in 2010 by the Biologics Price Competition and Innovation Act (BPCIA), sets out a complex scheme for evaluation of biosimilar[5] products. It also contains extensive provisions addressed to

---

4. The California Supreme Court recently held that pay-for-delay settlements can be challenged under state antitrust law, following the decision in *Actavis*. The court drew parallels between federal antitrust law and state antitrust law in making its decision, determining that nothing in California antitrust law precedent suggested that it was more limited than the federal law discussed in *Actavis*. The court instructed lower courts to use the rule-of-reason test to analyze these settlements. *In re Cipro Cases I & II*, No. S198616, 2015 WL 2125291 (Cal. Sup. Ct. 2015).

5. A "biosimilar" product is one that is "highly similar to the reference product notwithstanding minor differences in clinically inactive components," and as to which there

patent infringement litigation between the reference-product sponsor company and those seeking to produce a biosimilar product. Much as in the Hatch-Waxman context governing small-molecule drugs, the specialized statutory scheme governing biosimilar products has important implications for biosimilar patent case management.

Biosimilar patent disputes under the BPCIA differ from those governed by the Hatch-Waxman Act in a number of important ways, all of which are discussed in more detail in the following sections.

First, the BPCIA sets out a unique, bilateral, and complex prelitigation "patent dance," intended to provide robust exchange of information, and narrowing of issues, well in advance of litigation. However, whether and to what extent these prelitigation exchanges are mandatory is the subject of ongoing litigation.

Second, there is no central listing of relevant patents like the Orange Book in the biologics context; the statute contemplates that the patents to be litigated are defined in the prelitigation exchanges between the parties. In addition, there are no limitations on the types of patents (assuming that they potentially cover the biologic at issue) that can be asserted in these exchanges.[6]

Third, and related, the statute contemplates the possibility of a two-phase litigation, with different patents litigated in each phase. The parties select in prelitigation negotiations the patents to be litigated in each phase. Under the statute, the parties negotiate and determine the patents to be asserted in an initial phase of litigation. If there are relevant patents that were identified in the prelitigation exchanges but not litigated in the first phase of litigation, those patents may be litigated after the biosimilar sponsor provides a statutorily mandated notice that it intends to market its biosimilar product.

As can be seen from the above description, case management for BPCIA cases is likely to be complex and challenging. Active case management will be essential to successful disposition of these cases.

At the time of this writing, the biosimilar and patent litigation provisions of the BPCIA are largely untested in the courts, and the provisions, while detailed, leave many unanswered questions regarding how biosimilar patent cases will proceed. A number of recent cases squarely present some of these issues, and are discussed in detail below.

10.3.2 The Biosimilar Application Pathway

A background understanding of the pathway for biosimilar applications (codified as § 351(k) of the BPCIA) is helpful to contextualize and understand the timing and impact of the statute's patent litigation provisions.

---

are no clinically meaningful differences from the reference product in terms of safety, purity, or potency. 42 U.S.C. § 262(i), PHSA § 351(i)(2).

6. Both of these features suggest that more patents may be asserted in any given BPCIA matter than in a Hatch-Waxman matter.

10.3.2.1 Definition of a Biologic

Under the BPCIA, a biological product is "a virus, therapeutic serum, toxin, antitoxin, vaccine, blood, blood component or derivative, allergenic product, protein (except any chemically synthesized polypeptide), or analogous product, or arsphenamine or derivative of arsphenamine (or any other trivalent organic arsenic compound), applicable to the prevention, treatment, or cure of a disease or condition of human beings." 42 U.S.C. § 262(i)(1), BPCIA § 351(i)(1).[7] The FDA has defined a "protein" as "any alpha amino acid polymer with a specific defined sequence that is greater than 40 amino acids in size." Chemically synthesized polypeptides are "any alpha amino acid polymer that (1) is made entirely by chemical synthesis; and (2) is less than 100 amino acids in size." Biosimilars: Questions and Answers Regarding Implementation of the Biologics Price Competition and Innovation Act of 2009 (Guidance for Industry) (Apr. 2015), http://www.fda.gov/downloads/Drugs/GuidanceComplianceRegulatoryInformation/Guidances/UCM444661.pdf

In other words, biologics generally are manufactured through biologic synthesis—they are manufactured in or extracted from living systems. Such biological products also are usually "drugs" for purposes of the Food and Drug Cosmetic Act (FDCA). They are exempted from the NDA provisions of that Act, although they are subject to the other FDCA provisions that apply to drugs and to those provisions that expressly apply to biologics. 42 U.S.C. § 262(j), BPCIA § 351(j). Certain biologics have in the past been the subject of approved NDAs under the FDCA, rather than BLAs, and will shift to the BLA pathway in 2020 pursuant to transition provisions included in the BPCIA.

10.3.2.2 The Pioneer Biologic License Application (BLA)

A pioneering company seeking to market a new biologic shall submit to the FDA a Biologic License Application (BLA), analogous to an NDA in the drug context, called a § 351(a) BLA. 42 U.S.C. § 262(a), BPCIA § 351(a). A § 351(a) BLA normally includes exhaustive data demonstrating the proposed product's safety, purity, and potency, as well as manufacturing data and consent to the inspection of the manufacturing facility. *Id.* If the § 351(a) BLA is approved, the approved drug is referred to as the "reference product" for purposes of any subsequent biosimilar BLA.[8] 42 U.S.C. § 262(i)(4), BPCIA § 351(i)(4).

10.3.2.3 Period of Exclusivity for the Pioneering Company ("Reference-Product Exclusivity")

A § 351(k) BLA may not be filed until four years after the approval of the reference product, and may not be approved until twelve years after approval of the refer-

---

7. For ease of reference, citations in this section will be to both Title 42 of the U.S. Code and the corresponding section of the BPCIA.

8. The biosimilar BLA pathway is set out in the BPCIA's § 351(k), and is referred to as a "section 351(k) BLA."

ence product. 42 U.S.C. § 262(k)(7)(A)–(B), BPCIA § 351(k)(7)(A)–(B).[9] This period of exclusivity is wholly independent of patent protection. *Id.*

The BPCIA prevents the sponsor of a reference drug from extending exclusivity based on small changes to the biologic where the sponsor or a related entity seeks a subsequent § 351(a) BLA on (1) a nonstructural change resulting in a new indication, dosage form, dosing schedule, delivery device or system, route of administration, or strength, or (2) a structural change that does not result in a difference in safety, purity, or potency. 42 U.S.C. § 262(k)(7)(C); BPCIA § 351(k)(7)(C).[10] This provision prevents multiple extensions of exclusivity based on small changes to the original biologic.

10.3.2.4 Approval of the § 351(k) Biosimilar or Interchangeable BLA

A § 351(k) applicant may file an application for licensure as a biosimilar or interchangeable biological product. 42 U.S.C. § 262(k); BPCIA § 351(k). The application is intended to demonstrate sufficient similarity between the reference and biosimilar biologic product to permit reliance on the approval of the reference product BLA. To that end, to determine biosimilarity, the FDA shall determine whether the proposed biologic is "highly similar" to the reference product "notwithstanding minor differences in clinically inactive components" and "has no clinically meaningful differences from the reference product in safety, purity, or potency." 42 U.S.C. § 262(i)(2); BPCIA § 351(i)(2).[11]

The statutory scheme also provides for approval of biologics that are "interchangeable" with the reference product. 42 U.S.C. § 262(k)(4); BPCIA § 351(k)(4). To be determined interchangeable with the reference product, the biologic shall be (1) biosimilar and (2) expected to produce the same clinical result as the reference product in any given patient. *Id.* In addition, if the product is to be administered more than once, there must be no greater risk in terms of safety or diminished efficacy in switching between the reference product and the product under examination than there is in using the reference product without such a switch.

A biological product found to be interchangeable is entitled to a period of exclusivity, during which no other product may be approved as an interchangeable under the statute. 42 U.S.C. § 262(k)(6); BPCIA § 351(k)(6).

---

9. Under certain circumstances, an additional six months of exclusivity based on pediatric testing extends these periods. 42 U.S.C. § 262(k)(7)(A) & (B). Seven-year orphan exclusivity, which runs concurrently with reference-product exclusivity, also may apply.

10. The FDA has indicated it may not issue exclusivity decisions at the time of licensure, particularly in difficult or complex cases, and as a result duration of exclusivity may not be settled prior to litigation. FDA, Draft Guidance for Industry, Reference Product Exclusivity for Biological Products Filed Under Section 351(a) of the PHS Act (Aug. 2014) at 7.

11. Such differences, permissible under the statute, may lead to more claims of non-infringement in the BPCIA context than in the Hatch-Waxman context.

10.3.3 Pre-Market Litigation Procedures Under § 351(*l*) of the Public Health Services Act (42 U.S.C. § 262(*l*))

An application submitted under § 351(k) of the BPCIA is subject to the patent litigation provisions of § 351(*l*) of that Act.[12] As discussed above, those provisions are quite different from the prelitigation procedures of the Hatch-Waxman Act.

Broadly speaking, § 351(*l*) sets out three stages of prelitigation procedures. First, the biosimilar applicant shall provide its application and information about its manufacturing process to the reference-product sponsor, subject to default statutory confidentiality provisions. Second, the parties may engage in detailed exchanges of contentions relating to patents potentially covering the biosimilar product. Finally, the parties identify a set of patents for a first phase of litigation.[13] The U.S. Court of Appeals for the Federal Circuit has held that these prelitigation procedures are not mandatory and that it is permissible under the statute for a biosimilar applicant to decline to participate in the prelitigation procedures. *Amgen Inc. v. Sandoz Inc.*, 794 F.3d 1347, 1354–57 (Fed. Cir. 2015).

Where followed, the exchanges pursuant to the prelitigation provisions of the BPCIA force the parties to develop and test their contentions, and identify critical issues, prior to litigation. Moreover, the exchanges under § 351(*l*) are bilateral and the information provided to the reference-product sponsor significantly more complete than in the Hatch-Waxman context, discussed earlier. As a result, the parties should be even better situated to resolve the matter with minimal delay.

The exchanges also set the stage for the litigation in important ways. They define the patents that may be litigated, the timing of the litigation, and the remedies that may be sought by the reference-product sponsor.

To the extent that the biosimilar applicant declines to engage in the statute's prelitigation procedures, the consequence is exposure on the part of the biosimilar applicant to an immediate infringement suit brought by the reference-product sponsor.[14]

Tables 10.1 and 10.2 provide a visual diagram of the steps of patent litigation outlined in further detail.

---

12. The BPCIA does not contemplate reliance on the litigation provisions of § 351(*l*) by § 351(a) applicants, despite the fact that patent infringement actions may arise out of products licensed under § 351(a).

13. Ultimately, if there are any remaining relevant patents, those patents may be litigated in the months before market entry by the biosimilar product.

14. *See id.*

Table 10.1
First Phase of Litigation Steps: Immediate Patent Infringement Action After Applicant Is Notified that FDA Has Accepted Biosimilar Application

Time	Action	Notes
Within 20 days	Applicant provides application and manufacturing information (42 U.S.C. § 262(*l*)(2); BPCIA § 351(*l*)(2))	N/A
Within 60 days	Reference-product sponsor discloses patent list (42 U.S.C. § 262(l)(3)(A); BPCIA § 351(*l*)(3)(A))	Later-issued or licensed patents must be identified in a supplemental list no later than 30 days from the issuance/ licensing (42 U.S.C. § 262(*l*)(7); BPCIA § 351(*l*)(7))
Within 60 days	Applicant discloses patent list and detailed statement(s) (42 U.S.C. § 262(*l*)(3)(B); BPCIA § 351(*l*)(3)(B))	Reference-product sponsor shall supplement BPCIA § 351(*l*)(3) list with later-issued or exclusively licensed patents within 30 days of issuance or licensing; applicant shall respond with detailed statement(s) within 30 days (42 U.S.C. § 262(*l*)(7); BPCIA § 351(*l*)(7))
Within 60 days	Reference-product sponsor responds to applicant detailed statement(s) (42 U.S.C. § 262(*l*)(3)(C); BPCIA § 351(*l*)(3)(C)) Parties negotiate on list of patents for immediate infringement action (42 U.S.C. § 262(*l*)(4); BPCIA § 351(*l*)(4))	
Within 15 days from start of negotiation	If no agreement, exchange lists based on number of patents applicant listed (42 U.S.C. § 262(*l*)(5); BPCIA § 351(*l*)(5))	
Within 30 days	First phase patent litigation commences (42 U.S.C. § 262(*l*)(6); BPCIA § 351(*l*)(6))	

Table 10.2
Second Phase of Litigation Steps

• Applicant provides notice to the reference-product sponsor no later than 180 days before the date of first commercial marketing (42 U.S.C. § 262(*l*)(8)(A); BPCIA § 351(*l*)(8)(A))
• After receiving notice of commercial marketing, the reference-product sponsor may seek a preliminary injunction on the basis of any patent that was listed under (*l*)(3) or (*l*)(7) and not included on the lists for BPCIA § 351(*l*)(4) or (*l*)(5) (42 U.S.C. § 262(*l*)(8)(B); BPCIA § 351(*l*)(8)(B))

10.3.3.1 Information Provided by the Biosimilar Applicant

Under the patent litigation provisions of § 351(*l*), a § 351(k) applicant shall provide a copy of its application and information about its manufacturing process to the reference-product sponsor within twenty days after the FDA notifies the applicant that its application has been accepted for review. 42 U.S.C. § 262(*l*)(2); BPCIA § 351(*l*)(2). Until adoption of a protective order governing confidentiality, the materials provided to the reference-product sponsor are subject to default confidentiality provisions under § 351(*l*)(1)(A), though the parties can agree to modifications of the rules. 42 U.S.C. § 262(*l*)(1)(A); BPCIA § 351(*l*)(1)(A).

The statute provides that, if a § 351(k) applicant provides the relevant materials, neither the applicant nor the reference-product sponsor may bring a declaratory judgment action until the reference-product sponsor receives a notice of commercial marketing under the statute or the applicant fails to comply with certain of the patent litigation provisions under § 351(*l*). 42 U.S.C. § 262(*l*)(9); BPCIA § 351(*l*)(9).

However, if the § 351(k) applicant "fails" to provide the materials required by the statute to the reference-product sponsor, the reference-product sponsor can bring an immediate declaratory judgment action. BPCIA § 351(*l*)(9)(C); 42 U.S.C. § 262(*l*)(9)(C).

As discussed below in § 10.3.4, the Federal Circuit has found that the exchange detailed in § 351(*l*)(2)(A) is permissive and not mandatory. *Amgen Inc.*, 794 F.3d at 1354–57.

10.3.3.2 Exchange of Patent Contentions

Within sixty days of receipt of the § 351(k) applicant's application and manufacturing information, the reference-product sponsor shall provide a list of patents it believes that it could reasonably assert against the applicant (the reference-product sponsor's "initial list"). BPCIA § 351(*l*)(3)(A); 42 U.S.C. § 262(*l*)(3)(A). It shall also indicate whether it would be willing to license the patents listed. *Id.* The reference-product sponsor's initial list is of critical importance, as the owner of a patent that should have been, but was not, included on the reference-product sponsor's list will be precluded from bringing suit on that patent as to the biologic at issue. § 271(e)(6)(C).[15]

Within sixty days of receipt of the reference-product sponsor's initial list, the biosimilar applicant shall respond with either (1) detailed, claim-by-claim contentions regarding any claim of noninfringement, invalidity, or unenforceability; or (2) a statement that it will not market its product until patent expiry. BPCIA § 351(*l*)(3)(B); 42 U.S.C. § 262(*l*)(3)(B). It may also provide a list of patents upon which it believes the reference-product sponsor could bring an infringement claim (the biosimilar applicant's "initial list"). BPCIA § 351(*l*)(3)(A); 42 U.S.C. § 262(*l*)(3)(A). If the reference-product sponsor has made an offer to license, the biosimilar applicant shall respond to the offer. BPCIA § 351(*l*)(3)(B)(iii); 42 U.S.C. § 262(*l*)(3)(B)(iii). Failure by the § 351(k) applicant to provide this response can form the basis for a declaratory judgment action. BPCIA § 351(*l*)(9); 42 U.S.C. § 262(*l*)(9).

Within sixty days of receiving the applicant's contentions, the reference-product sponsor shall in turn respond with detailed contentions regarding infringement, validity, and enforceability. BPCIA § 351(*l*)(3)(C); 42 U.S.C. § 262(*l*)(3)(C). These contentions shall also be set out on a claim-by-claim basis. *Id.*

10.3.3.3 Supplementation of Patent Contentions

If, after the reference-product sponsor provides its initial list of patents to the applicant, a relevant patent issues or is exclusively licensed to the reference-product sponsor, the reference-product sponsor shall supplement its list within thirty days. BPCIA § 351(*l*)(7); 42 U.S.C. § 262(*l*)(7). The biosimilar applicant shall respond within thirty days, providing detailed noninfringement, invalidity and/or unenforceability contentions. Any patents on the supplemental list will not be litigated in the first phase of litigation, but will be addressed, if at all, in the second phase of litigation. BPCIA § 351(*l*)(7); 42 U.S.C. § 262(*l*)(7).

10.3.3.4 Selection of Patents for First Phase of Litigation

From the exchanges described above, the parties identify a set of patents for the first phase of litigation. For the fifteen days following the response of the reference-product sponsor, the parties shall negotiate in good faith to identify the patents that will be litigated immediately. BPCIA §§ 351(*l*)(4)(A), (B); 42 U.S.C. §§ 262(*l*)(4)(A), (B). If they agree, the reference-product sponsor shall bring suit on those patents within thirty days (the "agreed list for litigation"). BPCIA § 351(*l*)(6)(A); 42 U.S.C. § 262(*l*)(6)(A).

If the parties cannot agree on the patents to be litigated in the first round, they again exchange patent lists (the "separate lists for litigation"). Before the exchange of lists, the biosimilar applicant shall notify the reference-product sponsor of the number of patents it will list. BPCIA § 351(*l*)(5)(A); 42 U.S.C. § 262(*l*)(5)(A). Then, with-

15. It appears that the section is written to bind both the reference-product sponsor and any third party who had granted an exclusive license to the patent owner. § 271(e)(6)(C).

in five days of providing this number, the parties simultaneously exchange their respective lists of patents that they believe should be the subject of immediate litigation. BPCIA § 351(*l*)(5)(B); 42 U.S.C. § 262(*l*)(5)(B). The reference-patent sponsor may not include more patents on its list than the applicant includes, except in the case where the applicant includes none. Where the applicant includes none, the reference-product sponsor may include one. BPCIA § 351(*l*)(5)(B); 42 U.S.C. § 262(*l*)(5)(B).

10.3.3.5 Litigation of the First-Phase Patents

The reference-product sponsor shall, within thirty days of the final patent list exchange, bring an infringement action with respect to each patent included on the agreed or separate list for litigation. BPCIA § 351(*l*)(6)(B); 42 U.S.C. § 262(*l*)(6)(B).

The biosimilar applicant shall then provide the complaint to the FDA, which is published in the Federal Register. BPCIA § 351(*l*)(6)(C); 42 U.S.C. § 262(*l*)(6)(C). If the applicant fails to do so, the reference-product sponsor may bring an immediate declaratory judgment action on any of the patents in its initial or supplemental patent lists. BPCIA § 351(*l*)(9)(B); 42 U.S.C. § 262(*l*)(9)(B).

10.3.3.6 Notice of Commercial Marketing and Second Phase of Litigation

Not later than 180 days before "the first commercial marketing of the biological product licensed under subsection (k)," the applicant shall provide the reference-product sponsor with notice of intent to market the biosimilar. BPCIA § 351(*l*)(8); 42 U.S.C. § 262(*l*)(8). The reference-product sponsor may then initiate a second phase of litigation. In this action, the reference-product sponsor may seek a preliminary injunction on patents included in the reference-product sponsor's initial list, but not included in the lists of patents to be litigated that were exchanged by the parties. BPCIA § 351(*l*)(8)(B); 42 U.S.C. § 262(*l*)(8)(B).

The timing of the second phase of litigation has been disputed. The statute provides that the notice should come "not later than" 180 days before commercial marketing; thus, there is a question whether the biosimilar applicant can provide the notice years before any product is actually sold and potentially disrupt the statutory litigation scheme.

This question arose at the district court level in *Sandoz Inc. v. Amgen Inc.*, 2013 WL 6000069 (N.D. Cal. Nov. 12, 2013), a patent infringement matter concerning the biologic etanercept. In that matter, the biosimilar applicant argued that the statute permitted it to provide a notice of commercial marketing and bring a declaratory judgment action, prior to submitting its § 351(k) application. *Id.* at *2. In this manner, it essentially bypassed the prelitigation procedures of § 351(*l*) altogether. *See id.* The district court disagreed, finding that the notice of commercial marketing did not properly issue because the product was not "licensed under subsection (k)," as required by the statutory provision. *Id.* In other words, the district court found that the notice can only issue after the FDA approves the biosimilar product. *See id.* Because the biosimilar cannot be approved until the end of the exclusivity period, this approach arguably may have the effect of adding an additional six months before the biosimilar applicant may market its product. *See id.* at *2.[16] The Federal Circuit did not address the issue on review. *Sandoz Inc. v. Amgen Inc.*, 773 F.3d 1274 (Fed. Cir. 2014).

Recently, however, the Federal Circuit had another opportunity to address this question in a different matter involving these same parties. In *Amgen Inc.*, 794 F.3d at 1357–58, the Federal Circuit held the notice of commercial marketing is effective only after licensure of the biosimilar, and that such notice is mandatory under the BPCIA (see discussion in § 10.3.4).

10.3.3.7 Remedies

Assuming that the prelitigation procedures are invoked, the remedies available to the reference-product sponsor in the event of a finding of infringement and validity will depend upon the reference-product sponsor's compliance with the prelitigation provisions. As discussed above, if the reference-product sponsor fails to include a patent in its initial list, suit by the patent owner on that patent will be barred. § 271(e)(6)(C).[17]

If a patent was included in the agreed or separate lists for litigation, and the reference-product sponsor brought suit on the patent within thirty days of the production of the lists, injunctive relief is available. Where there has been a final court decision of infringement and validity, and the exclusivity period for the reference-product has not yet expired, injunctive relief is mandatory. § 271(e)(4)(D).

If the patent owner does not bring suit within thirty days on a patent included in the separate or agreed lists for litigation, the patent owner may only seek a reasonable royalty as to those patents, and injunctive relief is not available. § 271(e)(6)(B). Likewise, only a reasonable royalty may be recovered if an action on such patents was dismissed without prejudice or was not prosecuted in good faith. *Id.*

10.3.4 Current Cases Testing the Boundaries of the BPCIA Prelitigation Procedures

At the time of writing, only a handful of cases have addressed the BPCIA's prelitigation procedures.

The first case on the BPCIA's prelitigation provisions considered by the Federal Circuit was *Sandoz Inc. v. Amgen Inc.*, 773 F.3d 1274 (Fed. Cir. 2014). As discussed above, in this matter, a § 351(k) applicant, before filing its biosimilar application, brought an action for declaratory judgment on patents potentially covering its biosimilar product. At the time it filed suit, biosimilar applicant Sandoz was in clinical trials to test a biologic containing etanercept. Etanercept is the nonproprietary name for Amgen's product Enbrel, a human tumor necrosis factor receptor. Sandoz argued

---

16. The district court also rejected the biosimilar's attempt to bring a declaratory judgment action on a number of other bases.

17. The language of the statute suggests that the patent owner will be barred even if the owner is not the reference-product sponsor, but the reference-product sponsor is instead an exclusive licensee.

that it intended to file a § 351(k) application for its etanercept product as a biosimilar to Enbrel at the conclusion of clinical trials.

Amgen moved to dismiss on the basis that the action was barred both by the Article III case-and-controversy requirement and by the provisions of the BPCIA. The district court agreed on both points. *Sandoz Inc. v. Amgen Inc.*, 2013 WL 6000069 at *1 (N.D. Cal. Nov. 12, 2013). The district court found that there was no case or controversy because Amgen had never threatened to sue Sandoz, and Sandoz's intent to file an application with the FDA was insufficient to create a case or controversy between the parties. *Id.* at *2. It also found that a biosimilar applicant is not entitled to bring a declaratory judgment action under the BPCIA until it has complied with its obligation to participate in the initial prelitigation exchange of information. *Id.*

The Federal Circuit affirmed, but did not address the district court's interpretation of the BPCIA. Instead, it addressed whether, on the facts presented, Sandoz showed a case or controversy. It found that Sandoz had not, pointing to the lack of a § 351(k) application, as well as the potential for failure of Sandoz's clinical trial. It also raised the possibility that, particularly if the clinical trial failed, the content of the potential application could change, affecting the content of any patent dispute. *Sandoz Inc. v. Amgen Inc.*, 773 F.3d at 1280. The Federal Circuit also noted that Sandoz failed to show any immediate adverse impact from not being able to pursue its declaratory judgment action. *Id.* at 1281–82.

In two other cases predating the Federal Circuit's opinion in the *Sandoz* matter by a few days, the Southern District of New York considered similar issues in a similar factual posture. In the first matter, *Celltrion Healthcare Co., Ltd. v. Kennedy Trust for Rheumatology Research*, the court evaluated a motion to dismiss a declaratory judgment action brought by a biosimilar applicant that had not, at the time it filed its complaint, yet submitted its § 351(k) application. Opinion & Order (S.D.N.Y. Dec. 1, 2014), Case No. 14 Civ. 2256 (PAC) (Dkt. No. 32). However, in contrast to the *Sandoz* matter, the biosimilar applicant sued not the reference-product sponsor, but the patent holder that had granted an exclusive license to the reference-product sponsor. *Id.* at 9. The district court found that this was a distinction without difference for purposes of the application of the BPCIA's patent litigation procedures. *Id.*

The district court ultimately held, consistent with the Federal Circuit's opinion in the *Sandoz* matter, no case or controversy under Article III. *Id.* at 8. The district court also considered the BPCIA and whether its prelitigation procedures barred the suit. The court stopped short of finding that the BPCIA categorically foreclosed the lawsuit. It held only that, if a case or controversy existed, it would exercise its discretion not to consider it, given that doing so would be contrary to the complex statutory structure and goals of the BPCIA.

In the related *Hospira, Inc. v. Janssen Biotech, Inc.* matter, the same district court considered the situation in which the coexclusive marketer of the Celltrion biosimilar brought a declaratory judgment action against the reference-product sponsor. Opinion & Order (S.D.N.Y. Dec. 1, 2014), Case No. 14 Civ. 7049 (PAC) (Dkt. No. 60). The district court dismissed this action on the same basis, finding that Hospira, despite not being the § 351(k) applicant, "seeks to utilize the BPCIA pathway for approval of its biosimilar drug, yet disavows the BPCIA's authority over patent disputes." *Id.* at 3.

It was not long before the Federal Circuit addressed the BPCIA prelitigation provisions head on. In another case involving Amgen and Sandoz—this time relating to Amgen's Neupogen (filgrastim) product—Sandoz submitted a § 351(k) application to FDA but did not provide a copy of its application and manufacturing process information to Amgen. Instead, Sandoz provided notice of its intent to market the biosimilar prior to the biosimilar's approval by the FDA.[18] In response, Amgen brought claims alleging violation of California's Unfair Competition Law ("UCL"), conversion, and patent infringement. Amgen argued that Sandoz's failure to comply with the statute's prelitigation procedures and its notice of intent to market prior to receiving approval from the FDA amounted to unlawful conduct sufficient to invoke the UCL. Amgen also argued that Sandoz's reliance on Amgen's FDA license for the reference product, without compliance with the statutory prelitigation procedures, constituted a "wrongful act" sufficient to maintain a claim for conversion.

The district court dismissed Amgen's UCL and conversion claims, finding that Sandoz was entitled under the statute to decline to follow the prelitigation procedures. *Amgen Inc. v. Sandoz Inc.*, Case No. 14-cv-04741-RS, 2015 WL 1264756, at *11 (N.D. Cal. Mar. 19, 2015). The court found that the statutory provisions, rather than setting out mandatory prelitigation procedures, set out a system providing two potential pathways, each with potential costs and benefits. *Id.* at *3. The district court also found that Sandoz's decision to provide notice of intent to market prior to approval by the FDA was permissible, as to hold otherwise would "tack an unconditional extra six months of market exclusivity onto the twelve years reference-product sponsors already enjoy under 42 U.S.C. § 262(k)(7)(A)." *Id.* at *8. Amgen appealed.

In a fractured opinion, the Federal Circuit affirmed in part and reversed in part the district court's decision. First, the court agreed that the BPCIA's exchange-of-information provisions are not mandatory, and thus a biosimilar applicant may choose whether to follow the prelitigation procedures in § 351(*l*). *Amgen Inc.*, 794 F.3d at 1354–57. The court noted that, when read in isolation, the "shall" provision in § 351(*l*)(2)(A) appeared to mean that a biosimilar applicant "must" disclose its application and manufacturing information to the reference-product sponsor by the statutory deadline. *Id.* at 1355. However, because the BPCIA expressly contemplates that a biosimilar applicant might fail to do this and provides a consequence for such a failure—that is, the reference-product sponsor, but not the biosimilar applicant, may bring a declaratory judgment action for patent infringement—the "shall" in § 351(*l*)(2)(A) does not mean "must" and the biosimilar applicant has the option of whether to engage in the BPCIA's prelitigation exchange-of-information procedures. *Id.* at 1355–56. The court affirmed the dismissal of Amgen's UCL and conversion claims on this ground. *Id.* at 1360–61.

Second, the Federal Circuit reversed the district's court ruling on the BPCIA's 180-day intent-to-market notification requirement, holding that a biosimilar applicant can provide effective notice of commercial marketing to the reference-product

18. On March 6, 2015, the FDA approved Sandoz's biosimilar application for Zarxio (filgrastim-sndz).

sponsor only after the biosimilar has been licensed by FDA. *Id.* at 1357–58. The court found instructive that the BPCIA's 180-day notification provision in § 351(*l*)(8)(A) refers to the product as "the biological product licensed under subsection (k)," rather than "'the biological product that is the subject of' the application," as the BPCIA does in other provisions in subsection (*l*). *Id.* The court also noted that it would be "counterintuitive to provide that notice of commercial marketing be given at a time before one knows when, or if, the product will be approved, or licensed." *Id.* at 1358. In contrast to its holding with respect to the prelitigation exchange-of-information procedures, the court held that the 180-day intent-to-market notification is mandatory under the BPCIA. *Id.*

Judge Newman concurred in part and dissented in part, agreeing that the 180-day notice is mandatory and must occur after licensure, but disagreeing that the BPCIA's prelitigation exchange-of-information procedures are optional. *Id.* at 1363. According to Judge Newman, "[t]his designated exchange of information is fundamental to the BPCIA purposes of efficient resolution of patent issues," and a biosimilar applicant must comply with these provisions. *Id.* at *1364. Judge Chen dissented in part, explaining that the 180-day marketing notification should not be read as a standalone provision, but rather as part of the optional procedures set forth in § 351(*l*). *Id.* at 1367–70. Similar to the district court's reasoning, Judge Chen concluded that to read the provision otherwise would afford reference-product sponsors "an inherent right to an automatic 180-day injunction," *id.* at 1370, and "an extra-statutory exclusivity windfall," *id.* at 1371. Petitions for certiorari were filed in early 2016 in this case.

On July 5, 2016, the Federal Circuit ruled in *Amgen Inc. v. Apotex Inc.* that all § 262(k) applicants must provide reference product sponsors with 180 days' notice under § 262(*l*)(8)(A) before commercially marketing a biosimilar product, regardless of whether the § 262(k) applicant provided the reference product sponsor with notice of FDA review under § 262(*l*)(2). No. 16-1308, __ F.3d __ (Fed. Cir. 2016). As noted above, the Federal Circuit had made clear in *Amgen v. Sandoz* that § 262(*l*)(8)(A) notice is mandatory when a § 262(k) applicant elects to not provide the required § 262(*l*)(2) notice, and furthermore that issuance of the commercial marketing notice under § 262(*l*)(8)(A) starting the 180-day clock must follow licensure. 794 F.3d at 1357–58. Now, the Federal Circuit has determined that "the commercial marketing provision [outlined in § 262(*l*)(8)(A)] is mandatory and enforceable by injunction even for an applicant" who has followed the steps outlined in § 262(l), including notice under § 262(*l*)(2). *Amgen Inc. v. Apotex Inc.*, No. 16-1308, __ F.3d __ (Fed. Cir. 2016) (slip op. at 4). In addition, the court rejected the argument that a declaratory judgment action is the exclusive remedy for a § 262(*l*)(8)(A) violation, based on the provisions of § 262(*l*)(9)(B). *Id.* at 21. Therefore, courts may grant injunctive relief to prevent a § 262(k) applicant from entering the market until (1) it has provided the reference product sponsor with notice after the FDA has issued the relevant license under § 262(l)(8)(A) violation, and (2) it has then waited 180 days. *Id.* at 25.

It is very likely that, in the coming months, additional relevant case law will develop as more § 351(k) applications are submitted and more disputes arise.

Appendix 10.1
Glossary of Hatch-Waxman Related Terms

180-day exclusive marketing period: The period awarded to certain ANDA filers as a reward for successfully challenging a patent holder's claim that marketing a drug would infringe the patent holder's Orange Book–listed patent. § 10.1.2.

abbreviated new drug application (ANDA): The FDA application filed by a generic drug manufacturer seeking approval to market a follow-on drug by showing it is the same as a Reference Listed Drug, and relying on the clinical trial and other safety and efficacy data submitted by the original drug filer in its New Drug Application. § 10.1.

artificial act of infringement: Filing a Paragraph IV certification in an ANDA application stating that an NDA-holder's listed patent will not be infringed or is invalid. § 10.1.

at-risk launch: Commencing marketing a generic drug pursuant to a finally-approved ANDA before litigation is final. § 10.1.

carve-out: A statement by an ANDA filer that it seeks to market the drug only for uses not encompassed by the use code descriptions of patents listed by the NDA holder in the Orange Book. Same as a *Section (viii) statement*. § 10.1.

civil action to obtain patent certainty (CAPC): A declaratory judgment counterclaim brought by an ANDA applicant seeking a judgment that a patent listed by the NDA holder in the Orange Book, but not sued on by the NDA holder, is invalid, unenforceable or not infringed. § 10.2.2.2.

final approval: FDA approval to begin commercial sales of a regulated drug. § 10.1.1.

new chemical entity (NCE): A chemical compound not previously approved for marketing by the FDA. § 10.1.1.

new drug application (NDA): The drug application filed by a pharmaceutical company seeking approval to market a new drug, and supported by clinical trials showing the drug's safety and efficacy. § 10.1.

offer for confidential access: An offer by a generic drug manufacturer to an NDA holder to allow the NDA holder to review the generic company's ANDA in order to determine whether the NDA holder wishes to file a suit asserting infringement of its patents. § 10.2.2.2.

Orange Book: The FDA publication and online website containing NDA patent owners' claimed patents covering each drug or its uses. § 10.1.1.

Paragraph IV certification: A statement in an ANDA that the generic drug infringes no Orange Book–listed patent, or that the listed patents are invalid. § 10.1.1.

pop-up patent: A patent added by an NDA holder to its Orange Book listing of patents after the date the relevant ANDA was filed. § 10.1.1.

reference listed drug (RLD): An innovative drug approved by the FDA pursuant to an NDA based on the applicants' human clinical trials. § 10.1.

reverse payments: Payments by an NDA holder to a generic drug company as part of a settlement in which the generic drug company agrees to withhold marketing its drug for a period. § 10.2.4.1.

Section (viii) statement: Same as a *carve-out*, above. § 10.1.

tentative approval: Substantive approval by FDA to market a generic drug, but precluding commercial sales of the drug until termination of patent (Paragraph III certification), expiration of thirty-month period (if Paragraph IV certification and litigation within 45-day window), expiration of 180-day exclusivity of prior ANDA filer, or expiration of a period of exclusivity for the brand name drug (*e.g.*, New Chemical Entity). § 10.1.

use code/use code description: a description filed by an NDA holder of which FDA-approved uses or indications of the drug are encompassed by an Orange-Book listed method of use patent. § 10.1.1.

Appendix 10.2
ANDA Scheduling Order from Chief Judge Stark

REVISED July l, 2014

REVISED PATENT FORM SCHEDULING ORDER (ANDA)

[NOTE: text in brackets is for guidance and should be deleted from proposed schedules submitted for the Court's consideration]

This __ day of _____ , 201_, the Court having conducted a Case Management Conference/Rule 16 scheduling and planning conference pursuant to Local Rule 16.2(a) and Judge Stark's Revised Procedures for Managing Patent Cases (which is posted at http://www.ded.uscourts.gov; see Chambers, Judge Leonard P. Stark, Patent Cases) on ______ 201_, and the parties having determined after discussion that the matter cannot be resolved at this juncture by settlement, voluntary mediation, or binding arbitration;

IT IS HEREBY ORDERED that:

1. Rule 26(a)(l) Initial Disclosures and E-Discovery Default Standard. Unless otherwise agreed to by the parties, the parties shall make their initial disclosures pursuant to Federal Rule of Civil Procedure 26(a)(l) within five (5) days of the date of this Order. If they have not already done so, the parties are to review the Court's Default Standard for Discovery, Including Discovery of Electronically Stored Information ("ESI") (which is posted at http://www.ded.uscourts.gov; see Other Resources, Default Standards for Discovery, and is incorporated herein by reference).

2. Joinder of Other Parties and Amendment of Pleadings. All motions to join other parties, and to amend or supplement the pleadings, shall be filed on or before ____________, 201_.

3. Application to Court for Protective Order. Should counsel find it will be necessary to apply to the Court for a protective order specifying terms and conditions for the disclosure of confidential information, counsel should confer and attempt to reach an agreement on a proposed form of order and submit it to the Court within ten (10) days from the date of this Order. Should counsel be unable to reach an agreement on a proposed form of order, counsel must follow the provisions of Paragraph 8(g) below.

Any proposed protective order must include the following paragraph:

Other Proceedings. By entering this order and limiting the disclosure of information in this case, the Court does not intend to preclude another court from finding that information may be relevant and subject to disclosure in another case. Any person or party subject to this order who becomes subject to a motion to disclose another party's information designated "confidential" [the parties should list any other level of designation, such as "highly confidential," which may be provided for in the protective order] pursuant to this order shall promptly notify that party of the motion so that the party may have an opportunity to appear and be heard on whether that information should be disclosed.

4. Papers Filed Under Seal. In accordance with section G of the Administrative Procedures Governing Filing and Service by Electronic Means, a redacted version of any sealed document shall be filed electronically within seven (7) days of the filing of the sealed document.

Should any party intend to request to seal or redact all or any portion of a transcript of a court proceeding (including a teleconference), such party should expressly note that intent at the start of the court proceeding. Should the party subsequently choose to make a request for sealing or redaction, it must, promptly after the completion of the transcript, file with the Court a motion for sealing/redaction, and include as attachments (1) a copy of the complete transcript highlighted so the Court can easily identify and read the text proposed to be sealed/redacted, and (2) a copy of the proposed redacted/sealed transcript. With their request, the party seeking redactions must demonstrate why there is good cause for the redactions and why disclosure of the redacted material would work a clearly defined and serious injury to the party seeking redaction.

5. Courtesy Copies. Other than with respect to "discovery matters," which are governed by paragraph 8(g), and the final pretrial order, which is governed by paragraph 20, the parties shall provide to the Court two (2) courtesy copies of all briefs and one (1) courtesy copy of any other document filed in support of any briefs (i.e., appendices, exhibits, declarations, affidavits etc.). This provision also applies to papers filed under seal.

6. ADR Process. This matter is referred to a magistrate judge to explore the possibility of alternative dispute resolution.

7. Discovery. Unless otherwise ordered by the Court, the limitations on discovery set forth in Local Rule 26.1 shall be strictly observed.

a. Discovery Cut Off. All discovery in this case shall be initiated so that it will be completed on or before ________, 201_.

b. Document Production. Document production shall be substantially complete by ________, 201_.

c. Requests for Admission. A maximum of ___ requests for admission are permitted for each side.

d. Interrogatories.

i. A maximum of ___ interrogatories, including contention interrogatories, are permitted for each side.

ii. The Court encourages the parties to serve and respond to contention interrogatories early in the case. In the absence of agreement among the parties, contention interrogatories, if filed, shall first be addressed by the party with the burden of proof. The adequacy of all interrogatory answers shall be judged by the level of detail each party provides; i.e., the more detail a party provides, the more detail a party shall receive.

e. Depositions.

i. Limitation on Hours for Deposition Discovery. Each side is limited to a total of ____ hours of taking testimony by deposition upon oral examination.

ii. Location of Depositions. Any party or representative (officer, director, or managing agent) of a party filing a civil action in this district court must ordinarily be required, upon request, to submit to a deposition at a place designated within this district. Exceptions to this general rule may be made by order of the Court. A defendant who becomes a counterclaimant, cross-claimant, or third-party plaintiff shall be considered as having filed an action in this Court for the purpose of this provision.

f. Disclosure of Expert Testimony.

i. Expert Reports. For the party who has the initial burden of proof on the subject matter, the initial Federal Rule 26(a)(2) disclosure of expert testimony is due on or before _______, 201_. The supplemental disclosure to contradict or rebut evidence on the same matter identified by another party is due on or before _______, 201_. Reply expert reports from the party with the initial burden of proof are due on or before _______, 201_. No other expert reports will be permitted without either the consent of all parties or leave of the Court. Along with the submissions of the expert reports, the parties shall advise of the dates and times of their experts' availability for deposition.

ii. Expert Report Supplementation. The parties agree they [will] [will not] [CHOOSE ONE] permit expert declarations to be filed in connection with motions briefing (including case-dispositive motions).

iii. Objections to Expert Testimony. To the extent any objection to expert testimony is made pursuant to the principles announced in *Daubert v. Merrell Dow Pharm., Inc.*, 509 U.S. 579 (1993), as incorporated in Federal Rule of Evidence 702, it shall be made by motion no later than the deadline for dispositive motions set forth herein, unless otherwise ordered by the Court. Briefing on such motions is subject to the page limits set out in connection with briefing of case dispositive motions.

g. Discovery Matters and Disputes Relating to Protective Orders.

i. Any discovery motion filed without first complying with the following procedures will be denied without prejudice to renew pursuant to these procedures.

ii. Should counsel find, after good faith efforts—including verbal communication among Delaware and Lead Counsel for all parties to the dispute—that they are unable to resolve a discovery matter or a dispute relating to a protective order, the parties involved in the discovery matter or protective order dispute shall submit a joint letter in substantially the following form:

Dear Judge Stark:

The parties in the above- referenced matter write to request the scheduling of a discovery teleconference.

The following attorneys, including at least one Delaware Counsel and at least one Lead Counsel per party, participated in a verbal meet-and-confer (in person and/or by telephone) on the following date(s): ______________________

Delaware Counsel: ______________________

Lead Counsel: ______________________

The disputes requiring judicial attention are listed below:
[provide here a non-argumentative list of disputes requiring judicial attention]

iii. On a date to be set by separate order, generally not less than forty-eight (48) hours prior to the conference, the party seeking relief shall file with the Court a letter, not to exceed three (3) pages, outlining the issues in dispute and its position on those issues. On a date to be set by separate order, but generally not less than twenty-four (24) hours prior to the conference, any party opposing the application for relief may file a letter, not to exceed three (3) pages, outlining that party's reasons for its opposition.

iv. Each party shall submit two (2) courtesy copies of its discovery letter and any attachments.

v. Should the Court find further briefing necessary upon conclusion of the telephone conference, the Court will order it. Alternatively, the Court may choose to resolve the dispute prior to the telephone conference and will, in that event, cancel the conference.

8. Motions to Amend.

a. Any motion to amend (including a motion for leave to amend) a pleading shall NOT be accompanied by an opening brief but shall, instead, be accompanied by a letter, not to exceed three (3) pages, describing the basis for the requested relief, and shall attach the proposed amended pleading as well as a "blackline" comparison to the prior pleading.

b. Within seven (7) days after the filing of a motion in compliance with this Order, any party opposing such a motion shall file a responsive letter, not to exceed five (5) pages.

c. Within three (3) days thereafter, the moving party may file a reply letter, not to exceed two (2) pages, and, by this same date, the parties shall file a letter requesting a teleconference to address the motion to amend.

9. Motions to Strike.

a. Any motion to strike any pleading or other document shall NOT be accompanied by an opening brief but shall, instead, be accompanied by a letter, not to exceed three (3) pages, describing the basis for the requested relief, and shall attach the document to be stricken.

b. Within seven (7) days after the filing of a motion in compliance with this Order, any party opposing such a motion shall file a responsive letter, not to exceed five (5) pages.

c. Within three (3) days thereafter, the moving party may file a reply letter, not to exceed two (2) pages, and, by this same date, the parties shall file a letter requesting a teleconference to address the motion to strike.

10. Tutorial Describing the Technology and Matters in Issue. Unless otherwise ordered by the Court, the parties shall provide the Court, no later than the date on which their opening claim-construction briefs are due, a tutorial on the technology at issue. In that regard, the parties may separately or jointly submit a DVD of not more than thirty (30) minutes. The tutorial should focus on the technology in issue and should not be used for argument. The parties may choose to file their tutorial(s)

under seal, subject to any protective order in effect. Each party may comment, in writing (in no more than five (5) pages) on the opposing party's tutorial. Any such comment shall be filed no later than the date on which the answering claim-construction briefs are due. As to the format selected, the parties should confirm the Court's technical abilities to access the information contained in the tutorial (currently best are "mpeg" or "quicktime").

11. Claim Construction Issue Identification. On ________, 201_, the parties shall exchange a list of those claim term(s)/phrase(s) that they believe need construction and their proposed claim construction of those term(s)/phrase(s). This document will not be filed with the Court. Subsequent to exchanging that list, the parties will meet and confer to prepare a Joint Claim Construction Chart to be submitted on ________, 201_. The parties' Joint Claim Construction Chart should identify for the Court the term(s)/phrase(s) of the claim(s) in issue, and should include each party's proposed construction of the disputed claim language with citation(s) only to the intrinsic evidence in support of their respective proposed constructions. A copy of the patent(s) in issue as well as those portions of the intrinsic record relied upon shall be submitted with this Joint Claim Construction Chart. In this joint submission, the parties shall not provide argument.

12. Claim Construction Briefing. The parties shall contemporaneously submit initial briefs on claim construction issues on ________, 201_. The parties' answering/responsive briefs shall be contemporaneously submitted on ________, 201_. No reply briefs or supplemental papers on claim construction shall be submitted without leave of the Court. Local Rule 7.1.3(4) shall control the page limitations for initial (opening) and responsive (answering) briefs.

13. Hearing on Claim Construction. Beginning at _______ __.m. on ________, 201_, the Court will hear argument on claim construction. The parties shall notify the Court, by joint letter submission, no later than the date on which their answering claim construction briefs are due: (i) whether they request leave to present testimony at the hearing; and (ii) the amount of time they are requesting be allocated to them for the hearing.

Provided that the parties comply with all portions of this Scheduling Order, and any other orders of the Court, the parties should anticipate that the Court will issue its claim construction order within sixty (60) days of the conclusion of the claim construction hearing. If the Court is unable to meet this goal, it will advise the parties no later than sixty (60) days after the conclusion of the claim construction hearing.

14. Interim Status Report. On ________, 201_, counsel shall submit a joint letter to the Court with an interim report on the nature of the matters in issue and the progress of discovery to date. Thereafter, if the Court deems it necessary, it will schedule a status conference.

15. Supplementation. Absent agreement among the parties, and approval of the Court, no later than the parties must finally supplement, *inter alia*, the identification of all accused products and of all invalidity references.

16. Case Dispositive Motions. [Absent agreement between the parties, the Court will generally not hear case dispositive motions in ANDA cases.]

17. Applications by Motion. Except as otherwise specified herein, any application to the Court shall be by written motion filed with the Clerk. Any non-dispositive motion should contain the statement required by Local Rule 7.1.1.

18. Pretrial Conference. On ________, 201_, the Court will hold a pretrial conference in Court with counsel beginning at ______ _m. [The parties should request a date approximately 2–4 weeks prior to their requested trial date.] Unless otherwise ordered by the Court, the parties should assume that filing the pretrial order satisfies the pretrial disclosure requirement of Federal Rule of Civil Procedure 26(a)(3). The parties shall file with the Court the joint proposed final pretrial order with the information required by the form of Revised Final Pretrial Order – Patent, which can be found on the Court's website (www.ded.uscourts.gov), on or before ________, 201_. [The parties should insert a date no less than seven (7) days before the requested pretrial conference date.] Unless otherwise ordered by the Court, the parties shall comply with the timeframes set forth in Local Rule 16.3(d)(1)–(3) for the preparation of the joint proposed final pretrial order.

The parties shall provide the Court two (2) courtesy copies of the joint proposed final pretrial order and all attachments.

As noted in the Revised Final Pretrial Order – Patent, the parties shall include in their joint proposed final pretrial order, among other things:

a request for a specific number of hours for their trial presentations, as well as a requested number of days, based on the assumption that in a typical bench trial day there will be 6 to 7 hours of trial time;

their position as to whether the Court should allow objections to efforts to impeach a witness with prior testimony, including objections based on lack of completeness and/or lack of inconsistency;

their position as to whether the Court should rule at trial on objections to expert testimony as beyond the scope of prior expert disclosures, taking time from the parties; trial presentation to argue and decide such objections, or defer ruling on all such objections unless renewed in writing following trial, subject to the proviso that a party prevailing on such a post-trial objection will be entitled to have all of its costs associated with a new trial paid for by the party that elicited the improper expert testimony at the earlier trial; and

their position as to how to make motions for judgment as a matter of law, whether it be immediately at the appropriate point during trial or at a subsequent break and whether such motions may be supplemented in writing.

19. Motions *in Limine*. Motions *in limine* shall not be separately filed. All *in limine* requests and responses thereto shall be set forth in the proposed pretrial order. Each ***SIDE*** shall be limited to three (3) *in limine* requests, unless otherwise permitted by the Court. The *in limine* request and any response shall contain the authorities relied upon; each *in limine* request may be supported by a maximum of three (3) pages of argument and may be opposed by a maximum of three (3) pages of argument, and the side making the *in limine* request may add a maximum of one (1) additional page in reply in support of its request. If more than one party is supporting or opposing an *in limine* request, such support or opposition shall be combined in a single three (3) page submission (and, if the moving party, a single one (1) page

reply), unless otherwise ordered by the Court. No separate briefing shall be submitted on *in limine* requests, unless otherwise permitted by the Court.

20. Trial. This matter is scheduled for a __ day bench trial beginning at 8:30 a.m. on ________, 201_, with the subsequent trial days also beginning at 8:30 a.m. The trial day will end no later than 5:00 p.m. each day.

21. Post-Trial Briefing. The parties will address the post-trial briefing schedule and page limits in the proposed final pretrial order.

____
UNITED STATES DISTRICT JUDGE

Appendix 10.3
ANDA-Specific Local Patent Rules

United States District Court: District of New Jersey Local Patent Rule 3.6

3.6 Disclosure Requirements for Patent Cases Arising Under 21 U.S.C. § 355 (commonly referred to as "the Hatch-Waxman Act").

The following applies to all patents subject to a Paragraph IV certification in cases arising under 21 U.S.C. § 355 (commonly referred to as "the Hatch-Waxman Act"). This rule takes precedence over any conflicting provisions in L. Pat. R. 3.1 to 3.5 for all cases arising under 21 U.S.C. § 355.

(a) On the date a party answers, moves, or otherwise responds, each party who is an ANDA filer shall produce to each party asserting patent infringement the entire Abbreviated New Drug Application or New Drug Application that is the basis of the case in question.

(b) Not more than seven days after the initial Scheduling Conference, each party asserting patent infringement shall serve on all parties a "Disclosure of Asserted Claims" that lists each claim of each patent that is allegedly infringed by each opposing party, including for each claim the applicable statutory subsections of 35 U.S.C. § 271 asserted.

(c) Not more than 14 days after the initial Scheduling Conference, each party opposing an assertion of patent infringement shall provide to each party asserting patent infringement the written basis for its "Invalidity Contentions," for any patents referred to in the opposing party's Paragraph IV Certification, which shall contain all disclosures required by L. Pat. R. 3.3.

(d) Any "Invalidity Contentions" disclosed under L. Pat. R. 3.6(c), shall be accompanied by the production of documents required under L. Pat. R. 3.4(b) and (c).

(e) Not more than 14 days after the initial Scheduling Conference, each party opposing an assertion of patent infringement shall provide to each party asserting patent infringement the written basis for its "Non-Infringement Contentions," for any patents referred to in the opposing party's Paragraph IV Certification which shall include a claim chart identifying each claim at issue in the case and each limitation of each claim at issue. The claim chart shall specifically identify for each claim which claim limitation(s) is/(are) literally absent from each opposing party's allegedly infringing Abbreviated New Drug Application or New Drug Application.

(f) Any "Non-Infringement Contentions" disclosed under L. Pat. R. 3.6(e), shall be accompanied by the production of any document or thing that each party who is an ANDA filer intends to rely on in defense against any infringement contentions by each party asserting patent infringement.

(g) Not more than 45 days after the disclosure of the "Non-Infringement Contentions" as required by L. Pat. R. 3.6(e), each party asserting patent infringement shall provide each opposing party with a "Disclosure of Infringement Contentions," for all patents referred to in each opposing party's Paragraph IV Certification, which shall contain all disclosures required by L. Pat. R. 3.1. The infringement contentions shall be limited to the claims identified in L. Pat. R. 3.6(b).

(h) Any "Disclosure of Asserted Claims and Infringement Contentions" disclosed under L. Pat. R. 3.6(g), shall be accompanied by the production of documents required under L. Pat. R. 3.2.

(i) Not more than 45 days after the disclosure of "Invalidity Contentions" as required by L. Pat. R. 3.6(c), the party defending the validity of the patent shall serve on each other party its "Responses to Invalidity Contentions" as required under L. Pat. R. 3.4A.

(j) Each party that has an ANDA application pending with the Food and Drug Administration ("FDA") that is the basis of the pending case shall: (1) notify the FDA of any and all motions for injunctive relief no later than three business days after the date on which such a motion is filed; and (2) provide a copy of all correspondence between itself and the FDA pertaining to the ANDA application to each party asserting infringement, or set forth the basis of any claim of privilege for such correspondence pursuant to L. Civ. R. 34.1, no later than seven days after the date it sends same to the FDA or receives same from the FDA.

United States District Court for the Eastern District of Texas Patent Rule 3-8

3-8. Disclosure Requirements for Patent Cases Arising Under 21 U.S.C. § 355 (Hatch-Waxman Act).

The following provision applies to all patents subject to a Paragraph IV certification in cases arising under 21 U.S.C. § 355 (commonly referred to as "the Hatch-Waxman Act"). This provision takes precedence over any conflicting provisions in P.R. 3-1 to 3-5 for all cases arising under 21 U.S.C. § 355.

(a) At or before the Initial Case Management Conference, the Defendant(s) shall produce to Plaintiff(s) the entire Abbreviated New Drug Application or New Drug Application that is the basis of the case in question.

(b) Not more than 14 days after the Initial Case Management Conference, the Defendant(s) shall provide to Plaintiff(s) the written basis for their "Invalidity Contentions" for any patents referred to in Defendant(s) Paragraph IV Certification. This written basis shall contain all disclosures required by P.R. 3-3 and shall be accompanied by the production of documents required by P.R. 3-4.

(c) Not more than 14 days after the Initial Case Management Conference, the Defendant(s) shall provide to Plaintiff(s) the written basis for any defense of noninfringement for any patent referred to in Defendant(s) Paragraph IV Certification. This written basis shall include a claim chart identifying each claim at issue in the case and each limitation of each claim at issue. The claim chart shall specifically identify for each claim those claim limitation(s) that are literally absent from the Defendant(s) allegedly infringing Abbreviated New Drug Application or New Drug Application. The written basis for any defense of noninfringement shall also be accompanied by the production of any document or thing that the Defendant(s) intend to rely upon in defense of any infringement allegations by Plaintiff(s).

(d) Not more than 45 days after the disclosure of the written basis for any defense of noninfringement as required by P.R. 3-8(c), Plaintiff(s) shall provide Defendant(s) with a "Disclosure of Asserted Claims and Infringement Contentions," for all patents referred to in Defendant(s) Paragraph IV Certification, which shall contain all disclosures required by P.R. 3-1 and shall be accompanied by the production of documents required by P.R. 3-2.

(e) Each party that has an ANDA application pending with the Food and Drug Administration ("FDA") that is the basis of the pending case shall: (1) notify the FDA of any and all motions for injunctive relief no later than three business days after the date on which such a motion is filed; and (2) provide a copy of all correspondence between itself and the FDA pertaining to the ANDA application to each party asserting infringement, or set forth the basis of any claim of privilege for such correspondence, no later than seven days after the date it sends or receives any such correspondence.

Northern District of Ohio Local Patent Rule 3.9

3.9 Disclosure Requirements for Patent Cases Arising Under 21 U.S.C. § 355 (commonly referred to as "the Hatch-Waxman Act").

The following provision applies to all patents subject to a Paragraph IV certification in cases arising under 21 U.S.C. § 355 (commonly referred to as "the Hatch-Waxman Act"). This provision takes precedence over any conflicting provisions in L. P. R. 3.1 to 3.8 for all cases arising under 21 U.S.C. § 355.

(a) At or before the Case Management Conference, the Defendant(s) shall produce to Plaintiff(s) the entire Abbreviated New Drug Application or New Drug Application that is the basis of the case in question.

(b) Not less than fifteen (15) calendar days after the Case Management Conference, the Defendant(s) shall provide to Plaintiff(s) written Invalidity Contentions, for any patents referred to in Defendant(s) Paragraph IV Certification. At a minimum, these Invalidity Contentions should include those items required by L. P. R. 3.5(a-d);

(c) Any Invalidity Contentions disclosed under L. P. R. 3.9(b) shall be accompanied by the production of any document or thing that each Defendant intends to rely on to show invalidity. At a minimum, this disclosure should comply with L. P. R. 3.6(a).

(d) Not less than thirty (30) calendar days after the Case Management Conference, the Defendant(s) shall provide to Plaintiff(s) the written basis for their Noninfringement Contentions for any patents referred to in Defendant(s) Paragraph IV Certification which shall include a claim chart as required by L. P. R. 3.3(a) identifying each claim at issue in the case and each limitation of each claim at issue. The claim chart shall specifically identify for each claim which claim limitation(s) are literally absent from the Defendant(s) allegedly infringing Abbreviated New Drug Application or New Drug Application

(e) Any Noninfringement Contentions disclosed under L. P. R. 3.9(d) shall be accompanied by the production of any document or thing that the Defendant(s) intend to rely on in defense against any infringement contentions by Plaintiff(s), including those items required by L. P. R. 3.4(a).

(f) Not less than forty-five (45) calendar days after the disclosure of the Noninfringement Contentions as required by L. P. R. 3.9(d), Plaintiff(s) shall provide Defendant(s) with Infringement Contentions for all patents referred to in Defendant(s)

Paragraph IV Certification, including, at a minimum, those items required by L. P. R. 3.1.

(g) Any Infringement Contentions disclosed under L. P. R. 3.9(f) shall be accompanied by the production of documents required under L. P. R. 3.2.

District of Idaho Local Patent Rule 3-6

3.6. Disclosure Requirements for Patent Cases Arising Under 21 U.S.C. § 355 (commonly referred to as "the Hatch-Waxman Act").

The requirements of this Dist. Idaho Loc. Patent R. 3.6 apply to all patents subject to a Paragraph IV certification in cases arising under 21 U.S.C. § 355 (commonly referred to as "the Hatch-Waxman Act"). This provision takes precedence over any conflicting provisions in Dist. Idaho Loc. Patent R. 3.1 to 3.5 for all cases arising under 21 U.S.C. § 355.

(a) At or before the initial scheduling conference, the Defendant(s) shall produce to Plaintiff(s) the entire Abbreviated New Drug Application or New Drug Application that is the basis of the case in question.

(b) Not more than 14 days after the initial scheduling conference, the Defendant(s) shall provide to Plaintiff(s) the written basis for their "Invalidity Contentions," for any patents referred to in Defendant(s) Paragraph IV Certification which shall contain all disclosures required by Dist. Idaho Loc. Patent R. 3.3.

(c) Any "Invalidity Contentions" disclosed under Dist. Idaho Loc. Patent R. 3-6(b), shall be accompanied by the production of documents required under Dist. Idaho Loc. Patent R. 3.4.

(d) Not more than 14 days after the initial scheduling conference, the Defendant(s) shall provide to Plaintiff(s) the written basis for their "Non-Infringement Contentions," for any patents referred to in Defendant(s) Paragraph IV Certification which shall include a claim chart identifying each claim at issue in the case and each limitation of each claim at issue. The claim chart shall specifically identify for each claim which claim limitation(s) are literally absent from the Defendant(s) allegedly infringing Abbreviated New Drug Application or New Drug Application.

(e) Any "Non-Infringement Contentions" disclosed under Dist. Idaho Loc. Patent R. 3.6(d), shall be accompanied by the production of any document or thing that the Defendant(s) intend to rely on in defense against any infringement contentions by Plaintiff(s).

(f) Not more than 42 days after the disclosure of the "Non-Infringement Contentions" as required by Dist. Idaho Loc. Patent R. 3.6(d), Plaintiff(s) shall provide Defendant(s) with a "Disclosure of Asserted Claims and Infringement Contentions," for all patents referred to in Defendant(s) Paragraph IV Certification, which shall contain all disclosures required by Dist. Idaho Loc. Patent R. 3.1.

(g) Any "Disclosure of Asserted Claims and Infringement Contentions" disclosed under Dist. Idaho Loc. Patent R. 3.6(f), shall be accompanied by the production of documents required under Dist. Idaho Loc. Patent R. 3.2.

District of Maryland Patent Local Rule 805.3

3. Cases Arising Under the Hatch-Waxman Act (21 U.S.C. § 355)

Unless otherwise ordered by the Court, in all cases alleging patent infringement based upon a Paragraph IV certification under 21 U.S.C. § 355:

a. Sixty (60) days from the date of the Scheduling Order, the Defendant shall serve the Plaintiff with a Claim Chart containing the following:

i. The identity of each item of prior art that allegedly anticipates each asserted claim or renders it obvious. Each prior art patent shall be identified by its number, country of origin, and date of issue. Each prior art publication shall be identified by its title, date of publication, and where feasible, author and publisher. Prior art under 35 U.S.C. § 102(b) shall be identified by specifying the item offered for sale or publicly used or known, the date the offer or use took place or the information became known, and the identity of the person or entity which made the use or which made and received the offer, or the person or entity which made the information known or to whom it was made known. Prior art under 35 U.S.C. § 102(f) shall be identified by providing the name of the person(s) from whom and the circumstances under which the invention or any part of it was derived. Prior art under 35 U.S.C. § 102(g) shall be identified by providing the identities of the person(s) or entities involved in and the circumstances surrounding the making of the invention before the patent applicant(s);

ii. Whether the prior art anticipates the claim or renders it obvious. If a combination of prior art references makes a claim obvious, that combination must be identified;

iii. Where, specifically, within each item of prior art each element of the claim is found; and

iv. All grounds of invalidity other than anticipation or obviousness. This identification must be as specific as possible. For example, each party asserting an enablement defense must set forth with particularity what is lacking in the specification to enable one skilled in the art to make or use the invention, specifically citing information or materials obtained in discovery to the extent feasible. Each party asserting an enablement defense must set forth with particularity what is lacking in the specification to enable one skilled in the art to make or use the invention.

b. Sixty (60) days from the date of the Scheduling Order, the Defendant shall serve the Plaintiff with a Proposed Claim Construction Statement containing the following information for each claim in issue:

i. Identification of any special or uncommon meanings of words or phrases in the claim;

ii. All references from the specification that support, describe, or explain each element of the claim;

iii. All material in the prosecution history that describes or explains each element of the claim; and

iv. Any extrinsic evidence that supports the proposed construction of the claim, including, but not limited to, expert testimony, inventor testimony, dictionary definitions and citations to learned treatises, as permitted by law.

c. Ninety (90) days from the date of the Scheduling Order, the Plaintiff shall serve upon the Defendant a Responsive Proposed Claim Construction Statement containing the following:

i. Identification of any special or uncommon meanings of words or phrases in the claim in addition to those disclosed in the Proposed Claim Construction Statement;

ii. All references from the specification that support, describe, or explain each element of the claim in addition to or contrary to those described in the Proposed Claim Construction Statement;

iii. All material in the prosecution history that describes or explains each element of the claim in addition to or contrary to those described in the Proposed Claim Construction Statement; and

iv. Any extrinsic evidence that supports the proposed construction of the claim, including, but not limited to, expert testimony, inventor testimony, dictionary definitions and citations to learned treatises, as permitted by law.

d. Amendment of a Claims Chart or a Responsive Claims Chart may be made only on stipulation of all parties or by Order of the Court, which shall be entered only upon a showing of excusable subsequent discovery of new information or extraordinary good cause.

e. One hundred twenty (120) days from the date of the Scheduling Order, the parties, having met and conferred on claim construction, the parties shall file a Joint Claim Construction Statement which shall contain the following information:

i. The construction of those claims and terms on which the parties agree;

ii. Each party's proposed construction of each disputed claim and term, supported by the same information that is required in the respective claim construction statements; and

iii. For any party who proposes to call one or more witnesses at any claim construction hearing, the identity of each such witness, the subject matter of his or her testimony, and an estimate of the time required for the testimony.

f. One hundred twenty (120) days from the date of the Scheduling Order, the parties shall file and serve opening briefs with supporting evidence and identification of any proposed Claim Construction Hearing witnesses.

g. One hundred fifty (150) days from the date of the Scheduling Order, the parties shall file and serve any responsive brief and supporting evidence directly rebutting their opponents supporting evidence and identifying any additional proposed Claim Construction Hearing witnesses.

Eastern District of Missouri Local Patent Rule 3-1(a)(viii)

(viii) In patent cases arising under 21 U.S.C. § 355, at or before the initial Rule 16 Scheduling Conference, the Alleged Infringer shall produce to the Patent Claimant the entire Abbreviated New Drug Application or New Drug Application that is the basis of the case. The Court recognizes that, in cases brought under 21 U.S.C. § 355, scheduling and sequencing provisions distinct from those set forth in these Local Patent Rules may be appropriate.

Western District of Tennessee Local Patent Rule 3.10

3.10 Disclosure Requirements for Patent Cases Arising Under 21 U.S.C. § 355 (commonly referred to as "the Hatch-Waxman Act").

The following provisions apply to all patents subject to a Paragraph IV certification in cases arising under 21 U.S.C. § 355 (commonly referred to as "the Hatch-Waxman Act").These provisions take precedence over any conflicting provisions in LPR 3.1–3.8 for all cases arising under 21 U.S.C. § 355.

(a) Production of New Drug Application. At or before the Patent Scheduling Conference, Defendant(s) shall produce to Plaintiff(s) the entire Abbreviated New Drug Application or New Drug Application that is the basis of the case in question.

(b) Invalidity Contentions. Within 14 days after the Patent Scheduling Conference, Defendant(s) shall provide to Plaintiff(s) written Invalidity Contentions for any patents referred to in Defendant(s) Paragraph IV Certification. At a minimum, these Invalidity Contentions should include those items required by LPR 3.5(a)-(d).

(c) Production of Materials Supporting Invalidity Contentions. Any Invalidity Contentions disclosed under LPR 3.10(b) shall be accompanied by the production of any document or thing that each Defendant intends to rely on to show invalidity. At a minimum, this disclosure should comply with LPR 3.6(a).

(d) Non-Infringement Contentions. Within 30 days after the Patent Scheduling Conference, Defendant(s) shall provide to Plaintiff(s) the written basis for their Non-Infringement Contentions for any patents referred to in Defendant(s) Paragraph IV Certification, which shall include a claim chart as required by LPR 3.3(a) identifying each claim at issue in the case and each limitation of each claim at issue. The claim chart shall specifically identify for each claim which claim limitation(s) are literally absent from the Defendant(s) allegedly infringing Abbreviated New Drug Application or New Drug Application.

(e) Production of Materials Supporting Non-Infringement Contentions. Any Non-infringement Contentions disclosed under LPR 3.10(d) shall be accompanied by the production of any document or thing that each Defendant intends to rely on in defense against any infringement contentions by Plaintiff(s), including those items required by LPR 3.4(a).

(f) Infringement Contentions. Within 45 days after the disclosure of the Non-Infringement Contentions as required by LPR 3.10(d), Plaintiff(s) shall provide Defendant(s) with Infringement Contentions for all patents referred to in Defendant(s) Paragraph IV Certification, including, at a minimum, those items required by LPR 3.1.

(g) Production of Materials Supporting Infringement Contentions. Any Infringement Contentions disclosed under LPR 3.10(f) shall be accompanied by the production of documents required under LPR 3.2.

Chapter 11
Design Patents

In 1842, Congress extended patent protection to "new and original designs for articles of manufacture" in a bill that borrowed heavily from the British Copyright of Designs Act.[1] The defined subject matter was

> any new and original design for a manufacture, whether of metal or other material or materials, or any new and original design for the printing of woolen, silk, cotton, or other fabrics, or any new and original design for a bust, statue, or bas relief or composition in alto or basso relievo, or any new original impression or ornament to be placed on any article of manufacture, the same being formed in marble or other material, or any new and useful pattern, or print, or picture, to be either worked into or worked on, or printed or painted or cast or otherwise fixed on any article of manufacture or any new and original shape or configuration of any article of manufacture.

Act of Aug. 29, 1842, ch. 263, § 3, 5 Stat. 543, 543–44 (1842). Congress amended the design patent statute in 1902 to define the subject matter as simply "any new, original, and ornamental design for an article of manufacture." Design patent protection was carried forward in the 1952 Patent Act without any substantive change. *See Falcon Indus., Inc. v. R. S. Herbert Co.*, 128 F. Supp. 204, 210 (E.D.N.Y. 1955).

---

1. See Jason J. Du Mont & Mark D. Janis, *The Origins of American Design Patent Protection,* 88 Ind. L.J. 837 (2013), for a fuller explication of the Act's origins and the blending of patent language and examination procedures with copyright concepts.

11.1 Substantive Law

11.1.1 Statutory Basis

Design patent protection is available for "any new, original and ornamental design for an article of manufacture." 35 U.S.C. § 171. Whereas the subject matter of a utility patent is how the article works or is used, the subject matter of a design patent is how the article looks—the overall *ornamental* appearance of an article. *L.A. Gear, Inc. v. Thom McAn Shoe Co.*, 988 F.2d 1117, 1123 (Fed. Cir. 1993). Like utility patents, design patents provide the exclusive rights to the ornamental features. § 171 ("The provisions of this title relating to patents for inventions shall apply to patents for designs, except as otherwise provided."). Under § 173, the term of design patents is fourteen years from the date of issuance for applications filed before May 13, 2015, and fifteen years for applications filed on or after May 13, 2015.

The United States joined the Hague Union, effective May 13, 2015. *See* Patent Law Treaties Implementation Act of 2012, Pub. L. 112-211, 126 Stat. 1527 (2012). The Hague Agreement permits applicants to file a single international design application with either the World Intellectual Property Office (WIPO) or the USPTO to obtain design protection in member states. To implement the Hague Agreement, the term of design patents has been extended to fifteen years from issuance.

Certain design patents have been granted perpetual or renewable rights. Congress renews protection for the seal of the American Legion (U.S. Patent No. D54,296) every fourteen years, while the Red Cross symbol (U.S. Patent No. D54,308) was made perpetual by 18 U.S.C. § 706 (2012).

11.1.2 Requirements for Patentability

11.1.2.1 Definition of a Design

A patentable design consists of the configuration, surface ornamentation, or both, embodied in or applied to an article of manufacture. A design must be definite and reproducible. Designs that change in appearance during an article's use—such as animated designs for graphical user interfaces—may be protected, typically by the use of illustrations that show the different stages of the design's appearance. A design may be embodied in or applied to an entire article of manufacture, or only a portion thereof. *See In re Zahn*, 617 F.2d 261, 267–69 (C.C.P.A. 1980).

11.1.2.2 Definition of an Article of Manufacture

A design must be embodied in or applied to an article of manufacture. "Article of manufacture" has been interpreted broadly to encompass tools, machines, and any "manufacture" within the meaning of § 101. *See In re Koehring*, 37 F.2d 421, 424 (C.C.P.A. 1930) (holding that a compact and symmetrical design for a concrete truck possessed "more grace and pleasing appearance than existed in the prior art" and thus should be accorded a design patent). A manufacture is "anything made 'by the hands of man' from raw materials, whether literally by hand or by machinery or by art." *In re Hruby*, 373 F.2d 997 (C.C.P.A. 1967) (upholding a design created by the flow of water in a fountain as patentable). A design may be for only part of an article. *See In re Zahn*, 617 F.2d at 267–69. After some initial resistance, the PTO adopted guidelines that recognize that "computer-generated icons" may constitute articles of manufacture. *See* Guidelines for Examination of Design Patent Applications for Computer-Generated Icons, 61 FR 11380 (1996); *see* William J. Seymour & Andrew W. Torrance, *(R)evolution in Design Patentable Subject Matter: The Shifting Meaning of "Article of Manufacture,"* 17 Stan. Tech. L. Rev. 183, 200–05 (2014).

11.1.2.3 Ornamentality

Although § 171 requires that designs be ornamental to be patentable, most courts have assessed ornamentality by asking whether the design is dictated by functional considerations. *See, e.g., Best Lock Corp. v. Ilco Unican Corp.*, 94 F.3d 1563 (Fed. Cir. 1996); *In re Carletti*, 328 F.2d 1020, 1022 (C.C.P.A. 1964); *see also* Jason J. Du Mont & Mark D. Janis, *Functionality in Design Protection Systems*, 19 J. Intell. Prop. L. 261 (2012) (analyzing the ornamentality cases). A design must be the product of "aesthetic skill and artistic conception." *Blisscraft of Hollywood v. United Plastics Co.*, 294 F.2d 694, 696 (2d Cir. 1961); *see also In re Koehring*, 37 F.2d 421 (C.C.P.A. 1930) (upholding the design for a concrete mixer as patentable because the design created a "more symmetrical and compact whole").

Patentability may be barred where designs are hidden or obscured while in use or where their appearance cannot be a matter of concern. *Compare Ex parte Jaffe*, 147 U.S.P.Q. 45 (PTO Bd. App. 1964) (denying a patent application for a functional circuit board covered during use) *with In re Webb*, 916 F.2d 1553 (Fed. Cir. 1990) (upholding patentability of the design for a femoral hip stem prosthesis because its appearance could be a matter of concern at the point of sale, even though it would ultimately be concealed). The patented design must be considered as a whole, encompassing all ornamental features *visible* at any time during normal use. *Contessa Food Prods., Inc. v. Conagra, Inc.*, 282 F.3d 1370, 1379 (Fed. Cir. 2002) (abrogated on other grounds). "Normal use" is not limited to only one phase or portion of the lifetime of a product. *See Int'l Seaway Trading Corp. v. Walgreens Corp.*, 589 F.3d 1233 (Fed. Cir. 2009). "'Normal use' in the design patent context extend[s] over 'a period in an article's life beginning after completion of manufacture or assembly and ending with the ultimate destruction, loss or disappearance of the article.'" *Contessa Food Prods.*, 282 F.3d at 1379 (quoting *In re Webb*, 916 F.2d 1553, 1557–58 (Fed. Cir. 1990)).

The USPTO's policy is to reject applications for designs that could be deemed offensive to any race, religion, sex, ethnic group, or nationality.

11.1.2.4 Inventorship

A design patent may be obtained by "whoever invents any new, original and ornamental design for an article of manufacture." *Hoop v. Hoop*, 279 F.3d 1004 (Fed. Cir. 2002). Merely suggesting a design concept is not sufficient. The standard of inventorship is the same for both utility and design patents. An inventor is the person who conceives the invention. A person who assists an inventor after the conception of the invention cannot gain inventorship. Similarly, after conception, an inventor may use the services, ideas, and aid of others in the process of perfecting his or her invention without losing inventorship. In the case of interference, the ultimate test for design-patent inventorship is whether the second asserted invention is "substantially similar" to the first. *See id.*

11.1.2.5 Double Patenting

As with utility patents, the double-patenting doctrine precludes a person from obtaining more than one design patent for the same invention or obvious modifications to his or her invention. For multiple design patents issued to the same inventor, "same invention"-type double patenting occurs if "identical designs with identical scope" are twice claimed. If the designs are not identical, the obviousness-type double-patenting inquiry is whether the two designs are patentably distinct. In the case of non-identical designs, an applicant may overcome an obviousness-type double-patenting rejection by filing a terminal disclaimer, whereby the applicant agrees that the later-filed application will expire at the same time as the prior patent (or application). *See* § 14.2.5.1. A same-invention-type double-patenting rejection is statutory and may not be overcome with a terminal disclaimer.

The doctrine of double patenting may also preclude separate design and utility patents on related subject matter. In the case of same invention-type double patenting and some instances of obviousness-type double patenting (those in which the application at issue is the earlier filed of the two), a two-way unpatentability standard is used to determine double patenting: the claimed subject matter of each patent must be identical or obvious in light of the subject matter of the other. *See In re Dembiczak*, 175 F.3d 994 (Fed. Cir. 1999); *Carman Indus., Inc. v. Wahl*, 724 F.2d 932 (Fed. Cir. 1983). Double patenting can be found in the case of a design patent application over an earlier-issued utility patent (*see, e.g.*, *In re Barber*, 81 F.2d 231, 28 U.S.P.Q. 187 (C.C.P.A. 1936)) or a utility patent application over an earlier-issued design patent (*see, e.g.*, *In re Thorington*, 418 F.2d 528 (C.C.P.A. 1969)).

11.1.3 Specification and Claim

Like utility patents and unlike copyrights, design patents are examined and not merely registered. *See* USPTO, Manual of Patent Examining Procedure, part 1500 *et seq*. The § 112 requirements of adequate disclosure and definite claiming also apply to design patents. *See In re Owens*, 710 F.3d 1362 (Fed. Cir. 2013). In the case of design patents, both disclosure and definiteness are accomplished through the drawings. Only one claim is permitted in design patent applications. This claim takes the form of "the ornamental design of the specified article as shown." Although only one claim is permitted, a design application may illustrate multiple embodiments of a design if they involve a single inventive concept. *See In re Rubenfield*, 270 F.2d 391 (C.C.P.A. 1959).

The USPTO requires an applicant to "designate the particular article" for which a design patent is sought, although the patent need not depict the article and can represent it generically (as in the case of surface ornamentation). The degree of specificity with which an applicant must describe and claim the article is not straightforward. *See Ex parte Fulda*, 1913 Comm'n Dec. 206 (Comm'r Dec. Pat. 1913); *Ex parte Cadey*, 1916 Comm'n Dec. 57 (Comm'r Dec. Pat. 1916); *Ex parte Andrews*, 1917 Comm'n Dec. 13 (Comm'r Dec. Pat. 1916); *Ex parte Ginzburg*, 1925 Comm'n Dec. 159 (Comm'r Dec. Pat. 1925). For designs of "an ornament, impression, print or picture to be applied to an article of manufacture," an applicant may make a broad claim to the use of the ornament on more than one article. *See In re Schnell*, 46 F.2d 203 (C.C.P.A. 1931). In this case, the applicant must teach the manner of applying the design to show reduction to practice. *Id.* For designs that consist of a shape or configuration for an article of manufacture, the claim and specification must be narrower. *Id.*

Drawings must contain a "sufficient number of views to constitute a complete disclosure of the appearance of the design." 37 C.F.R. § 1.152(a) (2014). If the drawings are insufficient, a patent may be declared invalid under § 112.

11.1.3.1 The Design Patent Claim

The solid lines of a drawing define the scope of the claimed invention. The dotted or dashed lines merely provide context; they do not limit the scope of the claimed design. The illustration below reflects a typical design patent:

Figure 1
U.S. Patent No. D517,789 S

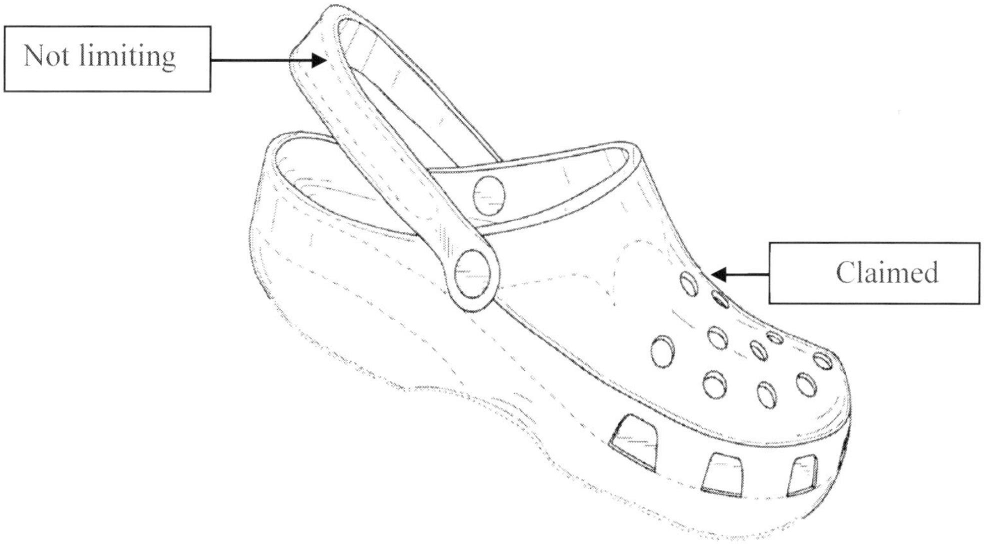

11.1.3.2 Intersection of Design Patents and Related IP Laws

Design patent protection and trade dress protection are conceptually similar in that both are ways of protecting the visual impression that products (or, sometimes, services) convey. Design patents and trade dress, however, serve different functions: a design patent encourages design innovation by rewarding inventors with a time-limited right to exclude infringers. Trade dress law instead protects consumers' expectation that a product with a particular configuration comes from a particular source. Thus, while design patent infringement requires only a showing that the accused product appears to embody the patented design as depicted in the patent's drawings, trade dress infringement further requires proof of secondary meaning (that is, that the design has come to identify its source of manufacture or supply) and a likelihood of consumer confusion.

At present, there is no requirement that a designer elect between design patent protection and trade dress protection for the same design. Several decades ago, the C.C.P.A. held that the existence of a design patent does not preclude an applicant from registering a product shape on the Principal Register (*see In re Mogen David Wine Corp.*, 328 F.2d 925, 929 (C.C.P.A. 1964), *aff'd*, 372 F.2d 539, 152 U.S.P.Q. 593 (C.C.P.A. 1967); *In re Morton-Norwich Prods., Inc.*, 671 F.2d 1322 (C.C.P.A. 1982)), and this remains the USPTO's practice. On the other hand, the Supreme Court has made clear that the obstacles to protecting product design through trade dress are substantial. *See Wal-Mart Stores, Inc. v. Samara Bros., Inc.*, 529 U.S. 205 (2000) (product design trade dress is distinctive only upon a showing of secondary meaning); *Traffix Devices, Inc. v. Mktg. Displays, Inc.*, 532 U.S. 23 (2001) (product design trade dress is nonfunctional only if it is not essential to the use or purpose of the product, and that it does not affect the cost or quality of the product). Accordingly, many designs that are protectable under design patent law might fail to satisfy the tests for protectable trade dress. *See, e.g., Apple Inc. v. Samsung Elecs. Co.*, 786 F.3d 983 (Fed. Cir. 2015) (upholding design patents against a functionality challenge but striking down trade dress on functionality grounds).

Design patents and copyrights protect similar types of works. The critical distinction here is that a copyright only extends to the actual sculptural work and derivations of it. Moreover, copyright infringement requires proof of *copying*, not merely of similarity of protectable features viewed as a whole. However, a design patent does not preclude protection for the same design under trademark and copyright law. *See Rosenthal v. Stein*, 205 F.2d 633, 635 (9th Cir. 1953) ("The area in which a thing would be either a copyrightable work of art or a patentable design, but not the other, is perhaps unsurveyable. Whether a thing is a work of art or a patentable design, or is a patentable design and not a work of art, cannot be determined by excluding one from the other. A thing is a work of art if it appears to be within the historical and ordinary conception of the term art. A thing is a design by the same token. The two are not necessarily distinct one from the other. Neither goes to the functioning of a utility."). Thus, the Statue of Liberty was formerly protected by U.S. Design Patent No. D11,023 as well as Copyright Registration No. 9939-G.

11.2 Case Management

11.2.1 Infringement

Design patent infringement is a question of fact, which must be proven by a preponderance of the evidence. *See L.A. Gear, Inc.*, 988 F.2d at 1124. Infringement of a design patent is determined by applying the "ordinary observer" test:

> [I]f, in the eye of an ordinary observer, giving such attention as a purchaser usually gives, two designs are substantially the same, if the resemblance is such as to deceive such an observer, inducing him to purchase one supposing it to be the other, the first one patented is infringed by the other.

Gorham Co. v. White, 81 U.S. 511, 528 (1871); *Egyptian Goddess, Inc. v. Swisa, Inc.*, 543 F.3d 665, 670 (Fed. Cir. 2008) (en banc). The ordinary observer is "deemed to view the differences between the patented design and the accused product in the context of the prior art." *Egyptian Goddess*, 543 F.3d at 676–77.

> When the differences between the claimed and accused design are viewed in light of the prior art, the attention of the hypothetical ordinary observer will be drawn to those aspects of the claimed design that differ from the prior art. And when the claimed design is close to the prior art designs, small differences between the accused design and the claimed design are likely to be important to the eye of the hypothetical ordinary observer.

Id. at 676.

Under *Egyptian Goddess*, where the accused design is not plainly dissimilar to the patented design, reference to the prior art can provide a useful tool to analyze infringement. *See id.* at 678. Particular care should be given in crowded fields with many prior-art designs. Even subtle differences may become significant. *Id.* There may also be instances where the accused design is sufficiently distinct from the patented design such that no comparison to the prior art is necessary. *Id.* It is typically useful for a court to review the nearest prior art, just as with utility patents. *Lytton Sys. Inc. v. Whirlpool*, 728 F.2d 1423, 1444 (Fed. Cir. 1984). By contrast, the analysis for design patents is purely visual, so the court should expect to compare exemplars of both the accused product and any relevant prior-art products. *See Richardson v. Stanley Works*, 597 F.3d 1288, 1296 (Fed. Cir. 2010) (emphasizing "the decisive importance of drawings in a design patent"). The design-patented product is less important because the infringement analysis compares the design patent *claims/drawings* and the accused product—not the patented *product* and the accused one. The court, therefore, should carefully consider how to ensure that the trier of fact has access to these embodiments and the appropriate comparisons.

It is customary in design patent cases to use a "visual claim chart," showing the patented images next to the accused products, using the same angles depicted in the design patent. For example:

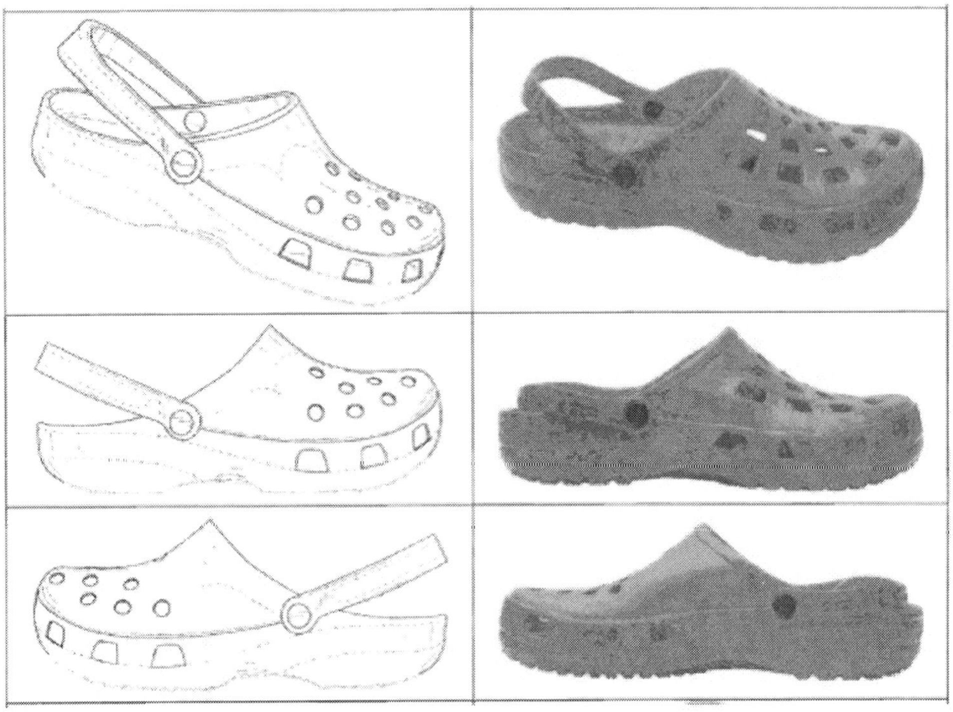

A visual claim chart will typically contain a comparison from each angle depicted in the design patent. *See Crocs, Inc. v. Int'l Trade Comm'n*, 598 F.3d 1294 (Fed. Cir. 2010); *see also Richardson*, 597 F.3d at 1296 ("design patents are typically claimed according to their drawings, and claim construction must be adapted to a pictorial setting").

A court should compare the overall effect of the patented and accused designs. *Crocs, Inc.*, 598 F.3d at 1303. "In other words, 'the deception that arises is a result of the similarities in the overall design, not of similarities in ornamental features in isolation.'" *Id.* (quoting *Amini Innovation Corp. v. Anthony Cal., Inc.*, 439 F.3d 1365, 1371 (Fed. Cir. 2006)). When a design contains functional elements alongside ornamental aspects, a court should exclude those functional elements provided the infringement test still evaluates the similarities in overall design between the accused product and claimed design, rather than comparing the two on an element-by-element basis. *See Richardson*, 597 F.3d at 1296.

Because the infringement test hinges on the reactions of an ordinary observer, courts have approved—but do not in all cases require—the use of customer surveys or other evidence of consumer motivation to establish infringement or injury. *Apple, Inc. v. Samsung Elecs. Co.*, 678 F.3d 1314, 1338–39 (Fed. Cir. 2012).

The principles of equivalency apply to design patents, according to the Federal Circuit, but not as a separate doctrine of equivalents. Rather, the notion of equivalency is subsumed within the *Gorham* substantial similarity standard and within the statutory language extending infringement liability to "colorable imitations" of the patented design. *Lee v. Dayton-Hudson Corp.*, 838 F.2d 1186, 1189 (Fed. Cir. 1988); § 289. Having decided that equivalency principles applied to design patents, the Federal Circuit has also decided that a version of the doctrine of prosecution history estoppel should likewise apply to design patents. *See Pac. Coast Marine Windshields Ltd. v. Malibu Boats, LLC*, 739 F.3d 694, 701 (Fed. Cir. 2014).

11.2.1.1 Ordinary Observer Test

Similarity between a patented design and an accused design is determined from the perspective of the "ordinary observer." The pertinent "observers" are the ordinary purchasers of the accused article. *Goodyear Tire & Rubber Co. v. Hercules Tire & Rubber Co., Inc.*, 162 F.3d 1113 (Fed. Cir. 1998).

The ordinary observer test is subject to several refinements and qualifications. Similarities must relate to the claimed design, not the plaintiff's particular embodiment. *See OddzOn Prods., Inc. v. Just Toys, Inc.*, 122 F.3d 1396 (Fed. Cir. 1997). Furthermore, similarity must arise from the nonfunctional aspects of a design. *See id.* at 1404–06. With respect to the determination of similarity, older authorities make clear that similarity between the patented and accused designs is not necessarily to be determined in a side-by-side comparison. *See, e.g., Ashley v. Weeks-Numan Co.*, 220 F. 899 (2d Cir. 1915). More recently, the Federal Circuit has seemed to signal a preference for a side-by-side comparison. *See, e.g., Arminak & Assoc., Inc. v. Saint-Gobain Calmar, Inc.*, 501 F.3d 1314, 1327 (Fed. Cir. 2007)

The Federal Circuit's en banc decision in *Egyptian Goddess* held that the *Gorham* ordinary observer test is the sole test for determining infringement of a design patent, specifically overturning the former "point of novelty" test. The Federal Circuit has held that *OddzOn*, which excluded functional elements of a design in an infringement analysis, is not undermined by *Egyptian Goddess. See Richardson*, 597 F.3d at 1293.

11.2.1.2 Claim Construction

Because design patents "typically are claimed as shown in drawings," trial courts are no longer required "to provide a detailed verbal description of the claimed design, as is typically done in the case of utility patents." *Egyptian Goddess*, 543 F.3d at 679 (citations omitted). *Egyptian Goddess* was an important change from prior law, in which the court was expected to describe the design-patented features in writing. *Egyptian Goddess* and its progeny make clear that a detailed verbal description of the asserted patent is unnecessary and that it is appropriate to "rely upon the illustrations set out in the [the patent], as they better represent the claimed design." *Arc'teryx Equip., Inc. v. Westcomb Outerwear, Inc.*, 2008 U.S. Dist. LEXIS 90228, 2008 WL 4838141 (D. Utah Nov. 4, 2008); *see also Dexas Int'l, Ltd. v. Office Max, Inc.*, 2009 WL 252164, 2009 U.S. Dist. LEXIS 6642, at *19–20 (E.D. Tex. Jan. 30, 2009) (same). The preferred approach is to limit the detail in any verbal description of a design patent. *Egyptian Goddess*, 543 F.3d at 679; *Crocs*, 598 F.3d at 1302 ("This court has cautioned, and continues to caution, trial courts about excessive reliance on a detailed verbal description in a design infringement case."). Nevertheless, the level of detail a court uses to describe a claimed design is a matter of discretion, and "absent a showing of prejudice, [a] court's decision to issue a relatively detailed claim construction will not be reversible error." *Egyptian Goddess*, 543 F.3d at 679.

A court may also, to the extent it would be helpful either to a jury or in the court's own analysis, describe the features of the claimed design as they relate to the accused product and prior art or to explain various conventions in design patent drafting, such as the use of solid and broken lines, aspects of the prosecution history, or any functional features. *Id.* at 680.

11.2.1.3 Product Scope

Section 289 provides that infringement occurs when the patented design is applied to "any article of manufacture." Design patent infringement may be found even when the accused infringer's products are not directly competitive with the patentee's. *See Avia Grp. Int'l, Inc. v. L.A. Gear Cal., Inc.*, 853 F.2d 1557, 1565 (Fed. Cir. 1988) ("To find infringement, the accused articles need only appropriate a patentee's protected design, not a patentee's market as well."). "[I]ndeed, an infringer is liable even when the patent owner puts out no product." *Id.*

11.2.2 Invalidity

Like utility patents, design patents are also subject to validity challenges, which must be proven by clear and convincing evidence. The same general invalidity arguments can apply, including written description, enablement, and indefiniteness challenges under § 112, as well as anticipation under § 102 and obviousness challenges under § 103. A design patent can also be deemed invalid for lacking ornamentality or for claiming a design that is purely functional. The most common challenges are functionality, anticipation, and obviousness.

11.2.2.1 Functionality

Design patents protect only ornamental or "nonfunctional" designs. The design of an article is deemed to be "functional" when the appearance is dictated by the use or purpose of the article. *See L.A. Gear,* 988 F.2d at 1123; *In re Carletti,* 328 F.2d 1020, 1022 (C.C.P.A. 1964) (when a configuration is the result of functional considerations only, the resulting design is not patentable as an ornamental design—even where the result is "pleasing to look upon"). A patent for a design that is primarily functional rather than ornamental is invalid. *See Richardson*, 597 F.3d at 1293–94.

While a design may be part of an object or device that has a function (e.g., a hammer with specific design), the design aspect itself must be nonfunctional. The determination of whether the patented design is dictated by the function of the article ultimately rests on an analysis of its overall appearance. *See PHG Techs., LLC v. St. John Cos.*, 469 F.3d 1361, 1366 (Fed. Cir. 2006). In determining whether a design feature is purely functional, courts consider factors such as: (1) whether there are alternate ways to design the article to achieve the same function, *see Seiko Epson Corp. v. Nu-Kote Int'l, Inc.*, 190 F.3d 1360, 1368 (Fed. Cir. 1999) and *Rosco, Inc. v.*

Mirror Lite Co., 304 F.3d 1373, 1378 (Fed. Cir. 2002); (2) the existence of any concomitant utility patents, see *Traffix Devices, Inc. v. Mktg. Displays, Inc.*, 532 U.S. 23, 29 (2001) ("A utility patent is strong evidence that the features therein claimed are functional."); (3) whether the design is aesthetically pleasing and not dictated by function alone, see *Bonito Boats, Inc. v. Thunder Craft Boats, Inc.*, 489 U.S. 141, 148 (1989); (4) whether alternative designs would adversely affect the utility of the article, see *PHG Techs.*, 469 F.3d at 1366; and (5) whether there are any elements in the design or an overall appearance clearly not dictated by function, see *id.*

11.2.2.2 Anticipation

In considering whether a design patent is anticipated by the prior art under § 102, the "ordinary observer" test is applied. *See Int'l Seaway Trading Corp. v. Walgreens Corp.*, 589 F.3d 1233, 1240 (Fed. Cir. 2009) (holding that the same tests must be applied to infringement and anticipation). As with infringement, the test applies only to those aspects of the design that are visible at some point during the "normal use lifetime" of the product and prior art, which includes from the point of sale through any use by consumers. *Id.* at 1241.

Anticipation requires a showing that a single prior-art reference is "identical in all material respects" to the claimed invention. *OddzOn Prods., Inc. v. Just Toys, Inc.*, 122 F.3d 1396, 1404 (Fed. Cir. 1997). First, the claim must be construed. Then the construed claim is compared to the design disclosed in the allegedly anticipatory prior-art reference, assuming that reference has qualified as prior art under the applicable provisions of § 102. If the claimed design and the alleged prior-art design are substantially the same, the alleged prior-art design anticipates the claimed design. Designs are "substantially the same" when their resemblance is deceptive to the extent that it would induce the ordinary observer to purchase an article, supposing it to be the other. *Door-Master Corp. v. Yorktowne, Inc.*, 256 F.3d 1308, 1313 (Fed. Cir. 2001). Once identity is established, a prior design will anticipate even if it is an article having a different use or is in a nonanalogous art. *See In re Glavas*, 230 F.2d 447, 450 (C.C.P.A. 1956).

The experimental use exception to the § 102(b) "public use" and "on sale" bars has limited application to design patents. *See* §§ 14.3.4.1.1, 14.3.4.1.5.1, 14.3.4.1.5.2. An ornamental design alone for an article of manufacture cannot qualify under the experimental use exception. *In re Mann*, 861 F.2d 1581 (Fed. Cir. 1988) ("obtaining the reactions of people to a design, whether they like it or not, is not experimentation"). However, where experimentation is directed to the functional features of an article, the use may fall within the experimental use exception. *See Tone Bros., Inc. v. Sysco Corp.*, 28 F.3d 1192 (Fed. Cir. 1994); § 14.3.4.1.5.1.

11.2.2.3 Obviousness

Like utility patents, design patents must also meet the nonobviousness requirement of § 103. *See Titan Tire Corp. v. Case New Holland, Inc.*, 566 F.3d 1372, 1380 (Fed. Cir. 2009). Challenges to a design patent under § 103 may include evidence from one skilled in the art regarding prior-art references and whether and how those references would be combined to form a design that compares to the claimed design.

The test for obviousness is different from the test for infringement and anticipation. Whereas the comparison of the claimed design to an accused article or potentially anticipatory prior art is seen through the eyes of the "ordinary observer," the comparison of the claimed design to the prior art for obviousness purposes is seen through the eyes of the "ordinary designer." *High Point Design LLC v. Buyers Direct, Inc.*, 730 F.3d 1301, 1311 (Fed. Cir. 2013); *Apple*, 678 F.3d at 1324 ("In addressing a claim of obviousness in a design patent, the ultimate inquiry is whether the claimed design would have been obvious to a designer of ordinary skill who designs articles of the type involved."). In *High Point Design*, the Federal Circuit held that it was error to apply the "ordinary observer" standard to assess obviousness, and suggested that *International Seaway* was not to the contrary. 730 F.3d at 1312 & n.2.

Federal Circuit decisions set forth a two-step process for the obviousness inquiry, which includes a "primary reference" requirement. In the first step, one must find a single prior-art reference that has design characteristics "basically the same as the claimed design" (the "primary reference"). In the second step, "other references may be used to modify it to create a design that has the same overall visual appearance as the claimed design." *High Point*, 730 F.3d at 1311 (quoting *Durling v. Spectrum Furniture Co.,* 101 F.3d 100, 103 (Fed. Cir. 1996)) (internal quotations omitted); *MRC Innovations, Inc. v. Hunter Mfg., LLP*, 747 F.3d 1326, 1331–32 (Fed. Cir. 2014).

The pertinent references sought to be combined to show obviousness need not be analogous arts in the mechanical sense, but must be so related that the "appearance of certain ornamental features in one would suggest the application of those features to another." *In re Glavas*, 230 F.2d 447 (C.C.P.A. 1956). It remains unsettled to what extent the Supreme Court's ruling in *KSR International v. Teleflex, Inc.*, 550 U.S. 398 (2007), should be applied to design patents. *See Titan Tire*, 566 F.3d at 1384-85; *see also* Petition for Writ of Certiorari at i, 5–6, *MRC Innovations, Inc. v. Hunter Mfg., LLP*, 135 S. Ct. 182 (2014) (No. 14-5), 2014 U.S. LEXIS 6444, 2014 WL 2986575, at *I, *5–*6 (presenting question whether *KSR* requires court to articulate a basis for combining known elements to find design patent invalid). In applying the "so related" requirement, the Federal Circuit has continued to rely on its pre-*KSR* jurisprudence. *See, e.g.*, *MRC Innovations*, 747 F.3d at 1334 (Fed. Cir. 2014) (quoting *In re Borden*, 90 F.3d 1570, 1574 (Fed. Cir. 1996) ("In order for secondary references to be considered, there must be some suggestion in the prior art to modify the basic design with features from the secondary references.")).

Some decisions suggest that more weight should be given to secondary considerations, particularly commercial success, than in the case of utility patents. Design patent law specifically aims "to encourage ornamentation and beautification in manufactured articles so as to increase their salability and satisfy the aesthetic sense of the purchasers." *Forestek Plating & Mfg. Co. v. Knapp-Monarch Co.*, 106 F.2d 554, 559 (6th Cir. 1939). However, it must be clear "that the commercial success is attributable to the design, and not to some other factor, such as a better-recognized brand name or improved function." *Litton Sys., Inc. v. Whirlpool Corp.*, 728 F.2d 1423, 1443 (Fed. Cir. 1984).

11.2.3 Patent Local Rules

Most patent local rules (PLRs) are directed to utility patent cases. *See, e.g.*, N.D. Ga. Pat. L.R. 1.2(b) (limiting PLRs to utility patent cases); N.D. Ill. Pat. L.R. 1.1 (same); E.D. Tex. Pat. L.R. 1-2 (same), E.D. Mo. Pat. L.R. 1-2(b) (same). Several districts allow parties to extend their PLRs to non-utility patent disputes where appropriate. *See, e.g.*, N.D. Cal. Pat. L.R. 1-2; S.D. Cal. Pat. L.R. 1-3, 1-4. The District of New Jersey specifically excludes design patents from the more detailed pretrial patent proceedings, including claim construction, infringement contentions, and invalidity contentions. *See* D.N.J. Pat. L.R. 3.1(c) & (e), 3.3(c), 3.4A(c), 4.1(c), 4.2(e), 4.3(g), 4.4, & 4.5(d) (2011). The District of New Jersey Local Patent Rules Committee noted that, in light of the Federal Circuit decision in *Egyptian Goddess v. Swisa*, 543 F.3d 665 (2008), a trial court should not provide a detailed verbal description of the claimed design and that it was not appropriate to apply "certain of the Local Patent Rules which call for a narrative claims chart, claim construction contentions and a claim construction hearing" to design patent cases. *See* District of New Jersey, Report of the Local Patent Rules Committee, Explanatory Notes for 2011 Amendments, *available at* http://www.njd.uscourts.gov/sites/njd/files/PatentRuleAmendment2011.pdf.

The Northern District of New York also excludes design patents from the more detailed claim-construction procedures (N.D.N.Y. Pat. L.R. 4.1), but requires design patent holders to provide specific infringement contentions (N.D.N.Y. Pat. L.R. 3.1(c)(ii)) ("For each design patent or variety of plant patent claim that is alleged, a chart displaying each view of the design or variety of plant patent drawings and a view of the accused design or variety of plant from every available angle for all embodiments.") and defendants must respond by explaining any denial of substantial similarity (N.D.N.Y. Pat. L.R. 3.3(a)) and by providing specific invalidity contentions. N.D.N.Y. Pat. L.R. 3.3(b)(1) (invalidity contentions must contain the "identity of each item of prior art that allegedly anticipates each asserted claim or renders it obvious, including in the case of a design or variety of plant patent a view from every available angle and all available embodiments").

11.2.4 Remedies

All of the remedies available for utility patent infringement are available for design patent infringement. § 171 (2012) ("The provisions of this title relating to patents for inventions shall apply to patents for designs, except as otherwise provided."). Design patentees can recover damages under § 284, obtain injunctive relief under § 283, reasonable attorney fees in exceptional cases under § 285, and so forth, so long as they comply with the same formalities (e.g., marking under § 287).

Section 289 provides a special additional damages remedy for design patent infringement, which is discussed below.

11.2.4.1 Injunctive Relief

A design patent plaintiff must satisfy the *eBay* test for preliminary or permanent injunctive relief, just as in a utility patent case. *See* §§ 3.2, 9.2.1. Because the analysis focuses on the *ornamental design* depicted in the patent, the patentee must make a slightly different factual showing with respect to the first *eBay* factor, irreparable injury: the design patentee must show "some causal nexus between" the defendant's *design* and the plaintiff's alleged injury. *Apple*, 678 F.3d at 1324; *cf.* §§ 3.2.2.2.4, 9.2.1.1. It also is possible to demonstrate irreparable harm by showing "design dilution," meaning that the presence of similar substitutes diminishes the value of the patented design. *Id.* at 1325 (noting, however, that the lower court properly had not found design dilution in the case at bar).

11.2.4.2 Damages

There is a special additional remedy available to design patentees:

> Whoever during the term of a patent for a design, without license of the owner, (1) applies the patented design, or any colorable imitation thereof, to any article of manufacture for the purpose of sale, or (2) sells or exposes for sale any article of manufacture to which such design or colorable imitation has been applied shall be liable to the owner to the extent of his *total* profit, but not less than $250, recoverable in any United States district court having jurisdiction of the parties.
>
> Nothing in this section shall prevent, lessen, or impeach any other remedy which an owner of an infringed patent has under the provisions of this title, but he shall not twice recover the profit made from the infringement.

§ 289 (emphasis added). Thus, a design patent owner can obtain the infringer's *total* profits for sale of an article to which the infringing design has been applied, but no less than $250. § 289; *see Apple Inc. v. Samsung Elecs. Co., Ltd.*, 786 F.3d 983 (Fed. Cir. 2015) (rejecting contention that § 289 incorporates an apportionment requirement under basic causation principles); *see also Schnadig Corp. v. Gaines Mfg. Co.*, 620 F.2d 1166, 1171 (6th Cir. 1980); *Henry Hanger & Display Fixture Corp. of Am. v. Sel-O-Rak Corp.*, 270 F.2d 635, 643–44 (5th Cir. 1959); *Bergstrom v. Sears, Roebuck & Co.*, 496 F. Supp. 476, 495 (D. Minn. 1980).

To establish profits under § 289, the patentee need only demonstrate the defendant's total sales. The defendant typically then demonstrates what portion of those sales is not attributable to the infringing design. Importantly, § 289(2) applies to any entity that "sells or exposes for sale any article of manufacture to which such design or colorable imitation has been applied." This means that distributors and retailers can be liable for *their* total profit, which likely far exceeds the manufacturer's total profit. Thus, design patent cases often give rise to indemnity disputes between manufacturers and retailers, because the possible total exposure for accused items with significant retail markups can easily surpass the manufacturer's total revenue, to say nothing of its total profit.

While § 289 is an additional remedy available to design patent holders, a design patentee cannot "twice recover" an infringer's profits. *See* § 289 ("Nothing in this section shall prevent, lessen, or impeach any other remedy which an owner of an infringed patent has under the provisions of this title, but he shall not twice recover the profit made from the infringement."). For example, a patentee is not entitled to both a reasonable royalty *and* the infringer's profits. *See Catalina Lighting, Inc. v. Lamps Plus, Inc.*, 295 F.3d 1277, 1291 (Fed. Cir. 2002). Similarly, when a utility patent and a design patent are asserted against the same accused product, a patentee can only recover damages for the single infringing act. *See id.* at 1292.

Chapter 12
Plant Patents

Prior to 1930, inventions in plants faced two obstacles to patentability. First, some commentators believed that plants might not qualify as eligible subject matter for patent protection because they are products of nature. *See, e.g., Ex parte Latimer*, 1889 Comm'n Dec. Pat. 123 (1889) (fiber from the needle of evergreen tree unpatentable product of nature). The second barrier was that plants were not thought amenable to patent law's "written description" requirement. Congress addressed these issues in enacting the Plant Patent Act of 1930, 46 Stat. 703, codified at §§ 161–164, which covers new varieties of plants, but excludes tuber-propagated plants. Congress enacted a second statutory system in 1970—the Plant Variety Protection Act, codified at 7 U.S.C. §§ 2321–2582 (2012)—to protect plant varieties that are sexually reproduced by seed.

12.1 Substantive Law

12.1.1 Statutory Basis

Three forms of intellectual property protection are available for plants in the United States: (1) plant patents, (2) plant variety protection, and (3) utility patents. *See* Mark D. Janis, Herbert H. Jervis, & Richard Peet, Intellectual Property Law of Plants (2014) (discussing these regimes in U.S. and foreign law).

12.1.1.1 Plant Patent Act

The Plant Patent Act (PPA) grants patent rights to "[w]hoever invents or discovers and asexually reproduces any distinct and new variety of plant, including cultivated sports, mutants, hybrids, and newly found seedlings, other than a tuber propagated plant or a plant found in an uncultivated state . . . ." § 161. Thus, to obtain a plant patent, the statute requires that the patentee (1) invent or discover a new and distinct variety of plant and (2) asexually reproduce the plant.

The PPA affords a patentee exclusive rights over *asexually* reproduced plants. Asexual reproduction includes reproduction by layering, budding, grafting, and inarching. The PPA does not grant rights over sexually reproduced plants—plants that are reproduced from seeds or propagated from tubers (such as the Irish potato and the Jerusalem artichoke). Moreover, the PPA does not cover plants found in an uncultivated state, which has generally been interpreted as the wild. No case law to date, however, defines "uncultivated state."

Plant patents are granted by the USPTO. Plant patents remain in effect for twenty years from the filing date of the application. Unlike utility patents, they are not subject to maintenance fees.

12.1.1.2 Plant Variety Protection Act

The Plant Variety Protection Act (PVPA) protects sexually reproduced and tuber propagated plant varieties. *See* §§ 2321–2582. Whereas the PPA authorizes the issuance of plant patents, the PVPA authorizes the issuance of Plant Variety Protection (PVP) certificates. PVP certificates are issued by the Secretary of Agriculture, rather than the USPTO.

A PVP certificate affords plant breeders the right "to exclude others from selling the variety, or offering it for sale, or reproducing it, or importing it, or exporting it, or using it in producing (as distinguished from developing) a hybrid or different variety . . . ." § 2483(a). A PVP certificate remains in effect for twenty years from the date of issuance, or twenty-five years in the case of a tree or vine. *See* § 2483(b). The United States adheres to the 1991 Convention of the International Union for the Protection of New Plant Varieties (UPOV), which the United States ratified in 1999. For an overview of UPOV systems, *see generally* Mark D. Janis, Herbert H. Jervis, & Richard Peet, Intellectual Property Law of Plants, ch. 4 (2014); *see also* § 12.2.4

12.1.1.3 Utility Patents

A novel plant variety can also be protected as a new "composition of matter" under the general utility Patent Act. *See* § 101. Utility patents offer the potential for broader protection for plants than do either the PPA or PVPA because utility patents can include trait claims, breeding method claims, seed deposit claims, and food product claims. For example, utility patents can protect plants bred to feature desirable traits such as heat tolerance. *See, e.g.*, U.S. Patent No. 6,294,715. Alternatively, utility patents can protect genetically engineered plants, such as plants designed to tolerate herbicide exposures, providing protection beyond the methods and tools for their production. *See, e.g.*, U.S. Patent No. 5,866,775.

Newly developed plant varieties are not limited to one statutory basis of protection. Specifically, the Supreme Court has held that neither the PPA nor the PVPA limits the scope of the coverage in § 101. *See J.E.M. Ag Supply, Inc. v. Pioneer Hi-Bred Int'l, Inc.*, 534 U.S. 124, 145 (2001). As such, sexually reproducing plants, for example, are patentable as utility patents and protectable under the PVPA.

12.1.2 The Plant Patent Claim

A plant patent consists of only one claim directed to a distinct and new variety of the plant specified, as described and illustrated in the specification, and can also recite the principal distinguishing characteristics. The claim must meet the requirements of § 101. The statute, however, relaxes the requirement of a § 112-compliant disclosure, recognizing that a written description in the case of plant patents may not enable one having skill in the art to reproduce the variety exactly. *See* § 162 ("No plant patent shall be declared invalid for noncompliance with section 112 of this title if the description is as complete as is reasonably possible.").

A typical plant patent claim is as follows: "1. A novel and distinct variety of grapevine rootstock plant designated '9365-85' having the characteristics described and illustrated herein." *See* U.S. Patent No. PP 021,358.

12.1.3 The PVP Certificate

Unlike plant and utility patents, PVP certificates have no claims. A PVP certificate is granted for a plant variety that is new, distinct, uniform, and stable. *See* 7 U.S.C. § 2402(a) (2012).

The "new" requirement is similar in some ways to the statutory bar rule as it existed in utility patent law under the 1952 Act, § 102(b). A "new" variety "has not been sold or otherwise disposed of to other persons, by or with the consent of the breeder, or the successor in interest of the breeder, for purposes of exploitation of the variety" more than a specified period of time before the application filing date. *See* 7 U.S.C. § 2402(a)(1). If the sale or disposal is in the United States, the specified period is one year. *See* 7 U.S.C. § 2402(a)(1)(A). If the sale or disposal is outside of the United States, the specified period is four years or six years in the case of a tree or vine. *See* 7 U.S.C. § 2402(a)(1)(B).

A "distinct" variety "is clearly distinguishable from any other variety the existence of which is publicly known or a matter of common knowledge" as of the application filing date. *See* 7 U.S.C. § 2402(a)(2).

A "uniform" variety is one wherein "any variations are describable, predictable, and commercially acceptable." *See* 7 U.S.C. § 2402(a)(3).

A "stable" variety is one, "when reproduced, will remain unchanged with regard to the essential and distinctive characteristics of the variety with a reasonable degree of reliability commensurate with that of varieties of the same category in which the same breeding method is employed." *See* 7 U.S.C. § 2402(a)(4).

The three requirements are often referred to collectively as the "DUS" requirements. Of the three, distinctness is perhaps the most technical. It relies on comparisons between physiological or other characteristics between the varieties. To facilitate these comparisons, UPOV has developed distinctness guidelines for nearly 300 species.

12.1.4 Utility Patent Claims Related to Plants

Utility plant patent claims may include seed deposit claims, claims directed to entire or parts of plants and isolated cells, trait claims, and breeding method claims.

An example of a seed deposit claim is as follows:

> Claim 1: A broccoli seed designated 393-2-19 and having ATCC Accession Number 203533.

See U.S. Patent No. 6,294,715.

An example of a claim directed at a plant and its parts is as follows:

> Claim 2: A broccoli plant or its parts produced by the seed of claim 1.

See U.S. Patent No. 6,294,715.

Typical trait claims are as follows:

> Claim 3: A regenerated broccoli plant regenerated from tissue culture of the broccoli plant of claim 2 wherein said regenerated plant comprises a center head having a diameter of 3 to 8 inches at maturity when said regenerated plant is exposed to a maximum temperature of at least 85° F for 15 days during the growth cycle of said regenerated plant.
>
> Claim 4: Progeny seed produced from crossing the plant of claim 2 with another broccoli plant wherein said progeny seed produces a progeny plant comprising a center head having a diameter of 3 to 8 inches at maturity when said progeny plant is exposed to a maximum temperature of at least 85° F for 15 days during the growth cycle of said progeny plant.

See U.S. Patent No. 6,294,715.

An example of a breeding method claim is as follows:

> Claim 9: A method for producing hybrid corn seed comprising the steps of a) planting in pollinating proximity seeds of corn inbred line NP982 having ATCC Accession No. 209453 and a second inbred line, not NP982.

See U.S. Patent No. 5,792,905.

12.2 Case Management

12.2.1 Plant Patents

12.2.1.1 Eligibility Requirements

Unlike the eligibility requirements for utility patents, § 161 provides that "[w]hoever invents or discovers and asexually reproduces any distinct and new variety of plant" may be eligible for a plant patent. Section 161 also specifies that the "distinct and new variety of plant" includes "cultivated sports, mutants, hybrids, and newly found seedlings" but does not include "a plant found in an uncultivated state." Both phrases were added to the statute in 1954 in an apparent effort to resolve a controversy over whether plants found by chance and then propagated could constitute eligible subject matter for a plant patent. The language seemed to distinguish between the act of finding a plant in a cultivated plot (an act that could potentially lead to a plant patent) and finding it in the wild (an act that could not lead to a plant patent). However, in *In re Beineke*, 690 F.3d 1344 (Fed. Cir. 2012), the Federal Circuit held that the subject matter at issue was ineligible because it could not have constituted a "cultivated" sport, mutant, or hybrid, nor could it have qualified as a "newly-found seedling." Mr. Beineke had observed two 100-year-old white oak trees growing in the front yard of a residence and had asexually reproduced these trees by planting acorns from each of these trees. *Id.* at 1346. Mr. Beineke certainly had not cultivated these trees from their inception, nor could he provide that anyone else had. According to the court, this disqualified the trees from constituting "cultivated" sports, mutants, or hybrids. Moreover, Mr. Beineke did not even attempt to argue that the mature trees were "seedlings," so he could not rely on that category either.

12.2.1.2 Determination of Infringement of Plant Patents

The PPA grants to plant patentees "the right to exclude others from asexually reproducing the plant, and from using, offering for sale, or selling the plant so reproduced, or any of its parts, throughout the United States, or from importing the plant so reproduced, or any parts thereof, into the United States." § 163. Each act specified in this section constitutes an independent act of infringement. *See Yoder Bros., Inc. v. Cal.-Fla. Plant Corp.*, 537 F.2d 1347, 1383 (5th Cir. 1976).

Prior to the Plant Patent Amendments Act of 1998, however, a plant patent covered the entire plant, and one did not directly infringe by selling or using the asexually reproduced plant. Congress extended the plant patent scope in 1998 to include using, offering to sell, selling, and importing an asexually reproduced plant or any of its parts. This amendment is effective for plant patents issued on or after October 27, 1998, the date the amendments were enacted. *See* Pub. L. 105-289, § 3, 112 Stat. 2781 (1998).

To prove infringement of a plant patent, the patentee must show that the alleged infringing plant resulted from asexual reproduction, i.e., that it is the progeny of the patented plant. *See Yoder*, 537 F.2d at 1380. The patentee, however, does not need to prove that one or more parts of the patented plant taken by the infringer, either directly or indirectly, actually matured into the patented plant variety. *See id.* at 1383.

Moreover, the alleged infringer does not need to know of the patent or the source of the plant. *See Kim Bros. v. Hagler*, 167 F. Supp. 665, 668 (S.D. Cal. 1958), *aff'd*, 276 F.2d 259 (9th Cir. 1960).

In determining infringement, courts consider the scope of protection of the plant patent and then compare the properly construed plant patent claim to that which is asserted to infringe. *See Imazio Nursery Inc. v. Dania Greenhouses*, 69 F.3d 1560, 1564–65 (Fed. Cir. 1995).

12.2.1.2.1 Meaning of the Term "Variety"

The meaning of the term "variety" informs the scope of protection of plant patents. Although the PPA does not specifically define the term "variety," the statute states that new plant varieties include "cultivated sports, mutants, hybrids, and newly found seedlings." § 161. "Sports" refers to plant varieties that result from bud variation rather than seed variation. "Mutants" refers to varieties that result from seedling variation by self-pollination of the species. "Hybrids" refers to varieties that result from seedlings of cross-pollination of two species, two varieties, or of a species and variety. "Newly found seedlings" refer to cultivated seedlings that have not previously been recognized as a new variety. *See Imazio Nursery*, 69 F.3d at 1566; *see also Ex parte Moore*, 115 U.S.P.Q. (BNA) 145, 147 (Pat. Off. Bd. App. 1957).

By contrast, the PVPA defines "variety" as a group of plants that have the same essential and distinctive characteristics. Courts, however, have rejected the argument that the term "variety" under the PPA should be interpreted in the same manner as defined under the PVPA. Even though the PPA and the PVPA both use the term "variety" and both grant some form of intellectual property protection for plant varieties, courts note that the two statutes differ significantly in their purposes.

> The term "variety" in both statutes cannot be read divorced from the very different circumstances in which that term is used. Those circumstances, asexual reproduction in the case of plant patents, and sexual reproduction in the case of plant variety protection, mandate the protection afforded under these different statutory provisions.

Imazio Nursery, 69 F.3d at 1568; *see also J.E.M. Ag Supply, Inc. v. Pioneer Hi-Bred Int'l, Inc.*, 534 U.S. 124 (2001); Mark D. Janis and Stephen Smith, *Technological Change and the Design of Plant Variety Protection Systems*, 82 Chi.-Kent L. Rev. 1557 (2008).

In light of this clear difference between the PPA and the PVPA, courts have focused on the meaning of "asexual reproduction" in determining the meaning of "variety" and the scope of plant patent protection.

12.2.1.2.2 Meaning of "Asexual Reproduction"

To assert plant patent infringement, the patentee must prove that the alleged infringing plant is either a direct or an indirect asexual reproduction of the patentee's original parent plant. A defendant does not infringe by sexually reproducing the patented plant, i.e., by reproducing the patented plant using seeds. Instead, the defendant has to physically take, either directly or indirectly, one or more parts from the patented plant to produce the progeny of the patented plant. For example, the defendant may grow a new plant from plant cuttings or graft a new plant from buds or nodes of the patented plant variety. The plant produced from asexual reproduction is the same plant, in contrast to sexual reproduction, which produces a different plant that may be like the parent plant. *See Yoder Bros., Inc. v. Cal.-Fla. Plant Corp.*, 537 F.2d 1347, 1380 (5th Cir. 1976) ("Asexual reproduction is literally the only way that a breeder can be sure he has reproduced a plant identical in every respect to the parent.").

A defendant, however, does not infringe by independently breeding a variety that closely resembles the characteristics of the patentee's variety. Independent creation is a defense to plant patent infringement. *See Imazio Nursery*, 69 F.3d at 1570.

12.2.1.3 Invalidity of Plant Patents

Like utility patents, plant patents are presumed valid. *See* § 282. Furthermore, validity challenges must be proven by clear and convincing evidence. *See Cal. Table Grape Comm'n v. RB Sandrini, Inc.*, No. 1:06-cv-00842-OWW-TAG, 2007 WL 1847631, 2007 U.S. Dist. LEXIS 48362, at *35 (E.D. Cal. June 27, 2007). The same general invalidity arguments for utility patents also apply to plant patents, although § 162 relaxes the written description for plant patents. *See* §§ 14.1.1.2–14.1.1.3.

12.2.1.3.1 Anticipation

The statutory bar provisions under § 102 apply to plant patents. Specifically, the public use or sale of a plant variety one year prior to the plant patent application date will bar a plant patent. Similar to utility patent cases, however, exceptions such as secret use may apply in plant patent cases. *See, e.g., Cal. Table Grape Comm'n v. RB Sandrini, Inc.*, 2007 U.S. Dist. LEXIS 48362 (E.D. Cal. 2007). An asexually reproduced plant variety cannot be perfected or improved in an ordinary sense and consequently any use must be of the complete invention. *Bourne v. Jones*, 114 F. Supp. 413, 419 (S.D. Fla. 1951), *aff'd*, 207 F.2d 173 (5th Cir. 1953).

In *Delano Farms Co. v. California Table Grape Commission*, 778 F.3d 1243 (Fed. Cir. 2015), the Federal Circuit considered whether plant varieties were "accessible to the public" more than one year before the plant patent applications were filed. The Federal Circuit held that the cultivation of the plant varieties openly in a field was not considered accessible to the public, because the growers had knowingly obtained the plant varieties without authorization and, in this case, had agreed not to reveal that they had possession of the varieties. Further, while the growers propagated the plant varieties in locations that were visible from the public road, the vines were not labeled such that members of the public would have been able to discern these plants from others in the field. Since the purpose of the public use bar is to prevent removal from the public domain of inventions the public has come to believe are freely available, the federal court stated that such bar does not apply when the public is not informed of the inventions and cannot readily discern the claimed features.

The printed publication provisions in § 102 present a special challenge when applied to plant varieties because a written description of a new plant variety may not be enough to enable one skilled in the art to reproduce the claimed variety. For example, the United States Court of Customs and Patent Appeals held that a publication with "a color picture of the rose clear enough to establish identity in appearance" was not an enabling disclosure of the new rose variety. *See In re LeGrice*, 301 F.2d 929, 944 (C.C.P.A. 1962) (reasoning that the instant publications were incapable of placing these roses in the public domain by their descriptions when interpreted in the light of the knowledge possessed by plant breeders). In another case, however, the Federal Circuit held that "evidence of the foreign sale of a claimed reproducible plant variety may enable an otherwise non-enabled printed publication disclosing that plant, thereby creating a § 102(b) bar." *In re Elsner*, 381 F.3d 1125, 1128 (Fed. Cir. 2004).

12.2.1.3.2 Obviousness

Like utility patents, plant patents must also meet the nonobviousness requirement of § 103. In *Yoder*, 537 F.2d at 1378, the Fifth Circuit Court of Appeals recognized the challenge of applying the traditional three-part test for obviousness, as set out in *Graham v. John Deere Co.*, 383 U.S. 1 (1966), to plants. With respect to the first two criteria of the *Graham* framework—the scope and content of the prior art, and the differences between the prior art and the claims at issue—the Fifth Circuit noted that they could consider the characteristics of prior plants of the same general type, and the differences between the prior plants and the claims at issue. *See Yoder*, 537 F.2d at 1379. The Fifth Circuit, however, saw "no meaningful way to apply the third criterion to plants—i.e. the level of ordinary skill in the prior art." *Id.* As a result, the Fifth Circuit applied an "invention" requirement to the obviousness analysis, recognizing that "the 'invention' of a new plant is the discovery of new traits *plus* the foresight and appreciation to take the step of asexual reproduction." *Id.* at 1380 (emphasis in original). Courts have yet to address the manner and extent to which the Supreme Court's ruling in *KSR International v. Teleflex, Inc.*, 550 U.S. 398 (2007), applies to plant patents.

12.2.1.4 Remedies Under the Plant Patent Act

All of the remedies available for utility patent infringement are available for plant patent infringement, including royalties, lost profits, injunctions, and treble damages. *See* §§ 161, 281–297. The calculation of damage awards and considerations of equity in plant patent infringement cases mirror the theories developed in the course of utility patent litigation. For example, courts are reluctant to award increased damages in cases where the issue of patentability is close and litigated in good faith. *See Yoder*, 537 F.2d at 1383.

12.2.2 Plant Variety Protection

12.2.2.1 Determination of Infringement Under the PVPA

To prove infringement of a PVP certificate, the plaintiff must show by a preponderance of the evidence that the defendant committed one or more of the acts constituting infringement defined in 7 U.S.C. § 2541. *See Delta & Pine Land Co. v. The Sinkers Corp.*, 177 F.3d 1343, 1347 (Fed. Cir. 1999). Infringing acts include, for example, selling, importing, or exporting novel plant varieties.

Furthermore, a plaintiff must show marking or actual notice. *See* 7 U.S.C. § 2567. Thus, a plaintiff can only sue under the PVPA once the variety is distributed with notice of PVP pending or after the PVP certificate issues. *See Syngenta Seeds v. Delta Cotton Co-operative, Inc.*, 457 F.3d 1269, 1276 (Fed. Cir. 2006).

12.2.2.1.1 Essentially Derived Varieties

Unlike the utility patent system, the PVPA affords certificate holders little scope beyond the "disclosed embodiment." Although infringement of PVP certificates may extend to a variety "essentially derived from a protected variety" under 7 U.S.C. § 2541(c), this provision does not operate analogously to patent law's doctrine of equivalents.

This "essentially derived" provision prevents infringers from escaping liability merely by making trivial changes to a protected variety. In other words, the "essentially derived infringement" provision prevents one party from identifying a successful PVPA-protected variety, altering a nonessential characteristic of that PVPA-protected variety, and then undercutting the PVPA-holder's rights by selling the copy.

The statute defines "essentially derived variety" as a variety that "is predominantly derived from another variety or from a variety that is predominantly derived from the initial variety, while retaining the expression of the essential characteristics that result from the genotype or combination of genotypes of the initial variety." 7 U.S.C. § 2401(a)(3)(A)(i). The statute specifies that the PVPA infringement provisions extend not only to the protected variety, but also to "any variety that is essentially derived from a protected variety, unless the protected variety is an essentially derived variety." 7 U.S.C. § 2541(c)(1). In other words, the PVPA establishes two tiers of protection: an initial variety "A" (meaning a variety that is not essentially derived from other varieties) gets PVPA protection for all EDVs of that variety (A(1), A(2), A(3), etc.); while an essentially derived variety (A(2), for example) does not get PVPA protection for varieties essentially derived from it (and so would not get protection over A(3), for example). This is referred to as a principle of limited dependency. *See* Mark D. Janis, Herbert H. Jervis, & Richard Peet, Intellectual Property Law of Plants, ¶¶ 4.95–4.106.

12.2.2.1.2 PVPA Exemptions

The PVPA exempts various acts that might otherwise be considered infringement under § 2541. *See* 7 U.S.C. §§ 2542–2545.

Section 2542, known as the "Grandfather Clause," authorizes a person to reproduce or sell a plant variety if he or she developed that variety more than one year before the effective filing date of the adverse application for a PVP certificate. For this section to apply, the person must at least have a good-faith claim to the seed variety at issue or be a successor in interest to the original developer. *See N. Star Genet-*

ics, Ltd. v. Bata, No. CIV. A3-00-57, 2001 WL 1820380, 2001 U.S. Dist. LEXIS 20065, at *5–6 (D.N.D. Aug. 9, 2001).

Section 2543 is the "saved seed" provision, also known as the crop exemption, and authorizes a person to save seeds of a legally purchased plant variety, if the seed is replanted on the purchaser's own property. The current provision came into effect in 1995 as a result of 1994 legislation. Prior to that time, some growers took the position that the saved seed exemption permitted growers to save and resell seed in unlimited amounts to other farmers, but that view was rejected even under the pre-1994 version of the provision in *Asgrow Seed Co. v. Winterboer*, 513 U.S. 179 (1995).

Section 2544, usually referred to as the breeder's exemption, exempts from infringement the "use and reproduction of a protected variety for plant breeding and other bona fide research." Because the PVPA includes a separate provision exempting "any act done privately and for noncommercial purposes," 7 U.S.C. § 2541(e), it is clear that the breeder's exemption extends to commercial activity in the form of plant breeding using a protected variety to create another variety. This section has been interpreted to permit a breeder's competitor to use the protected seed to create new varieties without permission. *See Monsanto Co. v. Byrd*, No. 7:99-CV-154-F1, 2000 WL 33952260, 2000 U.S. Dist. LEXIS 22793, at *10 (E.D.N.C. Dec. 11, 2000).

Section 2545 is directed to carriers and advertisers, the scope of which has yet to be determined by courts.

12.2.2.2 Invalidity of PVP Certificates

Similar to a utility or plant patent, a PVP certificate enjoys a presumption of validity. *See* 7 U.S.C. § 2561 ("If a variety is sold under the name of a variety shown in a certificate, there is a prima facie presumption that it is the same variety."). As a defense to infringement, the defendant bears the burden to establish invalidity of the PVP certificate. *See Genecorp, Inc. v. Progeny Advanced Genetics, Inc.*, No. C 97-20706 RMW, 1998 WL 1108155, 1998 U.S. Dist. LEXIS 21910, at *12–13 (N.D. Cal. Apr. 14, 1998).

12.2.2.3 Remedies Under the PVPA

Courts may issue an injunction under 7 U.S.C. § 2563, as well as award monetary damages, treble damages, and reasonable attorney fees under 7 U.S.C. § 2564. *See, e.g.*, *Heart Seed Co. v. Seeds, Inc.*, No. C-84-336-SPM, 1987 WL 41982, 1987 U.S. Dist. LEXIS 13969, at *9–10 (E.D. Wash. Jan. 29, 1987) (discussing injunctive relief, reasonable royalty, lost profits, treble damages, and attorney fees); *Bud Antle, Inc. v. Scattini Seed Co.*, No. C-85-20699-WAI, 1985 WL 6440, 1985 U.S. Dist. LEXIS 12587, at *6–8 (N.D. Cal. Dec. 20, 1985). Courts, however, are precluded from awarding damages for infringement prior to the issuance of the PVP certificate if the court finds that the infringer had innocent intentions. *See* 7 U.S.C. § 2564(d); *see also BASF Agrochemical Prods. v. Unkel*, No. 05 CV 1478, 2006 WL 3533133, 2006 U.S. Dist. LEXIS 88672, at *16 (W.D. La. Dec. 7, 2006).

12.2.3 Utility Patent Issues Related to Plants

As discussed in previous chapters, courts will often have to determine infringement or invalidity of a utility patent. Recent utility patent cases involving plants have also focused on several important patent law doctrines, including exhaustion, tying and patent misuse, and indirect infringement.

12.2.3.1 Patent Exhaustion

In *Monsanto Co. v. McFarling* (*McFarling I*), 302 F.3d 1291, 1299 (Fed. Cir. 2002), the Federal Circuit held that the first sale doctrine of exhaustion of the patent right was not implicated where new seeds grown from the original batch had never been sold. *Id.* Specifically, the original sale of the seeds did not confer a license to construct new seeds. Since the new seeds were not sold by the patentee, they entailed no principle of patent exhaustion. *Id.*

In *Bowman v. Monsanto*, 133 S. Ct. 1761 (2013), the Supreme Court affirmed the Federal Circuit's holding that one who purchases patented seeds may not "reproduce them through planting and harvesting without the patent holder's permission." The *Bowman* case involved the use of genetically modified soybean seeds. *Id.* at 1764. Soybeans are considered "self-replicating," because when soybean seeds are planted, additional soybean seeds are produced, and each new generation of soybean seeds will have substantially the same traits as the previous generation. *Id.* at 1768–69. This is because soybeans tend to be self-pollinating.

The Supreme Court rejected Bowman's argument that the authorized sale of a product exhausted Monsanto's patent rights in the product. According to the Court, the exhaustion doctrine "restricts a patentee's rights only as to the 'particular article' sold; it leaves untouched the patentee's ability to prevent a buyer from making new copies of the patented item." *Id.* at 1766. The Court rejected the argument that exhaustion applied because the seeds in question naturally self-replicate unless stored in a controlled manner and thus it was the soybeans and not Bowman that caused the invention to be practiced. The Court dismissed the "blame-the-seed" defense, noting that Bowman saved the seeds for replanting and replanted them, thereby controlling the reproduction of Monsanto's patented invention. *See id.* at 1768–69. The Court noted, however, that its holding was limited to these facts and did not necessarily govern how the exhaustion doctrine would apply to other self-replicating technologies. *See id.* at 1769.

12.2.3.2 Patent Misuse

The Federal Circuit addressed the issue of tying and patent misuse in *Monsanto Co. v. McFarling* (*McFarling II*), 363 F.3d 1336 (Fed. Cir. 2004). The court held that a contractual prohibition on the replanting of second generation seeds does not impermissibly extend a patentee's rights, where the patent at issue also reads on the second and all subsequent generations of seeds. *See id.* at 1343.

12.2.3.3 Indirect Infringement

Courts have also found indirect patent infringement of utility plant patents under an inducement theory. For example, the Northern District of Indiana addressed the issue of inducement in a plant case, holding that the cleaning of patent-protected seeds in furtherance of unauthorized replanting constituted an inducement of patent infringement. *See Monsanto Co. v. Parr*, 545 F. Supp. 2d 836, 842 (N.D. Ind. 2008) (issuing a permanent injunction to halt the unauthorized seed cleaning).

12.2.4 Other Plant-Related IP Issues: Variety Names and Trademarks

When dealing with plant-related intellectual property cases, courts often encounter variety name and trademark issues.

When a new plant variety is developed, the varietal name for the new variety is differentiated from a trademark or brand that is intended to be used ultimately to market the variety. The Convention of the International Union for the Protection of New Plant Varieties (UPOV), to which the United States is a party, requires that "each new plant variety shall be designated by a denomination which will be its generic designation." *See* Convention of the International Union for the Protection of New Plant Varieties, art. 20, Mar. 19, 1991, U.S.T. 104–17 [hereinafter UPOV]. UPOV further requires that each member of the Union register the generic designation of the new plant variety at the same time it issues the protection for the new variety. *Id.* Accordingly, under United States law, the generic or varietal designation must be listed in the plant patent application or application for a PVP certificate covering the new plant material. *See* USPTO, Manual of Patent Examining Procedure § 1612 (8th ed. 2010); *see also* U.S. Department of Agriculture, Agricultural Marketing Service, http://www.ams.usda.gov (providing information about the USDA guidelines for PVP applications).

UPOV provides criteria on the selection of the new varietal, which requires that it (1) not mislead or cause confusion concerning the nature of the variety of the identity of the breeder, (2) not interfere with prior rights of third parties, including trademark rights of third parties, and (3) differs from all other denominations used by other members of UPOV for the same or closely related categories of plants. UPOV, art. 20. Examination of varietal names is somewhat *ad hoc* in the United States as there is no registry of all varietal name designations that exist in the United States. UPOV has a database on CD-ROM of varietal names designated in plant variety protection applications that can be ordered from the UPOV site. *See* International Union for the Protection of New Varieties of Plants, http://www.upov.int. In addition, there are various databases specific to certain plant categories that may be examined to help locate conflicts.

The USPTO examiners will review the UPOV database and United States patent and trademark filings to determine whether a varietal designation can be accepted. Likewise, the USDA will "pre-clear" a varietal name intended to be included in an application for a PVP certificate. The failure of the USPTO or USDA to identify a conflict does not insulate the applicant from a challenge from a third party who might object to the use of the varietal name on the ground that it conflicts or causes confusion with respect to an existing varietal designation or trademark right.

While patent and PVP certificate holders may have exclusivity of use of the generic designation while the rights of the PVP or patent are valid and only those rights holders can market and sell the protected variety, when those rights expire the generic or varietal designation may be used by competitors in connection with their own use and sale of the formerly protected varietal. *See In re KRB Seed Co.*, 76 U.S.P.Q.2d (BNA) 1156 (T.T.A.B. 2005) (recognizing that the PVPA and UPOV require that once a breeder's protection period for a new plant expires, those who sell plants must be able to call the plant by its varietal name so that consumers will know what they are buying). It is not possible to extend the exclusivity in using the generic designation beyond the life of the plant protection by asserting trademark rights in the varietal designation. UPOV, art. 20 ("Each contracting state shall ensure that . . . no rights in the designation registered as the denomination of the variety shall hamper the free use of the denomination in connection with the variety, even after expiration of the breeder's right.").

Any application to register a trademark relating to a plant or varietal that consists of a term that was used as the varietal designation in a PVP certificate or plant patent for that plant or varietal will be rejected by the USPTO. *See* USPTO, Trademark Manual of Examining Procedure § 1202.12 (7th ed.) ("If the examining attorney determines that wording sought to be registered as a mark for live plants, agricultural seeds, fresh fruits or vegetables comprises a varietal or cultivar name, then the examining attorney must refuse registration, or require a disclaimer, on the ground that the matter is a varietal name of the goods and does not function as a trademark . . . ."); *see also In re Pennington Seed, Inc.*, 466 F.3d 1053 (Fed. Cir. 2006) (affirming the USPTO's refusal to register REBEL as a trademark for use on grass and grass seed owing to the fact that REBEL was designated in a PVP certificate as varietal name, despite evidence of extensive marketing and advertising of term by applicant).

Chapter 13
Patent Suits Against the United States

13.1 Introduction

13.1.1 Legal Foundation

For over a century, 28 U.S.C. § 1498 (2012) has allowed patent owners to assert patents against the United States for unauthorized use of patented inventions. Patent infringement claims against the United States are based in eminent domain, not tort.[1] Although patent infringement has long been understood as a tort, the United States has not consented to be sued for patent infringement on a tort theory. *See Schillinger v. United States*, 155 U.S. 163 (1894). And, as a sovereign entity, the United States is immune from suit without consent. *See United States v. Mitchell*, 445 U.S. 535, 538 (1980). Congress has instead "authorize[d] the Government to take, through exercise of its power of eminent domain, a license in any United States patent." *Decca Ltd. v. United States*, 640 F.2d 1156, 1166 (Ct. Cl. 1980). "[T]he sole

1. *See Leesona Corp. v. United States*, 599 F.2d 958 (Ct. Cl. 1979); *see also Crozier v. Fried. Krupp Aktiengesellschaft*, 224 U.S. 290, 307 (1912) ("[W]e think there is no room for doubt that [Section 1498] makes full and adequate provision for the exercise of the power of eminent domain for which considered in its final analysis it was the purpose of the statute to provide."); *Motorola, Inc. v. United States*, 729 F.2d 765, 768 (Fed. Cir. 1984) ("This is a 28 U.S.C. § 1498 action, and as such, the patent owner is seeking to recover just compensation for the Government's unauthorized taking and use of his invention. The theoretical basis for his recovery is the doctrine of eminent domain."); *Irving Air Chute Co. v. United States*, 93 F. Supp. 633, 635 (Ct. Cl. 1950) ("The Government urges, rightly, that 28 U.S.C.A. § 1498, is in effect, an eminent domain statute . . . .").

remedy available to a patentee for an eminent domain taking of a license in his patent" is an action for monetary recovery under § 1498. *Id.* That action must be brought in the United States Court of Federal Claims.

13.1.2 United States Court of Federal Claims

The United States Court of Federal Claims is an Article I court, with judges appointed to fifteen-year terms. Because there are no juries in the Court of Federal Claims, all patent cases are tried to the bench. Although the court is based in Washington, D.C., it has nationwide jurisdiction and subpoena power. Accordingly, it can, and often does, sit anywhere in the nation that makes sense—given the location of trial witnesses—to minimize plaintiffs' expenses. The court has also scheduled sessions out of town to hear a group of witnesses, such as those called in the plaintiff's case, and then reconvened in Washington, D.C., to hear the government's witnesses. When the court sits outside of Washington, D.C., it borrows other districts' courtrooms.

13.1.2.1 History

The U.S. Court of Federal Claims traces its existence to its predecessor, the United States Court of Claims,[2] which was created by the Act of February 24, 1855. Ch. 122, 10 Stat. 612 (1855) (amended by the Act of March 3, 1863, 12 Stat. 765 (1863) to permit the court to issue final judgments). The Court of Claims was intended to relieve pressure on Congress from claimants' requests for private bills providing for relief. *See* Stanton J. Peelle, *History and Jurisdiction of the United States Court of Claims*, 19 Recs. of the Colum. Hist. Soc. 1 (1916). At that time, however, it consisted of three judges who would investigate claims and provide proposed legislation to Congress to pay claims. James F. Davis, U.S. Court of Claims Patent Practice 2 (3d ed. Patent Res. Grp. 1970); *see also Pocono Pines Assembly Hotels Co. v. United States*, 73 Ct. Cl. 447 (1932). Thus, as originally established, it lacked the judicial power to enter judgments.

In the Act of March 3, 1863, at the urging of President Lincoln, Congress empowered the Court of Claims to adjudicate claims and enter judgments. 12 Stat. 765 (1863). It also increased the size of the court to four associate judges and a chief judge. *See Pocono Pines*, 73 Ct. Cl. at 467–68. In 1887, Congress passed the Tucker Act, which firmly established the Court of Claims' jurisdiction to hear cases arising under implied or express contracts, or under the Constitution or any statute, not

---

2. The United States Court of Appeals for the Federal Circuit also traces its existence to the Court of Claims. *See* Federal Courts Improvement Act of 1982, Pub. L. No. 97-164, § 133, 96 Stat. 40 (1982). The Federal Circuit assumed the appellate functions of the Court of Claims, while its trial responsibilities were passed on to the Court of Federal Claims (which was formerly known as the United States Claims Court). *See id.* §§ 101, 105(a), 96 Stat. 25, 27; Federal Courts Administration Act of 1992, Pub. L. No. 102-572, § 902, 106 Stat. 4506, 4516 (1992).

sounding in tort. Ch. 359, § 1, 24 Stat. 505 (1887) (codified at 28 U.S.C. § 1491 (2012)).

13.1.2.2 General Statistics

During fiscal year 2014, the Court of Federal Claims disposed of 703 complaints, as well as 562 petitions filed under the vaccine compensation program. *Report to the Administrative Office of U.S. Courts for FY 2014, available at* http://www.uscfc.uscourts.gov/sites/default/files/AO2014Stats.pdf. The total amount of judgments rendered by the court was nearly $13 billion. *Id.* In addition to monetary judgments, the court disposed of 124 contract cases in which injunctive or declaratory relief was sought. *Id.*

While the bulk of the court's caseload consists of contract cases (not including vaccine cases, which are handled by special masters), there were eighteen copyright and patent cases filed in Fiscal Year (FY) 2014. During FY 2014, there were fifteen copyright and patent cases disposed of, leaving thirty-eight such cases pending. *Id.* at 2.

There are eleven active judges on the Court of Federal Claims, along with seven senior judges. *See Judges – Biographies*, Fed. Cl., *available at* http://www.uscfc.uscourts.gov/judicial-officers (last visited Feb. 4, 2016). There are pending nominations for four others to become active judges. *See* U.S. Senate, *Judicial Nominations*, *available at* http://www.judiciary.senate.gov/nominations/judicial (last visited Feb. 4, 2016).

13.2 Jurisdiction

13.2.1 Scope of § 1498

Section 1498 confers upon the Court of Federal Claims exclusive jurisdiction for patent infringement actions against the United States. *See Crater Corp. v. Lucent Techs. Inc.*, 255 F.3d 1361, 1364 (Fed. Cir. 2001). This includes jurisdiction over use or manufacture of a patented invention "by" or "for" the United States. A government contractor's use of an invention shall be deemed use "for" the United States if the use was "for the Government and with the authorization and consent of the Government." 28 U.S.C. § 1498(a).

13.2.1.1 Historical Development

Prior to 1910, the Court of Claims did not have jurisdiction to hear patent infringement claims. 12 Stat. 765 (1863). While the Court of Claims had heard cases founded upon an implied contract with the patent owner under which an agreement to pay for use of an invention could be inferred, it lacked jurisdiction to hear general claims of patent infringement by the government. *Leesona Corp. v. United States*, 599 F.2d 958, 966 (Ct. Cl. 1979). In *Schillinger v. United States*, 155 U.S. 163 (1894), the Court held that patent infringement was a tort for which the Court of Claims lacked jurisdiction, and also held that it was not cognizable as a Fifth Amendment takings claim.

In 1910, Congress established a remedy for the recovery of reasonable compensation whenever an invention described in and covered by a patent was used by the United States without authorization or lawful right. 36 Stat. 851 (1910). Consistent with the Court of Claims' jurisdiction to render money judgments against the government, the remedy provided was reasonable compensation and not injunctive relief. *See Leesona*, 599 F.2d at 966–67. This remedy is based on the government's eminent domain power to take property, and reasonable compensation has been viewed as equivalent to just compensation under the Fifth Amendment. *Id.* at 967.

The Act of 1910, however, left the government's contractors also exposed to infringement suits, which could result in an injunction that could delay or prevent the government from obtaining needed materials or supplies. *See Cramp & Sons v. Int'l Curtis Marine Turbine*, 246 U.S. 28 (1918) (enjoining government contractor). During World War I, naval manufacturers expressed concern about patent infringement suits. *See Zoltek Corp. v. United States*, 672 F.3d 1309, 1315–16 (Fed. Cir. 2012). Acting Secretary of the Navy Franklin D. Roosevelt observed that these manufacturers faced the threat of "prohibitive injunction payment of royalties" and "punitive damages," instead of the "just and adequate compensation" available to patentees in the Court of Claims. *Id.* Congress reacted quickly, amending the Act of 1910:

> [W]henever an invention described in and covered by a United States patent shall . . . be used or manufactured by or for the United States without . . . lawful right . . . such owner's remedy shall be by suit in the United States Court of Claims for the recovery of his reasonable and entire compensation for such use and manufacture.

Act of July 1, 1918, Pub. L. No. 65-182, 40 Stat. 704, 705 (1918). In providing this remedy, Congress sought to avoid harm to the war effort by providing that the entire remedy for unauthorized use or manufacture of a patented invention lay against the government for the recovery of reasonable compensation. *See Leesona*, 599 F.2d at 967.

Courts considering claims under the Act of 1918 voiced some concerns over the government being subjected to liability for patent infringement that it did not intend. This led to the concept of authorization or consent as a limitation on the extent to which a government contractor might be insulated from any private suit for patent infringement. *See Wood v. Atl. Gulf & Pac. Co.*, 296 F. 718 (S.D. Ala. 1924). In turn, statutory language was added to § 1498(a) stating that

> the use or manufacture of an invention described in and covered by a patent of the United States by a contractor, subcontractor, or any person, firm or corporation for the Government and with the authorization or consent of the Government, shall be construed as use or manufacture for the United States.

13.2.1.2 Authorization and Consent

A common way to confer authorization and consent is to include a provision in the contract, which is required to be included ("flowed down") in subcontracts. The Federal Acquisition Regulations (FAR) prescribe two main authorization and consent provisions—a broad one used for research and development contracts, and a narrower one for procurement contracts. The "broad clause," referred to as FAR 52.227-1 Alternate I, is required for R&D contracts and simply confers authorization and consent for "all manufacture and use" of a patented invention in performance of the contract or any subcontract. The narrower clause in FAR 52.227-1 applies to contracts for procurement of supplies or services, and in its current form provides authorization and consent for manufacture or use of any patented invention (1) embodied in an article delivered to and accepted by the government, or (2) resulting from use of machinery, tools, methods required by contract specs and provisions, or a contracting officer's written direction.

In the absence of an express contractual provision, authorization and consent can be implied only in limited circumstances "where particular government specifications required a particular patent infringement." *Windsurfing Int'l v. Ostermann*, 534 F. Supp. 581, 588 (S.D.N.Y. 1982); *see also Auerbach v. Sverdrup Corp.*, 829 F.2d 175, 177 (D.C. Cir. 1987) ("[T]he government waiver of immunity by authorization and consent requires explicit acts or extrinsic evidence sufficient to prove the government's intention to accept liability for a specific act of infringement."); *Larson v. United States*, 26 Cl. Ct. 365, 368–69 (1992) (same). "[I]f the government requirements can be satisfied without an infringement, authorization or consent [for patent infringement] will not be implied," *Windsurfing Int'l*, 534 F. Supp. at 588, because "governmental waivers of liability must be construed narrowly," *Auerbach*, 829 F.2d at 179. Further, authorization and consent will not be implied if the governmental benefit from infringement is "too remote." *See Windsurfing Int'l*, 534 F. Supp. at 588 (holding that the government's general interest in the success of the Olympic Games was "simply too remote from the purposes underlying § 1498 to support the conclusion that the use of sailboards [at the Games] is use 'for' the United States entitling the patentee to sue the government for compensation."); *Larson*, 26 Cl. Ct. at 368–69 (holding that the federal government's general interest in Medicare did not mean that medical devices used to treat Medicare patients were used "for" the government); *see also Riles v. Amerada Hess Corp.*, 999 F. Supp. 938, 940 (S.D. Tex. 1998) (holding that even though the federal government had a national interest in developing public lands and derived a royalty from a lease for private drilling on those public lands, the drilling was not performed "for the government" under § 1498 because "the primary purpose of § 1498(a) is to allow the United States Government to purchase goods and services for performance of Governmental functions").

Where the government has accepted delivery of and used an allegedly infringing device, however, courts have found implied authorization and consent. *See, e.g.*, *Stelma, Inc. v. Bridge Elec. Co.*, 300 F.2d 761, 762 (3d Cir. 1962); *Bereslavsky v. ESSO Standard Oil Co.*, 175 F.2d 148, 151 (4th Cir. 1949); *Croydon Co., Inc. v. Unique Furnishings, Ltd.*, 831 F. Supp. 480, 484–85 (E.D.N.C. 1993). *See generally* 5 Donald Chisum, Chisum on Patents, § 16.06[3][c] at 16–289 (2004). In such a case, the government could be subject to suit under § 1498 for its use of an allegedly infringing device, so these holdings avoid the prospect of the government's supplier also being subject to suit for making the device that was delivered to the government.

Finally, courts have found authorization and consent where the government has intervened in an action and asserts that authorization and consent exists. *See Ad-*

vanced Software Design Corp. v. Fed. Reserve Bank of St. Louis, 583 F.3d 1371, 1377–78 (Fed. Cir. 2009); *see also IRIS Corp. v. Japan Airlines Corp.*, 769 F.3d 1359, 1362 (Fed. Cir. 2014) (holding that authorization and consent existed where the government agreed that the statute required performance of allegedly infringing activities).

13.2.2 Interplay with District Court Jurisdiction

13.2.2.1 Section 1500's Bar on Simultaneous Suits

One aspect of litigating patent claims against the government that differs from private infringement actions is 28 U.S.C. § 1500, which prevents a plaintiff from simultaneously pursuing cases "based on substantially the same operative facts" in multiple jurisdictions against the United States or its proxy. *United States v. Tohono O'Odham Nation*, 131 S. Ct. 1723, 1731 (2011). The statute provides:

> The United States Court of Federal Claims shall not have jurisdiction of any claim for or in respect to which the plaintiff or his assignee has pending in any other court any suit or process against the United States or any person who, at the time when the cause of action alleged in such suit or process arose, was, in respect thereto, acting or professing to act, directly or indirectly under the authority of the United States.

28 U.S.C. § 1500.

The combined effect of §§ 1498 and 1500 can limit plaintiffs' abilities to seek redress for injuries. For example, in *Croydon Co., Inc. v. Unique Furnishings, Ltd.*, 831 F. Supp. 480 (E.D.N.C. 1993), a plaintiff asserted claims against a government contractor for violating its patent rights, the Lanham Act, and state unfair-competition laws. The court held that it could not hear the patent count because § 1498 vested the Court of Federal Claims with exclusive jurisdiction over patent claims. *Id.* at 486–87. Section 1500, however, prevented the court from transferring the patent count to the Court of Federal Claims while the Lanham Act and unfair competition counts remained pending in the district court because all three counts arose out of the same operative facts. *Id.* at 489–90.

In *Trusted Integration, Inc. v. United States*, 659 F.3d 1159 (Fed. Cir. 2011), however, the Federal Circuit held that a previously filed district court complaint against the government, which alleged Lanham Act and breach of fiduciary duty counts, created a § 1500 bar to a suit in the Court of Federal Claims for counts alleging breach of implied contract and breach of the duty of good faith, but did not bar the suit from proceeding on a breach of express contract count. While there was some overlap in the allegations pleaded in both actions, the Federal Circuit held that the allegations in the district court complaint would not have sufficed to establish liability for the surviving count of the Court of Federal Claims action. *See id.* at 1170.

13.2.2.2 Section 1498 as a Defense

Government contractors sued outside the Court of Federal Claims can assert § 1498 as an "affirmative defense rather than a jurisdictional bar" to suit. *Toxgon Corp. v. BNFL, Inc.*, 312 F.3d 1379, 1381 (Fed. Cir. 2002). *But see O'Rourke v. Smith-*

sonian Inst. Press, 399 F.3d 113, 123 (2d Cir. 2005) (affirming dismissal based on lack of subject-matter jurisdiction).

13.3 Substantive Differences Between Patent Suits in District Court and the Court of Federal Claims

In § 1498(a) actions for unauthorized use or manufacture of a patented invention, the Court of Federal Claims applies the same principles and substantive law that governs private patent infringement actions. *Lemelson v. United States*, 752 F.2d 1538, 1548 (Fed. Cir. 1985). Many of the procedural practices in pretrial disclosure of infringement and invalidity contentions, and *Markman* hearing practice in the Court of Federal Claims, are similar, if not identical, to those used by district courts. However, the eminent domain underpinnings of § 1498 actions lead to several substantive differences between patent infringement actions in district courts and those in the Court of Federal Claims.

13.3.1 Infringement

Infringement suits against the government under § 1498 are limited to the types of infringement over which the government has consented to suit. *See, e.g.*, *Motorola, Inc. v. United States*, 729 F.2d 765, 769 n.3 (Fed. Cir. 1984) (holding that the United States has not consented to indirect infringement suits brought under 35 U.S.C. § 271(b) & (c) (2012)). The limited nature of this sovereign immunity waiver leaves open the possibility that a patentee may have no statutory remedy for acts defined as infringement under § 271 that do not find corresponding language in 28 U.S.C § 1498(a).

It is unsettled whether the Fifth Amendment provides such a patentee with a constitutional remedy. The Federal Circuit held that there was no Fifth Amendment remedy for such infringement. *Zoltek Corp. v. United States*, 442 F.3d 1345 (Fed. Cir. 2006), *vacated on other grounds*, *Zoltek Corp. v. United States*, 672 F.3d 1309, 1317 (Fed. Cir. 2012) (en banc in part). The reasoning contained in the now-vacated panel decision has been criticized for applying an obsolete understanding of the Fifth Amendment. *See* Justin Torres, Note, *The Government Giveth and The Government Taketh Away: Patents, Takings, and 28 U.S.C. § 1498*, 63 NYU Annual Survey of Am. L. 315 (2008). On the other hand, the government, in opposing a petition for certiorari from the *Zoltek* panel decision contended, *inter alia*, that because patent rights are a creature of federal statute, any statutory limitations on them define the property right, rather than constitute a taking of some preexisting right. Brief for the United States in Opposition at 19, *Zoltek Corp. v. United States* (No. 06-1155), *available at* http://www.justice.gov/sites/default/files/osg/briefs/2006/01/01/2006-1155.resp.pdf.

13.3.2 Third-Party Practice

Although the government assumes the liability of its contractors through § 1498, many contractors in turn indemnify the government for patent infringement. Court of Federal Claims Rule 14 offers a mechanism for providing notice to interested parties, such as third-party indemnitors. Because indemnitors may be bound by infringement and validity determinations reached in the Court of Federal Claims, government contractors frequently elect to join the case as third-party defendants by filing answers and asserting affirmative defenses. Third-party defendants, however, are not permitted to assert counterclaims. *Rolls-Royce Ltd. v. United States*, 364 F.2d 415, 417–18 (Ct. Cl. 1966).

The Federal Circuit, in *In re Uusi LLC*, 549 F. App'x 964 (Fed. Cir. 2013), reaffirmed the vitality of Rule 14(b) as a means of providing notice to a potentially interested third-party and affording an opportunity to enter the case, even though the prior statute that explicitly authorized this procedure, 41 U.S.C. § 114(b) (2012), had been repealed when Title 41 was reenacted.

In this regard a third-party defendant, while it may participate in the defense of a § 1498 action, has a more limited role than a third-party defendant has in a private infringement action. *In re Uusi*, 549 F. App'x at 967 (citing *Penda Corp. v. United States*, 44 F.3d 967, 970–71 (Fed. Cir. 1994)). The government will retain control of the litigation, as required by 28 U.S.C. § 516, but the third-party defendant can offer additional evidence and advance arguments on its behalf. *See Penda*, 44 F.3d at 970. A third-party defendant may not, however, appeal from an adverse judgment of the Court of Federal Claims where the government has declined to appeal. *See id.* at 971.

13.3.3 Damages

Section 1498's roots in eminent domain limit the damages theories available to patentees in the Court of Federal Claims. Damages claims under § 1498 usually cannot be based on the benefit the patented invention conferred on the government because "the proper measure in eminent domain is what the owner has lost, not what the taker has gained." *Leesona*, 599 F.2d at 969; *Dow Chem. Co. v. United States*, 226 F.3d 1334, 1338 (Fed. Cir. 2000). Thus, a reasonable royalty is the normal measure of compensation in § 1498 actions. Although lost profits have not been awarded in a § 1498 action since the 1930's, the Federal Circuit in *Gargoyles, Inc. v. United States*, 113 F.3d 1572, 1575–77 (Fed. Cir. 1997), declined to hold that lost profits could never be awarded in a § 1498 action.

Section 1498 establishes that patentees are entitled to "reasonable and entire compensation" for the unauthorized use of their inventions. That standard has been equated to just compensation under the Fifth Amendment, in light of the eminent domain foundation of § 1498. *See Motorola*, 729 F.2d at 768, n.3. Thus, reasonable compensation would include compensation for the taking of the patent license, normally in the form of a reasonable royalty, along with "delay compensation" as remuneration for the government's delay in taking the license. *See Decca Ltd. v. United States*, 640 F.2d 1156, 1167–68 (Ct. Cl. 1980). However, enhanced damages for willful infringement are not available against the government, and willfulness is not an issue in § 1498 cases. *See Leesona*, 599 F.2d at 969.

In determining a reasonable royalty, the Court of Federal Claims has considered the likely outcome of a hypothetical negotiation and weighed evidence relating to the

Georgia-Pacific factors. *See Gargoyles*, 113 F.3d at 1580–81. In this regard, a determination of a reasonable royalty in § 1498 cases parallels the same determination in a private infringement action. *See* § 14.4.3.2.1.4. Likewise, when plaintiffs have sought lost profits as the measure of reasonable compensation, the Court of Federal Claims has examined the various factors set forth in *Panduit Corp. v. Stahlin Bros. Fibre Works*, 575 F.2d 1152, 1156 (6th Cir. 1978) (the *Panduit* factors). *See, e.g.*, *Gargoyles*, 113 F.3d at 1577–79.

13.3.4 Costs and Attorney Fees

Section 1498(a) provides for an award of reasonable costs, including attorney and expert witness fees, to certain plaintiffs prevailing in patent cases. The award of reasonable costs is provided to successful claimants who are independent inventors, non-profit organizations, or entities having fewer than 500 employees during the five years preceding the date when the government first manufactured or used the patented invention.

However, where the action has been pending in the Court of Federal Claims for ten years or less, the statute only raises a presumption of entitlement to reasonable costs and attorneys' fees. The government may rebut this presumption by showing that the position of the United States was substantially justified or that specific circumstances exist that would make such an award unjust. The presumption of entitlement and the showing that is necessary to overcome that presumption are identical to the provisions of the Equal Access to Justice Act. *See* 28 U.S.C. § 2412(d). The presumption becomes irrebuttable when the case has been pending before the court for more than ten years.

The award of reasonable costs under § 1498 is made as part of the "reasonable and entire compensation" awarded for the government's manufacture or use of the patented invention. As such, the award of reasonable costs is made as part of a comprehensive judgment on the merits and not the result of a separate proceeding.

13.4 Early Case Management

The Court of Federal Claims has its own rules (RCFC), which largely mirror the Federal Rules of Civil Procedure. The current set of rules is available at http://www.uscfc.uscourts.gov/rules. RCFC 16 governs the Court of Federal Claims' scheduling and early case management. It, in turn, refers to submission of a Joint Preliminary Status Report (JPSR) within forty-nine days of the filing of an answer. RCFC 16(b)(1)(A); RCFC Appendix A § 4. The JPSR reflects the results of an early meeting of counsel to discuss various issues and attempt to arrive at a schedule to propose to the court.

The Court of Federal Claims will normally schedule a preliminary status conference, either in person if counsel are local or, more often, over the telephone. These conferences are individually arranged for each case. Unlike larger district courts, the Court of Federal Claims does not normally hold status calls in which multiple cases are scheduled for brief status conferences at the same time. At a preliminary status conference, the court will discuss proposed scheduling and attempt to resolve differences.

While the Court of Federal Claims does not have a uniform pretrial order governing the exchange of infringement and invalidity contentions, along with proposed constructions of claim terms, the parties will usually propose a schedule that calls for these exchanges and leads to a *Markman* hearing. Some judges have used a pretrial schedule based generally on the local rules of the Northern District of California. *See* § 2.1.3.2.

13.5 Discovery

Discovery issues in the Court of Federal Claims are similar to those in district court practice. *See* Chapter 4. Unlike district courts, however, the Court of Federal Claims judges do not have magistrate judges to handle discovery matters. Thus, judges directly resolve disputes based on their individual practices. A common approach is for one or both parties to request a telephonic status conference to raise a dispute. While this can ultimately require a motion to be filed, the judge can, where appropriate, forgo formal procedures and resolve the dispute informally. Some judges have invited the parties to call, particularly if a dispute arises during a deposition.

In § 1498 cases, the problem of asymmetric burdens can arise, since the government can have numerous agencies involved in a given case and voluminous (and possibly redundant) records. Similarly, e-discovery, particularly of e-mail, can pose a problem. In several cases, an e-discovery order has been entered along the lines of the Federal Circuit Advisory Council's model e-discovery order (contained in Appendix 4.2).

At the conclusion of discovery, the Court of Federal Claims will hold a post-discovery conference to determine how the case will proceed to resolution, either by trial or possibly by dispositive motions. RCFC Appendix A § 11. If the case will proceed to trial, Appendix A sets forth a series of steps to be taken, including the submission of pretrial findings of fact and conclusions of law. *Id.* §§ 13–17. The court may, and often does, call for the submission of posttrial briefs along with findings of fact that are annotated with citations to the record. *Id.* § 18.

Chapter 14
Patent Law Primer

This chapter surveys the procedures for obtaining patents and the substantive law governing patent litigation. It also provides an overview of the patent system and a starting point for researching patent law. After reviewing an actual patent document, the chapter summarizes prosecution, the process through which the U.S. Patent and Trademark Office (USPTO) grants patents to inventors. Patent cases often require courts to examine the prosecution history that led to the issuance of a patent.

The prosecution section provides a window into the USPTO to provide an appreciation of how patents are examined. The chapter then reviews the law regarding patent validity. The right to exclude others from practicing an invention is available only if several requirements are met. The chapter then discusses patent enforcement: infringement of a patent claim, defenses to a charge of infringement, and remedies. The chapter concludes by examining the wider battlefield for patent litigation existing outside of the district court—the appellate process and proceedings before the International Trade Commission, the USPTO, other U.S. courts, and foreign courts. Appendix A provides a glossary of patent law terms. Appendix B lists common acronyms.

14.1 The Patent

A patent grants its owner the right to exclude others from making, using, selling, offering to sell, importing, or offering to import the claimed invention within or into the United States. § 271.[1] Because a patent provides only a right to exclude, a patentee does not have an affirmative right to practice the invention. Inventors sometimes cannot make their patented inventions without infringing other patents on underlying technology. Such blocking patents in turn spur substantial licensing activity. As befits a right to exclude, a patent "ha[s] the attributes of personal property." § 261.

Unlike copyrights or trade secrets, a patent must issue from the USPTO after a proper application has been made by the inventor. The requirements of patentability are set forth in Title 35 of the U.S. Code, reflecting the omnibus codification of patent law completed in 1952 as well as numerous subsequent amendments, the most substantial of which is the Leahy-Smith America Invents Act, Pub. L. No. 112-29, 125 Stat. 284 (2011) (AIA), enacted on September 16, 2011.

14.1.1 The Patent Document

Patents issued by the USPTO follow a common format dictated by the World Intellectual Property Organization (WIPO).

1. Unless otherwise indicated, all section references are to the Patent Act (35 U.S.C. (2012)).

Figure 14.1
Page One of a Standard Patent Application

US005205473A

United States Patent [19]

Coffin, Sr.

[11] **Patent Number: 5,205,473**

[45] **Date of Patent: Apr. 27, 1993**

[54] **RECYCLABLE CORRUGATED BEVERAGE CONTAINER AND HOLDER**

[75] Inventor: **David W. Coffin, Sr., Fayetteville, N.Y.**

[73] Assignee: **Design By Us Company, Philadelphia, Pa.**

[21] Appl. No.: **854,425**

[22] Filed: **Mar. 19, 1992**

[51] **Int. Cl.**[5] **B65D 3/28**

[52] **U.S. Cl.** .... **229/1.5 B**; 206/813; 220/441; 220/DIG. 30; 229/1.5 H; 229/DIG. 2; 493/296; 493/907

[58] **Field of Search** .... 229/1.5 B, 1.5 H, 4.5, 229/DIG. 2; 220/441, 671, 737–739, DIG. 30; 493/287, 296, 907, 908; 209/8, 47, 215; 206/813

[56] **References Cited**

U.S. PATENT DOCUMENTS

1,732,322	10/1929	Wilson et al.	220/DIG. 30
1,771,765	7/1930	Benson	229/4.5
2,266,828	12/1941	Sykes	229/1.5 B
2,300,473	11/1942	Winkle	229/4.5
2,501,815	3/1950	Hamm .	
2,617,549	11/1952	Egger .	
2,641,402	6/1953	Bruun	229/4.5
2,661,889	12/1953	Phinney	229/4.5
2,969,901	1/1961	Behrens	229/1.5 B
3,237,834	3/1966	Davis et al.	229/1.5 B
3,779,157	12/1973	Ross, Jr. et al.	53/527
3,785,254	1/1974	Mann .	
3,890,762	6/1975	Ernst et al. .	
3,908,523	9/1975	Shikaya	229/1.5 B
4,080,880	3/1978	Shikay	493/296
4,146,660	3/1979	Hall et al. .	
4,176,054	11/1979	Kelley	209/8
5,009,326	4/1991	Reaves et al. .	
5,092,485	3/1992	Lee	229/1.5 B

OTHER PUBLICATIONS

"The Wiley Encyclopedia of Packaging Technology", John Wiley & Sons, pp. 66–69, 1986.

Primary Examiner—Gary E. Elkins
Attorney, Agent, or Firm—Synnestvedt & Lechner

[57] **ABSTRACT**

Corrugated beverage containers and holders are which employ recyclable materials, but provide fluting structures for containing insulating air. These products are easy to hold and have a lesser impact on the environment than polystyrene containers.

18 Claims, 8 Drawing Sheets

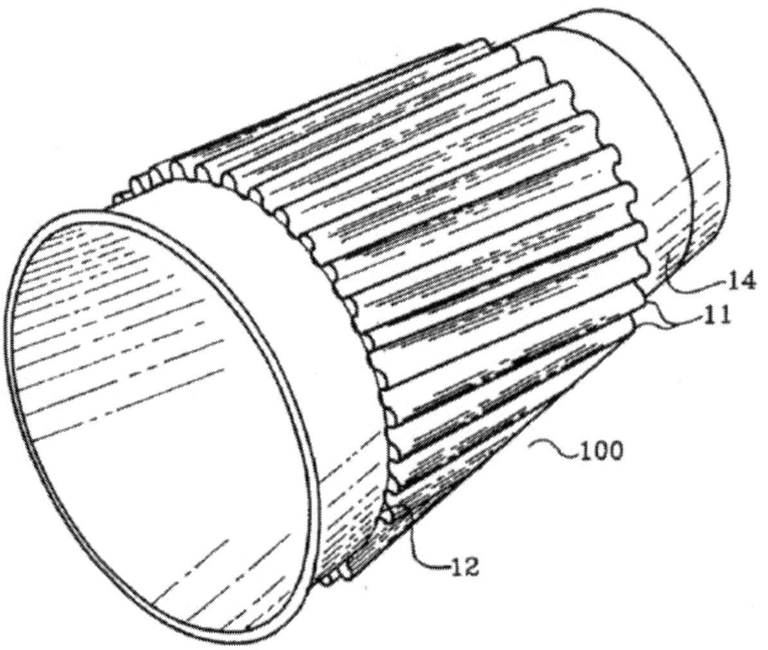

14.1.1.1 The First Page—Administrative Details

As reflected in Figure 14.1, the first page of a U.S. patent contains a header, an abstract, and a representative drawing. The header contains bibliographic information categorized using the Internationally (agreed) Numbers for the Identification of (bibliographic) Data (INID) classification system. Field 19 (labeled [19]) indicates the office or organization publishing the document, here the U.S. Patent Office. Field 11 shows the patent number. Every patent has a unique number assigned by the Patent Office in the order they issue. Parties often abbreviate patents to their last three numbers for convenience. Thus, Patent No. 5,205,473 becomes "the '473 patent." Field 45 contains the date the patent issued.

Fields 50–58 provide technical information, such as the domestic classification ([52]), title ([54]), a list of prior art documents cited during prosecution by the examiner or by the applicant ([56]), the abstract ([57]), and the technical field of search ([58]). The header also contains information showing the history and ownership of the patent. Fields 60–68 provide references to other legally or procedurally related domestic patent documents. (The '473 patent does not have any such references.) Fields 70–76 reveal the names of the inventors, assignees, and attorney or agents.

14.1.1.2 Drawings

Immediately following the first page are the drawings (if any), which illustrate the claimed invention. The drawings are routinely labeled with numbers to facilitate describing the invention and its components in the patent's specification.

14.1.1.3 The Specification

The specification describes the claimed invention. Section 112 lists a number of formal requirements that the specification must meet for a patent claim to be valid. *See* § 14.3.3. The specification begins by repeating the title of the invention, then listing any related patent applications. The specification typically proceeds by explaining the "field of the invention," another general description of the kind of invention the patent discloses. The "background of the invention" discusses the prior art in the field and the problems the prior art could not address. The "summary of the invention" briefly describes what the patentee has accomplished in the claimed invention. A "brief description of the drawings" commonly follows.

The "detailed description of the invention" is the heart of the specification and the "consideration" the public receives in exchange for the patent grant. It seeks to describe the invention in such detail that a person having ordinary skill in the art could practice the invention. It often explains the invention by explaining the drawings. All specifications must also disclose the "preferred embodiments" and "best mode" for practicing the invention.

14.1.1.3.1 Claims

The specification concludes with claims. The claims are commonly analogized to the "metes and bounds" of a property deed and serve the same purpose: to delineate the scope of the asset which, in the patent context, is an invention. Each claim represents the legal right to exclude others from making, using, selling, offering to sell, importing, or offering to import the claimed process, machine, manufacture, or composition of matter. A patent may, and often does, contain many claims, which usually become increasingly specific.

An "independent claim" stands on its own. A "dependent claim" refers to a single earlier claim or claims and adds further limitations. To understand all of the limitations of a dependent claim, it is necessary to read that claim together with the claim(s) on which it depends.

In a case for patent infringement, only some claims may be asserted. Some might not be infringed; further, some may even be invalid. It is important to recognize that each claim bestows distinct legal rights. Invalidity or noninfringement of one or more claims will not necessarily undermine other claims in the same patent.

Patent claims have a unique structure. Each claim must be stated as a single sentence. They begin with a preamble, which briefly describes the nature of the claimed invention. For example, a claim for a paper clip could begin, "A device for keeping papers together . . . ." In some circumstances, the preamble can act as an additional limitation on the scope of the claimed invention. *See* § 5.2.3.2.5.

The claim then has a transitional phrase, which demarcates the preamble from the list of restrictions or limitations that define the claimed invention. Patents often feature the same transitions, which have developed highly specific meanings in the case law. The transition "comprising" is understood to mean "including but not limited to"—that is, that the claim covers the listed limitations, as well as anything that includes all of the limitations and additional features. The transition "consisting of" means that the claim covers only the combination of the limitations listed and does not cover something that incorporates additional material along with all of the listed restrictions. The transition "consisting essentially of" covers not only products containing the recited limitations, but also those combining modest amounts of additional, unspecified substances, the presence of which would not materially affect the basic and novel properties of the expressly recited ingredients.

After the transition, the claim has a body that lists the limitations or restrictions of the claimed invention. Patentees typically use a method of peripheral claiming to delineate the outer boundaries of the claimed invention. Thus, the claim limitations or restrictions define what remains in the claim. The claim's body lists all of the features that must be present in the claimed invention and how these restrictions interact with each other.

As an illustration, consider a patent claim for a coffee cup insulator covered by the '473 patent illustrated in Table 14.1.

Table 14.1
Illustration of a Patent Claim

Preamble	A recyclable, insulating beverage container holder,
Transition	comprising
Body	a corrugated tubular member comprising cellulosic material and at least a first opening therein for receiving and retaining a beverage container, said corrugated tubular member comprising fluting means for containing insulating air; said fluting means comprising fluting adhesively attached to a liner with a recyclable adhesive.

Some claims contain words or structures, which, like the transitions, have specific, well-understood meanings. A means-plus-function claim defines one or more elements of the claim as a "means for [performing a] function," as allowed by § 112(f). This special type of claim format is interpreted based on how the structure, materials, or acts are described in the specification and to encompass "equivalents thereof" as of the time of filing. *See* §§ 5.2.3.5; 14.4.1.4.1.1.

Claims can follow other formats. As noted above, a dependent claim refers to one or several prior claim(s) and adds further limitations. A Jepson claim recites the elements of the prior art, then the transition "the improvement of which comprises," followed by the further restrictions that represent the advance over the prior art. A Markush claim covers a genus of related compositions sharing a common trait, such as "a chemical compound of the formula COOH–CH2-R, where R is selected from the group consisting of R_1, R_2, and R_3." Markush claims arise principally in the field of chemistry.

Interpreting the scope of claims is one of the principal challenges of patent litigation. The substantive law regarding how to interpret claim terms is presented in Chapter 5.

14.2 Patent Prosecution and the Patent Lifecycle

14.2.1 Institutional Aspects

14.2.1.1 The Patent Office

The USPTO is a federal agency in the Department of Commerce responsible for administering the patent and trademark laws. The USPTO's primary function is to examine inventors' applications and to determine whether to issue a patent. The USPTO also promulgates rules regarding the examination process and records all transfers of patent rights, in similar fashion to a state recordation office under Article 9 of the Uniform Commercial Code.

The USPTO employs over 7,000 scientists and engineers to examine patent applications. Examiners possess a science or engineering degree and are divided by Technology Centers (or group art units). A patent examiner need not hold a law degree, and the majority of patent examiners do not. The USPTO does, however, provide all examiners with training in patent law and procedure. New examiners also serve an apprenticeship period working with an experienced examiner.

The USPTO maintains an extensive website at http://www.uspto.gov/, which provides resources regarding the patent examination process and a searchable database of patents.

14.2.1.2 The Patent Bar

The USPTO requires practitioners who prepare and prosecute patent applications on behalf of others to pass a patent bar exam. To sit for the patent bar, applicants must possess scientific or technical training. One does not need to hold a law degree. Nonattorney members of the patent bar are called patent agents. Collectively, practitioners before the USPTO are known as patent prosecutors. The distinction between an inventor's prosecution counsel and trial counsel is critical to protective orders and the scope of attorney–client privilege. *See* §§ 4.2.5, 4.6.7–9.

Most litigated patents will have been drafted and prosecuted by a professional. Nonetheless, the USPTO does allow inventors to pursue their own application even if they have not passed the patent bar.

14.2.1.3 The Patent Trial and Appeal Board (PTAB)

The PTAB comprises the USPTO director, the deputy director, the commissioner for patents, the commissioner for trademarks, and administrative patent judges. Pursuant to the AIA § 7, the PTAB replaced the Board of Patent Appeals and Interferences (BPAI) as of September 16, 2012.[2] In addition to handling appeals from examiner rejections, the PTAB conducts several new administrative proceedings introduced under the AIA: postgrant review, covered business-method (CBM) review, inter partes review (IPR), and derivation proceedings. The PTAB also handles any interferences[3] or appeals of inter partes reexaminations that were filed before they were phased out under the AIA. Applicants may appeal decisions of the PTAB to the Federal Circuit.

The PTAB is often one of the first bodies to respond to changes in the substantive law of patent validity. For example, the PTAB was at the forefront of interpreting the Supreme Court's *KSR* opinion regarding obviousness. *KSR Int'l Co. v. Teleflex Inc.*, 550 U.S. 398 (2007). Despite the PTAB's familiarity with patent law, district courts owe its decisions no formal deference. Only the Federal Circuit creates binding precedent for the district courts when adjudicating patent cases. Nevertheless, the PTAB is an experienced and specialized agency tribunal such that a district court may find its rulings persuasive.

---

2. For the sake of consistency, this guide will use the acronym PTAB even when referring to the BPAI's decisions or actions before September 16, 2012.

3. An "interference proceeding" is an adversarial administrative adjudication that determines which of two or more inventors seeking a patent on the same invention has priority. *See* § 135. Any party to an interference proceeding that is dissatisfied with the PTAB decision can pursue a remedy in a district court. *See* § 146.

14.2.1.4 Laws Governing the USPTO and the Manual of Patent Examining Procedure (MPEP)

The patent statute is found in Title 35 of the U.S. Code. The USPTO's rules and regulations implementing the patent laws are codified in Title 37 of the Code of Federal Regulations.

The Manual of Patent Examining Procedure (MPEP) is the USPTO's operating manual for patent examiners. *See* http://www.uspto.gov/web/offices/pac/mpep/index.htm. Because most USPTO examiners are not attorneys, patent prosecutors will often cite the MPEP rather than case law during the course of patent prosecution. However, the MPEP does not carry the force of law.

Where the substantive patent law is uncertain, the USPTO issues guidelines to help examiners apply the law consistently. For example, there are guidelines governing the subject-matter requirement (MPEP § 2106), utility requirement (MPEP § 2107), and written description requirement (MPEP § 2163). Such guidelines represent the USPTO's interpretation of the law in those areas, but they are not substantive rulemaking and do not have the force and effect of law. While such guidelines may be persuasive on an issue, a district court is free to reach its own interpretation. Courts must, however, defer to USPTO interpretations of its procedures to the extent they are permissible under the governing statute. *See Cooper Techs. Co. v. Dudas*, 536 F.3d 1330, 1335–37 (Fed. Cir. 2008) (citing *Chevron U.S.A., Inc. v. Nat. Res. Def. Council, Inc.*, 467 U.S. 837 (1984)).

14.2.2 Filing a Patent Application

The process of patent procurement is commonly referred to as patent prosecution. Prosecution often consists of a lengthy and detailed interaction between the applicant and the USPTO examiner. During this process, the applicant attempts to convince the examiner that the applicant's invention meets the statutory requirements for patentability.

14.2.2.1 Overview of Patent Examination

Patent prosecution begins with an inventor having an idea that she believes is patentable. Although inventors may represent themselves before the USPTO, most retain a patent attorney or agent to prepare and prosecute their application. The application contains a description of the invention and claims outlining the bounds of the intellectual property right sought by the inventor. The prosecutor must also submit an Information Disclosure Statement (IDS) listing all prior art material to patentability of which the inventor or any person associated with prosecution is aware.

The USPTO assigns the application to an examiner in the most pertinent Technology Center. In addition to confirming that all formalities have been complied with, the examiner conducts a prior art search and assesses whether the proposed claims meet the requirements for patentability (§§ 101, 102, 103, and 112).

The first Office action almost always rejects the patent application. The examiner cites the relevant patent law authority and succinctly explains the reasons for rejection. At this point, the examiner bears the burden of establishing a prima facie case of unpatentability. The applicant then has the opportunity to respond to the Office action. *See* 37 C.F.R. § 1.111. Arguments made to overcome the examiner's rejections are commonly referred to as "traversing" the rejections. The applicant may argue that the examiner has mischaracterized the specification or the prior art and that the application, or portions thereof, should be allowed as submitted. In the alternative, the applicant may amend the claims.

The examiner may accept the applicant's amendments or arguments and allow the application in whole, or allow only some claims. If the applicant is unable to traverse, the examiner issues a so-called final rejection. In practice, the rejection is rarely the end of prosecution, which will generally continue until the applicant chooses to abandon the application or the examiner grants the claims. It is common for applicants to "continue" examination of the application, as discussed below. Alternatively, the applicant can appeal the examiner's rejection to the PTAB, and further still to the Federal Circuit.

Patent prosecution is an ex parte proceeding—only the applicant and the USPTO are directly involved. The examiner's actions play a significant role in shaping the contours of many patents. Patent prosecution operates much like a negotiation between the applicant and the USPTO.

The average prosecution pendency is three years, although it is not uncommon for prosecution to last five years or longer. The length of time required to prosecute the patent depends on any number of resource, strategic, and other factors and does not correlate with the "strength" of the patent claims.

Under the AIA, applicants may seek prioritized examination starting September 26, 2011 upon payment of an additional fee. AIA § 11. For applications considered important to the national economy or national competitiveness, the USPTO may prioritize examination at no extra cost to the applicant. AIA § 25.

14.2.2.2 The Application

Most applicants choose to file a nonprovisional patent application. Nonprovisional applications are the "regular" type of patent applications and are often referred to as "applications." Alternatively, applicants may file a provisional or Patent Cooperation Treaty (PCT) patent application prior to submission of the nonprovisional application. These types of applications are described further below.

14.2.2.2.1 Elements of a Nonprovisional Patent Application

The general requirements for a nonprovisional patent application include: (1) a written specification, including one or more claims; (2) an oath or declaration that the named inventor or inventors are believed to be the original and first inventor or inventors of the claimed subject matter; (3) drawings as required to support the application; and (4) applicable fees (e.g., filing fee, search fee, examination fee, and application-size fee). *See* 37 C.F.R. § 1.51; § 111; *see also* MPEP § 601.

Under the AIA, if an uncooperative or unavailable inventor is under an obligation to assign the invention, the assignee (who is typically the inventor's employer) may file a substitute statement in lieu of an oath or declaration. This provision became effective September 16, 2012, and applies to all applications filed on or after that date. AIA § 4.

14.2.2.2.2 Disclosure of Prior Art

14.2.2.2.2.1 Prior Art Disclosure by Applicant—Information Disclosure Statement

Applicants present prior art to the USPTO using an Information Disclosure Statement. *See* 37 C.F.R. § 1.97. The inventor and those assisting the inventor with the application process are not required to perform an exhaustive search of the prior art, but they must disclose all pertinent information of which they are aware. *See* 37 C.F.R. § 1.56. This requirement is part of the applicants' general duty of candor and good faith in dealing with the USPTO, which exists for the duration of patent prosecution. The USPTO will not issue a patent when faced with either fraudulent conduct or a failure to disclose material information through bad faith or intentional misconduct. *See id.* Such "inequitable conduct" can also render an issued patent unenforceable in later litigation. In some cases, applicants requesting accelerated examination must perform a preexamination search of the prior art and submit the results to the USPTO.

14.2.2.2.2.2 Prior Art Disclosure by Third Parties—Preissuance Submissions

The AIA provides a window during examination for third parties to submit prior art, along with a concise statement of relevance for each submitted document. These preissuance submissions became available September 16, 2012, for any applications pending on or filed after that date. AIA § 8.

14.2.2.2.3 Priority Date

The first filing of a patent application anywhere in the world describing an enabled invention usually establishes the "priority date" for that invention. The definition of prior art, which varies by country, is often keyed to the priority date. Some U.S. applications claim "foreign priority," which means that their priority date is derived from an earlier-filed foreign application.

With the enactment of the AIA, priority dates are treated differently for prior art purposes depending on whether the application was filed prior to March 16, 2013, under the first-to-invent regime, or on or after that date when the first-to-file rules govern. *See* § 14.3.4.

14.2.2.2.4 Nonstandard Applications

A patent application can also mature from several other types of filings. The most important is the provisional application. The USPTO began accepting provisional patent applications on June 8, 1995. *See* § 111(b). Provisional applications must contain a specification and required drawings, but need not contain claims or an oath or declaration. Provisional applications are less expensive to prepare and file than a nonprovisional application and preserve a priority filing date for a later filed nonprovisional application. Provisional applications are not examined by the USPTO and are subject to abandonment after twelve months.

An applicant can also file an application under the Patent Cooperation Treaty (PCT) to establish a priority date to an invention. Under the PCT, applicants can file a single application in a qualified patent office to initiate prosecution in all signatory countries. Over 130 nations have signed the PCT.

Finally, inventors can claim priority for U.S. patent applications based on filings in certain foreign countries, including any World Trade Organization (WTO) member state. *See* § 119. The applicant has twelve months from the time of the foreign filing to submit a U.S. national application claiming the same invention.

14.2.2.3 Restriction Requirements and Divisional Applications

If a nonprovisional application claims multiple independent and unique inventions, the examiner may "restrict" the application. *See* 37 C.F.R. § 1.142. Restriction requires the applicant to elect which invention it intends to pursue in the pending application. The other inventions can be examined in separate "divisional" applications that maintain the priority date of the original application. The examiner can also require a restriction if a reply to an office action introduces claims that are distinct from and independent of the invention previously claimed. *See* 37 C.F.R. § 1.145. The applicant can attempt to overcome the restriction requirement on the grounds that the examiner can assess all claims without performing an extra prior art search (*see* 37 C.F.R. § 1.143), but such arguments are typically unsuccessful. However, the examiner can also rejoin restricted claims upon allowance. Restriction is a procedural matter: a patent's validity does not depend on whether it claims multiple inventions. Restriction and division practice does, however, explain the typical manner in which one specification and written description can spawn a family of patents.

14.2.2.4 Publication

Until 2000, pending U.S. patent applications were held in secret by the USPTO until issuance. Under this system, patent applicants could draw out prosecution in secret for many years. Such "submarine" patents could emerge out of nowhere many years or even decades after filing, resulting in unfair surprise to others who began using the claimed invention during the secret pendency. Furthermore, if the patent did not issue or the inventor believed trade secrecy to be more advantageous than patenting, the applicant could abandon the application and maintain the invention as a trade secret.

The American Inventors Protection Act of 1999 brought the U.S. into harmony with most foreign patent offices by requiring the USPTO to publish nonprovisional patent applications eighteen months after their filing date. Published applications are available at the USPTO's website. *See* http://www.uspto.gov/patft/index.html. An applicant can opt out of publication only by certifying that the applicant has not and will not file any foreign applications on the same invention. Thus, applicants can maintain patent applications being pursued solely in the United States as trade secrets until issuance.

14.2.3 The Prosecution History or "File Wrapper"

The archive of written communications between the USPTO and the applicant during patent prosecution is called the "prosecution history" or "file wrapper." The file wrapper is available through the USPTO's Patent Application Information Retrieval (PAIR) system, *available at* http://portal.uspto.gov/external/portal/pair. This "procedural history" is important because, in addition to the patent's specification, correspondence between the patentee and the USPTO during prosecution is a primary source used to interpret claim language during litigation. *See Phillips v. AWH Corp.*, 415 F.3d 1303 (Fed. Cir. 2005) (en banc); § 5.2.2.1.1. Furthermore, the patentee is estopped from recovering through reexamination or during litigation (under the doctrine of equivalents) any subject matter surrendered during prosecution. The following sections explain the file wrapper's contents.

14.2.3.1 Office Actions

The patent examiner's responses are known as "office actions." These statements document the examiner's decisions and underlying reasons. The applicant can respond to the examiner's rejection arguments. This record of office actions and responses determines if and to what extent a patentee narrowed the scope of his or her claimed invention to overcome a rejection. It also bears on whether the patentee engaged in inequitable conduct. *See* § 14.4.2.3.1.

14.2.3.1.1 Affidavits

The applicant may attempt to overcome certain rejections through the use of affidavits. Rule 131 affidavits are used to establish inventorship before the date of prior art arising under § 102(a), (e), or (g). *See* 37 C.F.R. § 1.131. This process is known as "swearing behind" the prior art reference. Rule 131 requires an oath or declaration by the inventor along with supporting evidence. Misrepresentations in Rule 131 affidavits may violate the applicant's duty of good faith and candor, rendering the patent unenforceable. For patent applications subject to the first-to-file regime established under the AIA, "swearing behind" is not possible. *See* § 14.3.4.2.1.

Rule 132 affidavits contain information seeking to traverse rejections. *See* 37 C.F.R. § 1.132. These are commonly used to submit expert testimony responding to an obviousness rejection.

14.2.3.1.2 Interview Report

Applicants may request a telephone or face-to-face interview with the examiner. *See* 37 C.F.R. § 1.133. The applicant may be required to submit a written report of the meeting, although the report can be general. Many practitioners rely on interviews to expedite prosecution by personally engaging the examiner. Some practitioners also use interviews to limit the amount of written correspondence entering the prosecution history.

14.2.3.2 Request for Continued Examination (RCE)

Applicants generally have one opportunity to traverse the examiner's rejections before receiving a final rejection. After receiving a final rejection, applicants will often file a RCE in order to submit further arguments, claim amendments, or Information Disclosure Statements. *See* 37 C.F.R. § 1.114. An RCE provides applicants with another round of examination in the same application; it is not uncommon to see patents issue from applications in which multiple RCEs were filed. Instead of filing an RCE, applicants can pursue the rejected claims in a continuation application, or they can appeal the examiner's decision to the PTAB.

14.2.3.3 Continuation Applications

A continuation application is a second application for an invention claimed in a prior application. To qualify as a continuation application and claim the benefits of the earlier "parent" application's priority date, the application must be filed while the parent is still pending (i.e., not issued or abandoned), expressly refer to the parent application, identify at least one common inventor, and encompass the same disclosure of the parent application without adding any new matter. *See* § 120. The same invention must be claimed, but the scope of the claims can vary. However, the patent term of the continuation is limited to twenty years from the filing of the earliest application to which it claims priority.

Applicants often use continuation applications to pursue rejected claims or new claims that are different (usually broader) in scope from those in the parent application. A continuation application might also be used when the examiner allows some claims but rejects others: the applicant can cancel the rejected claims and pursue them in a continuation application, while allowing the remaining claims to issue as a patent.

14.2.3.4 Continuation-in-Part (CIP) Applications

A CIP is similar to a continuation application but introduces new subject matter to the parent application. For example, the inventor may add new data and descriptive material to support the claims. Alternatively, the inventor may have made improvements to the claimed invention and wish to add them in a CIP application. Claims to the new subject matter do not get the advantage of the priority date of the parent application. The relevant consideration is whether the claims are supported by the disclosure of the parent application under the test set forth in § 112. Claims that are so supported can rely on the parent application's priority date, whereas the other claims have the priority date of the CIP filing. Accordingly, some references might count as prior art for some of the claims in the CIP, but not qualify as prior art for other claims in the same application that are supported by the parent application's disclosure. Regardless of when material is added, all claims in a patent expire on the same date—typically twenty years from the earliest parent application's filing date. *See* § 14.2.4.

14.2.3.5 PTO Petition and Appeals

Applicants who reach an impasse with an examiner over procedural issues may petition the director of the USPTO. Such procedural issues include requests for time extensions, reviving abandoned applications, or reviewing a restriction requirement. Petitions are typically resolved in an informal manner by group directors in the USPTO.

An applicant may appeal a final rejection to the PTAB. *See* § 134. In upholding the rejection, the PTAB may consider any issue of patentability, including written description, enablement, novelty, and nonobviousness. The applicant may appeal adverse decisions of the PTAB to the Federal Circuit. *See* § 141. Alternately, the applicant may bring a civil action against the director to the U.S. District Court for the Eastern District of Virginia.[4] *See* § 145; AIA § 9. The district court can overturn PTAB decisions and order the USPTO to issue a patent. The Federal Circuit also hears appeals from the district court. A civil suit may be more expensive than a direct appeal to the Federal Circuit, but has the advantage that new evidence can be submitted to the district court, whereas the Federal Circuit only considers the USPTO record.

14.2.4 Patent Duration

A patent whose application was filed on or after June 8, 1995, expires twenty years after the earliest effective U.S. filing date, *see* § 154(a)(2), unless subject to various extensions discussed below. Prior to this date, patents expired seventeen years from the issuance date. For patents that were granted or pending before June 8, 1995, the patent expires either twenty years after the date of filing or seventeen years from issuance, whichever is later. *See* § 154(c)(1). All claims in a CIP application expire based on the effective filing date of the parent application, regardless of whether a claim's priority derives from the CIP application or its parent.

This change in the patent term harmonized the U.S. patent laws with those in most other nations. It also partially addressed the problem of "submarine patents." Under the old law, a patentee could use continuation practice to keep a patent application pending for years (or sometimes decades) until an unsuspecting third party began practicing the claimed invention. The patentee could then get the submarine patent issued and sue for infringement. The current law alleviates this abuse by tying patent duration to the filing date, thereby imposing the costs of delayed prosecution upon the applicant. In addition, the doctrine of prosecution laches can be raised as a defense in cases of undue prosecution delay. *See* § 14.4.2.3.4.1.

---

4. Prior to September 16, 2011, applicants were able to appeal a PTAB decision to the U.S. District Court for the District of Columbia.

The actual patent term commences the date that the patent issues. Thus, the effective term of the patent will be less than twenty years due to the pendency of prosecution. Nonetheless, provisional rights allow a patentee to collect a reasonable royalty from an infringer who had actual knowledge of a published patent application back to the date of actual notice. *See* § 154(d); § 14.4.3.2.

14.2.4.1 Patent-Term Adjustments

A patent's duration can be extended to account for certain delays occurring during prosecution. *See* § 154(b). Section 154(b)(1)(A) compensates the patentee for undue delays in prosecution: if the USPTO fails to deliver the first office action within fourteen months of the filing date or if the examiner fails to respond to an office action reply within four months, then additional time will be tacked on the patent term. Similarly, § 154(b)(1)(B) extends the patent term if patent prosecution lasts more than three years, not including continuations, interferences, and appeals. Section 154(b)(1)(C) extends the patent term if a patentee successfully overcomes adverse rulings at interference or appeals proceedings, or if the patent was subject to a secrecy order. Patent term adjustments are, however, limited by delays caused by the patentee. *See* § 154(b)(2).

14.2.4.2 Patent-Term Restoration

A patent's term can be extended by statutory patent-term restorations. For example, the Drug Price Competition and Patent Term Restoration Act of 1984, more commonly known as the Hatch-Waxman Act, extends the patent term for drug-related inventions up to five years when the commercial use of the claimed invention was delayed by regulatory approval. *See* § 156.

14.2.5 Postissuance Corrections and Administrative Proceedings

The failure of the patentee, or in some cases the USPTO, to properly address errors in an issued patent can result in adverse consequences at trial, such as the inability to receive damages or even complete loss of patent rights. Several administrative options exist at the USPTO for patentees to correct errors in the patent document after the patent has issued, as well as for third parties to challenge the validity of issued patents: disclaimer, certificate of correction, supplemental examination, post-grant review, covered business-method review (CBMR), reissue, reexamination, and inter partes review (IPR).

14.2.5.1 Disclaimers

Under § 253, a patentee (without deceptive intent) may disclaim any complete patent claim by filing a request with the USPTO. A patentee may also disclaim or dedicate to the public the entire patent term or any remaining portion of the patent term. The latter process is called a "terminal disclaimer." This process is frequently used when the USPTO rejects a patent application as obvious over an earlier patent or application by the same person. By filing the terminal disclaimer, the applicant agrees that the later filed application will expire at the same time as the prior patent (or application).

14.2.5.2 Certificate of Correction

Minor errors in an issued patent, such as typographical errors, omissions of an assignee, or printing of an original rather than amended claim, can be corrected with a Certificate of Correction. *See* §§ 254 (correction of USPTO mistake); 255 (correction of applicant mistake). These corrections cannot add new matter or change the scope of a patent claim such that reexamination would be required.[5]

Prior to the enactment of the AIA, a patent's named inventors could be corrected only upon showing that the error was made without deceptive intent. *See* § 256. Beginning September 16, 2012, inventorship errors may be corrected regardless of whether the error resulted from deceptive intent. AIA § 20.

Failure to inspect and correct an issued patent can be costly for the patentee. In *Southwest Software, Inc. v. Harlequin, Inc.*, 226 F.3d 1280 (Fed. Cir. 2000), the USPTO neglected to include a 330-page appendix with the issued patent. *Id.* at 1287. The accused infringer raised the issue during litigation. *Id.* at 1287–89. The patentee subsequently had the patent corrected under § 254. *Id.* at 1287. Nonetheless, the Federal Circuit held that a correction is only effective for causes of action arising after it was issued and remanded the case to determine whether the specification failed to satisfy the best mode and enablement requirements absent the appendix. *Id.* at 1295–97. The court stated, "[I]t does not seem to us to be asking too much to expect a patentee to check a patent when it is issued in order to determine whether it contains any errors that require the issuance of a certificate of correction." *Id.* at 1296.

14.2.5.3 Supplemental Examination

The AIA added § 257 to Title 35, under which a patentee may seek supplemental examination to have the USPTO consider any additional information relevant to patentability. AIA § 12. The USPTO will grant supplemental examination if a "substantial new question of patentability" exists. A patent cannot be held unenforceable based on conduct relating to information that had not been considered or was incorrect during a prior examination if the information was subsequently considered or corrected during a supplemental examination. This procedure allows patentees to submit additional information or prior art in order to avoid potential inequitable conduct claims so long as the supplemental examination is completed before the patentee files suit. However, supplemental examination cannot be used to cure pre-

5. For example, the Court of Customs and Patent Appeals, which handled appeals of PTO rejections prior to the creation of the Federal Circuit, held that a patentee could correct, through a Certificate of Correction, a chemical name in a specification whose errors resulted from translation from Japanese to English. *See In re Oda*, 443 F.2d 1200 (C.C.P.A. 1971).

existing allegations of inequitable conduct. Supplemental examination became available for all patents on September 16, 2012.

14.2.5.4 Reissue

Whereas certificates of correction address minor, nonsubstantive alterations of an issued patent, reissue proceedings allow a patentee to correct a substantive defect in the specification or to narrow or broaden the scope of an issued patent. Reissue may occur when, because of error without deceptive intent, a patent is "deemed wholly or partly inoperative or invalid, by reason of a defective specification or drawing, or by reason of the patentee claiming more or less than he had a right to claim in the patent." § 251. Under the AIA, reissue applications may be filed on or after September 16, 2012 without regard to deceptive intent. AIA § 20.

In pursuing reissuance of a patent, the patent owner files a reissue application and an oath attesting to the alleged error(s). The patent is then reprosecuted and may reissue in original or amended form. During the proceeding, the USPTO can reject any claims in the patent, not only those amended by the patentee. As a result, the entire patent loses its presumption of validity during the reissue process. The reissued patent is subject to invalidation in the same manner as the original patent (which is surrendered when the reissue patent is granted). Moreover, an accused infringer may defend on the grounds that the reissue itself was invalid.

The USPTO assigns reissued patents a new number, with the prefix "Re"—for example, "U.S. Patent No. Re. 50,000." Unlike the original proceedings, CIP applications (i.e., addition of new matter) are not allowed, and third parties are notified of the reissue request and may submit evidence and arguments. The duration of a reissued patent term cannot extend beyond that of the original patent.

The USPTO requires the patentee to provide an oath or declaration attesting to at least one error in the original patent. *See* 37 C.F.R. § 1.175.[6] Thus, reissue cannot be used to revive a patent rendered unenforceable because of inequitable conduct. The issued patent must contain "a defective specification or drawing," or the patentee must have claimed "more or less than he had a right to claim." § 251. Most patents are reissued to amend the claims, often to overcome newly discovered prior art that would invalidate one or more claims. Rather than filing a disclaimer that surrenders an entire claim or claims, the patentee can request reissuance with narrower claims that avoid the prior art. Furthermore, a reissue may be filed for the sole purpose of adding new dependent claims while leaving the original claims unchanged. *See In re*

---

6. The patentee is also held to a duty of candor regarding the reasons for the mistake. In *Hewlett-Packard Co. v. Bausch & Lomb, Inc.*, 882 F.2d 1556 (Fed. Cir. 1989), the patentee asserted a patent that was reissued with additional dependent claims. The original patent agent stated the additional claims were omitted from the original patent because of difficulty contacting the inventor, yet the record showed that the agent and inventor communicated regularly during prosecution. *Id.* at 1561. As a result, the Federal Circuit invalidated all claims added or amended during reissue, but did not disturb the unchanged claims from the original patent. *Id.* at 1566.

Tanaka, 640 F.3d 1246 (Fed. Cir. 2011). During the two-year window following issuance, a patentee can also attempt to broaden the scope of claim coverage, assuming that the original specification supports the amendments.

14.2.5.4.1 Narrowing Reissues

A patent owner may seek to narrow the scope of a patent at any point during the life of a patent.

14.2.5.4.2 Broadening Reissues

Broadening reissues are sought when the patentee's error is claiming less than the original specification, and presumably the prior art, would allow. The original specification must provide adequate written description for and must enable and disclose the best mode for the broader claim. A patentee has two years from the date of issuance to seek broader claims. § 251. The courts have construed this to mean "broader in any respect," so that an attempt to broaden a single claim limitation must be made within the two-year period, even if other amendments narrow the claim's overall scope. *See Ball Corp. v United States*, 729 F.2d 1429 (Fed. Cir. 1984). A patentee who has timely filed a broadening reissue application may continue to make broadening amendments outside the two-year window. *See In re Doll*, 419 F.2d 925 (C.C.P.A. 1970). But a patentee who sought a reissue within two years on other grounds cannot then seek to broaden claims outside the statutory period. *See In re Graff*, 111 F.3d 874 (Fed. Cir. 1997) (distinguishing *Doll* where the public was timely notified that the patentee sought broadened claims). A patentee's rights to enforce a broadening reissue are constrained by the doctrine of intervening rights. *See* § 252; § 14.2.5.5.2.2.

14.2.5.4.2.1 The Recapture Rule

The recapture rule is a judicially created limitation on broadening reissues that works similarly to prosecution history estoppel. *See* § 14.4.1.4.2.1.2. The rule bars a patentee from seeking reissue claims that regain subject matter that was surrendered to obtain allowance during the original prosecution. Surrendering subject matter to overcome patentability rejections does not constitute an "error" within the meaning of the patent laws. *See Ball Corp. v United States*, 729 F.2d 1429 (Fed. Cir. 1984).[7]

---

7. In *Mentor Corp. v. Coloplast, Inc.*, 998 F.2d 992 (Fed. Cir. 1993), Mentor had patented a condom catheter that transferred adhesive from the outer to inner surface during unrolling. The transfer limitation was added during prosecution to overcome an obviousness rejection. *Id.* at 995. After the patent issued, Mentor timely filed a broadening reissue application without the transfer limitation, asserting as error that it was entitled to the broader claim. *Id.* at 996. In a subsequent infringement action, the Federal Circuit held that Mentor's deliberate and intentional amendments made during initial prosecution to overcome issues of patentability were not errors within the meaning of the reissue statute and hence the broader reissued claim was invalid under the recapture rule. *Id.*

14.2.5.4.2.2 Intervening Rights

Although reissue claims that are "substantially identical" to those of the original patent "have effect continuously from the date of the original patent," § 252 ¶ 1, claims that were modified at reissue, for any reason, are subject to a reliance-type interest referred to as intervening rights. *See* § 252 ¶ 2. This doctrine recognizes that third parties may rely on the claims of an issued patent and thus provides a safe harbor to parties practicing subject matter covered by the amended claims. Unlike the recapture rule, which can invalidate claims in a reissued patent, intervening rights are applied on a party-by-party basis.

The patent laws codify two types of intervening rights: absolute and equitable. Under the absolute intervening rights doctrine, a court may allow a party who "made, purchased, offered to sell, or used" anything prior to reissue to continue to use or sell that thing. § 252. These rights do not allow a party to make new items after the reissue is granted, only to use or sell products that were already in existence. In addition, there are no intervening rights for subject matter that was claimed in the original patent.

Equitable intervening rights allow a court to authorize continued practice of an invention claimed in a reissue patent "to the extent and under such terms as the court deems equitable for the protection of investments made or business commenced before the grant of the reissue." *Id.* Again, these rights do not apply for inventions claimed in the original patent. As an example, a district court may provide equitable relief when a party has invested heavily in practicing the invention claimed at reissue. Such relief is subject to review by the Federal Circuit for abuse of discretion.[8]

Intervening rights can also apply when claims are narrowed. For example, a third party may practice a claimed invention in the belief that the applicable claims in the original patent are invalid. The patentee may later reissue the patent with narrowed claims that overcome the presumed invalidity arguments but still read on the third party's activities. Under such circumstances, a court may apply the intervening rights doctrine to the narrowed reissue patent.

---

8. In *Seattle Box Co. v. Industrial Crating & Packing, Inc.*, 756 F.2d 1574 (Fed. Cir. 1985), Seattle Box patented a system for bundling oil pipes. Industrial Crating acquired materials to bundle pipes in such a way that did not literally read on Seattle Box's claims. *Id.* at 1580. After bringing suit for infringement, Seattle Box obtained a broadening reissue that arguably covered Industrial Crating's system. *Id.* at 1575. Industrial Crating assembled its bundles after the reissue was granted, and the district court denied the defense of intervening rights. *Id.* at 1576. The Federal Circuit reversed, holding that equitable intervening rights applied. *Id.* The Federal Circuit noted that Industrial Crating relied on advice of counsel when designing around the original patent and that it had pending orders for the unassembled inventory before the reissue was granted. *Id.* at 1580. The court observed that "the new reissue claims in this case present a compelling case for the application of the doctrine of intervening rights because a person should be able to make business decisions secure in the knowledge that those actions which fall outside the original patent claims are protected." *Id.*

14.2.5.5 Reexamination

Reexamination is an administrative proceeding that can be initiated by the patentee, third parties, or the USPTO director, in which the USPTO reevaluates the validity of an issued patent. Prior to the AIA, the patent statute authorized two forms of reexamination: (1) ex parte, *see* §§ 302–307; and (2) inter partes, *see* pre-AIA §§ 311–318. The AIA left ex parte reexamination in place, but replaced inter partes reexamination with inter partes review (IPR), *see* § 14.2.5.6, though all inter partes reexaminations filed prior to September 16, 2012, will continue to completion. Reexaminations are limited to patentability issues raised by prior art patents and/or printed publications, as the USPTO is considered an expert in determining patentability over published prior art. Other issues affecting patentability, such as written description, enablement, "on sale" or public-use activities, or inequitable conduct, may require testimony and discovery, and thus are perceived as better handled through litigation.

14.2.5.5.1 The Reexamination Process

Reexaminations are handled by the USPTO's Central Reexamination Unit (CRU), which has its own staff of examiners. The USPTO created the CRU in 2005 to improve the quality of reexamination proceedings and to reduce their pendency. By statute, all reexaminations must be handled with "special dispatch." § 305; pre-AIA § 314.

A request for reexamination must provide new, noncumulative information affecting the patentability of a claim. Within three months of filing, the USPTO must issue a decision on whether to order a reexamination. For an ex parte reexamination, the threshold for ordering reexamination is whether the reexamination request raises a "substantial new question of patentability" (SNQ). § 303(a). Prior to the enactment of the AIA on September 16, 2011, the SNQ standard also applied to inter partes reexamination petitions. After the enactment of the AIA, however, the inter partes reexamination threshold was changed to "a reasonable likelihood that the requester would prevail with respect to at least 1 of the claims challenged in the request." AIA § 6. The new threshold applies to inter partes reexaminations filed after September 15, 2011.

Unlike regular prosecution or reissue proceedings, there is no continuation practice in reexaminations. The patentee can appeal adverse rulings to the PTAB, and thereafter to the Federal Circuit. *See* §§ 305–306; pre-AIA §§ 314–315.

A reexamination terminates with the issuance of a "Reexamination Certificate" that becomes part of the official patent document and states the result (cancelation, confirmation, and/or amendment of claims) of the reexamination proceeding. § 307; pre-AIA § 316. If a patent claim is reaffirmed in reexamination, courts are likely to view it as stronger, thus benefiting the patentee. As with reissue, the doctrine of intervening rights applies to any claims added or amended during reexamination. *See* § 307, pre-AIA § 316.

14.2.5.5.2 Ex Parte Reexamination

Anyone can file a request for an ex parte reexamination. Once the USPTO orders an ex parte reexamination, the patentee may file a preliminary statement including proposed amendments or new claims so long as the amendments are supported by the original filing (§ 304) and do not enlarge claim scope. *See Quantum Corp. v. Rodime, PLC*, 65 F.3d 1577 (Fed. Cir. 1995) (invalidating patent where the USPTO allowed broadened claim scope during reexamination). If a third party requested the reexamination, it may respond to the patentee's preliminary statement, but any further proceedings in the reexamination involve only the patentee and the examiner. § 305. In practice, patentees often decline to submit preliminary statements to limit third-party participation. After the preliminary statement and reply period, ex parte reexamination resembles regular prosecution between an examiner and the patentee.

14.2.5.5.3 Inter Partes Reexamination

As a result of the enactment of the AIA, inter partes reexamination was phased out over a one year transition period, beginning September 16, 2011. Starting September 16, 2012, inter partes review replaced inter partes reexamination. Inter partes reexaminations filed prior to September 16, 2012, will not, however, be converted into inter partes review proceedings, even if the proceedings have extended beyond September 16, 2012.

Inter partes reexamination was available only for patents granted on applications filed on or after November 29, 1999. *See* 37 C.F.R. § 1.913; *Cooper Techs. Co. v. Dudas*, 536 F.3d 1330, 1332–34 (2008). Unlike ex parte reexamination, requests for inter partes reexamination could not be filed by the patentee. Pre-AIA § 311; Pre-AIA 37 C.F.R. § 1.913. Inter partes reexamination allowed extensive involvement by the third-party requester throughout the proceedings, including appeal of adverse decisions to the PTAB and the Federal Circuit. Pre-AIA §§ 314–315.

Once the USPTO ordered an inter partes reexamination, the third-party requester was estopped from later arguing invalidity in a civil action on any ground that it raised, or could have raised, during the reexamination proceeding. Pre-AIA § 315(c). However, the third-party requester remained free to challenge the patent claims on other grounds, including newly discovered prior art unavailable to the third-party requester or the USPTO during the reexamination. *Id.*

14.2.5.5.4 Reexamination and Concurrent Litigation

It is not uncommon for an accused infringer to file a reexamination request for one or more of the patents-in-suit during litigation. Because reexaminations must proceed with "special dispatch" (§ 305; pre-AIA § 314), the USPTO Director cannot stay reexamination in light of concurrent litigation. *Ethicon, Inc. v. Quigg*, 849 F.2d 1422, 1426–27 (Fed. Cir. 1988). In contrast, district courts "have inherent power to manage their dockets and stay proceedings, including the authority to order a stay pending conclusion of a USPTO reexamination." *Id.* The USPTO prioritizes reexaminations of patents involved in litigation.

During a reexamination proceeding, the USPTO evaluates patentability issues under a "preponderance of the evidence" standard, whereas the district court must still apply the "clear and convincing" standard to invalidate a patent claim undergoing reexamination. *See Ethicon*, 849 F.2d at 1427.

A district court's finding that a patent was not proven invalid does not ordinarily create collateral estoppel effects on other courts or the USPTO during reexamination. *Ethicon*, 849 F.2d at 1429 n.3; *see also In re Swanson*, 540 F.3d 1368, 1379 (Fed. Cir. 2008) ("As properly interpreted a 'substantial new question of patentability' refers to a question which has never been considered by the USPTO; thus, a substantial new question can exist even if a federal court previously considered the question."). In contrast, a final, nonappealable court decision finding invalidity bars enforcement of the patent in subsequent proceedings (*see Blonder-Tongue Labs., Inc. v. Univ. of Ill. Found.*, 402 U.S. 313 (1971)), and the USPTO may discontinue the reexamination. *See Ethicon*, 849 F.2d at 1429.

14.2.5.6 Inter Partes Review (IPR)

IPR replaced inter partes reexaminations on September 16, 2012. AIA § 6 (amending §§ 311–319). In an IPR, a third party may seek cancellation of at least one claim based on § 102 or 103 using only prior art patents or printed publications. IPR may be requested by anyone who is not the patent owner, and who has not previously filed a declaratory judgment action challenging the validity of the patent. The USPTO will grant IPR if the petition shows "a reasonable likelihood" that the petitioner would prevail on at least one claim being challenged. The USPTO's decision on whether to institute an IPR is unappealable. *See In re Cuozzo Speed Techs., LLC*, 778 F.3d 1271 (Fed. Cir. 2015). IPR is handled by the PTAB rather than by the CRU, and appeals are taken directly to the Federal Circuit.

During IPR, the standard for proving invalidity is by a preponderance of the evidence, the parties may engage in limited discovery, and the patentee has an opportunity to provide comments and/or propose claim amendments that do not enlarge claim scope. With regard to patents filed under the AIA's first-to-file regime (and not patents filed prior to March 16, 2013), a petition for IPR cannot be filed until after the later of: (1) the closing of the postgrant review (PGR) window, that is, nine months after the grant (or reissue) of a patent, or (2) the termination of any PGR. The statute requires the USPTO to issue a final determination of the IPR no later than a year after instituting the proceeding; this deadline may be extended up to six months for good cause.

If, after filing a petition for IPR, the petitioner initiates a civil action seeking a declaratory judgment of invalidity of the same patent, the civil action is automatically stayed. The automatic stay is lifted if the patentee moves the court to lift the stay or asserts the patent against the petitioner in a civil action or in a counterclaim. Because the automatic stay provisions apply to "civil actions" rather than counterclaims, a petitioner is able to assert invalidity counterclaims while seeking IPR. A petition for IPR may not be filed more than one year after the date on which the patentee served the petitioner with a complaint for infringement of the patent.

In any subsequent proceeding in the USPTO, the district courts, or the ITC, the petitioner is estopped from raising issues that it had raised or reasonably could have raised during IPR. If the parties settle during IPR, there is no estoppel effect. In a manner similar to reissue claims, intervening rights attach to new or amended claims that emerge from IPR.

14.2.5.7 Postgrant Review (PGR)

Under §§ 321–329, AIA § 6, anyone other than the patentee may petition for postgrant review of a patent within nine months of grant or reissue based on any ground of invalidity. The PTAB will institute a postgrant review if it determines that it is more likely than not that at least one of the claims is unpatentable, or the petition raises a legal issue important to other patents or patent applications. If multiple postgrant review petitions are filed, the USPTO may consolidate them. The denial of a petition is unappealable.

The standard for proving invalidity in a postgrant review proceeding is by a preponderance of the evidence. The AIA provides limited discovery for the parties. The patentee has an opportunity to provide comments and/or propose claim amendments, but claim scope may not be enlarged. The statute requires the USPTO to issue a final determination no later than a year after instituting the proceeding; this deadline can be extended up to six months for good cause. In any subsequent proceeding in the USPTO, the district courts, or the ITC, the petitioner is estopped from raising issues that it had raised or reasonably could have raised during postgrant review. If the parties settle during postgrant review, there is no estoppel effect.

A party that has previously filed an action seeking a declaratory judgment of invalidity cannot petition for postgrant review. If, during the postgrant review proceeding, the petitioner files a declaratory judgment action, that action is stayed unless the patentee counterclaims for infringement. If the patentee files an action to assert the patent within three months of issuance, a court may not delay consideration of a motion for preliminary injunction on the ground that a postgrant review petition has been filed or that a postgrant review proceeding has been instituted. In a manner similar to reissue claims, intervening rights attach to new or amended claims that emerge from postgrant review. *See* § 14.2.5.4.2.2.

Postgrant review proceedings apply to claims with effective filing dates after March 15, 2013.

14.2.5.7.1 Covered Business-Method Review (CBMR)

The AIA provides for a variant of the postgrant review proceeding for business-method patents of all filing dates. Under the Transitional Program for Covered Business Method Patents, CBMR may be requested for a business-method patent that has been asserted against the requester, either in court or with allegations of infringement. AIA § 18. Courts may stay concurrent district court proceedings pending a CBMR, but the decision whether to grant a stay is subject to interlocutory review. This transitional program began September 16, 2012, and ends September 16, 2020.

Like postgrant review, and unlike IPR, patent validity can be challenged on any ground. Additionally, no time-bar exists in CBMR; a petitioner does not have to file within a certain period of time from being named defendant in a suit or from an accusation of patent infringement. The estoppel provision is also weakened. A petitioner is estopped from arguing any ground *actually* raised in CBMR in subsequent district court or ITC proceedings. However, a petitioner still faces estoppel based on anything that reasonably could have been raised in subsequent proceedings at the USPTO.

14.2.5.7.2 Postgrant, Inter Partes, and Covered Business-Method Review and Concurrent Litigation

Similar to reexamination, accused infringers commonly file a review request for one or more of the patents-in-suit during litigation. Reviews must ordinarily be completed within twelve months from an institution decision (with an outer bound of eighteen months upon showing of good cause) and cannot be stayed. Much of the analysis to stay a case pending a review is the same as with reexamination; however, one important exception applies.

In addition to the three traditional considerations courts weigh to decide whether to stay a case, Congress added a fourth to be considered when litigation is copending with CBMR of a patent: "whether a stay, or the denial thereof, will reduce the burden of litigation on the parties and the court." AIA § 18. As mentioned above, the grant or denial of a stay is subject to interlocutory review.

Table 14.2 summarizes the principal features of and differences between the AIA review procedures.

Table 14.2
Significant Differences Between AIA Reviews

AIA Review	Inter Partes	Postgrant	Business-Method
Evidentiary Standard	Petitioner to prove invalidity by the preponderance of the evidence		
Grounds for Review	§ 102, § 103	Any defense relating to invalidity	
Prior Art Limited to:	Patents and printed publications	No Limits	
Threshold to Institute Review	Reasonable likelihood that one or more claims invalid	More likely than not, at least one claim is unpatentable, or petition raises a novel legal question of patentability.	
Time to Institution	Maximum of 6 months		
Time to Decision	Maximum of 12–18 months from institution decision		
Claim Amendments	Patent owner may cancel claims or propose a reasonable number of substitute claims. Presumption that only one substitute claim will be required for each challenged claim		
Claim Construction	"Broadest reasonable construction in light of specification"		
Stay Considerations:	1) Stay simplify issues and streamline trial? 2) Is discovery complete, trial date set? 3) Stay tactically advantage moving party or unduly burden nonmoving party?		*AIA Consideration:* 4) Stay reduce burden on the parties and the court?
Estoppel in Subsequent Civil Action	Any ground raised or that reasonably could have been raised		Any ground *actually* raised
Effect of Settlement	Estoppel provisions do not apply.		

14.2.6 The Presumption of Validity

The 1952 Patent Act codified the judge-made presumption that the rigor of the USPTO's examination process should render an issued patent presumptively valid. Thus, a patent is presumed valid and a party asserting invalidity must prove the facts to establish a claim's invalidity by clear and convincing evidence. § 282; *Microsoft Corp. v. i4i Ltd. P'ship*, 131 S. Ct. 2238 (2011); *Kaufman Co. v. Lantech, Inc.*, 807 F.2d 970, 973–74 (Fed. Cir. 1986).

The "clear and convincing" standard applies to questions of fact and not to questions of law. The factual and legal aspects of an invalidity claim may be separated "by using instructions based on case-specific circumstances that help the jury make the distinction or by using interrogatories and special verdicts to make clear which specific factual findings underlie the jury's conclusions." *Microsoft*, 131 S. Ct. at 2253 (Breyer, J. concurring) (citing Fed. R. Civ. P. 49 and 51).

Where the references asserted against a claim's validity were not presented to the USPTO examiner, "the challenger's burden to persuade the jury of its invalidity defense by clear and convincing evidence may be easier to sustain." *Microsoft*, 131 S. Ct. at 2251. The Federal Circuit has similarly observed that the burden of proof may "be facilitated" or more easily met if the examiner never considered the asserted reference. *Kaufman*, 807 F.2d at 973; *Jervis B. Webb Co. v. S. Sys., Inc.*, 742 F.2d 1388, 1393 n.4 (Fed. Cir. 1984). In such situations, "the jury may be instructed to evaluate whether the evidence before it is materially new, and if so, to consider that fact when determining whether an invalidity defense has been proved by clear and convincing evidence." *Microsoft*, 131 S. Ct. at 2251.

14.3 Validity

A patent claim must meet five requirements to issue as part of a valid patent: (1) patentable subject matter, (2) utility, (3) disclosure, (4) novelty, and (5) nonobviousness. Failure to clear any one of these hurdles will invalidate the patent claim.

14.3.1 Patentable Subject Matter (§ 101)

Section 101 authorizes protection for "any" "process, machine, manufacture, or composition of matter" or "improvement thereof . . . subject to the conditions and requirements of this title." Although the Patent Act has not excluded any subject matter for much of U.S. history,[9] courts have long recognized subject-matter eligibility limitations. These limits emerged during the early to mid-nineteenth century as Anglo-American, common-law-trained jurists fleshed out the relatively terse patent law eligibility requirements.

Thus, the contours of these doctrines are found not in the text of the Patent Act but rather in two centuries of jurisprudence that has ebbed and flowed with technological advance, perspectives on scientific discovery, and concerns about the patent system stifling new inventions. Patent-eligibility doctrines lost salience from the early 1980s through 2009 as the Federal Circuit substantially liberalized the scope of patentable subject matter. The Supreme Court was dormant in patentable subject-matter jurisprudence during this period. The Supreme Court reentered the arena in 2010 and has since issued four significant opinions reinvigorating patentable subject-matter eligibility limitations and, in so doing, making this area ripe for litigation. *See Bilski v. Kappos*, 561 U.S. 593 (2010); *Mayo Collaborative Servs. v. Prometheus Labs., Inc.*, 132 S. Ct. 1289 (2012); *Ass'n for Molecular Pathology v. Myriad Genetics, Inc.*, 133 S. Ct. 2107 (2013); *Alice Corp. Pty. Ltd. v. CLS Bank Int'l*, 134 S. Ct. 2347 (2014). Most patents in effect today issued during the period in which subject-matter

---

9. As noted in §§ 14.3.1.3.1–2, the AIA excludes patents on tax strategies and human organisms.

eligibility was perceived to be very broad. Hence, the courts have seen a large and growing number of challenges to patent validity based on § 101 since 2010.

Navigating the boundaries of patentable subject matter entails careful study of the Supreme Court's recent decisions as well as the history leading up to those cases. The Supreme Court's predilection for considering all of its prior patentable subject-matter cases to be consistent poses notable interpretive challenges. Thus, it will be useful to examine the case law through a variety of lenses. The next section states the core principles undergirding modern Supreme Court jurisprudence. The following sections trace the history of these doctrines, examine particular subject-matter areas, and explore the challenges of applying patent-eligibility doctrines.

14.3.1.1 Modern Core Principles: Ineligible Subject Matter and Inventive Application

The Supreme Court's most recent patentable subject-matter decision, *Alice*, synthesizes two centuries of jurisprudence into a two-part test:

> Step 1: Does the patent claim a patent-ineligible law of nature, natural phenomena, or abstract idea?
>
> Step 2: If so, does the claim contain an inventive concept sufficient to transform the ineligible law of nature, natural, phenomena, or abstract idea into a patent-eligible application of the ineligible subject matter?

Alice, 134 S. Ct. at 2354. The exclusion of claims covering laws of nature, natural phenomena, and abstract ideas reflects the concern, sometimes referred to as the preemption rationale, that patents not unduly inhibit further discovery by tying up basic building blocks of human ingenuity. Step 2 requires that the patentee not merely *apply* the law of nature, natural phenomena, or abstract idea, but rather do so in an *inventive* manner. The application cannot be routine or conventional, but must be inventive above and beyond the discovery of the underlying law of nature, physical phenomena, or algorithm.

This characterization of patent eligibility potentially excludes some of the most important and difficult technological discoveries from patent protection: the discovery of laws of nature. During earlier eras, inventors could obtain patents on applications of such discoveries even if their *application* was conventional. The Supreme Court's recent jurisprudence, however, excludes routine or conventional applications of breakthrough scientific biomedical or algorithmic discoveries from patent eligibility. *See Ariosa Diagnostics, Inc. v. Sequenom, Inc.*, 788 F.3d 1371 (Fed. Cir. 2015) (invalidating a patent on noninvasive prenatal diagnostic methods on the ground that the *application* of the discovery that cell-free fetal DNA existed in maternal blood was not inventive); *cf. id.* at 1380 (Linn, J. concurring) (observing that "[t]his case represents the consequence—perhaps unintended—of that broad language [in the Supreme Court's *Mayo* decision] in excluding a meritorious invention from the patent protection it deserves and should have been entitled to retain").

The requirement of not merely *application* but *inventive* application of patent-ineligible subject matter overlaps with the § 103 nonobviousness requirement. Upon closer examination, however, the inventiveness required for § 101 eligibility is distinct from and arguably more demanding than § 103 nonobviousness analysis. According to *Mayo*, the inventive application requirement treats the patentees' discovery of the law of nature, physical phenomena, abstract ideas, or algorithms (in *Flook*) as known (even where it was not), whereas § 103 nonobviousness focuses on "the differences between the claimed invention and the prior art." *See* § 14.3.5.3.3. The rationale for this distinction apparently derives from the notion that laws of nature, physical phenomena, and abstract ideas are basic building blocks of human ingenuity. They are not invented by humans but merely discovered. The fact that § 101 of the Patent Act confers patent eligibility on "[w]hoever invents or *discovers* any new and useful process, machine, manufacture, or composition of matter, or any new and useful improvement thereof . . . ," however, only adds to the confusion.

As the evolution of these doctrines reveals, the Supreme Court's emphasis on *inventive* application rests on a questionable jurisprudential foundation. *See generally* Jeffrey A. Lefstin, 67 *Inventive Application: A History*, Fla. L. Rev. 565 (2015). Nonetheless, unless and until the doctrine's provenance is rectified, lower courts must work within this framework. Understanding the evolution of patent-eligibility jurisprudence illuminates the current state of the law and provides some guidance in applying the inventive application doctrine.

14.3.1.2 The Evolution of Patentable Subject-Matter Limitations

Like the modern Patent Act, the nation's first patent statutes authorized the granting of patents for a broad range of subject matter—"any new and useful art, machine, manufacture, or composition of matter"[10]—without express subject-matter limitations. Courts came to recognize that patentability of broad scientific principles and abstract claims created the need for patent-eligibility and scope limitations—what we today consider § 112 concerns. These concepts were intertwined in the early jurisprudence and continue to overlap today.

---

10. *See* Patent Act of 1793, Act of Feb. 21, 1793, 1 Stat. 318. This language parallels the modern subject matter categories with the replacement of the term "art" with "process." This shift reflects the evolution of language as opposed to substantive change. *See* H.R. Rep. No. 82-1923, A Bill to Revise and Codify the Laws Relating to Patents and the Patent Office, and to Enact into Law Title 35 of the United States Code Entitled "Patents," at 5–6, 82d Cong., 2d Sess. (1952). The concept of a "useful art" during the nation's formative period connoted guilds and trades utilizing what we would today call "technology." During the nineteenth century, courts defined "art" as "a new process or method of working or of producing an effect or result in matter." *See* George Ticknor Curtis, A Treatise on the Law of Patents for Useful Inventions, as Enacted and Administered in the Unites States of America 28 (3d ed. 1867). In explaining the substitution of "process" for "art," the drafters of the 1952 Act explained that the change was not substantive. Section 100 of the 1952 Act defined "process" to include "process, art or method, and includes a new use of a known process, machine, manufacture, composition of matter, or material." *See generally* Peter S. Menell, *Forty Years of Wondering in the Wilderness and No Closer to the Promised Land:* Bilski's *Superficial Textualism and the Missed Opportunity to Ground Patent Interpretation and Return Patent Law to Its Technology Mooring*, 63 Stan. L. Rev. 1289 (2011).

14.3.1.2.1 Early Development of Patent-Eligibility Limitations

In the years following the nation's founding, English cases substantially influenced American jurisprudence. The United States inherited many English legal traditions. This was especially true of intellectual property law, which closely followed English formulations and interpretations.

With the industrial revolution gaining momentum, courts on both sides of the Atlantic struggled to deal with the patentability and scope of path-breaking inventions such as the steam engine, hot blast furnace, sewing machine, telegraph, and telephone. The patenting of the hot blast process, which industrial historians came to view as "the most important single innovation in the industry in the age of iron," *see* Alan Birch, The Economic History of the British Iron and Steel Industry 1784–1879, 181 (1968), would prove especially important to patent-eligibility doctrine.

Scottish inventor James Beaumont Neilson challenged the conventional wisdom that hot-blast furnaces would function most effectively if they were fed cold air. Neilson's patent claimed preheating of air entering furnaces, and this preheating revolutionized the production of iron by substantially reducing the fuel required and enabling the use of raw coal and lower-quality ores. His brief specification provided few details and declared that "[t]he form or shape of the receptacle is immaterial to the effect," as were the composition of the air vessel and the manner of applying heat.

He would sue numerous ironmakers for patent infringement, leading to the important decision in the English Court of the Exchequer, *Neilson v. Harford* (1841), that continues to reverberate in U.S. patentable subject-matter jurisprudence today. The patent was attacked on two principal grounds: (1) that it was not sufficiently described; and (2) that a patent for injecting hot air into the furnace, instead of cold, and thereby increasing the intensity of the heat, was a patent for a principle, and that a principle was not patentable. The jury found that a skilled artisan could, based on the specification, construct an improved hot blast furnace. Therefore, the patent was sufficiently described.

The second issue would prove especially important. In upholding the patent, Judge Baron Parke explained:

> It is very difficult to distinguish it from the specification of a patent for a principle, and this at first created in the minds of the court much difficulty; but after full consideration we think that the plaintiff does not merely claim a principle, but a machine, embodying a principle, and a very valuable one. We think the case must be considered as if the principle being well known, the plaintiff had first invented a mode of applying it by a mechanical apparatus to furnaces, and his invention then consists in this: by interposing a receptacle for heated air between the blowing apparatus and the furnace. In this receptacle he directs the air to be heated by the application of heat externally to the receptacle, and thus he accomplishes the object of applying the blast, which was before cold air, in a heated state to the furnace.

The court reasoned that since the principle worked regardless of the dimensions of the receptacle in which the air was preheated before injection into the furnace, Neilson's invention applied the principle and hence, even though very broad (and arguably preemptive of the preheating principle), was patent-eligible. It is notable that the English court did *not* require *inventive* application of the law of nature (that preheating air before injection into a hot-blast furnace will allow for more efficient fuel usage and higher temperatures) for patent eligibility. The preheating receptacles and bellows were in the prior art. Rather it was recognition and application of the natural law that provided the basis for patent eligibility, not the inventiveness (or lack thereof) of the means of harnessing the natural law.

U.S. decisions followed this approach, barring protection for a mere "principle," "motive" force, or "new power" in the abstract. The Supreme Court explained in *Le Roy v. Tatham*, a case involving improved machinery for manufacturing lead pipe and a new property (the manufacture of wrought pipe from solid lead), that

> [a] principle, in the abstract, is a fundamental truth; an original cause; a motive; these cannot be patented, as no one can claim in either of them an exclusive right. Through the agency of machinery a new steam power may be said to have been generated. But no one can appropriate this power exclusively to himself, under the patent laws. The same may be said of electricity, and of any other power in nature, which is alike open to all, and may be applied to useful purposes by the use of machinery.
>
> In all such cases, the processes used to extract, modify, and concentrate natural agencies, constitute the invention. The elements of the power exist; the invention is not in discovering them, but in *applying* them to useful objects. . . .

55 U.S. 156, 1775 (1853) (emphasis added). The case approvingly discussed the *Neilson* case. *See id.* at 175–76; *see also id.* at 180–82, 185 (Nelson, J. dissenting).

The U.S. Supreme Court addressed *Neilson* in *O'Reilly v. Morse*, 56 U.S. 62 (1853), a case concerning the patenting of the telegraph. In addition to claims relating to the particular apparatus, Morse sought protection for "the use of the motive power of the electric of galvanic current, which I call electro-magnetism, however developed, for making or printing intelligible characters, letters, or signs, at any distances. . . ." *Id.* The breathtaking scope of this final claim led the Court to consider the principles enunciated in *Neilson v. Harford*. *Id.* at 62–63. While endorsing the requirement that patents must apply a law of nature, the Court nonetheless distinguished Neilson's claim from Morse's final claim. *Id.* Whereas the effect that Neilson claimed (improving the functioning of a hot-blast furnace) produced the desired effect for "whatever might be the form of the receptacle, or the mechanical contrivances for heating it, or for passing the current of air through it, and into the furnace," Moore had "not discovered, that the electric or galvanic current will always print at a distance, no matter what may be the form of the machinery or mechanical contrivances through which it passes." *Id.* at 116–17. Thus, Morse's final broad claim was invalid for reasons that we would today characterize as overbreadth (§ 112 written description), not ineligible subject matter (§ 101). Yet the Court's invocation of *Neilson* would take on great significance in American patent-eligibility jurisprudence a century later.

By the end of the nineteenth century, American patent-eligibility doctrine merely required that the patentee "carry the principle into effect, however simple and self-evident such means may be." *See* David Fulton, The Law and Practice Relating to Patents, Trade Marks and Designs 41 (1902); *see also* Robert Frost, A Treatise on the Law and Practice of Letters Patent for Inventions 36 (1891) ("Principles in a concrete form, together with a mode of applying them to a new and useful purpose, may form the subject of a grant of letters patent. . . . It is not necessary that the means, as well as the principle, should be new, for the novelty of the invention consists in applying the new principle by the means specified."). This view continued well into the twentieth century. *See* Caesar & Rivise, Patentability and Validity, §§ 33, 34 (1936) (observing that "[i]n the cases where the inventor was required to be also the discoverer of the law or force utilized, it appeared that the application or utilization of the law became self-evident as soon as the principle was formulated").

14.3.1.2.2 *Funk Brothers* (1948): The Emergence of Inventive Application

The *inventive* application eligibility concept first emerged in *Funk Brothers Seed Co. v. Kalo Inoculant Co.*, 333 U.S. 127 (1948). The claimed invention concerned bacteria cultures used to fix nitrogen in leguminous (pea and bean) plants, which is essential to promoting plant growth. At the time that the claimed invention was made, it was known that bacteria of the genus *Rhizobium* naturally exist in symbiotic association with leguminous plants. *Id.* at 128. Farmers routinely mixed *Rhizobium* cultures with leguminous plants to enhance nitrogen fixation. *Id.* at 129. Unfortunately, particular species of the *Rhizobium* genus infect only particular legumes. *Id.* Attempts at mixing different *Rhizobium* species into a single commercial product generally proved unsuccessful, as the bacteria species exerted inhibitory effects on each other when mixed together. *Id.* As a result, farmers would need to apply separate cultures for each leguminous crop, raising their costs and complicating the application of the bacteria. *Id.* at 129.

The inventor discovered that particular combinations of naturally occurring *Rhizobium* bacteria were not inhibitory and, therefore, could be packaged together into a product that could be applied across leguminous plant varieties more conveniently. *Id.* at 130. The patent broadly claimed the method of producing the bacteria mix as well as a broad composition of matter: "[a]n inoculant for leguminous plants comprising a plurality of selected mutually noninhibitive strains of different species of bacteria of the genus Rhizobium, said strains being unaffected by each other in respect to their ability to fix nitrogen in the leguminous plant for which they are specific." *Id.* at 128 n.1. The composition-of-matter claim covered all mutually noninhibitory combinations of the *Rhizobium* genus. *Id.* at 137.

A divided Supreme Court invalidated the patent on the ground that it did "not disclose an invention or discovery within the meaning of the patent statutes." *Funk Brothers*, 333 U.S. at 132. Justice Douglas's majority opinion began its analysis by restating well-established patent-eligibility jurisprudence:

> [P]atents cannot issue for the discovery of phenomena of nature. The qualities of these bacteria, like the heat of the sun, electricity, or the quality of metals, are part of the storehouse of knowledge of all men. They are manifestations of laws of nature, free to all men and reserved exclusively to none. He who discovers a hitherto unknown phenomenon of nature has no claim to a monopoly of it which the law recognizes. If

> there is to be invention from such a discovery, it must come from the *application* of the law of nature to a new and useful end.

Id. at 130 (citations omitted; emphasis added). The following paragraph, however, introduces the idea that merely applying a law of nature is insufficient.

> Discovery of the fact that certain strains of each species of these bacteria can be mixed without harmful effect to the properties of either is a discovery of their qualities of non-inhibition. It is no more than the discovery of some of the handiwork of nature and hence is not patentable. *The aggregation of select strains of the several species into one product is an application of that newly-discovered natural principle.* But however ingenious the discovery of that natural principle may have been, the application of it is hardly more than an advance in the packaging of the inoculants.

Id. at 131 (emphasis added). Justice Douglas acknowledged that the inventor had applied the law of nature, but nonetheless invalidated the claim as insufficiently inventive in its application of the newly discovered natural principle. *Id.* The Court noted that

> a product must be more than new and useful to be patented; it must also satisfy the requirements of invention or discovery. *Cuno Engineering Corp. v. Automatic Devices Corp.*, 314 U.S. 84, 90, 91 (1941), and cases cited; 35 U.S.C. § 31. The application of this newly-discovered natural principle to the problem of packaging of inoculants may well have been an important commercial advance. But once nature's secret of the non-inhibitive quality of certain strains of the species of Rhizobium was discovered, the state of the art made the production of a mixed inoculant a simple step. Even though it may have been the product of skill, it certainly was not the product of invention.

Id. at 131–32.

In a concurring opinion, Justice Frankfurter offered an alternative basis for invalidation reminiscent of the *Morse* decision. In his view, the patent was invalid not for unpatentable subject matter but rather for want of adequate identification of successful combinations of mutually noninhibitory bacteria. *Funk Brothers*, 333 U.S. at 133. He went on to observe that

> [i]t only confuses the issue . . . to introduce such terms as "the work of nature" and the "laws of nature." For these are vague and malleable terms infected with too much ambiguity and equivocation. Everything that happens may be deemed "the work of nature," and any patentable composite exemplifies in its properties "the laws of nature." Arguments drawn from such terms for ascertaining patentability could fairly be employed to challenge almost every patent.

Id. at 134–35.[11]

Following *Funk Brothers*, several appellate decisions implemented its holding, treating newly discovered scientific principles to be unpatentable and requiring *inventive* application of such principles. *See, e.g., Davison Chem. Corp. v. Joliet Chems., Inc.*, 179 F.2d 793 (7th Cir. 1950); *In re Arnold*, 185 F.2d 686 (C.C.P.A. 1950); *Nat'l Lead Co. v. W. Lead Prods. Co.*, 324 F.2d 539 (9th Cir. 1963).

---

11. Justices Burton and Jackson dissented, finding the product claims within the scope of patentable subject matter and adequately disclosed. *Funk Brothers*, 333 U.S. at 136.

14.3.1.2.3 The New Technological Age

With the dawning of the digital age, the Supreme Court returned to patent-eligibility cases. The inventor in *Gottschalk v. Benson*, 409 U.S. 63 (1972), claimed an algorithm for converting binary-coded decimal numerals into pure binary numerals. In upholding the USPTO's rejection of the patent on subject-matter grounds, a unanimous Court, drawing upon *Le Roy*, *Morse*, and *Funk Brothers*, articulated three principles for determining whether a process is patentable: (1) "[p]henomena of nature, though just discovered, mental processes, and abstract intellectual concepts are not patentable, as they are the basic tools of scientific and technological work," *id.* at 67; (2) "[t]ransformation and reduction of an article 'to a different state or thing' is the clue to the patentability of a process claim that does not include particular machines," *id.* at 70; and (3) algorithms may not be patented so as to avoid the practical effect of "wholly pre-empt[ing a] mathematical formula," *id.* at 71. Echoing concerns raised by various amicus briefs, the Court concluded by calling on Congress to take up the question of whether and to what extent computer programs ought to be patentable. *See id.* at 71–73.

Six years later in *Parker v. Flook*, 437 U.S. 584 (1978), the Supreme Court addressed whether a procedure for updating an alarm limit—measuring the present value of a process variable (such as temperature), using an algorithm to calculate an updated alarm-limit value, and adjusting the updated value—was eligible for patent protection. Writing for the majority in a sharply divided opinion, Justice Stevens expressly embraced the *inventive application* doctrine in upholding the USPTO's rejection of the claim. In an apparent misinterpretation, the Court grounded the doctrine on the statement in *Neilson* that "'*the case must be considered as if the principle being well known, the plaintiff had first invented a mode of applying it . . . .*'" *Flook*, 437 U.S. at 592 (quoting *Morse*, quoting *Neilson*). Based on this sentence from *Neilson*, the Supreme Court reasoned that "this case must also be considered as if the principle or mathematical formula were well known" and that patent eligibility required sufficient inventiveness beyond the application of the algorithm to be within the scope of patentable subject matter. *Id.* at 592, 594–95. As the Court declared:

> Even though a phenomenon of nature or mathematical formula may be well known, an *inventive application* of the principle may be patented. Conversely, the discovery of such a phenomenon cannot support a patent unless there is some other *inventive concept* in its application.

Id. at 594 (emphasis added).

Justice Stevens countered suggestions that such an approach "improperly imports considerations of 'inventiveness'" from §§ 102 and 103 into the § 101 analysis, noting that "[t]he obligation to determine what type of discovery is sought to be patented must precede the determination of whether that discovery is, in fact, new or obvious." *Id.* at 594.

Like the Court's opinion in *Benson*, the majority opinion concluded with a call for Congress, with its access to empirical evidence, rather than the courts, to take on the patentability of computer programs. *Id.* at 595–96. The opinion also invoked an interpretive principle of parsimony: "'[W]e should not expand patent rights by overruling or modifying our prior cases construing the patent statutes, unless the argument for expansion of privilege is based on more than mere inference from ambiguous statutory language.'" *Id.* at 595 (quoting *Deepsouth Packing Co. v. Laitram Corp.*, 406 U.S. 518, 531 (1972)).[12]

Justice Stewart, with whom Chief Justice Burger and Justice Rehnquist joined, did not see the patent at issue as preempting use of the algorithm, but rather as a potentially patentable application of it. *Id.* at 599. He criticized the majoring opinion for excluding a process from the scope of patentable subject matter because "*one step* in the process would not be patentable subject matter if considered in isolation," observing that "thousands of processes and combinations have been patented that contained one or more steps or elements that themselves would have been unpatentable subject matter." *Id.* (citation omitted; emphasis in original). The majority opinion responded to this contention by noting that the process is unpatentable "not because it contains a mathematical algorithm as one component, but because once that algorithm is assumed to be within the prior art, the application, considered as a whole, contains no patentable invention." *Id.* at 594.

In the midst of the controversy over the patentability of computer software, the Supreme Court confronted the patentability of genetically modified organisms. *See Diamond v. Chakrabarty*, 447 U.S. 303 (1980). The inventor claimed a self-replicating bacterium into which he had injected oil-degrading plasmids that could be used in dispersing oil spills. *Id.* at 305. The USPTO rejected the claim on the grounds that microorganisms are "products of nature" and living things, both of which make them ineligible for patent protection under § 101. *Id.* at 306. The Court of Customs and Patent Appeals reversed, upholding the claim under the standards set forth in *Flook. Id.*

The Supreme Court affirmed the appellate court decision, opening the way for patent protection for genetically modified organisms. *Id.* at 318. Writing for the majority, Chief Justice Burger characterized the Constitution's grant of patent legislative authority and § 101's text broadly. *Chakrabarty*, 447 U.S. at 307–08. While recognizing the unpatentability of "laws of nature, physical phenomena, and abstract ideas," the Court judged Chakrabarty's claim to a "nonnaturally occurring manufacture or composition of matter—a product of human ingenuity "having a distinctive name, character [and] use"—to "plainly" qualify for patent eligibility. *Id.* at 309–10 (quoting *Hartranft v. Wiegmann*, 121 U.S. 609, 615 (1887)). Drawing a contrast to *Funk Brothers*, the Court noted that Chakrabarty "has produced a new bacterium with markedly different characteristics from any found in nature and one having the po-

---

12. The Court was quite aware of the larger policy concerns surrounding the case. In discussing the procedural background to the case, the Court observed that "[t]he Acting Commissioner of Patents and Trademarks filed a petition for a writ of certiorari, urging that the decision of the Court of Customs and Patent Appeals will have a debilitating effect on the rapidly expanding computer 'software' industry, and will require him to process thousands of additional patent applications." *Flook*, 437 U.S. at 587–88.

tential for significant utility. His discovery is not nature's handiwork, but his own." *Id.* at 310.

Moreover, *Chakrabarty* interpreted the scope of patent-eligible subject matter expansively, stressing that § 101 encompasses any invention falling within the four designated categories. *Id.* at 308–09. The Supreme Court also looked to the legislative history of the 1952 Patent Act, from which it concluded that "Congress intended statutory subject matter to 'include anything under the sun that is made by man.'"[13] *Id.* at 309.

Propelled in part by *Chakrabarty*'s broad reading of patent eligibility, the pendulum swung decisively in the opposite direction of *Flook* three years after it was rendered. The USPTO rejected a patent application claiming a process for molding raw, uncured, synthetic rubber into cured precision products using a computer program, a known algorithm to calculate the cure time, and continuous measurement of the internal temperature. After the Court of Customs and Patent Appeals overturned the § 101 rejection, the USPTO sought certiorari based on the *Flook* decision:

---

13. The full passage from which this quotation was taken is arguably less expansive. The "anything under the sun" phrase arises in the section of the House Report describing "Part II" of Title 35, which "relates to patentability of inventions and the grant of patents." H.R. Rep. No. 82-1923, at 6. This discussion begins with four paragraphs explaining § 101: the first two deal with the subject matter categories; the second two focus on the final clause of § 101.

The first and longest paragraph begins by stating that Section 101 "specifies the type of material that can be the subject matter of a patent," thus implying that there are types of material that are not within the scope of patentable subject matter. The second paragraph explains that the definition of "process" was added in § 100 "to make it clear that 'process or method' is meant, and also to clarify the present law as to the patentability of certain types of processes or methods as to which some insubstantial doubts have been expressed." *See id.* The next two paragraphs explain the final clause of Section 101:

> Section 101 sets forth the subject matter that can be patented, "subject to the conditions and requirements of this title." The conditions under which a patent may be obtained follow, and section 102 covers the conditions relating to novelty.
>
> A person may have "invented" a machine or manufacture, which may include anything under the sun that is made by man, but it is not necessarily patentable under section 101 unless the conditions of the title are fulfilled.

H.R. Rep. No. 82-1923 at 6 (1952). Given the order of paragraphs as well as the transition, the final sentence, from which the Supreme Court draws in *Chakrabarty*, augments and reinforces the preceding paragraph—which addresses the final clause of § 101, not the preceding paragraphs that deal with the contours of patent eligible processes. Furthermore, the prefatory clause of that sentence appears to limit the dependent clause ("which may include anything under the sun that is made by man") to the statutory classes of "machine" or "manufacture." These categories plainly fall within the ambit of "useful Arts." Note that the prefatory clause does not include the other statutory categories: "process" and "composition of matter." Nor does this sentence call for maximal subject matter. Rather, it merely emphasizes the importance of meeting additional requirements for patentability.

> In both cases applicants seek to patent a process the only novel feature of which is an algorithm embodied in a computer program. The primary difference between the two cases is in the manner in which the claims have been drafted: although Flook's claims focused on the algorithm and recited only minor post-solution activity, the claims here recite in general terms the entire conventional rubber molding process.

Petitioner's Brief, *Diamond v. Diehr*, 6 No. 79-1112 (June 10, 1980) (summary of argument).

Writing for the majority, Justice Rehnquist explained that processes have been eligible for patent protection since the 1793 Act and referenced the statement from *Benson* that "[t]ransformation and reduction of an article 'to a different state or thing' is the clue to the patentability of a process claim that does not include particular machines." *Diamond v. Diehr*, 450 U.S. 175, 184 (1981) (quoting *Benson*, 409 U.S. at 70). The Court concluded that "a physical and chemical process for molding precision synthetic rubber products falls within the § 101 categories of possibly patentable subject matter." *Id.* Justice Rehnquist purported to distinguish *Benson* and *Flook* before proclaiming that "[o]ur earlier opinions lend support to our present conclusion that a claim drawn to subject matter otherwise statutory does not become nonstatutory simply because it uses a mathematical formula, computer program, or digital computer." *Id.* at 187. The Court emphasized that process claims are properly analyzed

> as a whole. It is inappropriate to dissect the claims into old and new elements and then to ignore the presence of the old elements in the analysis. This is particularly true in a process claim because a new combination of steps in a process may be patentable even though all the constituents of the combination were well known and in common use before the combination was made. The "novelty" of any element or steps in a process, or even of the process itself, is of no relevance in determining whether the subject matter of a claim falls within the § 101 categories of possibly patentable subject matter.

Id. at 188–89. In so doing, Justice Rehnquist swept away the requirement of *inventive* application. He reiterated, however, that "a mathematical formula as such" is not patentable nor is attempting to limit the use of a formula to a particular technological environment, citing *Benson* and *Flook*. *Id.* at 191. The touchstone for patentability of a process embodying a mathematical formula, according to the majority opinion, is significant postsolution activity—that is, "transforming or reducing an article to a different state or thing." *Id.* at 191–92.

Justice Stevens, joined by Justices Brennan, Marshall, and Blackmun, vehemently dissented, emphasizing that the majority eviscerated the inventive application doctrine. To the dissenters, if the inventor's "method is regarded as an 'algorithm' as that term was used" in *Benson* and *Flook*, "and if no other inventive concept is disclosed in the patent application," then the claim falls outside the scope of patentable processes under § 101. *Id.* at 213–14. Moreover, the dissenters contended that "the postsolution activity described in the *Flook* application was no less significant than the automatic opening of the curing mold involved in this case." *Id.* at 215.

14.3.1.2.4 The Rise of the Federal Circuit and Dismantling of Patentable Subject-Matter Limitations

Over the ensuing nearly three decades, the evolution of patent-eligibility doctrine shifted to the Court of Appeals for the Federal Circuit, established in 1982. Perhaps bearing out concerns that a national appellate patent tribunal would favor expansion of patent protection, the Federal Circuit gradually eroded patent-eligibility limitations. Building off of *Diehr*, the Federal Circuit gradually chipped away at the postsolution activity necessary to bring software-related claims within § 101. *See, e.g.*, *In re Alappat*, 33 F.3d 1526 (Fed. Cir. 1994). Similarly, the Federal Circuit endorsed the USPTO's policy of patent eligibility of DNA molecules. *See Amgen, Inc. v. Chugai Pharm. Co.*, 927 F.2d 1200 (Fed. Cir. 1991). In a departure from prior jurisprudence, the Federal Circuit "la[id the] ill-conceived [business-method] exception to rest." *State St. Bank & Tr. Co. v. Signature Fin. Grp., Inc.*, 149 F.3d 1368, 1375 (Fed. Cir. 1998). The Supreme Court declined to weigh in on these controversies.

The *State Street Bank* decision sent shockwaves through the financial community, sweeping away more than a century of jurisprudence holding that business methods were unpatentable. Financial institutions became concerned that their investment strategies, which were maintained as trade secrets and hence could not qualify as prior art, could be held to infringe later-developed patents. As a result, they sought legislation excluding business methods from the scope of patentable subject matter. Intellectual-property trade organizations, however, resisted any changes to § 101. As a compromise, Congress established the § 273 prior-user defense as a safe harbor for the financial community. *See* First Inventor Defense Act of 1999, Pub. L. 106-113, app. A, 113 Stat. 1501, 552, 555. The legislation did not take a position on the scope of patentable subject matter.

The Federal Circuit's loosening of patent-eligibility doctrines brought about a vast expansion in the range of patents being sought and granted. The USPTO shifted its position from skepticism about expansive patent eligibility to openness and even enthusiasm, resulting in a flood of software, DNA, and business-method patents. Entrepreneurs and venture capitalists came to see patenting as a valuable tool for developing (or at least claiming) Internet-related businesses. The late 1990s witnessed an unprecedented growth of start-up businesses based on speculative initial public offerings secured, in part, on patent portfolios.

The bursting of the Internet stock bubble in the early 2000s produced a vast shake-out, causing widespread bankruptcies and the auctioning and sale of Internet-related patents. This led to the emergence of patent assertion entities—patent-holding companies and nonpracticing entities seeking to monetize Internet-related patents. Lawsuits by patent-assertion entities produced a tidal wave of patent-eligibility challenges as well as calls by Silicon Valley companies, policy makers, and scholars for policy reform.

The Federal Circuit issued several decisions cautiously reinvigorating patent-eligibility limitations. *See, e.g.*, *In re Nuijten*, 500 F.3d 1346 (Fed. Cir. 2007) (holding that a watermarked electromagnetic signal does not fall into any of the four categories of patent-eligible subject matter); *In re Comiskey*, 499 F.3d 1365 (Fed. Cir. 2007), *amended by* 554 F.3d 967 (Fed. Cir. 2009) (noting the "'[t]he *obligation* to determine what type of discovery is sought to be patented [so as to determine whether it is 'the kind of "discoveries" that the statute was enacted to protect'] *must precede* the determination of whether that discovery is, in fact, new or obvious'" (citing *Parker v. Flook*, 437 U.S. 584, 593 (1978) (emphasis added by Federal Circuit); and affirming rejection of a business-method patent under § 101 as merely relying on mental steps). Most notably, the Federal Circuit, sitting en banc, attempted to clarify the boundaries of patentable subject matter under § 101. *See In re Bilski*, 545 F.3d 943 (Fed. Cir. 2008) (en banc).

Bilski claimed a method of managing risk of commodity prices—a business method that could be implemented using a computer. *Id.* at 949. In an effort to harmonize the Supreme Court's *Benson*, *Flook*, and *Diehr* precedents, the Federal Circuit devised the "machine-or-transformation" ("MoT") test "to determine whether a process claim is tailored narrowly enough to encompass only a particular application of a fundamental principle rather than to pre-empt the principle itself." *Id.* at 954. Under the MoT test, a claimed process is patent-eligible under § 101 if: "(1) it is tied to a particular machine or apparatus, or (2) it transforms a particular article into a different state or thing." *Id.* The court concluded that the Bilski patent failed both prongs—it was not tied to a "particular" machine, and transformation of legal obligations or relationships, business risks, or other abstractions were not within the types of tangible changes eligible for patent protection—and it hence was unpatentable. *Id.* at 963–66.

14.3.1.2.5 The Supreme Court's Revival of Subject-Matter Limitations

The Supreme opened a new chapter in patent-eligibility jurisprudence with its grant of review in the *Bilski* case. Many groups and individuals filed amicus briefs, with arguments ranging from the unpatentability of business methods as falling outside of the "useful arts" and hence beyond Congress's legislative authority to a textual argument that § 101 encompasses "any" process. The Court's ultimate decision in *Bilski* would prove anticlimactic and unilluminating. *See Bilski v. Kappos*, 561 U.S. 593 (2010); Peter S. Menell, *Forty Years of Wondering in the Wilderness and No Closer to the Promised Land:* Bilski*'s Superficial Textualism and the Missed Opportunity to Return Patent Law to Its Technology Mooring*, 63 Stan. L. Rev. 1289 (2011).

While affirming the Federal Circuit's decision holding Bilski's hedging patent application invalid, the Supreme Court rejected the MoT test as the *sole* test of patent eligibility of process claims. *Bilski,* 561 U.S. at 603. The Supreme Court characterized the MoT test as a "useful and important clue, an investigative tool, for determining whether some claimed inventions are processes under § 101," but too rigid in view of the broad statutory definition in § 100(b) of "process." *Id.* at 603–04. While recognizing the jurisprudentially developed exclusions for laws of nature, natural phenomena, and abstract ideas, the Court nonetheless warned that the judiciary does not have "*carte blanche* to impose other limitations that are inconsistent with the text and the statute's purpose and design." *Id.* at 603.[14] On similar grounds, the majority rejected the argument that business methods are categorically excluded from patent eligibility.[15] *Id.* at 606–08.

The majority ruled that Bilski's broad independent claim to hedging was "an unpatentable abstract idea, just like the algorithms at issue in *Benson* and *Flook*. Allowing petitioners to patent risk hedging would pre-empt use of this approach in all fields, and would effectively grant a monopoly over an abstract idea." *Id.* at 611–12. The Court further rejected Bilski's narrower dependent claims as unpatentable by reference to *Flook*, which "established that limiting an abstract idea to one field of use or adding token postsolution components did not make the concept patentable." *Id.*

Justice Stevens, joined by Justices Ginsburg, Breyer, and Sotomayor, filed an extensive opinion concurring in the judgment, but contending that the Patent Act and jurisprudence have long categorically excluded business methods from patent eligibility. *Id.* at 613.

In contrast to the cautious ruling in *Bilski*, the Supreme Court's next patentable subject-matter case, *Mayo Collaborative Servs. v. Prometheus Laboratories, Inc.*, 132 S. Ct. 1289 (2012), strongly reinvigorated patent-eligibility limitations. The patentee claimed a process for administering a particular drug, determining the resulting level of the drug in the patient's blood, and setting forth ranges for decreasing, maintaining, or increasing the dosage of the drug. *Id.* at 1295. Writing for a unanimous Court, Justice Breyer held the patent invalid on the ground that the claimed invention does little more than apply a law of nature. *Id.* at 1294.

The decision revives the inventive application framework set forth in *Flook*, a test that had been supplanted by *Diehr*. In so doing, the Court based the decision, as it did in *Flook*, on a misreading of *Neilson v. Harford*, stating that "the claimed process [in *Neilson*] included not only a law of nature but also several unconventional

---

14. The Supreme Court stressed that "[i]n disapproving an exclusive machine-or-transformation test, we by no means foreclose the Federal Circuit's development of other limiting criteria that further the purposes of the Patent Act and are not inconsistent with its text." *Id.* at 612–13. The Court emphasized, however, that "nothing in today's opinion should be read as endorsing interpretations of § 101 that the Court of Appeals for the Federal Circuit has used in the past." *Id.* at 612.

15. It reinforced this textual focus with the inference that Congress would not have enacted the § 273 prior-user defense if it did not consider business methods patentable. *Id.* at 607. A more plausible inference is that Congress side-stepped the scope of § 101 and created the prior-user defense as a way to defuse a politically divisive question quickly. Congress placed § 273 in Part III of Title 35, which addresses enforcement rights, not the conditions under which a patent may be obtained. Furthermore, in defining the term "method" for purposes of the prior-user defense, Congress avoided altering the definitions governing patentable subject matter in § 100. *See* 35 U.S.C. § 100(a) (providing definitions of terms "[w]hen used in this title"). Instead, Congress included a definition of "method" in § 273(a), "[f]or purposes of *this* section," which deals only with the limited defense. *Id.* (emphasis added).

steps (such as inserting the receptacle, applying heat to the receptacle externally, and blowing the air into the furnace) that confined the claims to a particular, useful application of the principle." *See id.* at 1300. To the contrary, the *Neilson* case upheld the broad claim to an application of a law of nature notwithstanding that the application of the natural law was conventional. *See* §§ 14.3.1.2.1, 14.3.1.2.3. Beyond this misapprehension, the Court glossed over the undeniable tension between *Flook* and *Diehr*.

The Supreme Court turned to the patent eligibility of genetic sequences in the following term. The patentee in *Association for Molecular Pathology v. Myriad Genetics, Inc.*, 133 S. Ct. 2107 (2013), had obtained patents on claims to isolated deoxyribonucleic acid (DNA) sequences associated with predisposition to breast cancers and ovarian cancers and for diagnostic methods of identifying mutations in those DNA sequences. *Id.* at 2112–13. The patentee also obtained claims on complementary DNA (cDNA) compositions derived from the naturally occurring DNA molecules.[16] *Id.* Writing for a unanimous Supreme Court, Justice Thomas held that isolated DNA involving a naturally occurring genomic DNA segment was unpatentable as a natural phenomenon, but that cDNA derived from such genomic DNA was patentable due to human intervention.[17] *Id.* at 2116–19.

The Court did not reach step two of the *Mayo/Alice* test on the ground that cDNA was not naturally occurring and therefore not drawn to a judicial exception. cDNA, however, contains the same genetic information as naturally occurring mRNA and Myriad did not create or alter this information. Moreover, the act of reverse-transcribing natural mRNA into cDNA was known, routine, and conventional when the Myriad patents were filed in 1994. *See* Jeffrey A. Lefstin, *The Three Faces of Prometheus: A Post-*Alice *Jurisprudence of Abstractions*, 16 N.C. J.L. & Tech. 647, 678–79 (2015).

The Supreme Court took another patent-eligibility case the following term. In *Alice Corp. Pty. Ltd. v. CLS Bank International*, 134 S. Ct. 2347 (2014), the Supreme Court addressed patent claims reminiscent of those at issue in *Bilski*. The patentee had obtained patents for mitigating settlement risk in financial transactions using a computer system as a third-party intermediary. The en banc Federal Circuit was

---

16. The PTO and the Federal Circuit considered DNA sequences derived from living organisms to be patentable so long as the patentee could establish credible utility. *See, e.g.*, *In re Fisher*, 421 F.3d 1365 (Fed. Cir. 2005). The legal basis for this view traces back a century to a Judge Learned Hand decision upholding a patent on a purified form of adrenaline (isolating the extract in the form of a chemical base) as distinct from the natural substance, *Parke-Davis & Co. v. H.K. Mulford & Co.*, 189 F. 95 (S.D.N.Y. 1911), *aff'd*, 196 F. 496 (2d Cir. 1912) (reasoning that the purified form of the naturally occurring substance "became for every practical purpose a new thing commercially and therapeutically").

17. DNA sequences are composed of regions that code for proteins (exons) and regions that do not (introns). cDNA molecules are synthesized by removing introns. cDNA is most often synthesized from mature (fully spliced) messenger RNA (mRNA) using the enzyme reverse transcriptase. *See* Complementary DNA, Wikipedia <https://en.wikipedia.org/wiki/Complementary_DNA>.

deeply divided on the interpretation of *Bilski* and *Mayo*. Writing for a unanimous Supreme Court, Justice Thomas reaffirmed the inventive application approach revived in *Mayo*: "We have described step two of this analysis as a search for an "'inventive concept'"—i.e., an element or combination of elements that is "sufficient to ensure that the patent in practice amounts to significantly more than a patent upon the [ineligible concept] itself."" *Id.* at 2355. Applying this framework, the Court concluded that the representative method claim does no more than implement the abstract idea of intermediated settlement on a generic computer and that the system and media claims add nothing of substance to the underlying abstract idea. *Id.* at 2355–60.[18]

14.3.1.3 Patent-Eligibility Conundrums

Notwithstanding the Supreme Court's renewed attention to patent eligibility, the *Bilski*, *Mayo*, *Myriad*, and *Alice* decisions provide relatively little guidance on how to determine whether a claim contains a patent-ineligible natural law, physical phenomenon, or abstract idea and, if so, whether there is a sufficient inventive concept or inventive application to bring the claim within § 101 eligibility. The Federal Circuit's early applications of this regime reinforce the "know it when you see it" quality of the Supreme Court's two-step test. *See, e.g.*, *DDR Holdings, LLC v. Hotels.com, L.P.*, 773 F.3d 1245 (Fed. Cir. 2014) (emphasizing under step 1 that the claim is "rooted in the computer technology" and hence not abstract; and basing step 2 analysis on a bald assertion that the claimed invention is "not merely the routine or conventional use of the Internet" without discussion of prior art); *Ultramercial, Inc. v. Hulu, LLC*, 772 F.3d 709, 715 (2014) (noting that "[a]s the Court stated in *Alice*, '[a]t some level, "all inventions . . . embody, use, reflect, rest upon, or apply laws of nature, natural phenomena, or abstract ideas"'); *Alice*, 134 S. Ct. at 2354 (quoting *Mayo*, 132 S. Ct. at 1293). We acknowledge this reality, and we do not purport to state that all claims in all software-based patents will necessarily be directed to an abstract idea. Future cases may turn out differently."). Several district court decisions have grappled with these issues. *See, e.g.*, *Ameritox Ltd. v. Millennium Health, LLC*, 88 F. Supp. 3d 885 (W.D. Wisc. 2015); *Cal. Inst. of Tech. v. Hughes Commc'ns, Inc.*, 59 F. Supp. 3d 974 (C.D. Cal. 2014); *Cogent Med., Inc. v. Elsevier Inc.*, 70 F. Supp. 3d 1058 (N.D. Cal. 2014).

Among the issues that remain to be resolved are: (1) to what extent does § 101 eligibility turn on subsidiary factual determinations (e.g., whether an application of a natural law is routine or conventional) and claim construction; (2) at what stage of litigation should district courts address § 101 eligibility; and (3) what is the continuing relevance of *Diehr* and can it be reconciled with *Flook*, *Mayo*, *Myriad*, and *Alice*. What is clear is that we are at the beginning of a new patent-eligibility era in which lower courts will need to develop case-management techniques for assessing whether

---

18. Echoing Justice Stevens' concurrence in *Bilski*, Justice Sotomayor, joined by Justices Ginsburg and Breyer, concurred in the holding based on the view that business methods do not qualify as a "process" under § 101. *Id.* at 2360.

patent claims involving natural laws, physical phenomena, and abstract ideas can surmount the § 101 inventive application hurdle and when and on what basis that determination should be made.

14.3.1.4 Subject Matter Expressly Excluded by Statute

For the first time in U.S. history, the AIA introduced two statutory exclusions to patentable subject matter, effective September 16, 2011.

14.3.1.4.1 Tax Strategies

Strategies for "reducing, avoiding, or deferring tax liability" are deemed to be within the prior art. This does not apply to claims directed to preparing tax returns or inventions "used solely for financial management" to the extent that they are severable from any tax strategy. AIA § 14. This provision is effective September 16, 2011, and applies to applications pending or filed on or after that date.

14.3.1.4.2 Human Organisms

Claims "directed to or encompassing a human organism" are barred. This provision is effective September 16, 2011, and applies to applications pending or filed on or after that date. AIA § 33.

14.3.2 Utility (§ 101)

Section 101 requires that an invention be "useful" to be patentable. Whether an invention meets the utility requirement is decided from the perspective of a person having ordinary skill in the art. Because most inventions have a clear utility (and "inventions" of questionable utility will typically be flagged during prosecution), the utility requirement rarely arises in litigation. Utility can arise where a claimed invention does not work for its intended purpose. The two areas in which utility tends to arise in litigation with some frequency are in the fields of chemistry and biotechnology, where inventors seek to obtain patents on compositions of matter before they have conclusive evidence of their utility.

The Supreme Court provided the framework for addressing this question in *Brenner v. Manson*, 383 U.S. 519 (1966). The patentee sought protection for an adjacent homologue[19] of a steroid demonstrated to have tumor-inhibiting effects in mice. *Id.* at 520–22. The inventor had yet to establish such properties for the compound at issue and there was high unpredictability of compounds in the relevant field of chemistry. *Id.* at 532. In rejecting the patent on the basis of lack of proven utility, the Supreme Court commented that

19. A homologue is a member of a chemical series whose compounds differ structurally from each other only by a repeating unit, such as a methylene bridge—CH_2—or a peptide residue. Homologues that are "adjacent" differ from each other by just one of the repeating unit.

> the basic quid pro quo contemplated by the Constitution and the Congress for granting a patent monopoly is the benefit derived by the public from an invention with substantial utility. Unless and until a process is refined and developed to this point—where specific benefit exists in currently available form—there is insufficient justification for permitting an applicant to engross what may prove to be a broad field.

Id. at 534–35. The Court required patentees to establish credible, specific, and substantial utility.

Thus, chemical compounds are not rendered useful merely because they have analogues that are useful. Utility in such cases will depend on the degree of predictability within the art and structural similarity between the claimed compound and others known to have useful properties. Clinical data is not generally required to show the utility of chemical compounds.

An invention must be useful for something more than further research on the product of the invention. If an invented chemical compound, for instance, is being studied extensively as a possible cancer treatment, but no potential to treat cancer has actually been shown, the chemical does not meet the utility requirement, nor is a process to make that chemical useful. The product of the process must have utility for the process to have utility. "Until the process claim has been reduced to production of a product shown to be useful, the metes and bounds of the monopoly are not capable of precise delineation. . . . Such a patent may confer power to block whole areas of scientific development, without compensating benefit to the public." *Id.* at 534. Additionally, an invention must have proven usefulness beyond use as a chemical probe where the results of such a probe are unknown or where the results of that probe are known to lack utility. *In re Fisher*, 421 F.3d 1365, 1371 (Fed. Cir. 2005).

Note, however, that an invention does not need to be better than other technology, nor must it show commercial success to possess substantial utility. Nor do courts judge the morality of a claimed invention in assessing utility. *See Juicy Whip, Inc. v. Orange Bang, Inc.*, 292 F.3d 728 (Fed. Cir. 2002).

14.3.3 Disclosure (§ 112)

Paragraph 1 of § 112 sets forth the disclosure requirement:

> The specification shall contain a *written description* of the invention, and of the manner and process of making and using it, in such full, clear, concise, and exact terms as *to enable* any person skilled in the art to which it pertains, or with which it is most nearly connected, to make and use the same, and shall set forth the *best mode* contemplated by the inventor of carrying out his invention (emphases added).

As interpreted by the Federal Circuit, this provision comprises three distinct requirements: (1) written description—that the specification conveys to a person having ordinary skill in the art that the inventor "possessed" the claimed invention as of the time of filing the application; (2) enablement—that the specification enables a person having ordinary skill in the art to make and use the invention; and (3) best mode—that the specification reveals the best mode of which the inventor is aware of making and using the invention.

14.3.3.1 Written Description

The written description requirement serves to "prevent an applicant from later asserting that he invented that which he did not." *Amgen Inc. v. Hoechst Marion Roussel, Inc.*, 314 F.3d 1313, 1330 (Fed. Cir. 2003). The patentee must "convey with reasonable clarity to those skilled in the art that, as of the filing date sought, he or she was in possession of the invention." *Vas-Cath Inc. v. Mahurkar*, 935 F.2d 1555, 1563–64 (Fed. Cir. 1991). Having "possession of the invention" means that the patentee invented what is claimed. *LizardTech, Inc. v. Earth Res. Mapping, Inc.*, 424 F.3d 1336, 1345 (Fed. Cir. 2005).

Although written description and enablement issues often rise and fall together, the written description requirement is separate and distinct from enablement. *Ariad Pharm., Inc. v. Eli Lilly & Co.*, 598 F.3d 1336, 1351 (Fed. Cir. 2010) (en banc) ("Since its inception, this court has consistently held that § 112, first paragraph, contains a written description requirement separate from enablement."). As a result, an invention may be described without being enabled, and vice versa. The written description requirement "plays a vital role in curtailing claims that do not require undue experimentation to make and use, and thus satisfy enablement, but that have not been invented, and thus cannot be described." *Id.* at 1352.

Compliance with the written description requirement is "an objective inquiry into the four corners of the specification from the perspective of a person of ordinary skill in the art." *Ariad*, 598 F.3d at 1351. The adequacy of the written description is a question of fact, and is highly dependent on the context; the nature and scope of the claims; the complexity and predictability of the relevant technology; the extent and content of the prior art; and the maturity of the science or technology. *Id.*

The patentee need not follow any specific form of disclosure in providing a written description of the invention. *In re Alton*, 76 F.3d 1168, 1172 (Fed. Cir. 1996). However, a description that merely renders the invention obvious is insufficient. *See Goeddel v. Sugano*, 617 F.3d 1350, 1356 (Fed. Cir. 2010) ("The question is not whether one skilled in this field of science might have been able to produce [the claimed subject matter] by building upon the teachings of the [prior art], but rather whether that application 'convey[ed] to those skilled in the art that the inventor had possession of the claimed subject matter as of the filing date.'") (*quoting Ariad*, 598 F.3d at 1351). In some cases, the drawings alone may be adequate to satisfy the written description requirement. *Vas-Cath*, 935 F.2d at 1564.

14.3.3.1.1 Policing Continuation Practice

The Federal Circuit has applied the written description requirement to police efforts by patentees to expand the scope of their patent beyond what they had initially contemplated as their invention. Some patentees will keep continuation and/or continuation-in-part applications pending for several years in order to pursue additional claims that capture their rivals' products introduced into the marketplace during the pendency of those applications. If the subject matter of the additional claims does not have written-description support in the specification of a prior related application from which priority is accorded, the additional claims will be invalid (even if the specification enables one skilled in the art to make and use the claimed subject matter). *See Centocor Ortho Biotech, Inc. v. Abbott Labs.*, 636 F.3d 1341 (Fed. Cir. 2011) (claims added eight years after priority date lacked support in written description); *see also* § 132(a).

14.3.3.1.2 Biotechnology Patents

Beginning in the mid-1990s, the Federal Circuit required that biotechnology patents disclose specific gene sequences in the application even when the functional properties of the gene (such as the protein it codes for) were already known. *See Regents of the Univ. of Cal. v. Eli Lilly & Co.*, 119 F.3d 1559 (Fed. Cir. 1997); *Fiers v. Revel*, 984 F.2d 1164, 1170–71 (Fed. Cir. 1993). Some have characterized these cases as erecting a "super-enablement" standard for biotechnology inventions. *See* Janice M. Mueller, *The Evolving Application of the Written Description to Biotechnological Inventions*, 13 Berkeley Tech. L.J. 615 (1998). More recently, the Federal Circuit has eased this standard by allowing patentees to satisfy the written description requirement by placing several versions of the claimed nucleotide sequences in a public depository. *See Enzo Biochem, Inc. v. Gen-Probe, Inc.*, 323 F.3d 956 (Fed. Cir. 2002); *see also Capon v. Eshhar*, 418 F.3d 1349 (Fed. Cir. 2005) (noting that the requirements for "written description" evolve with the fields of invention).

Demonstrating adequate written-description support for a genus is "a problem that is particularly acute in the biological arts." *Ariad Pharm., Inc. v. Eli Lilly & Co.*, 598 F.3d 1336, 1352–53 (Fed. Cir. 2010) (en banc). "[A] sufficient description of a genus . . . requires the disclosure of either a representative number of species falling within the scope of the genus or structural features common to the members of the genus so that one of skill in the art can 'visualize or recognize' the members of the genus." *Id.* at 1350 (citation omitted). "[M]erely drawing a fence around the outer limits of a purported genus is not an adequate substitute for describing a variety of materials constituting the genus and showing that one has invented a genus and not just a species." *Id.* ("The claims here recite methods encompassing a genus of materials achieving a stated useful result, i.e., reducing NF-[K]B binding to NF-[K]B recognition sites in response to external influences. But the specification does not disclose a variety of species that accomplish the result.").

14.3.3.2 Enablement

To satisfy the enablement requirement, the specification must set forth the "manner and process of making and using [the invention], in such full, clear, concise and exact terms as to enable any person skilled in the art to which it pertains, or with which it is most nearly connected, to make and use the same." § 112, ¶ 1. The purpose of the enablement provision is to ensure that "the public knowledge is enriched by the patent specification to a degree at least commensurate with the scope of the claims. The scope of the claims must be less than or equal to the scope of the enablement." *Nat'l Recovery Techs., Inc. v. Magnetic Separation Sys., Inc.*, 166 F.3d 1190,

1195–96 (Fed. Cir. 1999). Enablement is determined as of the effective filing date of the patent.[20] *See Plant Genetic Sys., N.V. v. DeKalb Genetics Corp.*, 315 F.3d 1335, 1339 (Fed. Cir. 2003). Accordingly, after-arising technology should not be considered in the enablement inquiry. Enablement is a question of law based on underlying findings of fact. *See In re Vaeck*, 947 F.2d 488, 495 (Fed. Cir. 1991).

Enablement is often a matter of degree. Courts evaluate compliance with the enablement requirement by considering whether the specification teaches those skilled in the art to make and use the invention without "undue experimentation." *In re Vaeck*, 947 F.2d at 495 (quoting *In re Wands*, 858 F.2d 731, 737 (Fed. Cir. 1988)). As the Federal Circuit has noted, "[t]hat some experimentation may be required is not fatal; the issue is whether the amount of experimentation required is 'undue.'" *Id.* In determining what constitutes undue experimentation, courts apply a standard of reasonableness, taking into account the nature of the invention and the state of the art. Factors to be considered in making such a determination include:

(1) The quantity of experimentation necessary,

(2) The amount of direction or guidance presented,

(3) The presence or absence of working examples,

(4) The nature of the invention,

(5) The state of the prior art,

(6) The relative skill of those in the art,

(7) The predictability or unpredictability of the art, and

(8) The breadth of the claims.

In re Wands, 858 F.2d at 737. These factors are "illustrative, not mandatory." *Amgen, Inc. v. Chugai Pharm. Co.*, 927 F.2d 1200, 1213 (Fed. Cir. 1991). It is not necessary that the patent specification teach what is well known in the art. *See Hybritech Inc. v. Monoclonal Antibodies, Inc.*, 802 F.2d 1367, 1384 (Fed. Cir. 1986).

A broad claim construction can result in invalidity due to lack of enablement. When two embodiments are "distinctly different," each must be separately enabled. *See Auto. Tech. Int'l v. BMW*, 501 F.3d 1274 (Fed. Cir. 2007) (comparing two columns and five figures of specification for a mechanical sensor with one short paragraph and one figure for an electronic sensor, with uncontradicted expert testimony indicating undue experimentation was required to enable the electronic sensor).

Furthermore, courts have interpreted the "how to use" prong of § 112 as incorporating the utility requirement of § 101. *Rasmusson v. Smithkline Beecham Corp.*, 413 F.3d 1318, 1322–23 (Fed. Cir. 2005). Accordingly, an applicant's failure to disclose how to use an invention may be rejected under either § 112 for lack of enablement or § 101 for lack of utility. *Id.* at 1323.

20. The "effective filing date" of an application is the earlier of the actual filing date or the filing date of an application from which priority is accorded.

14.3.3.3 Best Mode

For proceedings commenced on or after September 16, 2011, the AIA eliminates the failure to disclose the best mode as a basis for invalidating the patent during litigation. AIA § 15. This does not affect USPTO examination, such that the USPTO may still reject an application for failure to disclose the best mode.

The best mode requirement of § 112(a) demands that the specification set forth "the best mode contemplated by the inventor of carrying out his invention." This requirement restrains inventors from applying for patents while concealing known preferred embodiments of their inventions from the public. *See Teleflex, Inc. v. Ficosa N. Am. Corp.*, 299 F.3d 1313, 1330 (Fed. Cir. 2002). The Federal Circuit has interpreted best mode to require "an inventor to disclose the best mode contemplated by him, as of the time he executes the application, of carrying out the invention" defined by the claims. *See Bayer AG v. Schein Pharm., Inc.*, 301 F.3d 1306, 1314–15 (Fed. Cir. 2002) (quoting *In re Gay*, 309 F.2d 769, 772 (C.C.P.A. 1962)).

Compliance with the best mode requirement is a question of fact. *Bayer*, 301 F.3d at 1312. The test for compliance involves a two-prong inquiry: (1) did the inventor possess a best mode for practicing the invention at the time of filing the application; and (2) if the inventor possessed a best mode, is his disclosure adequate to enable a person having ordinary skill in the art to practice the best mode of the invention. *See Chemcast Corp. v. Arco Indus. Corp.*, 913 F.2d 923, 927–28 (Fed. Cir. 1990). While the first prong is subjective and examines the inventor's state of mind at the time of filing, the second prong is objective and focuses on the scope of the claimed invention and the level of skill in the art. *Eli Lilly & Co. v. Barr Labs., Inc.*, 251 F.3d 955, 963 (Fed. Cir. 2001). Best mode violations are found where there is either a "failure to disclose a preferred embodiment, or else failure to disclose a preference that materially affected making or using the invention." *Bayer*, 301 F.3d at 1316.

An inventor is typically not required to update the best mode disclosure based on findings made subsequent to the filing date, even if his or her patent application is still pending. Regarding continuation applications, the inventor need not update the best mode disclosure if the material in a continuation application is "common subject matter" with that of the original application. *See Transco v. Performance Contracting, Inc.*, 38 F.3d 551 (Fed. Cir. 1994). An inventor need only update the best mode in a continuation application if the claim feature associated with that best mode first appeared or first received adequate written description in that later filing.

14.3.3.4 Claim Definiteness

Section 112(b), formerly § 112, ¶ 2, provides that "[t]he specification shall conclude with one or more claims particularly pointing out and distinctly claiming the subject matter which the applicant regards as his invention." This requirement ensures that the patentee adequately notify the public of the scope of his or her invention. "A patent is invalid for indefiniteness if its claims, read in light of the specification delineating the patent, and the prosecution history, fail to inform, with reasonable certainty, those skilled in the art about the scope of the invention." *Nautilus v.*

Biosig Instruments, Inc., 134 S. Ct. 2120, 2123 (2014). The definiteness standard recognizes that "absolute precision is unattainable." *Id.* It "must take into account the inherent limitations of language" and allow a "modicum of uncertainty" so as to provide appropriate incentives for innovation. *Id.* at 2128. For example, terms of degree such as "substantially," "about," or "closely approximate" do not necessarily render the claim indefinite, so long as the term "provide[s] enough certainty to one of skill in the art when read in the context of the invention." *Interval Licensing LLC v. AOL, Inc.*, 766 F.3d 1364, 1370 (Fed. Cir. 2014). Nonetheless, the Supreme Court recognized that a patent must be precise enough to afford public notice of claim scope, otherwise there would be a "zone of uncertainty which enterprise and experimentation may enter only at the risk of infringement claims." *Nautilus*, 134 S. Ct. at 2128.

14.3.4 Novelty and Statutory Bars (§ 102)

With the enactment of the AIA, the regime under which patents are awarded in the U.S. changed on March 16, 2013, from a first-to-invent system (i.e., awarding a patent to the inventor having the earliest date of invention) to a first-to-file system (i.e., awarding a patent to the inventor who files his application first). AIA § 3. The change from a first-to-invent system to a first-to-file system is not retroactive. As a result, the first-to-invent regime will coexist in parallel with the first-to-file regime for at least the next couple of decades.

To establish a first-to-file system, § 102 was completely rewritten under the AIA. The amended version of § 102 will apply to any application having at least one claim with an effective filing date on or after March 16, 2013. The version of § 102 that was in effect under the first-to-invent regime prior to the enactment of the AIA will apply to applications in which all claims have effective filing dates before March 16, 2013. Accordingly, the discussion of novelty requirements under § 102 in this section will be presented separately for each regime: § 14.3.4.1 covers the first-to-invent regime, while § 14.3.4.2 covers the first-to-file regime.

14.3.4.1 The First-to-Invent Regime

For patent applications in which all claims have effective filing dates prior to March 16, 2013, the novelty requirement is governed by the pre-AIA version of § 102. Accordingly, all references to § 102 in this subsection (§ 14.3.4.1), will refer to the pre-AIA version.

Section 102 sets forth two sets of novelty requirements for a patent to issue: (1) that the inventor was the first to invent (§ 102(a), (e), (f), and (g)); and (2) that the inventor filed their application in a timely manner (§ 102 (b), (c), and (d)).

The first set of requirements, referred to as the anticipation or lack of novelty bars, seeks to ensure that a patent issues only to the first inventor. This goal is accomplished by using the applicant's date of invention as the relevant baseline for analysis. Prior art containing all elements of the claimed invention that became publicly available (or filed as part of a patent application or known, but not abandoned, suppressed, or concealed) will anticipate, and thereby defeat, the patent claim. By contrast, the second set of requirements, known as statutory bars, and related timely filing provisions promote prompt disclosure by requiring that the patentee file an application within one year of various triggering events.

Whether a reference anticipates the applicant's invention is a question of fact. *See Elan Pharm., Inc. v. Mayo Found. for Med. Educ. and Research*, 346 F.3d 1051, 1054 (Fed. Cir. 2003). A finding of anticipation requires the reference to contain each and every limitation of the claimed invention either expressly or inherently.[21] If even one limitation of the claimed invention is missing from the prior art reference, § 102 does not invalidate the claim—although the claim may still be vulnerable under the nonobviousness requirement. *See* § 14.3.5.

If a single reference discloses a species of a claimed genus,[22] a claim to the entire genus is anticipated. *See Eli Lilly & Co. v. Barr Labs., Inc.*, 222 F.3d 973, 987 (Fed. Cir. 2000); *Titanium Metals Corp. v. Banner*, 778 F.2d 775 (Fed. Cir. 1985). The opposite is not always true; the disclosure of a genus in a single prior art reference does not necessarily anticipate a claimed species that is a member of that genus. *See Atofina v. Great Lakes Chem. Co.*, 441 F.3d 991, 999 (Fed. Cir. 2006).

14.3.4.1.1 First to Invent—§ 102(a)

Section 102(a) precludes patentability where the "invention was known or used by others in this country, or patented or described in a printed publication in this or a foreign country," before the applicant's date of invention. Note the geographic limitations on the prior art covered by § 102(a): whereas knowledge or use must occur

---

21. A finding of anticipation requires that a prior art reference enable a person having ordinary skill in the art to make or use the claimed invention. *See Impax Labs., Inc. v. Aventis Pharm. Inc.*, 468 F.3d 1366 (Fed. Cir. 2006). This "enablement" standard is not as strict as that applied under § 112. Unlike that enablement requirement, an enabling reference under § 102 need not disclose utility, only the claimed invention's limitations. *Id.* A claim is anticipated if each element of the claim is found, either expressly or inherently, in a single prior art reference. *See Verdegaal Bros., Inc. v. Union Oil Co. of Cal.*, 814 F.2d 628, 631 (Fed. Cir. 1987). There are, however, several exceptions to the inherency doctrine. In *Tilghman v. Proctor*, 102 U.S. 707 (1880), the Supreme Court declined to invalidate a patent based on a prior art machine (a steam engine) that might have accidentally and unwittingly produced a claimed fatty acid that proved useful as a cleansing substance. Nor does mere probabilistic inherency, *see Continental Can Co. USA v. Monsanto Co.*, 948 F.2d 1264, 1269 (Fed. Cir. 1991), nor the presence of an unrecognized de minimis quantity of a claimed substance in the prior art, *see In re Seaborg*, 328 F.2d 996 (C.C.P.A. 1964), anticipate later patent applications. *See also Eibel Process Co. v. Minn. & Ontario Paper Co.*, 261 U.S. 45 (1923). The Federal Circuit has, however, interpreted these exceptions and qualifications to the inherency rule narrowly. *See Schering Corp. v. Geneva Pharm., Inc.*, 339 F.3d 1373, 1377 (Fed. Cir. 2003) (observing that "[c]ases dealing with 'accidental, unwitting, and unappreciated' anticipation . . . do not show that inherency requires recognition").

22. A genus is a category made up of multiple species that share a common characteristic. Chemical and biotechnology inventions are often claimed using genus and species formats.

in the United States to bar patentability, a patent or printed publication from anywhere in the world can invalidate a patent. The courts have developed nuanced interpretations of § 102(a), particularly the phrases "known or used" and "printed publication."

14.3.4.1.1.1 "Known or Used"

Knowledge or use must have been available to the public to qualify as prior art under § 102. *See Woodland Tr. v. Flowertree Nursery, Inc.*, 148 F.3d 1368, 1370 (Fed. Cir. 1998). Courts generally balance several factors—the number and credibility of observers, the intent of the discloser (i.e., whether the inventor sought to keep the information secret), the number of disclosures, and the extent to which the observers understood the invention—in determining whether a disclosure or use was "public." The evidence that knowledge or use was public is judged by the clear-and-convincing standard. In addition, "[t]he nonsecret use of a claimed process in the usual course of producing articles for commercial purposes is a public use." *W.L. Gore & Assocs., Inc. v. Garlock, Inc.*, 721 F.2d 1540, 1548 (Fed. Cir. 1983). Secret knowledge or use (including classified government research and articles under submission to journals) does not qualify for purposes of § 102(a). The effective date of a knowledge or use reference is the day on which it was presented to the public. Because it is aimed at determining whether anyone preempted the patentee, § 102(a) does not treat knowledge or use by the applicants themselves as a reference; it only refers to knowledge or use "by others."

14.3.4.1.1.2 Printed Publication

A printed publication has been interpreted to mean a reference that is "sufficiently accessible to the public interested in the art." *See Constant v. Advanced Micro-Devices, Inc.*, 848 F.2d 1560, 1568 (Fed. Cir. 1988). Accordingly, dissemination and public accessibility are the determinative factors regarding whether a reference is "published." "Accessibility goes to the issue of whether interested members of the relevant public could obtain the information if they wanted to. If accessibility is proved, there is no requirement to show that particular members of the public actually received the information." *Id.* at 1569. Whether a reference qualifies as a printed publication under § 102 is a question of law based on underlying factual determinations. *See Cooper Cameron Corp. v. Kvaerner Oilfield Prods., Inc.*, 291 F.3d 1317, 1321 (Fed. Cir. 2002).

The Federal Circuit has construed sufficient accessibility broadly, finding a single thesis cataloged (by subject matter) in a German university library accessible to those interested in the art exercising reasonable diligence constituted "sufficient accessibility" to bar patentability under § 102(b). *In re Hall*, 781 F.2d 897, 900 (Fed. Cir. 1986). Even a temporarily displayed reference that was neither distributed nor indexed may be sufficiently accessible to constitute a printed publication. *See In re Klopfenstein*, 380 F.3d 1345, 1350 (Fed. Cir. 2004). Relevant factors to analyze include:

(1) the length of time the display was exhibited,

(2) the expertise of the target audience,

(3) the existence (or lack thereof) of reasonable expectations that the material displayed would not be copied, and

(4) the simplicity or ease with which the material displayed could have been copied.

Id. Whether "printed publication" encompasses new technologies such as websites remains to be conclusively decided, but the Federal Circuit has noted that the phrase "has been interpreted to give effect to ongoing advances in the technologies of data storage, retrieval, and dissemination." *In re Hall*, 781 F.2d at 898.

14.3.4.1.2 Novelty—First to Invent—§ 102(g)

Section 102(g) addresses situations where two or more researchers independently discover the same invention, with the goal of granting a patent only to the first person to "invent" who does not abandon, suppress, or conceal the invention from the public. The somewhat opaque statutory provision provides that a patent shall issue unless:

> (1) during the course of an interference conducted under section 135 or section 291, another inventor involved therein establishes, to the extent permitted in section 104, that before such person's invention thereof the invention was made by such other inventor and not abandoned, suppressed, or concealed, or (2) before such person's invention thereof, the invention was made in this country by another inventor who had not abandoned, suppressed, or concealed it. In determining priority of invention under this subsection, there shall be considered not only the respective dates of conception and reduction to practice of the invention, but also the reasonable diligence of one who was first to conceive and last to reduce to practice, from a time prior to conception by the other.

The following schematic representation of § 102(g) shows how courts interpret this language:

(1) during the course of an interference conducted under section 135 or section 291, another inventor involved therein establishes, to the extent permitted in section 104, that

   a. before such person's invention thereof the invention was

   b. made by such other inventor and

   c. not abandoned, suppressed, or concealed, or

(2) [in the context of an invalidity defense to patent infringement]

   a. before such person's invention thereof, the invention was

   b. made in this country by another inventor who

   c. had not abandoned, suppressed, or concealed it.

(3) In determining priority of invention [under either branch] of this subsection, there shall be considered not only

   a. the respective dates of conception and reduction to practice of the invention, but also

b. the reasonable diligence of one who was first to conceive and last to reduce to practice, from a time prior to conception by the other.

Subsection (1) deals with interferences, proceedings ordinarily conducted within the Patent Office (and only rarely in federal district court) when multiple inventors simultaneously claim the same invention. Subsection (2) is the more relevant provision for district courts. Defendants in infringement proceedings typically scour the field of technology to identify evidence that someone other than the patentee invented the claimed invention prior to the patentee's date of invention. Such evidence invalidates the issued patent claim if the invention was made in the United States before the patentee's date of invention and the first inventor did not abandon, suppress, or conceal the invention.

To make these principles operational, we need precise definitions of the following terms: (i) "conception," (ii) "reduction to practice," (iii) "reasonable diligence," and (iv) "abandoned, suppressed, or concealed."

14.3.4.1.2.1 Conception

A conception of the claimed invention is "the complete performance of the mental part of the inventive art," a "definite and permanent idea of the complete and operative invention." *See Townsend v. Smith*, 36 F.2d 292, 295 (C.C.P.A. 1929). It represents the idea of the invention and does not require tests, models, or prototypes. Nonetheless, it must contain all limitations of the claimed invention as it is thereafter reduced to practice. To deter fraud, the law requires corroboration of any inventor testimony regarding conception, reduction to practice, or diligence. *See Mahurkar v. C.R. Bard Inc.*, 79 F.3d 1572, 1577–78 (Fed. Cir. 1996). Often this corroborating evidence takes the form of contemporaneous witnessed notebooks or records by someone skilled in the art. *See, e.g., Hahn v. Wong*, 892 F.2d 1028, 1032–33 (Fed. Cir. 1989). Without some form of corroborating evidence, an inventor's testimony is ignored. While before the Patent Office, an inventor may file a Rule 131 affidavit (*see* 37 C.F.R. § 1.131) to establish a date of invention. The patentee must corroborate this date.

14.3.4.1.2.2 Reduction to Practice

A reduction to practice can be actual or constructive. A prototype or working embodiment of the claimed invention that is "suitable for [the invention's] intended purpose" serves as an actual reduction to practice. *See Mahurkar v. C.R. Bard Inc.*, 79 F.3d 1572, 1578 (Fed. Cir. 1996). Proving that a prototype was "suitable for its intended purpose" will vary, depending on the complexity of the invention. A simple mechanical device may require only a drawing, while a chemical invention may require extensive experimental data. Patent law recognizes a patent application as a constructive reduction to practice, provided it describes and enables a person of ordinary skill in the art to practice the invention without undue experimentation.

14.3.4.1.2.3 Reasonable Diligence

"Reasonable diligence" is only at issue when the inventor was first to conceive but second to reduce to practice. In this specific context, the first-to-conceive inventor must have been reasonably diligent in working to reduce the invention to practice between the time "just prior" to the later inventor's date of conception until the first-to-conceive inventor's reduction to practice. *See, e.g.*, *Griffith v. Kanamaru*, 816 F.2d 624 (Fed. Cir. 1987). Once the first-to-conceive has reduced to practice, their further diligence is no longer relevant, although they must not abandon the invention through undue delay in filing a patent application. *See* § 14.3.4.1.2.4.

Whether an inventor was reasonably diligent is a case-by-case determination, but prior cases establish some guideposts. *Griffith* held that a delay of three months after conception before embarking on efforts to reduce the invention to practice while waiting for additional funding and the arrival of a graduate student was not reasonable. 816 F.2d at 628–29. Other factors to consider include the complexity of the invention, the need for other experiments, work on similar inventions, and the inventor's health.

14.3.4.1.2.4 Abandoned, Suppressed, or Concealed

Section 102(g) nullifies evidence of prior invention if such earlier inventor abandoned, suppressed, or concealed the invention. Whether an invention has been abandoned, suppressed, or concealed is a question of intent, but an unreasonably long delay in filing for a patent creates an inference that the inventor intended to suppress the invention. *See Dow Chem. Co. v. Astro-Valcour, Inc.*, 267 F.3d 1334 (Fed. Cir. 2001) (a two-and-a-half-year delay did not); *Peeler v. Miller*, 535 F.2d 647 (C.C.P.A. 1976) (a four-year delay in applying for a patent destroyed priority). While § 102(g) prevents an inventor from claiming an early priority date on an invention he or she later suppressed, it does not prevent an inventor from claiming a later date when he or she resumes work on the invention. In such cases, the earlier, suppressed work is ignored and the inventor can rely on the resumed work to establish new dates of conception and reduction to practice. *See Paulik v. Rizkalla*, 760 F.2d 1270 (Fed. Cir. 1985) (en banc).

By invalidating a claimed invention because of a prior invention that might not have been publicly disclosed, § 102(g) cuts against the principle that novelty is judged on the basis of public knowledge. The invention priority rule of § 102(g) seeks to balance that principle with the "first to invent" principle. The requirement that prior invention not have been "abandoned, suppressed, or concealed" provides the fulcrum for effectuating this balance.

14.3.4.1.2.5 Section 102(g)—Summary

The § 102(g) invention priority rule can be restated as follows:

(1) The first to reduce the invention to practice has priority by default.

(2) Filing a valid patent application is a constructive reduction to practice.

(3) The second person to reduce to practice can prevail only if they were the first to conceive and were diligent from a time prior to the other inventor's conception through to their own reduction to practice.

(4) Any reduction to practice that was abandoned, suppressed, or concealed cannot defeat patentability by another.

14.3.4.1.3 Novelty—"Secret Prior Art"—§ 102(e)

The possibility of secret prior art invalidating a patent also arises under § 102(e) whereby confidential patent applications within the Patent Office can be used to invalidate later filings.[23] If a patent application discloses but does not claim a later filed claimed invention and is later published, the application constitutes § 102(e)(1) prior art as of its filing date.[24] If the application later issues as a patent, such application constitutes § 102(e)(2) prior art as of its filing date. The policy rationale behind § 102(e) is that if another's earlier filed patent application describes the applicant's claimed invention, the applicant was not the first inventor of that subject matter. The fact that the knowledge was not publicly known is outweighed by the Patent Office's knowledge of the invention and its unique role in making patent determinations.

14.3.4.1.4 Novelty—Derivation—§ 102(f)

Section 102(f) precludes an applicant from obtaining a patent on inventions that he did not invent. This section is referred to as the "derivation" provision, meaning that an applicant may not patent subject matter derived from another. *See OddzOn Prods., Inc. v. Just Toys, Inc.*, 122 F.3d 1396, 1401 (Fed. Cir. 1997). Section 102(f) is not limited to public knowledge but may also concern private communications between the applicant and another. *Id.* at 1401–02. Proof that another derived the invention requires showing both prior conception of the invention and disclosure of that conception to the applicant. *See Gambro Lundia AB v. Baxter Healthcare Corp.*, 110 F.3d 1573, 1576 (Fed. Cir. 1997). Because there are no geographic limitations in § 102(f), prior conception and disclosure to the applicant can occur anywhere in the world.

14.3.4.1.5 Statutory Bars—Timely Filing—§ 102(b)

Section 102(b) arises frequently in patent litigation. The provision encourages timely filing of patent applications to expand the public's knowledge more quickly and prevent inventors from extending the effective life of their patent through delay in filing for protection. Section 102(b) states that a person shall be entitled to a pa-

---

23. A patent is considered "secret prior art" when its contents cannot become known until the date of publication or issuance, even though its effective date is the filing date. *Sun Studs, Inc. v. ATA Equip. Leasing, Inc.*, 872 F.2d 978, 982 n.3 (Fed. Cir. 1989).

24. If the pending application *claims* (and not merely discloses) the same invention, then it constitutes § 102(g) prior art and will provoke an interference if such conflict is recognized by an examiner.

tent unless "the invention was patented or described in a printed publication in this or a foreign country or in public use or on sale in this country, more than one year prior to the date of the application for patent in the United States. . . ."

The section recognizes three types of prior art: "printed publication," "public use," and offers for sale. Printed publications can come from anywhere in the world. The second and third categories of reference, public use or offers for sale, only invalidate the claimed invention if they occur in the U.S. The second salient feature of this provision is the critical date: one year prior to the date of the application. Any reference before the critical date—whether originating from the inventor or a third party—invalidates the patent claims that "read on" the reference. Each of these concepts has generated substantial jurisprudence. "Printed publication" and "public use" were discussed above with respect to § 102(a), *see* § 14.3.4.1.1, and their meanings are the same under § 102(b). "On sale" is unique to § 102(b).

14.3.4.1.5.1 Experimental Use

To accommodate circumstances in which inventors need to experiment in publicly accessible areas in making certain types of inventions, courts developed an "experimental use" exception to § 102(b)'s "public use" bar. *See City of Elizabeth v. Am. Nicholson Pavement Co.*, 97 U.S. 126 (1877).[25] The determination of whether an otherwise public use is experimental depends on balancing the following circumstances: "the number of prototypes and duration of testing, whether records or progress reports were made concerning the testing, the existence of a secrecy agreement between the patentee and the party performing the testing, whether the patentee received compensation for the use of the invention, and the extent of control the inventor maintained over the testing." *Lough v. Brunswick Corp.*, 86 F.3d 1113, 1120–21 (Fed. Cir. 1996). Of these factors, the Federal Circuit has emphasized the degree of control the inventor maintained because if it is absent, the inventor "is not experimenting." *Id.* at 1120. Any experimentation must be in regard to establishing that the claimed invention works for its intended purpose, and not, for example, for refining a product to improve marketability. *See In re Smith*, 714 F.2d 1127 (Fed. Cir. 1983). Once reduction to practice is achieved, the experimental use exception ends and § 102(b)'s one-year grace period begins to run.

14.3.4.1.5.2 On Sale Bar

Section 102(b)'s "on-sale bar" can be triggered by behavior that also runs afoul of the "public use" bar, in which case both provisions invalidate the claim. The more difficult and contentious cases involve offers or sales that do not occur in public. Such information is typically revealed through pretrial discovery.

The on-sale bar can be strict in its application. A single offer to sell technology can invalidate the patent, and it can be made by anyone, even a third party unknown

---

25. This type of "experimental use" applicable to § 102(b) is distinct from the "experimental use" defense to patent infringement. *See* § 14.4.2.2.2.

to the patentee. *See, e.g.*, *Abbott Labs. v. Geneva Pharm.*, 182 F.3d 1315 (Fed. Cir. 1999). The invention does not even have to be built. The Supreme Court interpreted the on-sale bar to require only that the invention be "ready for patenting" when subject to a commercial offer for sale. *Pfaff v. Wells Elecs.*, 525 U.S. 55 (1998). An invention is "ready for patenting" if it has been actually reduced to practice by being physically constructed or if there are "drawings or other descriptions of the invention sufficiently detailed to enable a person skilled in the art to practice the invention." *Id.* at 67.

Some additional nuances in the jurisprudence favor the patentee. First, the statute states that the "invention" must be placed on sale. The courts have interpreted this to mean that the offer for sale must involve an embodiment of the invention. Licensing activity does not trigger the on-sale bar so long as there is no embodiment of the invention at issue. *See In re Kollar*, 286 F.3d 1326 (Fed. Cir. 2002). For process claims, the process has to be carried out or performed to constitute a sale. *Kollar*, 286 F.3d at 1332–33 ("[B]ecause the . . . Agreement did not involve the sale of a product of the claimed process, but rather provided . . . a license to practice the claimed process and 'information defining an embodiment' of that process, that agreement did not trigger the on-sale bar.") (footnote omitted). Second, the invention must be subject to a genuine commercial offer for sale. A patentee does not violate the on-sale bar by distributing advertisements and data sheets to prospective buyers while fielding requests for samples from salesmen in the field because this behavior does not rise to the level of an "offer." *See, e.g.*, *Linear Tech. Corp. v. Micrel Inc.*, 275 F.3d 1040 (Fed. Cir. 2001).[26] The Federal Circuit has incorporated the Uniform Commercial Code and "traditional contract law principles" to determine whether an offer is genuine for purposes of applying the on-sale bar. Third, an offer to sell must be between unrelated parties. Hence, offers between a parent and a subsidiary do not trigger the bar. *See Ferag AG v. Quipp Inc.*, 45 F.3d 1562 (Fed. Cir. 1995).

The on-sale bar is subject to a territorial restriction. Only if the claimed invention is "on sale in this country" is the patent claim invalid. Determining whether an invention is "on sale in this country" can be difficult in the rapidly globalizing economy. For example, a foreign supplier's response that it was ready to fulfill a purchase order request of a patented invention before the critical date triggers the on-sale bar. *Hamilton Beach Brands v. Sunbeam Prods., Inc.*, 726 F.3d 1370 (Fed. Cir. 2013). As with deciding whether an offer was made, courts look to "traditional contract law principles" to determine the locus of an offer.

---

26. But note that a detailed advertisement can constitute a printed publication if it enables the invention.

14.3.4.1.6 Statutory Bars—Abandonment—§ 102(c)

Under § 102(c), an applicant is entitled to a patent unless he or she "has abandoned the invention."[27] This section is a loss-of-right provision. *See OddzOn Prods., Inc. v. Just Toys, Inc.*, 122 F.3d 1396, 1402 (Fed. Cir. 1997). It refers to an inventor's express dedication of his or her invention to the public through either deliberate surrender or conduct showing an intent not to pursue patent protection. Abandonment under § 102(c) occurs only based on actions by the inventor after he or she has made the invention but before he or she has filed the patent application. *See id.* at 1404.

14.3.4.1.7 Statutory Bars—International Filing—§ 102(d)

Under § 102(d), a patent may not issue where (1) the inventor filed a foreign patent application more than twelve months prior to filing the U.S. patent application, and (2) a patent issued from that foreign application prior to the U.S. filing date.[28] This provision encourages applicants to file their U.S. applications promptly after filing foreign applications. *See In re Kathawala*, 9 F.3d 942, 946 (Fed. Cir. 1993). Like § 102(c), violation of this provision results in the loss of right. *See OddzOn Prods, Inc.*, 122 F.3d at 1402. Owing to the Patent Cooperation Treaty (PCT), which facilitates and coordinates international patent prosecutions, patent invalidations under § 102(d) rarely occur today.

Validity of the foreign claims is immaterial to the § 102(d) determination. What matters to the inquiry is that the foreign patent issued "with claims directed to the same invention as the U.S. application." *In re Kathawala*, 9 F.3d at 945.

14.3.4.2 The First-to-File Regime

For patent applications having at least one claim with an effective filing date on or after March 16, 2013, the novelty requirement is governed by the amendments to Title 35 introduced in the AIA. *See* AIA § 3. Accordingly, all references to § 102 and other statutory provisions in Title 35 in § 14.3.4.2 will refer to the AIA-amended version, unless specified otherwise.

14.3.4.2.1 Novelty and Prior Art—§ 102(a)

Section 102(a), as amended by the AIA, provides as follows:

> (a) NOVELTY; PRIOR ART.—A person shall be entitled to a patent unless—
>
> (1) the claimed invention was patented, described in a printed publication, or in public use, on sale, or otherwise available to the public before the effective filing date of the claimed invention; or

---

27. Abandonment under § 102(c) and that under § 102(g) are separate concepts. While § 102(c) relates to abandonment of the right to receive a patent, § 102(g) refers to abandonment of the invention itself. *See* § 14.3.4.1.2.4.

28. Foreign patents of others can constitute prior art references under § 102(a) and (b).

> (2) the claimed invention was described in a patent issued under section 151, or in an application for patent published or deemed published under section 122(b), in which the patent or application, as the case may be, names another inventor and was effectively filed before the effective filing date of the claimed invention.

§ 102(a) (as amended by AIA § 3). Section 102(a) establishes novelty and awards priority based on the "effective filing date" of the claimed invention, which is "the filing date of the earliest application for which the patent or application is entitled, as to such invention, to a right of priority. . . ." § 100(i)(1)(B) (as amended by AIA § 3). In essence, the "effective filing date" (also called the "priority date") for a claimed invention is the filing date of the earliest application in a family of related applications that provides support under § 112 for that claimed invention. If a U.S. application claims priority from a foreign application, the "effective filing date" may be the date on which that foreign application was initially filed.

Compared to the first-to-invent regime, the first-to-file version of § 102(a) broadens the scope of prior art and novelty-defeating events in several key respects: (1) it eliminates the ability to "swear behind" a prior art reference based on the date of invention; (2) it provides a novelty-defeating catch-all category ("or otherwise available to the public"); (3) novelty-defeating prior public use or "on-sale" events are not limited to activities in the U.S.; and (4) because the effective filing date includes the foreign priority date, U.S. patents and published applications claiming priority to a foreign application are considered prior art as of their foreign priority date (rather than their later U.S. filing date under the pre-AIA version of § 102). *See also* § 102(d) (as amended by AIA § 3). Nonetheless, the USPTO has interpreted the "or otherwise available to the public" language as limiting the other art referenced in 102(a)(1) to be only art that is "available to the public." Therefore, "secret sales," which were considered prior art prior to the AIA, are no longer considered prior art by the PTO.

14.3.4.2.2 Novelty—Grace Period and Exceptions to Prior Art—§ 102(b)

Section 102(b), as amended by the AIA, provides for a grace period as well as certain exceptions to prior art, as follows:

> (b) EXCEPTIONS.—
>
> (1) DISCLOSURES MADE 1 YEAR OR LESS BEFORE THE EFFECTIVE FILING DATE OF THE CLAIMED INVENTION.—A disclosure made 1 year or less before the effective filing date of a claimed invention shall not be prior art to the claimed invention under subsection (a)(1) if—
>
> (A) the disclosure was made by the inventor or joint inventor or by another who obtained the subject matter disclosed directly or indirectly from the inventor or a joint inventor; or
>
> (B) the subject matter disclosed had, before such disclosure, been publicly disclosed by the inventor or a joint inventor or another who obtained the subject matter disclosed directly or indirectly from the inventor or a joint inventor.

(2) DISCLOSURES APPEARING IN APPLICATIONS AND PATENTS.—A disclosure shall not be prior art to a claimed invention under subsection (a)(2) if—

(A) the subject matter disclosed was obtained directly or indirectly from the inventor or a joint inventor;

(B) the subject matter disclosed had, before such subject matter was effectively filed under subsection (a)(2), been publicly disclosed by the inventor or a joint inventor or another who obtained the subject matter disclosed directly or indirectly from the inventor or a joint inventor; or

(C) the subject matter disclosed and the claimed invention, not later than the effective filing date of the claimed invention, were owned by the same person or subject to an obligation of assignment to the same person.

§ 102(b) (as amended by AIA § 3). Section 102(b)(1) gives priority to the first inventor to "disclose" the invention, whether directly or indirectly (e.g., by another who derived the invention from the applicant), if the inventor files an application within a year of the disclosure. If the U.S. application claims priority from a foreign application, the one-year grace period is measured from the foreign priority date. Notably, the statute does not define what qualifies as a "disclosure" for purposes of the grace period, thereby leaving it open to development through case law.

Section 102(b)(2) disqualifies certain patents and patent applications as prior art if the disclosed subject matter was derived from or previously "publicly disclosed" by the inventor (or a joint inventor), or shares a common owner with the claimed invention.

14.3.4.2.3 Novelty—Joint Research—§ 102(c)

Section § 102(c) provides that subject matter developed under a joint research agreement is deemed "commonly owned" for the purposes of the "common ownership" exception to prior art under § 102(b)(2)(C):

(c) COMMON OWNERSHIP UNDER JOINT RESEARCH AGREEMENTS.— Subject matter disclosed and a claimed invention shall be deemed to have been owned by the same person or subject to an obligation of assignment to the same person in applying the provisions of subsection (b)(2)(C) if—

(1) the subject matter disclosed was developed and the claimed invention was made by, or on behalf of, 1 or more parties to a joint research agreement that was in effect on or before the effective filing date of the claimed invention;

(2) the claimed invention was made as a result of activities undertaken within the scope of the joint research agreement; and

(3) the application for patent for the claimed invention discloses or is amended to disclose the names of the parties to the joint research agreement.

§ 102(c) (as amended by AIA § 3). The § 102(c) "joint research" exception to prior art applies if: (1) the joint research agreement was in effect before the effective filing date; (2) the invention resulted from activities within the scope of the joint research agreement; and (3) the patent application discloses the parties to the joint research agreement. Notably, the § 102(c) "joint research" exception introduced under the AIA is analogous to the pre-AIA version of § 103(c) applicable to obviousness issues.

14.3.4.2.4 Effective Date of Patent Prior Art—§ 102(d)

Section 102(d) defines when patents and published applications may qualify as prior art:

> (d) PATENTS AND PUBLISHED APPLICATIONS EFFECTIVE AS PRIOR ART.—For purposes of determining whether a patent or application for patent is prior art to a claimed invention under subsection (a)(2), such patent or application shall be considered to have been effectively filed, with respect to any subject matter described in the patent or application—
>
> (1) if paragraph (2) does not apply, as of the actual filing date of the patent or the application for patent; or
>
> (2) if the patent or application for patent is entitled to claim a right of priority under Section 119, 365(a), or 365(b), or to claim the benefit of an earlier filing date under Section 120, 121, or 365(c), based upon 1 or more prior filed applications for patent, as of the filing date of the earliest such application that describes the subject matter.

§ 102(d) (as amended by AIA § 3). Compared to the first-to-invent regime, the universe of patent prior art in the first-to-file regime is broader in a couple of major respects: (1) an applicant cannot "swear behind" a prior art patent or published application based on a prior invention date; and (2) U.S. patents and published applications claiming priority to a foreign application may qualify as prior art as of their foreign priority date (rather than being restricted to the U.S. filing date under the pre-AIA version of § 102).

14.3.4.2.5 Derivation Proceedings

Under the first-to-file regime, interference proceedings are replaced by "derivation proceedings" in which an inventor may challenge an earlier-filed third-party application or patent claiming subject matter that was derived from the inventor's own work. *See* AIA § 3 (amending §§ 135 and 291).

Derivation proceedings have timing restrictions. In the USPTO, a derivation proceeding must be requested within one year of the publication of a claim directed to the allegedly derived invention. *See* § 135. If a derivation proceeding is pursued as a civil action under § 146, the suit must be filed within a year of the issuance of the patent containing a claim to the allegedly derived invention. *See* § 291.

14.3.5 Nonobviousness—§ 103

14.3.5.1 Historical Development

Some measure of inventiveness has been required to receive a patent since the seminal case of *Hotchkiss v. Greenwood*, 52 U.S. 248 (1850), where the Supreme Court held that the patent law's concept of "invention" required going beyond the skill or ingenuity of an "ordinary mechanic acquainted with the business." *Id.* at 267. Over the following century, the "invention" requirement grew more stringent, leading to the controversial "flash of creative genius" test, *see Cuno Engineering Corp. v. Automatic Devices Corp.*, 314 U.S. 84, 91 (1941), and the "unusual or surprising consequences" test, *see Great A & P Tea Co. v. Supermarket Equipment Corp.*, 340 U.S. 147 (1950). This high bar to patentability was ultimately replaced with a less stringent nonobviousness standard in the Patent Act of 1952.

14.3.5.2 Nonobviousness Standard

As explained in the previous section on novelty and statutory bars under § 102, *see* § 14.3.4, the regime under which patents are granted in the U.S. changed on March 16, 2013, from a first-to-invent system to a first-to-file system. AIA § 3. Under the AIA, § 103 was rewritten to conform to the first-to-file framework set forth in the amended version of § 102. The primary substantive difference in the two filing regimes for analyzing obviousness under § 103 is the relevant time at which obviousness is evaluated: Under the first-to-invent regime, obviousness is evaluated at the time of invention, whereas under the first-to-file regime, it is evaluated as of the effective filing date.

14.3.5.2.1 Nonobviousness Under the First-to-Invent Regime

The pre-AIA version of § 103(a) states that:

> A patent may not be obtained though the invention is not identically disclosed or described as set forth in section 102 of this title, if the differences between the subject matter sought to be patented and the prior art are such that the subject matter as a whole would have been obvious at the time the invention was made to a person having ordinary skill in the art to which said subject matter pertains. Patentability shall not be negatived by the manner in which the invention was made.

Id. The text provides some structure for the nonobviousness inquiry. Under the first-to-invent regime, obviousness must be determined at the time of invention from the perspective of a person having ordinary skill in the art. As suggested by the last sentence, the manner of invention is irrelevant. An invention is eligible for patent protection whether accidental or nearly instantaneous so long as it meets the test set forth in the first sentence of § 103(a).

The Supreme Court provided an analytical framework for nonobviousness in *Graham v. John Deere Co. of Kan. City*, 383 U.S. 1 (1966), which required courts to make findings regarding the "scope and content of prior art," the "differences between the prior art and claims at issue," and the "level of ordinary skill in the pertinent art." *Id.* at 17. The Court also brought consideration of secondary factors—what might be deemed circumstantial evidence of inventiveness (such as long-felt need, failure of others, praise for the invention, and unexpected results)—into the determination of whether an invention was obvious at the time it was made. *Id.* at 17–18. In 2007, the Supreme Court reaffirmed the *Graham* framework and emphasized that the inquiry under § 103 is flexible, "broad" and open-ended. *KSR Int'l Co. v. Teleflex, Inc.*, 550 U.S. 398 (2007).

14.3.5.2.2 Nonobviousness Under the First-to-File Regime

Section 103, as amended under the AIA, states:

> A patent for a claimed invention may not be obtained, notwithstanding that the claimed invention is not identically disclosed as set forth in section 102, if the differences between the claimed invention and the prior art are such that the claimed invention as a whole would have been obvious before the effective filing date of the claimed invention to a person having ordinary skill in the art to which the claimed invention pertains. Patentability shall not be negated by the manner in which the invention was made.

§ 103 (as amended by AIA § 3). Compared to the pre-AIA version of § 103 that is applicable under the first-to-invent regime, the amended version of § 103 that is applicable to the first-to-file regime is a single paragraph that focuses the nonobviousness inquiry as of the effective filing date.

Much of the case law developed under the first-to-invent regime for evaluating obviousness is generally applicable under the first-to-file regime as well, by substituting the relevant time for evaluating obviousness to be the effective filing date rather than the date of invention.

14.3.5.3 Applying § 103

Courts generally assess nonobviousness by first ascertaining the level of ordinary skill in the art, then analyzing the pertinent prior art, and finally assessing the difference between the baseline of prior art and the claimed invention from the standpoint of a person having ordinary skill in the art as of the relevant time. Under the first-to-invent regime, obviousness is evaluated at the time the invention was made, whereas under the first-to-file regime, obviousness is evaluated as of the effective filing date.

14.3.5.3.1 Determining the Level of Ordinary Skill in the Art

In determining the level of ordinary skill in the art, courts look to the inventor's educational level, the nature of the field's typical problems, the skill required to grapple with the prior solutions to the field's problems, the pace of innovation in the field, the sophistication of technology, and the educational level of people working in the field. *See Envtl. Designs, Ltd. v. Union Oil Co.*, 713 F.2d 693, 696 (Fed. Cir. 1983). In practice, the alleged infringer will argue that the level of ordinary skill is very high, so that the invention appears obvious to the person of ordinary skill, whereas the patentee will often suggest a very low level of ordinary skill, so that the invention instead appears nonobvious.

Some opinions make explicit determinations of the person of ordinary skill, as did the district court in *KSR* ("an undergraduate degree in mechanical engineering (or an equivalent amount of industry experience) [and] familiarity with pedal control systems for vehicles," *Teleflex Inc. v. KSR Int'l*, 298 F. Supp. 2d 581, 590 (E.D. Mich. 2003)), although it is not uncommon for courts to leave this determination somewhat vague. For example, in *Environmental Designs, Ltd. v. Union Oil Co.*, 713 F.2d 693 (Fed. Cir. 1983), the parties conceded that each side's experts were persons of ordinary skill in the art. Moreover, "a specific finding on the level of skill in the art is not . . . required where the prior art itself reflects an appropriate level and a need for testimony is not shown." *Litton Indus. Prods., Inc. v. Solid State Sys., Corp.*, 755 F.2d 158, 163–64 (Fed. Cir. 1985). Table 14.3 provides illustrative findings of the person of ordinary skill in the context of particular fields of invention:

Table 14.3
Illustrative Findings of a Person Having Ordinary Skill

Case	Field of Invention	Person Having Ordinary Skill
Micro Motion, Inc. v. Exac Corp., 741 F. Supp. 1426 (N.D. Cal. 1990)	devices that measure the flow rate of fluids, for example, in a pipeline	"A design engineer with a college degree in mechanical engineering or the equivalent, and who had several years of experience in the design and development of flow measurement and control instruments."
Sud-Chemie, Inc. v. CSP Techs., Inc., 2006 U.S. Dist. LEXIS 54873, 2006 WL 2246404 (S.D. Ind. Aug. 4, 2006)	polymer blends with specific structural qualities	"A Ph.D.-level scientist [in the field of polymer chemistry]."
Imperial Chem. Indus., PLC v. Danbury Pharmacal, Inc., 777 F. Supp. 330 (D. Del. 1991)	method for treating patients suffering from hypertension	"A person of ordinary skill in the art would be an individual with a Ph.D. degree in organic chemistry, with an emphasis in medicinal chemistry and experience with the techniques of drug development in general and specific experience with the development of beta-blockers."
Eli Lilly & Co. v. Teva Pharm. USA, Inc., 2004 U.S. Dist. LEXIS 14724, 2004 WL 1724632 (July 29, 2004)	method of treating patients suffering from premenstrual syndrome	"A hypothetical medical doctor (an OB/GYN, a family practice physician, or a psychiatrist) who: (1) regularly sees and treats patients suffering from PMS, and (2) is familiar with the relevant prior art."

Case	Field of Invention	Person Having Ordinary Skill
Rosen Enter. Sys., LP v. Icon Enters., Inc., 359 F. Supp. 2d 902 (C.D. Cal. 2005)	flip-down screens for cars	"The level of ordinary skill here is a technical knowledge of the design and installation of overhead flip-down display units for automobiles."
Windsurfing Int'l, Inc. v. Fred Ostermann GmbH, 613 F. Supp. 913 (S.D.N.Y. 1985), *aff'd in relevant part, Windsurfing Int'l, Inc. v. AMF, Inc.*, 782 F.2d 995 (Fed. Cir. 1986)	sails	"The hypothetical person of ordinary skill in the art of sailboat design in 1967 had either a combination of several years sailing experience and several years of practical experience designing and/or constructing sailboats or, alternatively, he possessed a college degree in design or engineering as well as a general knowledge of sailing."

14.3.5.3.2 Scope and Content of the Prior Art

Because § 103 does not expressly define what constitutes "prior art," courts have looked to § 102 for the classes of references that can qualify as "prior art" references for the § 103 inquiry. In most cases, a reference that could be prior art under § 102 can qualify as a reference for § 103 purposes. *See OddzOn Prods., Inc. v. Just Toys, Inc.*, 122 F.3d 1396 (Fed. Cir. 1997). However, the range of prior art available for an obviousness analysis will be slightly different depending on whether the claim at issue was filed under the first-to-invent regime or the first-to-file regime.

Under the first-to-invent regime, it is worth noting that, notwithstanding the test of § 103, which measures obviousness as of the time of invention, § 102(b) references can also apply in making § 103 obviousness determinations, even though they are effective as of one year prior to the application filing date (and hence may postdate the time of invention). *See OddzOn Products*, 122 F.3d at 1402; *In re Foster*, 343 F.2d 980 (C.C.P.A. 1965); 2 Donald S. Chisum, Chisum on Patents § 5.03[2][b].

Both the first-to-invent and first-to-file regimes provide "joint research" exceptions to prior art. To prevent companies from having one group of employees' nonpublic research used as prior art against other employees' inventions, § 103(c), under the first-to-invent regime, excludes consideration of §§ 102(e), (f), and/or (g) references if it comes from the inventor, his or her firm, or someone with an assignment obligation to the patenting enterprise. The analogous provision under the first-to-file regime is provided under § 102(c).

A § 103 reference must also come from an "analogous art" to satisfy the presumption that a person having ordinary skill in the art would be familiar with it. Courts base this determination upon whether the reference is "from the same field of endeavor, regardless of the problem addressed," and if not, whether the reference is "reasonably pertinent to the particular problem with which the inventor is involved." *See In re Clay*, 966 F.2d 656 (Fed. Cir. 1992); *see also In re Paulsen*, 30 F.3d 1475 (Fed. Cir. 1994). A prior art reference qualifies as analogous art if it satisfies either inquiry. Table 14.4 illustrates this mode of analysis:

Table 14.4
Assessing Whether Prior Art Is Analogous

Case	Field of Invention	Reference	Same Field?	Same Problem?
AstraZeneca Pharms., LP v. Mayne Pharma (USA) Inc., 2005 U.S. Dist. LEXIS 26196, 2005 WL 2864666 (S.D.N.Y. Nov. 2, 2005)	Pharmaceutical formulation	Patent related to sludge formation in fuel	No	No
Festo Corp. v. Shoketsu Kinzoku Kogyo Kabushiki Co., Ltd., 2005 U.S. Dist. LEXIS 11621, 2005 WL 1398528 (D. Mass. June 10, 2005)	Sealing rings for large magnetic devices	Sealing rings for small magnetic devices	Yes	Yes

14.3.5.3.3 Differences Between Invention and Prior Art

Once the level of ordinary skill in the art and the applicable prior art have been identified, the trier of fact assesses the differences between the claimed invention and the prior art.

14.3.5.3.4 Secondary Considerations

The Supreme Court in *Graham* suggested a number of secondary considerations to guide the obviousness inquiry. As the Court reaffirmed in *KSR*, the list of secondary considerations is not exclusive; a court may look to "any secondary considerations that would prove instructive" as to whether an invention was obvious. *KSR*, 550 U.S. at 415. The Federal Circuit requires that there be a nexus between the proffered secondary consideration and the claimed invention. The Federal Circuit requires district courts to make findings regarding secondary considerations. *See Custom Accessories, Inc. v. Jeffrey-Allen Indus., Inc.*, 807 F.2d 955 (Fed. Cir. 1986). Below are the most widely cited secondary considerations.

14.3.5.3.4.1 Long-Felt Need and Failure by Others

The *Graham* Court suggested that a claimed invention that solves a "long-felt need" within an industry would likely be nonobvious. Evidence that many others within the field have tried and failed to make the claimed invention suggests that the claimed invention was not obvious to a person of ordinary skill in the art. For example, in *Texas Instruments, Inc. v. United States International Trade Commission*, 988 F.2d 1165, 1178 (Fed. Cir. 1993), the evidence showed that the semiconductor industry had attempted but failed to package semiconductors in plastic for over six years prior to the invention. The patentee's invention solved the problem of damaged components by insulating semiconductors in plastic. *Id.*

14.3.5.3.4.2 Awards and Praise

Awards or praise for an invention may suggest that it represents a significant advance. For example, in *W.L. Gore & Associates, Inc. v. Garlock, Inc.*, 721 F.2d 1540 (Fed. Cir. 1983), the Federal Circuit noted the industry's characterization of Gore-Tex as "magical" and "a remarkable new material," along with other secondary indicia (commercial success, long-felt need), to find the invention nonobvious. When analyzing patent claims that cover a component of a larger system, the only awards or praise that are relevant for § 103 are those specifically relating to the patented component, rather than to the system as a whole.

14.3.5.3.4.3 Skepticism, "Teaching Away," and Unexpected Results

If the literature in the relevant field suggested prior to the relevant time for evaluating obviousness that the claimed solution was impossible, that suggests that the invention was nonobvious. *See, e.g., United States v. Adams*, 383 U.S. 39, 51–52 (1966). In *Adams*, the prior art discouraged experimenting with the combination that led to the patented invention as risky and unlikely to be successful.[29] *Id.* The Court relied on this background evidence to find that a person having ordinary skill in the art would have found it nonobvious. *Id.* The record in *Adams* also showed that many experts disbelieved Adams's results, only to later apply for patents on improvements on Adams's invention. *Id.* at 52.

Unexpected results that contradict long-held industry assumptions or beliefs can also demonstrate that the claimed invention was nonobvious at the relevant time. In *American Hoist & Derrick Co. v. Sowa & Sons*, 725 F.2d 1350 (Fed. Cir. 1984), the patentee demonstrated that a thin coating of chemicals could produce stronger safety glass than a thick coating, which was contrary to accepted beliefs in the industry at the time.

29. This discouragement is referred to as "teaching away" from the invention.

14.3.5.3.4.4 Licensing Activity

Extensive licensing may suggest that industry actors consider the patented invention nonobvious. *See, e.g.*, *Eibel Process Co. v. Minn. & Ont. Paper Co.*, 261 U.S. 45, 53–56 (1923). However, patent holders routinely cross-license portfolios of patents without considering individual claims. Accordingly, a court should examine whether a nexus exists between the decision to license and the claimed invention.

14.3.5.3.4.5 Copying

Copying by others may give rise to an inference that an invention is nonobvious. *See, e.g.*, *Diamond Rubber Co. v. Consol. Rubber Tire Co.*, 220 U.S. 428, 440–41 (1911). Courts should exercise caution in evaluating this factor because patentees routinely accuse alleged infringers of "copying" their invention. In addition, some alleged infringers may copy the invention believing that the patent is invalid; accordingly, the mere fact of copying should not defeat alternative arguments of obviousness.

14.3.5.3.4.6 Commercial Success

If a claimed invention is successful in the marketplace because of its patented features, the invention may be nonobvious. *See, e.g.*, *Hybritech, Inc. v. Monoclonal Antibodies, Inc.*, 802 F.2d 1367 (Fed. Cir. 1986). When looking at commercial success as an indication of nonobviousness, courts should carefully assess the nexus between the success and the patent claim. This is particularly important when the patented technology is but one component in a larger system. Consider a patented air bag that an automaker installs on all of its new vehicles. The automaker cannot point to its overall car sales as evidence of nonobviousness unless it can show that the improved airbag is a key factor in car sales. It is likely, however, that consumers are basing their purchasing decisions on a wide variety of factors, such as engine performance, fuel economy, and body design. If, on the other hand, the automaker can demonstrate that safety-conscious buyers bought its cars in large numbers because of the new airbag technology, that evidence would favor a finding that the claimed invention is nonobvious.

14.3.5.3.5 The Ultimate Conclusion and Combining References

With these factual predicates—the level of ordinary skill in the art, the analogous prior art, the differences between the invention and the prior art, and the pertinent secondary considerations—the court then determines as a question of law whether the claimed invention as a whole would have been obvious to a person having ordinary skill in the art as of the relevant time. *KSR Int'l Co. v. Teleflex, Inc.*, 550 U.S. 398 (2007); *Graham*, 383 U.S. at 17–18; *Pharmastem Therapeutics, Inc. v. Viacell, Inc.*, 491 F.3d 1342 (Fed. Cir. 2007); *see generally* § 7.3.4.4. The person having ordinary skill in the art is presumed to know all analogous prior art.

Many cases raising nonobviousness will involve a claimed invention that is a combination of preexisting elements or components. Where all of the limitations were known in the prior art, the question becomes whether it was obvious for a person having ordinary skill in the art to combine those features to address a known problem. Prior to *KSR*, the Federal Circuit applied a doctrine referred to as the "teaching, suggestion, or motivation" or "TSM" test which required evidence of an explicit cross-reference linking the preexisting restrictions from disparate references and that a person having ordinary skill in the art would not have to engage in undue experimentation to create the combination. The *KSR* Court rejected this "rigid formulation." 550 U.S. at 415. Instead, the Court suggested that in many fields "market demand" may compel an inventor to combine prior art elements. *Id.* at 419. The *KSR* Court stressed that nonobviousness cannot be reduced to a single inquiry. Instead, the inquiry is expansive, flexible, and functional. For example, the Court suggested that, "[o]ne of the ways in which a patent's subject matter can be proved obvious is by noting that there existed at the [relevant time] a known problem for which there was an obvious solution encompassed by the patent's claims." *Id.* at 1742.

Since *KSR*, the Federal Circuit has held that merely replacing known mechanical components of an invention with electronic parts is likely to be obvious. *See Leapfrog Enters., Inc. v. Fisher-Price, Inc.*, 485 F.3d 1157 (Fed. Cir. 2007). Often, advances in collateral technologies—such as advances in digital technology or the development of the Internet—or the emergence of market demand (as occurred in *KSR*) will enable persons having ordinary skill in the art to apply known technologies or skills in new but obvious ways that have tremendous value. Section 103 bars patents on such techniques.

The flexible, broad, and open-ended nonobviousness inquiry adopted by the Federal Circuit in its post-*KSR* decisions has been synthesized by the USPTO in a set of examination guidelines for its patent examiners. Examination Guidelines Update: Developments in the Obviousness Inquiry after *KSR v. Teleflex*, 75 Fed. Reg. 53643 (2010). Table 14.5–14.8 summarize those guidelines:

Table 14.5
Combining Prior Art Elements

Case	Teaching Point
In re Omeprazole Patent Litig., 536 F.3d 1361 (Fed. Cir. 2008)	Even where a general method that could have been applied to make the claimed product was known and within the level of skill of the ordinary artisan, the claim may nevertheless be nonobvious if the problem which had suggested use of the method had been previously unknown.
Crocs, Inc. v. U.S. Int'l Trade Comm'n., 598 F.3d 1294 (Fed. Cir. 2010)	A claimed combination of prior art elements may be nonobvious where the prior art teaches away from the claimed combination and the combination yields more than predictable results.

Case	Teaching Point
Sundance, Inc. v. DeMonte Fabricating Ltd., 550 F.3d 1356 (Fed. Cir. 2008)	A claimed invention is likely to be obvious if it is a combination of known prior art elements that would reasonably have been expected to maintain their respective properties or functions after they have been combined.
Ecolab, Inc. v. FMC Corp., 569 F.3d 1335 (Fed. Cir. 2009)	A combination of known elements would have been *prima facie* obvious if an ordinarily skilled artisan would have recognized an apparent reason to combine those elements and would have known how to do so.
Wyers v. Master Lock Co., 616 F.3d 1231 (Fed. Cir. 2010)	The scope of analogous art is to be construed broadly and includes references that are reasonably pertinent to the problem that the inventor was trying to solve. Common sense may be used to support a legal conclusion of obviousness so long as it is explained with sufficient reasoning.
DePuy Spine, Inc. v. Medtronic Sofamor Danek, Inc., 567 F.3d 1314 (Fed. Cir. 2009)	Predictability as discussed in *KSR* encompasses the expectation that prior art elements are capable of being combined, as well as the expectation that the combination would have worked for its intended purpose. An inference that a claimed combination would not have been obvious is especially strong where the prior art's teachings undermine the very reason being proffered as to why a person of ordinary skill would have combined the known elements.

Table 14.6
Substituting One Known Element for Another

Case	Teaching Point
In re ICON Health & Fitness, Inc., 496 F.3d 1374 (Fed. Cir. 2007)	When determining whether a reference in a different field of endeavor may be used to support a case of obviousness (i.e., is analogous), it is necessary to consider the problem to be solved.
Agrizap, Inc. v. Woodstream Corp., 520 F.3d 1337 (Fed. Cir. 2008)	Analogous art is not limited to references in the field of endeavor of the invention, but also includes references that would have been recognized by those of ordinary skill in the art as useful for applicant's purpose.
Muniauction, Inc. v. Thomson Corp., 532 F.3d 1318 (Fed. Cir. 2008)	Because Internet and web browser technologies had become commonplace for communicating and displaying information, it would have been obvious to adapt existing processes to incorporate them for those functions.

Case	Teaching Point
Aventis Pharma Deutschland v. Lupin, Ltd., 499 F.3d 1293 (Fed. Cir. 2007)	A chemical compound would have been obvious over a mixture containing that compound as well as other compounds where it was known or the skilled artisan had reason to believe that some desirable property of the mixture was derived in whole or in part from the claimed compound, and separating the claimed compound from the mixture was routine in the art.
Eisai Co. Ltd. v. Dr. Reddy's Labs., Ltd., 533 F.3d 1353 (Fed. Cir. 2008)	A claimed compound would not have been obvious where there was no reason to modify the closest prior art lead compound to obtain the claimed compound and the prior art taught that modifying the lead compound would destroy its advantageous property. Any known compound may serve as a lead compound when there is some reason for starting with that lead compound and modifying it to obtain the claimed compound.
Procter & Gamble Co. v. Teva Pharm. USA, Inc., 566 F.3d 989 (Fed. Cir. 2009)	It is not necessary to select a single compound as a "lead compound" in order to support an obviousness rejection. However, where there was reason to select and modify the lead compound to obtain the claimed compound, but no reasonable expectation of success, the claimed compound would not have been obvious.
Altana Pharma AG v. Teva Pharms. USA, Inc., 566 F.3d 999 (Fed. Cir. 2009)	Obviousness of a chemical compound in view of its structural similarity to a prior art compound may be shown by identifying some line of reasoning that would have led one of ordinary skill in the art to select and modify a prior art lead compound in a particular way to produce the claimed compound. It is not necessary for the reasoning to be explicitly found in the prior art of record, nor is it necessary for the prior art to point to only a single lead compound.

Table 14.7
The Obvious-to-Try Rationale[30]

Case	Teaching Point
In re Kubin, 561 F.3d 1351 (Fed. Cir. 2009)	A claimed polynucleotide would have been obvious over the known protein that it encodes where the skilled artisan would have had a reasonable expectation of success in deriving the claimed polynucleotide using standard biochemical techniques, and the skilled artisan would have had a reason to try to isolate the claimed polynucleotide. *KSR* applies to all technologies, rather than just the "predictable" arts.
Takeda Chem. Indus. v. Alphapharm Pty., Ltd., 492 F.3d 1350 (Fed. Cir. 2007)	A claimed compound would not have been obvious where it was not obvious to try to obtain it from a broad range of compounds, any one of which could have been selected as the lead compound for further investigation, and the prior art taught away from using a particular lead compound, and there was no predictability or reasonable expectation of success in making the particular modifications necessary to transform the lead compound into the claimed compound.
Ortho-McNeil Pharm., Inc. v. Mylan Labs, Inc., 520 F.3d 1358 (Fed. Cir. 2008)	Where the claimed anticonvulsant drug had been discovered somewhat serendipitously in the course of research aimed at finding a new antidiabetic drug, it would not have been obvious to try to obtain a claimed compound where the prior art did not present a finite and easily traversed number of potential starting compounds, and there was no apparent reason for selecting a particular starting compound from among a number of unpredictable alternatives.
Bayer Schering Pharma A.G. v. Barr Labs., Inc., 575 F.3d 1341 (Fed. Cir. 2009)	A claimed compound would have been obvious where it was obvious to try to obtain it from a finite and easily traversed number of options that was narrowed down from a larger set of possibilities by the prior art, and the outcome of obtaining the claimed compound was reasonably predictable.
Sanofi-Synthelabo v. Apotex, Inc., 550 F.3d 1075 (Fed. Cir. 2008)	A claimed, isolated stereoisomer would not have been obvious where the claimed stereoisomer exhibits unexpectedly strong therapeutic advantages over the prior art racemic mixture without the correspondingly expected toxicity, and the resulting properties of the enantiomers separated from the racemic mixture were unpredictable.

30. Prior to *KSR*, the Federal Circuit had consistently ruled that "obvious-to-try" was not a legitimate test of patentability. *In re Fine*, 837 F.2d 1071, 1075 (Fed. Cir. 1988). *KSR* held that the Federal Circuit had been too rigid for precluding "obvious-to-try" considerations. *KSR*, 550 U.S. at 402.

Case	Teaching Point
Rolls-Royce, PLC v. United Techs. Corp., 603 F.3d 1325 (Fed. Cir. 2010)	An obvious-to-try rationale may be proper when the possible options for solving a problem were known and finite. However, if the possible options were not either known or finite, then an obvious-to-try rationale cannot be used to support a conclusion of obviousness.
Perfect Web Techs., Inc. v. InfoUSA, Inc., 587 F.3d 1324 (Fed. Cir. 2009)	Where there were a finite number of identified, predictable solutions and there is no evidence of unexpected results, an obvious-to-try inquiry may properly lead to a legal conclusion of obviousness. Common sense may be used to support a legal conclusion of obviousness so long as it is explained with sufficient reasoning.

Table 14.8
Consideration of Evidence

Case	Teaching Point
PharmaStem Therapeutics, Inc. v. ViaCell, Inc., 491 F.3d 1342 (Fed. Cir. 2007)	Even though all evidence must be considered in an obviousness analysis, evidence of nonobviousness may be outweighed by contradictory evidence in the record or by what is in the specification. Although a reasonable expectation of success is needed to support a case of obviousness, absolute predictability is not required.
In re Sullivan, 498 F.3d 1345 (Fed. Cir. 2007)	All evidence, including evidence rebutting a prima facie case of obviousness, must be considered when properly presented.
Hearing Components, Inc. v. Shure Inc., 600 F.3d 1357 (Fed. Cir. 2010)	Evidence that has been properly presented in a timely manner must be considered on the record. Evidence of commercial success is pertinent where a nexus between the success of the product and the claimed invention has been demonstrated.
Asyst Techs., Inc. v. Emtrak, Inc., 544 F.3d 1310 (Fed. Cir. 2008)	Evidence of secondary considerations of obviousness such as commercial success and long-felt need may be insufficient to overcome a prima facie case of obviousness if the prima facie case is strong. An argument for nonobviousness based on commercial success or long-felt need is undermined when there is a failure to link the commercial success or long-felt need to a claimed feature that distinguishes over the prior art.

14.3.6 Inventorship

The Patent Act requires that the patent application list all of the inventors. This section discusses who qualifies as an "inventor," the legal effect of that determination, and how the question arises in litigation.

14.3.6.1 Inventive Entities

Section 116 requires each inventor to apply jointly for a patent on their invention. The statute does not define inventor. Instead, it suggests that multiple people can be joint inventors even if (1) they did not work together in the same space or at the same time, (2) they made unequal contributions to the invention, or (3) they did not contribute to all of the claims of the patent.

For a person to be a joint inventor, they have to contribute to the "conception" of the invention. Testing the invention to make sure it works is not sufficient. *See Burroughs Wellcome Co. v. Barr Labs., Inc.*, 40 F.3d 1223 (Fed. Cir. 1994). Although § 116 does not require that all coinventors work at the same time or in the same place, there must be some collaborative effort. *See Kimberly-Clark Corp. v. Proctor & Gamble Distrib. Co.*, 973 F.2d 911 (Fed. Cir. 1992).

An "inventive entity" is the group of inventors behind any given patent. An inventive entity can be a lone inventor A, or it can be a group, for example, A, B, and C. The inventive entity in these two situations is different, despite sharing an inventor. The significance of this difference requires understanding the various statutory rules governing patent validity. Some rules, like § 102(a)'s novelty bar and § 103's nonobviousness requirement, only invalidate a claim based on prior art attributable to other inventive entities. This seems logical when the other inventive entity is a competitor or stranger, but note that the solo work of inventive entity A is distinct from the work of inventive entity A, B, and C. For an application of this principle, *see In re O'Farrell,* 853 F.2d 894 (Fed. Cir. 1988).

14.3.6.2 Default Rights of Owners

The question of inventorship often arises because inventors receive a potentially powerful and valuable set of rights in their patents. Each inventor is a co-owner of the patent and may freely grant nonexclusive licenses. Alleged infringers have exploited this technicality by searching for an unlisted coinventor of any of the claims of the patent and obtaining a license from them. *See, e.g., Ethicon, Inc. v. U.S. Surgical Corp.*, 135 F.3d 1456 (Fed. Cir. 1998). Additionally, each joint inventor may freely practice the invention without accounting to the other inventors. *See* § 262.

In general, companies avoid "rogue" inventor problems by obtaining assignment agreements from everyone they employ. The construction and validity of these assignment agreements depend on state contract law, introducing a choice-of-law wrinkle to patent litigation. Some research institutions are more lax in binding researchers and may not have comprehensive assignment agreements. Such contexts, like a university research setting or a collaborative industry meeting, can give rise to knotty inventorship disputes.

14.3.6.3 Correction of Inventorship

The district court can order corrections to address errors in inventorship. § 256. The Federal Circuit has interpreted this provision broadly, allowing for wide-ranging correction of inventorship. *See Stark v. Advanced Magnetics, Inc.*, 119 F.3d 1551 (Fed. Cir. 1997). The Federal Circuit was careful to note, however, that any "mistakes" in inventorship designed to avoid the problems created by misaligned inventive entities discussed above could support a finding of "inequitable conduct" and render the patent unenforceable.

14.4 Enforcement: Infringement, Defenses, and Remedies

The second major aspect of most patent litigations relates to the determination of whether infringement has occurred or will occur. Unlike the validity determination—in which the alleged infringer bears the burden of proof (as a result of the presumption of validity)—the patentee bears the burden of proving infringement by a preponderance of the evidence. The alleged infringer then has the opportunity to assert a broad range of legal and equitable defenses. The final aspect of most patent litigations concerns remedies—injunctive relief, damages (including the possibility of enhanced damages), and attorneys' fees.

14.4.1 Infringement

14.4.1.1 Section 271

Section 271 defines patent liability to include both direct and indirect infringement. Direct infringement exists where an individual violates one of the exclusive rights granted to the patentee under § 271(a). Indirect infringement occurs where a person induces infringement under § 271(b) or contributes to infringement under § 271(c). In either case, the patent holder bears the burden of proving infringement by a preponderance of the evidence. *See Centricut, LLC v. Esab Grp., Inc.*, 390 F.3d 1361, 1367 (Fed. Cir. 2004).

14.4.1.2 Direct Infringement

A person is liable for direct infringement if he "without authority makes, uses, offers to sell, or sells any patented invention, within the United States or imports into the United States any patented invention during the term of the patent therefore." § 271(a). An accused infringer's intent is immaterial, as patent infringement is a strict liability offense.

14.4.1.3 Indirect Infringement

Indirect infringement covers conduct by a person who assists or supports another's direct infringement of a patented invention. Direct infringement must be established as a predicate for each act of indirect infringement. *See Dynacore Holding Corp. v. U.S. Philips Corp.*, 363 F.3d 1263, 1272 (Fed. Cir. 2004) ("Indirect infringement . . . can only arise in the presence of direct infringement, though the direct infringer is typically someone other than the defendant accused of indirect infringement."). Both the direct infringer and indirect infringer are jointly and severally liable for the infringement.

The Patent Act recognizes both inducement (§ 271(b)) and contributory infringement (§ 271(c)). A third theory of indirect infringement, whereby multiple parties are conjoined in order to prove that all of the steps of a patented process were practiced, was rejected by the Supreme Court in *Akamai Techs., Inc. v. Limelight Networks, Inc.*, 134 S. Ct. 2111 (2014).

14.4.1.3.1 Inducement

Section 271(b) provides that "[w]hoever actively induces infringement of a patent shall be liable as an infringer." A finding of inducement requires that a patent owner establish evidence of culpable conduct directed toward encouraging another's infringement. "[I]nduced infringement under § 271(b) requires knowledge [by the inducer] that the induced acts constitute patent infringement." *Global-Tech Appliances, Inc. v. SEB S.A.*, 131 S. Ct. 2060, 2068 (2011). Thus, the inducer must have "actively and knowingly aid[ed] and abet[ted] another's direct infringement." *Water Techs. Corp. v. Calco, Ltd.*, 850 F.2d 660, 668 (Fed. Cir. 1988) (emphasis in original) (noting that "[a]lthough section 271(b) does not use the word 'knowing,' the case law and legislative history uniformly assert such a requirement").

To satisfy the knowledge requirement, the patentee must show that the inducer had actual or constructive knowledge of the patent, *see Insituform Techs., Inc. v. Cat Contracting, Inc.*, 161 F.3d 688, 695 (Fed. Cir. 1998), or acted with "willful blindness." *Global-Tech*, 131 S. Ct. at 2070–71. Under the doctrine of "willful blindness," the inducer must have: (1) subjectively believed that there was a high probability of infringement; and (2) taken deliberate actions to avoid learning of that fact. *Id.* at 2070.

Regarding requisite specific intent, the Federal Circuit commented that "it is clear that a good-faith belief of noninfringement is relevant evidence that tends to show that an accused inducer lacked the intent required to be held liable for induced infringement." *Commil USA, LLC v. Cisco Sys., Inc.*, 720 F.3d 1361, 1367–68 (Fed. Cir. 2013). The same standard does not, however, apply to a good-faith belief that a patent is invalid. In *Commil USA, LLC v. Cisco Sys., Inc.*, 135 S. Ct. 1920 (2015), the Supreme Court ruled that because induced infringement and validity are separate issues and have separate defenses under the Patent Act, belief regarding validity cannot negate § 271(b)'s scienter requirement of "actively induce[d] infringement."

Inducement liability often arises from supplier/customer relationships. A finding that a single party is responsible for direct infringement under § 271(a) is required before any party can liable for inducement under § 271(b). Thus, a single party must either have performed every step of the patent, or directed or controlled others who performed them. *See Limelight Networks, Inc. v. Akamai Techs. Inc.*, 134 S. Ct. 2111 (2014).

Section 298, added by the AIA, provides that an accused infringer's failure to obtain or present advice of counsel may not be used to prove that the accused infringer intended to induce infringement. AIA § 17. Section 298 is applicable to patents issued on or after September 16, 2012.

14.4.1.3.2 Contributory Infringement

Section 271(c) imposes liability under the following circumstances:[31]

> [1] Whoever offers to sell or sells within the United States or imports into the United States a component of a patented machine, manufacture, combination or composition, or a material or apparatus for use in practicing a patented process, [2] constituting a material part of the invention, [3] knowing the same to be especially made or especially adapted for use in an infringement of such patent, [4] and not a staple article or commodity of commerce suitable for substantial noninfringing use, [5] shall be liable as a contributory infringer.

The alleged contributory infringer must have knowledge of the patent. *See Aro Mfg. Co. v. Convertible Top Replacement Co.*, 377 U.S. 476, 488 (1964). Element [4] serves as an important defense, immunizing the sale of staple articles of commerce, that is, products that have substantial noninfringing uses. Thus, absent evidence of inducing conduct, sellers of nonpatented goods are shielded from liability unless the good "has no commercial use except in connection with . . . [the] patented invention." *Dawson Chem. Co. v. Rohm & Haas Co.*, 448 U.S. 176, 184 (1980).

14.4.1.3.3 Joint Infringement

Patent law has struggled to deal with scenarios in which multiple parties carry out the steps of a claimed method or the elements of a claimed system. The traditional rule in patent law has been that an infringer must practice every limitation of a claim to infringe it. If no single entity practices each step or element, there can be no infringement. Nonetheless, liability can be found where one party controlled or directed each step in a patented process. *See Akamai Techs., Inc. v. Limelight Networks, Inc.*, 134 S. Ct. 2111, 2117 (2014) (holding that "a method's steps have not all been performed as claimed by the patent unless they are all attributable to the same defendant, either because the defendant actually performed those steps or because he directed or controlled others who performed them"); *Centillion Data Sys., LLC v. Qwest Commc'ns Int'l*, 631 F.3d 1279, 1284 (Fed. Cir. 2011) (holding that direct infringement for "use" of the claimed system is possible where a single party does not physically possess or own some elements of the system, if that party "put[s] the invention into service, i.e., control[s] the system as a whole and obtain[s] benefit from it").

The Federal Circuit has expanded the scope of direct infringement under § 271(a) in situations to encompass circumstances where

> an alleged infringer conditions participation in an activity or receipt of a benefit upon performance of a step or steps of a patented method and establishes the manner or timing of that performance. *Cf. Metro-Goldwyn-Mayer Studios Inc. v. Grokster, Ltd.*, 545 U.S. 913, 930 (2005) (stating that an actor 'infringes vicariously by profiting from direct infringement' if that actor has the right and ability to stop or limit the infringement). In those instances, the third party's actions are attributed to the alleged infring-

31. The section is reproduced in subdivided form to highlight its essential elements.

> er such that the alleged infringer becomes the single actor chargeable with direct infringement.
>
> Whether a single actor directed or controlled the acts of one or more third parties is a question of fact, reviewable on appeal for substantial evidence, when tried to a jury.

Akamai Techs., Inc. v. Limelight Networks, Inc., 797 F.3d 1020, 1023 (Fed. Cir. 2015) (en banc) (following remand). In addition, the Federal Circuit held that participants in a joint enterprise can be charged with the acts of the other for purposes of direct infringement. *Id.* at 1023 (citing Restatement (Second) of Torts § 491 cmt. b ("The law . . . considers that each is the agent or servant of the others, and that the act of any one within the scope of the enterprise is to be charged vicariously against the rest.").

A joint enterprise requires proof of four elements: "(1) an agreement, express or implied, among the members of the group; (2) a common purpose to be carried out by the group; (3) a community of pecuniary interest in that purpose, among the members; and (4) an equal right to a voice in the direction of the enterprise, which gives an equal right of control." Restatement (Second) of Torts § 491 cmt. c. As with direction or control, whether actors entered into a joint enterprise is a question of fact, reviewable on appeal for substantial evidence. 797 F.3d at 1023 (citing Restatement (Second) of Torts § 491 cmt. c).

14.4.1.4 Infringement Analysis

Infringement analysis involves two steps: (1) claim construction and (2) comparison of properly construed claims with the accused product or process. *See Cybor Corp. v. FAS Techs., Inc.*, 138 F.3d 1448, 1454 (Fed. Cir. 1998) (en banc). The first step, interpreting the claims, was covered in Chapter 5. We now turn to the second step.

14.4.1.4.1 Literal Infringement

Literal infringement exists when the accused product or process contains each and every limitation recited in a claim, "*i.e.* when the properly construed claim reads on the accused device exactly." *Cole v. Kimberly-Clark Corp.*, 102 F.3d 524, 532 (Fed. Cir. 1996). Accordingly, there can be no literal infringement if the accused product or process lacks any claim limitation. The standards for anticipation under § 102 and literal infringement are identical. As the Federal Circuit has observed, "that which would literally infringe if later anticipates if earlier." *Bristol-Myers Squibb Co. v. Ben Venue Labs., Inc.*, 246 F.3d 1368, 1378 (Fed. Cir. 2001).

One special category of literal claim interpretation relates to so-called means plus function or functional claim formats.

14.4.1.4.1.1 Interpreting the Literal Scope of Means-Plus-Function Claims (§ 112(f))

In *Halliburton Oil Well Cementing Co. v. Walker*, 329 U.S. 1 (1946), the patentee had claimed an apparatus for measuring the depth of oil wells using functional claim limitations: "means communicating with said well for creating a pressure pulse" and "echo receiving means." *Id.* at 9 n.7. The patentee did not want to limit itself to a specific means, and instead sought to define the claim through the functions sought. Such claiming formats were relatively common in patent practice. Nonetheless, the Supreme Court invalidated the claims for failing to reveal specific structures. *Id.* at 11–14. The Court believed that such claims were overbroad, indefinite, and could discourage experimentation by others.

The patent bar promptly persuaded Congress to remove the cloud over the many functional claims in issued and pending patents the Halliburton decision created. The provision, which is now codified in § 112(f), authorizes the use of the means-plus-function claim format while limiting the scope of such claims to all embodiments set forth in the specification "and equivalents thereof." The determination of "equivalents thereof" is based on the state of technology as of the date that the patent issues. This characterization of "equivalents" differs from the meaning under the "doctrine of equivalents." *See* § 14.4.1.4.2.

14.4.1.4.1.1.1 Determining Whether a Claim Limitation Is Governed by § 112(f)

The use of the term "means" in a claim limitation typically implies that the inventor used the "means-plus-function" claim format, which invokes the associated statutory limits on the literal scope of that claim limitation. *See Greenberg v. Ethicon Endo-Surgery, Inc.*, 91 F.3d 1580, 1584 (Fed. Cir. 1996); *cf. Williamson v. Citrix Online LLC*, 2015 U.S. App. LEXIS 10082, 2015 WL 3687459 at *7 (Fed. Cir. 2015) (en banc) (revoking prior cases holding that there is a strong, but rebuttable, presumption that a term lacking the word "means" does not invoke § 112(f)); § 5.2.3.5.1. Nonetheless, this implication does not apply where the claim language itself provides the structure that performs the recited function. *See Phillips v. AWH Corp.*, 415 F.3d 1303 (Fed. Cir. 2005) (en banc) (finding that a claim limitation stating "means disposed inside the shell for increasing its load bearing capacity comprising internal steel baffles" provides the relevant structure ("internal steel baffles") and hence is not limited to the embodiments in the specification and equivalents thereof); *Cole v. Kimberly-Clark Corp.*, 102 F.3d 524, 531 (Fed. Cir. 1996) (finding that use of the phrase "perforation means" does not invoke § 112(f)).

Conversely, merely because a claim does not include the word "means" does not prevent a claim limitation from being construed as a means-plus-function limitation. The *Williamson* decision holds that

> [t]he standard is whether the words of the claim are understood by persons of ordinary skill in the art to have a sufficiently definite meaning as the name for structure. *Greenberg*, 91 F.3d at 1583. When a claim term lacks the word "means," the presumption can be overcome and § 112[(f)] will apply if the challenger demonstrates that the claim term fails to "recite sufficiently definite structure" or else recites "function without reciting sufficient structure for performing that function." *Watts*, 232 F.3d at 880. The converse presumption remains unaffected: "use of the word 'means' creates a presumption that § 112[(f)] applies." *Personalized Media*, 161 F.3d at 703.

Williamson v. Citrix Online LLC, 792 F.3d. 1339, 1349 (2015). The focus is on the claim language as a whole, not just the isolated term that is akin to "means." *Id.* at *8. Generic terms such as "mechanism," "element," "device" and other such terms that do not connote sufficiently definite structure in the context of the overall claim are tantamount to stating "means," and therefore may be construed pursuant to 112(f) if nothing else in the claim provides sufficient structure. *Id.* at *8. Whether a claim invokes § 112(f) is decided on a limitation-by-limitation basis looking to the patent and the prosecution history. *See Cole*, 102 F.3d at 531.

14.4.1.4.2 Nonliteral Infringement—The Doctrine of Equivalents

The doctrine of equivalents allows for a finding of infringement where the accused product or process is close to the patented invention, but does not literally infringe. The doctrine of equivalents evolved in response to the concern that an "unscrupulous copyist" could avoid literal infringement of a patented invention by making insubstantial changes to the invention. *Graver Tank & Mfg. Co. v. Linde Air Prods. Co.*, 339 U.S. 605, 607–08 (1950). The doctrine is judge-made and has long served to provide courts some leeway to ensure that insubstantial variations do not destroy the value of patents. The doctrine of equivalents has increasingly come under scrutiny on the grounds that it introduces tremendous uncertainty into the scope of patents and makes it difficult for competitors to determine where they can legitimately tread. As a result, the Supreme Court and the Federal Circuit have revisited the contours of this doctrine frequently over the past decade. The process of judicial tinkering appears to have come to rest.

There are two tests for determining equivalence: (1) the function-way-result test and (2) the insubstantial differences test. The use of either test is case-dependent. *See Warner-Jenkinson Co. v. Hilton Davis Chem. Co.*, 520 U.S. 17, 40 (1997). Under the function-way-result test, an accused element is equivalent to a claim limitation "if it performs substantially the same function in substantially the same way to obtain the same result." *Graver Tank*, 339 U.S. at 608 (quoting *Sanitary Refrigerator Co. v. Winters*, 280 U.S. 30, 42 (1929)). Under this test, a finding of equivalence requires that all three prongs be satisfied. Under the insubstantial differences test, equivalence exists where the differences between the element in the accused product or process and the claim limitation are insubstantial. *See* Kenneth D. Bassinger, *Unsettled Expectations in Patent Law:* Festo *and the Moving Target of Claim Equivalence*, 48 How. L.J. 685, 695 (2005). Under either test, nonliteral infringement is a question of fact for the jury to decide. *See Cook Biotech Inc. v. Acell, Inc.*, 460 F.3d 1365, 1373 (Fed. Cir. 2006). The doctrine of equivalents determination is judged on the state of technology as of the time of the infringement, not (as in the case of means-plus-function claims) as of the time the patent issued.

14.4.1.4.2.1 Limiting Principles

While the doctrine of equivalents is a question of fact, the courts have developed various legal doctrines that limit its applicability: (1) the all-elements rule, along with the claim vitiation corollary; (2) prosecution history estoppel, along with the specific exclusion corollary; (3) the prior art rule; and (4) the public dedication rule. These limiting doctrines are not mutually exclusive—the patentee must satisfy all of them to establish infringement under the doctrine of equivalents.

14.4.1.4.2.1.1 The All-Elements (All-Limitations) Rule

The all-elements rule[32] provides that the test for equivalence under the doctrine of equivalents must be applied on an element-by-element (or limitation-by-limitation) basis. A finding of infringement therefore requires that the accused product or process contain each claim limitation or its equivalent. Under the all-elements rule, the trier of fact performs an equivalence analysis to determine whether each claim limitation exists in the accused product or process either literally or as an equivalent. However, if no reasonable jury could find an equivalent element in the accused product or process to the claim limitation, the court must grant summary judgment as to noninfringement. *Warner-Jenkinson Co. v. Hilton Davis Chem. Co.*, 520 U.S. 17, 39 n.8 (1997).

14.4.1.4.2.1.1.1 Claim Vitiation

The claim vitiation doctrine is a corollary of the all-elements rule: an accused device cannot be infringing if it would effectively vitiate (or eliminate) any claim limitation. *See Freedman Seating Co. v. Am. Seating Co.*, 420 F.3d 1350, 1358 (Fed. Cir. 2005). The Federal Circuit has applied the claim vitiation rule in varying ways, leading to somewhat unpredictable results. *See* Daniel H. Shulman & Donald W. Rupert, *"Vitiating" the Doctrine of Equivalents: A New Patent Law Doctrine*, 12 Fed. Cir. B.J. 457 (2003). In *Cadence Pharmaceuticals Inc. v. Exela PharmSci Inc.*, 780 F.3d 1364, 1371 (Fed. Cir. 2015), the Federal Circuit clarified that "'vitiation' is not an exception or threshold determination that forecloses resort to the doctrine of equivalents, but is instead a legal conclusion of a lack of equivalence based on the evidence presented and the theory of equivalence asserted." The court explained that equivalence should not depend on "labels like 'vitiation' . . . but on the proper assessment of the language of the claimed limitation and the substantiality of whatever relevant differences may exist in the accused structure."

14.4.1.4.2.1.2 Prosecution History Estoppel

Prosecution history estoppel can preclude a patent holder from using the doctrine of equivalents to reclaim subject matter relinquished expressly or by operation of law during patent prosecution. *See Eagle Comtronics, Inc. v. Arrow Commc'n*

---

32. The Federal Circuit prefers to use "limitation" when referring to claim language and "element" when referring to the accused product. *Festo Corp. v. Shoketsu Kinzoku Kabushiki Co.*, 234 F.3d 558, 563 n.1 (Fed. Cir. 2000). Along those lines, the all-elements rule is also known as the all-limitations rule. *Ethicon Endo-Surgery, Inc. v. U.S. Surgical Corp.*, 149 F.3d 1309, 1317 n.1 (Fed. Cir. 1998).

Labs., Inc., 305 F.3d 1303, 1315 (Fed. Cir. 2002). Prosecution history estoppel is most often applied where a patent applicant amended or canceled a claim that the patent examiner rejected as unpatentable in light of prior art. Whether prosecution history estoppel applies in a particular case is a question of law. *See Panduit Corp. v. Hellermanntyton Corp.*, 451 F.3d 819, 826 (Fed. Cir. 2006).

In *Festo Corp. v. Shoketsu Kinzoku Kabushiki Co.*, 535 U.S. 722 (2002), the Supreme Court adopted a rebuttable presumption that amendments made to narrow a claim limitation foreclose later stretching of that limitation to reach an accused technology under the doctrine of equivalents. The patentee can rebut this presumption under three scenarios: (1) the equivalent was unforeseeable to a person having ordinary skill in the art at the time of the amendment; (2) the rationale for the amendment was no more than tangentially related to the equivalent at issue; or (3) another reason suggesting that the patentee could not reasonably be expected to have described the alleged equivalent. *Id.* at 740–41. Table 14.9 summarizes guidelines outlined by the Federal Circuit for applying the three rebuttal criteria. *See Festo Corp. v. Shoketsu Kinzoku Kabushiki Co.*, 344 F.3d 1359, 1368–70 (Fed. Cir. 2003) (en banc).

Table 14.9
Rebuttal Criteria for Presumptive *Festo* Bar

Rebuttal Criteria	Application	Focus of Inquiry	Evidence the Court May Consider
The equivalent was unforeseeable at the time of the application.	Unforeseeable equivalent: later-developed technologies or technology unknown in the relevant art. Foreseeable equivalent: old technology or equivalent was known in the prior art in the relevant field of the invention.	Underlying factual issues such as the state of the art and understanding of one skilled in the art at the time of the amendment.	Expert testimony and other extrinsic evidence relating to relevant factual inquiries.
The rationale for the amendment was no more than tangentially related to the equivalent at issue.	Tangential means peripheral or not directly relevant Not tangential: amendment made to avoid prior art containing the alleged equivalent.	Patentee's objective apparent reason for the narrowing amendment, including the context in which the amendment was made.	Prosecution history record and no additional evidence except when expert testimony is necessary for interpretation of that record.

Rebuttal Criteria	Application	Focus of Inquiry	Evidence the Court May Consider
Another reason suggesting that the patentee could not reasonably be expected to have described the alleged equivalent.	Another reason: shortcomings in language.	[No cases yet on point.]	Should be limited to prosecution history record.

14.4.1.4.2.1.2.1 Specific Exclusion

The specific exclusion principle is a corollary to the doctrine of prosecution history estoppel. It provides that a patentee cannot use the doctrine of equivalents to reclaim subject matter which he clearly excluded. *SciMed Life Sys., Inc. v. Advanced Cardiovascular Sys., Inc.*, 242 F.3d 1337, 1347 (Fed. Cir. 2001). A patent may specifically exclude a proposed equivalent from the scope of the claimed invention either implicitly or explicitly. The rule ensures that the public may rely on clear disclaimers in the patent to conclude that the patentee did not seek patent rights for this excluded subject matter.

The specific exclusion doctrine applies where the patentee clearly disclaims subject matter from the scope of the claimed invention in the specification or the claims. Cases involving specific exclusion in the specification focus on explicit disclaimers, such as where the patentee criticizes the equivalent or requires that the invention contain the specific element claimed. *See Gaus v. Conair Corp.*, 363 F.3d 1284, 1291 (Fed. Cir. 2004); *SciMed*, 242 F.3d at 1345. Specific exclusion is rarely applied on the basis of a claim, but where the patentee claims one option in a binary choice setting, specific exclusion precludes the patent holder's assertion that the other option is equivalent. *See Senior Techs., Inc. v. R.F. Techs. Inc.*, 76 F. App'x 318, 321 (Fed. Cir. 2003). The binary choice setting does not simply involve the negation of a claim limitation (i.e., "suede" versus "not suede" or "blue" versus "not blue"), but requires that the claim limitation be one of only two options.

14.4.1.4.2.1.3 Prior Art Rule

A third limiting principle of nonliteral infringement analysis, the prior art rule, provides that a patentee may not use the doctrine of equivalents to obtain coverage of subject matter in the prior art, that is, "coverage which he could not lawfully have obtained from the USPTO by literal claims." *Wilson Sporting Goods Co. v. David Geoffrey & Assocs.*, 904 F.2d 677, 683–84 (Fed. Cir. 1990). Accordingly, an accused infringer who merely practices the prior art cannot infringe under the doctrine of equivalents. This principle is applied by constructing a hypothetical claim based on the accused technology. *See id.* at 684. If the USPTO could have allowed the hypothetical claim over the prior art (i.e., if the prior art did not anticipate or render the hypothetical claim obvious, *Abbott Labs. v. Dey, L.P.*, 287 F.3d 1097, 1105–06 (Fed. Cir. 2002)), the prior art does not preclude infringement under the doctrine of equivalents. The patent holder bears the burden of proving that the range of equivalents sought does not cover the prior art. *See Wilson Sporting Goods*, 904 F.2d at 685. This determination is a question of law. *See id.* at 683.

14.4.1.4.2.1.4 The Public Dedication Rule

The public dedication rule (or disclosure-dedication rule) provides that a patent holder cannot invoke the doctrine of equivalents to recapture subject matter disclosed but not claimed in a patent. *See Johnson & Johnston Assocs. Inc. v. R.E. Serv. Co.*, 285 F.3d 1046, 1054 (Fed. Cir. 2002) (en banc) (per curiam). The Federal Circuit stated that to hold otherwise would "conflict with the primacy of the claims in defining the scope of the patentee's exclusive right." *Id.* (quoting *Sage Prods. Inc. v. Devon Indus., Inc.*, 126 F.3d 1420, 1424 (Fed. Cir. 1997)). The public dedication rule derives from and promotes the patent system's notice function. The test for determining whether a disclosure has been dedicated to the public is whether "one of ordinary skill in the art can understand the unclaimed disclosed teaching upon reading the written description." *PSC Comput. Prods., Inc. v. Foxconn Int'l, Inc.*, 355 F.3d 1353, 1360 (Fed. Cir. 2004). Like prosecution history estoppel, the public dedication rule is a question of law. *See Toro Co. v. White Consol. Indus., Inc.*, 383 F.3d 1326, 1331 (Fed. Cir. 2004). Patentees are free to broaden the scope of their patent under the broadening reissue provision, § 251, for up to two years following issuance. *See* § 14.2.5.4.2.

14.4.1.4.2.2 Interpreting the Nonliteral Scope of Means-Plus-Function Claims

The question arises whether means-plus-function claims are entitled to one or two stretches for "equivalents"—one as a part of literal infringement analysis under § 112(f) (to reach "equivalents thereof" relating to embodiments set forth in the specification) and a second under the doctrine of equivalents. Since the § 112(f) literal "equivalents" analysis is based on the state of technology as of the time the patent issues, the doctrine of equivalents provides a second stretch to the extent that the accused device employs "after-arising" technology—means that were not known in the art at the time that the patent issued. *See Al-Site Corp. v. VSI Int'l, Inc.*, 174 F.3d 1308, 1320 (Fed. Cir. 1999).

Even with regard to technology that was known as of the time that the patent issued, the patentee is entitled to additional scope under the doctrine of equivalents to the extent that the function of the accused device is substantially the same as the function of the claimed invention. *See id.* at 1320–21; *see also WMS Gaming v. Int'l Game Tech.*, 184 F.3d 1339, 1353 (Fed. Cir. 1999). This is because § 112(f) requires that the function of the accused element be identical to the function of the claim limitation, whereas the doctrine of equivalents is broader—allowing substantially similar function.

Nonetheless, the patentee cannot invoke the doctrine of equivalents to reach a substantially similar "structure, material, or act" that did not fall within the scope of the § 112(f) "equivalents thereof" with regard to technology that was known as of the time that the patent issued. The Patent Act will not permit an "equivalent of an equivalent" by applying both § 112(f) and the doctrine of equivalents to the structure of a given claim element with regard to technology that the patent draftsperson was fully capable of capturing when preparing the application. *Al-Site*, 174 F.3d at 1320 n.2; *Chiuminatta Concrete Concepts, Inc. v. Cardinal Indus., Inc.*, 145 F.3d 1303, 1310–11 (Fed. Cir. 1998).

14.4.1.4.3 The Reverse Doctrine of Equivalents

The reverse doctrine of equivalents is an equitable doctrine designed "to prevent unwarranted extension of the claims beyond a fair scope of the patentee's invention." *Scripps Clinic & Research Found. v. Genentech, Inc.*, 927 F.2d 1565, 1581 (Fed. Cir. 1991). More than a century ago, the Supreme Court recognized that there may be circumstances in which an accused device that literally infringes a patent should nonetheless be excused from liability because it substantially differs in operative principle and results. Although the so-called reverse doctrine of equivalents has rarely been found, it nonetheless continues to be raised. In *Boyden Power-Brake Co. v. Westinghouse*, 170 U.S. 537 (1898), George Westinghouse had invented a train brake that used a central reservoir of compressed air for stopping power in 1869. *Id.* at 545–46. Further advances in his design, primarily the addition of an air reservoir in each brake cylinder, resulted in a brake that was patented in 1887. *Id.* at 558–60. An improvement on this 1887 brake, invented by George Boyden, added an ingenious mechanism for pushing compressed air into the brake piston from both the central reservoir and a local reservoir in each brake cylinder. (Westinghouse's brake required a complicated series of passageways to supply air from the two sources.) With the added stopping power of the Boyden brake, engineers could safely operate the increasingly long trains of the late nineteenth century.

The Westinghouse patent included a claim for "the combination of a main air-pipe, an auxiliary reservoir, a brake-cylinder, a triple valve [the device that coordinated the airflows from the main reservoir and the individual brake reservoir] and an auxiliary-valve device, actuated by the piston of the triple-valve . . . for admitting air in the application of the brake." *Id.* at 553–54. The Court noted that the literal wording of the Westinghouse patent could be read to cover Boyden's brake since it included a "triple valve." But it refused to find infringement on the ground that Boyden's device was a significant contribution that took the invention outside the equitable bounds of the patent, explaining:

> a charge of infringement is sometimes made out, though the letter of the claims be avoided . . . [t]he converse is equally true. The patentee may bring the defendant within the letter of his claims, but if the latter has so far changed the principle of the device that the claims of the patent, literally construed, have ceased to represent his actual invention, he is as little subject to be adjudged an infringer as one who has violated the letter of a statute has to be convicted, when he has done nothing in conflict with its spirit and intent.

Id. at 562.

The reverse doctrine of equivalents was recognized—but not applied—once again by the Supreme Court in *Graver Tank & Mfg. Co. v. Linde Air Prods. Co.*, 339 U.S. 605, 608–609 (1950). But since 1898, no case has squarely applied the doctrine to excuse infringement. According to the Federal Circuit, "because products on which patent claims are readable word for word often are in fact the same, perform the same function in the same way, and achieve the same result, as the claimed invention, a defense based on the reverse doctrine of equivalents is rarely offered." *SRI Int'l v. Matsushita Elec. Corp. of Am.*, 775 F.2d 1107, 1123 n.19 (Fed. Cir. 1985); *See Monsanto Co. v. Mycogen Plant Sci., Inc.*, 61 F. Supp. 2d 133, 187–88 (D. Del. 1999) (granting JMOL overturning jury's exoneration of accused infringer under reverse doctrine of equivalents). Indeed, the Federal Circuit has observed that "[t]he reverse doctrine of equivalents is rarely applied, and this court has never affirmed a finding of noninfringement under the reverse doctrine of equivalents." *See Roche Palo Alto LLC v. Apotex, Inc.*, 531 F.3d 1372, 1378 (Fed. Cir. 2008) (*citing Tate Access Floors, Inc. v. Interface Architectural Resources, Inc.*, 279 F.3d 1357 (Fed. Cir. 2002)).

14.4.1.5 Extraterritorial Infringement

14.4.1.5.1 Manufacturing Components Within the United States for Assembly Abroad—§ 271(f)

The rights conferred under patent law generally apply only to inventions made, used, sold, or imported into the United States. § 271(a). After the Supreme Court held that there could be no liability for shipping the components of a patented device outside of the United States for purposes of assembly abroad, *see Deepsouth Packing Co. v. Laitram Corp.*, 406 U.S. 518 (1972), Congress added § 271(f) to extend liability for supplying unassembled "components" from the United States for "combination" outside the United States, where the same combination would infringe a patent if it occurred within the United States. The two prongs of infringement under § 271(f) are similar to active inducement and contributory infringement found in § 271(b) and (c).

Applying § 271(f) poses several challenges in the digital age. One particularly thorny issue has been the meaning of "component." For example, a "component" does not include the supply of blueprints, plans, or instructions. *Pellegrini v. Analog Devices, Inc.*, 275 F.3d 1113 (Fed. Cir. 2004). Nor does it include software; instead only a tangible, computer-readable medium like a CD can be a "component." *See Microsoft Corp. v. AT&T Corp.*, 550 U.S. 437 (2007). The term "supply" has also been controversial. In *Microsoft*, the Court held that to "supply" a component from the United States means to ship it from the United States; making copies abroad does not constitute "supplying." *Id.* at 452–53.

Notably, § 271(f) is inapplicable to method claims. *Cardiac Pacemakers, Inc. v. St. Jude Med., Inc.*, 576 F.3d 1348, 1364 (Fed. Cir. 2009) (en banc in relevant part) ("[B]ecause one cannot supply the step of a method, Section 271(f) cannot apply to method or process patents."). Accordingly, "Section 271(f) does not encompass devices that may be used to practice a patented method." *Id.* at 1366.

14.4.1.5.2 Importing Products Made Using Patented Processes—§ 271(g)

Section 271(g) was also added in the 1980s to close a loophole pertaining to products imported into the United States made using patented processes. It establishes liability for importing, making, using, or selling within the United States a nonpatented product made abroad using a process that is patented in the United States. A "product" under subsection (g) must be a manufactured physical article; it does not include intangible information produced or transmitted by a patented process. *See NTP, Inc. v. Research in Motion, Ltd.*, 418 F.3d 1282 (Fed. Cir. 2005). Furthermore, there is no liability if the product is "materially changed by subsequent processes." § 271(g)(1). The Federal Circuit has held that "in the chemical context a 'material' change . . . is a significant change in the compound's structure and properties." *Eli Lilly & Co. v. Am. Cyanamid Co.*, 82 F.3d 1568, 1573 (Fed. Cir. 1996).

14.4.2 Defenses

Section 282 of the Patent Act provides for the following defenses:

> (1) Noninfringement, absence of liability for infringement or unenforceability;
>
> (2) Invalidity of the patent or any claim in suit on any ground specified in part II [of the Patent Act] as a condition for patentability;
>
> (3) Invalidity of the patent or any claim in suit for failure to comply with any requirement of sections 112 or 251 [of the Patent Act];
>
> (4) Any other fact or act made a defense by [the Patent Act].

14.4.2.1 Noninfringement

An accused infringer may contend that he does not infringe the asserted patent either literally or under the doctrine of equivalents. Noninfringement exists where the patent holder does not meet the burden of proving infringement by a preponderance of the evidence.

14.4.2.2 Absence of Liability

Even if the accused technology is found to read on the claimed invention, the defendant can prevail by establishing consent, experimental use, or several other legal and equitable defenses.

14.4.2.2.1 Consent or License

An alleged infringer can defend on the ground that the patentee has consented to their use of the technology by, for example, granting a license. A patent license is an agreement or covenant between the patent holder and the licensee stipulating that the patent holder will not sue the licensee for otherwise infringing acts. If such an agreement covers the acts in question, the accused infringer cannot be liable for infringement because his or her acts were not "without authority" as required by § 271(a).

Patent licenses can be express or implied. An implied license arises by acquiescence, conduct, equitable estoppel, or legal estoppel. *Wang Labs., Inc. v. Mitsubishi Elecs. Am., Inc.*, 103 F.3d 1571, 1580 (Fed. Cir. 1997). Such licenses are generally revocable. The existence and scope of licenses are generally governed by state contract law.

14.4.2.2.1.1 First-Sale Doctrine/Exhaustion Principle

Under the first-sale doctrine (sometimes referred to as the exhaustion principle), a form of implied license by operation of law, the first unrestricted sale of a patented product exhausts the patentee's control over that product, and it can be resold and repaired without implicating the patent owner's rights. *See Aro Mfg. Co. v. Convertible Top Replacement Co.*, 377 U.S. 476, 484 (1964) (stating that "it is fundamental that sale of a patented article by the patentee . . . carries with it an 'implied license to use.'"). The line between permitted repair and impermissible reconstruction is not easily determined, resulting in rather vague, context-specific rulings. *See, e.g.*, *Hewlett-Packard Co. v. Repeat-O-Type Stencil Mfg. Co.*, 123 F.3d 1445 (Fed. Cir. 1997). Such issues frequently arise in the context of contributory infringement claims, where the alleged infringer is providing specialized replacement parts.

Contractual restrictions on resale or reuse can provoke patent misuse allegations and antitrust counterclaims. *See Lexmark International, Inc. v. Impression Prods., Inc.*, — F.3d —, 2016 WL 559042 (Fed. Cir. 2016); *Monsanto Co. v. McFarling*, 363 F.3d 1336, 1341 (Fed. Cir. 2004); *Mallinckrodt, Inc. v. Medipart, Inc.*, 976 F.2d 700 (Fed. Cir. 1992); *see also* § 14.4.2.3.2. Unlike other forms of implied licenses, patent exhaustion cannot be disclaimed. Nonetheless, patent exhaustion does not prevent the owner of a patent on a self-replicating product from using contractual restrictions to bar use of self-replicated progeny. Patent exhaustion only applies to "the particular item sold, and not to reproductions" made within the purchaser's control. *Bowman v. Monsanto Co.*, 133 S. Ct. 1761, 1768 (2013).

Exhaustion is determined on a patent-by-patent, as opposed to a claim-by-claim, basis. *See Keurig, Inc. v. Sturm Foods, Inc.*, 732 F.3d 1370 (Fed. Cir. 2013); *but see id.* at 1375 (O'Malley, J., concurring in the result) (noting that because each patent claim represents a separate invention, patent exhaustion should apply on a claim-by-claim basis).

The doctrine of patent exhaustion applies to method claims and the method patent is exhausted by sale of the item that embodies the method. *See Quanta Comput., Inc. v. LG Elecs., Inc.*, 553 U.S. 617 (2008). Although repair of a patented product that has been sold is permissible, reconstruction of the patented technology crosses the line into the patentee's "make" right. Furthermore, sale of a component that does not completely practice or embody a patent claim can still exhaust the patent if the product has no substantial noninfringing use or if the component substantially embodies the claim. *See id.*

The Federal Circuit held in *Jazz Photo Corp. v. International Trade Commission*, 264 F.3d 1094 (Fed. Cir. 2001), that where a licensee sells a product outside the U.S., such sale does not exhaust the licensor's U.S. patents if that product is subsequently imported and sold in the U.S. The Federal Circuit reaffirmed the *Jazz Photo* rule in *Lexmark International, Inc. v. Impression Products, Inc.*, — F.3d —, 2016 WL 559042 (Fed. Cir. 2016) (en banc) (distinguishing the Supreme Court's holding in *Kirtsaeng v. John Wiley & Sons, Inc.*, 133 S. Ct 1351 (2013), holding that international exhaustion applies under the Copyright Act notwithstanding the importation right).

14.4.2.2.1.2 Shop Right

Based on state law, a "shop right" entitles an employer to use patented technology developed by an employee in the employer's "shop." *See McElmurry v. Ark. Power & Light Co.*, 995 F.2d 1576, 1580 (Fed. Cir. 1993). An employer has a shop right where it has provided wages, materials, tools, and workspace to finance its employee's invention. An employee's consent, acquiescence, inducement, or assistance to the employer in using the invention without seeking payment or restricting its use also creates a shop right. *Id.* at 1582. The defense is an equitable doctrine. *Schroeder v. Tracor, Inc.*, No. 99-1281, 1999 U.S. App. LEXIS 30386, at *4–5, 1999 WL 1021055 (Fed. Cir. Nov. 5, 1999). To determine whether an employer has a shop right to an invention, courts "look to the totality of the circumstances on a case by case basis and determine whether the facts of a particular case demand, under principles of equity and fairness, a finding that a 'shop right' exists." *McElmurry*, 995 F.2d at 1581–82. A shop right is personal to an employer and cannot be assigned or transferred. *See Francklyn v. Guilford Packing Co.*, 695 F.2d 1158, 1163 (9th Cir. 1983). However, a shop right will pass to the purchaser of the employer's entire business. *See Cal. E. Labs., Inc. v. Gould*, 896 F.2d 400, 402 (9th Cir. 1990).

14.4.2.2.2 Experimental Use Defense

Courts have long recognized a common-law defense of experimental use. The Federal Circuit has, however, interpreted this doctrine quite narrowly, limiting it to uses "for amusement, to satisfy idle curiosity, or for strictly philosophical inquiry." *See Madey v. Duke Univ.*, 307 F.3d 1351, 1361–62 (Fed. Cir. 2002). If the use has the "slightest commercial implication," the experimental use defense does not apply. *Id.* at 1362. Additionally, conduct in keeping with the legitimate business of the accused infringer does not qualify for the defense, regardless of the commercial implications. *Id.* Furthermore, whether a user is a profit or nonprofit entity is not determinative. *Id.*

In addition to the common-law doctrine of experimental use, § 271(e) creates a limited experimental use exception for submitting information for regulatory purposes. Adopted in 1984 as part of the Drug Price Competition Act (also known as the Hatch-Waxman Act), § 271(e)(1) provides a safe harbor for using a patented drug in testing before the end of the patent term "solely for uses reasonably related to the development and submission" of regulatory information. Without this safe harbor, a competitor seeking to get advance approval of a generic version of a particular drug would infringe if they tested their alternative before the patent term expired, which would effectively lengthen the patent term by the amount of time necessary to test the generic drug for FDA approval. *See Roche Prods. Inc. v. Bolar Pharm. Co.*, 733 F.2d 858 (Fed. Cir. 1984). While the safe harbor is not so expansive as to include "basic scientific research . . . performed without the intent to develop a particular drug," its scope has been interpreted broadly to cover drug testing, human clinical trials, and preclinical laboratory testing, or any reasonable research that might be "appropriate to include in a submission to the FDA." *Merck KGaA v. Integra Lifesciences I, Ltd.*, 545 U.S. 193, 205–06 (2005); *see also Integra Lifesciences I, Ltd. v. Merck KGaA*, 496 F.3d 1334 (Fed. Cir. 2007). In addition to pharmaceuticals, § 271(e)(1) covers experimental testing of medical devices. *See Eli Lilly & Co. v. Medtronic Inc.*, 872 F.2d 402 (Fed. Cir. 1989), *aff'd*, 496 U.S. 661 (1990).

14.4.2.2.3 Prior-Use Right

Section 273 of the Patent Act, added by the First Inventor Defense Act of 1999, provides an infringement defense for an earlier inventor of a business method which was subsequently patented by another. This defense is available if the accused infringer "had, acting in good faith, actually reduced the subject matter to practice at least 1 year before the effective filing date of such patent, and commercially used the subject matter before the effective filing date of such patent." § 273(b)(1). The party asserting a prior-use defense need not prove that it invented the business method before the patentee in accordance with § 102(g). Section 273(e) limits the transfer of the prior-use right except as "an ancillary and subordinate part of a good-faith assignment or transfer for other reasons of the entire enterprise or line of business to which the defense relates."

Effective September 16, 2011, to patents issued on or after that date, the AIA expands the scope of prior-use rights to also include "subject matter consisting of a process, or consisting of a machine, manufacture, or composition of matter used in a manufacturing or other commercial process." AIA § 5. For this defense to apply, the prior use must have been a prior commercial use in the U.S. by the party asserting the defense. In addition, the prior use must have occurred at least one year before the earlier of either: (1) the effective filing date, or (2) the date of the first public disclosure of the claimed invention. The prior-use defense must be established by clear and convincing evidence. In certain cases, this defense does not apply to patents held by universities.

14.4.2.2.4 Bar Against Remedies for Infringement of Medical Procedure Patents by Doctors and Hospitals

Following a lawsuit against a doctor to enforce a patent on a cataract surgery procedure in 1993, the American Medical Association lobbied Congress to exclude medical procedure patents from the scope of patentable subject matter. While declining to curtail the scope of § 101, Congress enacted § 287(c) which bars the enforcement of medical procedure patents against medical practitioners or related health-care entities. This provision does not, however, insulate sellers of medical devices from indirect (inducement or contributory) infringement of medical procedure patents.

14.4.2.2.5 Sovereign Immunity

During the 1980s, intellectual property owners became concerned that states and state agencies, including public universities, might escape or at least frustrate enforcement of federal intellectual property rights by invoking state sovereign immunity under the Eleventh Amendment of the U.S. Constitution. In the early 1990s, Congress enacted a series of laws expressly abrogating state sovereign immunity for intellectual property infringement, including patent violations. The Supreme Court struck down one such act, the Patent and Plant Variety Remedy Clarification Act, on the grounds that Congress cannot abrogate state sovereign immunity on the basis of its Article I powers under the Constitution and that Congress had not established an adequate basis for abrogation of state sovereign immunity pursuant to the Fourteenth Amendment. *Fla. Prepaid Postsecondary Educ. Expense Bd. v. Coll. Sav. Bank*, 527 U.S. 627 (1999). As a result, states and state instrumentalities cannot be sued in federal court for patent infringement without their consent.

14.4.2.3 Unenforceability

A finding that a patent is unenforceable renders each and every claim of that patent unenforceable. By contrast, a finding of invalidity is assessed on a claim-by-claim basis, the result of which may be that some claims are held invalid whereas others are sustained and may continue to be enforceable.

14.4.2.3.1 Inequitable Conduct

Where a patent applicant breaches the duty to prosecute a patent application in good faith and candor, it may result in a finding of inequitable conduct. *See* 37 C.F.R. § 1.56 (2013); *Purdue Pharma L.P. v. Endo Pharm. Inc.*, 410 F.3d 690, 695 (Fed. Cir. 2005). Inequitable conduct may "arise from an affirmative misrepresentation of a material fact, failure to disclose material information, or submission of false material information, coupled with an intent to deceive or mislead the USPTO." *Id.* A determination that inequitable conduct occurred in relation to one or more claims will render the entire patent unenforceable. *Kingsdown Med. Consultants, Ltd. v. Hollister, Inc.*, 863 F.2d 867, 877 (Fed. Cir. 1988) (en banc in relevant part). Furthermore, inequitable conduct is not limited to the patent-in-suit; it may also render related patents unenforceable where the inequitable conduct had an "immediate and necessary relation" to other patents. *See Consol. Aluminum Corp. v. Foseco Int'l Ltd.*, 910 F.2d 804, 810–12 (Fed. Cir. 1990) (*quoting Keystone Driller Co. v. Gen. Excavator Co.*, 290 U.S. 240, 245 (1933)).

Inequitable conduct claims must be pled with particularity under Federal Rule of Civil Procedure 9(b), and "requires identification of the specific who, what, when, where, and how of the material misrepresentation or omission committed before the USPTO." *Exergen Corp. v. Wal-Mart Stores, Inc.*, 575 F.3d 1312, 1327 (Fed. Cir. 2009). The accused infringer must prove both materiality and intent by clear and convincing evidence. *See Purdue Pharma*, 410 F.3d at 695. Once these threshold findings are established, the court "must weigh them to determine whether the equities warrant a conclusion that inequitable conduct occurred." *Id.* at 696. "Intent and materiality are separate requirements. A district court should not use a 'sliding scale,' where a weak showing of intent may be found sufficient based on a strong showing of materiality and vice versa." *Therasense, Inc. v. Becton, Dickinson & Co.*, 649 F.3d 1276, 1290 (Fed. Cir. 2011) (en banc) (internal citation omitted).

The level of materiality required to establish inequitable conduct is "but-for" materiality. *Id.* at 1291. "[P]rior art is but-for material if the USPTO would not have allowed a claim had it been aware of the undisclosed prior art." *Id.* at 1291–92. To determine whether the USPTO would have allowed the claim, "the court should apply the preponderance of the evidence standard and give claims their broadest reasonable construction." *Id.* (citing Manual of Patent Examining Procedure (MPEP) §§ 706, 2111 (8th ed. Rev. 8, July 2010)). Even if the withheld prior art does not invalidate a claim under the clear-and-convincing standard, it may be "but-for" material if it would have blocked patent issuance under the USPTO's evidentiary standards. *Id.* at 1292 (citing MPEP §§ 706 (preponderance of the evidence), 2111 (broadest reasonable construction)). In addition, "[a]lthough but-for materiality generally must be proved to satisfy the materiality prong of inequitable conduct, [the Federal Circuit] recognizes an exception in cases of affirmative egregious misconduct," such as the filing of an unmistakably false affidavit. *Id.*

Intent to mislead or deceive the USPTO may be shown by direct evidence or inferred from clear and convincing evidence of the surrounding circumstances. *See Purdue Pharma*, 410 F.3d at 700. A court may not infer intent solely from materiality. *Therasense*, 649 F.3d at 1290. Rather, it must weigh the evidence of intent independent of its analysis of materiality. *Id.* "[T]o meet the clear and convincing evidence standard, the specific intent to deceive must be 'the single most reasonable inference able to be drawn from the evidence.'" *Id.* (quoting *Star Sci., Inc. v. R.J. Reynolds Tobacco Co.*, 537 F.3d 1357, 1366 (Fed. Cir. 2008)). Otherwise, if multiple reasonable inferences may be drawn, intent to deceive cannot be found. *Id.* at 1290–91.

14.4.2.3.2 Patent Misuse

The affirmative defense of patent misuse exists to prevent harm to the market caused by a patentee extending a patent's right to exclude beyond its legal scope. The underlying principle of misuse is that an alleged infringer must prove by clear and convincing evidence that a patentee has both "impermissibly broadened the physical or temporal scope of the patent grant" and caused some "anticompetitive effect." *See Va. Panel Corp. v. MAC Panel Co.*, 133 F.3d 860 (Fed. Cir. 1997). Where the patentee's behavior remains within the grant of the patent right to exclude, however, there can never be patent misuse. *See Monsanto Co. v. McFarling*, 363 F.3d 1336, 1341 (Fed. Cir. 2004). In response to concern that this judge-made doctrine was vague, unpredictable, and overbroad, Congress exempted several specific behaviors from the doctrine by adding § 271(d). For example, enforcing a patent or refusing to license cannot constitute patent misuse. *See* §§ 271(d)(3)–(4). Courts scrutinize other behavior under antitrust's familiar levels of review: per se and rule of reason.

Many behaviors can theoretically constitute patent misuse. Tying sales of a patented good and an unpatented good, package licenses, extending royalties beyond the patent term, grantback clauses, field-of-use restrictions, horizontal arrangements like patent pools, price discrimination, and market division can all constitute patent misuse if they improperly expand a patent right to anticompetitive effect. A detailed discussion of this doctrine can be found in 1 Herbert Hovenkamp, Mark D. Janis & Mark A. Lemley, IP and Antitrust § 3.3 (2006).

14.4.2.3.2.1 Postexpiration Royalties

The Supreme Court held in *Brulotte v. Thys Co.*, 379 U.S. 29, 32 (1964), that license agreements providing for payment of patent royalties beyond the expiration of a patent are per se patent unlawful. The Supreme Court reaffirmed that decision in *Kimble v. Marvel Entertainment, LLC*, 135 S. Ct. 2401 (2015).

14.4.2.3.3 Equitable Estoppel

Equitable estoppel arises where a patentee misleads an alleged infringer into believing that he or she would not be sued for using the patented technology. The defense may bar all relief on an infringement claim. *See A.C. Aukerman Co. v. R.L. Chaides Constr. Co.*, 960 F.2d 1020, 1041 (Fed. Cir. 1992) (en banc). Three elements must be established to prove equitable estoppel:

> (1) The actor, who usually must have knowledge of the true facts, communicates something in a misleading way, either by words, conduct or silence.
>
> (2) The other relies upon that communication.
>
> (3) And the other would be harmed materially if the actor is later permitted to assert any claim inconsistent with his earlier conduct.

Id. (quoting D.B. Dobbs, Handbook on the Law of Remedies § 2.3, at 42 (1973)). In the patent infringement context, the "something" communicated is that the plaintiff will not bring an infringement claim against the accused infringer. *See id.* at 1042. Accordingly, the defendant must not only be aware of the patentee and/or his patent but also know or reasonably be able to infer that the patentee has been aware of the accused infringer's acts for some time. A plaintiff's inaction may give rise to the inference that he abandoned his infringement claim when combined with other facts regarding the parties' relationship or contracts with each other. Regarding the third factor, material harm may include a change of economic position or loss of evidence. *See id.* at 1043.

Even where the defendant proves all three elements of the estoppel defense, the court must consider "any other evidence and facts respecting the equities of the parties in exercising its discretion and deciding whether to allow the defense of equitable estoppel to bar the suit." *Id.* The defense does not require an unreasonable delay in filing suit, as is necessary for laches. *See id.* at 1041–42. However, such a delay may be evidence relevant to determining whether the plaintiff's conduct was misleading.

14.4.2.3.4 Laches

The equitable defense of laches may be available where the plaintiff unreasonably delayed filing his or her infringement suit. *See A.C. Aukerman Co. v. R.L. Chaides Constr. Co.*, 960 F.2d 1020, 1032 (Fed. Cir. 1992) (holding that Congress codified a laches defense in § 282(b)(1)); *see also SCA Hygiene Products Aktiebolag v. First Quality Baby Products, LLC*, 807 F.3d 1311 (Fed. Cir. 2015) (en banc) (holding that *Petrella v. Metro-Goldwyn-Mayer, Inc.*, 134 S. Ct. 1962 (2014) does not disturb the patent laches doctrine articulated in *A.C. Aukerman Co.*). The defense is applicable where the accused infringer proves two factors:

> (1) the plaintiff delayed filing suit for an unreasonable and inexcusable length of time from the time the plaintiff knew or reasonably should have known of its claim against the defendant, and
>
> (2) the delay operated to the prejudice or injury of the defendant.

A.C. Aukerman Co., 960 F.2d at 1028. The period of delay is defined as the time from when the plaintiff knew or reasonably should have known of the defendant's alleged infringing acts until the date of suit. *Id.* This period may not begin until after the patent issues. *Id.* Regarding the second factor, prejudice to the defendant may be either economic or evidentiary. *See id.* at 1033. A laches defense may be defeated where the infringer "has engaged in particularly egregious conduct which would change the equities significantly in plaintiff's favor." *Id.* (quoting *TWM Mfg. Co. v. Dura Corp.*, 592 F.2d 346, 349 (6th Cir. 1979)). Laches only bars damages accrued prior to suit. *See id.* at 1041.

A rebuttable presumption of laches exists where the accused infringer proves that the plaintiff delayed filing suit for more than six years after actual or constructive knowledge of the defendant's alleged infringing acts. *See id.* at 1035–36, 1038. The defendant's burden of persuasion does not shift as a result of the plaintiff's six-year delay. *See id.* at 1039.

14.4.2.3.4.1 Prosecution Laches

A special form of laches—prosecution laches—renders a patent unenforceable where the patentee unreasonably delayed in prosecuting the patent, and the accused infringer or others suffered prejudice by the delay. *Cancer Research Tech. Ltd. v. Barr Labs., Inc.*, 625 F.3d 724, 729 (Fed. Cir. 2010). "[T]o establish prejudice[,] an accused infringer must show evidence of intervening rights, *i.e.*, that either the accused infringer or others invested in, worked on, or used the claimed technology during the period of delay." *Id.* The Federal Circuit reviews a determination of prosecution laches for abuse of discretion. *Id.* at 728–29. The Federal Circuit has left the threshold for applying prosecution laches somewhat vague, but stressed that it should only be invoked in "egregious cases of misuse of the statutory patent system." *Symbol Techs., Inc. v. Lemelson Med., Educ. & Research Found., L.P.*, 422 F.3d 1378, 1385 (Fed. Cir. 2005) (affirming judgment of unenforceability due to prosecution laches where patent applications were pending between eighteen to thirty-nine years, the applicant had engaged in "culpable neglect" in allowing them to linger, and intervening rights had developed).

14.4.2.4 Invalidity

The invalidity defense may be asserted where the patent fails to comply with any of the statutory requirements provided in §§ 101, 102, 103, and 112. Under § 282, a patent is presumed to be valid. "The presumption of validity is based on the presumption of administrative correctness of actions of the agency charged with examination of patentability." *Applied Materials, Inc. v. Advanced Semiconductor Materials Am., Inc.*, 98 F.3d 1563, 1569 (Fed. Cir. 1996). Accordingly, the burden of proving invalidity of a claim rests on the accused infringer, who must prove invalidity by clear and convincing evidence. *Microsoft Corp. v. i4i Ltd. P'ship*, 131 S. Ct. 2238 (2011).

Once a claim is declared invalid, patentees are collaterally estopped from asserting the claim unless they can show that they did not have "a fair opportunity procedurally, substantively and evidentially to pursue [their] claim the first time." *Blonder-Tongue Labs., Inc. v. Univ. of Ill. Found.*, 402 U.S. 313, 332–33, 350 (1971).

14.4.2.4.1 Double Patenting

Courts have interpreted patent law to forbid a second patent from covering the same invention or an obvious variation of it so as to prevent patentees from extending the duration of their patents by patenting the same subject matter more than once. The cases distinguish between two forms of double patenting: (1) so-called statutory or same-invention double patenting; and (2) obviousness-type or non-statutory double patenting. The former draws upon the language of § 101 stating that "[w]hoever invents or discovers any new and useful [invention] may obtain a patent therefore . . . ." Use of the singular implies that inventors are entitled to only one patent per invention. The latter is a judicial doctrine intended to prevent prolongation of the patent term through the assertion of claims that were made obvious by a prior patent of the same inventor. A patent which merely discloses a prior invention does not double patent—only the claims matter.

14.4.2.4.1.1 Statutory, or Same-Invention

Statutory double patenting occurs when the claims of a later patent would infringe an earlier-issued patent by the same inventor. This can happen where multiple patents derive from a common application. The courts have interpreted § 121 (relating to divisional applications, *see* § 14.2.2.3) as shielding applicants subject to a restriction requirement from the double-patenting doctrine. *See Eli Lilly & Co. v. Barr Labs., Inc.*, 251 F.3d 955 (Fed. Cir. 2001) (holding that a species patent that issues before an earlier-filed genus patent is not a double patent if the order of issue was due solely to USPTO delay); *Gerber Garment Tech., Inc. v. Letra Sys.*, 916 F.2d 683 (Fed. Cir. 1990) (holding that divisional application from a USPTO restriction requirement is not a double patent as long as divisional claims have not materially changed).

14.4.2.4.1.2 Nonstatutory or Obviousness-Type

Obviousness-type double patenting occurs when a later patent is made obvious by an earlier patent of the same inventor. Thus, where a prior patent for "pork" packing exists, a later patent which claims technology for "meat" packing is an obviousness-type double patent, but not a same-invention double patent. *See Eli Lilly & Co. v. Barr Labs., Inc.*, 251 F.3d 955, 967–72 (Fed. Cir. 2001); *In re Vogel*, 422 F.2d 438 (C.C.P.A. 1970). Where double patenting allegations arise, patentees often elect to shorten the term of their second patent so that it expires with the first, precluding concern over double patenting as long as each subsequent patent remains commonly owned. *See* § 253; 37 C.F.R. § 1.321(c)(3); § 14.2.5.1 (terminal disclaimer).

In addition, "a later-issued, but earlier-expiring patent could qualify as a double patenting reference, and thus invalidate an earlier-issued but later-expiring patent." *AbbVie Inc. v. Kennedy Inst. of Rheumatology*, 764 F.3d 1366, 1374 (Fed. Cir. 2014) (citing *Gilead Scis., Inc. v. Natco Pharma Ltd.*, 753 F.3d 1208, 1217 (Fed. Cir. 2014)).

14.4.2.4.2 Estoppel by Transfer of Ownership

Although patent validity may generally be challenged by third parties, courts have developed doctrines affecting whether patent invalidity may be asserted by those in privity with the patent owner. These doctrines derived from principles holding that parties to contracts relating to property ought not to be permitted to question the consideration on which the deeds or other property conveyances were based. These doctrines have been reassessed in light of patent-law policies.

14.4.2.4.2.1 Assignor Estoppel

Under the doctrine of assignor estoppel, a seller of a patent or patent application may not, absent exceptional circumstances, attack the validity of that patent in a subsequent patent-infringement litigation. *See Mentor Graphics Corp. v. Quickturn Design Systems, Inc.*, 150 F.3d 1374, 1378 (Fed. Cir. 1998); *Diamond Scientific Co. v. Ambico, Inc.*, 848 F.2d 1220, 1223 (Fed. Cir. 1988). The doctrine derives from legal estoppel (or estoppel by deed), which prohibits a grantor of property from challenging the validity of the grant. *See Westinghouse Elec. & Mfg. Co. v. Formica Insulation Co.*, 266 U.S. 342, 348–49 (1924). Notwithstanding dicta in *Lear, Inc. v. Adkins*, 395 U.S. 653, 670–71 (1969) ("Surely the equities of the licensor do not weigh very heavily when they are balanced against the important public interest in permitting full and free competition in the use of ideas which are in reality a part of the public domain."), *see* § 14.4.2.4.2.2 (discussing rejection of licensee estoppel); *see e.g.*, *Coastal Dynamics Corp. v. Symbolic Displays, Inc.*, 469 F.2d 79 (9th Cir. 1972) (per curiam) (holding that dicta in *Lear* indicates that the assignor estoppel doctrine is no longer valid), the Federal Circuit continues to uphold the assignor estoppel doctrine. *See Diamond Scientific*, 848 F.2d at 1223 (Fed. Cir. 1988) ("Beyond the questioning dicta in *Lear*, the Court has left assignment estoppel untouched . . ."). The considerations supporting the assignor estoppel doctrine (encouraging fair dealing) differ from those motivating the licensee estoppel doctrine (fostering free competition). *Cf. id.* at 1224 ("Unlike the licensee, who, without *Lear* might be forced to continue to pay for a potentially invalid patent, the assignor who would challenge the patent has already been fully paid for the patent rights.").

The doctrine of assignor estoppel is not absolute and courts have allowed assignors to challenge patent validity in exceptional circumstances. "A determination whether assignor estoppel applies in a particular case requires a balancing of the equities between the parties." *See Carroll Touch, Inc. v. Electro Mechanical Systems, Inc.*, 15 F.3d 1573, 1579 (Fed. Cir. 1993). Such balancing is a matter committed to the discretion of the trial court. *See id.* (analogizing to laches defense; nonetheless overturning the determination that assignor estoppel did not apply where the trial court's findings—that the controlling owner of defendant, a named inventor and former employee of the firm that assigned the patent, played only a minimal role in the invention and was misled as to the scope of the patent at issue—were not adequately supported by the entire record).

Exceptional circumstances disfavoring application of the assignor estoppel doctrine include: an express reservation by the assignor of the right to challenge the validity of the patent or an express waiver by the assignee of the right to assert assignor estoppel, *cf. Mentor Graphics Corp. v. Quickturn Design Systems, Inc.*, 150 F.3d 1374, 1378 (Fed. Cir. 1998); where the assignor's participation was under duress, *cf. Shamrock Technologies, Inc. v. Medical Sterilization, Inc.*, 903 F.2d 789, 793 (Fed. Cir. 1990); or where the rights were assigned prior to the invention being completed (and hence it might not be reasonable to presume the assignor's representation that the patent was valid).

14.4.2.4.2.2 No Licensee Estoppel

Under traditional contract and property principles, "one receiving bargained-for benefits under a contract may not question the consideration he has received." *See* Robert B. Orr, Note, *The Doctrine of Licensee Repudiation in Patent Law*, 63 Yale L.J. 125 (1953). Courts applied this doctrine to bar patent licensees from challenging the validity of the patents supporting their bargain since the mid-nineteenth century. *See Automatic Radio Manufacturing Co. v. Hazeltine Research, Inc.*, 339 U.S. 827, 836 (1950); *United States v. Harvey Steel Co.*, 196 U.S. 310, 317 (1905); 3 William C. Robinson, A Treatise on the Law of Patents for Useful Inventions § 1252 (1890) ("The licensee, in his defense, cannot attack the patent or the title of his licensor."); *but cf. Lear, Inc. v. Adkins*, 395 U.S. 653, 663–64 (1969) (observing that "[l]ong before *Hazeltine* was decided, the estoppel doctrine had been so eroded that it could no longer be considered the 'general rule,' but was only to be invoked in an ever narrowing set of circumstances"). The applicability of this doctrine to patents came under scrutiny for failing to account for the larger public-policy considerations surrounding patents. *See* James M. Treece, *Licensee Estoppel in Patent and Trademark Cases*, 53 Iowa L. Rev. 525, 542 (1967); *cf. Sears, Roebuck & Company v. Stiffel Company*, 376 U.S. 225, 229–31 (1964) (emphasizing the public interest in a robust public domain); *Compco Corporation v. Day-Brite Lighting, Inc.*, 376 U.S. 234 (1964) (same); *cf. Brulotte v. Thys Company*, 379 U.S. 29 (1964) (declaring as per se unlawful a patentee's agreement projecting royalty payments beyond the patent's expiration); *Kimble v. Marvel Entertainment, LLC*, 135 S. Ct. 2401 (2015) (reaffirming *Brulotte*).

The Supreme Court looked to "the strong federal policy favoring free competition in ideas which do not merit patent protection" reflected in these cases in overturning more than a century of jurisprudence and rejecting the doctrine of licensee estoppel. *See Lear, Inc. v. Adkins*, 395 U.S. 653, 670–71 (1969). The Court emphasized:

> Licensees may often be the only individuals with enough economic incentive to challenge the patentability of an inventor's discovery. If they are muzzled, the public may continually be required to pay tribute to would-be monopolists without need or justification. We think it plain that the technical requirements of contract doctrine must give way before the demands of the public interest in the typical situation involving the negotiation of a license after a patent has issued.

Id.

14.4.2.4.2.3 Assignee Estoppel

Although the basic rationale of *Lear v. Adkins* (*see* § 14.4.2.4.2.2) would appear to apply to assignees (*see* 6 Moy's Walker on Patents § 17:42 (4th ed.)), a few courts have declined to extend the doctrine. *See, e.g., Coast Metals, Inc. v. Cape*, 205 U.S.P.Q. 154 (D.N.J. 1979); *Baladevon, Inc. v. Abbott Laboratories, Inc.*, 871 F. Supp. 89, 95 (D. Mass. 1994) ("Outside of licensee estoppel, which is commonly understood to have been abolished by *Lear*, the status of estoppel doctrines in patent law has not been definitively settled. The weight of authority holds that the doctrine of assignee estoppel survived *Lear*."); *see also Diamond Scientific Co. v. Ambico, Inc.*, 848 F.2d 1220, 1224–25 (Fed. Cir. 1988) (citing two decisions holding that an assignee may be estopped from challenging the validity of the assigned patent: *Roberts v. Sears, Roebuck & Co.*, 573 F.2d 976 (7th Cir. 1978), and *Coast Metals, Inc. v. Cape*, 205 U.S.P.Q. 154 (D.N.J. 1979)).

14.4.2.5 Antitrust Counterclaims

While not technically a defense, antitrust counterclaims frequently arise in patent cases. *See* 1 Herbert Hovenkamp, Mark D. Janis & Mark A. Lemley, IP and Antitrust § 13.1, 11–12 (2006) (observing that between 1993 and 2000, there were more than 100 reported decisions regarding counterclaims alleging the original suit was anticompetitive behavior in violation of the antitrust laws). Patent litigation can constitute an attempt to monopolize in violation of § 2 of the Sherman Act in two contexts: (1) where the counterclaimant can show that the patentee obtained the patent through fraud on the Patent Office, *see, e.g., Walker Process Equip., Inc. v. Food Mach. & Chem. Corp.*, 382 U.S. 172 (1965); and (2) where the counterclaimant can establish that the litigation is a "mere sham," which requires proving that the initial suit is objectively baseless and motivated by a desire to impose harm. *See In re Indep. Serv. Orgs. Antitrust Litig.*, 203 F.3d 1322, 1326 (Fed. Cir. 2000); *Nobelpharma AB v. Implant Innovations, Inc.*, 141 F.3d 1059 (Fed. Cir. 1998); *Handgards, Inc. v. Ethicon, Inc.*, 601 F.2d 986 (9th Cir. 1979).

Most antitrust counterclaims ultimately fail. *See* David R. Steinman & Danielle S. Fitzpatrick, *Antitrust Counterclaims in Patent Infringement Cases: A Guide to* Walker

Process *and Sham-Litigation Claims*, 10 Tex. Intell. Prop. L.J. 95, 99 & n.22 (2001). Because of the Federal Circuit's strict requirements for stating a Sherman Act § 2 claim, and the Supreme Court's concern about the scope of discovery in antitrust cases, these counterclaims can potentially be dismissed on the pleadings or on summary judgment. *See Bell Atlantic Corp. v. Twombly*, 550 U.S. 544 (2007).

14.4.3 Remedies

Patent law provides a potent arsenal of remedies, including injunctive relief, damages (which can be enhanced based on an infringer's conduct), costs, prejudgment interest, and attorneys' fees.

14.4.3.1 Injunctive Relief

Section 283 of the Patent Act provides that courts "may grant injunctions in accordance with the principles of equity to prevent the violation of any right secured by patent, on such terms as the court deems reasonable." Injunctive relief serves to protect and uphold the right to exclude granted by a patent. *Smith Int'l v. Hughes Tool Co.*, 718 F.2d 1573, 1577–78 (Fed. Cir. 1983). The law permits both preliminary and permanent injunctions.

14.4.3.1.1 Preliminary Injunction

In assessing whether to grant a preliminary injunction, the court must consider four factors, with the burden of proof on the moving party:

(1) the likelihood of the movant's success on the merits (validity, enforceability, and infringement),

(2) the irreparability of harm to the movant without an injunction,

(3) the balance of hardships between the parties, and

(4) the demands of the public interest.

AstraZeneca LP v. Apotex, Inc., 633 F.3d 1042 (Fed. Cir. 2010); *see generally* Chapter 3. The court must balance these factors in the interests of equity. No one factor is dispositive. *FMC Corp. v. United States*, 3 F.3d 424, 427 (Fed. Cir. 1993). Prior to the establishment of the Federal Circuit in 1982, courts rarely granted preliminary injunctive relief in patent cases on the grounds that likelihood of success on the merits typically required prior judicial determination of validity and the difficulty of establishing irreparable harm due to the availability of compensatory damages after trial. The Federal Circuit substantially eased these requirements soon after its creation by emphasizing the role of equity to protect the right to exclude and erecting a rebuttable presumption of irreparable harm once validity and continuing infringement were established. *See Smith Int'l v. Hughes Tool Co.*, 718 F.2d 1573 (Fed. Cir. 1983). A decade later, the Federal Circuit shifted toward a higher burden on movants, noting that a preliminary injunction "is a drastic and extraordinary remedy . . . not to be routinely granted." *See Intel v. ULSI*, 995 F.2d 1566, 1568 (Fed. Cir. 1993). The Supreme Court's decision in *eBay Inc. v. MercExchange, L.L.C.*, 547 U.S. 388 (2006), discussed in § 14.4.3.1.2, provides the most authoritative word on the exercise of discretion in assessing injunctive relief in patent cases. Although the case involved the granting of permanent injunctive relief, its analysis applies with extra force in the context of preliminary injunctions—where caution in granting relief is especially important.

The Federal Circuit has since further restricted the grant of preliminary and permanent injunctions on multifeatured products by introducing a "causal nexus" requirement to inform the irreparable harm inquiry. A patentee must show a "casual nexus" between its alleged harm and the defendant's infringement before a court can issue an injunction on a multifeature product. *See Apple Inc. v. Samsung Elecs. Co.*, 678 F.3d 1314, 1324 (Fed. Cir. 2012); *Apple Inc. v. Samsung Elecs. Co. (Apple III)*, 735 F.3d 1352 (Fed. Cir. 2013) (extending the "causal nexus" requirement to permanent injunctions). To satisfy the "causal nexus" inquiry, the patentee must prove that the infringing feature drove demand for the entire product. *See Apple, Inc. v. Samsung Elecs. Co.*, 695 F.3d 1370, 1374–75 (Fed. Cir. 2012); *see also* § 3.2.2.2.4.

The patent holder has the burden of proof to demonstrate the predicates for a preliminary injunction. *See Abbott Labs. v. Andrx Pharm., Inc.,* 452 F.3d 1331, 1334 (Fed. Cir. 2006). This includes the burden of showing that the asserted patents likely are infringed and the absence of any substantial question that the asserted patent claims are valid (*Trebro Mfg., Inc. v. Firefly Equip., LLC,* 748 F.3d 1159, 1166–67 (Fed. Cir. 2014)) or that the patent is enforceable (*Purdue Pharma L.P. v. Boehringer Ingelheim GmbH*, 237 F.3d 1359, 1366 (Fed. Cir. 2001)). On the other hand, an accused infringer challenging a preliminary injunction can be successful on evidence that would not suffice to support an invalidity judgment at trial, but merely raises a substantial question concerning either infringement or validity. *Id.* The showing of a substantial question as to invalidity requires less proof than a clear and convincing showing necessary to establish invalidity itself. *Id.* "Vulnerability is the issue at the preliminary injunction stage, while validity is the issue at trial." *Id.*

14.4.3.1.2 Permanent Injunction

A court may enter a permanent injunction after a final judgment of infringement in accord with principles of equity. § 283. To obtain a permanent injunction, the plaintiff must satisfy a four-factor test, similar to the test used for preliminary injunctions. *See eBay Inc. v. MercExchange, L.L.C.*, 547 U.S. 388, 391 (2006). The plaintiff must show:

(1) That it has suffered an irreparable injury;

(2) That remedies available at law, such as monetary damages, are inadequate to compensate for that injury;

(3) That, considering the balance of hardships between the plaintiff and defendant, a remedy in equity is warranted; and

(4) That the public interest would not be disserved by a permanent injunction.

In the past, courts routinely issued permanent injunctions once infringement had been found. *See id.* at 393–94 ("The [Federal Circuit] articulated a 'general rule,' unique to patent disputes, 'that a permanent injunction will issue once infringement and validity have been adjudged.'"). However, in *eBay*, the Supreme Court explicitly overruled such categorical granting of injunctive relief. *See id.* at 394. Accordingly, courts must carefully apply the four-factor test in determining whether to grant a permanent injunction. As with all injunctions, the district court's order is reviewed for abuse of discretion.

eBay eliminates any presumption of irreparable injury to a patent holder after a judgment of infringement and no invalidity. *Robert Bosch LLC v. Pylon Mfg. Corp.*, 659 F.3d 1142, 1149 (2011). The Federal Circuit also has also held that there must be a "causal nexus" between any such irreparable injury and patent infringement. *Apple III*, 735 F.3d at 1360. In a case in which the harm stems from lost sales owing to a competitor's infringement, this requires proof that "the patented features impact consumers' decisions to purchase the accused devices" even if they are not "the exclusive or predominant reason why consumers bought ... [the infringing] products." *Apple Inc. v. Samsung Elecs. Co.*, 801 F.3d 1352, 1360 (Fed. Cir. 2015).

14.4.3.2 Damages

Section 284 of the Patent Act provides:

> Upon finding for the claimant the court shall award the claimant damages adequate to compensate for the infringement but in no event less than a reasonable royalty for the use made of the invention by the infringer, together with interest and costs as fixed by the court.
>
> When the damages are not found by a jury, the court shall assess them. In either event the court may increase the damages up to three times the amount found or assessed. Increased damages under this paragraph shall not apply to provisional rights under section 154(d) of this title.
>
> The court may receive expert testimony as an aid to the determination of damages or of what royalty would be reasonable under the circumstances.

Section 286 establishes a six-year statute of limitations, barring patentees from recovering damages for any infringing acts committed more than six years prior to the filing of the complaint or counterclaim for infringement.

14.4.3.2.1 Compensatory Damages

Courts apply several approaches for measuring damages "adequate to compensate" for a defendant's infringement.

14.4.3.2.1.1 Lost Profits

To recover lost-profits damages, the patentee must prove a causal relation between the infringement and its lost profits. *See Crystal Semiconductor Corp. v. Tritech Microelectronics Int'l, Inc.*, 246 F.3d 1336, 1354 (Fed. Cir. 2001). Accordingly, the patentee must show "a reasonable probability that 'but for' the infringing activity, the patentee would have made the infringer's sales." *Id.* An accepted, "but non-exclusive" method for establishing "but-for" causation is the four-factor "DAMP" test, under which the patentee must prove:

(1) Demand for the patented product;

(2) Absence of acceptable noninfringing substitutes;

(3) Manufacturing and marketing capability to exploit the demand; and

(4) Profit he would have made.

Rite-Hite Corp. v. Kelley Co., 56 F.3d 1538, 1545 (Fed. Cir. 1995) (en banc) (citing *Panduit Corp. v. Stahlin Bros. Fibre Works, Inc.*, 575 F.2d 1152, 1156 (6th Cir. 1978)). Additionally, the patentee is required to show that the damages were or should have been reasonably foreseeable by an infringing competitor in the relevant market. *See id.* at 1546.

14.4.3.2.1.2 Convoyed Sales

"A 'convoyed sale' refers to the relationship between the sale of a patented product and a functionally associated nonpatented product. A patentee may recover lost profits on unpatented components sold with a patented item, a convoyed sale, if both the patented and unpatented products 'together were considered to be components of a single assembly or parts of a complete machine, or they together constituted a functional unit.'" *Am. Seating Co. v. USSC Grp., Inc.*, 514 F.3d 1262, 1268 (Fed. Cir. 2008) (citing *Rite-Hite*, 56 F.3d at 1550). "A functional relationship does not exist when independently operating patented and unpatented products are purchased as a package solely because of customer demand." *Id.*

14.4.3.2.1.3 Price Erosion

The patentee may also recover additional lost profits damages under a price-erosion theory. *See Crystal Semiconductor Corp. v. TriTech Microelectronics Int'l, Inc.*, 246 F.3d 1336, 1357 (Fed. Cir. 2001). To recover for price-erosion damages, patentees are required to prove that "but for" the infringement, they would have sold their patented invention at a higher price. *Id.* Furthermore, patentees must prove the number of products they would have sold at this price. *Id.* Accordingly, "the patentee's price erosion theory must account for the nature, or definition, of the market, similarities between any benchmark market and the market in which price erosion is alleged, and the effect of the hypothetically increased price on the likely number of sales at that price in that market." *Id.*

Because lost sales and price erosion are "inextricably linked," patentees must show how a price increase would have affected their profits due to lost sales. *See id.* at 1360. Consequently, the court should not independently analyze lost profits and price-erosion damages. *See id.*

14.4.3.2.1.4 Reasonable Royalty

Under § 284, the patentee may recover no less than a reasonable royalty on the infringer's sales for which the patentee has not shown entitlement to lost profits. *See Rite-Hite Corp. v. Kelley Co.*, 56 F.3d 1538, 1554 (Fed. Cir. 1995) (en banc). A reasonable royalty may be derived from an established royalty (if one exists) or, more commonly, from a hypothetical negotiation between the patentee and the infringer when the infringement began. *Id.*

The hypothetical negotiation (during which the asserted patent claims are assumed to be valid and infringed) tries "to recreate the *ex ante* licensing negotiation scenario and to describe the resulting agreement." *Lucent Techs., Inc. v. Gateway, Inc.*, 580 F.3d 1301, 1325 (Fed. Cir. 2009). Evidence relevant to calculating the reasonable royalty may include not only factual developments before the date of the hypothetical negotiation, but also events occurring after that date. *Id.* at 1333–34.

Determining the reasonable royalty based on the hypothetical negotiation commonly involves an analysis of the factors set forth in *Georgia-Pacific Corp. v. U.S. Plywood Corp.*, 318 F. Supp. 1116 (S.D.N.Y. 1970):

> (1) The royalties received by the patentee for the licensing of the patent in suit, proving or tending to prove an established royalty.
>
> (2) The rates paid by the licensee for the use of other patents comparable to the patent in suit.
>
> (3) The nature and scope of the license, as exclusive or non-exclusive; or as restricted or non-restricted in terms of territory or with respect to whom the manufactured product may be sold.
>
> (4) The licensor's established policy and marketing program to maintain his patent monopoly by not licensing others to use the invention or by granting licenses under special conditions designed to preserve that monopoly.
>
> (5) The commercial relationship between the licensor and licensee, such as, whether they are competitors in the same territory in the same line of business; or whether they are inventor and promoter.
>
> (6) The effect of selling the patented specialty in promoting sales of other products of the licensee; the existing value of the invention to the licensor as a generator of sales of his non-patented items; and the extent of such derivative or convoyed sales.
>
> (7) The duration of the patent and the term of the license.
>
> (8) The established profitability of the product made under the patent; its commercial success; and its current popularity.
>
> (9) The utility and advantages of the patent property over the old modes or devices, if any, that had been used for working out similar results.
>
> (10) The nature of the patented invention; the character of the commercial embodiment of it as owned and produced by the

licensor; and the benefits to those who have used the invention.

(11) The extent to which the infringer has made use of the invention; and any evidence probative of the value of that use.

(12) The portion of the profit or of the selling price that may be customary in the particular business or in comparable businesses to allow for the use of the invention or analogous inventions.

(13) The portion of the realizable profit that should be credited to the invention as distinguished from non-patented elements, the manufacturing process, business risks, or significant features or improvements added by the infringer.

(14) The opinion testimony of qualified experts.

(15) The amount that a licensor (such as the patentee) and a licensee (such as the infringer) would have agreed upon (at the time the infringement began) if both had been reasonably and voluntarily trying to reach an agreement; that is, the amount which a prudent licensee—who desired, as a business proposition, to obtain a license to manufacture and sell a particular article embodying the patented invention—would have been willing to pay as a royalty and yet be able to make a reasonable profit and which amount would have been acceptable by a prudent patentee who was willing to grant a license.

Id. at 1120. The *Georgia-Pacific* factors are unprioritized, and some factors may overlap. *See ResQNet.com, Inc. v. Lansa, Inc.*, 594 F.3d 860, 869 (Fed. Cir. 2010).

14.4.3.2.1.4.1 Damages Theories

A reasonable royalty calculation will typically require determining the royalty base and the royalty rate. The determination is relatively straightforward where the demand for a final product comprises a single patented technology, such as a drug with a patented active ingredient. The most sensible royalty base would typically be total sales revenue for the final product, what is often referred to as the entire market value. *See Fonar Corp. v. Gen. Elec. Co.*, 107 F.3d 1543, 1552 (Fed. Cir. 1997) (citing *Rite-Hite Corp. v. Kelley Co.*, 56 F.3d 1538, 1549 (Fed. Cir. 1995) (en banc)). The royalty rate would account for alternative treatments (of which there may be few), marketing costs, and manufacturing costs.

Patent law has long struggled to deal with apportioning patent value where a patent covers only one component of a larger product. *See Cincinnati Car Co. v. New York Rapid Transit Corp.*, 66 F.2d 592, 593 (2d Cir. 1933) (Learned Hand, J.) (observing that the allocation of profits among multiple components "is in its nature unanswerable"). The problem has become particularly acute in modern patent litigation as a result of the growing use of juries called upon to apportion value based on complex and often widely divergent economic expert analyses.

In theory, a wide range of royalty bases can be appropriate with an appropriately calibrated royalty rate to account for the myriad factors affecting consumer demand. In practice, however, the open-ended nature of the *Georgia-Pacific* framework can lead to wildly divergent royalty calculations by expert economists. Especially in a jury trial, such testimony can produce outsize damage awards. As the Supreme Court recognized long ago, it would be "very grave error to instruct a jury 'that as to the measure of damages the same rule is to govern, whether the patent covers an entire machine or an improvement on a machine.'" *Seymore v. McCormick*, 57 U.S. 480, 491 (1853); *see also Westinghouse Elec. & Mfg. Co. v. Wagner Co.*, 225 U.S. 604, 614–15 (1912) ("[The] invention may have been used in combination with valuable improvements made, or other patents appropriated by the infringer, and each may have jointly, but unequally contributed to the profits. In such case, if plaintiff's patent only created a part of the profits, he is only entitled to recover that part of the net gains."); *Garretson v. Clark*, 111 U.S. 120, 121 (1884) ("When a patent is for an improvement, and not for an entirely new machine or contrivance, the patentee must show in what particulars his improvement has added to the usefulness of the machine or contrivance.)

While estimating a reasonable royalty is not an "exact science" in that there may be more than one reliable method, *Apple Inc. v. Motorola, Inc.*, 757 F.3d 1286, 1315 (Fed. Cir. 2014), the Federal Circuit has enhanced the judge's gatekeeping role in order to prevent excessive awards. Recent decisions have sought to align the royalty base to the patented component of a product, exclude unreliable damages theories, scrutinize the admissibility of various forms of evidence, and provide limiting jury instructions.

In general, a patent holder seeking a reasonable royalty must provide substantial evidence supporting both its choice of royalty base and royalty rate. "[W]here multi-component products are involved, the governing rule is that the ultimate combination of royalty base and royalty rate must reflect the value attributable to the infringing features of the product, and no more." *Ericsson, Inc. v. D-Link Sys., Inc.*, 773 F.3d 1201, 1226 (Fed. Cir. 2014) (citing *VirnetX, Inc. v. Cisco Sys., Inc.*, 767 F.3d 1308 (Fed. Cir. 2014)).

As the Federal Circuit has warned, "reliance on the entire market value might mislead the jury, who may be less equipped to understand the extent to which the royalty rate would need to do the work in such instances." *Ericsson*, 773 F.3d at 1227 (citing *LaserDynamics, Inc. v. Quanta Computer, Inc.*, 694 F.3d 51, 67, 68 (Fed. Cir. 2012) (barring the use of too high a royalty base—even if mathematically offset by a "'low enough royalty rate'"—because such a base "carries a considerable risk" of misleading a jury into overcompensating, stating that such a base "'cannot help but skew the damages horizon for the jury'" and "make a patentee's proffered damages amount appear modest by comparison" (quoting *Uniloc USA, Inc. v. Microsoft Corp.*, 632 F.3d 1292, 1320 (Fed. Cir. 2011)))).

To cabin the risk of outsize awards in multicomponent cases, the Federal Circuit has pushed the royalty base toward the smallest salable patent-practicing unit or "SSPPU." *See Cornell Univ. v. Hewlett-Packard Co.*, 609 F. Supp. 2d 279 (N.D.N.Y. 2009) (Rader, J., sitting by designation). The Federal Circuit embraced the SSPPU framework in *LaserDynamics Inc. v. Quanta Computer, Inc.*, 694 F.3d 51 (Fed. Cir. 2012), holding that "it is generally required that royalties be based not on the entire product, but instead on the 'smallest salable patent-practicing unit.' . . . The entire market value rule is a narrow exception to this general rule." *Id.* at 67; *see also VirnetX, Inc. v. Cisco Sys., Inc.*, 767 F.3d 1308, 1328–29 (Fed. Cir. 2014); *LaserDynamics, Inc. v. Quanta Comput., Inc.*, 694 F.3d 51, 66–70 (Fed. Cir. 2012); *Uniloc USA, Inc. v. Microsoft Corp.*, 632 F.3d 1292, 1320 (Fed. Cir. 2011); *Lucent Techs., Inc. v. Gateway, Inc.*, 580 F.3d 1301, 1336 (Fed. Cir. 2009).

Beyond calibrating the royalty base to the scale of the patent-practicing unit, courts seek to ensure that the royalty rate is based on sound economic methodology and grounded in reliable and pertinent evidence. Using the construct of the hypothetical negotiation between a willing licensor and licensee, experts use the *Georgia-Pacific* factors to determine a license rate that would have been agreed upon just before the infringement began (and based on the assumption that the patent was valid, infringed, and enforceable). The proof of an appropriate royalty rate using this method allows for necessary "approximation and uncertainty." *Aqua Shield v. Inter Pool Cover Team*, 774 F.3d 766, 771 (Fed. Cir. 2014). Nevertheless, it must be supported by substantial evidence, which usually will be based on the application of the relevant, but not necessarily the complete list of fifteen, *Georgia-Pacific* factors. *See WhitServe, LLC v. Computer Packages, Inc.*, 694 F.3d 10, 31–32 (Fed. Cir. 2012).

The open-ended *Georgia-Pacific* framework affords economic experts substantial leeway in determining a royalty rate. The most pertinent evidence usually comprises past licenses to the infringing or comparable technology, the value of comparable features in the marketplace, an estimate of the value of the benefit provided by the infringed features by comparison to noninfringing alternatives, or an estimate of the cost to design around the patent. *See, e.g.*, *Ericsson*, 773 F.3d at 1227 (citing *Monsanto Co. v. McFarling*, 488 F.3d 973, 978 (Fed. Cir. 2007) ("An established royalty is usually the best measure of a 'reasonable' royalty for a given use of an invention . . . ."). However, license agreements that are unrelated to the claimed invention cannot form the basis of a reasonable royalty calculation. *See, e.g.*, *Lucent*, 580 F.3d at 1327; *see also ResQNet*, 594 F.3d at 869 ("Any evidence unrelated to the claimed invention does not support compensation for infringement but punishes beyond the reach of the statute."). The Federal Circuit has observed that licenses arising out of litigation might be reliable in certain circumstances, but has cautioned that "litigation itself can skew the results of the hypothetical negotiation." *ResQNet*, 594 F.3d at 872.

In many cases, the technology either has not been previously licensed or the licenses cover a broader range of technologies than the patented invention and/or multiple product or product components. As an alternative or shortcut to considering the *Georgia-Pacific* factors, some patentees have put forward general royalty theories such as the 25% rule and the Nash Bargaining Solution (50% split of net product value). The Federal Circuit has rejected the application of these generalized "rules of thumb." *See Apple*, 757 F.3d at 1324–25; *VirnetX*, 767 F.3d at 1331–34 (rejecting the Nash Bargaining Solution); *Uniloc*, 632 F.3d at 1312 (rejecting the "25% Rule"); *but cf. Summit 6, LLC v. Samsung Electronics Co., Ltd.*, 802 F.3d 1283 (Fed.

Cir. 2015) (allowing limited use of the Nash Bargaining Solution as part of a multi-faceted expert analysis).

Damages experts have begun to deploy consumer surveys to allocate value within multicomponent patented products. *See* Zelin Yang, Note, *Damaging Royalties: An Overview of Reasonable Royalty Damages*, 29 Berkeley Tech. L.J. 647, 664 (2014); S. Christian Platt & Bob Chen, *Recent Trends and Approaches in Calculating Patent Damages: Nash Bargaining Solution and Conjoint Surveys*, 86 Patent, Trademark & Copyright J. (BNA) 909 (Aug. 30, 2013). Marketing researchers have long used "conjoint analysis" to differentiate value within product configurations. *See* Paul E. Green, Abba M. Krieger & Yoram Wind, *Thirty Years of Conjoint Analysis: Reflections and Prospects*, 31 Interfaces 56 (2001); Paul E. Green and V. Srinivasan, *Conjoint Analysis in Marketing: New Developments with Implications for Research and Practice*, 54(4) J. of Marketing 3 (1990).

Conjoint analysis draws upon consumer ranking of products with different features. Researchers use statistical methods to estimate consumers' willingness to pay for particular attributes. While these methods provide a logical framework for differentiating value, the technique can be limited in practice. *See* Patricia Dyck, *Beyond Confusion—Survey Evidence of Consumer Demand and the Entire Market Value Rule*, 4 Hastings Sci. & Tech. L.J. 209, 226 (2012) (noting sensitivity to data collection methods and algorithms and the problem of combinatorial explosion); Lisa Cameron, Michael Cragg & Daniel McFadden, *The Role of Conjoint Surveys in Reasonable Royalty Cases*, Law360 (Oct. 16, 2013), http://www.law360.com/articles/475390/the-role-of-conjoint-surveys-in-reasonable-royalty-cases.

Courts have shown cautious receptivity to conjoint analysis. Recognizing the general admissibility of consumer surveys in *Oracle America, Inc. v. Google, Inc.*, No. C 10-03571 WHA, 2012 WL 850705, at *10 (N.D. Cal. Mar. 13, 2012), Judge Alsup nonetheless rejected some of Oracle's expert's conjoint analysis as unreliable while allowing some of it to be admitted. *Id.* *10–14. In *TV Interactive Data Corp. v. Sony Corp.*, 929 F. Supp. 2d 1006 (N.D. Cal. 2013), Magistrate Judge Joseph Spero held the patentee's expert testimony using conjoint analysis to be admissible. *Id.* at 1019–25.

14.4.3.2.1.4.2 FRAND Licensing of Standard Essential Patents

A growing number of technologies arise within the context of network industries in which standard protocols and interfaces promote technological innovation and greater consumer value. Industry standard-setting organizations such as the Institute of Electrical Electronics Engineers (IEEE) and the International Telecommunication Union (ITU) bring together company representatives to develop industry standards. To ensure that the industry standards reflect the best technologies while avoiding (or at least postponing) licensing disputes, the participants typically commit to license standard-essential patents (SEPs) on "reasonable and non-discriminatory" (RAND) or "fair, reasonable and non-discriminatory" (FRAND) terms. The standard-setting organizations have typically left the parameters for determining FRAND license terms undefined, *see* Mark A. Lemley, *Intellectual Property Rights and Standard-Setting Organizations*, 90 Cal. L. Rev. 1889, 1906 (2002), leaving courts with the difficult task of determining licensing rates for highly complex products involving potentially hundreds of patents.

The valuation of SEPs presents distinct problems. Industry standards can encompass hundreds of patented technologies of carrying significance. Not surprisingly, owners of patents within a SEP pool often see their patents as particularly valuable, thereby risking hold-up and undue royalty stacking. The challenge lies in separating the value of the particular technology from the often tremendous value from standardization. Once consumers adopt a product, they become locked into the standard to varying degrees. This could provide the patentee tremendous leverage in a negotiation. With potentially hundreds of SEPs and dozens of patent owners, the problem becomes intractable if patent owners stake out aggressive positions or refuse to propose licensing terms.

In a series of recent cases, courts have surmounted this challenge by interpreting the principal goal of standard-setting agreements to be widespread adoption of the standard by barring FRAND licensors from capturing the coordination and network value of the standard. *See* § 14.4.3.2.1.4.2; *Commonwealth Sci. and Indus. Research Org. (CSIRO) v. Cisco Sys., Inc.*, 809 F.3d 1295 (Fed. Cir. 2015); *Microsoft Corp. v. Motorola, Inc.*, No. C10-1823JLR, 2013 U.S. Dist. LEXIS 60233, 2013 WL 2111217 (W.D. Wash. Apr. 25, 2013); *see also Ericsson*, 773 F.3d at 1229–35; *In re Innovatio IP Ventures LLC Patent Litig.*, No. 11 C 9308, 2013 U.S. Dist. LEXIS 144061, 2013 WL 5593609 (N.D. Ill. Oct. 3, 2013). The courts have adapted the *Georgia-Pacific* factors to serve the standard-setting context.

14.4.3.2.1.5 Marking

The Patent Act encourages patentees and persons who make, sell, or import any patented article to provide notice to the public by marking the article or, if the article cannot be marked, to label the package containing it with "patent" or "pat." and the patent number. *See* § 287(a). To further facilitate marking, § 287 has been amended under the AIA to allow patentees to "virtually mark" a product by providing the address of a webpage containing a list of the patents covering the product. The virtual-marking provision became effective September 16, 2011, and applies to any case pending or filed on or after that date. AIA § 16.

While marking is not required for patent protection, the failure to mark may limit the award of damages unless the infringer was notified of the infringement and subsequently continued to infringe. In such a case, damages may be awarded only for infringing acts performed after such notice (which includes the filing of an infringement action). "Actual notice [under the second prong of § 287(a)] requires the affirmative communication of a specific charge of infringement by a specific accused product or device." *See Amsted Indus. Inc. v. Buckeye Steel Castings Co.*, 24 F.3d 178, 187 (Fed. Cir. 1994). Mere notice of the patent itself or its ownership does not constitute sufficient notice for purposes of the actual notice prong of § 287(a). The notice inquiry must focus on the patentee's actions as opposed to the infringer's knowledge.

The marking provision of § 287(a) does not apply to patents claiming only processes or methods. *See Am. Med. Sys., Inc. v. Med. Eng'g Corp.*, 6 F.3d 1523, 1538

(Fed. Cir. 1993). Furthermore, the marking provisions do not apply to patents that contain both method and apparatus claims if the plaintiff elects to assert only the method claims in such patents. *See Crown Packaging Tech. v. Reexam Beverage Can, Co.*, 559 F.3d 1308 (Fed. Cir. 2009); *Hanson v. Alpine Valley Ski Area*, 718 F.2d 1082 (Fed. Cir. 1983). The provisions do apply, however, "[w]here the patent contains both apparatus and method claims . . . to the extent that there is a tangible item to mark by which notice of the asserted method claims can be given." *Id.* at 1538–39.

Several district courts have interpreted the marking provision to apply to websites offering or running patented software. In *IMX, Inc. v. Lendingtree, LLC*, 79 U.S.P.Q.2d 1373, 2005 U.S. Dist. LEXIS 33179, 2005 WL 3465555 (D. Del. Dec. 14, 2005), *motion for reconsideration denied*, 2006 U.S. Dist. LEXIS 551, 2006 WL 47066 (D. Del. Jan. 10, 2006), the court held that Internet vendors of downloadable patented software must mark their websites in order to satisfy § 287(a): "[a]lthough IMX did not make or sell the computer components through which its patented system is processed, and although the IMX website itself was not the patented invention, nevertheless . . . the website is intrinsic to the patented system and constitutes a 'tangible item to mark by which notice of the asserted method claims can be given.'" Similarly, the court in *Soverain Software LLC v. Amazon.com, Inc.*, 383 F. Supp. 2d 904 (E.D. Tex. 2005), held that websites were "tangible items," and thus the patentee was required to mark its websites in order to comply with the marking provision and establish entitlement to damages for willful infringement.

14.4.3.2.2 Enhanced Damages

Under § 284, the court may increase damages up to three times the compensatory award. An award of enhanced damages and the extent of the enhancement are within the court's discretion. *See Read Corp. v. Portec, Inc.*, 970 F.2d 816, 826 (Fed. Cir. 1992), abrogated on other grounds; *Markman v. Westview Instruments, Inc.*, 52 F.3d 967 (Fed. Cir. 1995) (en banc). In *Halo Electronics, Inc. v. Pulse Electronics, Inc.*, 579 U.S. ___ (2016), the Supreme Court rejected as "unduly rigid" the two-prong test that the Federal Circuit adopted in *In re Seagate Technology, LLC*, 497 F.3d 1360 (Fed. Cir. 2007). *Seagate* had required a patentee to first "show by clear and convincing evidence that the infringer acted despite an objectively high likelihood that its actions constituted infringement of a valid patent," and then "demonstrate that this objectively-defined risk . . . was either known or so obvious that it should have been known to the accused infringer." *Id.* at 1371.

The Supreme Court did not adopt a specific test for enhanced damages, but rather gave broad guidelines within which the district court should exercise its discretion. Damages should not be enhanced in "garden-variety" infringement cases. They are "generally ... reserved for egregious cases typified by willful misconduct," such as "deliberate or wanton" infringement, "malicious pira[cy]," or objective recklessness. Nonetheless, willfulness is not a per se requirement for enhanced damages and enhanced damages need not follow a finding of egregious misconduct. *Halo*, slip op. at 11, 15. "[C]ourts should continue to take into account the particular circumstances of each case in deciding whether to award damages, and in what amount." *Id.* Willful infringement must be proven by a preponderance of evidence, *id.* at 12, and usually is based the infringer's knowledge and conduct at the time of infringement, not, for example, the merit of arguments later asserted in litigation, *id.* at 10.

14.4.3.2.3 Prejudgment Interest

Section 284 authorizes the patentee to recover prejudgment interest. The Supreme Court has held that prejudgment interest "should be awarded . . . absent some justification for withholding such an award." *Gen. Motors Corp. v. Devex Corp.*, 461 U.S. 648, 657 (1983). The court may award prejudgment interest only on compensatory damages and not on enhanced damages. *See Underwater Devices Inc. v. Morrison-Knudsen Co.*, 717 F.2d 1380, 1389 (Fed. Cir. 1983), overruled on other grounds by *Knorr-Bremse Systeme Fuer Nutzfahrzeuge GmbH v. Dana Corp.*, 383 F.3d 1337 (Fed. Cir. 2004) (en banc), and *In re Seagate*, 497 F.3d 1360 (Fed. Cir. 2007) (en banc). Interest is calculated from the time of infringement until the date judgment is rendered. *See General Motors*, 461 U.S. at 656. The district court has substantial discretion to determine both the prejudgment interest rate and the assessment of simple or compound interest to the damages. *See Gyromat Corp. v. Champion Spark Plug Co.*, 735 F.2d 549, 556–57 (Fed. Cir. 1984).

14.4.3.3 Costs

The award of costs under § 284 refers to Federal Rule of Civil Procedure 54(d)(1), which provides that "costs other than attorneys' fees shall be allowed as of course to the prevailing party unless the court otherwise directs." Fed. R. Civ. P. 54(d)(1). Section 1920, title 28 of the U.S. Code, lists the types of costs the prevailing party may recover under Federal Rule of Civil Procedure 54(d)(1), some of which include court reporter fees, docket fees, and compensation for court-appointed experts.

14.4.3.4 Attorneys' Fees

Section 285 provides that the "court in exceptional cases may award reasonable attorney fees to the prevailing party." The Supreme Court has interpreted this standard to afford district judges discretion to award attorneys' fees where it finds that the case "simply . . . stands out from others with respect to the substantive strength of a party's litigating position . . . or the unreasonable manner in which the case was litigated." *Octane Fitness LLC v. Icon Health & Fitness Inc.*, 134 S. Ct. 1749, 1755–76 (2014) (rejecting the Federal Circuit's rule that a defendant may only be awarded fees where it demonstrates that the patentee litigated with subjective bad faith and that the suit was objectively baseless). The Court directed district courts to consider the totality of the circumstances. Such determinations are reviewable for abuse of discretion. *Highmark Inc. v. Allcare Health Mgmt. Sys., Inc.*, 134 S. Ct. 1744, 1749 (2014).

14.5 Other Patent-Related Causes of Action

This section provides an overview of other patent-related causes of action that do not relate to enforcement, such as false marking and civil actions challenging decisions of the USPTO's Patent Trial and Appeal Board (PTAB).

14.5.1 False Marking

While § 287 encourages the marking of patented products with the patent number, § 292 imposes a civil penalty for false marking. A party asserting false marking must show by a preponderance of the evidence that an unpatented article was marked with intent to deceive the public. *Forest Grp., Inc. v. Bon Tool Co.*, 590 F.3d 1295, 1300 (Fed. Cir. 2009). False marking claims must be pled with particularity under Federal Rule of Civil Procedure 9(b). *In re BP Lubricants USA Inc.*, 637 F.3d 1307, 1309 (Fed. Cir. 2011).

Prior to the enactment of the AIA on September 16, 2011, the false marking statute had been enforceable as a *qui tam* action, in which anyone may bring suit on behalf of the government and retain one-half of the recovery. As a response to the proliferation of false marking suits in recent years, the AIA amended § 292 to eliminate the *qui tam* provision so that only the U.S. government may sue to recover the statutory penalty. AIA § 16. In addition, private parties may bring false marking actions only if they have suffered a "competitive injury" as a result of false marking, and damages are limited to an amount "adequate to compensate for the injury." *Id.* Marking with an expired patent number is no longer deemed a false marking violation. The amendment to § 292 became effective September 16, 2011, and applies to any case pending or filed on or after that date.

14.5.2 Civil Actions Under §§ 145 and 146

In most instances, a party dissatisfied with a PTAB decision files an appeal to the Federal Circuit under § 141. Alternatively, a party may challenge the PTAB decision in a civil action filed against the USPTO in federal district court. *See* §§ 145 (civil action to obtain patent), 146 (civil action for interference/derivation proceedings).

Actions brought under §§ 145 or 146 have a "hybrid" nature of an appeal and a trial de novo: while new evidence may be introduced, issues that were not raised during the USPTO proceedings cannot be raised in the district court action absent compelling circumstances. *Conservolite, Inc. v. Widmayer*, 21 F.3d 1098, 1102–03 (Fed. Cir. 1994). If a party introduces new evidence, the district court can make de novo findings with respect to factual issues to which the new evidence relates. *Mazzari v. Rogan*, 323 F.3d 1000, 1005 (Fed. Cir. 2003) ("If the parties choose to present additional evidence . . . the district court would make de novo factual findings if the evidence is conflicting."). However, if no new evidence is introduced, the district court reviews the USPTO's fact findings under the "substantial evidence" standard of review. *Id.* at 1004–05.

In *Hyatt v. Kappos*, the Supreme Court unanimously held that parties may present new evidence in the district court action without regard to whether the evidence could have been presented during the USPTO proceeding. 132 S. Ct. 1690, 1700 (2012). In addition, the district court must make de novo factual findings based on the new evidence and evidentiary record from the USPTO. *Id.*

14.6 Appeals and Parallel Litigation

The blockbuster patent case can unfold before multiple judicial and quasi-judicial bodies. As discussed in §§ 14.2.5.5–6, parties can request the USPTO to reexamine issued patents. The following section discusses the appellate process and its consequences for patent cases as well as the various forms of parallel litigation that can occur.

14.6.1 Appeals to the Federal Circuit

In 1982, Congress created the U.S. Court of Appeals for the Federal Circuit and gave it exclusive jurisdiction over all appeals in patent cases. *See* 28 U.S.C. § 1295 (2000). The Federal Circuit was deemed necessary because patent cases were "inconsistently adjudicated," which led to forum shopping. S. Rep. No. 97-275 at 5 (1981). Congress believed that unpredictability of patent law hampered technological innovation.

14.6.1.1 Appellate Jurisdiction

The Federal Circuit has jurisdiction over any final judgment of a district court if the district court's jurisdiction was based on 28 U.S.C. § 1338. 28 U.S.C. § 1295(a)(1). Section 1338 in turn provides that the district courts have original, exclusive jurisdiction over cases arising under the Patent Act. *See* 28 U.S.C. § 1338(a).

14.6.1.2 Choice of Law

One of the many complications arising from patent cases stems from this "exclusive" subject-matter jurisdiction. Unlike other cases, patent cases involve intercircuit choice-of-law questions because of the Federal Circuit's subject matter, as opposed to regional, appellate jurisdiction. This limited jurisdiction has led the Federal Circuit to create a choice-of-law jurisprudence reminiscent of the *Erie* doctrine.

Where a question of law relates to the Federal Circuit's exclusive patent-law jurisdiction, courts should apply Federal Circuit law. *See Lab. Corp. of Am. Holdings v. Chiron Corp.*, 384 F.3d 1326, 1330 (Fed. Cir. 2004) (regarding the interlocutory appealability of an injunction order). If not, courts should apply the regional circuit's law. Hence, substantive matters like claim construction require the district court to follow Federal Circuit precedent. Procedural matters like whether a party waived an issue by not moving for judgment as a matter of law require the district court to apply its regional circuit's precedent. Difficulties arise when courts face a procedural issue that potentially implicates a substantive patent law issue. Federal Circuit law controls such an issue if "the issue pertains to patent law, if it bears an essential relationship to matters committed to [the Federal Circuit's] exclusive control by statute, or if it clearly implicates the jurisprudential responsibilities of [the Federal Circuit] in a field within its exclusive jurisdiction." *Midwest Indus., Inc. v. Karavan Trailers, Inc.*, 175 F.3d 1356, 1359 (Fed. Cir. 1999) (en banc in relevant part) (internal quotation marks omitted). The Federal Circuit decides whether an issue pertains to patent law on an issue-by-issue basis. *See Mars Inc. v. Kabushiki-Kaisha Nippon Conlux*, 24 F.3d 1368 (Fed. Cir. 1994).

Table 14.10 presents a sampling of the issues requiring choice-of-law analysis and the Federal Circuit's rationale in deciding which law to apply. In general, if there is a cognizable argument that allowing differences in the procedural law will undermine the uniformity of patent law, the Federal Circuit will hold that its body of precedent controls the outcome.

Table 14.10
Choice of Law

Issue	Does Federal Circuit Law Govern?/Reasoning
Whether the district court had subject-matter jurisdiction to hear a claim of Japanese patent infringement. *Mars Inc. v. Kabushiki-Kaisha Nippon Conlux*, 24 F.3d 1368, 1371 (Fed. Cir. 1994).	Yes: "[The issue] is of importance to the development of the patent law and is clearly a matter that falls within the exclusive subject matter responsibility of this court."
Whether a party waived its right to dispute the sufficiency of the evidence supporting the jury's antitrust verdict. *Unitherm Food Sys. v. Swift-Eckrich, Inc.*, 375 F.3d 1341, 1365 n.7 (Fed. Cir. 2004), *rev'd on other grounds*, 546 U.S. 394 (2006).	No: "Because we decide antitrust issues that do not implicate patent law, including market definition, under the law of the regional circuits, . . . we similarly apply [regional circuit] law to determine whether or not [the party] has preserved its right to appeal."
Whether an injunction against copending patent litigation in another district court is immediately appealable. *Lab. Corp. of Am. Holdings v. Chiron Corp.*, 384 F.3d 1326, 1330 (Fed. Cir. 2004).	Yes: "Because of the importance of national uniformity in patent cases, we hold that injunctions arbitrating between copending patent declaratory judgment and infringement cases in different district courts are reviewed under the law of the Federal Circuit."

Prior to September 16, 2011, the well-pleaded complaint rule introduced an additional wrinkle to the choice-of-law analysis. Where the district court's original jurisdiction did not stem from § 1338 because, for example, the plaintiff did not assert a patent claim, the Federal Circuit had no appellate jurisdiction and the district court was instead bound by its regional circuit law. This situation could arise where the patent case stemmed from the defendant's counterclaim to a nonpatent cause of action. *See, e.g.*, *Holmes Grp., Inc. v. Vornado Air Circulation Sys., Inc.*, 535 U.S. 826 (2002). The AIA closed this gap in the Federal Circuit's jurisdiction by amending § 1295 so as to provide the Federal Circuit with exclusive jurisdiction over all patent appeals, including those cases where the patent-related cause of action exists only as a counterclaim. AIA § 19. This statutory amendment, which overrules the holding in *Holmes Group*, applies to actions filed on or after September 16, 2011.

14.6.1.3 Interlocutory Appeals

The Federal Circuit has appellate jurisdiction over any interlocutory appeal from a case based on the district court's original jurisdiction over patent cases. § 1292(c)(1). As with other federal courts of appeals, the Federal Circuit has discretion to decline an interlocutory appeal. *See, e.g.*, *In re Convertible Rowing Exerciser Patent Litig.*, 903 F.2d 822 (Fed. Cir. 1990).

District courts most frequently encounter the question of interlocutory appealability with respect to claim construction issues. However, the Federal Circuit almost always refuses to entertain interlocutory appeals on claim construction orders. *See Nystrom v. TREX Co., Inc.*, 339 F.3d 1347, 1351 (Fed. Cir. 2003) ("Such appeals are rarely granted."). Nevertheless, the Federal Circuit may grant an appeal on a claim construction order if it already has jurisdiction over a prior claim construction order, for example, if a preliminary injunction is already on appeal. *See, e.g.*, *Regents of the Univ. of Cal. v. Dako N. Am., Inc.*, 477 F.3d 1335 (Fed. Cir. 2007).

14.6.2 Parallel Litigation Forums

Some patent cases spawn parallel litigation, presenting a host of issues regarding stays and coordination of discovery that was dealt with in prior chapters. A district court should be aware of the potential for parallel litigation and where it might be filed.

14.6.2.1 International Trade Commission

Under 19 U.S.C. § 1337, the U.S. International Trade Commission (ITC) has jurisdiction to bar importation of articles that infringe a valid and enforceable U.S. patent (as well as other federal intellectual property rights). *See generally* Peter S. Menell, et al., Section 337 Patent Investigation Management Guide (Lexis 2012). The ITC has become increasingly popular over the past decade due to its speed and expertise in patent litigation. The typical ITC proceeding is completed in under eighteen months. Although the ITC may not award damages, it can issue exclusion orders preventing the importation of infringing goods into the United States.

ITC cases are heard by an administrative law judge (ALJ), who conducts an evidentiary hearing that resembles a bench trial. The ALJ's determinations are reviewed by the ITC's six-member commission, whose decisions are subject to review by the President. If the President fails to disapprove the ITC's determination within sixty days, it becomes final, and the losing party may file an appeal to the Federal Circuit.

Because ITC proceedings are governed by the Administrative Procedure Act, the Federal Circuit reviews the ITC's factual findings for substantial evidence and its legal conclusions de novo. 5 U.S.C. § 706(2)(A), (E). ITC decisions are not binding on district courts, and have no *res judicata* or collateral estoppel effect. *See Tex. Instruments v. Cypress Semiconductor Corp.*, 90 F.3d 1558, 1569 (Fed. Cir. 1996). Patent actions may proceed simultaneously in district court and in the ITC, especially if the patentee seeks both damages (only available in the district court) and an exclusion order (only available from the ITC). Under 28 U.S.C. § 1659(a), parties to a civil action that are also respondents in a parallel proceeding before the ITC can move for a stay of the district court proceedings as a matter of right. *See* § 2.2.6.2.1.

14.6.2.2 Patent Office Reexamination or Review

As discussed previously (*see* §§ 14.2.5.5–7) litigants can request that the USPTO reexamine or review the validity of issued patents. High-stakes patent litigation often leads to requests for reexamination or review to invalidate a patent or alter its scope. To avoid duplicative proceedings, district courts may decide to stay the litigation pending reexamination or review. *See* § 2.2.6.4.1.

14.6.2.3 Other District Courts and MDL Proceedings

Patent litigation can lead to the proverbial "race to the courthouse," especially where declaratory judgment jurisdiction is available. In other instances, a defendant may choose to file a countersuit for infringement of its own patents in a different jurisdiction. Lastly, the Judicial Panel on Multidistrict Litigation occasionally consolidates patent cases nationwide before a single judge for pretrial proceedings. *See* § 2.2.6.3; U.S. Judicial Panel on Multidistrict Litigation, Pending MDLs, http://www.jpml.uscourts.gov/pending-mdls-0.

14.6.2.4 Foreign Courts

Complex patent litigation may be occurring simultaneously overseas because each nation operates its own patent system. While many nations have harmonized their patent laws to a significant extent, it is an abuse of discretion for a district judge to take jurisdiction over infringement claims based on other nation's patents. *See Voda v. Cordis Corp.*, 476 F.3d 887 (Fed. Cir. 2007). Indeed, the Federal Circuit's holding that the U.S. district courts cannot consolidate patent-infringement claims from multiple countries ensures that parallel litigation will occur over particularly valuable inventions. In such cases, district courts should be sensitive to the potential for strategic effects that certain types of motions (for example, regarding depositions or privileged documents) can create.

Appendix A
Patent Glossary

Note: Many of these definitions are derived from the USPTO glossary, available at http://www.uspto.gov/main/glossary/index.html.

abandonment: A patent application becomes abandoned for failure to file a complete and proper reply within the time period provided under 37 C.F.R. § 1.134 and § 1.136 unless an office action indicates otherwise. Abandonment may be either of the invention or of an application. An abandoned application, in accordance with 37 C.F.R. §§ 1.135 and 1.138, is one which is removed from the Patent Office docket of pending applications. *See* § 14.3.4.1.6.

abstract of the disclosure: A concise statement of the technical disclosure, including that which is new in the art to which the invention pertains.

agent (practitioner, representative): One who is not an attorney but is authorized to act for or in place of the applicant(s) before the USPTO, that is, an individual who is registered to practice before the USPTO.

all-limitation rule (all-elements rule): A doctrine requiring that an allegedly infringing device contain every element of a claim to establish infringement, either literally or under the doctrine of equivalents. *See* § 14.4.1.4.2.1.1.

analogous art (pertinent art, relevant art): In a nonobviousness analysis, art that a person having ordinary skill in the art would have consulted in attempting to solve the problem addressed by the innovation. Analogous art must be either within the same field of endeavor as the invention, or from a different field but reasonably pertinent to the same problem. *See* § 14.3.5.3.2.

antedate (swearing behind a reference): A procedure whereby a patent applicant can establish an invention date earlier than the effective date of prior art that has been cited against his claims in a rejection for non-obviousness (§ 103) or lack of novelty (§§ 102(a) or (e)).

anticipation: A single prior art reference anticipates a claim when it contains all the elements of the claim. The claim is rejected for lack of novelty under § 102.

assignment: A transfer of ownership of a patent application or patent from one entity to another. Record all assignments with the USPTO Assignment Services Division to maintain clear title to pending patent applications and patents.

benefit claim: The claiming by an applicant in a nonprovisional application of a benefit of an invention disclosed in a prior-filed, co-pending (under examination at the same time), provisional, or nonprovisional application, or international application designating the United States for the purposes of securing an earlier effective filing date for the nonprovisional application.

best mode: The specification must set forth the best mode, or preferred embodiment, contemplated by the inventor at the time of filing, of making and using his or her invention (§ 112), or the patent may be declared invalid. *See* § 14.3.3.3. The AIA eliminated failure to set forth best mode as a basis for patent invalidity.

blocking patent: Two or more patented inventions block each other when one cannot be practiced without infringing the other, and vice versa. Blocking patents often arise when an improvement on an invention is patented: the improvement cannot be practiced without infringing the original patent, and the original inventor cannot practice the improvement without infringing the improvement patent. The parties commonly agree to a cross-license to resolve the issue.

central claiming: A claiming regime in which a claim recites the preferred embodiment of the invention but is deemed to cover a range of equivalents to that preferred embodiment.

Certificate of Correction: Minor errors in an issued patent can be corrected with a Certificate of Correction. *See* § 254 (correction of USPTO mistake); § 255 (correction of applicant mistake).

claim restriction: A discretely claimed component of a patent claim. *See also element.*

claim vitiation: An accused device cannot be infringing if it would effectively vitiate (or eliminate) any claim limitation. This doctrine is a corollary of the all-elements rule. *See* § 14.4.1.4.2.1.1.1.

claims: Claims delineate the patented invention. The patent specification must conclude with a claim or claims particularly pointing out and distinctly claiming the subject matter that the applicant regards as his or her invention or discovery.

classification: Patents are classified by a system using a three-digit class and a three-digit subclass to describe every similar grouping of patent art. Multiple classification codes may describe a single invention.

combination patent: A patent granted for an invention that unites existing components in a novel way.

composed of (used when defining the scope of a claim): A transitional phrase that is interpreted in the same manner as either *consisting of* or *consisting essentially of*, depending on the facts of the particular case.

comprising (used when defining the scope of a claim): A transitional phrase that is synonymous with *including*, *containing* or *characterized by*; is inclusive or open-ended and does not exclude additional, unrecited elements or method steps. *Comprising* is a term of art used in claim language that means that the named elements are essential in describing the invention.

conception: The formation in the mind of the inventor of the definite and permanent idea of the complete invention that is thereafter reduced to practice. *See* § 14.3.4.1.2.1.

consisting essentially of (used when defining the scope of a claim): A transitional phrase that limits the scope of a claim to the specified materials or steps and those that do not materially affect the basic and novel characteristics of the claimed invention. For the purposes of searching for and applying prior art under §§ 102 and 103, absent a clear indication in the specification or claims of what the basic and novel characteristics actually are, *consisting essentially of* will be construed as equivalent to *comprising*.

consisting of (used when defining the scope of a claim): A transitional phrase that is closed and excludes any element, step, or ingredient not specified in the claim.

continuation: A second application for the same invention claimed in a prior nonprovisional application and filed before the first application becomes abandoned or patented.

continuation-in-part (CIP): An application filed during the lifetime of an earlier nonprovisional application that repeats some substantial portion or all of the earlier nonprovisional application and adds matter not disclosed in the earlier nonprovisional application. *See* § 14.2.3.4.

contributory infringement: Section 271(c) imposes liability when a party "offers to sell or sell within the United States or imports into the United States a component of a patented machine, manufacture, combination or composition, or a material or apparatus for use in practicing a patented process, constituting a material part of the invention, knowing the same to be especially made or especially adapted for use in an infringement of such patent, and not a staple article or commodity of commerce suitable for substantial noninfringing use, shall be liable as a contributory infringer." *See* § 14.4.1.3.2.

counterpart: An application filed in a foreign patent office that is substantially similar to the patent application filed with the USPTO and is based on some or all of the same invention. The two applications would generally have the same applicant.

covered business method review (CBMR): The America Invents Act instituted a variant of the postgrant review process for business method patents of all filing dates. Patent validity can be challenged on any ground, and covered business method review is broader than inter partes review. *See* § 14.2.5.8.1.

critical date: The date one year prior to the date a patent application is filed. The patent will be invalid for lack of novelty if the invention was in public use in the United States, or patented or described anywhere in the world, prior to the critical date. *See* § 102(b); § 14.3.4.1.5.

declaration (of inventor): A document in which an applicant for patent declares that he or she (1) made or authorized the application, (2) believes that he or she is the original inventor or an original joint inventor of a claimed invention in the application; and (3) acknowledges that any willful false statement made in the declaration is punishable under 18 U.S.C. § 1001 by fine or imprisonment of not more than five (5) years, or both. These requirements apply to applications filed after September 15, 2012. *See* M.P.E.P § 602.01(a)–(b). For applications filed prior to that date, the declaration also required the inventor's country of citizenship. An oath or declaration must be filed in each nonprovisional patent application.

definiteness: Shorthand for the requirement, under § 112(b), that the claims particularly point out and distinctly claim the subject matter that the applicant regards as his or her invention. *See* § 14.3.3.4.

dependent claim: A claim that refers back to and further limits a preceding dependent or independent claim. A dependent claim includes by reference every limitation of the claim from which it depends.

derivation proceeding: The AIA established this new proceeding to allow an inventor to challenge an earlier-filed third-party application or patent claiming subject matter that was derived from the inventor's own work. This proceeding partially substitutes for interference proceedings. *See* § 14.3.4.2.5.

design patent: A patent for a new, original, and ornamental design for an article of manufacture.

designation: A selection made by the applicant, in the Request for an International Application filed under the Patent Cooperation Treaty (PCT), as to the countries in which protection for an invention is desired.

diligence: To establish a conception date as the date of invention, the inventor must have worked diligently following conception to reduce the invention to practice. In the course of an interference, a party can establish its conception date as the date of invention by showing reasonable diligence from before the other's conception until their own reduction to practice date. *See* § 102(g); § 14.3.4.1.2.3.

direct infringement: A person is liable for direct infringement if he or she "without authority makes, uses, offers to sell, or sells any patented invention, within the United States or imports into the United States any patented invention during the term of the patent therefore." § 271(a). An accused infringer's intent is immaterial, as patent infringement is a strict liability offense. *See* § 14.4.1.1.

disclaimer: There are two types of disclaimers under § 253: statutory disclaimers and terminal disclaimers. A patentee may make a statutory disclaimer of any complete claim, stating therein the extent of his or her interest in such patent. A patentee may make a terminal disclaimer to disclaim or dedicate to the public the remaining time of the term of the patent granted. A terminal disclaimer may be filed for the purpose of overcoming a judicially created double-patenting rejection. Disclaimers are required to be in writing and recorded in the USPTO, and are considered part of the original patent to the extent of the interest actually possessed by the disclaimant and by those claiming under him or her.

disclosure: In return for a patent, the inventor gives as consideration a complete disclosure of the invention for which protection is sought. *See* § 14.3.3.

divisional application: A later application for an independent or distinct invention disclosing and claiming only a portion of the subject matter disclosed in the earlier or parent application.

doctrine of equivalents: A judicially developed principle for finding patent infringement when the accused process or product falls outside the literal scope of the patent claims. The essential objective inquiry is: "Does the accused product or process contain elements equivalent to each claimed element of the patented invention?" *See* § 14.4.1.4.2.

double patenting: An inventor may not obtain claims in more than one patent directed either to the same invention or an obvious variation of the same invention. A rejection by the USPTO based on obviousness can be overcome by filing a terminal disclaimer stating that the additional patents will expire on the same date as the first patent. A terminal disclaimer, therefore, eliminates any improper extension of the initial patent term. *See* § 14.4.2.4.1.

effective filing date: The filing date of an earlier-filed application accorded under §§ 119/365(a)/365(b) (foreign filing or domestic provisional application), 120/365(c) (earlier U.S. filing date), or 121 (divisional applications), or if none of these sections is satisfied, the actual filing date of the patent.

electronic file wrapper: A system that provides a way to access electronic copies of the correspondence, documents, and other pertinent records used in considering a particular patent application.

element: A discretely claimed component of a patent claim. *See also claim restriction.*

embodiment: A manner in which an invention can be made, used, practiced, or expressed. *See best mode.*

enablement: The specification must describe in "full, clear, concise, and exact terms" how to make and use the invention such that any person skilled in the art can do so without undue experimentation. *See* § 14.3.3.2.

ex parte reexamination: A procedure whereby patentees and third parties can seek reexamination of issued patents. *See* § 14.2.5.5.2.

experimental use: Experimental use has two distinct meanings within patent law. First, experimental use is an exception to the public-use statutory bar under § 102(b). So long as the public use was to test or experiment with the invention, it is not counted in computing the one-year statutory bar. Second, experimental use is a defense to infringement and requires that the construction and use of the patented invention be for scientific purposes only. *See* § 14.3.4.1.5.1.

express abandonment: *See abandonment.*

file wrapper: The folder into which papers for a particular application are collected and maintained. It contains a complete record of proceedings in the USPTO from the filing of the initial patent application to the issued patent. The file wrapper of a patent application that is maintained by the USPTO is the official record.

file wrapper estoppel: *See prosecution history estoppel.*

filing date: The date of receipt in the USPTO of an application which includes (1) a specification containing a description and, if the application is a nonprovisional application, at least one claim, and (2) any required drawings.

final office action: A USPTO action on the second or any subsequent examination or consideration by an examiner that is intended to close the prosecution of a nonprovisional patent application.

First Sale Doctrine/Exhaustion Principle: The first unrestricted sale of a patented product exhausts the patentee's control over that product, and it can be resold and repaired without implicating the patent owner's rights. This is a form of implied license. *See* § 14.4.2.2.1.1.

grace period: The one-year period between the critical date and the filing date, during which the invention may be offered for sale or used publicly in the United States, or described in a printed publication or patented anywhere in the world without invalidating the patent under § 102(b).

***Handgards* claim**: An antitrust counterclaim to a patent infringement suit, alleging that the patentee either knew the patent was invalid or was not being infringed. *See Handgards, Inc. v. Ethicon, Inc.*, 601 F.2d 986 (9th Cir. 1979).

having (used when defining the scope of a claim): A transitional phrase that is synonymous with *including*, *containing*, or *characterized by*; is inclusive or open-ended and does not exclude additional, unrecited elements or method steps.

improvement patent: A patent based on an improvement to a preexisting invention.

indefiniteness: *See definiteness.*

independent claim: A claim that does not refer back to or depend on another claim.

indirect infringement: Indirect infringement covers conduct by a person who assists or supports another's direct infringement of a patented invention. Direct infringement must be established as a predicate for each act of indirect infringement. *See* § 14.4.1.3.

inducement: Section 271(b) provides that "[w]hoever actively induces infringement of a patent shall be liable as an infringer." A finding of inducement requires that a patent owner establish evidence of culpable conduct directed toward encouraging another's infringement. *See* § 14.4.1.3.1.

inequitable conduct: Where a patent applicant breaches the duty to prosecute a patent application in good faith and candor. *See* 37 C.F.R. § 1.56; *see also* § 14.4.2.3.1.

information disclosure statement (IDS): A list of patents, publications, U.S. applications, or other information submitted for consideration by the USPTO in a nonprovisional patent application filed under § 111(a) to comply with applicant's duty to submit information that is material to the patentability of the claimed invention. *See* § 14.2.2.1.

inter partes reexamination: A procedure allowing third parties to seek invalidation by the USPTO of patents granted on applications filed on or after November 29, 1999. It was phased out beginning on September 16, 2011, and replaced by the AIA's inter partes review procedure. *See* § 14.2.5.5.3.

inter partes review (IPR): A procedure established by the AIA for third parties to seek invalidation of patents. *See* § 14.2.5.6.

interference: A proceeding, typically conducted before the Board of Patent Appeals and Interferences or in certain circumstances before a district court, to determine priority of invention between a pending application and/or one or more unexpired patents.

intervening rights: Claims that were modified at reissue, for any reason, are subject to a reliance-type interest (intervening rights). Third parties may rely on the claims of an issued patent. *See* § 14.2.5.4.2.2.

invention: Any art or process, machine, manufacture, design, or composition of matter, or any new and useful improvement thereof, or any variety of plant, which is or may be patentable under the patent laws of the United States.

invention date: The date either on which an invention is reduced to practice or conceived, so long as the inventor can show reasonable diligence from conception until reduction to practice.

issue date: The date that a patent application becomes a U.S. patent. The issue date is the date that patent rights can be exercised.

***Jepson* claim format**: A claim containing a preamble explaining the current state of the art, followed by a description of the claimed patentable improvement.

joint infringement: Liability for joint infringement can be found only where one party controlled or directed each step in the process. *See* § 14.4.1.3.3.

joint inventor: An inventor who is named with at least one other inventor in a patent application, wherein each inventor contributes to the conception of the invention set forth in at least one claim in a patent application.

laches: An equitable defense that the plaintiff unreasonably delayed in asserting an infringement claim. If a patentee files suit more than six years after he or she became (or reasonably should have become) aware of the alleged infringement, a presumption of laches arises, and the patentee must establish legitimate reasons for the delay. This defense does not bar the plaintiff's action entirely, but prevents the recovery of any damages accrued prior to the filing of the action. *See* § 14.4.2.3.4.

license: An agreement between a patent owner and a licensee that the patent owner will not sue the licensee for acts that would otherwise constitute infringement.

limitation: A component of an invention described in a patent claim. *See element.*

literal infringement: Literal infringement requires an accused device to satisfy every element of the asserted patent claim precisely. *See* § 14.4.1.4.1.

***Markush* claim format**: A *Markush* claim claims a genus of inventions in a single claim where the family of inventions all share a common trait, for example, "a chemical compound of the formula COOH–CH2-R, where R is selected from the group consisting of ________." *Markush* claims normally do not occur outside of the field of chemistry.

means-plus-function claim format: A means-plus-function claim defines one or more elements of the claim as a "means for [performing a function]." This special type of limitation is interpreted to cover the structure(s) described in the specification for performing the claimed function as well as equivalents of that/those structure(s) as of the time of filing. *See* § 112(f); § 14.4.1.4.1.1.

method claim: A claim covering a way of doing something, typically conveyed as a series of steps.

multiple dependent claim: A dependent claim that further limits and refers back in the alternative to more than one preceding independent or dependent claim. Acceptable multiple dependent claims shall refer to preceding claims using the terms *or*, *any one of*, *one of*, *any of*, *either*. A multiple dependent claim may not depend on another multiple dependent claim, either directly or indirectly.

national stage application: An application that has entered the national phase of the Patent Cooperation Treaty by the fulfillment of certain requirements in a national patent office. Such an application is filed under § 371 in the United States and is referred to as a "371 application."

new matter: Information in an amendment to a pending patent that departs from the original disclosure. Under § 132, amendments cannot introduce new matter into the disclosure of the invention.

nonfinal office action: An office action made by the examiner where the applicant is entitled to reply and request reconsideration or further examination, with or without making an amendment.

nonobviousness: The requirement that to be patentable, an invention be sufficiently different from the prior art that, at the time it was made, it would not have been obvious to a person having ordinary skill in the art. *See* § 14.3.5.

nonpatent literature: Documents and publications that are not patents or published patent applications but are cited as references for being relevant in a patent prosecution. For example, a magazine article or doctoral thesis relevant to a claimed invention might be cited as nonpatent literature. Typically, references cited in an application are grouped into domestic patents and patent application publications, foreign patents, and nonpatent literature.

nonprovisional application: The "regular" type of patent applications, as distinct from provisional applications filed under § 111(b), often referred to simply as "applications." *See* § 14.2.2.2.1.

nonresponsive amendment: An amendment filed by the applicant that does not fully respond to the examiner's office action in accordance with 37 C.F.R. § 1.111.

normal publication: Regular 18-month publication or redacted publication of a nonprovisional application.

notice: The practice of marking a patented article with the word *patent* followed by the patent number. Without notice, the patentee may recover only for damages that occurred after the infringer received a charge of patent infringement.

notice of abandonment: A written notification from the USPTO that an application has been declared abandoned or, in other words, is no longer pending. If the application was abandoned unintentionally or due to USPTO error, the applicant has a deadline of two months from the issue date of the notice of abandonment to file either (1) a petition to revive the application or (2) a request to reinstate the application.

notice of allowance: A notification to the applicant that he or she is entitled to a patent under the law and requesting payment of a specified issue fee (and possibly a publication fee as well) within three months (non-extendable) from the mailing date of the notice of allowance.

notice of references cited (also known as a PTO-892 form): A list of relevant references cited by a patent examiner in an office action. The following are some examples of such references: domestic patents, domestic patent application publications, foreign patents or patent publications, publications, electronic documents, and affidavits.

novelty: The requirement under § 102 that an invention be sufficiently new relative to the prior art. *See* § 14.3.4.

oath: *See declaration (of inventor).*

obviousness: *See nonobviousness.*

office action: The patent examiner's responses to the patent application and subsequent amendments.

on-sale bar: Section 102(b) specifies an on-sale bar, such that if an invention has been on sale for over one year, it is no longer patentable. *See* § 14.3.4.1.5.2.

opposition: A procedure allowing a third party to request a patent application's refusal or an issued patent's annulment.

original application: *Original* is used in the patent statute and rules to refer to an application that is not a reissue application. An original application may be a first filing or a continuing application.

parent application: The term *parent* is applied to an earlier application of the inventor disclosing a given invention.

patent: A quasi-property right granted by the government of the United States to an inventor "to exclude others from making, using, offering for sale, or selling the invention throughout the United States or importing the invention into the United States" for a limited time in exchange for public disclosure of the invention.

Patent Cooperation Treaty (PCT): A mechanism by which an applicant can file a single application that, when certain requirements have been fulfilled, is equivalent to a regular national filing in each designated country. There are currently over 130 PCT contracting states.

patent pending: A phrase that often appears on manufactured items. It means that someone has applied for a patent on an invention that is contained in the manufactured item. It serves as a warning that a patent may issue that would cover the item and that copiers should be careful because they might infringe if the patent issues. Once the patent issues, the patent owner will stop using the phrase "patent pending" and start using a phrase such as "covered by U.S. Patent Number XXXXXXX."

patent term: The period of time during which a patent is enforceable. For patent applications filed after June 8, 1995, the expiration date is twenty years from the earliest effective filing date, subject to various extensions for delays occurring during prosecution and regulatory approval for drug-related patents. *See* § 14.2.4.

Patent Trial and Appeal Board (PTAB): The AIA created this administrative body to replace the Board of Patent Appeals and Interferences (BPAI). It hears appeals by a patent applicant from a USPTO patent examiner's final refusal to allow a patent application or adverse decision in an ex parte patent reexamination proceeding, inter partes and postgrant review proceedings filed by a party challenging the validity of an issued patent, derivation proceedings filed by a subsequent patent applicant claiming that an earlier patent applicant for the same invention derived the invention from the subsequent patent applicant, and interference proceedings to determine the first inventor of an invention commenced before September 16, 2012. PTAB decisions concerning inter partes and postgrant reviews and ex parte reexamination proceedings may be appealed only to the U.S. Court of Appeals for the Federal Circuit. In several circumstances, a civil action against the USPTO in the U.S. District Court for the Eastern District of Virginia may be instituted after a final

PTAB decision: (1) where a patent applicant is dissatisfied with a PTAB decision concerning the final rejection of the patent application unless the applicant has appealed to the Federal Circuit (*see* § 145); (2) in a derivation proceeding where the losing party initially filed a notice of appeal from the PTAB decision to the Federal Circuit, the adverse party may request that further proceedings instead be conducted in the Eastern District of Virginia (*see* AIA § 7); and (3) where a party is dissatisfied with the decision in an interference proceeding over which the PTAB has jurisdiction, unless that party has appealed to the Federal Circuit (*see* § 146).

peripheral claiming: A regime in which an applicant delineates the precise boundaries of the claimed area of exclusivity, in contrast to central claiming in which the applicant defines the claim directly.

person: For purposes of small entity determination, a person is defined as any inventor or other individual (e.g., an individual to whom an inventor has transferred some rights in the invention) who has not assigned, granted, conveyed, or licensed, and is under no obligation under contract or law to assign, grant, convey, or license any rights in the invention.

person having ordinary skill in the art (PHOSITA): A hypothetical person with knowledge of all analogous art from whose perspective nonobviousness, written description, and enablement are analyzed. *See* §§ 103, 112; *see also* §§ 14.3.3, 14.3.5.3.1.

petition to make special (PTMS): An applicant may petition the USPTO to examine his or her application ahead of other pending applications. A petition to make special may be granted on the basis of an inventor's age or poor health, that the patent will enable manufacture of the invention, is presently being infringed, relates to certain fields including superconductivity, HIV/AIDS, and counter-terrorism, or several other reasons.

post-grant review (PGR): Under this new procedure added by the AIA, third parties may file a petition seeking to cancel one or more patent claims within nine months of a patent's issue or reissue date. *See* § 14.2.5.8.

preferred embodiment: How the inventor sets forth the best mode for carrying out the claimed invention in the application.

printed publication: A reference that is sufficiently accessible to the public interested in the invention. *See* § 14.3.4.1.1.2.

prior art: The general category of technologies and events against which novelty and nonobviousness are evaluated. What qualifies as prior art is specified in §§ 102 and 103.

priority claim: Claims under §§ 119(a)–(e) and 120 for the benefit of the filing date of earlier filed applications.

priority date: The first filing of a patent application anywhere in the world describing an enabled invention usually establishes the priority date for that invention. *See* § 14.2.2.2.3.

pro se: Used to designate an independent inventor who has elected to file an application by himself or herself without the services of a licensed representative.

prosecution: The process for applying for and obtaining a patent from the USPTO.

prosecution history estoppel: A doctrine that prevents a patentee from obtaining coverage through the doctrine of equivalents over subject matter that was surrendered during prosecution. *See* § 14.4.1.4.2.1.2.

provisional application: A provisional application for patent is a U.S. national application for patent filed in the USPTO under § 111(b), which allows filing without a formal patent claim, oath or declaration, or any information disclosure (prior art) statement. A provisional application can establish an early effective filing date in a nonprovisional patent application filed under § 111(a) and automatically becomes abandoned after one year. It also allows the term *patent pending* to be applied. *See* § 14.2.2.2.4.

reads on: An accused device, manufacture, composition, or process "reads on" (and hence infringes) a patent claim if it embodies each of the claim limitations. Similarly, a patent claim "reads on" a prior art reference (and hence is invalid) if the prior art reference contains each of the claim limitations.

reasonable diligence: First-to-conceive inventor must have been reasonably diligent in working to reduce the invention to practice between the time "just prior" to the later inventor's date of conception until the first-to-conceive inventor's reduction to practice. Reasonable diligence is only at issue when the inventor was first to conceive but second to reduce to practice. *See* § 14.3.4.1.2.3.

recapture rule: Bars a patentee from seeking reissue claims that regain subject matter that was surrendered to obtain allowance during the original prosecution. *See* § 14.2.5.4.2.1. This rule is similar to prosecution history estoppel. *See* § 14.4.1.4.2.1.2.

record copy: Original copy of an international application filed under the Patent Cooperation Treaty maintained by the International Bureau of the World Intellectual Property Organization.

redacted publication: A patent application publication that omits material that was present in the specification or claims of the nonprovisional patent application filed in the USPTO. *See* 37 C.F.R. § 1.217 and MPEP § 1132.

reduction to practice: Following conception, reduction to practice is the final step in the inventive process. Reduction to practice can be actual (by constructing a physical embodiment of the invention) or constructive (by filing a patent application that satisfies the disclosure requirements of § 112). *See* § 14.3.4.1.2.2.

reexamination proceeding: At any time during the enforceability of a patent, any person may file a request for the USPTO to conduct a second examination of any claim of the patent on the basis of prior art patents or printed publications which that person states to be pertinent and applicable to the patent and believes to have a bearing on the patentability (*see* 37 C.F.R. § 1.501). For the request for reexamination to be granted, a substantial new question of patentability must be present with regard to at least one patent claim. The request must be in writing and must be accompanied by payment of a reexamination request filing fee as set forth in 37 C.F.R. § 1.20(c). *See* § 14.2.5.5.

reference: *See prior art.*

reissue application: An application for a patent to take the place of an unexpired patent that is defective in one or more particulars. Resissues may narrow or broaden the application. *See* § 14.2.5.4.

rejoinder: The returning to active consideration of claims previously withdrawn from consideration to due to a restriction requirement—i.e., a determination by the USPTO that an application contains more than one invention.

request for continued examination (RCE): A request filed in an application in which prosecution is closed (e.g., the application is under final rejection or a notice of allowance) that is filed to reopen prosecution and continue examination of the application.

restriction: If two or more independent and distinct inventions are claimed in a single application, the examiner may require the applicant to elect a single invention to which the claims will be restricted. This requirement is known as a requirement for restriction (also known as a requirement for division). Such requirement will normally be made before any action on the merits; however, it may be made at any time before final action (final rejection).

reverse doctrine of equivalents: A doctrine excusing infringement where an accused device literally infringes a patent, but should nonetheless be excused because it substantially differs in operative principle and results. Although it has not been applied in over a century to excuse infringement, it continues to be raised. *See* § 14.4.1.4.3.

specification: A written description of the invention and the manner and process of making and using the same.

statutory disclaimer: *See disclaimer.*

submarine patent: An informal term for a patent that is intentionally delayed in prosecution by the applicant to let an infringing user continue to develop its business, with the intention of claiming later-invented technology once the patent finally "surfaces" from the PTO. As of November 29, 2000, most patent applications must be published within eighteen months of filing, so submarine patents have become less common.

substitute patent application: An application that is, in essence, a duplicate of a prior application by the same applicant abandoned before the filing of the substitute application. A substitute application does not obtain the benefit of the filing date of the prior application.

supplemental Examination: A procedure added by the AIA authorizing a patentee to seek further consideration of additional information relevant to patentability. *See* § 14.2.5.3.

terminal disclaimer: *See disclaimer.*

utility: To be patentable, an invention must have specific, substantial, and credible utility. *See* § 14.3.2.

***Walker Process* claim**: An antitrust counterclaim to a patent infringement suit, alleging that the patent was fraudulently obtained so as to exert monopolistic power and is therefore invalid. *See Walker Process Equip., Inc. v. Food Mach. & Chem. Corp.*, 382 U.S. 172 (1965).

written description: The portion of a patent specification, as required by § 112(a), describing the background of the invention, a summary of the invention, and a detailed description of the invention. The patentee must convey with reasonable clarity to those skilled in the art that, as of the filing date sought, he or she was in possession of the invention, and the written description must enable a person having ordinary skill in the art to practice the invention without undue experimentation. *See* § 14.3.3.1.

Appendix B
Acronyms

AIA: America Invents Act
AIPA: American Inventors Protection Act of 1999
AIPLA: American Intellectual Property Law Association
ANDA: Abbreviated New Drug Application
AOUSC: Administrative Office of the United States Courts
AU: (Group) Art Unit
BLA: Biologic License Application
BPAI: Board of Patent Appeals and Interferences
BPCIA: Biologics Price Competition and Innovation Act
CAPC: civil action to obtain patent certainty
CBM: covered business method
CBMR: covered business method review
CC: claim construction
CCPA: United States Court of Customs and Patent Appeals
CIP: continuation-in-part
CMC: case-management conference
CPA: continued prosecution application
CRU: Central Reexamination Unit
DOE: Doctrine of Equivalents
EAST: examiner automated search tools
EFD: effective filing date
EFS: electronic filing system
ePAS: Electronic Patent Assignment System
EPO: European Patent Office
ESD: examination support document
ESI: electronically stored information
FAR: Federal Acquisitions Regulations
FCBA: Federal Circuit Bar Association
FDA: Food and Drug Administration
FDCA: Food, Drug, and Cosmetic Act
FRAND: fair, reasonable and non-discriminatory
FTC: Federal Trade Commission
FTF: first-to-file
FTI: first-to-invent
GAU: Group Art Unit
IDS: information disclosure statement
INID: Internationally agreed Numbers for the Identification of bibliographic Data
IPR: inter partes review
IT: information technology
ITC: International Trade Commission

JMDL: Judicial Panel on Multidistrict Litigation
JSPR: joint preliminary status report
MDL: multidistrict litigation
MPEP: Manual of Patent Examining Procedure
MSJ: motion for summary judgment
NCE: new chemical entity
NDA: new drug application
NOA: notice of allowance
NPE: nonpracticing entity
NPL: non-patent literature
OG: Official Gazette
OIPE: Office of Initial Patent Examination
PAIR: Patent Application Information Retrieval
PCT: Patent Cooperation Treaty
PGR: postgrant review
PHOSITA: person having ordinary skill in the art
PHSA: Public Health and Safety Act
PLR(s): patent local rule(s)
PPA: Plant Patent Act
PTA: patent term adjustment
PTAB: Patent Trial and Appeal Board
PTE: patent term extension
PTMS: petition to make special
PTO: Patent and Trademark Office
PVP: plant variety protection
PVPA: Plant Variety Protection Act
RAND: reasonable and nondiscriminatory
RCE: request for continued examination
RCFC: Rules of the United States Court of Federal Claims
RLD: Reference Listed Drug
SEP: standard-essential patents
SNQ: substantial new question of patentability
SSO: standard setting organization
TD: terminal disclaimer
TSM: teaching, suggestion, or motivation
UPOV: Convention of the International Union for the Protection of New Plant Varieties
USITC: United States International Trade Commission
USPTO: United States Patent and Trademark Office
WIPO: World Intellectual Property Organization
WTO: World Trade Organization

Table of Cases

Schering Corp. v. Amgen, Inc., 35 F. Supp. 2d 375 (D. Del. 1999), 5-96

Schering Corp. v. Geneva Pharm., Inc., 339 F.3d 1373 (Fed. Cir. 2003), 14-52

Schering Corp. v. Roussel-UCLAF SA, 104 F.3d 341 (Fed. Cir. 1997), 2-30

Schering-Plough Corp. v. FTC, 402 F.3d 1056 (11th Cir. 2005), 2-91, 10-20

Schering-Plough Corp., *In re*, 136 F.T.C. 956 (2003), 10-20

Schillinger v. United States, 155 U.S. 163 (1894), 13-1, 13-3

Schnadig Corp. v. Collezione Europa U.S.A., 2001 U.S. Dist. LEXIS 9208, 2001 WL 766898 (N.D. Ill. July 3, 2001), 2-52

Schnadig Corp. v. Gaines Mfg. Co., 620 F.2d 1166 (6th Cir. 1980), 11-14

Schnell, *In re*, 46 F.2d 203 (C.C.P.A. 1931), 11-5

Schoenhaus v. Genesco, Inc., 440 F.3d 1354 (Fed. Cir. 2006), 6-11

Schrieber v. Federal Express Corp., No. 09-CV-128-JHPPJC, 2010 WL 1078463 (N.D. Okla. Mar. 18, 2010), 4-44

Schroeder v. Tracor, Inc., No. 99-1281, 1999 U.S. App. LEXIS 30386, 1999 WL 1021055 (Fed. Cir. Nov. 5, 1999), 14-91

Sciele Pharma Inc. v. Lupin Ltd., 684 F.3d 1253 (Fed. Cir. 2012), 3-10, 3-16

SciMed Life Systems, Inc. v. Advanced Cardiovascular Systems, Inc., 242 F.3d 1337 (Fed. Cir. 2001), 5-60, 14-85

Scripps Clinic & Research Foundation v. Genentech, Inc., 927 F.2d 1565 (Fed. Cir. 1991), 5-82, 6-12, 7-51, 14-87

Seaborg, *In re*, 328 F.2d 996 (C.C.P.A. 1964), 14-52

Seachange Int'l, Inc. v. C-COR, Inc., 413 F.3d 1361 (Fed. Cir. 2005), 5-70

Seagate Tech., LLC, *In re*, 497 F.3d 1360 (Fed. Cir. 2007), 1-10, 2-43, 3-6, 3-10, 4-28, 6-45, 7-14, 7-56, 9-10, 14-111, 14-112

Sears Petroleum & Transp. Corp. v. Archer Daniels Midland Co., 2007 U.S. Dist. LEXIS 53576, 2007 WL 2156251 (N.D.N.Y. July 24, 2007), 5-100

Sears, Roebuck & Company v. Stiffel Company, 376 U.S. 225 (1964), 14-99

Seattle Box Co. v. Industrial Crating & Packing, Inc., 756 F.2d 1574 (Fed. Cir. 1985), 14-22

Seattle Box Co., Inc. v. Indus. Crating & Packing, Inc., 731 F.2d 818 (Fed. Cir. 1984), 5-49

SEB S.A. v. Montgomery Ward & Co., 137 F. Supp. 2d 285 (S.D.N.Y. 2001), 3-28

Seiko Epson Corp. v. Nu-Kote Int'l, Inc., 190 F.3d 1360 (Fed. Cir. 1999), 2-47, 11-10

Sekisui Am. Corp. v. Hart, No. 12 Civ. 3479 (SAS) (FM), 2013 WL 4116322 (S.D.N.Y. Aug. 15, 2013), 4-20

Semiconductor Energy Lab. Co. v. Chimei Innolux Corp., 2012 U.S. Dist. LEXIS 186322, 2012 WL 7170593 (C.D. Cal. Dec. 19, 2012), 2-56

Semiconductor Energy Laboratory Co. v. Nagata, 706 F.3d 1365 (Fed. Cir. 2013), 2-35

Semitool, Inc. v. Tokyo Elec. Am., 208 F.R.D. 273 (N.D. Cal. 2002), 3-21

Senior Technologies, Inc. v. R.F. Techs. Inc., 76 F. App'x 318 (Fed. Cir. 2003), 14-85

Senju Pharmaceuticals Co. v. Metrics, Inc., Civ. No. 14-3962 (JBS/KMW), 2015 WL 1472123 (D.N.J. Mar. 31, 2015), 10-11

Serco Services Co., L.P. v. Kelley Co., Inc., 51 F.3d 1037 (Fed. Cir. 1995), 2-52

Serio-US Indus., Inc. v. Plastic Recovery Techs. Corp., 459 F.3d 1311 (Fed. Cir. 2006), 8-17, 9-17

Seymore v. McCormick, 57 U.S. 480 (1853), 7-21, 14-107

SFA Systems, LLC v. 1-800-Flowers.com, Inc., No. 09-cv-340, 2014 U.S. Dist. LEXIS 184311 (E.D. Tex. July 7, 2014), 9-15

Author Biographies

Peter S. Menell is the Koret Professor of Law at the University of California, Berkeley School of Law, where he specializes in intellectual property law. In 1995, he co-founded the Berkeley Center for Law & Technology, which has been instrumental in Berkeley Law being named the top intellectual property program in the nation for nearly two decades. Professor Menell earned his B.S. from M.I.T., M.A. and Ph.D. in Economics from Stanford University, and J.D. from Harvard Law School, where he served as an editor of the *Harvard Law Review*. After graduating from law school, he clerked for Judge Jon O. Newman of the Court of Appeals for the Second Circuit. Professor Menell has written more than 70 articles and 10 books, including *Intellectual Property in the New Technological Age* (with R. Merges and M. Lemley, now in its eighth edition, 2016) and *Software and Internet Law* (with M. Lemley, R. Merges, P. Samuelson, and B. Carver, 4th ed. 2011). Professor Menell has organized more than 50 intellectual property education programs for the Federal Judicial Center since 1998. Professor Menell founded and supervises the *Annual Review of Law and Technology* (now in its nineteenth year, published by the *Berkeley Technology Law Journal*). He has advised the U.S. Congress, federal agencies, state attorneys general, and technology and entertainment companies on a wide range of intellectual property and antitrust matters. He is a member of the District of New Jersey Local Patent Rules Advisory Committee and the Court of Federal Claims Advisory Council. He served from 2012–2013 as one of the inaugural scholars in the USPTO's Thomas Alva Edison Visiting Professionals Program.

Lynn H. Pasahow is a partner in the Litigation Group at Fenwick & West, where he specializes in patent litigation. He has represented cutting-edge technology companies and universities and their Nobel laureate and other inventors in patent and other intellectual property litigation in the software, Internet, and biotech industries. Mr. Pasahow is a coauthor, with Judge William W Schwarzer, of *Civil Discovery: A Guide to Efficient Practice*. He co-teaches an intellectual property course at the University of California, San Francisco, and regularly lectures about intellectual property law subjects to groups that have included the Federal Judicial Center, the American Association for the Advancement of Science, the American Law Institute, the Practising Law Institute, and the University of California, Berkeley School of Law. Mr. Pasahow earned his B.A. from Stanford University and his J.D. from the University of California, Berkeley School of Law.

James Pooley advises clients on patent and trade secret matters in Silicon Valley. He served from 2009 through 2014 as deputy director general, Innovation and Technology Section, at the World Intellectual Property Organization (WIPO). Prior to that appointment, Mr. Pooley was a partner at Morrison and Foerster, where he specialized in intellectual property and technology-related commercial litigation. Mr. Pooley is the author of the treatise *Trade Secrets* (Law Journal Press), *Secrets: Managing Information Assets in the Age of Cyberespionage* (Verus Press 2015), and numerous other professional publications in the field of intellectual property. He is a former president of the American Intellectual Property Law Association and the National Inventors Hall of Fame. Mr. Pooley has taught as an adjunct professor of law at the University of California, Berkeley School of Law. He is a fellow of the California Council on Science and Technology and a member of the National Academy of Sciences Committee on Intellectual Property Rights. Mr. Pooley conceived and scripted an instructional video for jurors in patent cases that was produced by the Federal Judicial Center. Mr. Pooley earned his B.A. from Lafayette College and his J.D. from Columbia University School of Law.

Matthew D. Powers is the lead partner at Tensegrity Law Group, LLP. He is one of the nation's most experienced patent trial lawyers. He has litigated and tried cases in jurisdictions nationwide involving a wide range of technologies, including semiconductor, biomedical, computer, computer peripherals, cellular, holographic, digital media and specialty chemical products. He has published articles on various aspects of intellectual property law and litigation. Mr. Powers has taught as an adjunct professor of law at the University of California, Berkeley School of Law. Mr. Powers earned his B.S. from Northwestern University and his J.D. from Harvard Law School.

Steven C. Carlson is managing partner in the Silicon Valley office of Kasowitz, Benson, Torres & Friedman LLP, where he specializes in patent litigation. He served as a judicial law clerk to Judge Roderick R. McKelvie of the U.S. District Court for the District of Delaware and to Judge Paul R. Michel of the U.S. Court of Appeals for the Federal Circuit. He earned his B.A. from Reed College and his J.D. from Yale Law School, where he served as an editor of the *Yale Law Journal*.

Jeffrey G. Homrig is a partner in the Silicon Valley office of Latham & Watkins LLP. He has extensive experience as a litigator and trial lawyer in complex and high-stakes patent cases for leading technology companies. He graduated from University of California, Berkeley School of Law, and holds a B.A. from the University of California, Berkeley.

George F. Pappas is a partner at Covington & Burling LLP, where he specializes in patent litigation. He is a fellow of the American College of Trial Lawyers and the chair of its Complex Litigation Committee. He also chairs the Editorial Committee and is one of the coauthors of *Anatomy of a Patent Case* (2d ed. 2012), published in conjunction with the Federal Judicial Center. He received his undergraduate and law degrees from the University of Maryland.

Carolyn Chang is a partner at Fenwick & West's Silicon Valley office, where she specializes in patent litigation. She received her B.A. from the University of California, Berkeley, and her J.D. from the University of California, Hastings College of the Law.

Colette Reiner Mayer is a partner at Morrison & Foerster's Silicon Valley office, where she specializes in patent litigation. She earned her B.S. from M.I.T. and her J.D. from Cardozo School of Law.

Marc David Peters is a partner at Morrison & Foerster's Silicon Valley office, where he specializes in patent and trade secret litigation. He earned his B.A. from Harvard University, his M.A. and Ph.D. in Physics from the University of California, Berkeley, and his J.D. from Stanford Law School.

Collaborator Profiles

Anita Choi is an associate at Morrison & Foerster's Silicon Valley office, where she focuses on clean technology, biofuels, agricultural biotechnology, life sciences, biotechnology, pharmaceuticals, molecular diagnostics, and material sciences. She earned her B.S. from the California Institute of Technology, her M.B.A. from the Wharton School of Business, and her J.D. from the University of Pennsylvania Law School.

John Fargo serves as the director of the Intellectual Property Staff within the Commercial Litigation Branch of the Civil Division at the U.S. Department of Justice. He specializes in intellectual property litigation at the Federal Court of Claims. He earned his B.S. in Industrial Engineering and his J.D. at the State University of New York at Buffalo.

Michael Sawyer is an associate in the Washington, D.C., office of Covington & Burling where he specializes in patent litigation. He served as a judicial law clerk to Judge William C. Bryson of the U.S. Court of Appeals for the Federal Circuit. He earned his B.S. in Computer Science and Mathematics at the University of Scranton and his J.D. from the University of California, Berkeley School of Law.

Allison A. Schmitt currently serves as a law clerk to the Honorable Stanley R. Chesler at the U.S. District Court for the District of New Jersey, after which she will be clerking for Judge Kathleen M. O'Malley of the U.S. Court of Appeals for the Federal Circuit. She earned her B.S. in Chemistry and Biochemistry from the University of Washington, her Ph.D. in Chemistry from Duke University, and her J.D. from the University of California, Berkeley School of Law.

Michael R. Ward is a partner at Morrison & Foerster's San Francisco office, where he specializes in intellectual property relating to plants and biotechnology. He earned his B.S. from the University of California, Berkeley, his M.S. in Agronomy and Ph.D. in Plant Physiology/Biochemistry from the University of California, Davis, and his J.D. from Golden Gate University School of Law.

Patricia Young is an associate at Latham & Watkins LLP, where she specializes in patent litigation. She received her S.B. from M.I.T. and her J.D. from Harvard Law School.

Made in United States
Orlando, FL
04 November 2026

90203569R00236